D0162817

A CONSTITUTIONAL AND LEGAL HISTORY OF MEDIEVAL ENGLAND

Second Edition

A CONSTITUTIONAL AND LEGAL HISTORY OF MEDIEVAL ENGLAND

Second Edition

BRYCE LYON

BROWN UNIVERSITY

W · W · NORTON & COMPANY

New York London

To Mary

Published simultaneously in Canada by George J. McLeod Limited, Toronto. Printed in the United States of America.

Second Edition

Library of Congress Cataloging in Publication Data
Lyon, Bryce Dale, 1920–
A constitutional and legal history of medieval England.
Bibliography: p.
Includes index.
1. Great Britain—Politics and government—To 1485.
2. Law—Great Britain—History and criticism.
I. Title.
JN137.L9 1980 342'.42'029 79-21455
ISBN 0-393-95132-4

1 2 3 4 5 6 7 8 9 0

CONTENTS

PART TWO. THE NORMAN KINGS

PART THREE. HENRY II AND HIS SONS

PART FIVE. EDWARD II, EDWARD III, AND RICHARD II

PART SIX. THE HOUSES OF LANCASTER AND YORK

PREFACE TO SECOND EDITION

The first edition of this book, in 1960, appeared at a time already little sympathetic to the study of history, especially constitutional and legal history. The precocious growth of the social sciences after World War II offered many alternative disciplines for studying human society, some seemingly far more relevant than history, then under attack for having failed to guide men toward more intelligent, realistic, and just objectives. There had been the decade of the Great Depression and the failure of the western democracies to thwart the challenges of nazism, fascism, and communism. Why had not historical knowledge prevented or at least alleviated these preludes to war. To make history appear even more irrelevant as a body of knowledge there followed the long American involvement in Vietnam and the student discontent and civil rights movements of the sixties and early seventies.

The damage to constitutional and legal history from these unfavorable tides was even greater than to history in general. Increasingly the new historical fields and methodologies spawned after the war caught the interest of historian and student. Rightly there was more emphasis upon Russian, Chinese, Japanese, and Middle Eastern history. The knowledge and methodologies of the social sciences brought more social, economic, and cultural history, all considered more relevant to human problems than political and constitutional history. It was not easy to refute the argument that all the knowledge in the world about such matters as parliamentary procedure, juries, and governmental administration had no applicability to starvation, the underprivileged, and the minorities deprived of their rights as citizens.

For an historian living in the midst of all this to say that he now sees change and a better future for history may be unrealistic, but what explains the steady demand throughout the twenty years following 1960 for this book and the current demand for a new edition? American constitutional and legal history since the war partly explains this demand. Although the demonstrations and movements of the sixties and seventies had an effect upon the social, economic, political, and legal fabric of the United States, it is now coming to be recognized that what really altered it were certain landmark decisions in the federal courts that demanded legislative and administrative action. To follow the cases in the federal courts is to see how vitally they have influenced our society. The publicity given key decisions by the Supreme Court, as on admissions policies of universities or on environmental issues or on desegregation of schools, has awakened people to the significance of the judicial system for their daily lives. With this shift in perspective on the judicature has also come that on the executive and legislative. Starkly seen in the Vietnam War and Watergate is the power that presidents were able to accrue protected by the umbrella of executive privilege. Now fifty years after continuous growth in the powers of the American presidency, congress, recognizing the danger, has moved to challenge and trim presidential power through its investigative committees, its legislation, its hold over the purse, and its ultimate resort to impeachment.

These recent judicial, executive, and legislative developments have refocussed the attention of historian and layman on the enduring importance of constitutional and legal history. Most of the medieval legal and governmental problems—due process, an independent judiciary, and law enforcement—concern us today as do also executive privilege (called the royal prerogative in the Middle Ages), a responsible bureaucracy, and the taxes levied by federal, state, and local government. These and other issues, fundamental as long ago as Magna Carta or before, illustrate how much our lives are influenced and controlled by the courts, the presidency, and congress.

A response to the reviving interest in constitutional and legal history, this new edition also answers the need to update what was written twenty years ago. Subsequent research has revised fact and interpretation, especially for that period from the late fourteenth century to 1485. Long neglected by constitutional and legal historians, this century of history has now received its due as a transitional period when the Middle Ages were waning, when medieval ways of life and modes of thought were giving way to others characteristic of a more modern age. This edition reflects, therefore, new interpretations reached and information unearthed during the past twenty years. Since there have now appeared a number of fine bibliographical guides and works that comprehensively note all the pertinent books and articles, it has been possible to delete the many articles originally included in the bibliographies for the various sections and to include only the principal books and a few articles either particularly seminal or concerned with subjects not treated in books. These bibliographical guides are noted in the General Bibliography. Because the organization of the first edition was generally appreciated, it has been retained. So also have the references to the *Sources of English Constitutional History* by Stephenson and Marcham because the new collections of sources in English translation that have appeared are not as easy to use.

Hopefully this revised edition will remind the student that history does not repeat itself but that people have always had to face similar problems. Ignorance of the past is also ignorance of the present, that time of which one is a part.

BRYCE LYON

George Washington's Birthday, 1979

PREFACE TO FIRST EDITION

The task of writing a book on English constitutional and legal history fell to me as the result of a chance remark made one day to the late Professor Carl Stephenson that there was need for such a book and that he was the one to write it. He was asked to write such a history only a few years before his death but, already in poor health, he felt unable to accept the invitation and persuaded me to attempt the book. Though beset with misgivings, I undertook the task out of a strong feeling that it would fill a need for students still courageous enough to register for the formidable subject of English constitutional history. Not since the second edition of A. B. White's *The Making of the English Constitution* appeared in 1925 has an American scholar written a text on the constitutional history of medieval England. There has long been need for a treatment of this subject more advanced than that found in the usual surveys by American scholars and less difficult than that written by the majority of English scholars. Somewhere between these two approaches I have set my course.

No claim is made for new viewpoints or interpretations of English constitutional history. My objective has been to summarize the best modern scholarly opinion on the numerous problems connected with English medieval institutions. Only in a few cases where I have made a special study of certain institutions have I advanced ideas and arguments solely my own. This book differs from others mainly in its emphasis upon the importance of administrative history. Since the great studies of Tout, Willard, and others we have come to understand the advantage in knowing something about English medieval administration. I have strived to emphasize the close relation between routine government administration and the development of the law courts, parliament, and various departments of state.

This text, written as a companion volume to Stephenson and Marcham, *Sources of English Constitutional History*, is the first to make extensive use of the documents in this collection of sources. By referring the student to the documents when they are discussed, I have hoped that he will come to learn that there is a relation between what the documents say and what he reads in the text. Perhaps he will also come to realize that the great story of English constitutional history can be comprehended only after the significant records have been read, studied, and pondered. To facilitate use of the source book of Stephenson and Marcham I have followed its general organization. There are six parts: The Anglo-Saxon Period; The Norman Kings;

Henry II and His Sons; Henry III and Edward I; Edward II, Edward III, and Richard II; and The Houses of Lancaster and York. Each part is systematically arranged into chapters that deal with the principal themes of English constitutional history during the Middle Ages. For each part there is a chapter explaining the nature of the principal sources so that the student will have some idea of the purpose served by the records and of their importance for constitutional history. Then follows a brief chapter on political history intended to give the student some grasp of the background before which the institutions and the law were taking form. Each part then has a chapter on central administration, on local government, and on the law. Where there has been need for variation in this organization and where chapters on special subjects have been required, I have felt free to modify and to add. Obviously the Norman period cannot be understood satisfactorily unless one knows what is meant by Norman feudalism; I have therefore included a chapter on the feudalization of England. In the parts on the fourteenth and fifteenth centuries when the development of parliament was the principal theme of constitutional history, I have devoted long chapters to the maturing and elaboration of parliamentary institutions. Constant attention has thus been given to arrangement and organization with the aim of helping the student to sort out the main threads from the tangled skein that is English constitutional history and to carry away with him after his final examination some orderly impressions about the common law, king, and parliament.

Finally, I want to say a few words about the bibliography. To the teacher and to the seasoned student it will be obvious that I have been very selective. I have been so for good reason. I see no sense in perpetuating what amounts to a fairy story comparable to *The Emperor's New Clothes*, that extensive and detailed bibliographies are of great service to the teacher and the student. To parade hundreds of learned monographs and articles before the reader is folly. The teacher should be relatively familiar with many of the books and articles. And, from the books here cited, the eager student can soon obtain references to more books than he will ever have time to read. Fully cognizant that I will be criticized for not including the most obscure note in some learned journal on an unnoticed charter of William the Conqueror, I have arranged a selective bibliography into seven parts. The first, which immediately follows the preface, lists the standard books that treat the entire medieval period. Then at the end of each of the six parts appears a more specialized bibliography on the institutions peculiar to the period under consideration. This arrangement has rendered unnecessary a bibliography for each chapter and has precluded the repetition of works pertinent for numerous chapters.

To indicate specifically my debt to the learned books and articles from which this book has been constructed is impossible. The discerning reader will recognize how great is the debt to Stubbs, Maitland, Tout, Holdsworth, and the scores of other masters who have labored in the field of English constitutional history and who have contributed to its formidable corpus of historical literature. To all who have written on the constitutional history of medieval England I express my gratitude. But even with such excellent scholarly assistance this book would have foundered had it not been for my wife, who edited and typed the manuscript. What merit it has in style and accuracy is due to her.

BRYCE LYON

Saint Hilary's Day, 1959

GENERAL BIBLIOGRAPHY

Bibliographical Guides

Since most of the standard works cited in the bibliographies for the various sections of this book contain excellent references to the voluminous writing on English constitutional history, only more recent guides will be noted here. The most comprehensive, *A Bibliography of English History to 1485*, E. B. Graves, ed. (Oxford, 1975), is a revision of Charles Gross, *The Sources and Literature of English History from the Earliest Times to about 1485*, a work not revised since 1915. The Conference on British Studies is beginning to issue a series of *Bibliographical Handbooks* of which two on medieval England have appeared: Michael Altschul, *Anglo-Norman England, 1066–1154* (Cambridge, 1969) and Bertie Wilkinson, *The High Middle Ages in England, 1154–1377* (Cambridge, 1978). Also published under its auspices is *Changing Views on British History: Essays on Historical Writing since 1939*, E. C. Furber, ed. (Cambridge, Mass., 1966), a volume especially valuable because the essays discuss and place in perspective the writings. The medieval period is dealt with by Bryce Lyon, "From Hengist and Horsa to Edward of Caernarvon," and by Margaret Hastings, "High History or Hack History: England in the Later Middle Ages." See also S. B. Chrimes and I. A. Roots, *English Constitutional History: A Select Bibliography*, Historical Association Helps, No. 58 (London, 1958).

General Histories of Medieval England

The most scholarly and comprehensive history of medieval England is *The Oxford History of England* edited by G. N. Clark. All the volumes on the period before 1485 have appeared: R. G. Collingwood and J. N. L. Myres, *Roman Britain and the English Settlements*, 2d ed. (Oxford, 1937), F. M. Stenton, *Anglo-Saxon England, c. 550–1087*, 3d ed. (Oxford, 1970), A. L. Poole, *From Domesday Book to Magna Carta, 1087–1216*, 2d ed. (Oxford, 1955), F. M. Powicke, *The Thirteenth Century, 1216–1307*, 2d ed. (Oxford, 1962), May McKisack, *The Fourteenth Century, 1307–1399* (Oxford, 1959), and E. F. Jacob, *The Fifteenth Century, 1399–1485* (Oxford, 1961). Shorter and less comprehensive is the Nelson Series edited by Christopher Brooke and D. M. Smith: P. H. Blair, *Roman Britain and Early England: 55 B.C.–A.D. 871* (Edinburgh, 1963), Christopher Brooke, *From Alfred to Henry III: 871–1272* (Edinburgh, 1961), and George Holmes, *The Later Middle Ages, 1272–1485* (Edinburgh, 1962). Even shorter but very readable are the volumes in *The Pelican History of England*: I. A. Richmond, *Roman Britain* (Harmondsworth, 1955), Dorothy Whitelock, *The Beginnings of English Society* (Harmondsworth, 1952), D. M. Stenton, *English Society in the Early Middle Ages* (Harmondsworth, 1951), and A.

R. Myers, *England in the Later Middle Ages* (Harmondsworth, 1952). Another good series is the Longmans Green edited by W. N. Medlicott: D. J. V. Fisher, *The Anglo-Saxon Age* (London, 1973), Frank Barlow, *The Feudal Kingdom of England, 1042–1216* (London, 1955), and Bertie Wilkinson, *The Later Middle Ages in England, 1216–1485* (London, 1969). Good surveys are V. H. Green, *The Later Plantagenets* (London, 1955) and J. R. Lander, *Ancient and Medieval England: Beginnings to 1509* (New York, 1973).

Constitutional History

The classic work on the constitutional history of England with which any consideration of the subject must begin is William Stubbs, *The Constitutional History of England* (Oxford, 1874–1878), 3 vols. Although much of what Stubbs wrote, especially in vol. I, has been revised by subsequent research, his insights into constitutional history will never be superseded. Some sections of his history were revised by Charles Petit-Dutaillis and Georges Lefebvre, *Studies and Notes Supplementary to Stubbs' Constitutional History* (Manchester, 1923–1929), 3 vols., itself in need of revision. For an evaluation of the work of Stubbs see Helen Cam, "Stubbs Seventy Years Later," *Cambridge Historical Journal*, IX (1948), 129–147, and J. G. Edwards, *William Stubbs*, Historical Association Helps, No. 22 (London, 1952). The short classic by F. W. Maitland, *The Constitutional History of England* (London, 1908) has a directness and simplicity in its explanation of English institutions not found in most works. For advanced students there is J. E. A. Joliffe, *The Constitutional History of Medieval England*, 4th ed. (London, 1961). The most recent comprehensive history with a pronounced Stubbsian flavor is Bertie Wilkinson's *The Constitutional History of England 1216–1399* (London, 1948–1958), 3 vols. Appearing later was another volume entitled *Constitutional History of England in the Fifteenth Century* (New York, 1964). These four volumes are of particular worth because they contain translations of pertinent records. The best short history by an English scholar, which unfortunately goes only to 1272, is that of G. O. Sayles, *The Medieval Foundations of England*, rev. ed. (London, 1950). Still important are A. B. White, *The Making of the English Constitution*, 2d ed. (New York, 1925), W. A. Morris, *Constitutional History of England to 1216* (New York, 1930), and S. B. Chrimes, *English Constitutional History*, 2d ed. (London, 1953).

Administrative History

The pioneer and indispensable work on administrative history is T. F. Tout, *Chapters in the Administrative History of Mediaeval England* (Manchester, 1920–1933), 6 vols. S. B. Chrimes offers a brief and scholarly treatment of the subject in his *Introduction to the Administrative History of Medieval England*, 3d ed. (Oxford, 1966).

Legal History

An incomparable history of English law from the Anglo-Saxons to the reign of Edward I is Frederick Pollock and F. W. Maitland, *The History of English Law Before the Time of Edward I*, 2d ed. (Cambridge, 1895), 2 vols. When reissued in paperback at Cambridge in 1968 it included an introduction by S. F. C. Milsom showing Maitland's influence on legal study and the ways in which he has been revised. For an evaluation of Maitland as an historian see T. F. T. Plucknett, "Maitland's View of Law and History," *Law Quarterly Review*, LXVII (1951), 179–194, Helen Cam, *Selected Essays of F. W. Maitland* (Cambridge, 1957), and the introduction by Bryce Lyon to the paperback edition of Maitland's *Domesday Book and Beyond* (New York, 1966). Also good for medieval English law is W. S. Holdsworth, *A History of English Law*, 7th rev. ed. (London, 1956), vol. I; 3d rev. ed. (London, 1923), vols. II and III. For a shorter treatment see T. F. T. Plucknett, *A Concise History of the Common Law*, 5th rev. ed. (London, 1956). For the common law's development see S. F. C. Milsom, *Historical Foundations of the Common Law* (London, 1969) and R. C. van Caenegem, *The Birth of the Common Law* (Cambridge, 1973). See also Alan Harding, *The Law Courts of Medieval England* (London, 1973) and *Social History of English Law* (London, 1966).

Collections of Sources

Those desiring to read more extensively in the sources than is possible in the source book of Stephenson and Marcham should turn to the following good collections with translations of the records. The most comprehensive, complete with bibliographies and critical introductions, is *English Historical Documents* under the general editorship of D. C. Douglas. All the volumes on the Middle Ages have now appeared: Dorothy Whitelock, *English Historical Documents, c. 500–1042* (London, 1955), Douglas and G. W. Greenaway, *English Historical Documents, 1042–1189* (London, 1953), Harry Rothwell, *English Historical Documents, 1189–1327* (London, 1975), and A. R. Myers, *English Historical Documents, 1327–1485* (London, 1969). On the later Middle Ages is the collection by S. B. Chrimes and A. L. Brown, *Select Documents of English Constitutional History, 1307–1485* (Oxford, 1961). Those who read Latin and Old French should consult William Stubbs, *Select Charters and Other Illustrations of English Constitutional History*, 9th rev. ed., H. W. C. Davis, ed. (Oxford, 1929). Many good translations are in the series *Medieval Classics* under the general editorship of V. H. Galbraith, R. A. B. Mynors, and C. N. L. Brooke. There are two fine introductions on the nature of constitutional and legal records: V. H. Galbraith, *An Introduction to the Use of the Public Records* (Oxford, 1934) and *Studies in the Public Records* (London, 1948). Even more detailed are *Guide to the Contents of the Public Record Office*, Her Majesty's Stationery Office (London, 1963), 2 vols., and Hilary Jenkinson, *Guide to the Public Records* (London, 1949).

Part One

THE ANGLO-SAXON PERIOD

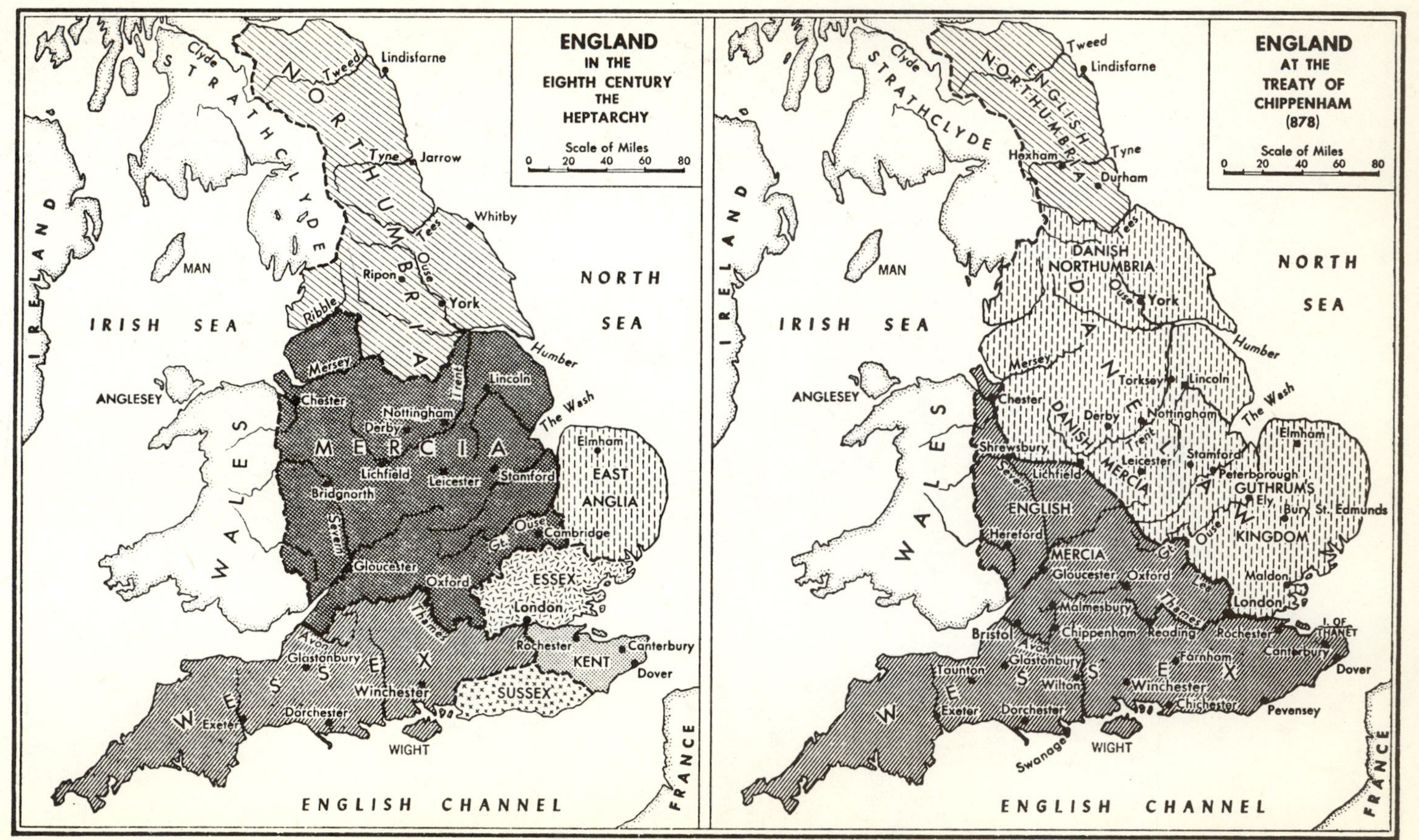
ENGLAND
IN THE
EIGHTH CENTURY
THE
HEPTARCHY
Scale of Miles
0 20 40 60 80
NORTHUMBRIA
STRATHCLYDE
MERCIA
EAST ANGLIA
ESSEX
KENT
SUSSEX
WESSEX
WALES
IRELAND
IRISH SEA
NORTH SEA
ENGLISH CHANNEL
FRANCE
MAN
ANGLESEY
WIGHT
Clyde
Tweed
Lindisfarne
Tyne
Jarrow
Tees
Whitby
Ouse
Ripon
York
Ribble
Humber
Mersey
Trent
Lincoln
Chester
Nottingham
Derby
The Wash
Elmham
Lichfield
Leicester
Stamford
Bridgnorth
Severn
Gt. Ouse
Cambridge
Gloucester
Oxford
London
Thames
Avon
Rochester
Canterbury
Dover
Glastonbury
Winchester
Dorchester
Exeter
ENGLAND
AT THE
TREATY OF
CHIPPENHAM
(878)
Scale of Miles
0 20 40 60 80
ENGLISH NORTHUMBRIA
STRATHCLYDE
DANISH NORTHUMBRIA
DANELAW
DANISH MERCIA
GUTHRUM'S KINGDOM
ENGLISH MERCIA
WESSEX
WALES
IRELAND
IRISH SEA
NORTH SEA
ENGLISH CHANNEL
FRANCE
MAN
ANGLESEY
WIGHT
I. OF THANET
Clyde
Tweed
Lindisfarne
Hexham
Tyne
Durham
Tees
Ouse
York
Humber
Mersey
Torksey
Lincoln
Chester
Derby
Nottingham
The Wash
Trent
Shrewsbury
Leicester
Stamford
Elmham
Peterborough
Ely
Bury St. Edmunds
Severn
Lichfield
Hereford
Gt. Ouse
Gloucester
Oxford
Lea
Maldon
London
Malmesbury
Thames
Bristol
Chippenham
Reading
Rochester
Canterbury
Dover
Avon
Taunton
Glastonbury
Wilton
Farnham
Winchester
Chichester
Pevensey
Exeter
Dorchester
Swanage

I

The Sources for Early English Institutions

THE historical obscurity of the early Middle Ages has led modern scholars to welcome many new techniques in historical research. The written records, always the standard medium for historians, have been supplemented by archaeological, geographical, and linguistic evidence. Disciplines such as sociology, economics, anthropology, and agronomy have uncovered new evidence and given importance to that hitherto neglected as arid. Such development has relegated numerous books to historical limbo and demanded extensive revision of the classics. And yet this revision of English institutional history necessitated by new evidence is minor when compared to that caused by changing interpretation. The historian today cannot write history as did his Victorian predecessors who labored enthusiastically under the influence of romanticism, nationalism, and democracy; nor can he accept as confidently as did historians of several decades ago economic cause as the principal explanation for the growth of such English institutions as parliament. He is more inclined to be eclectic, giving due recognition to any explanation based upon solid evidence. To keep pace with the age and to maintain relevance the history of English institutions will thus continue to be rewritten. Though new techniques of research and new interpretations will vary the pattern and emphasis, fundamentally such history must always rest upon written evidence.

1. NONNARRATIVE SOURCES

The evidence for early English institutions may be classified as narrative (for example, chronicles and biographies) and nonnarrative (for example, charters and laws), the latter being far more important. Unsurpassed as nonnarrative evidence are the dooms or laws of the Anglo-Saxon kings beginning with Ethelbert, first Christian king of Kent.[1] Composed about 602–603 in the form of a code, these laws expressed the unwritten custom of centuries, custom similar to that governing the principal Germanic tribes on the Continent. There was a code drawn up between 673 and 685 by two other Kent-

[1] For the dooms see Stephenson and Marcham, *Sources of English Constitutional History*, nos. 1–9, 11–13. Henceforth this book will be cited as SM.

ish kings, Hlothhere and Eadric, and yet another for Kent by King Wihtred in 695. A fine collection of laws (688–694) has been preserved from the reign of Ine, the king of Wessex. Two centuries later the great Alfred, also king of Wessex (871–899), published more laws including Ine's code and certain laws of Ethelbert and Offa, king of the Mercians (757–796). Offa's laws have all disappeared except those preserved by Alfred. There then follows a series of laws promulgated by Alfred's successors in the tenth century, the most noteworthy being those of Edward the Elder (899–925), Athelstan (925–939), Edmund (939–946), Edgar (959–975), and Ethelred the Redeless (979–1016). This impressive list is terminated by the laws of Canute (1016–1035) that are mainly a collection of those previously published. As Wessex came to control all of England in the tenth century, so too did her laws come to have force throughout the island, although never to the exclusion of local custom. Unlike the so-called *leges barbarorum*, which were a codification of Germanic custom written in Latin, the Anglo-Saxon laws were drawn up in the vernacular. In addition to the laws themselves there is scattered information about Anglo-Saxon law in private compilations of customs and formularies (custumals) written in the century after the Norman Conquest to help explain Anglo-Saxon law to the new rulers. The *Laws of Edward the Confessor* is perhaps the best-known compilation of this type.

Second in importance to the laws are the charters or landbooks which record the donation of land and its appurtenances by kings and lesser persons.[2] These donations went most frequently to the church, which preserved by the meticulous care of its records most of the charters we now have. Private individuals also received charters but only a few are extant. In the Anglo-Saxon period both royal and private charters generally took the form of a diploma written in Latin and describing in a very solemn and artificial manner the creation or transfer of an estate of land. Modeled at first upon the private deeds of the later Roman Empire, the charter gradually acquired a pronounced ecclesiastical flavor. The preamble containing the grantor's reason for the donation abounded in pious references proving the blessedness of giving, and in references to classical mythology. The dispositive proper set forth in minute detail the boundaries of the land. Lastly came the sanction, which appealed to any and all ecclesiastical penalties should the will of the grantor be thwarted. We thus find a sanction in a charter of 846 stating: "If anyone . . . shall with sacrilegious presumption attempt to pervert or to make invalid the conferment of this munificence, may he be separated from the community of the Church of Christ and from the fellowship of the saints here and in the future, and may his part be set with misers and robbers and may he be associated with Judas Iscariot who betrayed the Lord." Undoubtedly the practice of drawing up charters to record donations stemmed from the influence of the church and such of its leaders

[2] SM, no. 15.

as Theodore of Tarsus, archbishop of Canterbury (668–690), whose education in the eastern part of the Roman Empire familiarized him with Roman legal tradition and practice. The first royal charter dates from 679 and from the period down to 1066 hundreds of others are extant.

During the course of the eleventh century another form of charter gradually superseded the diploma; this was the writ.[3] Couched in the form of a simple letter, it was brief and authenticated by a seal which, by the eleventh century, had become pendant, that is, hanging down from the bottom. Towards the end of the tenth century Bishop Oswald of Worcester used the writ for leasing land, and about the same time one finds wills, testaments, and deeds in the same form. The first extant royal writ is one of Ethelred the Redeless addressed to local officials concerned with the administration of an area which has received a royal grant or privilege. Compared to the cumbersome diploma, the writ was an amazingly efficient document, able to do in a few lines what a diploma could scarcely do in scores. Unknown to the Continent before the Normans adopted it, the writ became one of the chief instruments of the strong Norman-Angevin administration both in England and on the Continent. If the dooms indicate the substance of early English law, the charters allow us to see how the law operated in civil cases, to reconstruct legal procedure in court, and to learn of royal rights and of the relation between king and local administrative officers.

The single most valuable record of the Middle Ages for social and economic institutions is *Domesday Book*. Compiled as a result of an inquest ordered by William the Conqueror in 1086, it was to provide him with an estimate of the annual revenue due from his new realm. A reservoir of information on the manorial economy and its social classes, *Domesday Book* is also valuable for early urban institutions and the royal rights throughout England. It supplies us with a picture of England for 1066 when Edward the Confessor still lived as well as for the year 1086. We can thus, as Maitland expressed it, look "beyond" *Domesday Book* into Anglo-Saxon history and at times follow the technique of Seebohm, who worked "from the known to the unknown." In addition to *Domesday Book* we have certain records such as the *Cambridgeshire Survey* and the *Ely Inquest* which are actually the returns made in response to the inquest by tenants holding land of William and from which *Domesday Book* was compiled. Other miscellaneous records of an economic nature help to enlarge our picture of Anglo-Saxon society. Probably the most informative is one drawn up some time before the Conquest called *The Rights and Ranks of People* which provides a detailed description of manorial organization during the reign of Edward the Confessor. We learn of social conditions from surveys made by religious establishments such as that of the abbey of Bury Saint Edmunds (1045–1098). A particularly noteworthy document, known as the *Burghal Hidage*,

[3] SM, no. 15E.

supplies one of the few clues we have for understanding the Anglo-Saxon borough; it lists all the boroughs under the rule of Edward the Elder in the first quarter of the tenth century. This magnificent collection of documents, a collection unequaled on the Continent except during the reigns of Charlemagne and his son Louis the Pious, helps one to pursue the course of early English institutions. To bring life to this skeleton of documents, however, the narrative records are required; in them we can observe the efficient Alfred at work and discern the weakness of Ethelred the Redeless.

2. NARRATIVE SOURCES

For a knowledge of the social, economic, and political organization of the Angles, Saxons, and Jutes before they came to England in the fifth century, we can but assume that what Caesar and Tacitus said about other Germanic tribes is valid also for them. Writing his *Gallic Wars* in 51 B.C. Caesar described in five short passages the tribes he encountered while fighting in Gaul. This evidence, providing a glimpse of a small segment of the Germans beyond the Rhine River, is scarcely basis for wide generalization. A century and a half later the famous historian Tacitus described the Germans far more adequately. His *Germania* is the principal source on the Germans until the barbarian codes are set down some five hundred years later. At least twenty-four chapters bear directly on law and institutions. We must discount as propaganda many of his eloquent tributes to the noble German savage, but his remarks on the tribal government seem accurate when tested against later evidence. Our knowledge of the Germans is further increased by the excellent *History* of the Roman soldier Ammianus Marcellinus composed towards the end of the fourth century, the *Gallic Chronicle* (c. 450), Zosimus' *History* (c. 500), and the work of the Greek historian Procopius, completed in the middle of the sixth century.

Unmatched as an English narrative source is *The Anglo-Saxon Chronicle*. Written in Anglo-Saxon, it records the yearly events of Britain from Caesar's invasion in 54 B.C. to the end of King Stephen's reign in 1154. There are seven extant manuscripts of the *Chronicle*. Down to 891 all were apparently derived from a set of English annals composed during Alfred's reign. After 891 each manuscript begins to differ, no doubt because from this time on the *Chronicle* was continued by scribes located in churches scattered about England. It is also apparent that the manuscripts were circulated yearly from church to church to facilitate a broader coverage of news. This practice produced a uniformity of content for certain periods even after 891. Without doubt the intellectual revival sparked by the energetic Alfred was responsible for the conception of this fine annalistic history, but Alfred himself cannot be credited with founding the *Chronicle*. Regardless of origin, we are thankful to have this record; without it we would be hard pressed to reconstruct the political history of Anglo-Saxon England.

The information imparted by the British priest Gildas some time before 547 in the work *On the Destruction and Conquest of Britain* is often too vague and unreliable for help in solving the chief problems connected with the settlement of Britain, but the work deserves mention because of its references to the Angles and Saxons during the fifth and sixth centuries when they were winning Britain away from the Celts. If used with caution, because of its numerous errors of fact and inconsistencies, the *History of the Britons* is a useful source in the form of notes on Northumbrian history and regnal lists for the early English kingdoms. It is now fairly well established that the author was a writer called Nennius, who may have written his work as early as the latter part of the eighth century, although some scholars would date it as late as the second half of the tenth. Although some doubt has recently been expressed about Asser's *Life of King Alfred* being a contemporary record, it does appear to have been written about 893. Asser was an ecclesiastic referred to by Alfred as "my Bishop Asser" and as one who helped in the chores of governing. Though inferior in perspective, organization, and style to Einhard's *Life of Charlemagne*, Asser's biography is a good portrait of an Anglo-Saxon king and, like Einhard's work, particularly valuable because written by a close companion of the king. Through it we can see what lay behind Alfred's extensive reorganization of government and can learn of his relations with court and household.

There is little reason to discuss such post-Conquest Latin histories as the *History of the Kings* ascribed to Simeon of Durham, Roger of Hoveden's *Annals*, Roger of Wendover's *Flowers of History*, William of Malmesbury's *On the Acts of Kings*, Florence of Worcester's *Chronicon ex Chronicis*, and Henry of Huntingdon's *History of the English*, except that in addition to drawing much information from the works just described they also made use of various annals and other sources bearing upon the history of northern England which have long since disappeared and incorporated traditions which otherwise would not have come down to us. To these chroniclers should be added the Norman historians who while concentrating on Normandy still supplied many important details on the last years of Anglo-Saxon history. The works of two contemporaries of William the Conqueror are of particular value for this period; William of Jumièges' *History of the Normans* covers the years between 1028 and 1072, and the biography of the Conqueror by William of Poitiers, entitled *The Deeds of William, Duke of the Normans and King of the English*, helps to interpret the events leading up to the Conquest of 1066. Even more important, however, is *The Ecclesiastical History* of Ordericus Vitalis, a monk of the Norman abbey of Saint Evroul. Ordericus writes best on the period after 1066 but he still enables us to verify the writings of his two predecessors.

Not to be overlooked as a historical source is the rich body of Anglo-Saxon and Scandinavian literature, predominantly in the form of poetry.

Though contributing little to our knowledge of English institutions, the Scandinavian scaldic verse enriches our concept of the Danish and Norwegian conquerors of England from the eighth century through the reign of Canute and his two successors. Like such Anglo-Saxon epic poetry as the familiar *Beowulf* and *The Battle of Maldon* or the lesser-known *The Wanderer* and *The Seafarer*, the scaldic verse introduces us to the customs and ideals of aristocratic society and to the closely knit organization called the *comitatus*.

The ecclesiastical sources, although primarily concerned with church affairs, frequently refer to contemporary politics. Without Bede's *Ecclesiastical History of the English Nation* the period to 731 would be only a hodgepodge of ill-assorted facts gathered mainly from *The Anglo-Saxon Chronicle* and other rather unreliable sources. A man of encyclopedic knowledge, Bede was the most remarkable scholar of western Europe in the eighth century. Before he composed the *History* between 725 and 731 he had already established himself as an authority in theology and ecclesiastical administration, in science and chronology; he thoroughly knew his Greek and Latin. Reared by the beneficent and sage Benedict Biscop in the Northumbrian monastery of Jarrow, he spent almost his entire life there. In many respects Bede was a captive of the eighth-century climate of opinion; he believed in the miraculous, in the outlandish cures for maladies, and in the superstitions so rife in that age. All this we could expect; what is remarkable in such a milieu is his obvious intellectual maturity and use of common sense. He tells us the source for most of his stories, he establishes his evidence for us, and when he is uncertain of a tradition or source he so informs us. He, and others for him, ransacked libraries and archives tracking down reliable information. He was a discriminating man in an undiscriminating age; it was a long time before the Middle Ages again saw his equal. Stenton has said that the quality which makes Bede great is "his astonishing power of co-ordinating the fragments of information which came to him through tradition, the relation of friends, or documentary evidence. In an age when little was attempted beyond the registration of fact, he had reached the conception of history."

This summary of the written evidence has naturally been selective; other sources less significant have been neglected. Sources such as saints' lives, the correspondence of holy men like Boniface and the learned Alcuin, and the papal bulls contribute little to a history of institutions. More rewarding is a study of other types of evidence to supplement the written records.

3. SUPPLEMENTARY EVIDENCE

For the pre-Alfredian period archaeological evidence is essential for helping to fill in gaps and for substantiating or refuting facts and ideas gleaned from the only written evidence at that time—a few miscellaneous records for scattered periods of time and areas. Neither Tacitus nor Bede, each writing three hundred years from the period of the migration of the Angles,

Saxons, and Jutes, describes satisfactorily their location on the Continent. Tacitus merely mentions the Angles when giving a long list of German tribes; Bede vaguely located the Jutes in Jutland and the Angles and Saxons in Frisia (modern Holland), in Denmark, and along the northern coast of Germany between the Elbe and Rhine rivers. As a result of extensive archaeological field work and study by German and Dutch scholars we now know that the Jutes did not come from Jutland but from the Elbe-Weser region inhabited also by Saxons in the fifth century. The Saxons, originally from Holstein, not only held the Elbe-Weser region which they occupied during the third century but took over Frisia and went farther west into Flanders and the area around Boulogne (northern Belgium and northeastern France). The Angles started from Schleswig about the same time and moved southward to mingle with the Saxons; the result was a close amalgamation of the two tribes which makes it difficult to distinguish between them when they arrived in Britain. The archaeologist has, furthermore, helped to pinpoint the settlement of these tribes in Britain. A specialist familiar with the artifacts and customs of these people has relatively little trouble in establishing, for example, that the Jutes occupied Kent and that the Saxons spread into southwestern England. And, indeed, a rich discovery such as the Sutton Hoo burial ship found in East Anglia in 1939 greatly aids the historian in evaluating the level of Angle culture in the early seventh century before it was influenced by the Christian.

With the appearance in 1895 of August Meitzen's fundamental work on medieval agrarian history, historians have been more sensitive to the value of topographical study to explain medieval field systems. In the last forty years such study has also been successfully applied to castles and towns. With towns it has helped to determine more precisely urban expansion as well as the date of origin. In regard to Anglo-Saxon boroughs or towns it has tended to show that real towns, that is, areas with true urban life, developed much later than previously supposed. Since the First World War aerial photography has greatly facilitated topographical study, especially in the reconstruction of field patterns and the outlines of castles, marked now merely by earthen embankments where once stood powerful wooden or stone fortifications. More than any other work Marc Bloch's study in 1931 on French medieval agrarian history shows the benefits of aerial photography. The technological advances resulting from the Second World War have made possible even more extensive application of photography to historical research.

Physical geography and agronomy offer much vital information for plotting the early conquest of Britain. To determine the distribution of settlements one must have a knowledge of the terrain, that is, where were the principal forests, fens, marshes, and rivers, and of the quality of the soil. For example, the poor clay of the Midlands would seem to account for its sparse population, and this may in turn explain the eclipse of both the Mercian and the Northumbrian kingdoms. Other kingdoms were long permitted to develop in isolation because surrounded by natural barriers of wood and water. Knowing from agronomic research that the Saxon economy on the Continent was based upon winter fodder secured from alluvial water meadows, we can thus understand why the Saxons never originally settled on upland sites in Wessex but invariably concentrated in the river valleys where water meadows provided winter fodder. Such knowledge helps us to trace the advance of the Saxon invaders up the rivers and streams of southwestern England.

In the years after the First World War great emphasis was put upon the study of personal and place names. By delving into the origin of names peculiar to certain regions one can often account for distribution of settlements. Bede, for instance, stated that the Jutes settled in Kent and southern Hampshire. The old Jute place names found in Hampshire are like those of Kent and so verify Bede. We have noted that the Angles and Saxons mingled while still on the Continent, eventually blending their cultures. After they arrived in Britain the process continued by means of intertribal migration and settlement; a *mélange* of Angle and Saxon personal and place names reflects this close association. But place-name study has proved most rewarding when focused upon the problem of the survival of Celtic culture and its influence after the Conquest. Here and there Celtic names survived but by and large they disappeared. This does not mean that the Celtic population was wiped out but strongly indicates that there was no Celtic influence on Anglo-Saxon institutions.

The sources summarized in this chapter are the principal ones with which the historian must deal when studying the development of early English institutions. If in the following chapters questions and problems frequently seem to be posed to which satisfactory answers are not given, it should be borne in mind that the Anglo-Saxons were not as record-conscious as their descendants. Furthermore, it should be emphasized that the custom and life they saw fit to put into writing were not intended as a collection for the use of historians. The information set down, whether in law or in charter, was deemed sufficient to convey to men of that day what was meant or intended; there is no detailed apparatus explaining the legal sense of a doom which to us may seem totally without rhyme or reason. But why should there be? These men knew their dooms as we are expected to know our most common statutes. Actually such shortcomings in the evidence are not without their compensations. Except for forgeries we are certain that the documentary records faithfully reflect the intent of the men responsible for them. Seldom are we burdened with the impediments to research in the modern age—underlying causes, propaganda, deceitful memoirs, and the double-talk of politicians and statesmen. These Ango-Saxon politicians and administrators were infinitely more forthright than their counterparts of today and for this we should be grateful even as we sweat our way through sac and soc, toll and team, infangenetheof and utfangenetheof.

II

Germanic Foundations of English Institutions

HOW much did Roman civilization influence English institutions? Like the explanation for the fall of the Roman Empire in the West, this has been a classic problem of historiography. It involves various aspects of Roman survival for which numerous theories have been advanced. Traditionally, historians who have seen Roman civilization as a force in the development of English institutions have been labeled Romanists; those who have seen only German origins, Germanists. In the late nineteenth century there was a no man's land between the two schools of historians and each advanced extravagant theories for which there was no evidence. In 1878, for example, the work of Coote entitled *The Romans of Britain* built many castles in the air. Only a vivid imagination could derive the Anglo-Saxon shires and their administrative officers from the Roman provincial organization and the *comites*. And even the most ardent Germanists could not subscribe to the thesis of Kemble that the mark was "the original basis on which all Teutonic societies are founded." During the twentieth century both schools have abandoned much ground but the Germanists have retreated less; the available evidence still shows that they are correct in seeing a predominantly Germanic strain in English institutions. There will be opportunity later to evaluate much of the evidence bearing upon this problem but let us now see why English institutions were built upon a Germanic foundation.

The Visigoths, Ostrogoths, Franks, Lombards, and Burgundians, who established kingdoms upon the remnants of the Roman Empire in the West during the course of the fifth, sixth, and seventh centuries, had long been familiar with Roman civilization. Before entering the Empire they had lived along the frontier, coming into contact with the Romans through trade and war. As military allies (*foederati*), they were further introduced to Roman life; as conquerors, they took over a culture of which they at least had some appreciation and which they recognized as superior to their own. And in winning such lands as Italy, France, and Spain they settled in the core of the Empire, that part most intensely Romanized. The result was, at first, two cultures living side by side each with its own law. In this age the concept of the "personality of the law" prevailed. There was Roman law for the Roman, but for the Visigoth and Burgundian there was Germanic custom. The Germans might be political masters but they did not exterminate the Romans, who for a time certainly remained in the majority. Gradually the two cultures blended and in the process the Ostrogoths and Visigoths in particular abandoned much of their culture for the Roman. Though the other Germans were less Romanized, with all of them the Roman influence was strong. There was intermarriage, and as distinction between Roman and German was erased "personality of the law" gave way to "territoriality of the law." If one lived in Ostrogothic Italy, he was governed by the law prevailing there. Assuredly, even in Italy, southern France, and Spain, Germanic custom came to prevail and yet in numerous cases it incorporated or was influenced by Roman law.

The German chieftains became kings with Roman titles and surrounded themselves with functionaries and the paraphernalia of imperial pomp. Here and there the purple was donned. Court officials were given Roman titles like those of the officers sent out to govern the old Roman provinces. As under the Roman administration, the city-state (*civitas*) was retained as the principal unit of local government. Here were concentrated the bureaus and officers responsible for justice, finance, and daily administration. The late imperial system of taxation in kind, the *annona*, was continued and the Roman coinage remained in force or was mimicked. It would be tedious to elaborate further on the influence wielded by Roman institutions over the German; enough evidence has been presented to show that it was considerable. In no respect, however, were these kingdoms any more than pseudo copies of the Roman original; the Roman influence failed to penetrate below the top crust of German aristocracy. But there was Roman or imperial influence that survived the darkest days of Italy in the sixth century and the equally degenerate age of the last Merovingians. The coronation of Charlemagne as emperor at Rome on Christmas day 800 attests to the irresistible hold Rome still had over men. Largely responsible for the survival of Roman institutions after their initial glow had rubbed off was the Christian church, the one force that outlived the Empire. Having borrowed most of its ecclesiastical organization from Roman government, the church was admirably equipped to preserve the Roman heritage among the barbarians whom it proceeded to Christianize. From the first crossing of the Germans into the Empire the Classical-Christian-Germanic fusion that was to create the civilization of the Middle Ages was at work.

Across the Channel matters were to proceed much differently for centuries. In looking at the geographical disposition of the three principal conquerors of Britain—the Angles, Saxons, and Jutes—one notes that they were concentrated in northern Germany, Denmark, and Holland. These regions had never been a part of the Roman Empire nor had these tribes ever been in direct contact with the Romans. During the migrations between the second and fourth centuries the Franks, Lombards, and Burgundians had always been buffers between them and the Empire. The Germans who went to

Britain, therefore, were strangers to Rome and were thoroughly Teutonic in culture. It should be remembered that Caesar does not mention them and that Tacitus only vaguely admits to having known of the Angles. None of these tribes had as yet heard of Christianity.

What, then, awaited these Germans in Britain, a Roman province since its conquest in the middle of the first century A.D. by the Emperor Claudius? The same situation, one would assume, that awaited the Germans in the Roman provinces on the Continent. But in so far as we can determine, this was not the case. In southern and central Britain one finds evidence of strong Romanization. Archaeological study points to urban centers and villas on the Gallic pattern. The degree of civilization seems to have equaled that of the Continent. The fine mosaics, baths, houses, and artifacts compare favorably to those at the general Roman level. The urban centers were not, however, as dense as those on the Continent. Towards Scotland in the north, and Wales in the west, Roman civilization thins. In no part of Britain were the subjected Celts as Romanized as the Gauls; Roman culture and language seem hardly to have seeped down to them. The most satisfactory explanation for this cultural lag appears to be that Britain, last to be brought into the Empire, had consequently far less contact with the Romans than had, for example, Gaul. The distance from Rome was another factor. This province always seems to have been considered a military outpost, an island conquered to put an end to its being a refuge for rebellious Gallic leaders organizing revolt against Roman rule. We must admit that even if the Germans had landed in Roman Britain at the peak of its prosperity in the second century they would not have found the high level of civilization that existed on the Continent.

But the Germans did not land in Britain until the middle of the fifth century and in these 250 years Roman culture had undergone radical change. Long before effective Roman rule ceased in Britain, be the date A.D. 311, 350, 410, or 430, evidence points to a deteriorating civilization, just as it does on the Continent. Following the economic pattern of the western half of the Roman Empire, the economy of Britain degenerated in the third and fourth centuries. The towns—the heart and strength of the Roman system—ceased to be centers of flourishing commerce and industry. As economic communication ceased, the towns became isolated and gave way to the countryside. An urban money economy was replaced by an agrarian economy dominated by the large estate (*latifundium*) controlled by the powerful landowner and worked by free but economically dependent farmers, called *coloni*, who were supplemented by slaves. We must assume that the labor came from the Celtic population and a large segment of small Roman proprietors whose desperate economic status forced them to hand over their land and promise their services to the powerful man of the locality in return for minimal economic security and protection. We must also remember that as the economy fell apart so, too, did the local and central government. Deprived of adequate taxes, the administrative system decayed. For a time taxation in kind sufficed to pay the government officials but it was only a stopgap measure. Reduced to forcing senators (*curiales*) of the local municipal *curia* to fulfil the tasks of governing and making them responsible and financially liable for the collection of a stipulated annual tax from their *civitas*, the government ruined these men and drove them to the countryside. Towns became deserted except for the churches and their functionaries, military personnel, and a few stragglers. The towns completely lost their urban characteristics and survived only in fortification, decayed dwellings, and name. With no effective contact with the central government, which was often nonexistent for long periods when generals, governors, and legions fought for control of Rome or against the barbarians on the Continent, the local communities came under both the economic and the political control of the great landlord. He provided what law and order there was and all too frequently was nothing but a gangster surrounded by armed retainers. His fortified villa had replaced the town. Public power and law had become a matter of private power and law.

In the fifty years before the Germans started to conquer Britain it apparently was governed by the landlords, who succeeded in extending their power over large areas. No longer held in check by strong government, the Celts began to organize and to group themselves under leaders. Throughout the island civil wars raged between Roman and Celt, between Celt and Celt. Occasionally one leader would make himself overlord of most of Britain. The Celtic ruler Vortigern did this just prior to 450. The sources depict him as "a proud tyrant" fighting against the Picts and Scots in the north and arranging to settle Saxons in eastern Britain in order to secure military assistance. To such political instability came the Germans; effective Roman rule had long ceased. How could it be otherwise when there was no Roman government even in Italy? There was a survival of Roman culture and institutions but, as our examination of the evidence has shown, only on a level of bare subsistence. The upsurge of the Celts reveals how superficial had been the Roman occupation. There seems to be no other conclusion but that the Germans found an emaciated Roman culture which had been wasting away far more rapidly than on the Continent.

Now, we may ask, how much of the Roman culture was preserved by the Germans? Did Roman law influence Germanic custom? Did the chieftains model their newly won kingdoms upon the Roman administrative system? Did the urban remains and the villa system find a place in the German scheme of settlement and agrarian economy? Was the church a bridge between the old and the new? Numerous arguments have adduced evidence for the influence of Roman law upon Germanic; some scholars have even claimed to find Celtic elements in German law. The best answer to these claims is Maitland's well-known declaration: "Now the mere coincidence of particulars in early bodies of laws proves nothing beyond the resemblance of all institutions in certain ages." Beyond Celtic coincidences no scholar has been able to present any evidence that the Germans borrowed from Celtic custom, nor has anyone shown similarities in Celtic, early English, and Germanic laws of the Continent. The earliest records of Celtic law are, moreover, of a much later date than the Anglo-Saxon dooms. The Celtic argument rests upon not a scrap of solid evidence. Roman elements can be found in the Anglo-Saxon laws but not nearly to the extent that they appear, for instance, in the Visigothic and Ostrogothic. What elements of Roman legal influence are found, however, come from sources other than the province of Roman Britain; the infiltration was of a later date.

The first Roman influence stems from the introduction of Christianity into Anglo-Saxon England at the end of the sixth century. As all England was gradually Christianized and closer ties were established with the church on the Continent, particularly with the Holy See, we can detect a growing body of Roman legal ideas. But we should emphasize that it always appears in an ecclesiastical guise. Later such law was to be called canon law, that is, law meant for the guidance of the church but derived in great part from the Roman civil law. We must conclude that the imperial Roman law of the province of Britain had no influence upon Germanic custom, which remained for 150 years as purely Teutonic as it had been in northern Germany. This is indeed a striking contrast to what we have found in southern Europe. In England between 450 and 1066 there were six hundred years of predominantly, or rather exclusively, Anglo-Saxon law reinforced from time to time by other Germanic infusions. In the ninth and eleventh centuries the Germanic custom of the Danes was added; the relations with the Carolingians opened England to Frankish influence; and the Normans brought not only some Danish custom but what they had absorbed of the Frankish.

Nothing of the Roman administrative system can be found in the Anglo-Saxon kingdoms. In no respect is the continental development reproduced. The *civitas* cannot be equated with the shire or any other Anglo-Saxon administrative unit as it can be with a county or duchy on the Continent. It was many years before towns became important centers of local government. In England one finds neither the pseudo-Roman pomp nor the courts characteristic of the German kings on the Continent. When later the Anglo-Saxon kings affected Roman titles in their charters it resulted from ecclesiastical influence. The break between Roman imperial administration and German administration was complete.

We have already hinted that Roman towns played a negligible role in early English history. It has been noted that only in name, fortification, and reduced population did the town continue its existence. And such continuity is no evidence for real urban continuity. We cannot find what Myres would call "a continuity of civic consciousness" or what most historians would consider commercial or industrial life. The towns that the Germans found were dead and it was some time before they were to breathe new life into them.

Although topographical study of Roman urban sites is not nearly as complete as we should like, it does show that the Germans avoided towns for a long time, preferring to live outside them. Diggings have uncovered no Anglo-Saxon objects from Roman towns in the period of settlement during the fifth and sixth centuries; inevitably the remains are found outside the towns, evidence which confirms those early writers who tell us that the Germans seemed to fear walls and houses and avoided them like the plague. The Germans, therefore, seem not to have invigorated the rotting towns. Gildas particularly emphasizes a general destruction of towns in the fifth and sixth centuries when the Germans were in the midst of the conquest. Admittedly Gildas overdrew his picture of destruction and panic for the purpose of teaching a moral to his degenerate countrymen, but it appears that for the western part of Britain, with which he was familiar, his statements must be heeded. The evidence of Gildas is reinforced by Nennius and *The Anglo-Saxon Chronicle;* even in Kent where Britain was most urbanized such Roman towns as Canterbury and Rochester are not mentioned in the period of settlement. Colchester and London share a like fate; indeed, no attempts however ingenious have established any kind of urban continuity in London. We must wait until the time of Bede for evidence of economic activity. Until better evidence can be produced, we must accept Myres' conclusion that "the evidence for urban survival in these years has led . . . to a negative verdict." In the words of the historian Ammianus Marcellinus the towns were only "tombs surrounded by nets."

Archaeological and place-name evidence relative to Roman and British villas supports what we have said about the towns. In the first place the estate names of the villas have disappeared. If the invaders had taken over these estates, as they generally did on the Continent, certainly some of the names would have come down to us, even if in a German form. Numerous Gallo-Roman estates have given their names to small agrarian villages of modern France. A second and even better proof for the disintegration of the villa system is the fact that scarcely a site of a Roman villa has yielded up Saxon objects for the fifth and sixth centuries. The evidence of Saxons' taking over the Roman villa of Withington and retaining its organization seems to be an exceptional case. There is no reason why the Germans should not have settled upon the large estates but archaeological and place-name evidence so annuls this idea that one is not justified in thinking that they often did. For the present discussion the question involving the influence of Roman and British agrarian techniques such as the field systems is somewhat irrelevant. But it still should be noted that consensus of modern opinion sees no major influence over the German agrarian pattern. If there are similarities it is not so much because the Roman remained to guide the German but because the Germans found a system of agriculture not too foreign to their own.

On the Continent the church was the principal medium for the transfer of Roman culture to the Germans; in Britain not even this medium remained. It is still an open question whether during the height of the Roman occupation in Britain the church was as strong as it was in Italy, Gaul, and Spain; probably not. But however we argue, it is undeniable that the church almost disappeared from Britain in the fifth and sixth centuries. During that time the episcopal organization centered about the *civitas* cannot be found. This disintegration points also to the end of urban life. On the Continent urban life also came to a halt, but even in the darkest days bishops and their staffs resided in the fortified shells that once had been the heart of flourishing *civitates* and dioceses. In Britain Christianity was driven to the countryside as the Germans advanced. When the migrations ended, only in the Welsh west did the church survive, and there to continue without the episcopal form that was to distinguish it and the later Irish Christianity from the orthodox organization reintroduced by Augustine in 597. The heathens had supplanted the Christians. But the missionary zeal of Pope Gregory the Great sparked the work that finally united the Anglo-Saxon kingdoms to the community of orthodox Christianity in the seventh century. And even then there remained large pockets of heathen Germans to whom the missionaries had not yet brought the Christian faith.

But what happened to the Celts? We have already seen that having absorbed little Roman culture they were incapable of passing it on. As for their own culture, was it significant enough to influence the new masters? We know in law that it was not. But good work in archaeology plus some common sense has disposed of the old view of Freeman and the Germanists that the "English at the end of the sixth century had been as nearly extirpated as a nation can be." Evidently enough Celts remained to influence the Angles and Saxons in burial custom; excavations show that instead of cremating their dead they began to inhume some of them as was customary with the Celts. A marked revival of Celtic art that influenced the Germanic also points to survival of the Celts. Indeed, why should we look for the elimination of a people who characteristically occupied the lowest stratum of society, furnishing the large proportion of laborers for the landed estates? Such people never have much to win or lose by a change of masters; they suffer much less than men of substance who have to be eliminated by the conqueror. Is it not reasonable to suppose that the bands of Angles and Saxons who initially spread out over Britain found the Celts more useful alive than dead? Certainly for a time the invaders had no men to spare for agrarian duties. From the first they needed men to work the land for them while they got on with the business of fighting. After disposing of the Roman masters and those bands of Celts who fought them, the Angles and Saxons saw to it that the Celts produced food for them and did the menial labor. But in spite of believing in the survival of a considerable Celtic population, especially in the west, we must admit that the Celts passed on practically nothing of their own culture. What patterns of culture and organization we find corresponding to the Anglo-Saxon have to be ascribed to "coincidences."

In summarizing the results of our investigation of Roman influence on early English institutions we must concede that the Germanist school of historians has established a convincing case for the disappearance of Roman civilization. On the other hand, the conclusion of Kemble and Freeman, that the German invasions produced a "clean slate" as a result of their destroying Roman civilization, is not tenable. The decline of Roman institutions had long preceded the landing of the first boatload of Saxons in the fifth century. All that was needed on the part of the Germans was a gentle push to send this decaying structure tumbling to the ground. A comparatively "clean slate" was the end result, but it was not brought about solely by the Germans; their part was more of a mopping-up operation. What survived of Rome upon their arrival was not vital enough, as it was on the Continent, to make an initial imprint. Whereas on the Continent a *mélange* of Roman-German culture finally ended in the Germanic state of Charlemagne in the late eighth century, in England the Germans started out with what one may consider an almost exclusively Teutonic culture; and so it remained until 1066. In our study of early English institutions it will be useful to bear in mind this distinction between the German kingdoms of England and the Continent; it will help to account for the divergence between English and continental institutions. For Anglo-Saxon England we shall have to unlearn that elementary school maxim that the Romans are to be remembered for their roads and law. For a long time in English history we shall have to remember only Roman roads.

III

Anglo-Saxon England, 450–1066

FORTUNATELY a study of early English institutions requires no detailed account of political history. This statement should relieve those who have attempted to guide themselves through the maze of archaeological, linguistic, and written evidence, the price for understanding the early English settlements, or those who have floundered amidst the lists of kings of the so-called Heptarchy. All that is needed in the way of a background for understanding the growth of English institutions is a sketch of the most significant historical movements between the arrival of the Saxons in the middle of the fifth century and the death of the last Saxon king Harold at Hastings in 1066.

Why did the Angles, Saxons, and Jutes come to Britain? Because, so scholars tell us, the weakness of the Roman Empire enabled them to occupy its provinces, because piratical raids had shown Britain to be a more agreeable and rich land than northern Germany, and because, being overpopulated, they were land-hungry. To these causes we could also add daring and adventure. Although these answers are basically correct, we are still left wondering why these particular Germans turned north across the sea rather than south towards Rome and why their migration began in full force about the middle of the fifth century. Geographic location is largely responsible for the fortunes of these peoples. In looking at a map of fifth-century Europe one discovers that the three principal Germanic invaders of Britain lived along the North Sea coast from Denmark to the mouth of the River Meuse, with scattered groups of Saxons extending as far south as Boulogne in northeast Gaul. The Angles, Saxons, Jutes, and Salian Franks, located in what is now Belgium, were the tribes closest to Britain. On looking further one observes that the Saxons to the south along the coast of maritime Flanders and northeastern Gaul were between the Franks and the Channel. In fact all the Saxons, Angles, and Jutes to the north were hemmed in lower Germany by such tribes as the Salian and Ripuarian Franks, Thuringians, Sueves, and Burgundians who lived to the south. Such was the position of these tribes after almost four centuries of movement. Blocked by these larger and better-organized tribes, the invaders of Britain had no choice but to turn across the sea. Centuries of experience had made them skilled and fearless sailors; indeed the word "Saxon" had become a synonym for pirate. Since the third century they had conducted raids against Britain and were consequently familiar with its topography and defenses. When Roman government and military defense completely cracked during the early fifth century, only the Roman masters and Celts remained to resist invasion. Within twenty years raids had turned into settlement, first by small bands, and then by constantly swelling numbers. The end of effective defense constituted an invitation to conquest.

But we must still determine why such large numbers moved into Britain during the second half of the fifth century. Ferdinand Lot has often warned us against overestimating the numbers of Germans that came over the imperial frontier between the fourth and sixth centuries and has effectively argued that Germany was not overpopulated. In general his conclusion is valid. Referring again to the map, however, we can see that unlike the other tribes, who had room to maneuver, the Angles, Saxons, and Jutes were cooped up in a small area. It is quite possible that in 450–451 when Attila with his army of Huns and subject Germans moved northwestward from Rumania and Hungary across Germany and into northern Gaul he may have pushed these people farther against the coast. Certainly the sack of such towns as Troyes and Metz proves the proximity of the Huns to the Franks and neighboring tribes, who may have adjusted their location northward to escape the horde of Attila. There must be some connection between the *adventus Saxonum* of 450 in Britain and the continental events of 450–451. Such a movement cannot have failed to cause, at least temporarily, displacement of some tribes. Crowded into an even smaller area, the Saxons and their neighbors reacted as one would expect; they manned their boats and sailed to a prostrate Britain.

But this argument cannot be pressed too far. Other than human forces may also have been at work. A combination of archaeological work and some exacting study in physical geography by German, Dutch, and Belgian scholars has established that the coast of northern Germany and the Low Countries began to change radically in the fourth century. Following a cycle shown by geologists to have been in operation for millenniums, the coastal areas began to sink under the rising waters of the North Sea. Low even in normal times and cut through by numerous rivers such as the Elbe, Weser, Ems, Ijssel, Rhine, Meuse, and Scheldt, this northwestern section seems to have been more severely affected than other parts of northern Europe. Reaching a peak in the fifth century, the high waters remained at an abnormal level at least to the tenth century. New rivers, gulfs, and bays were created; one of these was the Zuider Zee. How many thousand square miles of land and marsh were inundated no one will ever know. No attempt was made to go back into this area and reclaim it from the sea until the eleventh century. The artificial mounds (*Terpen*) thrown up out of the marshes were not large enough for the people to live on, and even most of them were submerged. And as they never could have provided more than a living space, the problem of obtaining food must have been acute. Only one course was open—large-scale evacuation, either farther inland or to the sea. It was to the sea that these people turned from their desolate sodden homes. Though we must again beware of overemphasizing this evidence as a cause for migration, there is no doubt that as research in physical geography continues it will more fully confirm the inundation of the coasts of northern Germany as a major reason for the journey of the Saxons to Britain.

1. THE ANGLO-SAXON CONQUEST (450–600)

Having suggested the reasons for the coming of the Germans to Britain we may now proceed with the main events of the settlement. We have seen that in the first half of the fifth century a local Celtic leader, Vortigern, established his authority over much of Britain and, while engaged in fighting the Picts and Scots from the north, arranged to settle some German war bands in the south in return for their assistance. It was then, some time around 450, that the Saxon or Jutish chieftains Hengist and Horsa with three boatloads of followers established a beachhead. Other Germans poured in under similar arrangements. Legend has it that Vortigern lost his head over the ravishingly beautiful daughter of Hengist and offered the chieftain all Kent in return for the hand of his daughter. We read of the arrival of sixteen and then forty ships of Germans. Hereafter the events are muddled. Vortigern temporarily lost his power to a son, who attempted to drive out the Germans. When the son died suddenly, Vortigern came back to power, and so did the Germans, who continued to take over more land. Then Vortigern fell again from power and disappeared from history. As the area around Kent fell to the Germans similar events were occurring throughout southeastern Britain. Various chieftains and their bands continued to consolidate their gains and win new ground until defeated by the Britons under their leader Ambrosius Aurelianus some time between 490 and 516 at the Battle of Mount Badon, a site on the upper Thames. With this battle and other heroic Celtic resistance to the German advance, legend has connected the mythical Arthur. This battle ended the first stage of the Germans' conquest. For a time their expansion ceased, we hear of no raiding war bands probing deeper inland, and they seem to have established themselves around the coast and streams of Kent, Essex, Sussex, Surrey, Middlesex, and Hampshire in southeastern Britain. During this peaceful interval, extending to the second quarter of the sixth century, the leading chieftains installed their families as dynasties in the small states that developed.

Expanding our investigation to other parts of Britain, we find that the river systems of the Wash and the Thames facilitated the conquest of the eastern Midlands and the southwestern region. Entering East Anglia, various Angle bands then carved it up into small states. This particularism remained until the first quarter of the seventh century when a powerful chief, Redwald, called a Bretwalda by Bede, established his overlordship over the other petty states to form the temporary kingdom of East Anglia. Meanwhile other Angles went west into the central Midlands, where they teamed up with more Angles who were working their way down from the Humber and the River Trent. How this large area called Mercia was settled and divided by these bands, our pitifully scant sources do not say. The best we can do is to imagine a period of consolidation in the sixth century like that in southeastern Britain. Not until 626 do we hear of Penda, the first historical king of Mercia.

There is as yet no agreement on the principal route of the Saxons into southwestern Britain. Archaeological and written evidence suggests three possible routes, two by water and one by land. Arguing that Saxon remains at Dorchester on the upper Thames were already extensive by the year 500, some archaeologists envisage the Saxons landing in East Anglia and following the Wash River inland as far as Cambridge. From there they went overland towards the Thames, concentrating at Dorchester for further expansion to the west and south. Other scholars see the Thames as the more logical route. The narrative sources relate that two Saxon chiefs, Cerdic and Cynric, landed in 495 near Southampton and fought their way inland through Hampshire and Wiltshire towards the upper Thames. There is no reason why the Saxons could not have used all three routes, converging finally in the region of Dorchester. In the last half of the sixth century Cerdic's successors succeeded in establishing their hegemony over the other Saxon groups and initiated unity among bands that had been mere raiders and pillagers. During his reign (560–591) the ambitious Ceawlin not only strengthened his rule in this region but established the Saxons as far west as Bath and as far east as to include Surrey in his Bretwaldship. It was the Saxon conquest of Surrey that blocked the drive of King Ethelbert of Kent in this direction. Like other early overlordships this West Saxon one forged from Dorchester collapsed. A shift of power brought the Mercians south to the upper Thames in the seventh century. By 661 they had conquered Dorchester; henceforth the West Saxons concentrated their power at their new capital of Winchester to the south. From there the more powerful kingdom of Wessex was to emerge.

The Anglo-Saxons never conquered Wales, which stubborn Celtic resistance saved, or Scotland, which remained to the fierce Picts and Scots, but they did settle in Britain north of the Humber, in the area that Bede called Northumbria. As with Mercia, our evidence for the early period of settlement is meager. It is clear, however, that as with northern Mercia the Humber and its tributaries radiating off to the south and north served as a base for the Angles who conquered this northern land. The kingdom of Northumbria was derived from two settlements. The southern half called Deira, located between the Humber in the south and the Tees River in the north, was occupied by Angles coming in by sea during the fifth century. The poorer half, Bernicia, stretching from the Tees River north to the Firth of Forth, was not settled by Angles until 547 when the leader Ida and his followers fought their way in from the east coast. The bands fanned out from two points of concentration, the Tyne and Tweed rivers. Scholars formerly concluded that the Angles had come directly by sea from the Continent. Other opinion held that they pushed overland north from Mercia. Neither view is tenable; large-scale migration from the Continent was over by the middle of the sixth century and movement overland was beset by too many natural obstacles such as water and dense forests. What seems more likely is that Angles from Mercia followed their leaders by boat to natural points of assembly at the mouths of the Rivers Tyne and Tweed. Partitioned into small states both Bernicia and Deira remained apart until the last quarter of the seventh century when Ethelfrith (593–616) reduced both to his rule, becoming another early Bretwalda.

From 450 to approximately 600 the Anglo-Saxons were occupied solely with subjecting the native population of Britain and carving out their kingdoms. In this struggle only the strongest chiefs survived; into their hands fell the lands originally won by the weaker. After 150 years of fighting, the most successful chiefs had established dynasties in seven fairly well-defined regions of Britain—Northumbria, Mercia, East Anglia, Essex, Kent, Sussex, and Wessex; these kingdoms formed what some historians have called the Heptarchy.

2. THE SUPREMACY OF NORTHUMBRIA AND MERCIA

The next 250 years witnessed the emergence of three kingdoms—Northumbria, Mercia, and Wessex—each in its turn to dominate the history of Britain. The kingdom of Northumbria reached its apogee in the seventh century. First, Ethelfrith had established a kingdom between the Irish and North seas and the Humber, Firth of Forth, and Clyde River. Luck had it that three extraordinary successors were to carry on in his tradition. In fact, Edwin (616–632) and Oswald (633–641) were overly ambitious and stretched the resources of their newly formed kingdom too thin. Penetrating south into Mercia, Edwin was slain by the Mercian king Penda in 632 with the result that Northumbria temporarily relapsed into a mosaic of small kingdoms. Oswald managed to restore Northumbrian unity, but when he was killed in battle by Penda in 641 even Deira fell under the lordship of Penda. It was Oswy (641–670) who finally rallied his people to so striking a victory over Penda in 654 that Northumbria remained the dominant power in the north to the end of the century. The death of Oswy's son Aldrith in 704 marks the end of this kingdom as a power. In the eighth century the records speak only of anarchy. Northumbria was not a rich land; she never could support the population needed to keep her a dynamic power. This deficiency plus lack of an established rule for succession destined Northumbria to impotency. The ablest member of the royal family was considered the best candidate. But who was the ablest member? Only civil war could answer this question.

Mercia, the successor to Northumbrian power and the dominant kingdom of Britain in the eighth century, had no historian like Bede to recount its history. Biased entries from *The Anglo-Saxon Chronicle*, charters, correspondence from the Continent, and a document called the *Tribal Hidage* comprise our only evidence. The latter document, drawn up some time in the hundred years following Penda's reign (626–655), records the amount of land belonging to the small tribal states of Mercia in the sixth and seventh centuries, presumably for an evaluation of the taxes due Bretwaldas who had established their rule over a group of small states. From this evidence we know Mercia remained a land of predominantly independent states down to Penda. Beyond this fact all we know of the sixth-century Mercians is that they spread west to the Irish Sea, conquering the forest as they advanced. The remarkable Penda, a leader of striking military talent, not only kept the Northumbrian power north of the Humber but established his overlordship throughout all Mercia to the Thames; for the first time Mercian unity had been achieved. Even Wessex and East Anglia recognized his supremacy. Penda's son Wulfhere (657–674) continued the work of expansion. Forcing Essex to recognize his rule, he acquired the strategic site of London. Both Kent and Sussex recognized him as lord; in acquiring Oxfordshire, Wulfhere pushed Wessex south of the Thames and thus established a natural line of defense between the two kingdoms. But Mercian power declined after his death, an eclipse due partly to the temporary revival of West Saxon power in the next half-century. The foundation laid by Penda and Wulfhere would be finished only in the eighth century.

The history of Mercia in the eighth century is that of its two great kings Ethelbald (716–757) and Offa (757–796). One of the few bits of information the Northumbrian Bede gives us about the rival Mercian power is that in 731 all the kingdoms south of "the boundary formed by the River Humber, with their kings, are subject to Ethelbald, king of the Mercians." We do not know how or when, but Ethelbald had achieved a lordship over all Britain except Northumbria; even Wessex and the other southern kingdoms came under his power. Offa's success was more striking. He married members of his family into the dynasties of the subject kingdoms and easily subdued all revolt. A keystone of his policy was a *Drang nach Osten* to facilitate relations with the Carolingian Continent and to secure access to the richer lands of southeastern Britain. Kent remained a kingdom recognizing Offa's lordship, but Sussex, Essex, and East Anglia were incorporated into Mercia. Such political reconstruction gave Offa control of London, a center of political strength; Canterbury, the ecclesiastical capital of Britain; and ports near the Carolingian Empire.

The great power of Offa is reflected in developments other than his conquests. He considered himself more than the king of Mercia and overlord of the remainder of Britain. He conceived of himself as ruler of all England and styled himself "king of the English" (*Rex Anglorum* or *Rex totius Anglorum patriae*). His subjects also regarded him as a superior sort of king and his successor King Cenwulf referred to him as the "king and glory of Britain." Heptarchial provincialism was receding before the concept of a territorial state and royal power including all Britain; the idea of an Anglo-Saxon kingdom was in the air. The subject kings had to secure Offa's permission for all important acts such as the alienation of land and privileges. Many dynasties even disappeared, as happened in Sussex, Essex, Kent, and East Anglia. Offa's power was recognized beyond the shores of Britain; he was the first king in Britain to enter into continental affairs. Relations of an intimate nature were established with Rome; in 786 the first legate was sent to Britain by the pope and the church universal had finally recognized the political and ecclesiastical importance of this northern island. Although the mighty Charlemagne disdained a marriage agreement with Offa's family, he concluded commercial agreements with Offa relative to safe-conducts for English merchants in Frankish ports and Franks in English ports. He expressed also a keen interest in the church affairs of Offa's kingdom. Without doubt Offa was the predecessor of the strong kings of Wessex who were to forge the kingdom of England.

Though Offa's successor Cenwulf (796–821) upheld the Mercian hegemony over Britain, a later successor Beornwulf threw it away at the Battle of Ellendum in 825 where he was defeated by the West Saxons under their king Egbert. Mercia soon lost most of the subject kingdoms and was reduced to its original boundaries plus East Anglia. We lack the evidence required to explain satisfactorily the sudden fall of Mercia. A major cause, however, as we have previously hinted, seemed to be underpopulation and poor land opposed to the superior population and resources of the south.

We have noted that in the last years of the sixth century Wessex, under Ceawlin, extended from Bath to Surrey and from the Thames to the Channel. This political construction collapsed, however, under Mercian pressure. What remained of Wessex was to develop around the area of Hampshire, Wiltshire, and Dorset. Almost until the end of the seventh century Wessex was a conglomeration of small states ruled by subkings who recognized the theoretical lordship of a Bretwalda. The old German custom of splitting up land to provide for all royal successors seems to have produced this loose political confederacy, in which there was no strength to oppose Mercia. A temporary renaissance came between 685 and 726. We lack details as to how King Cadwalla began the restoration of West Saxon fortunes, but within three years he had eradicated all subkings, centralized his rule over their lands, and forced the kingdoms of Sussex, Kent, and Surrey to recognize him as Bretwalda. After such a strenuous three years Cadwalla retired to go on a pilgrimage to Rome.

Cadwalla was followed by Ine (688–726), whom Stenton calls "the most important king of Wessex between Ceawlin and Egbert." We have the dooms that Ine published, but little other evidence for his remarkable reign. Perhaps the silence of the records stems from a reign relatively peaceful;

seldom were there any large-scale campaigns or conquests by force. Ine was content to consolidate the gains of his predecessor and to encourage the peaceful settlement of Devon and East Cornwall by Saxon colonists. When he resorted to force it was to eliminate rivals, of whom there were many among the subkings. That he could compile a collection of laws which reflect a fairly adequate administrative system testifies to his ability. The darkness of Wessex history in the century after Ine's death serves to emphasize the accomplishments of this Saxon king.

From the death of Ine to the ninth century Wessex was under Mercian domination. It retained its kings but they were often subkings under the lordship of such as Offa. With King Egbert (802–839), however, Wessex again played a leading role in Britain. Tracing his descent back to the brother of Ine, Egbert first appeared as a candidate for the throne of Wessex in 789. Offa, however, supported a rival and Egbert was forced to live as an exile in Charlemagne's lands until 802. Perhaps it was there that he observed the efficient Carolingian administration and took some lessons in kingship from the great Charles. Certainly it was a special influence that produced the first strong West Saxon king since Ine. At the death of his rival in 802 Egbert was recalled by the West Saxons to be their king; this move amounted to a repudiation of Mercian dominance. Egbert never recognized Mercian lordship and for twenty years worked unobtrusively to restore West Saxon power and to expand his lands farther to the southwest. In 825 he met an invading Mercian army at Ellendum and routed it. This was one of the decisive battles of Anglo-Saxon history, marking the end of Mercian supremacy in Britain and placing all Britain below the Thames under West Saxon power. Immediately the kings of East Anglia, Kent, Surrey, Sussex, and Essex recognized the rule of Egbert. Just before his death he even occupied Mercia temporarily and it is said that the king of Northumbria swore loyalty to him. Mercia soon regained her independence and at the time of Egbert's death there still remained three Anglo-Saxon kingdoms. The balance of power, however, had shifted from Northumbria in the north, through Mercia, and south to Wessex, around which the fortunes of England were to revolve for the next two centuries. Just in time had Egbert created a kingdom that would give England a dynamic leadership, for there were signs even before his death that sterner challenges than the unification of England were to be met.

3. THE VIKING INVASIONS

In the last quarter of the eighth century western Europe was introduced to what was to be the last great offensive westward until the Ottoman Turks began their fearsome drive through central Europe in the fifteenth and sixteenth centuries. Between the third and sixth centuries there had been the Germanic invasions, in the seventh and early eighth centuries, the Moslem threat to southern Europe; and now began the Viking invasions that paralyzed not only western Europe but much of the known world. Coming from Scandinavian lands these fierce fighters belonged to three kingdoms that were well formed by the end of the eighth century—Sweden, Norway, and Denmark. As with the Germanic migrations many reasons have been advanced for their far-flung expeditions. The Vikings lived in lands that were mostly cold and rocky; to eke out a living must have been difficult. This explains why the Norwegians and Danes were such skilled sailors and shipbuilders. They survived by fishing, by trading with the Frisians, and by piracy. To such people the more temperate and rich lands to the south must have looked inviting. From their trading activities they were familiar with conditions in these lands and when the political climate was favorable may have decided to probe their riches. Some historians have thought that overpopulation forced the Vikings to migrate, a cause that, easily thought up, always seems to be the last resort of historians who find no real evidence to explain migration, or of modern imperialists in need of propaganda to justify their expansionist goals. For the Norwegians, forced by the mountainous and rocky terrain of the interior to cluster about the coastal fjords, this explanation may have some element of truth, but not for the Swedes or Danes. It has also been suggested that the aristocratic landowners, limited in the amount of good land at their disposal, could not adequately provide for all their sons. The younger ones consequently took to their boats with their followers in search of land, adventure, and plunder. Other historians believe that King Horik's strong government in Denmark during the middle of the ninth century may have been too peaceful and restrictive for the adventurous and warlike aristocrats, whose favorite pastime seems to have been civil war and raiding parties. Deprived of these pleasures, some apparently gathered their bands and went sailing for adventure to the south.

It may also have been that the Frisians with their ships had served as a buffer between the north and south. For years they had been the trading intermediaries between the Vikings and the Frankish kingdom. But when Charlemagne incorporated Frisia into his Empire and completed the conquest of the Saxons, he eliminated this buffer, and apparently the Frisian fleet. Such encroachment towards Denmark was bound to lead to border incidents and bad feeling between the Danes and Carolingians. With the North Sea cleared of the Frisian fleet the Danes as well as their Scandinavian neighbors could sail it with impunity. Before the death of Horik Danish raiding of the Carolingian coast was held in check. But upon his death in 854 a flood was let loose throughout the lands that rimmed the North Sea. Louis the Pious (814–840) had managed to settle some of the Danes in Frisia and Saxony, to play the chiefs off against each other and to bribe them to stop their raids farther south. But civil war among his three sons for the crown left the Empire completely at the mercy of the Vikings; all restraints had been removed. Even the small fleet Charlemagne had built to meet such raids had been forgotten and scrapped. The landlocked Empire was like an elephant clumsily defending itself against a horde of hornets.

The Viking bravery and daring of the sea command admiration. We all are familiar with reproductions of the Vikings' long, sleek, open ships with single masts and sixteen oars. Carrying usually about forty men they sailed not only the open sea but also, because their draught was shallow, far up the rivers. Sometimes the Vikings made portage to other streams. When portage was impossible, they beached their ships, rounded up all the horses in the neighborhood, and rode forth in all directions plundering the rich monasteries, churches, and manor houses. Putting all to the sword or holding them for ransom, they were likewise a scourge to the poor peasants whose crops they destroyed or stole. Their mobility was phenomenal. They avoided pitched battles, and no large armies could be mobilized fast enough to deal with them. Having loaded themselves with plunder, they returned unscathed to their ships and the open sea. They had no fear of the unknown and uncharted sea. They sailed around France into the Bay of Biscay, around Spain, through the Strait of Gibraltar, into the Mediterranean where they raided Marseilles and Rome, and even somehow reached the Alps. In the north they sailed across the North Sea to the Shetland and Orkney Islands, then on to Ireland and the Isle of Man. By 860 they had reached Iceland. Under Eric the Red they colonized Greenland in 985. About 1000 Eric's son Leif advanced to Labrador and Nova Scotia; from there he went as far south as the mouth of the Hudson River. Later voyagers revisited this area. Some scholars are still debating whether the Vikings sailed the Great Lakes as far west as Wisconsin. Meanwhile, beginning in the middle of the ninth century, the Swedes, or Russ or Varangians as they were called, turned east and south and reached the Dnieper River, sailing down it to Constantinople. By the tenth century they had established a strong kingdom around Kiev and had concluded commercial and political treaties with the Byzantine emperors. For centuries they were commercial intermediaries between Byzantium and the North Sea region and acquired fame as the Varangian Guard of the emperors at Constantinople.

Admittedly these remarks on the Vikings are somewhat irrelevant for English history, but they show well what is sometimes forgotten, that the invasions of England were only a part of a vast movement. As we follow the gallant defense of Alfred against the Vikings, we must beware of overestimating its significance. Statements that Alfred saved western Christian civilization assuredly are overdrawn. Though the Carolingians provided no defense for their beleaguered people, the local officers such as the counts and dukes of the frontier marches did; the dismal failure of the Vikings to establish themselves in the Low Countries and Germany is a tribute to the military ability of such as the counts of Flanders. We should not let the donation of Normandy to the Vikings in 911 blind us to the fact that the rest of France merely suffered raids. And even in Normandy the Vikings were gradually assimilated, Christianized, and won over to Frankish culture. It is indeed erroneous to consider Alfred and his faithful the last beacon light of civilization in the West.

Word of Viking raids against England first comes from *The Anglo-Saxon Chronicle*. Relating the events of 789 the *Chronicle* states that "there came [to the Dorset coast] for the first time three ships of Northmen and then the reeve rode to them and wished to force them to the king's residence, for he did not know what they were; and they slew him. Those were the first ships of Danish men which came to the land of the English." In 793 "the ravages of heathen men miserably destroyed God's church on Lindisfarne, with plunder and slaughter." From this time on entries like these become common. Striking England always at different points, the Danes were a foe too elusive for battle. Egbert did manage to defeat a group of Norwegians in southwestern England but such instances were rare. Until 850 the Vikings had always raided in the summer and returned home for the winter; in that year, however, about 350 ships wintered on the Isle of Thanet. The raids had ended; a period of conquest had begun. The Danish forces were constantly augmented and by 865 there was formed the Great Army. It started a systematic conquest of England; by 870 all England had been reduced except Wessex. Ireland meanwhile had been subjugated and turned into a Norwegian kingdom that lasted until 1014. When the Great Army invaded Oxfordshire in 870, Wessex and indeed the whole of England was fortunate in seeing Alfred become king of the West Saxons.

An evaluation of the versatile qualities and many achievements of Alfred the Great is beyond the scope of this book; it suffices to remark that he and Charlemagne were the two greatest rulers between the end of the Roman Empire and the eleventh century. A summary of his military exploits fully substantiates this judgment. After a few inconclusive skirmishes in Berkshire, the Vikings upon payment of tribute from Alfred turned their energies northward for a few years. This interval gave Alfred an opportunity to organize his defense, a task facilitated by the division of the Great Army. One half occupied northern England with York as headquarters, while the other half took over the rest of England with its base of operations in the Midlands. In 876 Guthrum, the leader of the southern Danish force, reinforced by recruits from the north and overseas, struck at Wessex. From what we can reconstruct of the campaign it was largely guerrilla warfare, each army attempting to ambush and catch the other by surprise. In 878 Alfred was surprised; he must have been badly defeated because he fled for refuge to the fen country where he reassembled his army and recruited more fighters. Later in the same year he attacked Guthrum at Edington and won a stunning victory, one that marked the end of the Danish advance and the advent of Wessex as the rallying ground for all England against the invader.

By the Treaty of Chippenham (878) Guthrum agreed to leave Wessex. To separate Danish territory (the Danelaw as it came to be called) from

Wessex a border was established that extended from London northwest above Oxford on towards Warwick to the Upper Severn River. Guthrum agreed also that he and his Danes would become Christian and give to the English of the Danelaw legal status equal to the Danes'. This treaty gave Alfred time to improve the efficiency of his army, the defense system of the boroughs (*burhs* or strongholds located strategically along the border), and local administration. He displayed his foresight in constructing a fleet to repel the Danes before they could land recruits from overseas and to block the transportation of Danes by water from one land point to another. This move greatly reduced the Danish mobility and equalized the military strength of the opposing forces. The wisdom of Alfred's defense is seen in the last serious Danish attempt to reduce England, in 892–896. Coming from France, a large army landed in Kent and attempted to recruit Danish settlers in this region under Alfred's rule. Unsuccessful, the army marched about Wessex trying to reduce the boroughs. Repulsed here also and harried by Alfred's fleet, some of the Danes went into the Danelaw while the rest returned to France. Alfred had saved Wessex and provided his able successors not only with a strategically located base of operations but also with a fine military and administrative system with which they could undertake the subjugation of the Danelaw in the tenth century.

4. WESSEX AND THE UNIFICATION OF ENGLAND

The first half of the tenth century witnessed unspectacular but steady reconquest of England from the Danes. Alfred had preserved Wessex, a task demanding all his energies; it now remained for Alfred's son Edward the Elder (899–925) and his successors to rewin most of England from a stubborn and resourceful opponent. Aided by Ethelred, the competent ruler of the Mercians, who was the husband of his sister Ethelfleda, Edward was able to begin operations from Mercia. Cooperating closely with Ethelred and Ethelfleda, who built boroughs along the frontier that bordered the Danelaw, Edward began to gnaw away at Danish territory region by region. In each region conquered, he built a borough to hold the new position. It was a frontier type of military strategy used with equal success in the tenth century by Henry the Fowler and Otto the Great of Germany in their campaigns against the Wends and Avars. So successful was Edward that at the end of his reign he was king of an England that reached to the Humber.

Athelstan (925–939) pushed into the Danish kingdom of York, which he annexed in 927. It was held, however, only after a bitter struggle. Securing the military assistance of the Scots, the Celts of Strathclyde, and the Norwegians from Ireland, the Yorkish Danes faced Athelstan with a formidable military coalition in 937. Athelstan's power was decisively established in the famous victory at Brunanburh near the Firth of Forth. Like his predecessors, the powerful Offa and the learned Alfred, he became a leading figure of western Europe, contracting marriages with the Carolingian, Saxon, and

Capetian families. It was left for Athelstan's two successors to consolidate his northern conquests, and by 955 the kingdom of England had been forged. In less than a century the kings of Wessex had made themselves rulers of England up to the Firth of Forth. Their kingdom included Mercia, Northumbria, and the Danelaw. Under Edgar the Peaceable (959–975) any idea of Danish revolt was forgotten and the kingdom of Anglo-Saxon England was at the peak of its power. One speaks now of institutions such as the king and witenagemot as common to all England; provincial kings and their institutions had been left behind and the Heptarchy was no more.

5. THE DANISH CONQUEST

The fantastically good fortune of England to have a string of powerful rulers from 871 to 975 could not in the nature of things continue indefinitely. When luck ran out, the strength of these men is more clearly apparent; one sees that only by their strong personalities and abilities was England welded together. Although the kingdom was not to fall apart again into separate entities, events show that it could not function efficiently under weak kings. Too many local customs, diversities, loyalties, and varying institutions remained for England to work as a team without a forceful captain. Edgar left behind a boy, Edward the Martyr (975–979), who seems to have been promptly assassinated with the connivance of Edgar's second wife, who wanted her son Ethelred the Redeless (979–1016) to be king. The events between 975 and 1016 read somewhat like the bloody and treacherous history of the Julio-Claudians portrayed so vividly in the *Annals* of Tacitus. Totally incapable of rule and burdened with an inferiority complex, Ethelred relieved his frustration by rationalization, fits of rage, indecision, acts of treachery, and flight to safety when a situation got out of control. To increase his woes the Danes began in 980 to raid England again, prompted no doubt by a repression of the carefree military and feuding habits of the landed aristocracy by the powerful Danish king Harold "Gormsson," who had established a strong kingdom of Denmark and Norway. To escape such discipline they turned with their retainers to England for adventure and conquest.

Ethelred was an ineffective leader, leaving the local officers to defend their districts just as the Carolingian counts did in the ninth century. Some resisted as best they could; others bribed the Danes to spare their lands. In 991 Ethelred followed the example of the latter; he paid the raiders a tribute of 22,000 pounds of gold and silver to leave his realm in peace. Thus began the famous blackmail called Danegeld. He hired Danes to fight Danes, but suspecting suddenly that they were plotting to kill him and his councillors he had many of them assassinated on Saint Brice's Day, 13 November 1002. An avenging army led by King Swein of Denmark invaded England in 1003 and conducted persistent raids to 1007; Ethelred appeared from time to time only to offer Swein more Danegeld. In 1009 an even more powerful army hit the coasts under the command of Thorkell the Tall, a lieutenant of Swein. After initial success, he betrayed Swein and went over to Ethelred in 1012. The following year Swein came to England with the intent of catching Thorkell and becoming king. Except for scattered resistance all England welcomed him as king; when he occupied London, Ethelred fled to Normandy to join his Norman wife Emma. Political fortunes now changed rapidly. Swein died almost immediately and his youthful son Canute, little experienced in leading an army, temporarily abandoned England to Ethelred, who was received back after swearing that he would be a true king and govern justly. In 1015, however, Canute returned, and by early 1016 he had reduced most of England. About this time Ethelred died. Edmund his son succeeded him and put up a stiff resistance, but after a few months he also died. At the end of 1016, then, Canute found himself king not only of Denmark and Norway but also of England.

Canute (1016–1035) was one of the most capable kings prior to 1066. Extremely diplomatic and sensitive to native Anglo-Saxon feeling, he ruled as an Anglo-Saxon and appeased hostile reaction. He made England the center of his North Sea empire, confirmed all Anglo-Saxon laws, re-established efficient administration, and became an ardent supporter of the Anglo-Saxon church, cooperating closely with the bishops and higher ecclesiastics. Then he climaxed this amazing program by marrying Ethelred's widow Emma, an act which would forestall Norman support for Emma's two sons by Ethelred. Meanwhile, having eliminated all possible rivals in England, he ruled peaceably and wisely until he died in bed one day in 1035. Neither of Canute's sons, Harold and Harthacanute, measured up to their father. They viewed England as a foreign land to be drained of as much revenue as they could extort. By surrounding themselves exclusively with Danes in the government, they forfeited the close rapport Canute had maintained with the English aristocracy. *The Anglo-Saxon Chronicle* recounts what most English must have thought a fitting end to Harthacanute. In 1041 he had "sent his housecarls [retainers] through all the provinces of his kingdom to collect the tax he had imposed. Two of them were killed . . . by the people of Worcestershire . . . when a riot broke out. Hence the king, moved to anger, sent there to avenge their slaying . . . a great army, ordering them to kill, if they could, all the men, to plunder and burn the city and to lay waste the whole province. . . . When the city had been burnt, everyone went off to his own parts with much booty, and the king's wrath was at once appeased." But soon thereafter, in 1042, Harthacanute attended a wedding celebration of one of his Danes and, "while he stood cheerful, in health and high spirits, drinking with the aforesaid bride and certain men, fell suddenly to the ground by a sad fall in the midst of his drinking, and remaining thus speechless, expired."

6. EDWARD THE CONFESSOR AND THE NORMAN CONQUEST

Dying without heirs, Harthacanute left the kingdom to three possible claimants. Canute's nephew, King Swein Estrithson of Denmark and Norway, was unavailable because of civil war in Norway. Edmund the Exile, the grandson of Ethelred the Redeless descended from a first marriage, was considered too foreign because of long exile in Hungary. This left Edward the Confessor, the son of Ethelred and Emma, a man of forty, who had spent his whole life in Normandy, for the most part in a monastery with the monks who had reared him. It was he whom the English aristocracy and church accepted as their ruler. A complete stranger to England and a Norman by speech and culture, Edward always remained a foreigner. As often as possible he appointed Normans to rich ecclesiastical posts and benefices, surrounded himself with Norman councillors, and rewarded them with English land. Never a worldly man Edward escaped the secular duties of kingship whenever possible and devoted his energies to prayer, good works, and the plans for building Westminster Abbey. Although pressed into marriage with an Anglo-Saxon woman he remained true to celibacy throughout his life; thus obviously he produced no heir. He was as unfit to govern as his father Ethelred but was saved from his father's excesses by a sincere faith which justly won him the title "Confessor."

With but a titular head it is not surprising that the most powerful Anglo-Saxon aristocrats, the earls who possessed vast areas of England, should hold actual control. In effect, during most of Edward's reign the real power resided in the house of Godwin, earl of Wessex. Until 1051 Godwin was virtual ruler of England. He married off his daughter Edith to Edward in 1045 to secure the gifts of land given by the king to his bride. Edward was persuaded to make earldoms for two of Godwin's sons, Swein and Harold. Rich grants went also to other members of Godwin's family. The witenagemot, the royal council, seems to have been dominated by Godwin. Meanwhile Edward surrounded himself with Normans and appointed them to bishoprics and abbacies. Two parties were in the making—a Norman and an Anglo-Saxon.

In 1051 when Edward appointed the Norman Robert of Jumièges to be archbishop of Canterbury, he overstepped himself. The appointment offended the Anglo-Saxons and also Godwin, whose chances for succession to the throne depended greatly upon a sympathetic archbishop. The ill feeling was heightened by another event of the same year. While traveling to London, Eustace of Boulogne, Edward's brother-in-law and a wealthy holder of Anglo-Saxon land, was assaulted by men of Dover and several of his men were killed. Edward immediately ordered Godwin, in whose lands Dover lay, to punish the offenders; his curt refusal indicates the strong Anglo-Saxon antipathy to the Normans. Edward, for once acting vigorously, ordered the other earls to help him punish the rebellious Godwin. Caught by surprise and unable to mobilize sufficient forces, Godwin was forced to accept the banishment proclaimed by Edward and the witenagemot. Godwin and some members of his family went to Flanders; the others went to Ireland.

Godwin's exile lasted only a year. Edward's support of Norman infiltration continued to alienate the English, and none of the earls seemed at all inclined to assume a dominant role in the central government. Thus, when Godwin sailed from Flanders in 1052 with a few ships and men, he had acquired a reputation as the leader of Anglo-Saxon opposition to the hated Normans. He established himself in England with little trouble. Numerous Normans took flight, including Robert of Jumièges, and Edward, lacking effective military support, had to take Godwin back and restore all lands and privileges to his family. From now until his death in 1066 Edward was dominated by the house of Godwin. He practically abdicated from his secular duties and devoted his life to ecclesiastical projects. Godwin died within the year and was succeeded as head of the family by Harold, a man of deep political insight and superior military talent who would certainly have been known as one of the three or four greatest Anglo-Saxon kings had he not met so untimely an end. He was the real ruler of England for the next thirteen years, supervising the central administration and repelling Welsh aggression in Gloucestershire and Herefordshire. Placing Anglo-Saxon unity above family loyalty, he permitted his brother Tostig, earl of Northumbria, to be banished in 1065 because of his corrupt and evil administration. Tostig took refuge in Flanders and was soon to be the cause of Harold's death.

When Edward died in January 1066 it was obvious to the leading men of the witenagemot that Harold was the man best qualified to rule. Even Edward must have concurred, for on his deathbed, ignoring the claims by members of his family, he seems to have indicated Harold as his successor. The day after Edward's death Harold was consecrated at Westminster; he had at his back a loyal Anglo-Saxon England. Bad luck, and that alone, limited the reign of this energetic man to nine months. Receiving news of Edward's death, William, duke of Normandy, laid claim to the English throne. Because William had no legitimate claim, this move can be explained only as an expression of that Viking daring and sense of adventure that had kept his ancestors roaming about the western world for three hundred years. William's claims to the throne were three: that he was a cousin of the Confessor by marriage; that upon his visit to England in 1052 Edward had promised him the throne; and that Harold, while enjoying his hospitality after being shipwrecked on the Norman coast in 1064, had promised upon his oath to support him. There is no evidence for the last two claims, and obviously none of them had any legality. The only mark of respectability that William could muster for his conquest of England was the papal blessing. The pope regarded the expedition as a sort of crusade on the pretext that the Anglo-Saxon church was not orthodox in all its organization and ritual. But in the eleventh century what church was? To a fighter like William such considerations were of little importance. He hastily recruited a large force of knights and mercenaries from all over western Europe and began to build a fleet. From William down to the lowliest fighter the adventure had one motive—land and power.

Informed of William's preparations, Harold mobilized his forces and kept a vigilant patrol along the Channel coast. But in September word from the north forced him to leave the south undefended. His brother, the exile Tostig, had persuaded the king of Norway to support him in an attempt to win England. Collecting a formidable fleet, they sailed into the Humber, defeated a local levy on 20 September, captured York, and established themselves in the country about. Within five days of this skirmish Harold had brought his army across England by forced marches to meet the invader. He threw his forces upon the Norwegian army and completely routed it, killing its king and Tostig. He then wheeled about for the south, reached London on 6 October, and on 14 October was at Hastings on the Channel. Such a feat equals some of the most celebrated campaigns found in military annals and again proves the extraordinary talents of Harold.

But meanwhile what was Duke William doing? For a month he had been waiting for a favorable wind. Ill luck would have it for Harold that the wind came when he was marching north. On 28 September William landed unopposed at Pevensey, marched a little inland, built a stronghold at Hastings, and established his base of operations around it. We do not know why Harold offered battle so soon with his depleted and battle-weary forces, but he managed to deploy them skillfully on an incline so that the Normans would have to attack uphill. Fighting on foot, the Saxons maintained an unbroken wall for six hours and probably would have won the battle had they not been deceived by a Norman ruse. Feigning to retreat, the Norman knights turned from the field; the Saxons, thinking the enemy was retiring, broke their defensive line in pursuit. The Normans then quickly faced about and proceeded to cut them down. Their line broken, the Saxon footsoldiers could no longer defend themselves against the mobile knight. The Saxons were routed and the Norman knight had demonstrated his superiority over the footsoldier. One of history's decisive battles had been won by William. His gallant opponent, surrounded by his faithful thegns, lay dead upon the field with an arrow through his body. With Harold's death the Anglo-Saxon kingdom came to an end. A sturdy Norman dynasty was henceforth in control.

IV

Central Administration

UNDERLYING all cultures, however primitive, has ever been the concept of the leader. Whether of royal blood and descended from the gods, whether the temporarily appointed war leader, or whether the priest, society has had to have him in one form or another. Needed little during routine and peace, he has been necessary to his people during conquest, migration, and defense. A leader known as king seems not to have existed among the German tribes described by Caesar. No central or common leader united the kindred divisions (*pagi*) of each tribe; each division had its chief (*princeps*), who was responsible for administration and justice. There were other private chiefs, who had no public function or recognition but who, on the basis of their valor, enlisted warriors into bands to conduct raids into the territories of neighboring tribes for plunder and military glory. They could, of course, aspire to become a public *princeps*. A general leader for the whole tribe was resorted to only during war; the divisions then appointed one or several temporary leaders to command them. It is uncertain whether this leader was appointed by the *principes* of the divisions from the most powerful among them or whether the free warriors of the tribe assembled to elect him, but evidence from later ages lends support to the more aristocratic approach.

I. KINGSHIP

One hundred and fifty years later when Tacitus wrote about the Germans it is difficult to ascertain whether their tribal organization had progressed or whether we are just more fully informed about it. At any rate a leader common to all the tribe in war and peace was more prevalent. Some tribes now had kings elected at tribal assemblies of the free warriors. There was a discussion preceding election and there the *principes* of the divisions, who constituted a nobility by virtue of war and political experience and amount of land held probably dominated the proceedings. Other tribes practiced hereditary succession. When one of the elected *principes* became powerful enough to impose his successor upon the tribe without an election, hereditary succession probably began; but it is at a later date that we hear of such dynasties' tracing their descent to Woden and other gods. When tribes had kings they were far from being absolute. For war special leaders called *duces* were elected and had an authority superior to the king's. At assemblies of the tribe the king had no more authority than the *principes*, whose experience and position gave their opinions equal weight. Like the *principes* the king held land, perhaps a trifle more because of his exalted title, and he received a share from the fines of justice. But beyond these few perquisites it is difficult to see the king as a more elevated person than the *principes* of the *pagi*. If he was an average man he would be nothing more than a figurehead and symbol of tribal unity. If, however, he was a strong man able to draw about him a powerful band of warriors (the *comitatus*) who would loyally support him in all ventures, he could convert his title into more than a symbol, perhaps into a right held exclusively by members of his family. With the tribes that remained nonmonarchic much the same system of government existed as in Caesar's time. The *principes* independently administered the affairs of their tribal division, obeying only during war a superior military commander. They presided over the local courts of justice and led the military forces of the *pagus* to serve under the *dux*.

Throughout the pages of Caesar and Tacitus is portrayed a fundamentally aristocratic society where the noble *principes* control the tribal divisions and steer general tribal affairs in assemblies of free warriors. Some tribes came to adopt kingship, a tendency that increases as we reach the fifth century. The temporarily appointed war leader was a competent and valorous *princeps*; he was the man most likely to become a king. The *principes* and lesser nobles had their own *comitatus* of privately recruited warriors loyal only to them while on a quest for glory and booty. These leaders competed for control of the *pagus*. Any successful warrior could have his *comitatus*. Throughout this structure the noble warrior dominates, aspires to, and wins all the great positions. The mobility within this aristocratic caste must have been considerable. In an extended period of war and conquest such as the Anglo-Saxons experienced in the fifth and sixth centuries, the fortunes of the *principes* had great opportunity to improve. During the conquests and settlements of land many a successful leader became not only a chief but a king of the area he and his faithful followers had won.

The obscure period for tracing the development of English kingship comes in the four hundred years after Tacitus. Although we know little of the evolution, by the fourth and fifth centuries most of the Germanic tribes had kings. There were, for example, kings of the Visigoths, Ostrogoths, Franks, and the other tribes that took over the Roman Empire. For such tribes the narrative sources and *leges barbarorum* supply the principal evidence. With the Germans who conquered Britain the problem is more complex. The Angles had kings but it appears that the Jutes and Saxons did not. The essential point is, however, that the earliest Germanic organizations in Britain were headed by kings regardless of whether or not these tribes had kings on the Continent. It is comparatively simple to reconstruct the transition. Britain was conquered not by tribes under kings as was the Empire on the Continent but by war bands under chieftains. Here and there a leader may also have been a king but in general we must visualize the leaders as *principes*, public and private, aspiring to higher rank and land of their own to rule. The successful chiefs like Hengist and Horsa in Kent, Cerdic in Wessex, Ida and Aelle in Northumbria established their families as dynasties over the lands they subdued; other chiefs did likewise. According to Germanic custom, upon the death of the father, his lands were divided among his sons, who then became kings. Some kings established their lordship over other kings; now there were Bretwaldas and subkings.

By the seventh century there were seven kingdoms which, in turn, were merged into larger kingdoms. Dynasties of subkings vanished; so, too, did dynasties of the larger kingdoms. Finally Wessex in its successful fight against the Danes united all Britain and its dynasty ruled Anglo-Saxon England in the tenth and eleventh centuries. During this tug of war for power there arose the fictions and customs that the founders of the dynasties were divinely descended from Woden, that only nobles could aspire to kingship, later that only members of the royal family could, and finally that the eldest son or the ablest member of the family should succeed to the kingship, which should not be partitioned into smaller kingdoms. Thus no elaborate theories are required to explain the origin of kingship in Britain. From the first, expediency called for rulers above the status of chieftain or *princeps*. Subsequent experiment plus pure force and ability established the West Saxon kings as kings of England.

But let us see how the institution of kingship developed. Brute force established the strong chiefs as kings and enabled them to make kingship hereditary in one family, excluding all other ambitious nobles such as ealdormen and earls from succession. Within a family many kinsmen might aspire to kingship, but as the period of settlement is left behind the tendency becomes marked for the king to designate his eldest son or nearest male relative as successor. In unsettled times this custom was overturned; on occasion a minor or incapable heir was passed over for the ablest member of the royal family. The Mercian king lists of the eighth century show eldest sons succeeding fathers just as they did in tenth-century Wessex. Of course there were many exceptions. In the ninth century, for example, King Ethelwulf of Wessex was succeeded by his four sons in the order of their birth. Alfred came to the throne in preference to a royal son. But such irregularity is probably explained by the strain of the Danish invasions. Political experience showed rulers that succession of the eldest son instead of partition preserved the royal territory intact and lessened the danger of civil war. When king was followed by son or close relative he governed with the knowledge that the fruit of his labor would be bestowed upon a blood successor who would continue the work; he therefore had more incentive to leave after him a strong and rich territory.

The earliest kings of England recognized the value of claiming descent from Woden and other gods. If such descent did not make them and their ancestors gods, at least it gave them divine qualities and set them above all other men. When Christianity became entrenched throughout England the pagan concept of divine descent was gradually superseded by Christian sanction; kings came to rule by the grace of God. Tangible evidence of such divine favor was the consecration ceremony with its coronation and unction. Since the dawn of history kings had worn crowns as a symbol of royalty. The Old Testament supplied the precedent for Christian coronation, a ceremony adopted by the Byzantine emperors and then copied by the German kings of the West. Before being Christianized, however, the Germans had a ceremony to symbolize royal succession. At the death of the king a solemn feast would be prepared while the son occupied the seat of his father and took possession of his residence and property as well as of his kingdom. Tacitus tells how amid loud acclaim the new chief was raised high upon a shield. The Merovingian rulers were drawn about the realm in an oxcart to see and be seen by their subjects. When the German kings occupied the Roman west, imperial symbols were aped; the purple was worn and the title of *imperator* added. The introduction of anointing to the ceremony of coronation cannot be easily traced. The Christian precedent was the anointing of Jewish kings by oil. But it is not known when Christian kings adopted it and when it became a part of the coronation ceremony. Some of the Ostrogoths were anointed, and so were most of the Visigoths, but not the early Franks. Some evidence points to the anointing of the Celtic kings of the fifth century. But no matter when the practice became general, it seems to have been regarded as a type of sacrament wherein the priest by the grace of the Holy Spirit so changed the character of the ruler that he then entered into a closer relation with God. He became God's chosen representative in this world and was set apart and beyond other men. Between the eighth and tenth centuries there was a blending of the pagan Germanic inauguration ceremony and the Christian coronation and anointing. When a king was consecrated the ceremony generally consisted of "anointing, investiture with insignia, coronation, enthronement, the coronation banquet, and subsidiary proceedings."

The first Christian coronation of an Anglo-Saxon king for which there is reliable evidence was in 785 when King Offa of Mercia had his son Ecgferth anointed and designated as his successor; thereafter consecration became customary in the succession of the Anglo-Saxon kings. A powerful influence must have been the Carolingian consecration as it was practiced by Pepin, Charlemagne, and their successors. Dunstan, archbishop of Canterbury, who resided in Frankish land in the tenth century, composed the first Anglo-Saxon coronation order and it shows definite Carolingian elements.[1] Written between 960 and 973 it provided for anointing and coronation as well as for investiture with scepter and rod; when this was done the assembled lords

[1] SM, no. 10.

were to thrice hail the king and swear loyalty to him. But apart from the Carolingian influence there was another element of the coronation order germinated on Anglo-Saxon soil—the royal oath at consecration. A pontifical of King Egbert of Wessex states that the new king should swear to preserve and protect the Christian church, to prevent inequities to all subjects, and to render good justice. In the coronation of King Edgar in 973 are not only all the elements just described, that is, the crowning, anointing, and investiture, but also the *promissio regis,* in which the king promised to protect the church and to administer good and lawful government and justice to his people. This coronation ceremony of Edgar became a model for succeeding kings. The oaths taken by Ethelred the Redeless at his coronation in 979 and upon his restoration in 1014 continued the *promissio regis.* In 1014 he swore that he would be to his people "a mild and devoted lord, would consent in all things to their will . . . if all with one mind and without perfidy would receive him to the kingdom." These oaths had great bearing upon the later relation of king and subject. They marked the beginning of the constitutional concept that the king should swear to do the will of his people and they set a precedent for later medieval coronation oaths.

Royal responsibility to subjects saw the parallel growth of a sense of duty and obedience to the kings. Personal loyalty to one's chief or lord, the *princeps* of Tacitus, had always been a strong characteristic of German society. Tacitus' famous account of the *comitatus* relation of *princeps* to his *comites* tells of the obligation of the chief to provide battle equipment, food, and war booty for his followers in return for their supreme loyalty. They were to defend and protect him and to equal or surpass his deeds. To have retired from a battlefield alive while the chief remained behind dead was the greatest disgrace. Repeatedly this close, private relation is echoed in Anglo-Saxon literature. It dominates *Beowulf* and *The Battle of Maldon;* there are constant allusions to it in *The Anglo-Saxon Chronicle.* From the first, all the Anglo-Saxon kings commanded a personal loyalty from the men about them. This loyalty is seen when King Cynewulf of Wessex was killed in 786. One night while he was "visiting his mistress" a noble Cyneheard surrounded the lovers' chamber with his thegns and killed the king. Awakened by the woman's cries the royal thegns sprang to the defense of their king. They were greatly outnumbered and therefore Cyneheard offered them their life and some money as a bribe. "Not one of them would accept it. But they continued to fight until they all lay dead except for one British hostage, and he was severely wounded." The concept difficult to establish, however, was that of a public, nonpersonal loyalty to the king by men who had no personal tie with him. It meant building a loyalty higher than other lords could command and one which cut across the personal and private bond of lord and man. We know that the Merovingians toured their realm after accession and received an oath of fealty from all freemen; but not until the laws of Edmund in the middle of the tenth century is this concept clearly expressed in England. It was laid down that "all shall swear, in the name of the Lord, fealty to King Edmund as a man ought to be faithful to his lord, without any controversy or quarrel, in open and in secret, in loving what he shall love, and in not willing what he shall not will."[2] Coinciding with the unification of England under the West Saxon kings this law marked a definite advance in placing the king above all other lords and binding all Anglo-Saxons to him by oath of fealty.

Certainly the oath of Edmund had its antecedent in the doom of Alfred that expressed for the first time the idea that certain actions against the king were treasonable. The doom provided that if anyone directly plotted against the royal life or harbored exiles he was liable to forfeiture of life and possessions.[3] In their dooms Alfred's successors continued to elaborate on the crimes considered treasonable. The background for the concept of treason is found, however, much earlier than Alfred's doom. In the earliest dooms the kings already appear as persons whose superiority is protected by stringent enactments and fines. Inherent in Anglo-Saxon thinking was the idea that every man's house had a peace which if broken entitled him to a special payment by the intruder. This peace was called a *mundbyrd* and was scaled according to a man's rank. The dooms of King Ethelbert of Kent fixed the royal *mundbyrd* at 50*s*., the *eorl's* at 12*s*., and the *ceorl's* at 6*s*. Members of the royal household were included in the *mundbyrd*. King Ine of Wessex stiffened breach of the royal *mundbyrd*. When anyone fought in the royal household he was at the mercy of the king for his life and property. For invading the royal residence a man was liable to a *burhbryce* of 120*s*. By the reign of Alfred the royal *mundbyrd* was £5, a sum greatly exceeding that of other nobles.[4] The king's wergeld (fine paid when a man was killed) was set so high that practically no one could pay it and, in reality, it amounted to stipulating death for such a crime. It has been suggested that because the fines were so high they referred to settlements struck between factions and kingdoms at war. Since 120 West Saxon shillings were equivalent to twenty oxen the suggestion appears quite possible. Mercian law stipulated 7200*s*. as the royal wergeld and a fine called a *cynebot* consisted of an equal amount which had to be paid to the subjects.

With their pre-eminence established by law the kings further accentuated their majestic position by the use of material and titular symbols. They sat upon an elevated throne wearing a royal crown or helmet and holding a scepter or special lance. Court etiquette and ceremony offered another medium for royal display. In addition to the previously mentioned use of titles such as *Rex Anglorum* by Offa and the kings of Wessex, kings gave further expression to their territorial sway with titles such as *Rex Britanniae, Imperator Britanniae,* and *Basileus* employed by Edmund and his successors.

[2] SM, no. 9.
[3] SM, no. 5.
[4] SM, nos. 1, 4, 5.

The title *Rex Angliae* used by Canute does not appear regularly until the reign of John at the beginning of the thirteenth century.

Once royal power had been attained, had been expressed by law, ceremony, and title, and had expanded in territorial sway, it accrued numerous obligations and rights. No longer could the king be just a war leader. Nowhere were his powers more forcefully exhibited than in his responsibility for justice. In fact, royal power and justice supported each other and developed apace. In the complicated system of fines for infractions of the law the king assumed an expanding role. Minor infractions were atoned for by payment of compensation or a *bot* to the injured party and a duplicate amount to the king in order to get back into the king's good grace.[5] For crimes too enormous to be compensated by fines, the malefactor was put beyond the law, unprotected against anyone who might harm or kill him; only the king could restore him to the pale of justice. Crimes of a public rather than a private nature were the sole concern of the king, who collected all the fines paid; the king's peace pertained especially to such offenses. This royal peace should not be confused with the king's general or public peace (*frith*), which is comparable to our modern expression "law and order."[6] When a man was accused of violating the king's general peace, it was in a political rather than a legal sense and no particular legal action could be taken against the individual in court. The words *mund* or *grith* referred, however, to a more limited or special royal peace for which there was legal action. We have seen that the homes of all freemen had a peace but that the king's residence had a very high peace; and so it was with all objects or persons that came under the king's special peace. Infraction against it incurred fines to the king called *wites*. We thus start with a concept of the king's peace limited to his residence. But as the royal power and functions increased so did his *mund*. Wherever he resided while traveling, his *mund* held. Slowly this peace was extended over places and areas which did not know the king's presence but required special protection. Highways, rivers, bridges, churches, monasteries, markets, and towns came under the royal *mund*. Not only the royal court but the hundred and shire courts were put in the royal peace. It was considered that theoretically he was present at these courts and other places.

By the eleventh century it was possible for royal officers such as sheriffs to proclaim the king's peace wherever suitable. Even included were festivals and special occasions of the year such as Christmas, Lent, Easter, and Whitsuntide. The personal royal peace is now becoming a general peace. One day it will include all England for 365 days a year. Persons in the royal presence, as, for example, his household officers and members of the witenagemot, were under his *mund*. But the king's presence could not be everywhere and because certain individuals required more than territorial protection they

[5] SM, no. 2.
[6] SM, no. 1.

came to be safeguarded by a personal peace (*grith*) put over their persons by the king. The members of the witenagemot, for example, were so protected while traveling to and from the assemblies.[7] At first the *grith* was given orally; later it was granted in writing under the royal seal. Very high fines protected such fortunate individuals against the serious offenses of assault and murder. And yet in no sense did any of the Anglo-Saxon kings reserve serious offenses for their special jurisdiction. They had only begun to put their peace over special places and persons and times. A category of crimes reserved for royal jurisdiction, called pleas of the crown, was a development of the twelfth century. The influence that the king could exert in spreading and strengthening law and justice was just beginning to realize its potential power; the justice of a Henry II was still far distant. Yet the Anglo-Saxon kings comprehended that their laws and commands must be efficiently and justly executed by subordinates. From the reign of Edward the Elder fines called *oferhyrnes* were levied against officers who did not obey the royal command and carry out the law.[8] At times they were removed from office.

Even before Christian influence caused the Anglo-Saxon kings to put custom into writing, they had declared the law for the tribe and were considered its symbol and fountainhead. Never, however, did they declare the custom arbitrarily. It was done only after consultation with the chief men of the tribe and generally in the presence of all the freemen in an assembly. After the custom became written dooms and was supplemented by new law the kings continued to declare the law or legislate with the advice of the great men of the realm.[9] In 695 King Wihtred of Kent issued his dooms in "a deliberative assembly of leading men," and "there, with the consent of all, the leading men devised these decrees and added them to the lawful usages of the people of Kent." Restricted though he might be in legislating, the king must be considered the driving force behind the collecting of the dooms and the making of new ones. His was the order that put the ecclesiastics to writing down the custom and his was the experience and perception that called for new laws. By his order the great men assembled to give advice and consent. To adjust heathen custom to the Christian faith, the early kings put the dooms into writing. When conquests were made such as those completed by the West Saxon kings in the tenth century, laws had to be adjusted and enacted in order to incorporate new people and their custom. Laws had to bring the Danes into the fabric of Anglo-Saxon society. Concurrent with the necessity of new law to ease such adjustment was the need to extend its jurisdiction. The laws of Wessex expanded with every new conquest. Edward the Elder legislated for Wessex and Mercia; his successors legislated for Wessex and the Danelaw; Canute could legislate for all England. The political

[7] SM, nos. 1, 4, 5, 13.
[8] SM, no. 13.
[9] SM, no. 4.

and territorial power of the king was reflected step by step in its advance by the law.

Passing outside the realm of law we come to powers and privileges of the king that were fiscal, administrative, and appointive. To the king fell the fines for the breach of his peace and also those collected in courts dealing with ordinary criminal and civil cases.[10] He and his household were entitled to hospitality and maintenance as they traveled around the realm. A night spent at a lord's manor house or at a monastery entailed a tremendous amount of food and drink for the royal party. The king had exclusive rights to salvage from shipwreck and to treasure-trove. He had a monopoly over the products of mines and saltworks. Indirect taxes came to him from tolls and dues of markets, ports, and the routes by land and by river. The successor of a man having been granted land by the king had to pay a heriot to acquire possession of the land. Down to 1066, heriot was paid predominantly in kind, principally in horses and weapons. The dooms of Canute give in detail the amount of heriot for different ranks of nobles. Today we would call such a payment an inheritance tax.[11] When the king so desired, he could remit or grant to another person any of the rights noted above. Beyond these pecuniary rights the king had sole responsibility for the protection of strangers. As commercial and political relations increased with the Continent and the North Sea area this task became a major concern of the kings. Treaties were concluded to insure special protection for merchants and envoys; letters were issued to proclaim safe-conducts and privileges to strangers; and laws were made to regulate the relations of foreigners with the English. Another right of the king was the construction of bridges and strongholds (boroughs). All royal officers were appointed by the king and were removable upon the royal will. Lastly we should mention that the king was the greatest landowner of the realm; from the royal estates came the bulk of his income, customarily composed until the eleventh century of produce and payments in kind by tenants. Although these are not all the royal rights, obligations, and revenues that pertained to kingship, the rest are more conveniently discussed when we come to examine the other institutions of central administration.

2. THE WITENAGEMOT

Literally witenagemot means an assembly or gathering of wise men. This was the name of the group of important lords who composed a part of the Anglo-Saxon central administration. To trace the origin of this group would be fruitless; the evidence is too scant until the tenth century and by this time the witenagemot was a body different from any of its antecedents. All that may be safely said is that the German tribes had assemblies which dis-

[10] SM, no. 2.
[11] SM, no. 13.

cussed and acted upon important tribal affairs. According to Tacitus tribal assemblies of all freemen under arms were held periodically such as at the full and new moon. The assembly wielded the central power of the tribe. After silence had been proclaimed by the priests, discussion began, dominated by the king, *principes*, and other men of political and military prowess. Opposition to a speech or proposal was in the form of shouts. If there was agreement spears were flourished. If a proposal was enthusiastically received the men would clash their spears and shields. All important business and proposals were arranged prior to the assembly by the *principes*. Routine affairs were handled by meetings of the *principes* alone. The whole assembly passed upon war, peace, alliances, and appointment of tribal officers such as *duces* and *principes*. In a judicial capacity it received complaints and rendered the highest sentences. From tribe to tribe this organization may have varied and for the fifth and sixth centuries it would be risky to speculate much on the nature of the assemblies that helped the early Anglo-Saxon kings govern their newly won kingdoms. From the Tacitean description, however, it appears likely that the meetings were dominated by the king and his most powerful nobles. About all that the ordinary freeman could expect to do was give his assent to a previously formulated decision.

Nineteenth-century opinion that the witenagemot developed out of a folk court of the shire is supported by no evidence; the witenagemot had no connection with local administration and justice. If some of the earliest kingdoms corresponded in territorial extent to what later were shires, it was only coincidence. Kingdoms like Wessex, Mercia, and Northumbria were composed of numerous shires. Until England was united by Wessex in the tenth century each of the seven kingdoms had its own witenagemot; the witenagemots of the Northumbrian and Mercian kings may have extended over other kingdoms. The only assemblies which included members from all of England prior to the tenth century were the ecclesiastical synods called from time to time by a king such as Oswy or Offa or a prelate such as Theodore of Tarsus or Dunstan, both archbishops of Canterbury. The witenagemots of England in the tenth and eleventh centuries were not the heritage of these ecclesiastical synods but we must admit that the synods must have set an example for large territorial meetings, familiarizing the kings and great men with meetings that included all England. The ecclesiastics who were an important component of the witenagemot were certainly aware of this church precedent.

We have not yet defined an Anglo-Saxon witenagemot of the tenth and eleventh centuries. Definitions based upon size, frequency, components, place and time of assembly, and business treated end in contradiction. This confusion is understandable when one realizes that the witenagemot was an amoebic sort of organization with no definite composition or function. It was not just a large assembly of the great men of England upon festive occasions such as the crown-wearing and Christmas nor was it just a small council of constant and intimate officers and advisers of the king; it could be either. Whenever the king consulted with either body of men and it cooperated in the royal business of governing, that body can be considered a witenagemot. The nature of the business could be major or minor, and the king could consult at any place and at any time, though he favored certain towns like London and Winchester and preferred to consider major items of business at Christmas, Lent, and Easter when his court would have the greatest number of nobles present. In defining the nature of the witenagemot the most one can say is that it was an arbitrarily organized assembly completely undefined in composition. When any number, great or small, of the aristocrats were asked by the king to give him counsel and consent or to witness and license a royal act, this seemed to constitute a witenagemot. It is certain that on all important matters the king consulted with the witenagemot to secure its advice and consent.

That the witenagemot was a democratic national assembly representing the interests of all freemen of the realm is a figment of the imagination of nineteenth-century romantic and nationalistic historians who saw democracy in just about any medieval institution or document. There is not a shred of evidence to support this fantastic view; the witenagemot was aristocratic and totally unrepresentative. The king was the most important member, followed by relatives of the royal family. Next in importance were high-ranking ecclesiastics; the two archbishops were often present, as were bishops and abbots of the leading monasteries.[12] Though a few of the lesser clergy, such as the royal chaplains, attended, they had no great influence; they were undoubtedly there to serve as clerks. The lay nobility was headed by the earls or their early predecessors, the *eorls* or ealdormen. Then there were the lesser nobles, the thegns, who as members of the royal household or local officers such as the sheriffs attended the witenagemot when it assembled in the region where their lands lay. Occasionally thegns with no direct ties with the king attended. But always thegns were inferior in number to the greater lords and played a decidedly subordinate role in the assembly.

An attempt to establish the average number of lords who attended is of no value; it would not reflect the normal composition for there was none. The king always had some lords with him as members or officers of the royal household; if he consulted with them or used them in the task of governing, they would be a witenagemot. When the king met with many lords from various parts of the kingdom, the members of the household merely became a part of a much larger witenagemot. For routine business the king used the lords of the household plus what lords happened to be in the neighborhood of the royal residence; important matters were discussed upon festive occasions when the lords of the kingdom would normally be with the king. But if affairs became urgent the king could summon the great lords to meet with him at London or wherever he chanced to be. Some lords, especially the

[12] SM, no. 4.

greater prelates and earls, were summoned more often than others, yet none had to be summoned nor was the king obligated to summon certain ones. When the lords met with the king it was not as representatives of their local area and its inhabitants but as representatives of their own interests; they came to the witenagemot by virtue of their social position and the amount of land they held. The ordinary freeman never appears and there is no reason to believe that his superiors bothered about working for his interests.

The functions of the witenagemot were varied. We no longer believe that the Anglo-Saxons did not legislate. The theory that Anglo-Saxon custom was fundamental law, unalterable and existing from time out of mind of man, does not tally with the facts. The kings and the doomsmen did more than declare the law; they made it. Even where the kings declared that they had merely collected or confirmed custom and put it in writing, legislation was involved; a group of laws had been selected and were henceforth to be obeyed. We have no proof that any of the codes were exhaustive; much custom, as for example that governing marriage, was never written down. No one, however, who reads the dooms can deny that new law was made; it had to be made in order to control the problems that arose with a growing kingdom and society. And although the king could make the law alone, generally he consulted with a large witenagemot; he seemed to feel that to consult with men from all parts of the kingdom produced a wider sampling of opinion and gave the law more solid support. If only for purposes of good public relations and propaganda the king would make law with as many of his nobles as possible. Occasionally some of them may have proposed laws but in general it seems that the king and his intimate advisers drafted most of the laws and consulted the witenagemot for its opinion and consent.

A study of the dooms shows that the legislation was both secular and ecclesiastical. That king and witenagemot should legislate for the church was unquestioned when the leading members were ecclesiastics; there was no time or thought for fine and impractical distinctions. The ecclesiastics were, however, chiefly responsible for the preparation of laws relative to the church, and the lay nobility merely gave its consent. To cite at random a few ecclesiastical laws, we find King Wihtred and the witenagemot declaring that "if a priest permits an illicit union, or neglects the baptism of a sick person, or is so drunk that he cannot [perform it], he is to abstain from his ministration until the bishop's sentence."[13] According to the laws of King Ine of Wessex a "child is to be baptized within 30 days." The dooms of Ethelred the Redeless ordered that "bishops and abbots, monks and nuns, priests and women devoted to God, are to submit to their duty and to live according to their rule and to intercede zealously for all Christian people." Previously noted was the cooperation of the witenagemot with King Wihtred of Kent in the publication of his dooms. King Ine stated in a prologue to his dooms that he had consulted with the churchmen and great nobles of the kingdom,

[13] SM, no. 3.

and that they had inquired into secular and spiritual matters so that "true law and true statutes might be established and strengthened throughout our people." Alfred collected and published previous laws with the advice of his witenagemot. King Athelstan issued laws "along with the councillors who have been with me at Christmas at Exeter." Canute's laws were made with "the advice of councillors . . . at the holy Christmas season at Winchester."[14]

Just as the witenagemot could not legislate except by invitation of the king, neither could it give unsolicited advice and consent on other royal business. In general, however, the king felt out its opinion before taking major decisions on war, peace, and treaties; and even for routine business, consultation was normal. This cooperation reflected the king's bid for wide public support for his actions. When Alfred concluded a treaty some time between 886 and 890 with King Guthrum of the Danes, he did so with the "councillors of all the English race." Bede tells us that in 627 King Edwin accepted the Christian faith with the consent of the witenagemot. Occasionally the king consulted with the witenagemot in planning military and naval operations. In 996 Ethelred the Redeless and the witenagemot decided to assemble the fleet at London and appointed certain commanders to lead it against the Danes. Edward the Confessor seems to have disbanded some of his fleet and sailors in 1050 and 1051 upon the advice of the witenagemot; the following year he secured its advice for the appointment of naval commanders. For minor military decisions only a few of the witenagemot were consulted, probably just the members of the household.

The king lived principally upon the income from his lands and from the various indirect taxes and profits of justice. Many public services were performed gratuitously by men whose land so obligated them. We thus do not hear much of taxation in the witenagemot and, when we do, it usually concerns consent and advice regarding extraordinary taxation. In 991 when Ethelred the Redeless decided to bribe the Danes with Danegeld, the tax was approved by the witenagemot. Three years later it gave consent to a Danegeld of £16,000. In 1002 "the king and councillors determined that tribute should be paid"; they reached the same conclusion in 1007 and 1011. For extraordinary taxes that put a heavy strain upon the lands of all nobles, the king must have felt obliged to secure the consent of as many men as possible. The only regular (not annual) tax levied by king and witenagemot was the *heregeld*. In 1012–1013 the Danish king Swein demanded money and provisions for his army (*here*). In the same year Thorkell the Tall made similar demands for his fleet of forty-five ships then in the service of Ethelred the Redeless. To meet these two demands the king and witenagemot levied the *heregeld*. It continued to be levied by king and witenagemot to support standing naval and military forces until abolished in 1051 by Edward the Confessor.

[14] SM, nos. 4, 5, 9, 12, 13.

The judicial business of the witenagemot was not burdensome. It was a court of the first instance, that is, it had jurisdiction over cases concerning the king and the great men of the realm. This original jurisdiction dealt almost exclusively with disputes over bookland, the land which the king had created by charter.[15] Often the cases involved bishops and abbots whose claims to lands conflicted and needed to be settled by king and witenagemot. Seldom did the witenagemot act as a court of appeal; cases from lower courts came to it only when some local condition prevented justice from being obtained. The extent of the witenagemot's participation in cases involving treason and exile is hard to determine. The difficulty is to know when as members of a witenagemot the great lords declared treason and exile. We are certain of only a few cases. In 680 Bishop Wilfrid of Northumbria, who had been deprived of his bishopric and expelled from the kingdom by King Ecgfrith, brought his case before the witenagemot and produced a papal bull ordering his reinstatement. The assembly, however, imprisoned him for a time and then sent him into exile. *The Anglo-Saxon Chronicle* reports that in 1020 King Canute held a witenagemot at Easter and that outlawry was proclaimed against the ealdorman Ethelweard and the etheling Edwig. There is debate as to whether with his army or with his witenagemot Edward the Confessor outlawed Earl Godwin's son Swein in 1049. Evidence favors the view that Swein was outlawed by the army. In 1051 when Earl Godwin failed to obey the Confessor's order to punish those men of Dover who had attacked Count Eustace of Boulogne, Edward called a witenagemot at London and then exiled Godwin for treason.

Grants of land were made by the king in consultation with the witenagemot. These grants were known as bookland, that land granted by charter in outright ownership and exempted from most public burdens that fell on other land. Generally on these occasions the witenagemot was composed only of household officers and what lords happened to be with the king at the moment; all that the king sought was the sanction of the witenagemot and for this it was not necessary to call together a large number of lords. Such grants were not made indiscriminately because they might deprive the king of too much revenue and necessitate extraordinary taxation. Besides consenting to these grants the members of the witenagemot served as witnesses to the charter that made official recognition of the grant, and in so doing gave the charter a legal validity that could be appealed to should dispute over the land ever arise.[16] Moreover, the granting of land in the presence of the witenagemot gave the act official recognition and publicity; it was a good way to spread the news that such and such a man had come into ownership of certain land and rights.

In the appointment of ecclesiastical and lay officers the witenagemot had a minor role. Less important church posts were filled through election by

[15] SM, no. 5.
[16] SM, no. 5.

the clergy. With the major appointments such as archbishops, bishops, and abbots of great monasteries the will of the king was decisive. Though in making such appointments the king ordinarily consulted with ecclesiastical members of the witenagemot and a few great lords, he was not compelled to accept their advice; he could and did make appointments that were contrary to their will. In deposition of ecclesiastics the witenagemot possibly carried more weight. For such a step the king needed the support of ecclesiastical and lay backing. In 1043 Stigand, bishop of Elmham, was deposed by the Confessor and witenagemot because he supported the candidacy of Magnus, king of Norway, to the English throne. Upon Earl Godwin's return to power in 1052, Edward the Confessor was persuaded to hold at London a witenagemot which deposed and outlawed Robert of Jumièges, archbishop of Canterbury, and Ulf, bishop of Dorchester. Except with a weak king to whom a great lord like Earl Godwin could dictate, the appointment as well as the dismissal of lay officials such as ealdormen, earls, and sheriffs was a matter of the royal will. Of course the king could and sometimes did get advice, but apparently this was not a regular practice.

The right to kingship, as we have noted, came to rest upon heritable succession within one family. If there were no heirs or only ones incapable of rule, the fittest member of the family customarily became king. Whenever possible the king designated his eldest son or someone of his choice. This was done by King Ethelwulf of Wessex. Edward the Elder designated his son Athelstan as successor; Canute divided his North Sea kingdom between sons; and the Confessor, upon his deathbed, probably nominated Harold as successor. In most cases, therefore, the witenagemot did not select or elect the king. Undoubtedly it consulted with the king upon a successor when it was difficult to find a suitable one, and obviously it played an essential part in choosing a successor if the king died leaving no close heir and without having made previous disposition for succession. But the witenagemot was still limited in its choice by the fittest member of the royal family. Normally, then, the witenagemot did not elect a king but merely recognized a king who came to the throne by heritable right or by previous disposition. For strong kingship it could not be otherwise. No one could legally style himself king without the consent of the witenagemot, but consent was generally given; seldom was there any trouble.

There are some historians who believe that at times, usually during duress or war, the witenagemot elected the king. But certainly when the witenagemot accepted Canute and William the Conqueror as kings no real election was involved; conquest forced acceptance. Those members of the witenagemot who accepted the son of Ethelred the Redeless, Edmund Ironside, instead of Canute were not electing but merely consenting to the son of the former king. In spite of some claim that the witenagemot elected the Confessor, evidence points to Harthacanute's designating Edward as his successor in preference to any Danish candidates. Although, as we have seen,

Harold claimed to have received Edward's deathbed blessing, there is some reason to believe that he was elected. Edgar the Etheling, who traced his descent through Edward the Exile back to Ethelred the Redeless and thus to the West Saxon kings, had the best heritable claim, but, a sickly youth who had lived practically all his life outside England, he could not cope with the tasks of kingship. The witenagemot, therefore, turned to the most capable man, Harold, and elected him king. There was little choice, to be sure, but still it was an election. The election of Edgar the Etheling after Harold's death can hardly be counted; he never really ruled because William the Conqueror never gave him that opportunity.

Evidence that the witenagemot deposed kings is scanty and is limited to the Heptarchic period. In 774 King Alcred of Northumbria was deposed by "the counsel and consent of all his people," meaning, perhaps, by a witenagemot. Another vague reference of about the same time suggests the deposition of another Northumbrian king. In 775 *The Anglo-Saxon Chronicle* notes that King Sigebert of Wessex was deprived of his kingdom by "Cynewulf and the councillors of the West Saxons." Obviously no generalization can be made from this meager evidence. What it seems to suggest is that a powerful lord gathered a strong faction of other lords around him and then proceeded to remove the king. But the times were too anarchical when these so-called depositions occurred to regard them as being conducted in a calm and judicial atmosphere. All that can be said is that if a king was so bad or incompetent that he could not control the great lords, they rose up and removed him by force, often replacing him with the leader of the opposition.

A witenagemot, then, can be defined as an assembly of the king with the men who constituted his household and the aristocracy at large for consultation on any sort of business. The most important members were the great prelates, earls, and royal household officers, but the composition was not defined or limited. The members had no definite rights and functions and consulted with the king only when he so wished. The king controlled the witenagemot and initiated most of the business. In no respect can it be viewed as a democratic national assembly. It was strongest when the kings were weak or during periods of minority and interregnum. And yet the king felt obliged to consult with the witenagemot; no king would have ruled for long without its support and confidence. By meeting with the king, the lords had an opportunity to voice their opinions and to discuss matters of common interest. Here, at least, was a precedent for future cooperation between king and lords in governing the realm. But it is too early to see the witenagemot as a defined or established part of royal government.

3. THE ROYAL HOUSEHOLD

The earliest Germanic kings had about them more than the members of their immediate family. The royal household began with the first kings.

Tasks had to be performed for the king by men constantly at his side. Because the first duties were military, it is therefore reasonably certain that the antecedent of the household organization is to be found in the *comitatus* of Tacitus. Warriors close to the king's person provided constant military support. The earliest Anglo-Saxon kings were attended by such a *comitatus*, with perhaps some modifications in its organization. By the seventh century there is evidence that a noble class of warriors called *gesiths* supplied a military entourage for the king. Seemingly the *gesiths* did not receive land but were directly maintained by the king. It was not long, perhaps even in the early tenth century, until the *gesith* disappeared as a legally recognized class, giving way to an elevated rank of the noble class which went under the general name of thegns. Henceforth we hear of the king's thegns who performed the household service. All nobles were thegns but only royal thegns were members of the household. Unlike their predecessors, the *gesiths*, they were rewarded for their service with land, a development that may explain why thegns were a legally recognized class. When Canute became king he brought with him a royal bodyguard of Danish warriors called *huscarls*. At the outset they may have been necessary to protect a foreign king, but they continued as the royal bodyguard to 1066. At first they were maintained like the *gesiths* but gradually they came to receive land.

In origin, then, the household was military and it remained so down to 1066. Meanwhile the kings became involved in duties other than fighting; they became occupied with the administration of their land, finance, and justice. Unable to handle all the tasks personally, they began to delegate such work to members of the household. It is with this delegation of authority that the household became a royal organ of administration. Though evidence for the organization of the household prior to the tenth century is negligible, we must still assume that households were in existence. The king required food, drink, and clothing; his horses needed provisions and care. Multifarious services were required to insure the travel of the king, his family, and his household from residence to residence. From an early time members of the household were given specific domestic functions to perform. When these domestic functions combined with related public duties the men performing them became also officers of the state.

Traditionally historians have compared the Anglo-Saxon household to the Merovingian and Carolingian; some have looked to the continental household as the model for the English. Generally they are correct. Both developed out of the *comitatus* and were composed of officers responsible first for domestic duties and later for public ones. Undeniably the household of Charlemagne and his successors influenced the Anglo-Saxon household but we cannot press this comparison too far. The Merovingian and Carolingian household was modified in some respects by the imperial court organization of the Late Roman Empire; this is not true with the Anglo-Saxon household. Although the titles and functions of the households corresponded, the Anglo-Saxon showed certain unique characteristics. The Merovingian household came to be dominated by an officer styled *major domus*, called traditionally by historians, mayor of the palace. While holding the office of *major domus* the Carolingians became powerful enough to supersede the Merovingians as kings of the Franks. The Anglo-Saxon household had no such officer. In the eighth century a royal reeve called *praefectus regis* appears for an instant, but it would be rash to identify him as the head of the household. From first to last the Anglo-Saxon kings remained the masters of their household. The Carolingian household consisted of four chief officers—the seneschal or steward, butler, chamberlain, and marshal—who fulfilled domestic and public administrative functions. The Anglo-Saxon household had comparable officers, frequently with two or three bearing the same title, but not until the tenth century do they fulfil public functions. Probably these officers took turns at court; perhaps they became honorary officers and the menial domestic work was accomplished by ordinary servants. Some scholars have thought the plurality of officers was a willful design of Alfred and his successors to restrain any of the officers from becoming too powerful.

The *discthegns* (seneschals) were responsible for provisioning the royal household, but, unlike the Carolingian seneschals, they had no pre-eminence over other functionaries. The first evidence of a *discthegn* comes from the reign of Athelstan. The *byrel* (butler or cupbearer) kept the royal thirst quenched. The chamberlains (*burthegns, bedthegns, cubicularii, camerarii*) were charged with the supervision of the royal bedchamber or chamber (*camera*) and dressing room or wardrobe (*garderoba*). The *horsthegns* (marshals) supervised the royal stables and took charge of the royal itinerary. Canute introduced a Danish household officer called a *staller*. Sometimes there were as many as eight *stallers*, and evidence indicates they held a more elevated position than the other officers. Their tasks seem to have been military and they may have been officers in command of *huscarls*. Their importance, however, was transitory; after 1066 we hear no more of them. The last members of the household were the priests who administered to the spiritual needs of the king and royal family. At first responsible solely for domestic duties, these royal officers, *intimates* and *familiares* as the records call them, gradually came to assume public administrative tasks. They formed a corps of experts around the king, a type of executive organ that initiated and supervised royal government. They were more than a witenagemot that consulted with the king because day in and day out they fulfilled the royal will. Most members of the witenagemot, even the royal officers (*ministri*) concerned with local administration, saw the king only sporadically, and none were solely occupied with royal government. It was, therefore, mainly from the household that the later permanent royal council was to emerge. For the present our concern lies only with those domestic officers whose functions became important in royal administration. The seneschal, butler, marshal, and *stallers* were never important; the key officials were the chamberlains and royal priests.

The chamber, as we have seen, was a bedroom; adjacent to it was a dressing room called the wardrobe where the king stored his valuables. Being near the royal person the chamber was considered the most secure place to keep strongboxes and chests for the storage of robes of silk and fur, money and bullion, jewels, religious ornaments, books, and documents. The first reference to the chamberlains who cared for the chamber and wardrobe is in a will of King Edred in 955; he left some money to his *hraegethegns*. To the end of the Anglo-Saxon period each king seems to have had two or three chamberlains. Edgar the Elder had three; Edmund Ironside, two; and Edward the Confessor, three. In addition to the duties of the chamber and wardrobe, these officers gradually undertook official assignments. There had to be deposits and disbursements of the precious items under their care and so they became involved in finance. The idea that a man's chamber was the safest place for his treasure turned domestic servants into public servants. The intimate relation between private and public business during this period is vividly illustrated by a story about Hugh, the chamberlain of King Edward the Confessor. One day while Edward was taking his nap Hugh quietly entered the royal chamber to take some money out of a chest to pay for the current expenses of the household. In a hurry, he forgot to lock the chest, thus giving a scullion from the kitchen an opportunity to sneak in and steal some of the money.

For expediency in making deposits and disbursements as well as for additional storage space some of the kings resorted to putting part of their treasure in other secure places. King Edred stored money and records in Dunstan's abbey; both Canute and Edward the Confessor put money at Winchester, which by then may have been a permanent place of deposit or treasury (*thesaurus*). No separate financial department with a single treasurer was organized prior to 1066. The chamber or wardrobe was the royal treasury and the chamberlains guarded, received, and disbursed all the royal treasure besides being responsible for domestic duties. Under these conditions we could not expect to find a well-developed financial department. As yet there was no distinction between public revenue and the personal revenue of the king; everything went to his chamber. *Domesday Book* does prove, however, that there was some organized royal financial machinery before the Conquest.

To the chamber came the revenues of indirect taxation such as tolls and duties, the royal fines (*wites* and *oferhyrnes*) from the courts, salvage from shipwrecks, and treasure-trove. Large sums of money had to be accounted for when the Danegeld and *heregeld* were levied. In turn, this money had to be paid out for tribute or for military service. The management of these revenues must have entailed a considerable administration. Our best evidence for such organization comes in connection with the rendering of the royal farm (*feorm*). When the Anglo-Saxon kings lived an itinerant life, constantly moving about their kingdom, they lived off the land. We have already seen that if the king decided to stop with his household for a night or so with some prelate, earl, or thegn, it was their obligation to feed and lodge the royal entourage. The king also stayed at his own estates, which supported him with food rents (*feorm*). Such a primitive arrangement lasted until the king became less itinerant and from choice or press of business came to reside for the most part at London, Winchester, or one of his favorite residences. Then the farm had to be reorganized. Some of the royal estates were responsible for a complete day's maintenance (*firma unius diei* or *noctis*) as their annual rent; others for only three-quarters or a half day's maintenance. Sometimes a group of estates were combined to pay a day's farm. From local storehouses the food would be transported to the royal residence. Such an arrangement was clumsy and provided ample opportunity for food to disappear before it got into the royal mouth.

Although down to 1066 the kings still received some food rents in wheat, meat, and drink, constantly the rents in kind were commuted into money rents until by the eleventh century, whether paid in kind or money, they were always evaluated in terms of money. *Domesday Book*, for example, shows that the royal manors of Basingstoke, Kingsclere, and Hurstbourn in Hampshire were grouped together to pay one day's farm. On the other hand the manors of Barton Stacey and Eling each paid a sum of £38 8*s*. 4*d*. for a half day's farm. We thus find that the officers in charge of the royal manors were responsible for a certain sum per annum and that, unless the king resided at the manor and ate up the sum, they paid it to the sheriff who administered the shire in which the manor was located. The next administrative advance was to total up the sums due from all the royal manors in a shire and make the sheriff responsible for paying a set amount yearly into the chamber. By the reign of Edward the Confessor each sheriff paid a fixed yearly farm. If the king should grant some of his land to another person, the sheriff in whose shire the land lay was authorized to deduct from the fixed yearly farm the annual value of this land.

From *Domesday Book* comes another interesting fact about Anglo-Saxon royal finance. When the sheriffs paid their annual farm into the chamber, the money was frequently put to a test. The silver pennies, the only coins in circulation, were examined to see if they were of standard weight, that is, 240 good pennies to a pound. An assay was made and if 240 pennies did not weigh a pound, an additional number of pennies had to be added to make good the deficiency. Such a method was termed payment in blanch. By 1066, then, was developed an embyronic financial administration centered about the chamber and able to deal with a variety of transactions; it received the annual farms rendered by sheriffs and credited them with deductions made when lands were granted away, and it disbursed money for private and public business, keeping record of where the money went. Perhaps already it was using wooden tallies to keep these accounts. Indeed, it was sophisticated enough to check against clipping and counterfeiting and had initiated a primitive test to help the king get 240 good pennies for each pound. Out of the royal bedroom had come a department of finance.

The clergy attached to the royal household always looked after the royal spiritual needs, a function that became less important as they came to be pressed into other work. From the ecclesiastics who could read and write and who had been brought up in the long church tradition of the written record came the principal motivation for the king's use of the written document. It was a natural step for the kings to employ them to draw up their documents, of which the earliest examples are charters from the late seventh century. The priests of the royal chapel formed the first writing office (*scriptorium*) of the king. Until the tenth century, however, there is no evidence that the work of the royal clerks was extensive. They were still mainly concerned with the chapel plus witnessing royal charters. As on the Continent it was common in the early period for the kings not to draw up their own charters, only to ratify them. Frequently the interested parties drew up the charter and then presented it to the king for his confirmation. It is only with the reign of Athelstan that we can confidently assert the existence of an organized writing office. A uniformity of royal formulas and techniques of authentication prove that a royal secretariat was at work. To insure against forgery the clerks began to use the chirograph or indenture. A document would be copied two or three times on a piece of parchment and then the copies cut apart in a wavy or saw-toothed line. Each party would get a copy and to authenticate it he would have to match up the cut edge with the edges of the other copies. But this early medieval form of a jigsaw puzzle was extremely clumsy, and as the writing office became burdened with increased secretarial work it could not use it for the major part of the charters drawn up. It was the genius of the Anglo-Saxon royal secretariat to devise the royal writ. This simple and short instrument became the chief method of expressing the royal will in writing. To authenticate the writs a new technique was developed.

In medieval Italy the primary method to authenticate documents was the notarial. Certain well-qualified scribes came to be granted special recognition and authority by ecclesiastical and secular princes so that acts composed by them had a public and official character. These scribes or notaries formed special corporations that upheld a professional tradition and training. The validity of a document written by a member of such an organization was established by the special phraseology and script employed and by the peculiar signs placed on it by the notary. The notarial method, however, never gained much prominence outside Italy; western Europe remained primarily the land of the seal. Although the signet ring had authenticated documents of the Roman Empire, this technique was forgotten in the dark centuries after the Empire's fall, when validation was provided only by signature, crosses of witnesses, and other peculiar marks. Not until the Carolingian period did the seal again become the method for authenticating documents. By the eleventh century it was the prevailing method. Made from wax and imprinted with a symbol and other marks depicting the authority of the prince responsible for the charter, the seal hung to the charter by being pressed onto a strip of parchment cut generally from the lower margin of the document. Soon the great territorial prince expressed his political power by imprinting on his seal a likeness of himself sitting on a throne or a horse, garbed in princely robes, and holding symbols of authority. Larger than the usual seals, this type was called the great seal.

By the early eleventh century all the powerful rulers such as the emperors of Germany, the kings of France, the counts of Flanders, and the dukes of Normandy had their great seals. In general this evolution was followed at the English court. From the ninth century to the reign of Edward the Confessor the smaller royal seal was attached to the writ. Seals may also have been put to the longer charters (diplomas) but there are none extant for the Anglo-Saxon period. Under Edward the Confessor the great seal first appears. It differed from the continental ones in that rather than being a single-faced pendant seal it was imprinted on both sides; such a seal does not appear in France until the reign of Louis VI (1108–1137). Probably Edward's seal imitated the lead *bulla* of papal and Byzantine documents, which had two faces and had been in use since the seventh century.

The increase in secretarial work forced the household to expand and organize its personnel more efficiently. The priests or clerks who staffed the writing office were skilled, clever men. By the eleventh century some were rewarded for their good service with appointments as bishops and abbots. But it is impossible to pin down the organization to anything very definite. On the Continent since Carolingian times there had developed in the better-organized states and bishoprics a secretariat supervised by an officer, originally just a clerk, who came to be styled chancellor in the tenth century and who by the eleventh not only supervised the writing staffs but also authenticated documents with the great seal, then under his custody. Though this development undoubtedly influenced the English court and though Edward the Confessor's employment of Norman churchmen must have familiarized the household with the chancellor and his functions, we still cannot find any evidence of a chancellor. We know of several men under the Confessor who supervised the secretariat and served as a type of chancellor but they did not guard the great seal. Despite our lack of evidence for specific terms, we may still conclude that in all but name a chancellor and chancery existed in England before 1066. The essential fact is that a well-organized writing office with responsible officials operated in the last days of Edward the Confessor just as it did on the Continent. The Normans introduced many innovations but they had a solid foundation upon which to build.

By 1066 the Anglo-Saxon kings had established political unity in England.

Over the kingdom shaped by incessant struggle had been superimposed a fairly well-defined central administration. To attempt precise definition of the parts that constituted this central administration would be folly. The functions were still too vague in the minds of those who performed them, and there was not yet any conception of separation or specialization of powers. There were, nevertheless, clearly defined tendencies and opinions nurtured by centuries of experience and custom that influenced and circumscribed the central power. To flout this opinion for long was to invite political disaster. The strong and intelligent kings knew what was expected of them and how far they could press their power without consulting their household officers and lords who composed the membership of the witenagemot. The support and consent of this body assured the king that widely dispersed opinion condoned what he did and that he was acting within the bounds of accepted custom. Were he to ignore this custom, consent and cooperation would be withheld and he would be faced with an opposition that could forcibly remove him if pushed to that extreme. From the household with its domestic functions came an executive core which could carry out the royal will in government. Private functions turned into public ones. And in the chamber and writing office there emerged financial and secretarial units that anticipated the exchequer and chancery of the Norman-Angevin kings.

V

Local Administration

ALWAYS there are chronicles and records of kings and their esteemed associates, but for men of lesser estate the historian meets with no such fortune. More often than not their history must be gleaned from inferences in sources whose primary purpose is the recording of other facts—areas of land, tenures, revenue, the law, services, and the like. The commonplace in history has always been slighted and local Anglo-Saxon government reflects this lacuna because it was a government of local and common men. In that a small core of fact plus considerable deduction must form the basis of any account of this government, generalizations, however cautious, will have their contradictions. What follows is an attempt to present the historical generalizations that have lived longest with the fewest contradictions.

Going again to Tacitus, we find that his vaguest words are on local organization of the German tribes. Each tribe was divided into *pagi* and each *pagus* was composed of villages called *vici*. Apparently these divisions were not in terms of land allotment but based on numbers of men, of which the figure one hundred seems to underlie all calculations. Perhaps a *pagus* was composed of one hundred households and perhaps it had to supply one hundred warriors or one hundred judges. In turn the *vici* may have been subdivisions of the area allotted to support the number one hundred, of whatever it may have consisted. Beyond these few remarks all that can be learned from Tacitus is that the *principes* administered the *pagi* and were assisted in the work of justice by men from the *vici*. The village, a community of cultivators, may have been a division of the *pagus* for the administration of justice.

To fit the only account of early Germanic local government into the scheme of government found after German kingdoms had been established on the old Roman Empire is tricky. How much was their own and how much was taken from the Roman organization? The Ostrogoths in Italy and later the Lombards, as well as the Visigoths in Septimania and Spain, were strongly influenced by Roman provincial organization. Generally the provinces (*provinciae*) were retained and over them the kings appointed dukes (*duces*) with financial, judicial, military, and administrative powers. The provinces were divided into city-states (*civitates*) over each of which there was a subordinate official called a count (*comes*) with powers similar to those of the dukes. Commonly the senators (*curiales*) of the city-state were retained to provide local administration and collect taxes. Though at first Germanic organization of *pagus* and *vicus* may have been retained, once the roots of settlement took hold these divisions seem to have been absorbed into the Roman scheme.

The early Frankish organization was somewhat different and a knowledge of it is more relevant for us because of the light it throws on Anglo-Saxon government. The Salic Law, composed during the last years of Clovis (507–511), is the first and best source after Tacitus. The territory in Gaul conquered by Clovis was arranged in *pagi* where the royal authority was represented by an officer called *grafio* (later *comes*). The *pagi* were subdivided into hundreds (*centenae*) which had courts of justice presided over by the hundred-man (*centenarius*), who pronounced judgments with the help of selected landed men called *rachineburgi.* In the sixth and seventh centuries a slight change occurred. Where at first the *pagi* seem to have corresponded to the Roman city-states, now, particularly in northern Gaul, they were so numerous that a number of them composed a city-state. The *comes*, though still representing the king in all financial, judicial, military, and administrative matters, was now assisted in such business by a subordinate called a vicar who came to administer a subdivision of the *pagus* called a vicariate. It would seem that the hundred-man had become identified with the vicar. Less Romanized than the Germans to the south and farther from the core of things Roman, the Franks lagged behind in adapting their local tribal government to the Roman. Never did it become as Roman as, for example, that of the Ostrogoths. In summary, apparently Roman influence and permanent settlement of vast new lands considerably altered German tribal government. It is impossible to compare in area or numbers the old *pagus* to the new one, which was now either a province, city-state, or division of a city-state. The tribe had become a kingdom composed of larger territorial divisions. As for the old number of one hundred, it appears only in the form of the Frankish hundred-man, who presided over the court of the hundred and later of the vicariate. It is obviously incorrect to regard the Tacitean description as underlying the local organization that developed in the German kingdoms between the fifth and seventh centuries.

Untouched by Roman culture before their migration and coming into contact with only a dying remnant of Roman civilization when they arrived in Britain, the Anglo-Saxons made no striking alteration in their local government. Roman provincial government was not copied and a purely Germanic organization developed. The new political configurations were unlike the ones found in Tacitus but still resembled them more than those on the Continent. Conquest and permanent settlement changed tribes into kingdoms; chiefs became kings and allotted the land to their faithful followers who eventually settled down in various parts. For some time the men with the most land must have been responsible for the administration of local government but only in the capacity of men faithful to their lord; as yet there were no officers. Administrative districts were still undefined, at most corresponding roughly to the territorial power and sway of the great lords. As kingdom succeeded kingdom and as some disappeared, local organization reflected these changes. As the early kingdoms were absorbed into the Heptarchy, as Northumbria and Mercia became dominant, and as the West Saxon kings unified the kingdom of England, kingdoms became administrative districts.

To imagine the Anglo-Saxons coming to Britain in *pagi* of one hundred households or warriors under their *principes* and then meticulously allotting the land after conquest is just an academic hobby. It is like conceiving of Hengist and Horsa arriving in command of two forces divided into regiments and battalions and accompanied by a team of civil government experts whose task was to organize local government after conquest. Local government in Anglo-Saxon England was indebted to ancient tradition and custom on the Continent but much more to the fortunes of war, conquest, and settlement.

1. THE SHIRE

Literally shire means a share or division of a larger whole; its origins were diverse. Kent, Sussex, Essex, Middlesex, and Surrey in southern and eastern England, which were the first shires, were originally kingdoms. They first fell to other kings or Bretwaldas and became subkingdoms under subkings and, later, shires administered by officials of the Bretwaldas. The shires of Norfolk and Suffolk were probably formed from tribal divisions of East Anglia. Many shires in Wessex were organized around early points of settlement; the shire Somerset was thus set up around Somerton, Hampshire around Southampton, Dorset around Dorchester, and Wiltshire around Wilton. This type of local organization probably stems from the fact that the kings of Wessex established their hegemony over various chieftains whose lands had hitherto not been separated by precise borders but merely by forests, streams, and waste. Mercia and Northumbria were not organized into real shires until conquered by the Danes. Previous to Danish occupation Northumbria was divided into two districts, Lancashire and Yorkshire. The kingdom of Mercia, ruled by Penda and his successors, had been formed from five large districts which were probably the original settlements.

It cannot be proven that these settlements, divisions, and shires were modeled upon or corresponded to the old *pagi*. The Danes, conquering the north and east of England in the ninth century, ignored the existing divisions and set up administrative areas around strongholds (boroughs) built to hold the country in subjugation. Thus arose the so-called Five Boroughs of Leicester, Lincoln, Nottingham, Stamford, and Derby. United into a confederacy these boroughs sent Danes to a general assembly that constituted a high court pronouncing Danish law.

Meanwhile the kings of Wessex set up shires as burghal districts around boroughs or strategically situated communities. When the kings acquired all the lands below the Thames, they incorporated small kingdoms first as subkingdoms under subkings and then as shires under royal officials. There is evidence that such organization began at least a century before Alfred's reign and continued until Wessex had unified England. After Alfred had halted the Danes his successors struck out into the western Midlands, where they built boroughs surrounded by territory arranged into shires. This process continued until most of England had been put into shires. Conquering the Danelaw, the kings converted the Five Boroughs into shires along with the land still outside such division.

But more should be said about the burghal organization of shires. Alfred had been rearranging his shires for military and financial purposes long before his successors began organizing shires to the north. The *Burghal Hidage* from Edward the Elder's reign suggests that most of the shires had been put into districts surrounding boroughs. These burghal districts were based upon fiscal rather than territorial assessment. Each borough and the area about was assessed in so many units called hides for the support of military service. Although the hide was generally a measurement of land equivalent to 120 acres, in this case it was used as a fiscal measurement. There seems to be no equation between the hides of land of a burghal area and the number of fiscal hides for which it was assessed. For taxes each burghal area was assessed in so many round figures of fiscal hides. By totaling up the number of boroughs in a shire and the number of hides for which each was assessed, one can determine the number of fiscal hides in a shire. Wiltshire, for example, contained five boroughs respectively assessed for 1400, 300, 700, 1500, and 1300 hides. This gives a total of 5200 hides for the shire. The kings applied this fiscal assessment to the shires established in the Midlands when they moved towards the Danelaw. Throughout this area one finds a symmetrical assessment of hides in figures of one hundred; burghal districts of hides made up the shires. The shires of Anglo-Saxon England were derived, therefore, from a combination of primitive settlements, kingdoms, and the artificial organization of the Danes and the West Saxon kings.

Until the reign of Edward the Elder the administrative districts and shires were headed by officials styled ealdormen.[1] They probably came originally from royal families who had ruled over territories converted into districts of a larger kingdom; at times they were relatives of the king appointed to the office. The ealdormen had been appointed because the king needed officials who could exercise delegated powers locally; he needed assistance in the business of governing. The ealdorman was thus the royal representative in the shire. He mustered and led the men to combat, he presided over the shire court, he executed all royal commands. He was the principal contact of the king with the shires of his realm. For these services the ealdorman was

[1] SM, nos. 4, 5, 11.

richly rewarded. He received grants of land; he could claim hospitality and maintenance for himself, his officers, and his servants; he received a third of the fines from the profits of justice and collected as well a third of the revenues derived from tolls and duties levied in the boroughs of his shire. If anyone disturbed a meeting where he was presiding, he was entitled to a fine of 120s.[2] His house was protected by a special peace, and higher compensation had to be paid to him for infraction of this peace.

Essentially the ealdormen were royal officials responsible to the king's will. The theory that ascribes the origin of the ealdorman to an elected tribal representative as, for example, the *princeps* of Tacitus rests on no sound evidence. The ealdorman could be removed when the king so willed; the evidence always portrays an official carrying out the royal command and not the will of the men of the shire. Though the earliest ealdormanships and those of the eleventh century tended to be hereditary, they were mainly appointive offices. Whereas in the last quarter of the ninth century Wessex had an ealdorman for each shire, Mercia had less than six. The expansion of Wessex changed this pattern. Edward the Elder combined three or four shires under one ealdorman, and by the reign of Edmund three ealdormen headed all the shires below the Thames and five all those in the Midlands and East Anglia. In the tenth century a few great families provided the ealdormen. Under Canute all England was controlled by a few powerful men who came to be called earls rather than ealdormen.[3] By the eleventh century the office had accrued so much power that it was dangerous to the authority of the king. Earl Leofric, for example, controlled Mercia, and Earl Godwin, Wessex. Their power was immense and the office was passed on to their sons. Their interests had long ceased to be local; their stakes were now control of the royal government. Earl Godwin obtained this, and Harold after him. Inevitably these extensive interests drew them away from their primary tasks of administering the shire.

When groups of shires were put under the control of one ealdorman he could no longer attend personally to all the duties; this situation gave rise to a new royal officer to help the ealdorman—the sheriff. Henceforth the shire was to become his special preserve. The antecedents of the sheriff are found among the royal officials called reeves (*gerefas*) who had an administrative rank inferior to that of the ealdorman. As early as the reign of King Ine of Wessex we find a royal reeve serving in the household. Not until around 800, however, are royal reeves found representing the king locally. It was a royal reeve who rode down to the sea to the first Danes, presumably for collecting tolls from men he thought to be merchants. Throughout the ninth century, especially at the time of Alfred, we hear more of the royal reeves. We see them acting as subordinates of the ealdorman, collecting dues and labor services from royal estates, presiding over courts, and per-

[2] SM, no. 5.
[3] SM, nos. 5, 13.

forming military functions.[4] By the tenth century they have become extremely important judicial officers at royal manors (*tuns*) and at boroughs. With the help of subordinates they enforced royal rights and, as official witnesses, supervised commercial transactions.[5] These reeves, however, cannot yet be identified as shire reeves or sheriffs; their duties did not yet embrace the whole shire. But though the ealdorman still administered the shire and presided over its court, most of his duties were fulfilled by the reeves.

The first evidence of a reeve's administering a shire is in an enactment of Athelstan. It designates the shire as the district headed by a reeve (*gerefa*) and states that he presided over the folk court and received pledges for the observance of peace.[6] By the reign of Edgar the shire had become a financial district headed by the reeve, and a document between 964 and 988 shows the reeve presiding over a shire court. Definitely, then, the sheriff had come into being by the middle of the tenth century. His appearance coincides with the expansion of Wessex and the centralization of local government. The ealdorman now headed a group of shires, and the reeve, who had been the ealdorman's subordinate and had concentrated his activities on the burghal districts about the boroughs which had been the local royal financial units, now came to administer the shire, which had supplanted the burghal district as the financial unit of local government.

The king appointed the sheriff during pleasure. Some sheriffs held office for many years and were retained by succeeding kings. Edward the Confessor began to place some sheriffs over two shires as, for example, Norfolk and Suffolk. The perquisites of the office consisted of grants of land from the king and the privilege of farming royal estates and keeping some of the profits. Theoretically the ealdorman was still to preside over the shire court held twice a year and the sheriff was to remain his judicial deputy. But as whole regions of England came under control of the ealdorman, he presided less frequently. By the reign of Edward the Confessor the sheriff regularly presided over shire courts and exercised all the judicial powers of the ealdorman. In the eleventh century the sheriff was also presiding over subordinate judicial sessions termed hundred courts. Although he was not present at all twelve courts held each year, he or a deputy called a *motgerefa* headed each session. The military obligations of the shire were now the sheriff's care. He could claim bodyguard for his tours around the shire. He received orders to assemble the shire levy and led it to fight under the king. In the western shires sheriffs directed the defense against Welsh incursions; in others they defended towns when necessary. As an officer of justice the sheriff proclaimed the king's peace in the shire and led men in pursuit of criminals. His financial functions were of great importance. Already we have seen how he collected the annual farm of the shire, accounted for it at the

[4] SM, no. 5.
[5] SM, nos. 6, 7.
[6] SM, no. 7.

chamber, and made disbursements from the shire revenue. By the reign of Edward the Confessor judicial profits had come to be lumped in with the farm of the royal manors and all these had to be collected by the sheriff. Special fines for breaking the royal peace were collected and accounted for separately. Land forfeited to the king was taken over by the sheriff and administered until its disposition. The royal income from boroughs was accounted for by the sheriff and he helped to assess and collect Danegelds when the king levied them. All sorts of miscellaneous service due the king was the sheriff's responsibility. When the king traveled through a shire, a special bodyguard was provided; while he resided in a borough, guards were supplied to protect his residence. When Edward the Confessor hunted around Shrewsbury, men of the town with horses guarded him, and the sheriff supplied thirty-six men on foot to stalk the deer. Special requisitions were made for the king and for royal service; one finds the sheriff securing plow service, supervising the cutting and gathering of hay, and assembling guards to protect the royal fields from wandering cattle.

By 1066 the sheriff was a key official and an important person; he was entitled to a bodyguard. When he presided over the shire court, he proclaimed royal commands and enactments and then executed them. As head of the hundred and shire courts he held jurisdiction over criminal justice. He had become a responsible military official in local and national defense. He had almost exclusive control of the shire finances. He helped to supervise royal estates and provided the king comfort and protection when honored by the royal presence. The sheriff was, in fact, responsible for shire government. His power made him a prototype for the later unscrupulous Norman sheriffs. At times he usurped royal rights, used royal estates for his own purposes, encroached on private land and rights, and collected revenues with a view only to lining his own pockets.

Constitutionally the sheriff is most interesting for his relation to earl and king. He generally worked for the king and was controlled by him, although under Edward the Confessor there was danger that the powerful earls might make the sheriff a tool of their local interests. But the government of the Anglo-Saxon shire was dualistic. The sheriff was, on the one hand, a royal representative and, on the other, the judicial and financial deputy of the earl, who never abdicated his power in local government but held to his financial and judicial perquisites to the end. Gradually, however, the sheriff was to become the chief royal officer in the shire and one of the royal centralizing forces. Through him kings were to direct administration on the local level. In the sheriff had been found a bridge between the central and local institutions, a bridge that was to be essential in the growth of English constitutional government.

The shire court, which will be discussed in detail when we treat the law, was an administrative and judicial assembly. At times it was convened to hear proclaimed the commands and enactments of the king and to help the sheriff provide the machinery for implementing these commands. Twice a year it was a judicial court assembled to deal with criminal, civil, and ecclesiastical cases.[7] It was the highest such court and few cases went above it to the king. Theoretically the men who attended the court were all the freemen of the shire. Actually they were only the great lords of the shire—the bishops, earls, and thegns. They helped to carry out the royal will and provided the suitors of the court, who declared the law and indicated what form of proof the accused party had to undergo to prove his innocence or guilt. The shire court was completely dominated by the aristocratic landowner. To see in it all the freemen assembling to elect officers, to govern themselves, and to judge themselves is but a misconception of democratic enthusiasts of the nineteenth century.

2. THE HUNDRED

When the expansion of the Anglo-Saxon kingdom in the tenth century required an administrative division into shires, such reorganization must have influenced the development of the hundred, the unit into which shires were divided. For convenience we shall call all these divisions hundreds, even though in the shires of Lincoln, Derby, Leicester, Nottingham, and parts of York they were called wapentakes, a word of Danish origin which once denoted the flashing of weapons to symbolize assent to decisions in assemblies. We can establish no direct connection between the Anglo-Saxon hundred and the hundred warriors or households of Tacitus, but we have seen that the Franks retained a hundredal organization in which *pagi* were divided into administrative districts called hundreds with courts presided over by a hundred-man where the law was declared by law-worthy men. Hundredal organization was definitely characteristic of German local government. For the historian the problem has been to determine what constituted a hundred. Was it an area that had to supply one hundred men for military service, did it hold one hundred households, did it have an area of one hundred hides of land with each hide containing 120 acres, or was it an area assessed as one hundred fiscal hides for purposes of taxation? As yet there is no one answer to these questions. In the Midlands it is correct to say that areas called hundreds were assessed exactly at one hundred fiscal hides. But no such assessment held in other parts of England. In the south it appears that hundreds may have been organized earlier, perhaps on the basis of one hundred warriors or households. Within one shire the assessment of hundreds varied from 20 to 150 hides, and the number of hundreds in a shire varied from one shire to another; Sussex had fifty hundreds while Staffordshire had but five. The French historian Marc Bloch has justifiably called the hide one of the most mysterious units of the early Middle Ages. And Stenton,

[7] SM, no. 11.

the English authority on Anglo-Saxon history, has called the origin of the hundred "one of the most difficult problems of Anglo-Saxon history."

Skipping over the hundreds of the Midlands, which we know were created in the tenth century, we find that from quite an early time a need was felt for a small unit of government to handle justice, finance, and policing. As kingdoms came to embrace a considerable area it was impossible for men to meet with the king or to gather in large assemblies to settle their affairs. They therefore began to organize government locally, probably limiting their local unit to an area that could supply one hundred fighters or that contained one hundred households, each perhaps holding one hide of land (120 acres). Upon this scheme was organized a court, a policing system, and a tax structure. This arrangement endured until some time before Alfred when the kings desired to have a more precise fiscal and military organization. They seem to have split up and reassessed the local regions (*regiones*) at one hundred fiscal hides, the number liable for paying the royal farm and supplying military service. Evidence also points to the king's allocating a group of these assessed areas to a royal manor which served as administrative headquarters. In the eleventh century many hundreds still were attached to royal manors where formerly the royal farm was collected. For example, the six hundreds of Basingstoke, in existence even after the Conquest, seem to represent a survival of the time when six areas assessed at one hundred fiscal hides were lumped into an administrative area around the royal manor of Basingstoke. Almost wherever we look, therefore, the fiscal or areal hide seems to have been at the bottom of the hundredal organization.

This hypothesis when related to other developments of local administration becomes even more convincing. The laws of King Ine of Wessex show royal reeves not only supervising royal estates (*tuns*) but also performing such public functions as collecting revenue, policing, and executing orders of the king. They must also have come to preside over local courts whose jurisdiction was over areas smaller than a shire. We see this in the Laws of Edward the Elder.[8] Meanwhile territory around the royal manors assessed, as we have seen, in hundreds of hides was attached to the manor and formed a defined administrative district. This grouping was soon to be known as the hundred.

Although some historians have linked the folk courts of Alfred's day with the hundred, and others have regarded the *popularia concilia* under King Cenwulf of Mercia as a hundred court, evidence that speaks only of a people's court is too slim to use as proof for an organized hundred. We can only surmise that these were courts held by the royal officials heading the royal manors and the areas about them. The first real evidence of an organized hundred is supplied by a royal ordinance issued some time between 939

[8] SM, no. 6.

and 961; it suggests that hundreds came into existence in the first half of the tenth century. In stipulating that men of the hundred should assemble every four weeks to mete out justice, the ordinance indicates that a hundred-man was in charge. Men were also grouped into tens (tithings), perhaps to act as surety for each other's good conduct. More likely, however, the tithings were but territorial divisions of the hundred with tithingmen at their head. Upon summons all had to follow the hundred-man in the pursuit of criminals and wrongdoers. In the dooms, regulations for the holding of court and fines for failure to attend are stipulated, procedures to deal with stolen cattle and property are established, and rules for vouching to warranty are set up. About the same time laws of Edmund, concerned with the preservation of the public peace, provided that anyone engaging in a feud would incur a fine of 30s. payable to the hundred.[9] It is possible that earlier mention in the Laws of Edward the Elder to a reeve holding "a meeting every four weeks" may refer to a hundred court.[10]

In some respects the organization of the hundred resembled that of the shire. The court convened out of doors every fourth Sunday; the sheriff presided at least two or three times a year, and his subordinate (*motgerefa* or *gingran*) presided over the remaining sessions. The court was attended by lords of the hundred (thegns) or by their bailiffs representing them, by the parish priest, and by four respectable men from each agrarian community. The suitors to the court, who declared the law and ordered the form of proof, were customarily thegns, often twelve in number. Jurisdiction was over criminal and civil cases; here criminals were tried, disputes over land settled, and transfers of land witnessed. Profits of justice were shared with the king and with the local lords of manors whose rights or property had suffered harm. No case could be appealed to the shire court until fully dealt with at the hundred level. All men traveling to and from court were protected with a special peace and those who failed to answer a summons were fined. Though all freemen possessing land could attend the hundred court, those with the most land controlled the hundredal machinery, as was the case in the shire court. It should be observed that thegns declared the law, received some of the profits of justice as *landrica,* and helped the sheriff carry out administrative functions. For rendering a bad doom it is stated that a doomsman would lose his rank of thegn.[11] No rural democracy composed of small independent farmers is at work here. From the beginning the hand of the king and his royal officials can be seen in the growth of the hundred; it was seconded by the great landowners, who controlled and operated the machinery.

[9] SM, no. 9.
[10] SM, no. 6.
[11] SM, nos. 11, 13.

3. THE BOROUGH

Passing to the next lowest division of local government, one finds communities called boroughs whose inhabitants just prior to 1066 had acquired special privileges and a status far better than that of the mass of men. Despite the numerous theories advanced to explain why the borough attained such a privileged place, few satisfactorily account for its origin and peculiar characteristics. In summarizing these theories we should bear in mind that the word "borough," derived from the Anglo-Saxon *burh*, could mean two things. Originally it meant simply a fortified place, be it an old Roman camp, a fortified manor house or monastery, or the wood and earthen forts constructed by the kings in the tenth century. By the eleventh century borough had come to signify a town with inhabitants enjoying rights not held by men of the countryside; it had urban characteristics that we associate with towns today. The problem is to discover what changed the meaning of borough from fortress to town. No Roman towns survived to provide the basis for Anglo-Saxon town life. There is no evidence for the theory that derives towns from communities under bishops who, through royal grants of immunities, had come to exercise special privileges. According to this theory, when the communities won their independence they also exercised special privileges. Towns did not slowly evolve out of servile manorial villages and come to be governed by former manorial officers. Nor did towns develop from an agrarian community free from the outset. Such a community, called a *Landgemeinde* by German historians, was known as a township by English historians such as Kemble, Green, and Stubbs, all of whom enthusiastically endorsed this theory as best explaining the origin of the English town. Adherents to the theory can still be found. Some historians saw the origin of the town in social and religious associations that developed economic and political interests; but this deriving a town from a guild is putting the cart before the horse. Also untenable is the theory that explains towns as arising on market sites granted a special peace and mercantile privileges. Maitland's ingenious theory that towns grew from the fortified garrison sites and administrative centers built by Alfred and his successors is partially correct, and yet it falls short of explaining how a fort became a town.

The most plausible explanation seems to be the mercantile-settlement theory advanced by Pirenne and Rietschel and applied to England by Stephenson. They argued that old Roman camps, fortified monasteries or manor houses, or castles or boroughs strategically located at crossroads, at the confluence of streams, and on busy routes were the sites where towns first appeared, and that this development occurred only after trade and commerce revived in the tenth and eleventh centuries. The merchants who did the trading naturally passed through these places and soon settled around them for protection and because of their advantageous location. Because their profession was totally different from that of the inhabitants of the agrarian countryside, the merchants had to have special rights as, for example, freedom of mobility. They gradually won these privileges, which encompassed their settlement as well as the fortified stronghold. At this stage the borough was no longer a fort but a town with men and privileges totally different from those in the countryside. Thus understood, the borough was the product of social and economic forces rather than the descendant of a Germanic free village community or the recipient of special legal privileges. But the debatable point with this theory is when the transformation occurred. Certainly those historians err who place it as early as the eighth and ninth centuries. The evidence of these centuries depicts the borough as still a military and administrative site subject to the same custom governing the countryside; its inhabitants had no special privileges. On the other hand, those who credit the Norman Conquest with bringing England into the stream of continental economic life and thus causing the transformation are probably placing it too late. We have enough evidence to conclude that by the late tenth and early eleventh centuries many of the boroughs such as London, York, Lincoln, Rochester, Canterbury, and Bristol were real towns with urban characteristics differentiating them from the countryside.

The place occupied by the borough in the scheme of local administration presents another problem. Until at least the late tenth century the borough was primarily a military and administrative center of an agrarian territory with which it shared the same law. The evidence is slight for burgesses who pursued the life of merchants carrying on trade and commerce. Monotonously the dooms tell only of local markets where the primary item of commerce was cattle and agrarian produce. But because of the fortification and strategic location of some boroughs the kings selected them as primitive administrative headquarters. The development of the burghal organization to provide military service made the borough a natural place for such a headquarters. Then, too, the kings often had royal residences in boroughs, and reeves there to administer them. As early as the late seventh century the dooms of Hlothere and Eadric of Kent provided that trading transactions of Kentishmen in London had to be conducted in the king's hall in the presence of a royal reeve and other trustworthy witnesses. About the same time King Ine of Wessex published a law stating that a royal reeve was to preside over a local court of justice located at royal residences. In the last quarter of the ninth century Alfred's dooms again refer to the local judicial responsibilities of royal reeves at boroughs.[12]

By the early tenth century the borough can be recognized not only as the military center of a burghal district but also as the administrative headquarters. Such boroughs were called *ports* and were headed by royal officers called portreeves who, we may assume, had been the reeves formerly managing the

[12] SM, nos. 2, 4, 5.

royal estates and supervising justice and trading transactions. The borough had become an official center at which certain designated business must be transacted. Edward the Elder ordered that no one could trade except in a *port*, where witnesses must include the portreeve or other reliable men.[13] Athelstan renewed this law with the amendment that trading transactions involving less than 20*d.* (a cow's price) could be carried on outside a *port*. He forbade coining money outside a *port* and placed thirty-seven moneyers at twelve *ports*, among them the boroughs of London, Canterbury, Rochester, and Winchester. He also provided for one moneyer at all other boroughs. Dooms of Athelstan also indicate the importance of the borough for territorial administration. Church tithes from all royal estates within a burghal district were to be collected by the portreeve. Under various circumstances a man clearing himself of a charge was to be provided with six oath-helpers from the burghal district in which he lived. Any man who failed three times to answer a summons to court was fined the royal *oferhyrnes;* if he refused to pay the fine all the leading men of the borough were to ride after him, take all his property, and place him under surety.[14] Thus by the middle of the tenth century boroughs had become not only military but administrative centers. Here were official mints, and markets, and a court of justice. Here resided the portreeve, who was responsible for the administration of the whole burghal district.

The court of justice held in the borough requires a few remarks. It was not, as some scholars believe, the borough court of the twelfth century, where a special law governed burgesses setting them above the ordinary inhabitants of the countryside. What then was it? In some cases it was the hundred court, as when a burghal district was the equivalent of a hundred or when the burghal district was a part of a hundred and its court met in the borough. The shire courts held twice a year generally met in boroughs but they clearly had no connection with the borough or its burghal district. There was a third court, however, called a borough court, which assembled three times a year. Into what scheme of justice did it fit? The most reasonable suggestion regards it as a court originally held in a borough which was the judicial center of a district not yet brought into the shire by Alfred and his successors. Such a district might include a group of hundreds, and its court would be superior in jurisdiction to the hundred courts. Thus in the ninth and early tenth centuries there could be three courts held in a borough and all were territorial. None of them dealt with law expressly adapted to fit the needs of the burgesses, whose primary occupation was trade and commerce. There were not yet enough such men to secure special law and justice. In the tenth century when England was shired, the borough courts held three times a year disappeared; they were absorbed into the shire courts.

Boroughs remained a part of territorial organization until the later tenth

[13] SM, no. 6.
[14] SM, no. 7.

and eleventh centuries when the commercial revival of western Europe produced a new grouping of men. From the late eighth and ninth centuries we begin to have evidence testifying to trade beyond that of local markets and in items other than cattle and produce. In the tenth century this body of evidence bulks large. Bishop Aelfric's *Colloquy* listing the imports of merchants notes "purple robes and silk, precious stones and gold, rare apparel and tin, sulphur and glass, and many such things." Dooms of Edgar established prices for wool and standardized weights and measures.[15] Athelstan laid prohibitions on certain exports. A treaty of Ethelred the Redeless with the Danes makes provision for protection of English trading ships and their cargos in Scandinavian harbors, and English coins of Ethelred and Canute are found in significant quantities not only in Denmark and Norway but in other areas of western Europe. When Canute took his pilgrimage to Rome he met the emperor of Germany and the duke of Burgundy and talked them into giving his merchants and subjects more protection and a reduction of tolls. Meanwhile evidence from ports scattered about England shows a steady rise in trade in the late tenth and eleventh centuries. Some towns like Dover were securing freedom of toll for their merchants throughout England. At Chester regulations were decreed for entrance of ships to the harbor. If a ship entered or departed without royal permission each man on the ship had to pay 40s. to the king and earl. If the ship docked despite royal prohibition, ship, cargo, and men were confiscated. Our best evidence, however, is an ordinance of Ethelred in the late tenth century regulating trade and tolls at London. Here we are introduced to merchants from Flanders, Ponthieu, Normandy, France, Liège, and the Empire, and from towns such as Rouen, Huy, Nivelles, Ghent, Bruges, and Cologne. Their ships were loaded with lumber, fish, blubber, cloth, gloves, pepper, wine, and vinegar; they took back wool, cattle, and grease. Certain merchants such as those from Rouen, Ghent, and Bruges enjoyed special privileges. The merchants of Germany were to enjoy the same rights as English merchants. A new mercantile life was affecting many boroughs of England and their inhabitants who traded not just with each other but with all western Europe; they were developing into a new type of burgess living in a privileged community.

By virtue of their profession the merchants had to secure rights and liberties not provided by an agrarian economy; they required what the tillers of the soil did not—personal freedom and mobility to carry on their trade. Thus in some of the English boroughs an economic and legal revolution was under way; personal freedom was becoming the rule, seignorial obligations were disintegrating, and there was evolving a new peace, land tenure, law, and burgess status. This is not the place to trace in detail how these burgess privileges were acquired but we should at least summarize the ones found in English boroughs prior to 1066. *Domesday Book* and other records show that

[15] SM, no. 11.

burgesses of the leading boroughs were definitely separated from the peasants who lived under seignorial custom; they did not have to perform the agrarian services that typified the peasant's lot. The essential features of burgage tenure were beginning to appear. The house and land of a burgess became heritable and a nominal quitrent called a *landgable* was paid for their use. With some restrictions the land and house could be sold or mortgaged. Some borough courts distinct from the shire and hundred courts now appear. In these urban courts, which gave justice only to the merchants, a type of law merchant regulated the economic and legal relations, guaranteeing some of the rights and liberties that a mercantile life demanded. The courts also formed administrative bodies for regulation of borough affairs. Until the Conquest a royal reeve presided over this court and in reality administered the borough. Gradually he came to be aided in his task by the rich merchants who dominated the membership. Often these men were members of a merchant guild, a social and economic organization which had developed in the eleventh century to facilitate and protect the merchants' economic ventures and through which they worked to secure privileges and to win a court for the regulation of their legal, economic, and administrative affairs.

By the middle of the eleventh century the more important boroughs had secured a legal and economic status that set them apart from the rest of the agrarian communities. Through their courts and guilds merchant the burgesses were learning to cooperate in the business of local government and to bargain with the king for wider privileges. Some boroughs were obtaining freedom from tolls throughout England. Others along the Channel won even greater concessions from Edward the Confessor. *Domesday Book* tells us that Dover, Sandwich, Romney, and Hythe promised Edward quotas of ships for the royal navy in return for special privileges. They were granted freedom from toll for their merchants throughout the kingdom, they were exempted from payment of Danegeld, and they were permitted to enjoy some of the profits of justice. This agreement suggests that to supply and staff the fleet and to collect and account for the profits of justice the burgesses had organized a primitive borough government. The increasing privileges obtained by the boroughs, and the evidence of borough government anticipate the emergence of the commune that was to characterize the reign of Henry I. Already the burgesses, well versed in the art of business negotiation, were beginning to bargain with the king for privileges in return for their services and money. The mutual need for each other's services and a long tradition of bargaining was eventually to produce the English parliament.

4. THE AGRARIAN COMMUNITY

The boroughs constituted only a small part of the territory that composed a hundred. Predominantly agrarian, Anglo-Saxon England was made up of agrarian communities known under various names such as *tuns*, townships, vills, and manors. In these local agrarian units or villages lived the great mass of the population—the cultivators of the soil. To determine their legal and economic position and the form of community in which they lived has been one of the most complicated historical problems of the early Middle Ages. It involves questions as to whether the typical inhabitant of these agrarian communities was free or unfree; whether he was an independent proprietor of land or an economic dependent; whether or not, like the famous Roman citizen Cincinnatus, he fought, governed, and farmed; and whether or not he held and exercised some political power.

Most English historians are of the opinion that from the outset English society was characterized by free, independent landowners who lived in free villages and democratically ordered their local economic and political life, held folk courts to settle their disputes, and left their farming when summoned to go and fight with the king. This view adopted by English historians came originally from a group of German historians of the eighteenth and nineteenth centuries who conceived of early Germanic society as founded upon the principle of the *Mark*. Pre-Carolingian Germany, so the theory runs, was filled with free agrarian proprietors who voluntarily organized themselves into associations for the ordering of their local economic and political affairs. These members met in open-air assemblies, discussed their agrarian interests, and elected headmen to enforce their economic and political enactments and to act as military leaders. The territory occupied by such a democratic association was called a *Mark*. Some scholars argued that the typical member of such a community possessed his own house and land and shared with his associates the use of forests, streams, pasture, waste, and meadows. A larger group of scholars, however, insisted that all was held in common; to them the *Mark* was a form of primeval communism, not unlike that natural society so vividly portrayed by Jean Jacques Rousseau. This utopian organization lasted down to the Carolingians and the advent of the feudal regime. Then the feudal aristocrat by destroying the local self-governing communities and taking away the freedom and land of the proprietors inaugurated the seignorial regime of the Middle Ages, typified by a dependent peasantry working the land of manors held by feudal lords.

According to the *Mark* theorists, when the Anglo-Saxons came to Britain from their home in northern Germany, they brought along the *Mark* organization and used it as the basis of their settlements. Thus, fundamentally, English society was founded upon the *Mark*. We must envisage free warriors conquering the land and then in a democratic assembly partitioning it among themselves and organizing themselves into a community for the regulation of their economic, political, and legal interests. English historians, preferring to call these communities townships rather than *Marken* or marks, found in them the same principles as in the German associations with but one variation—the free English community or township survived far longer.

Some, in fact, lasted down to the Norman Conquest and others were not broken up into manors and deprived of their freedom until the late tenth and eleventh centuries. According to Stubbs "the unit of the constitutional machinery is the township." Originally when all townships were communities of free farmers they elected their headman (*tun-gerefa*) and sent their priest and four law-worthy men to represent them at a monthly hundred court. When townships were acquired by lords and converted into manors they became dependent townships whose headman, priest, and four men were appointed by the lord. It has also been suggested that the early township courts were the result of a primitive need for courts smaller and more local than "the meeting of the whole folk," and that they were the antecedents of the later hundred courts of which their representatives became members. At this stage the independent township court was absorbed by the hundred court and only the dependent township court (manorial court) controlled by the lord continued to function. According to this theory, therefore, two sets of townships existed down to 1066. The independent townships became part of the hundred, which took over most of their functions. The dependent township held by a lord, though also a unit of the hundred, continued to have its own court, the manorial court, with jurisdiction over a certain category of justice.

This theory of the *Mark* as the cell of local government from which larger units developed, however appealing, is not supported by any substantial evidence. Restricting ourselves for the moment to Germany, we find that in the records of the early Middle Ages *Mark* never meant anything except a border or boundary. By the twelfth century when it appears in land grants of charters it merely designates the manor and the rights held in common by the peasants to certain parts such as woods and pasture. For the rest of western Europe it is even more impossible to consider the *Mark* as the basis of Germanic land settlement. From the outset of the German occupation most agrarian communities were dominated by a dependent peasantry under control of a powerful lord. Fundamentally the society of western Europe was aristocratic. The lord possessed most of the land and did the governing and fighting; the ordinary inhabitant devoted his efforts to rendering economic service to his lord. In England there is no evidence to the contrary. It is impossible to find a local unit of government called a *Mark* or a township. The dooms, charters, and Anglo-Saxon literature portray an aristocratic society in which the king, church, earls, and thegns controlled the land, governed the people, and did the fighting.

Though legally the Anglo-Saxon peasant or freeman (*ceorl*) was free and might have his rights in the hundred and shire court, economically he was the dependent of a lord from whom he held land and for whom he worked it. Dooms from Ethelbert to Canute repeatedly testify to the large element of freemen (*ceorls*) who comprised the mass of ordinary Anglo-Saxon inhabitants but afford no evidence of a free and independent township organization.[16] A doom often cited to prove such an organization is one of King Ine: "If *ceorls* have a common meadow or other land divided in shares to fence, and some have fenced their portion and some have not, and [if cattle] eat up their common crops or grass, those who are responsible for the gap are to go and pay to the others, who have fenced their part, compensation for the damage that has been done there. They are to demand with regard to those cattle such reparation as is proper."[17] Such evidence, and it is the best we have, hardly proves a township. It merely asserts that pasture rights are held in common, as on any manor, and that if the peasants do not fulfil their common obligations they will incur a fine. To be sure, no lord is mentioned, but neither is he excluded. As for the folk court of the supposed township, there is no evidence to prove that it was other than that of the shire or hundred. The most we can claim for the supposed township is that it was an agrarian community of peasants, many of them free, who lived under the economic control of a lord. Their common agrarian concerns were discussed in meetings under a leader from their own ranks, most likely a reeve appointed by the lord. There must also have been a primitive organization or court to implement the custom that governed the agrarian routine of such a community. But, note well, economic and not political matters were the subject of discussion, enactment, and fine.

The evidence thus far shows that the township was not a political unit and that consequently it cannot be regarded as a division of the hundred. It was an agrarian community or village of free and unfree men living under some sort of control by a lord. But how were the villages organized and how did lords acquire power over them? There is no written evidence throwing light on these questions until the late seventh century. We can, however, suggest some answers for the preceding period provided we are willing to accept English society as emerging from a social and economic scheme other than that of the free village community of warrior-peasants who democratically ordered their political and economic affairs. Upon settling in Britain the Anglo-Saxon conquerors divided up the spoils. Kings and chiefs kept much of the land for their estates and apportioned the remainder to the lesser lords, who in turn allotted portions of their estates to ordinary freemen, both those who accompanied the expeditions and those who followed later. Men of lower status such as freedmen also secured some land, and slaves helped to work it. What seems likely is that from the outset the lords of large estates exerted authority over the villages of men among whom they had divided the land and that they had an interest in the machinery of justice and of village administration. A court for the settlement of ordinary misdemeanors would be organized with the lord's appointed reeve presiding while the village freemen declared the time-honored custom. This court would also handle the administration of the economic routine of the com-

[16] SM, no. 1.
[17] SM, no. 4.

munity with its fields, pastures, streams, and woods. Profits of justice would go to the lord. The more serious crimes such as stealing, assault, ambush, murder, and manslaughter would come before the court held by the royal reeve at the nearest estate of the king in the region.

By the late seventh century the charters and dooms are beginning to give us some details. The charters show that the kings created bookland out of their royal land and gave along with it the food rents and services formerly paid to the king by the inhabitants of the donated estates. The principal recipients of bookland were the church and the greater lords. Certainly the courts along with minor jurisdiction fell also to the recipients of the charters. The only rights always reserved by the kings were the *trimoda necessitas*, which entailed the privilege of exacting from the inhabitants *fyrd* (army service), work on bridges, and work on fortifications.[18] The king and his officers could demand nothing beyond these three exactions. By charter the king had created an immunity. During the nineteenth century scholars were convinced that kings with the consent of the great lords created bookland out of folkland (*ager publicus*), that land belonging collectively to the people. This interpretation, though based on slight evidence—the word folkland appears only four times in all Anglo-Saxon history—prevailed until revised towards the end of the century. Without becoming involved in the complex arguments of this revision we can say that most scholars would now agree that too much has been said about folkland; it was in reality nothing other than the land belonging to the king which came to be known later as the royal domain.

About the time we begin to have written evidence describing the type of authority lords came to acquire over agrarian villages, we also have a few references to the relation between lord and peasant. Except that lords are found directing village justice and administration we know nothing as yet of the bond between lord and village inhabitants. A doom of Ine begins to clarify the issue. It states that peasants are receiving land, a virgate in area (thirty acres) from lords in return for rent and labor services.[19] The peasant retains his legal freedom but is acquiring an economic unfreedom similar to that of the seignorial system. Such grants of land must have come from the land of the lord hitherto directly worked by himself with the help of freedmen and slaves. There is every reason to suppose that such a practice served as a precedent for peasants already owning their own land to give it to the lord and then receive back its possession or use with the lord's promise that he would guarantee its security and give to the peasant his protection. In turn the peasant had to pay rent and perform labor service. Thus, by the late seventh century we are certain that kings were putting whole villages or groups of villages under the control of lords through the creation

[18] SM, nos. 7, 12.
[19] SM, no. 4.

of bookland and that, concurrently, certain tenurial bonds were developing informally between lord and free peasant.

From the eighth into the eleventh century these two developments proceeded with increasing momentum. Along the way we receive information that enables us to say more definitely what authority and bonds lords were securing over the men on their land. The bare level of subsistence of most free peasants gave them no extra margin of safety when lean years or war destroyed their crops and cattle. A few bad years inevitably forced the peasant, as yet under no tenurial bond with a lord, to establish one for protection and security; the peasant already with such a bond generally substituted labor services for the food rent he could not pay. The tendency was, therefore, for lords to secure tighter control over the peasants, to collect more of their land, and to receive their labor to work the land in lordly domain. We hear more and more of peasants commending themselves with their land to lords. By the time of the Conquest commendation (*commendatio*) seems to have governed the relation of large numbers of peasants with lords.

We do not possess the records needed to estimate how rapidly these tenurial relations spread over England, but when *Domesday Book* describes the lands of Anglo-Saxon England hundred by hundred it tells us that by 1066 the general land pattern was a manorial one and that the countryside was dominated by manors (*maneria*) of lords whose authority extended over any number of agrarian villages of peasants. At this point, legally, there were still free peasants and all sorts of men who were said to be able to commend themselves with their land to any lord they wished. Such freedom was, however, more theoretical than real. Few were the peasants who actually transferred their land and selves to the lordship of another man and few were those who could be seen any more at the hundred and shire court. Increasingly lords substituted their private manorial courts for the public courts, a process that during the twelfth century blocked most peasants from obtaining justice in public courts.

How and when private justice came to supplant public justice for large masses of peasants is a knotty problem. The first charters that definitely say kings granted the exercise of public justice to the church and lords come from the middle of the tenth century. They declare that a lord is granted an estate of land with *sacu* and *socn* (the modern sac and soc) over it.[20] Such a phrase literally means "cause and suit" but in effect meant that the recipient of such a grant had the right to hold a court to which his tenants must come. Supplementary evidence from an earlier date has convinced most authorities of Anglo-Saxon history that royal grants of sac and soc go back into the eighth century. There is a difference, however, as to how the phrase should be interpreted. Sac and soc meant the right to hold a court but could also mean the right merely to receive the profits of justice collected from a neighboring shire or hundred court. At times it is difficult or

[20] SM, no. 15E and G.

even impossible to ascertain which right a lord had. Stenton and Maitland are convinced, however, that lords received the right to exercise public jurisdiction as early as the eighth century.

We do not know precisely of what this public justice consisted. We have already assumed for the period before the late seventh century that a lord could hold a court to settle the economic misdemeanors and infractions of agrarian routine that were a commonplace of manorial justice. Later, when we have records, we find our hunch confirmed; this type of justice was indeed exercised by all lords. But public justice is a different matter. By the eleventh century, some charters are becoming specific to the point of elaborating what justice sac and soc included. Along with sac and soc they begin to tack on the phrase "with toll and team, and with infangenetheof."[21] Toll signified the lord's right to collect a payment on the sale of cattle and property within his manor. Team gave the lord the right to hold a court to determine the honesty of a man accused of illegal possession of cattle. At the court men who had acted as witnesses to the cattle transaction would give testimony. Such testimony generally settled the guilt or innocence of the accused. Infangenetheof signified the right of bringing to justice in the lord's court any thief caught with stolen property on the lord's lands. By the eleventh century almost every church and lord possessed such rights of justice.

A favored few secured even higher rights of justice from the king. Since at least Canute's reign certain great prelates and lords had been permitted to receive the forfeitures incurred by their own men who had committed certain serious offenses, forfeitures that had hitherto gone only to the king. By 1066 such grants by Edward the Confessor were quite common. On rare occasions the kings even permitted these offenses to be tried in the lordly courts. Canute, for example, granted to Archbishop Ethelnoth of Canterbury sac and soc, justice over thieves apprehended in the act, and jurisdiction over the crimes of harboring outlaws, ambush, breaking into a house, and infraction of the king's special peace. By the Confessor's reign the number of offenses granted over to the jurisdiction of great lords had increased; it now included breach of the royal peace, ambush and treacherous manslaughter, harboring of outlaws, forced entry into a residence, and failure to answer a military summons. Jurisdiction was generally held by prelates or lords who had come to control hundred courts by virtue of royal grant. By the reign of the Confessor there were numerous instances in which a whole hundred court or more had passed under the jurisdiction of an abbot, bishop, or earl. The abbot of Abingdon, for example, held the hundred of Hormer in Berkshire; the bishop of Worcester, the triple hundred of Oswaldslow; and the abbot of Bury Saint Edmunds, eight and a half hundreds in west Suffolk over which he had sac and soc "and all royal customs over the land of every man, whoever may possess it." Though in their grants the kings reserved this high justice for only the greatest lords, the right to hold a court for the

[21] SM, no. 15G.

lesser misdemeanors belonged to practically every thegn by 1066. The hundred still remained the great public court but deep inroads had been made into the scope of its justice.

What may we conclude about the so-called township and its free peasants? Free in that they were not slaves and that they had the right to suit in the hundred and shire courts, they nevertheless had no real freedom. By the eleventh century most of them held their land from lords and worked it as well as the lord's lands in return for his protection. Even those peasants who were said to be able to go wheresoever they desired with their land certainly did not. Once commended to a lord they stayed commended. One cannot envisage the lords' permitting their commended men to switch lords whenever they desired. Such freedom and mobility did not exist in medieval agrarian life. Rather than being a free agent participating in the political and legal affairs of a free village community (township), the peasant was a member of a manorial community and was firmly attached to the soil. His only participation in group affairs was economic. His lord did the worrying about justice and politics. Even the freedom of the peasant to plead his cases in the hundred court was being cut off in the eleventh century. Many knew only of a hundred court under the private control of their lord. Such a state as we have described is the seignorial system in almost its full vigor. To see the township or free village community at any time in Anglo-Saxon history as the local cell of English government with its legal and political affairs organized in a democratic fashion is an act of faith. As of now no one has produced convincing evidence for the famous "township."

The agrarian community was not a political division of the hundred but it eventually developed into a territorial subdivision with the responsibility of producing and punishing criminals. One of the most serious problems of the early Middle Ages was to apprehend criminals and bring them to justice. Constantly in the dooms one meets the kings' attempts to devise some sort of police organization. Gradually they formed a system whereby the people policed themselves. First the kings legislated that all freemen must have a surety (*borh*), that is, other persons who would be responsible for producing them in court in case of crime or failure to pay a debt. The *borh* could be one's family or lord. A doom of Athelstan directed that every lordless man should be placed by his kindred under a lord who would be responsible for his appearance in court. Those who were not produced for justice and were not put under lords became fugitives and could be struck down with impunity.[22] Later dooms of Edgar enlarged upon this enactment. They required that every man in and outside boroughs should have a *borh* responsible for producing him at court, or answering for him if he was not produced: "if anyone commits a crime and escapes, the surety is to incur what he [the criminal] would have incurred."[23] Finally a doom of Canute ordered

[22] SM, no. 7.
[23] SM, nos. 9, 11.

every man of a hundred to be under surety, "and the surety is to hold him and bring him to every legal duty."[24]

The *borh* system, however efficient, was not liked by the lords, upon whom the greatest burden fell. It put them in the position of being responsible for their own men's crimes and generally having to pay the fines incurred. If the lord enjoyed the profits of justice from the hundred court or held the court himself, he found himself paying fines to himself. It was no wonder, then, that the lords attempted to evade this responsibility and consequently substituted a system whereby they would be relieved of such an onerous duty and stand to reap greater profits of justice. They began to force their men to obtain *borh* from among themselves; such a system came to be called a tithing. The dooms made this the principal system for bringing criminals to justice. Except for lords with considerable landed property, each man was placed in a group of ten headed by a principal guarantor called the tithingman. If one of them became involved in a crime, the other nine had to produce him in court and even pay the fine incurred if the individual was found guilty and could not pay it. If they could not produce the man, the nine received a fine and, in addition, had to pay the forfeiture to the injured party. Dooms of Edgar directed that all men of the hundred had to pursue thieves in groups of ten under their tithingmen and that no strange cattle could be kept by any man without the knowledge of the tithingman.[25] A doom of Canute decreed that all men over twelve had to be in a tithing or hundred or lose their rights as freemen.[26] Perhaps from the dooms of Edgar and Canute developed the famous Norman system of frankpledge, the efficient police system of England in the Middle Ages. Just how and when we are not certain, but in some areas of England the tithing also came to be regarded as a territorial unit of an agrarian community. If one can visualize the hundred completely broken down into agrarian communities whose lands were composed of areal tithings for policing, he may be looking at the smallest unit of local government in Anglo-Saxon England.

The well-developed local government of Anglo-Saxon England cannot be matched in any other part of western Europe. It was the work of the West Saxon kings to put the finishing touches to local government with the object of insuring that royal authority would be respected in the smallest village. The kings were not motivated by an innate sense of justice and desire for orderly government; they were primarily interested in a strong law and order because it brought peace and unity to their realm, gave them military strength, and produced a steady flow of income into the royal chamber. Beyond the royal officers who made the local machinery work and were rewarded with land and privileges were a multitude of ordinary lords and men who helped to carry on local government and justice without remuneration.

[24] SM, no. 13.
[25] SM, no. 11.
[26] SM, no. 13.

Theirs was an obligation imposed by royal command, an obligation that was the beginning of self-government by the royal command. One must not lose sight of the fact that the fabric of local government was imposed from above by the king and then carried out chiefly by the aristocratic thegn; it did not originate with the free and democratic folk of the "township." But local government there was, strong and relatively efficient; later in the Middle Ages it was to cooperate with the central government in producing those English institutions that we characterize as constitutional.

VI
Anglo-Saxon Society and the Law

1. THE KINDRED

PRIMITIVELY all the German tribes based their organization on the kindred (*maegth*). How far the ties of the kindred spread is uncertain, yet we know that it did not include all the Joneses and Browns but just the more immediate members of the family. Before artificial protections were devised, the individual secured his protection and rights through the kindred. Should he be slain it was the responsibility of the kindred to avenge his death through feud against the slayer and his kindred. In lieu of such vengeance it became acceptable for the slayer and his kindred to pay compensation to the dead man's kindred. This was the wergeld (man-price). If a man was killed the composition of the kindred would vary from what it was if his wife was killed. Husband and wife were not responsible for each other's kindred because there was no blood relationship; the husband's kin were responsible for his crimes and the wife's for hers. From Tacitus to Edward the Confessor the kindred is one of the principal bonds of Anglo-Saxon society and one of the foundations of its law. Tacitus tells us that the kindred had a share in the fines paid for crimes committed against one of its kinsmen. Canute's dooms are filled with references to the rights of the kindred. The man who slays a priest must pay his wergeld to the kindred. In case of murder the murderer has to be handed over to the kindred of the slain man. The kindred's was not just the right and honor of avenging its wronged member but also its duty; so too was it a duty to make amends for his crimes or to protect and support him by carrying on the feud. Only through the kindred did custom find expression and force; the individual without kinsmen was in a precarious state.

The kindred was a group so powerful and so entrenched by custom and tradition that it never completely yielded priority to government. There was a constant struggle for ascendancy. At first government could only attempt to direct and legalize the actions of the kindred. Gradually the kings began to place the feud within bounds. The dooms defined when physical force could be used. Feuds could not be pursued against an individual who had done homicide while fighting for his lord, while protecting his men or relations from attack, or while defending his wife, daughter, sister, or mother against attempted violation. In this latter case, however, he had to kill the offender at the scene of the offense. The kindred could not engage in feud if one of its members was killed in the act of stealing property, committing other capital crimes, or resisting capture; in such cases the kindred had to swear that it would not avenge his death. King Ine forbade revenge upon penalty of a fine if it was carried out before justice was sought; anyone suspected of wrongdoing but not caught in it could not be attacked but must be taken to a court.[1] In this connection it was finally ordered that a slayer had to be proven guilty before vengeance could be obtained against him. He could deny homicide by swearing a prescribed oath and obtaining other men to give their oaths that he was guiltless. A man guilty of homicide generally did not attempt to conceal it; such an act would turn his crime into murder, which fell into the category of secret slaying as by poison or witchcraft. Crimes of this type could not be compensated for by a wergeld but entailed death.

After the kings had enacted dooms regulating the occasions when it was lawful to conduct a feud, the next step was to acclimate the kindred to accept a composition instead of demanding revenge for a wrong done against it. The feud was never eradicated but the dooms gave inducement enough for the kindred to forego it. We have already seen how the kings were supplanting the duties of the kindred in protection and policing by introducing the *borh* and the tithing. The first extant dooms, those of King Ethelbert of Kent, largely concern a tariff of wergelds; it is found in almost all the dooms that follow.[2] A man's wergeld was determined by his rank. A plain freeman (*ceorl*) was worth 200s. while a nobleman (thegn) was worth 1200s. Commonly one reads of men referred to as two hundred and twelve hundred men.[3] Although at first the wergeld was expressed in terms of cattle and then later in money, we must assume that payments were predominantly in cattle or kind. Alfred seems to have been the first king to attempt halting the feud. A group of dooms lays down restrictions against violence under various conditions. For example, a man who knew his adversary to be at home was to do no violence to him until justice had been demanded. It was also ordered that if any wrongdoer surrendered his weapons and offered no resistance, violence was to be avoided.[4]

However much the kings tried to eradicate the feud, neither their power nor Anglo-Saxon society was ready for such a change. Repeated prohibitions in the dooms against violence and references to feuds in Anglo-Saxon literature prove that private warfare was prevalent down to 1066. After expressing his distress over "illegal and manifold" fights, King Edmund enacted dooms to reinforce Alfred's. When a feud broke out only the actual offender could be slain. When the offender agreed to pay a compensation, elaborate

[1] SM, no. 4.
[2] SM, no. 1.
[3] SM, no. 5.
[4] SM, no. 5.

precautions were taken so that the kindred of the slain would not spoil the offender's peaceful advances by lapsing into violence. The slayer who decided to pay a wergeld was to secure an intermediary to negotiate with the kindred of the slain. The intermediary was to obtain the promise of safe-conduct for the slayer so that he could meet with the kindred and give pledges and security for payment of the wergeld. If any of the kindred should then resort to violence, they would incur a very steep fine because the slayer was considered as being under the royal protection.[5] But in the late tenth and eleventh centuries the literature continues to give us vivid accounts of feuds, especially in the north, where there was a large Danish population with whom the feud was a particularly strong ingredient of their society. Enactments of Ethelred the Redeless prove that powerful kindreds still flouted royal authority and pushed feuds when and wherever they desired. Sometimes, in fact, the levies of three shires had to be summoned to bring members of such kindreds to justice. A feud that erupted in 1016 between Earl Uhtred of Northumbria and his kindred and the noble Thurbrand of a great family from Yorkshire smoldered down to 1073 when almost all the male descendants of Thurbrand were assassinated.

By 1066, however, the feud was a much more anemic affair than it had been in the seventh century. Working constantly the kings had finally established public authority over the rights of the kindred; in this hard fight they had been supported by the church. Conflict between the strong right of the Germanic kindred and the claims of Christian ethics was inevitable. In the earliest records churchmen can be found throwing their influence behind the kings to starve out feuds and substitute compositions. Influenced by Christian doctrine, Ethelbert must have felt the need to adjust custom to the teachings of the church and to publish a tariff of wergelds that could be substituted for the feud. Such church influence partly explains the first written dooms. Orientation of the kindred to Christian ideas on violence did not proceed at all smoothly in the early centuries and evidence shows that the kings who swallowed Christian ideas on nonviolence too readily were themselves the victims of kindreds fighting to preserve the feud. Never did the church get to the place where it could fight for the principle that homicide could not be atoned for by vengeance or by composition. It had to content itself with pushing the claims of composition over feud. Theodore of Tarsus, archbishop of Canterbury, declared that a man who killed in vengeance had to do penance for seven to ten years. To popularize composition, however, Theodore waived half the penance if the slayer was willing to pay a wergeld to the aggrieved kindred. The prelates, moreover, used their good services to arrange compromises and truces between kindreds who were feuding. The clergy itself was so much a part of secular Anglo-Saxon society and its custom that it could not isolate itself from the system; for its own protection it participated in the system of

[5] SM, no. 9.

composition. The different ranks of clergy were worked into the tariffs of wergelds. Bishops and archbishops had wergelds equal to those of the greatest lords; a thegn's wergeld was that of a priest. Like the kings, the church could advance only so far against custom and human passion.[6] It was a bond more tangible and practical that was to weaken the kindred and almost supplant it by 1066.

2. LORDSHIP

In Tacitus is found the earliest account of the personal relation between lord and man that, along with the kindred, provided the principal bond of Germanic society. Like kinship the tie of lordship was not tribal; it was a personal bond that seldom took second place even to the kindred. By 1066 the paramount bond of Anglo-Saxon society among freemen was lordship. The lordship depicted by Tacitus in the *comitatus* was a bond between free warriors who devoted their lives to fighting. For a man's military support and highest loyalty the lord offered adventure, glory, protection, and booty. The spoils of war plus maintenance constituted the lord's reward for loyalty and service. Throughout the Anglo-Saxon period the dooms and poems testify to the vitality of this bond. If modified at all, it was in the substitution of land for booty and maintenance. The poem *The Battle of Maldon* portrays the personal bond of lordship at its best, resembling that in the *comitatus* of Tacitus. The men of the lord Brihtnoth fought to the end for their dead lord, even after the flight of his army and without hope of victory or survival. They fought to avenge his death and to fulfil their oath of loyalty to him. With the advent of Christianity there was not the conflict between it and the Germanic lordship that there had been between it and the kindred. Battle between lords and their men simply for the sake of adventure and material reward the church could not condone, but Christian doctrine could encompass the noble concept that bound man to man and, with its holy sanctions, reinforce the oath of loyalty sworn by man to lord. The bond of lordship as described by Tacitus and the later poems concerns only the relations between free and noble warriors; the ordinary freeman had no part in such a relation. He was, however, enmeshed in a lordship that bound him as tightly to his lord as did the other more noble bond. We have previously discussed how the free peasant out of economic necessity could receive land from a lord and could hand his land over to a lord in return for protection and security. The bond of lordship was thus inaugurated on a lower level. The service required for the lord's protection was nonnoble and nonmilitary; it was economic, the tilling of the soil and the harvesting of the crops. A tight lordship had been established, however, and a man's dependence upon land was so fundamental that if conflict arose between lordship and the kindred it was the former that had to take priority. We must understand that the bond of commendation,

[6] SM, no. 6.

therefore, was a bond on a noble and on a nonnoble level but that it still set up the strong tie of lordship.

But to return momentarily to the higher level of lordship, it will be remembered that when the king granted bookland to a lord he relieved it of all obligations except the *trimoda necessitas*—military service and the repair of bridges and fortifications.[7] But such land did cement the allegiance owed by Anglo-Saxon lords to their king. There were, however, other grants of land called loanland that definitely entailed service. Whereas bookland was granted in outright ownership like allodial land and without having specific service and conditions imposed upon it, loanland was so granted that the grantor did not lose his rights over it. It was in truth loaned to a man in return for specific service and on special conditions.[8] The land was loaned only for the duration of three lives and if the lord so desired it reverted back to him after this period. Moreover, if the services laid upon the land were not rendered, it could be seized. The conditions imposed on loanland were much more precarious than those upon bookland; they resemble those laid upon the land held by peasants. In both cases the recipient could be deprived of his land if he failed to perform stipulated service. There still existed, nevertheless, a great distinction between noble and nonnoble service.

Though it is possible to find examples of loanland as early as the reign of King Ine of Wessex in the late seventh century, it is not until the tenth century that evidence becomes specific and plentiful enough to comment upon loanland in detail. Our best evidence is afforded by the grants of loanland made by Bishop Oswald of Worcester between 962 and 992. Some seventy grants were made to men, generally of the thegnly class, for a period of three lives in return for stipulated services. Oswald did not specify the service in the grants but he did in a letter to King Edgar telling him what he was doing. Recipients had to perform riding service, delivery and execution of messages, repairs on bridges, and had to render hospitality to Oswald and certain payments to the church. The bond of lordship was clearly expressed when Oswald wrote that all recipients "shall with all humility and subjection be obedient to his domination and to his will, in consideration of the benefice that has been loaned to them, and according to the quantity of the land that each of them possesses." We do not know how prevalent loanland became throughout England before 1066, but we are certain that men were very familiar with it and its obligations. By its very nature it made lordship a strong and constant bond.

Originally a purely personal bond with no relation to land, lordship came in the long period between Tacitus and Edward the Confessor to be bound to land and strengthened by it. Whether on the noble or nonnoble level, land was the tangible and material element that catapulted the bond of lordship over that of the kindred with the result that the bond of lordship gov-

[7] SM, no. 15B and G.
[8] SM, no. 15C.

erned the relations of Anglo-Saxon society. When Anglo-Saxon government was again obliged to step in and regulate the bond, it was, in this case, with a willingness and cooperation not found with the kindred. The king was the general lord of all men and by virtue of all sorts of relations he was the personal lord of many men. As general overlord and personal lord he understood lordship and saw what benefits could be reaped from it if woven into the law by his dooms. Through the concept of lordship and the obligations demanded by it, the king could secure the services of government on all levels. As Maitland has so well put it, the relation of lord and man became "formally recognized as a necessary part of public order." From the dooms of Ine to those of Canute the kings made provision for the bond of lordship and worked it into the government and public order. In Ine's dooms lords are not to work their men on Sundays, men who steal away into other districts without their lord's permission are to pay him 60s., and if a lord has not restrained his men from wrongdoing he cannot share in the profits of justice received from fines levied against them.[9] By the reign of Athelstan a lordless man was a suspicious and dangerous individual who had to be put under a lord; a lordless man was as much beyond the law as the kinless man. It was assumed that all men, noble and nonnoble, had lords.[10] We have seen how lords were forced to provide *borh* for their men. The principles of lordship, like those inherent in the kindred, involved revenge if lord or man was slain. If vengeance was not done, the survivor could demand a composition in line with the rank of the dead man; this principle held firm even on the nonnoble level. There are cases of peasants' avenging their lord's death. The dooms provided that a lord could demand a "man-composition" for the slaying of any of his men. Such a payment was in addition to what had to be paid to the kindred. Lordship and its meshing with land tenure, noble and nonnoble, led to its triumph over the kindred and to its recognition by law. Some scholars have seen in this development what they call feudalism. Though it did resemble such a system and though England in 1066 was close to the feudalism of the Continent, no real feudalism existed prior to the Conquest; it was left for the Normans to introduce it. Anglo-Saxon England knew only seignorialism.

3. WEALTH AND PROPERTY

We have already had occasion to remark that among freemen the concept of nobility put a select group of individuals above the rest. Individual prowess and military ability originally won some men the prestige and land that enabled them to set themselves apart as kings and nobles and then to transfer nobility into a matter of blood descent. Throughout Anglo-Saxon history royal service gave a man nobility and an elevated rank. The dooms of Ine differentiate the royal companions and servants, the *gesiths*, from ordinary

[9] SM, no. 4.
[10] SM, no. 7.

nobles and *ceorls*.[11] The ealdormen and later the earls held the highest noble rank because of their royal offices. Bishops, archbishops, and abbots were well up in rank because of their high church position. Basically, however, the right of a man to belong to the noble class rested on possession of a certain amount of land and property. Generally the man who held five hides of land was considered a thegn and set apart from the *ceorl*. Occasionally the successful trader who had crossed the sea so many times and had acquired a certain amount of wealth was admitted to thegnhood. As the possession of land and wealth became a more important concept it dictated the position men held in society and their role in government. Ultimately it counted for everything. The substratum of Anglo-Saxon society consisted, then, of the bonds of the kindred and lordship, noble blood, royal service, and possession of land and wealth. Classes of men were founded upon these elements and they expressed themselves through the law.

4. CLASSES OF MEN

When the Anglo-Saxon law distinguished classes it did so by referring to the price each man had on his head; it spoke of a man's wergeld, which was determined by one of the elements discussed above. Among freemen there was a vast difference between thegn and *ceorl*. In seventh-century Kent the noble, then called an earl, had a wergeld of 300s.; the *ceorl*, one of 100s. At one time these amounts were equivalent to 300 and 100 oxen. Ordinarily throughout England the thegn had a wergeld of 1200s. and the *ceorl* one of 200s. We shall not worry over the various wergelds held by earls and *gesiths* when these words still denoted nobility or over the wergelds held by all the various and intermediate ranks of freemen; it suffices to emphasize that all freemen had a wergeld. One should note that the clergy too had its ranks and appropriate wergelds. But let us examine the nobility and learn the connotation of its different ranks. At first *eorl* meant a nobleman but under Danish influence it came to denote only an office. Thus, like its predecessor ealdorman, the tenth- and eleventh-century earl designated an officer. Probably *gesith* was the Anglo-Saxon equivalent for the *comes* of Tacitus and literally meant companion. In actual usage before the late ninth century *gesith* stood for a nobleman attached to the king by military service. During Alfred's reign it seems to have meant a noble who had inherited noble rank and possessed much land. Alfred's reign saw *gesith* and *eorl* supplanted by the word "thegn." Henceforth it designated all noblemen although originally it had meant only household officers serving great nobles and the king.

Innumerable were the variations in rank among the *ceorls*. The Kentish *ceorls* had higher wergelds than those in the rest of England and held more land. Throughout England there were the *laets*, whose wergeld was two- to four-fifths that of the *ceorl*. In Wessex the dooms refer to Welsh peasants

[11] SM, no. 4.

with lower wergelds.[12] By the tenth century the records are speaking of *geburs*, who are freemen but are of much lower status than the *ceorl*. They held only a virgate (thirty acres) of land instead of one or two hides and performed more onerous labor services. Yet freedom knew even lower classes of men. There were the *cotsetlan* (cottage dwellers), who possessed on the average five acres and paid rent instead of rendering labor services. Below them were homeless laborers to whom the lord gave food and clothing for their service. In the tenth and eleventh centuries we meet men a little more elevated than the *ceorl*. An eleventh-century document on manorial management entitled *Rights and Ranks of People* speaks of *geneats* who "ride and perform carrying service and furnish means of carriage . . . bring strangers to the village, pay church dues and alms money, act as guard to his lord, take care of the horses, and carry messages far and near wheresoever he is directed." Literally *geneat* meant courtier or companion; he was a man primarily engaged in riding service. His work was much more elevated than the *ceorl's* and his labor services were greatly reduced. The west Midlands knew the *geneats* as *radcnihts*.[13]

We have only scratched the surface of the ranks of freemen; there were ranks below the *ceorl*, but a discussion of them as well as of the rights and labor services of *ceorl*, *gebur*, and cottar belongs in the domain of economic history. Among the classes of freemen there were further distinctions. For example, offenses committed against men and places under the protection of freemen had to be atoned for according to the importance of the freeman. Similarly fines varied for housebreaking and fighting in a freeman's house. When freemen committed crimes the fines varied according to their degree of rank; this is particularly evident in the worth of a man's oath. The thegn's oath was equivalent to the oaths of six *ceorls* because his wergeld was 1200*s*. and the *ceorl's* but 200*s*.

There were, lastly, the men who had no wergelds—the unfree or the slaves. Many records of manumissions and references to the slave trade prove that slavery was widespread. Dooms of Ine forbade the sale of English beyond the seas; this was repeated with added provisions in dooms of Ethelred the Redeless and Canute. The churchmen denounced slave trade in sermons and actively worked to eradicate it in infamous centers of the trade such as Bristol. One observes, however, that the emphasis was upon the evil of slave trade rather than the holding of slaves. As an institution slavery was accepted and regulated by law. Treated as a piece of property, the slave obviously could have no wergeld. If he was killed, the slayer only had to pay his purchase price—ordinarily a pound or eight oxen. Vouching to warranty accompanied the sale of slaves just as with cattle and other property, and tolls were collected from the transaction. The dooms show the slave as an individual without property who could therefore not be fined for crimes

[12] SM, nos. 1, 4.
[13] SM, no. 4.

committed; he must undergo some form of corporal punishment from flogging to mutilation and even to death for grave offenses.

Numerous types of unhappy individuals could be found in the slave markets. There were the conquered British population and their descendants, the captives of war, and occasionally the children and kindred of a man who, because of economic distress, was reduced to selling them into captivity. Sometimes individuals voluntarily became slaves in order to keep on living. The penalty for some crimes was slavery. Also slavery was often the fate of a man and his family when he could not pay his debts or fines and compensations. If he was not bought out of slavery in a year, he remained a slave to the end of his life and lost his wergeld. Slavery was heritable. The church held slaves but nevertheless did all in its power to mitigate their lot. It advocated kind treatment, restriction on the amount of labor, and sufficient food and quarters. Above all it taught that manumission was one of the best of Christian deeds and it often set an example for others. Wills are our best sources for manumission although it was not necessary to record the act in writing. The individual either freed his own slave or purchased the freedom of a slave owned by another person. The ceremony of emancipation was performed before law-worthy men so that there would be adequate proof for the individual's new freedom. Sometimes the act was performed at the church altar but more often at a crossroads because the location symbolized the freed person's ability to choose whatever path of life he desired. Somehow slaves managed to acquire some property for occasionally they bought their freedom. In any event the former master or individual responsible for manumission retained right to the man's inheritance and wergeld. In this manner the freedman was protected because often he had no kindred to help him obtain his rights. Apparently only second- and third-generation descendants of manumitted slaves could hope to enjoy all the privileges of an ordinary freeman.

5. THE LAW AND ITS PENALTIES

Much has already been said about Anglo-Saxon courts. For our discussion of the law we need only jog our memory and repeat that the public courts, in order of precedence and dignity, were those of the king and his witenagemot, the shire, the hundred, and the borough. The borough court need not detain us; it dealt in a law merchant for burgesses of a particular borough, and the law varied from court to court. Before it became such a special court it, too, had been a public court like the hundred and shire. The hundred was the busiest court for all types of justice; it handled more criminal justice than the shire, which concerned itself more with land disputes. Occasionally the shire court received cases from the hundred when satisfactory justice could not be obtained on that level. The witenagemot had jurisdiction over cases affecting the king and his great lords plus a few cases that were appealed from the shire. Manorial or private courts merely dealt with the routine disputes common to an agrarian community. The grant of public justice by the king transformed the manorial court into a public court controlled by a private individual. When a hundred or a group of hundreds fell under the power of a lord, his private court became the hundred court with all its jurisdiction. As for the subject matter of Anglo-Saxon law we shall presently see that the substantive rules (rules of right administered by a court) dealt almost exclusively with offenses and wrongs connected with violence and stealing.

We come now to the matter of penalties. If the kindred of a slain man could be so persuaded, it would accept a wergeld from the slayer and his kindred. Compensation also had to be paid to the lord of the slain. A fine (*wite*) was also paid to the king and the lords who shared with him the profits of justice from the public courts. If a hundred court was held by a lord, then the profits of justice from such fines would fall to him. The most serious offenses, such as murder, treachery to one's lord, arson, housebreaking, and open theft, could not be atoned for by the payment of compensation. These were the botless crimes (the word *bot* literally denoted compensation) punishable by death and forfeiture of all property. The most common form of execution was by hanging on a gallows situated on the boundaries between villages or local administrative districts; less prevalent was beheading. A woman convicted of causing death by witchcraft could be drowned. In London, witches were thrown from London Bridge. Male slaves convicted of thievery were stoned; female slaves were burned. As we have seen, some crimes were punished by slavery, and on a few occasions men were imprisoned on royal estates. Of prisons and imprisonment, however, we hear little. The church shared the profits of justice when offenses bearing on its teachings were involved. For example, the king shared with the church fines collected when perjury or incest was committed and when the marriage customs of the church were broken. The individual who contemplated crime was wiser to perpetrate it during normal periods of the year and at places and occasions not under a special peace. All fines were much stiffer for crimes committed during Lent and other special church seasons and days, or in a church or public court. The king's special peace prevailed when *fyrd* service was summoned and when men traveled to and from public courts and meetings.

A reading of the dooms leaves one with the impression that the Anglo-Saxons devoted much of their time to inflicting injuries upon each other. In almost every collection of dooms there is a long list of tariffs that had to be paid for inflicting body injuries. In each instance the fine for the injury was determined by the law and not by the court. If a man was found to have caused an injury, the court levied the fine prescribed by the law for that specific injury. In such a manner did the courts declare the law for all offenses. It would be tedious to describe here all the offenses that Anglo-Saxons were prone to commit, but let us note a few typical ones. When we delve beneath the impersonal record, we find that men and women in that age were not much different from those of today; they seem only to have been more open and uninhibited in their actions and passions. The dooms of Alfred give us a fair idea of the misdemeanors of the Anglo-Saxons. We come first to the injuries. If a wound an inch long was inflicted under the hair, the compensation was 1s. For striking off an ear, 30s. had to be paid. For knocking out a man's eye, 66s. 6*d*. was the penalty; if the eye still remained in the head, only two-thirds compensation was due. For cutting off a nose, one had to pay 60s. A front tooth was worth 8*s*.; a back tooth, 4*s*.; and a man's canine tooth, 15*s*. For tearing a man's tongue out of his mouth, 60s. was demanded. For the breaking and cutting off of the various limbs of a man, a penalty was prescribed from little finger, to big toe, to leg. Fighting in any freeman's house was penalized by fines varying with the rank of the house owner. It was the same with housebreaking, where the scale ran from king to *ceorl*. As for insults and slanders, if anyone uttered public slander and it was proven against him, he lost his tongue or, in lieu, the value of his wergeld. For scourging a *ceorl* the penalty was 20s. If you cut his hair in order to spoil his appearance or to insult him, you paid 10s. A beard-cutting cost one 20*s*. There were, as in our time, lustful individuals. For stealing a nun out of a nunnery, the fine was 120s. For committing adultery with another man's wife, fines were regulated by that man's wergeld. If he was a 1200*s*. man, 120*s*. was the fine; if he was a *ceorl*, only 40*s*. Unmarried young women were less protected. For seizing an ordinary woman, the fine was 5s. to her. The fine was 60s. for sexual intercourse. If the woman had previously had intercourse with another man, the fine was but 30s.[14]

Theft was the crime with which the dooms were mostly concerned. From Hlothere to Canute there was legislation to make it more difficult for thieves to dispose of their goods and to make it easier for the man losing his property to recover it. Cattle were usually the property involved although anything valuable was likely to be stolen—grain, money, jewels, and personal effects.[15] Already we have noted the elaborate precautions laid down to insure that all important business transactions would be conducted in the presence of royal officials or trustworthy witnesses. If later the buyer of cattle or other goods was accused of illegal possession, he could vouch to warranty these witnesses. Written evidence covering such dealings which would hold up in court was unknown. Athelstan was particularly occupied with legislation against cattle-stealing.[16] He enacted that no cattle could be traded unless witnessed by a reeve, priest, or trustworthy men. Goods valued at more than 20*d*. had to be purchased before witnesses. All men had to help their neighbor recover his cattle and to accompany him along the trail that led to the thief's residence. If the trail led out of one hundred into another, the men of the next hundred had to follow the trail. Men were to notify the com-

[14] SM, no. 5.
[15] SM, no. 2.
[16] SM, no. 7.

munity of all buying and selling done by them; they were to be constantly observant of new cattle in their neighborhood and to report them. Should cattle be destroyed, their value had to be paid to the offended party. When stolen cattle were found, the man who attached them must select one out of five men nominated by the community who would swear that the cattle had been attached according to law. The man found with the cattle had to select two out of ten men nominated who would swear that he rightfully possessed the cattle. At the court, possession would then be determined by rules of procedure that awarded proof. If it was found that the cattle had been stolen, the aggrieved person would receive the cattle and the court would receive a fine paid by the thief. If the accusation was proved false, then the plaintiff would pay a fine for false accusation.

Anglo-Saxon law never freed itself from the concept that the family of a man was an accomplice to his crime. If he could not return stolen property or make recompense for it, he and his family could be sold into slavery. A doom of Ine did state that a wife could clear herself as an accomplice if she took an oath swearing that she knew nothing about the cattle found on the land of her husband. Yet even in the eleventh century Bishop Wulfstan of Worcester complained that "cradle-children" were unjustly considered accomplices and sold into slavery with their parents.

6. THE LAW OF PROPERTY AND CONTRACT

We have been speaking of stolen property. The Anglo-Saxon law conceived of property much differently from the way the law of today regards it. If a law of property can be said to have existed, it did so only as unwritten custom; we must learn of it from charters and lawsuits in which rights to property were involved. What the law and lawyers call property and ownership did not exist in the Anglo-Saxon mind. The law was interested only in possession. Property is never at stake but always its possession, and this is what must be recovered or retained. The courts only determined possession, and a favorable decision only gave one possession of property without further liability of dispute. Such law held for both land and movable property such as cattle, jewels, implements, and arms. The laws of sale, delivery, and contract were also unwritten. Apparently transfer could be effected only by the actual delivery of the goods. A bargain was undoubtedly sealed by swearing one's faith, giving pledges and what is known as earnest-money (a deposit). Written contract did not exist; contracts were struck orally before qualified witnesses who could be called later to testify. Oaths were sworn principally because they put the contract under sanction of the church. Such procedure was, in fact, probably derived from ecclesiastical practice. It is likely that hundred courts did adjudicate some disputes over contracts, promises, and sales.

We are more fully informed by extant records of lawsuits on the procedure that determined the possession of land. About 990 a lawsuit occurred between the noblewoman Wynflaed and a certain man Leofwine. First

Wynflaed produced four witnesses—the archbishop of Canterbury, a bishop, Earl Elfric, and King Ethelred the Redeless' mother—all of whom swore that Earl Elfric had given Wynflaed the estates of Hagbourne and Bradfield in Berkshire in return for one at Datchet in Buckinghamshire. Notified of this by the four witnesses, King Ethelred immediately had them go to Leofwine and inform him of what they had sworn. But he would not recognize Wynflaed's possession unless it could be determined at the shire court. Thereupon the king ordered a shire court of Berkshire consisting of all the great lords to settle the case. The court informed Wynflaed that she might prove her possession. She was awarded this chance to substantiate her claim because, by her earlier transaction with Elfric, sworn to by him and three other witnesses, she had invalidated Leofwine's right of possession. Such an award by the court practically amounted to a decision for her because now she only had to produce a certain number of men to take an oath for her right of possession. This she did, producing apparently thirty-six individuals who were willing to swear that she had the right. The court, convinced by this number, dispensed with the oath, for if it had been taken Leofwine not only would have lost possession of the estates in question but would have had to pay a fine plus his wergeld to the king. This decision was agreeable to Leofwine, who "dispensed with the oath and handed over the estates uncontested."

Some time during Canute's reign the full shire court of Herefordshire consisting of the bishop, the earl, the sheriff, and the thegns heard a somewhat different lawsuit.[17] Edwin, the son of the noblewoman Enneawnes, came to the court and sued his mother for some land lying at Wellington and Cradley. Then the court asked who represented Enneawnes and up stood Thurkel the White, the husband of Enneawnes' kinswoman Leofflaed. But Thurkel was not well informed about the land or what disposition Enneawnes had made of it. The court, therefore, ordered three thegns to ride to Enneawnes and ask her "what claim she had to the lands for which her son was suing her." Upon hearing the three thegns she was greatly angered at her son, said that he had no claim to the land, and called Leofflaed before them. She then declared that it was to her that she granted all her land, gold, and clothing. Then she told the thegns: "Act like thegns, and duly announce my message to the meeting before all the worthy men, and tell them to whom I have granted my land and all my property, and not a thing to my own son, and ask them to be witness of this." This the thegns did. Thereupon Thurkel the White asked the court to give possession of the lands "unreservedly" to his wife. The court did so. Finally with the court's permission, Thurkel rode to the church of Saint Ethelbert and had the court decision recorded in a gospel book.

In these two lawsuits possession was determined by witnesses who had been present at the original grant of land or by those of the community who

[17] SM, no. 15F.

could swear that a certain individual had the best right of possession. Also the statement of the grantor before legal witnesses was used as evidence by the court. We note further in Thurkel's case that he left nothing in the future to the oaths of witnesses, he recorded the decision in the Holy Book and the next time trouble arose over possession it would be settled by written evidence. Needless to say those whose rights to possession were challenged produced charters if they had them. It did not take long for those possessing land to see the advantages of the charter.

Let us examine a few cases in which written evidence was used. In 824 in Mercia there was a lawsuit between the monastery of Berkeley and Heahberht, bishop of Worcester. The monastery sued the bishop to recover lands granted at Westbury by Ethelric. In the court, a witenagemot, the bishop fortunately was able to produce a title-deed that showed the lands granted to the church of Worcester by Ethelric. Upon this evidence the court awarded the proof or oath to the bishop, who made it successfully within thirty days. Obviously in this suit the written evidence practically decided the case; the oath was but a formality. Sometimes the courts dispensed with the formality when substantial written evidence was produced, as occurred at the witenagemot held by King Brihtwulf of Mercia in 840. Brihtwulf had previously taken certain lands possessed by the church of Worcester and granted them to other men. Because of this action Bishop Heahberht and his men rode to the witenagemot "having with them their privileges and charters of the lands . . . and they were read out there before the king and his nobles, and there the leading men of the Mercians gave judgment for him and that they had been wrongly and illegally despoiled of their own. Then their land was returned to them in peace." Such a decision was nothing other than the trial by charters that one meets after 1066.

There are no extant laws relating to inheritance of land. All we know from charters and wills and other stray references is that the old Germanic custom prevailed. A man divided his land among his sons or, lacking sons, among his daughters. Of marriage and the law we have little to say. A discussion of marriage law has scant relevance for English institutions and, moreover, we do not know too much about it because its customs were left unwritten. The arrangements for marriage were made orally and were well enough known so that no written laws were required. The church acquired wide jurisdiction over marriage and had much to say about illicit marriages among kinsmen, divorce, and second marriages. The marriage-gift brought by husband to wife was a constant source of trouble when she died and we hear of all sorts of arrangements made by noble families to provide for succession of land in case of either the husband's or the wife's death. We should emphasize that Anglo-Saxon women had great freedom in the possession and disposal of land. Their Norman successors were not to know such freedom.

7. MISADVENTURE AND RESPONSIBILITY FOR ACCIDENT

Rarely did the dooms deal rationally with death by pure accident. One of the few cases appears in the dooms of Alfred. It was enacted that men should carry their spears level on their shoulders to avoid blame if another person ran into the point. If, however, the point of the spear was the height of three fingers above the butt end of the spear so that it was at the level of a man's face, the bearer had to pay a wergeld if an accident occurred. The bearer was even more liable for accident if the point of the spear was in front of him for he could then see what was happening. Such thinking was quite reasonable and the doom almost attempts, as Holdsworth has said, to "establish a standard of diligence." The general rule of Anglo-Saxon law was, however, that a man acts at his own peril. Even if an act was accidental or committed in self-defense, compensation had to be paid. However innocent a man's intentions, he was liable and we can discern no question of negligence raised. These ideas of old German law expressed in the *Laws of Henry I* are our earliest evidence. One must be careful not to leave his arms unguarded for if someone should take them and kill a man, the owner was held responsible. A doom of Canute did state, however, that the person committing the act was responsible if the owner of the weapons could clear himself by oath from having any part in the crime.

Weapons were a dangerous property or possession. They were stolen, borrowed, taken forcibly, or secured fraudulently from an armorer, who might be repairing them for the owner, with the view to covering up evidence of manslaughter or for producing false evidence. Sometimes the armorer was bribed to cooperate. To the present-day lawyer it is quite amusing to read of one Anglo-Saxon swearing that he did not kill a man, followed by another who swore that no weapons of his killed a man. The dooms of Alfred are quite explicit on liability. If you lent your weapons to another man for the purpose of killing, then you had to help him pay the wergeld. If you lent your weapons to another without knowledge of the purpose, you still had to pay one-third of the wergeld and of the fine to the king. Armorers and smiths repairing weapons were bound to the owners for secure custody and return "unless it has been stipulated that there shall be no liability." It may be that the armorer was also held to return the weapons without any claim of unlawful use. There were other dangers in connection with weapons. If a man placed his weapons against a wall or tree and another person passed by and knocked them down so that they killed or injured a man, the owner was liable. Negligent custody of animals was a common subject of the dooms. Ine provided that any beast found breaking through hedges into common meadows and lands and eating the grass and destroying the crops could be killed by anyone discovering it.[18] The owner suffered the loss. A doom of Alfred stipulated in detail the compensation a

[18] SM, no. 4.

man had to pay when his dog bit someone: 6s. for the first bite, 12s. for the second, and 30s. for the third. More bites and injuries made the owner liable for paying a man's full wergeld. If a man lent his horse to another and injury or death resulted, the lender was held liable. Moreover, if one man asked another to go with him on a journey and the person invited was attacked along the way by his enemies, the man who asked the injured one to accompany him was liable. These examples well show that liability was based solely on the act causing the damage; negligence is not involved. Liability extended farther than the consequences resulting from negligence. The law considered only the person injured or killed whose misfortunes could be ultimately connected with the act.

In Roman law noxal actions (*noxa* meaning hurt or damage) were those done by persons and animals belonging to another. The owner was held liable unless he surrendered the person or beast. Such a principle is to be found also in Anglo-Saxon law where it appears as the rule of deodand. When a man was killed by accident the immediate cause, whether animate or inanimate, had to be handed over to the kindred of the dead man as the guilty party. This rule was associated with the idea that personal chattels causing death should be given to God as an expiatory offering. A doom of Alfred quite clearly expressed this rule when it declared that if a "man kills another unintentionally, [by allowing a tree to fall on him] while they are engaged in a common task, the tree shall be given to the [dead man's kindred], and they shall remove it within 30 days from the locality." A doom of Ine directed that if a Welsh slave killed a man of Wessex, the owner had to hand over the slave to the dead man's kindred and lord or purchase his life for 60s.[19] Another of Ine's dooms provided that a man's animal which had bitten or wounded another could be substituted for a composition in money.

These archaic ideas on misadventure and responsibility were, however, gradually modified. The influence of the church certainly made itself felt on those who declared and made the law. Christian doctrine was interested not in the act but in the motive and the state of mind of the individual sinning and committing evil. By the eleventh century we can detect the result of this influence in modification of the law and legal thinking. In one of his dooms Canute declared that in the past when stolen property was found in a man's house it had been customary "to treat a child which lay in the cradle, even though it had never tasted food," as also being guilty and as having an intelligence. He ordered that henceforth this should cease. Later it was recognized that lunatics could not be held responsible for their actions, though there was still some question over the liability of the man responsible for their custody. The law was definitely softening; at times wergelds and *wites* were dispensed with and we can even detect the beginning of the idea that the king could pardon liability and accident.

[19] SM, no. 4.

8. PROCEDURE

All early Germanic law attempted to regulate the conditions under which a man could resort to self-help to secure his rights. Self-help was not eliminated but was limited under numerous rules preventing a man from taking action that would not receive court approval. Much of the early Salic Law is devoted to rules regulating the occasions when a creditor can seize property owed to him. These early rules dealt not with the merit of cases but only with the rigid procedure that must be followed by persons resorting to self-help. Any error made in procedure lost the person his property. He had to restore all goods seized and pay a double fine. In so far as we can determine, distraint of property was not in the eyes of Anglo-Saxon law a remedy to obtain right. It but preceded court action and was allowed because it compelled the defendant's appearance in court. Equally rigid rules were devised to regulate the self-help taken by a man whose goods had been lost or stolen. Immediately he must raise the hue and cry, and all the community was liable to assist him.[20] Anyone who allowed a thief to escape or to conceal his stolen goods was liable for paying the thief's wergeld. If and when a man found his stolen property, he was allowed to claim it at once; if the thief refused to surrender it, the man could summon him to court to hear the charge. As creditor or owner of stolen property a man taking the course of self-help was but acting prior to court procedure; he was permitted such action only because it aided the law. Self-help was closely regulated in the case of thieves and criminals apprehended in the act or caught by the posse assembled through hue and cry. Upon capture, the criminal was hustled off to court with his stolen property or with his marks of guilt. Again this action was preliminary to court procedure but in such obvious instances of guilt the law took into account the feelings of the injured party. The criminal could utter no word of defense. Restitution of property and payment of fines were demanded immediately by the court and, should death be the penalty, the injured party was frequently the executioner.

We are not concerned chiefly with preliminary procedure but with the Anglo-Saxon legal machinery developed for administering differences of plaintiff and defendant and with the methods devised to decide between them. In the description of procedure that follows we should recognize how highly formalized were the rules which, if departed from, lost the suit. First the plaintiff had to summon the defendant to court to answer the charge. This summons must be done at the residence of the defendant before sunset and in the presence of witnesses. At the same time an agreement was reached setting the time for meeting in court, the date depending upon the distance and difficulty of the defendant in traveling there. Sometimes the law regulated the time. The defendant must then appear at the scheduled

[20] SM, no. 11.

time or supply an excuse (essoin) for not coming.[21] Essoins recognized as valid by Anglo-Saxon law were absence overseas, service for one's king or lord, sickness, and impossible travel conditions. If the defendant failed to appear in court and gave no valid essoin the next step was to compel appearance. He was fined and could be summoned three times with a higher fine for each summons. To collect the fine the court could authorize distress. Failure to appear after three summonses lost the defendant his suit.

In civil cases, then, the plaintiff could claim his land or goods. Only in the most serious criminal cases was a man outlawed. We should note that no trial occurred in the defendant's absence. According to the law the court had no right to hear a suit if defendant or plaintiff was absent; this rule was derived from the idea that recourse to court was a result of consent by both. If, for example, the defendant refused court procedure, the court had no jurisdiction. But in regard to the fines levied for nonappearance, it should be remarked that if the defendant and his kindred failed to pay them, he could be declared an outlaw. A "wolf's head" was said to be upon him and he could be killed with impunity. Any man who harbored him or avenged his death incurred very heavy fines. Only the king could restore the outlaw to the pale of law. When fines or distraint did produce the defendant, he had to give some security that he would appear hereafter when required at court. If he declined or was a suspicious character, he could be put in jail. Such action was rarely necessary because a man's tithing was ordinarily enough security.

We have now arrived at that point where either by volition or by compulsion defendant and plaintiff are at court. Normally the plaintiff was permitted to make a preliminary oath that his claim and accusation was made in all good faith. He must demonstrate that he acted not out of "hatred or malice or wrongful covetousness." The accusation must be made verbatim according to the prescribed oath; severe fines were levied for false accusation. Having made his oath the plaintiff was next expected to give pledges that he would prosecute the suit. Then he had to support his accusation with evidence or a sufficient number of oaths. The amount of evidence and number or value of the oaths required depended upon the seriousness of the accusation and the rank of the plaintiff. Should circumstances require the oath of a man or men worth 1200s., a plaintiff who was a thegn would require no oath-helpers or men to swear oaths for him. On the other hand a *ceorl* would require five other *ceorls* to make up the oath. Should the defendant be an outlaw or the circumstantial evidence be extremely strong, no oath was required. Next the defendant was permitted to make an oath of denial. In this connection the point should be made that to Anglo-Saxon law "denial is always stronger than accusation." The defendant's oath and the number of oath-helpers required was again determined by the nature of the charge and by his rank. If oath-helpers were needed, the defendant was usually

[21] SM, no. 11.

given time to round them up, sometimes up to thirty days. Before departing, however, he had to give a pledge (property, neighbors, or his lord) that he would accept the court's judgment and that he would produce the required oath. Only with those accused of capital crimes such as murder, house-breaking, and treason was an immediate oath demanded.

Assuming now that the defendant was ready to produce the oath by himself or with the help of oath-helpers (compurgators), he would swear first that he was guiltless of the crime charged and then the compurgators would swear that his oath was pure and not false. We should note that they only swore that his oath was valid and did not give any evidence on the case. When the oath had been suitably performed the suit was ended and the defendant cleared.[22] To us such a procedure seems incredibly simple and easy for the defendant. Actually proof by compurgation was more difficult than might be supposed. The compurgators who had to be secured all came from the defendant's community and none of them would consent to support his oath if they believed him guilty. Needless to say, in a small agrarian village neighbors knew each other's business extremely well. Bearing in mind that the compurgators were referred to in terms of so much money and so many hides of land, we will realize that they were not going to swear falsely and lose their wergeld or land. A defendant looked upon suspiciously or thought guilty simply could not collect compurgators and would lose his suit. In the procedure described thus far it can be seen that the Anglo-Saxons considered the award to a man to establish his proof a valuable right. It almost always meant that the person so awarded won the suit. Proof was not a burden but a boon.

There were, however, defendants not permitted to use the proof of compurgation. Suspicious characters with a record of numerous accusations and with conviction of perjury were not considered oath-worthy. If the man was caught in crime or in possession of stolen property for which he had no valid excuse, compurgation was closed to him. Under these circumstances the court awarded the opportunity of producing the oath to the plaintiff, who by himself or with compurgators swore the suitable oath. The plaintiff was also awarded the proof if he had seen the defendant commit the crime. After the plaintiff had successfully given his oath or when the defendant had been awarded the oath and could not produce it, he had to submit to another form of proof—the ordeal. At this point the church took over control of the proceedings. Proof by ordeal was a primitive practice based on the belief that the gods or God intervened with some sort of sign or miracle to settle the question of guilt or innocence. By the time we have records on the ordeal the church dominated the proceedings and had superimposed upon them Christian ritual. Prior to the ordeal the defendant fasted for three days, heard mass, and was requested to confess his guilt before being administered the sacrament.

[22] SM, nos. 6, 7, 8A, 13, 14.

There were three forms of ordeal and the plaintiff was commonly permitted to determine which the defendant must undergo. The ordeal of cold water involved the following procedure. The defendant was first given a drink of holy water and then thrown into some water previously blessed by the priest who prayed that God would accept the innocent in the water and throw or keep out the guilty. If a man sank he was innocent; if he floated he was guilty. We may be certain that a man's aquatic dexterity and his psychological behavior played a large if not determining part in his guilt or innocence. The other two ordeals were more severe and were conducted within the church. Both forms had to be prepared by the priest and his assistants and they were closely observed by witnesses of each party to insure that correct preparation was followed and that no favoritism was shown. With the ordeal of hot iron the defendant had to carry in his hand a glowing bar of iron, a pound in weight, for nine feet. With the ordeal of hot water he had to put his hand up to the wrist into a cauldron of boiling water and pull out a stone. In both cases the defendant's hand was bound up and after three days the bandage was removed. If the burned skin was healing properly the defendant was declared innocent. If his skin was festered and infected he was declared guilty. For the really serious charges, such as the capital crimes, the defendant had to submit to the threefold ordeal. With the hot iron the weight was increased to three pounds and with the boiling water he had to put his arm in up to his elbow.[23] We find that ordinarily the clergy could clear themselves of accusation more easily. Archbishops and bishops merely had to give their word that they were guiltless. Abbots, priests, and deacons could clear themselves by their own oaths, declaring at the altar "before Christ I speak the truth; I do not lie." Lesser ranks had to clear themselves with the oaths of three compurgators of their rank. Where accusation was serious enough to demand more proof the clergy underwent the ordeal of the consecrated morsel. After repeating a phrase or prayer stating that the morsel would choke him if he spoke falsely, the defendant swallowed the morsel. When a man was found guilty by compurgation or ordeal the court pronounced the penalty or punishment prescribed by the law for the crime. There were times when the courts tended to be more lenient in pronouncing the punishment. Though it was the law that murder by witchcraft and apprehended thievery were punishable by death, if witchcraft and theft were only proved by ordeal and the previous record of the defendant was clean, the punishment could be limited to imprisonment and pecuniary fines.

We have examined the general rules of procedure in court and for our purposes they are enough to know. There were variations in the procedures followed in claims and debts resulting from sales transactions, theft or loss of movable property, dispute over land, and criminal offenses, but the differences are not enough to warrant study of each procedure. Those who de-

[23] SM, nos. 7, 8A and B, 12.

sire to probe deeper may refer to the standard texts on English law. We must, however, linger over one more legal development if we would complete our picture of Anglo-Saxon law. Repeatedly we have referred to the problem of bringing men to justice, of getting them to court. The difficulty was especially acute during the reigns of ineffective kings and in the old Danelaw where new people were being assimilated. The Code of Ethelred the Redeless issued between 979 and 1008 at Wantage was enacted to suppress lawlessness in the north where the ordinary methods of bringing criminals to justice were totally ineffective. Powerful kindreds and unscrupulous lords protected men against innumerable sentences which had been handed down by shire and hundred courts. Some men never were brought to justice. The innovation in this Code makes it noteworthy for English law. After proclaiming that the laws issued were for the "improvement of public security," Ethelred ordered that "a meeting is to be held in each wapentake, and the twelve leading thegns, and with them the reeve, are to come forward and swear on the relics which are put into their hands that they will accuse no innocent man nor conceal any guilty one." Next the thegns were to seize all those men of ill repute who had been frequently accused of wrong; the men taken had to produce security that they would come to court. Each had to undergo the threefold ordeal or in its stead pay a fourfold fine. All those convicted were to be so struck that their necks were "broken."[24] Other provisions were included in the Code but its chief interest lies in the fact that the twelve leading thegns seem to be one of the antecedents of the famous presentment jury found under Henry II.

We are not yet able to compare the Anglo-Saxon system of law and jurisdiction with that built by the Norman-Angevin rulers; this we can do better after studying the innovations made by the new kings. We can, however, say here that there was no sharp change after 1066. In many respects the efficient Norman kings were innovators and brought along with them a sizable collection of law and procedure from the Continent which they grafted on to the Anglo-Saxon legal system. What made these hardheaded kings so efficient in the art of ruling was that they possessed an innate sense of knowing when they saw a good thing. Never did they destroy an effective Anglo-Saxon institution. What they grafted of the Norman law was the best of what they knew and it in turn served to invigorate and advance the efficiency of an already remarkable system of courts and law. Some of the first steps of William the Conqueror were to confirm Anglo-Saxon law and custom. The *Laws of Henry I* is a mine of information for Anglo-Saxon law and procedure. The hundred and shire courts were retained and converted into more efficient and rational tribunals of law. By 1066 a solid foundation had been poured for the erection of the independent and resilient English law.

[24] SM, no. 12.

BIBLIOGRAPHY

The principal Anglo-Saxon records are translated by Doris Whitelock in vol. I of *English Historical Documents* but for others and further analysis see F. M. Stenton, *The Latin Charters of the Anglo-Saxon Period* (Oxford, 1955), A. J. Robertson, *Anglo-Saxon Charters* (Cambridge, 1939), *The Laws of the Kings of England from Edmund to Henry I* (Cambridge, 1925), F. L. Attenborough, *The Laws of the Earliest English Kings* (Cambridge, 1922), H. G. Richardson and G. O. Sayles, *Law and Legislation from Aethelberht to Magna Carta* (Edinburgh, 1966), and F. E. Harmer, *Anglo-Saxon Writs* (Manchester, 1952).

For surveys of the period prior to 1066 see particularly Sheppard Frere, *Britannia: A History of Roman Britain* (London, 1967), D. P. Kirby, *The Making of Early England* (London, 1967), P. H. Sawyer, *From Roman Britain to Norman England* (London, 1978), H. R. Loyn, *Anglo-Saxon England and the Norman Conquest* (London, 1962). Loyn has also written a well-balanced account of *Alfred the Great* (Oxford, 1967). Frank Barlow in his scholarly *Edward the Confessor* (London, 1970) argues unconvincingly that Edward was an able king.

On the nature of the early Anglo-Saxon kings and their government see H. M. Chadwick, *Studies on Anglo-Saxon Institutions* (Oxford, 1905) and D. A. Binchy, *Celtic and Anglo-Saxon Kingship* (Oxford, 1970). A more specialized study is W. A. Chaney, *The Cult of Kingship in Anglo-Saxon England* (Berkeley, 1969). Also of interest is the broader study by Fritz Kern, *Kingship and Law in the Middle Ages*, S. B. Chrimes ed. and trans. (Oxford, 1939). In *A History of the English Coronation* (Oxford, 1937) Percy Schramm traces the coronation ceremony from the earliest times through the Middle Ages. See also the brief survey by Bertie Wilkinson, *The Coronation in History* (London, 1953). Still the best study on the royal household is L. M. Larson, *The King's Household in England before the Norman Conquest* (Madison, 1904). For many years the standard work on the witenagemot was Felix Liebermann, *The National Assembly in the Anglo-Saxon Period* (Halle, 1913) but its conclusions have been largely superseded by those of Tryggvi Oleson, *The Witenagemot in the Reign of Edward the Confessor* (Toronto, 1955).

Following are a few of the most important books on the structure of Anglo-Saxon society and on the agrarian system. The Germanist interpretation is found in F. W. Maitland, *Domesday Book and Beyond* (Cambridge, 1897), Paul Vinogradoff, *Villainage in England* (Oxford, 1892) and *The Growth of the Manor*, rev. ed. (Oxford, 1911). The Romanist position is defended by Frederic Seebohm, *The English Village Community* (London, 1905). For a criticism of these views see Carl Stephenson, *Mediaeval Institutions: Selected Essays*, Bryce Lyon, ed. (Ithaca, N.Y., 1954) and Eric John, *Orbis Britanniae and Other Studies* (Leicester, 1966).

On local government and courts the following studies are outstanding: H. M. Cam, *Local Government in Francia and England* (London, 1912), W. A. Morris, *The Early English County Court* (Berkeley, 1926), and *The Mediaeval

English Sheriff to 1300 (Manchester, 1927). For the Anglo-Saxon borough see the excellent work of Carl Stephenson, *Borough and Town* (Cambridge, Mass., 1933). The views of Stephenson on the origin of the town have been criticized by James Tait, *The Medieval English Borough* (Manchester, 1936). Still useful is F. W. Maitland, *Township and Borough* (Cambridge, 1898). For a good topographical study see Colin Platt, *The English Medieval Town* (London, 1976). A recent survey is Susan Reynolds, *An Introduction to the History of English Medieval Towns* (Oxford, 1977).

For the growth of the Christian church in early Anglo-Saxon England see Henry Mayr-Harting, *The Coming of Christianity to Anglo-Saxon England* (London, 1972). Other pertinent works that deal with all of medieval England are *The English Church and the Papacy in the Middle Ages*, C. H. Lawrence, ed. (London, 1965), R. E. Rodes, Jr., *Ecclesiastical Administration in Medieval England* (Notre Dame, Ind., 1977), and David Knowles, *The Monastic Order in England* (Cambridge, 1940).

Part Two

THE NORMAN KINGS

THE LANDS OF
WILLIAM I
IN 1086
English Counties and Normandy ruled by William I
English Palatinates and Earldoms
Lands held in Fief from William I
Archbishopric
Bishopric
Scale of Miles
0 20 40 60
SCOTLAND
Berwick
Tweed
NORTHUM-
BERLAND
Tyne
Newcastle
Carlisle
Durham
Ouse
YORKSHIRE
York
ISLE OF MAN
IRISH SEA
NORTH SEA
Humber
INTER
RIPAM ET
MERSHAM
St. Asaph
ANGLESEY
Bangor
NORTH
WALES
Chester
CHESHIRE
DERBY
Derby
NOTTINGHAM
Trent
Tetford
Lincoln
LINCOLN
The Wash
Nottingham
STAFFORD
Stafford
Lichfield
Shrewsbury
SHROP-
SHIRE
LEICESTER
Leicester
RUT
LAND
Stamford
NORFOLK
Norwich
HUN-
TINGDON
CAMBRIDGE
Ely
Huntingdon
SUFFOLK
Coventry
WARWICK
Warwick
NORTHAMPTON
Northampton
Cambridge
Ipswich
CARDIGAN
WORCES-
TER
Worcester
HEREFORD
Hereford
Bedford
BED
FORD
DYFED
BRECON
GLAMOR-
GAN
Gloucester
OXFORD
Oxford
BUCKINGHAM
HERTFORD
Hertford
Colchester
ESSEX
Severn
GLOUCESTER
Thames
Wallingford
Malmesbury
BERK
SHIRE
MIDDLE
SEX
London
Bristol Channel
Bristol
Bath
Windsor
Rochester
Sandwich
WILTSHIRE
SURREY
Canterbury
KENT
Wells
SOMERSET
Salisbury
HAMPSHIRE
Dover
Calais
Bruges
FLANDERS
DEVON
Winchester
SUSSEX
Hastings
Chichester
Southampton
Boulogne
DORSET
Exeter
Pevensey
CORNWALL
I. OF WIGHT
Dorchester
ENGLISH CHANNEL
Somme
PICARDY
Rouen
Jumièges
VEXIN
Bayeux
Caen
Seine
Coutances
ÎLE DE
NORMANDY
Paris
FRANCE
Tinchebrai
Dol
BRITTANY
MAINE
Rennes
LeMans
Orléans
ANJOU
Angers
Loire
Nantes
Tours

VII

The Norman Sources

RARELY after 1066 does the historian of English institutions have to turn to unwritten evidence. Rather than searching for sufficient evidence he suddenly is faced with selecting relevant information from the massive documentation left behind by the Normans and their kings. For the medieval scholar the glory of the English records is their great antiquity, bulk, continuity, and fine state of preservation. From his first look at *Domesday Book* in the museum of the Public Record Office at London and throughout the hours spent there with records in the Round Room the historian is ever aware that there are more official records for medieval England than for any other region of western Europe. So adequate, indeed, are the nonnarrative sources that English institutions can be explained almost exclusively from them. The narrative sources such as the chronicles assume a distinctly secondary role after 1066.

1. NONNARRATIVE SOURCES

Pre-eminent as a record for early Norman administration is *Domesday Book*, which we have previously discussed as a record for the Anglo-Saxon period.[1] From the returns supplied by the royal tenants to compile it, *Domesday Book* provides our surest description of finance, central and local administration, and the status of rural and urban inhabitant. Closely associated in purpose was the *Northamptonshire Geld Roll* (1072–1078), which tabulated the amount of Danegeld assessed to each hundred of Northamptonshire during the reigns of Edward the Confessor and William the Conqueror. As in the Anglo-Saxon period, manorial surveys conducted by the great abbeys afford supplementary information on the extent of lands and resources, their value, and the obligations of agrarian tenants. Of these surveys the most valuable are those made by the Abbeys of Bury Saint Edmunds, Burton, and Peterborough between 1045 and 1128. Pertinent for every aspect of Norman government are the royal and private charters, writs, confirmations, and wills.[2] The charters of Henry I and Stephen granted at the outset of their reigns were nothing but bids for support from their

[1] SM, nos. 21, 22.
[2] SM, nos. 27, 28.

subjects; though neither king kept the provisions of the charters, they did confirm good custom and grant new privileges. Thus they continued the Anglo-Saxon *promissio regis* and set valuable constitutional precedents.[3] Both charters and writs contain all sorts of information for central and local judicial organization and procedure; they are concerned with the machinery of local government. The writs in particular spell out the duties of the sheriffs and other local officials. By means of writs and charters the kings, private persons, and the church granted lands and privileges. From them as well as from wills and confirmations we can describe and explain the possession of land and the numerous tenures governing it. The wills, moreover, tell in detail about the status of feudal and manorial tenants, particularly about their obligations and rights. Charters and writs are the key to royal pecuniary rights and the financial exemptions granted by the kings to certain of their vassals and subjects. By charter the Norman kings granted urban privileges to well-established boroughs like London and founded new towns with elementary bourgeois privileges. Occasionally the royal writ inaugurated new policy to govern the relations of state and church. Indeed, it is from writ and charter that we are able to understand the principles of Anglo-Norman feudalism and to observe how they operated; here one finds pictured the basic ingredients of feudalism—the fief, homage, feudal tenure, and knight service.

Besides the magnificent collection of charters and writs we have two other excellent sources for judicial organization and the substance of the law. The *Laws of William the Conqueror*, ten in number, seems to represent an early twelfth-century compilation of the various legal enactments made by William during his reign. These laws supplemented and revised the Anglo-Saxon law confirmed by William in one of the enactments of the collection.[4] The other source, the *Laws of Henry I* compiled about 1118 by an anonymous author, is a legal treatise attempting to describe the English law as it was in the early twelfth century. Deficient in his knowledge of Latin and mentally unequipped to understand the collection of laws and treatises that he used, the author produced an extremely ill-organized and obscure book. He quotes inaccurately from all sorts of continental legal sources such as the *leges barbarorum*, the Carolingian capitularies, canons of the church, and stray treatises. Obviously a Norman unfamiliar with Anglo-Saxon, our author got into real trouble when he tried to explain the sense of the Anglo-Saxon dooms. Despite these shortcomings, however, he presents us with a fairly reasonable account of Anglo-Norman law; if one takes time to work carefully through the hodgepodge of stray quotations, laws, and interpretations, he gains an approximate idea of early twelfth-century law, which, at best, was in a confused state. How could it be otherwise with the Normans trying to fathom the mysteries of Anglo-

[3] SM, no. 23.
[4] SM, no. 18.

Saxon custom and procedure while adding to it law of their own? This industrious author deserves admiration for even attempting a law book, in itself a new venture in the early twelfth century.[5] To be studied along with the *Laws of Henry I* is another legal compilation entitled the *Liber Quadripartitus*. Apparently written also by a Norman clerk during the reign of Henry I it once contained four books. The first book was composed of a Latin translation of the Anglo-Saxon dooms; here are most of the dooms we have plus a few that otherwise would not have been preserved. We know that the second book contained important enactments, charters, and royal papers from the author's period, although it has come down to us with only Henry I's coronation charter and documents on the investiture struggle. There were two other books treating legal procedure and theft but they have not been preserved.

We come now to two works whose principal purpose was the description of Anglo-Saxon law under Edward the Confessor. In addition, both indicate how the Normans interpreted Anglo-Saxon custom and what legal divergence was occurring in the first fifty years after the Conquest. The *Les Williame* was a private compilation completed in the early twelfth century. We do not know what language it was composed in but it has been preserved both in Latin and in French; the Latin version differs slightly from the French and leads us to believe that it was derived from a text no longer extant. The work can be divided into three parts. The first part is the most valuable. It lists certain rules of the Anglo-Saxon law as the Normans understood them plus adding to them some of the Norman legal rules and innovations. A statement rather than a copy of the law, this part is a reliable account of some aspects of the fused Anglo-Norman law. The second part consists of a few maxims taken at random from Roman law. We are not sure of the purpose of these maxims; they may represent an urge to find and use some rational principles of jurisprudence to clear away the confusion of the irrational and customary Anglo-Saxon law. The last part is simply a partial translation of Canute's laws. The other law book, also in Latin and already noted as a source for Anglo-Saxon law, is the *Laws of Edward the Confessor*. Written by a Norman who probably completed his task towards the end of Henry I's reign, it is the most unreliable of such records we possess. Supposedly to describe the law of the Confessor's day, it discussed a law having more resemblance to that prevailing during the reign of William Rufus. The author, biased in favor of the church and filled with numerous prejudices, made remarks and expressed opinions that cannot be accepted literally. Only when supplemented by independent evidence can his statements be trusted. Maitland has ventured that the author was someone who "would have liked those statements to be true" in the twelfth century. But to sum up the value of all these legal compilations, they should be regarded as sources that help to explain the transformation undergone by Anglo-Saxon law in the first century of Norman rule.

[5] SM, no. 26.

However much the Anglo-Saxon dooms and charters portrayed the working of royal administration, it was always in an impersonal way; they leave most details to the imagination. Only with the Norman kings do we begin to get records specific enough to launch serious investigation of the royal court and its part in the government of the realm. Though it is common knowledge that the household formed the nucleus of royal and princely courts in western Europe, only in early twelfth-century England do we have a document describing the daily operation and organization of such an establishment. It marks out the lines along which certain of the domestic officers will develop and forecasts the specialized departments of the court that they will come to direct. In the reign of Henry I the greater domestic officers can still be seen in the company of the humble servants. By the reigns of Henry II and Richard I there was no longer this association. The specialization was already partially completed. *The Establishment of the King's Household* is a detailed account of the household under Henry I. It was probably written in 1136 for the guidance of Stephen in the management of his household; the composer was one with an intimate knowledge of such matters. The incorporation of a minute list of the wages and allowances received by the functionaries leads some scholars to name Nigel, bishop of Ely and Henry I's treasurer, as the author. This document is our first evidence of the role this nucleus of the royal court was to play in forging the powerful Norman central institutions.[6]

Until Henry I the English kings showed themselves hardly more advanced in the appreciation of orderly recordkeeping and of accurate methods of financial accounting than their princely contemporaries. What royal records there are before the twelfth century owe their preservation to the church and private persons. No systematic advance had yet been made in this domain of government. The reign of Henry I marks the beginning of elaborate royal records and at no time thereafter were the English kings to be excelled in this branch of administration. Typically the first of the great records were financial. If the money-conscious Norman rulers hoped to tap the resources of their realm efficiently, they had to devise a type of record that would provide an up-to-date and full account of what was owed to them and how well it was being collected; royal pecuniary interest rather than a sense of orderliness forced them to keep adequate records. In all respects this need was fulfilled by the Pipe Roll of the thirty-first regnal year of Henry I (1130).[7] It is the first we have of such rolls and there are no more for the rest of Henry's reign or for that of Stephen. With the second regnal year of Henry II the Pipe Rolls are again extant and continue in an almost unbroken procession for the next seven hundred years. Later when we have occasion to discuss the organization of the exchequer, we shall examine in detail the content of one of these Pipe Rolls; at present it is enough to

[6] SM, no. 29.
[7] SM, no. 25.

describe their chief characteristics. The Pipe Roll was a record of the accounts rendered yearly by all sheriffs and included all debts owed to the king and payable at the exchequer. Contemporaries referred to it as the roll of the treasury, as the great roll of the year, or as the great roll of accounts; later it became known as the great roll of pipe. It consisted of membranes of parchment, referred to as pipes. Its resemblance to a pipe or cylinder when rolled up seems to explain the etymology of the name. There is no evidence for the assertion that derives the name from a comparison of the royal treasury to the reservoir into which all the revenue flowed through a main pipe. Equally unhistorical is the explanation that derives the name from the roll's likeness to a wine cask. Each pipe consisted of two strips of parchment sewn together end to end to form one length. The length of a pipe was about three to four feet and on an average the width was fourteen inches. When all these pipes were sewn together endwise for filing at the end of the fiscal year, they produced a tremendous roll. A strikingly efficient record, the Pipe Rolls supply our best evidence on central and local administration in the twelfth century; they are a high testimonial to the advanced stage of administration in Norman England. For a like record on the Continent one has to wait another fifty years.

After severance of the close union and cooperation of the Anglo-Saxon church with the state by the Normans, and after the church was pushed full center into the stream of the Hildebrandine reform movement, church and state relations forged to the front as one of the most critical problems of the kings and prelates. Both church and state had to surrender or compromise on all sorts of powers, claims, and jurisdictions. Like the Continent, eleventh- and twelfth-century England was caught in the throes of the investiture struggle. Inevitably this bitter quarrel produced its records, of which we yet possess an amazingly large number. The papal bulls indicate the papal policy of interfering more in the secular and spiritual affairs of England. From them we learn of privileges bestowed upon the church and of papal policy towards the secular power. More numerous and informative is the correspondence between popes, kings, archbishops, papal legates, and royal envoys. From their expression of personal views on pressing issues we can clearly delineate the nature of the men and their attitude towards the problems raised by the investiture struggle. Most useful are the letters of Pope Gregory VII, the archbishops Lanfranc and Anslem, and Henry I. Occasionally such records can be supplemented by royal charters.

2. NARRATIVE SOURCES

Without *The Anglo-Saxon Chronicle* much of the period before 1066 would be lost to us. There are too few nonnarrative records to tell a large part of the story. The situation changes with the reign of Henry I, however, and despite the richness of the chronicles and biographies their value after 1066 lies chiefly in providing a general background of historical events that afford explanations for the development and modification of institutions. In that the royal character was a key element in successful government, we are grateful to the chroniclers and biographers for some good portraits of the kings. Perhaps if we had only the royal records for William the Conqueror's reign, we would deduce that he was a strong-willed and industrious man who prided himself upon orderly government, but the chronicler prepares us for the records or confirms our judgment of this remarkable man. In a few sentences an anonymous Norman monk of Caen fills in the background of William's character: "He never allowed himself to be deterred from prosecuting any enterprise because of the labour it entailed, and he was even undaunted by danger. . . . In speech he was fluent and persuasive, being skilled at all times in making clear his will."

So many chroniclers and biographers deal with Norman England that we can mention only the most notable. As valuable for the Norman as for the Anglo-Saxon period are the three Norman writers Ordericus Vitalis, William of Jumièges, and William of Poitiers. For the Anglo-Saxon attitude towards the Normans *The Anglo-Saxon Chronicle* is still useful. The role of Lanfranc and Anselm in the investiture struggle and in the reorganization of the church is seen in Eadmer's *History* and *Life of Anselm*. Eadmer was a monk of Canterbury and chaplain to Anselm. A contemporary of the events he recounts, Eadmer surpasses subsequent writers on these subjects. A more sophisticated and cosmopolitan view of history was held by William of Malmesbury, a contemporary of Eadmer. Malmesbury, who died in 1143, wrote of English history from Bede to 1142. His *History of the Kings of England* and *Modern History* provide authoritative accounts of Henry I's reign and of the first seven years of Stephen's. Florence of Worcester produced a world chronicle which has no great value for the period up to 1082 because he copied out of other works such as *The Anglo-Saxon Chronicle*. But from 1082 to 1118, the year of his death, his work is original and as such is reliable. Later another monk, John of Worcester, continued the chronicle of Florence to 1140; John was a witness to the numerous events which he describes. Simeon, a monk of Durham during Henry I's reign, also wrote a history of the English kings. Down to 1119 he copied Florence of Worcester, and from 1119 to 1129 he worked independently; a continuator carried his history down to 1154. Simeon is of value for his facts on northern England, facts gleaned from records no longer extant. The *History of England* by Henry of Huntingdon contains original material for the period from 1129 to 1154, but it owes its popularity primarily to its literary embellishments. The other principal contemporary source from the Norman period is a *History of Stephen*; it is the main reference for the troubled years between 1135 and 1154. The author was strongly pro-Stephen and one historian suggests that he was in the ecclesiastical service of Henry, bishop of Winchester, a brother of Stephen. There are other minor works of a miscellaneous nature for the Norman period, but the ones discussed form the base of the narrative evidence. Those histories produced after 1154 that deal also with Norman England can be discussed more advantageously when we come to the Angevin age.

VIII

Norman England, 1066–1154

I. WILLIAM THE CONQUEROR (1066–1087)

DUKE WILLIAM the Conqueror's victory at Hastings guaranteed to him and his army a permanent stay in England. Harold, the one Anglo-Saxon leader of great ability, had perished and no man or group of men left behind was equal to organizing successful resistance to the Normans. Thus, despite the fine opportunity that yet remained to inspire the mass of the Anglo-Saxons to heroic and stubborn resistance, there was no leadership to call it forth. It was now but a question of how long it would take the Normans to march around the island suppressing local and ill-organized defense. Rightfully, some Anglo-Saxon lords and prelates regarded London as the key to defense and rallied the surviving forces there. They immediately elected as king Edgar the Etheling, the last male descendant of the West Saxon dynasty, to provide a symbol of resistance and unity. But he was a mere youth with no flair for leadership. Within five days of Hastings, William had his army on the march towards London. Dover and Canterbury fell without resistance, but he failed to take London Bridge by assault. Not having the equipment necessary to storm London, William fell to devastating a band of land encircling London, blocking all approaches. Deprived of reinforcements and obviously impressed by the terrible and methodical thoroughness with which William laid waste the approaches, some of Edgar's followers soon lost heart; the first to offer submission to William was Stigand, the archbishop of Canterbury. The rest were soon to follow. A meeting was then held between William and the leading Anglo-Saxon lords and Londoners; the latter, realizing the futility of further fighting and the desirability of a strong ruler, agreed to cease resistance and surrender London. On Christmas day William was crowned king of England in Westminster Abbey and was acknowledged lawful sovereign by the verbal assent of the assembled Anglo-Saxons and Normans. Meanwhile William strengthened his hold upon the new land, starting construction of castles such as the Tower of London, levying taxes to pay for his army, receiving the homage of lords, and confiscating the lands of those who had resisted his invasion. By March of 1067 he was so completely in control that he felt able to return to Normandy, leaving England under the direction of trusted Norman lieutenants.

However much William's presence was required in his duchy, he had to neglect it for England within nine months. His lieutenants ruled a seething land too harshly and caused more discontent than order by their undiplomatic policies. The suppression of an abortive attempt by Kentishmen to make the Norman Eustace of Boulogne king signaled to William the urgency for return. During the next eight years he was to be sporadically occupied in stamping out the last embers of Anglo-Saxon resistance to foreign rule. After suppressing a revolt centered around Exeter in southwestern England, William concentrated his energies in the north where the core of resistance to his rule had gravitated. Easily able to secure the support of the Scottish kings, the Anglo-Saxon lords of this region forced William to organize repeated expeditions for service in Northumbria. In 1068 the flight of Edgar the Etheling to the Scottish court was the occasion of the first Northumbrian revolt, which William quickly suppressed; it was marked by the building of more castles at strategic points such as York. The next year the Northumbrian area rose up in a more severe revolt. It was strong enough to inflict defeats upon small Norman forces and garrisons and to secure the support of a Danish naval expedition sent by Swein Estrithson, king of Denmark, who laid claim to England by virtue of descent from Canute. The forces from 240 ships beached at the Humber River and united with the Anglo-Saxons near York, soon capturing this stronghold. Such initial success sparked revolt in Wessex and along the Welsh border. To combat this series of revolts William had to employ continental mercenaries. With his characteristic energy he moved first against the rebels in Wessex and the west and after pacifying these regions moved towards York. His revenge was terrible. After negotiating the withdrawal of the Danish forces he captured York and then so systematically wasted Yorkshire that *Domesday Book*, compiled in 1086–1087, still lists much of that region as wasteland. No such destruction had fallen on England since the Danes had pillaged it in the ninth century. The hope of renewed Danish support prolonged scattered uprisings during 1070 and into the summer of 1071 when finally the records tell us of a brief interlude of peace. William's work was not completed though until the Scottish kings were convinced that they should not offer asylum and support to Anglo-Saxon rebels of the north country. A brief march into Scotland in 1072 achieved this purpose; King Malcolm did homage to William and promised henceforth to offer no refuge to his enemies. Soon Edgar the Etheling was on his way to Flanders.

Until 1075 there was relative calm in England and then William was faced with the last serious revolt of Anglo-Saxon lords, this time supported by some French nobles plus a Danish fleet commanded by Canute, brother of the king of Denmark. The back of the revolt was crushed before the fleet arrived and it returned without seeing action. The Anglo-Saxon and

French lords who had led the revolt lost their lands and were executed, imprisoned, or exiled. Some of the earldoms were discontinued; others were put into the possession of Normans whom William completely trusted. Except for another short rebellion in Northumbria in 1080 and a brief expedition into Wales in 1081 to impress the Norman power upon the Welsh king and lords, William was annoyed by no further military efforts until 1085. To be sure, the northern frontier was not stable but his successors would have to wrestle with that problem. To the west a group of earldoms kept the Welsh in check, and in the rest of England the will to resist had been broken. The last serious threat to William was a coalition formed of the Danes, Norwegians, and Flemish in 1085. Canute, who had succeeded to the Danish kingdom, again laid claim to the English throne and collected an imposing fleet. William reinforced the east coast with continental mercenaries but civil war in Denmark delayed the sailing of the fleet and ended in Canute's death in 1086.

The year 1086 marks the climax of William's reign. Completely the master of England he now displayed his strength by two symbolic acts. *The Anglo-Saxon Chronicle* relates that he held his great court at Gloucester for five days to celebrate Christmas in 1085 and that he "had much thought and very deep discussion with his council about this country—how it was occupied or with what sort of people." Such "deep discussion" resulted the following year in the famous inquest that produced *Domesday Book*. Primarily a record that would give him an accurate account of the incomes due him yearly, *Domesday Book* also supplied him a wealth of detail about the condition of the land and the people who held and worked it. Its minuteness is all the proof we need for the amazingly efficient government William had constructed; no other country of western Europe had the machinery for making such a comprehensive survey. So exacting was the inquest that the *Chronicle* sourly complains "there was no single hide nor a yard of land, nor indeed (it is a shame to relate but it seemed no shame to him to do) one ox nor one cow nor one pig was there left out, and not put down in his record." In August of the same year William held another great council at Salisbury where he received from his tenants-in-chief and their most important tenants an oath of fealty. This procedure was remarkable not in demanding fealty from the royal tenants but in demanding it from undertenants. William recognized that undertenants owed fealty to their lords but nevertheless felt himself so strong that he could demand another oath of fealty to himself which entailed a higher loyalty than that owed to their lords (William's tenants-in-chief). William had become more than a strong feudal king; he had become a national ruler to whom all free subjects owed their supreme loyalty.

William's last months were spent in his duchy. It seems but natural that a ruler who had cut his teeth on Norman revolt should die amidst a Norman border skirmish. Our preoccupation with William's efforts to consolidate his conquest should not lead us to think that he looked upon Normandy as a subsidiary possession or that he neglected it; no king could, until John lost Normandy early in the thirteenth century. William devoted much time to his duchy, which was more vulnerable to attack from its warlike neighbors. Throughout much of his reign William had to fight the counts of Anjou to retain possession of the county of Maine, lying between the two feudal principalities. William's eldest son Robert Curthose was able to hold Maine only because it was agreed that he would do homage for it to the Angevin counts. A more serious danger to Norman security was the French king, who supported all enemies of William located about the perimeter of the duchy. To wrest English control from French land was to be the goal of the Capetians and Valois for the next four hundred years. Barons of Normandy, Maine, and Brittany, as well as the weak-willed Robert, who was in nominal control of Normandy and Maine, were baited by the French kings; they were periodically in revolt against William, who expended considerable time in quelling the risings. Down to his death William was not sure of Robert's faithfulness; no wonder William spent time in Normandy each year.

Trouble in the Vexin, a buffer area between Normandy and the French royal domain, called William to the Continent in 1087. William controlled the northern half of the Vexin but the French kings dominated the southern half and used this outpost to harry the Norman dukes. From the town of Mantes a French force invaded the Norman Évreux for this purpose and William retaliated by taking and burning Mantes. While conducting this operation William sustained an injury that apparently aggravated an internal disorder. Desperately ill he was taken to the peaceful abbey of Saint Gervais in the suburbs of Rouen and there on September 9 died. Before dying, however, he made provision for his three sons. Despite his faithlessness Robert as eldest son received the duchy of Normandy. It has been argued that William planned to have Robert succeed him as king of England to preserve unity of rule over Normandy and England, but this did not occur and William Rufus, his second son, received England, which could be freely disposed of because it had been acquired by conquest. The third son, Henry, received only a large grant of money and treasure, £5000 of silver. It is a testimony to William's efficient rule that the decidedly anti-Norman *Anglo-Saxon Chronicle* amidst the criticism it heaps upon him still admits his accomplishments. Perhaps he "poor men had oppressed . . . loved greediness above all . . . and loved the stags so much as if he were their father" but he was a "very wise man and very powerful and more worshipful and stronger than any predecessor of his had been." He was, moreover, dignified and "the good security he made in his country is not to be forgotten—so that any honest man could travel over his kingdom without injury with his bosom full of gold."

2. WILLIAM RUFUS (1087–1100)

In William Rufus England received a king with all the bad qualities of his family and none of the good, except for his prowess as a fighter and a hunter. He was greedy, hateful, and revengeful, inconstant in purpose, unfaithful to all, impious and a despoiler of the church, and highly irregular in his private life. This big but short and reddish man well deserves the nickname Rufus. If he gave England a stern but orderly government, it was only the better to tax her. Unloved by all except his unscrupulous minister Ranulf Flambard, he was mourned by none when luckily an arrow found him while hunting in the New Forest outside Winchester on 2 August 1100. His whole reign is characterized by the extortion of money from persons, private or corporate; most of it was lavished upon bribes and mercenaries used to win the duchy of Normandy from Robert. The folly of William the Conqueror in dividing his possessions led to thirteen years of war between the two brothers and has moved one historian to call the reign of William Rufus the Conquest of Normandy.

Only two revolts in England distracted William's attention from Normandy. In 1088 a group of Norman barons under the leadership of William's uncle, Odo of Bayeux, who had been freed by the Conqueror on his deathbed, revolted; their object, it seemed, was to put Robert on the English throne. The uprising was quickly suppressed by William, who received the wholehearted support of the church and the English people. To secure their help William promised all sorts of reforms—just government, good laws, a reduction of taxation, and the end of burdensome restrictions on hunting. This was the one time he was popular; his promises all unkept, he lapsed immediately back into his normal behavior. When Archbishop Lanfranc died in 1089 the last good and reasonable restraint was removed and for the next eleven years William was a law unto himself. Mild treatment of the rebellious barons of 1088 failed to convince them that revolt against William did not pay. Infuriated by the despotic government of William, another group of Norman barons revolted in 1095; again revolt failed. This time a mixture of heavy fines, confiscation of lands, exile, beating, blinding, castration, and hanging was the penalty; William was never troubled with another revolt.

The possession of Normandy depended upon personalities and Norman politics. Clearly the warlike William with his superior resources could prevail over the ineffective Robert, who succeeded at nothing except the First Crusade. He was a likable figure, to be sure, but could so little carry out any line of action that he was never in control of any situation. Under his rule Normandy fell victim to feudal anarchy at its worst; ducal authority became nonexistent and it was each baron for himself. Such a situation was obviously relished by the Norman barons, who profited from weak rule, as well as by the French king, who could expand the royal domain at the expense of a disunited duchy. Rather than forfeit such propitious conditions both Normans and French king frequently threw their support behind Robert; neither could see any benefit in the unification of England and Normandy. The only dependable weapon in William's hands was the money he lavished in bribes upon the Norman barons; not even desire for a weak duke could submerge their pecuniary greed. William wasted little time in starting trouble for Robert. A series of minor military ventures and expeditious bribes forced Robert to cede to William lands around Eu, Aumâle, and Fécamp to the northeast of the Seine, and around Conches to the west. From 1091 to the end of 1093 the brothers were at peace; William even cooperated for a short time to help return order to Normandy but soon left Robert in the lurch. In 1094 fighting was resumed, continuing inconclusively into 1095. In 1096 Robert practically presented Normandy to his royal brother. Anxious to go on the First Crusade but penniless, he arranged to pawn his duchy to William for three years in return for a sum of 10,000m. of silver. We may rest assured that William's forceful government in Normandy netted him a fat profit long before Robert's return from the Crusade in 1100. So well had William fared on this transaction that he was not inclined to return the pawn; only his untimely death enabled Robert once more to become duke of Normandy.

Towards sunset on 2 August 1100 William was engrossed in pursuing a deer he had wounded while hunting in the New Forest near Winchester. A hunting companion, Walter Tirel, lagging behind, saw at the same moment a stag not far from William and took aim. According to William of Malmesbury "thus it was that unknowing, and without power to prevent it (oh, gracious God!), he pierced the king's breast with a fatal arrow." An accident, possibly, but more likely a deliberate act. Walter was a member of the Clare family, which, along with William's brother Henry, was included in the royal hunting party. Far from demonstrating any grief over the dead king everyone scrambled away immediately, Walter to safety in Normandy and Henry to the royal treasure at Winchester. That a plot had been premeditated by Henry with the Clare family is supported by the preferential treatment he, as king, accorded to its members. No one was punished for William's death.

3. HENRY I (1100–1135)

The reign of Henry I was dominated by two objectives—the conquest and pacification of Normandy and the provision for peaceful succession to his Anglo-Norman realm. Immediately upon the death of his brother, Henry demonstrated the boundless energy that characterized his long rule. Though William was killed towards sunset, Henry seized the royal treasure that same day. The next day, 3 August, he had himself elected king by a small group of barons. On 5 August he was crowned at Westminster Abbey. The parallels in the characters of William and Henry are striking; only Henry's diplomatic moderation and higher sense of decency saved him from the cruder violence of William. With no time to be lost in consolidating his position over Robert in England, Henry issued a coronation charter promising an end to the injustices of William and a future government in accordance with the principles of justice and the established laws of England. Amicable relations were also inaugurated with the church. Henry never intended to fulfil all the charter promises and he never did; the charter only represented a bid for support. But his reign was such an improvement over the preceding one that his subjects were content to let matters well enough alone. Like William, Henry first had to suppress a baronial revolt staged in 1101 in support of Robert. Henry easily succeeded and won Robert's recognition of his regal title in return for an annuity of 3000 marks yearly. Henry quickly disposed of the revolting baronage, confiscating their lands and driving them into exile. Most conspicuous among those who so suffered was Robert of Bellême, earl of Shrewsbury. Henry captured his castles, confiscated the earldom, and drove him to Normandy. Henry was the uncontested master of England.

As with William, the shiftless rule of Robert in Normandy and its attendant anarchy played into Henry's hands. From the outset of his reign it is clear that he meant to take advantage of these conditions and acquire Normandy. Shrewdly bribing the Norman barons and concluding alliances with the counts of Flanders, Anjou, Maine, and Brittany and with other lords located around the Norman borders, Henry launched his campaign in 1104. That year he secured the county of Évreux. In 1105 he occupied Caen and Bayeux. Then on 26 September 1106 Henry met Robert outside the castle of Tinchebrai and administered a crushing defeat. Robert was captured and languished the remaining twenty-eight years of his life in captivity. He died at the age of eighty in Cardiff Castle. Henry was now duke of Normandy. In less than a year he had so restored orderly government to the duchy that he could leave it under the control of deputies while he returned to England.

However strong Henry's rule was in Normandy, continental politics forced him to spend more than half of his reign in the duchy. The union of one of the strongest feudal states on the Continent with England was not to the liking of such princes as the counts of Flanders and Anjou and King Louis VI of France, who was bent upon establishing order in the royal domain and expanding its borders. To his death Henry had to parry, militarily or diplomatically, the attempts of these rulers to weaken his hold on Normandy. Until 1128 Henry's enemies could stir up trouble by supporting as duke Robert's son William Clito. This unfortunate boy spent most of his life attempting to win his father's inheritance or the lordship of some feudal principality. While fighting in Flanders in 1128 to establish himself as count there, he was mortally wounded. But against William Clito, counts, French king, and discontented Norman barons, Henry was more than a match. He skillfully played one off against the other and when necessary conducted a campaign to throw them off balance. Although too much of his time was wasted on such matters, Henry never lost his grip on Normandy.

Of more concern than Normandy to Henry was the task of providing for a successor. He had children in abundance, twenty-two to be precise. But only two of them were legitimate. Until 1120 all Henry's hopes were centered on his son William. Then one stormy night in November while William and other distinguished members of the royal household were crossing the Channel from Normandy to England, their ship, the White Ship, hit a rock and sank. Only a Rouen butcher survived to tell the tale of horror. Ironically the accident probably would have been avoided if both passengers and crew had not been in a drunken stupor. This disaster suddenly deprived Henry of a male heir and led eventually to a war of succession and twenty years of anarchy. Henry's only other legitimate offspring was his daughter Matilda whom he had married off in 1109 to the emperor Henry V of Germany. Until Henry V's death in 1125, however, Henry was unable to present Matilda as his successor because England might fall into Henry V's hands. In 1126 Matilda returned to England and in 1127 Henry forced his barons to recognize her as the next lawful sovereign. The following year he married her off again, this time to Geoffrey, son of Count Fulk of Anjou. By this marriage Henry detached Anjou from the French alliance and provided Matilda a husband who could champion her cause if need be. The two were completely incompatible and seldom lived together. They did manage, however, to produce Henry Plantagenet, future heir of England, thereby laying the basis for the Angevin Empire in the second half of the twelfth century. In 1133 Henry left England to see his grandson; he was destined never to return. Forced to suppress a Norman rebellion, fomented this time by his son-in-law, Henry died amidst the exertions of war in December 1135. The chroniclers tell us that he ate too heavily of lampreys; severe indigestion seized him, followed by a fever that killed him. The last of the great Norman kings left behind him a collection of rich possessions on the Continent plus the kingdom of England. Order had been restored to Normandy. In England Henry had gone a long way towards giving her the strong centralized government that was to be the wonder of western Europe later in the century. Fate would have it that this industrious monarch should leave this heritage to a woman incapable of ruling it and deprived of baronial support. Soon thirty-five years of peace in England were to be replaced by almost two decades of war.

4. STEPHEN, MATILDA, AND THE ANARCHY (1135–1154)

The English baronage may have been forced to acknowledge Matilda as Henry's successor but few abided by their oath upon his death. They looked with distaste upon the rule of a woman, especially a woman who alienated them with her haughty, unsympathetic, and foreign behavior. Her marriage to the Angevin count Geoffrey was no asset. Most barons threw their support behind the man that beat other contenders in securing the crown. This man was Stephen, count of Boulogne and Mortain, and lord of English estates in Lancaster and Eye. His heritable claim was extremely tenuous; he was the son of Adela, William the Conqueror's daughter. It is only the quickness of action and energy in the first few months that explains Stephen's success in surprising the Angevin party and uniting England behind him. A coronation charter confirmed all the good and lawful usages of England and it was elaborated upon in a charter of liberties granted in 1136. Stephen could count on the support of the church because his brother Henry was bishop of Winchester and a leading prelate. Even the adherence of Robert, earl of Gloucester and Matilda's half brother, was initially secured. If Stephen had shown any of the purpose and industry of the hardheaded Norman kings he could have ruled England in peace. But he was their opposite in personal qualities. He was an excellent knight and brave fighter whose chivalrous conduct repeatedly lost him battles and political advantage. Naïve and generous, he was repeatedly the victim of his natural good nature. He hated to make decisions and therefore temporized and compromised. His frequent concessions to the church and baronage for their support weakened the royal authority and gave him the reputation of a man easily maneuvered into granting favors. In politics and government he could be counted on to do the undiplomatic thing. It is a shame that a man with basically decent impulses should be so incompetent. His incapacity was not long in manifesting itself. Though warmly supported by the Norman baronage in his attempt to take Normandy in 1137, he lost that adherence and with it the duchy because of his use of crude Flemish mercenaries. The following year under the leadership of Robert of Gloucester, Matilda opened her fight for the crown.

Matilda's bid for the crown could have been parried had not Stephen forfeited the support of the church. Anticipating trouble, many of the prelates and barons had looked to the fortification of their castles. Among these were Bishop Roger of Salisbury, justiciar of England; his son Roger the Poor, chancellor; his nephew Bishop Nigel of Ely, treasurer; and another nephew, Bishop Alexander of England. Though their position and wealth had been won under Henry I, they had remained loyal to Stephen, giving him a strong central administration and close ties with the church. Suspicious of their intent in fortifying their castles, Stephen took advantage of a minor difference with Bishop Roger to seize and confiscate the lands and offices of the four men. There is no evidence that Stephen was justified in this action, which immediately lost him church support in his struggle against Matilda. The fighting that followed intermittently down to 1153 was characterized by few pitched battles. Skirmishes, sieges, and baronial plundering comprised the bulk of the fighting. Both sides had to resort to mercenaries. Stephen relied in particular on the Flemish mercenaries of William of Ypres. The barons played both sides off against each other and accrued rich possessions and a plurality of offices. Loyal only to their own self-aggrandizement, they built adulterine castles (unlicensed), usurped royal authority, and bled the countryside white. John Horace Round, the great Norman authority, has familiarized all students of the period with the most unsavory of such characters, Geoffrey de Mandeville, sheriff of three shires and constable of the Tower of London. But this feudal anarchy should not lead us to conclude that law and order had completely disintegrated. That Stephen somehow received royal revenue supports our believing that royal financial machinery functioned. Evidence shows royal justices presiding over trials in various shires. Trade and industry, though hindered, continued almost as under Henry I. We may suspect that contemporaries exaggerated the feudal anarchy because it was so foreign to England. When we reflect that this anarchy was but routine in the French royal domain under Louis VI, not to mention the other French states, we are inclined to discount some of the evidence.

Ignoring most of the details of the struggle, we need only mention key events that constituted turning-points for Stephen and Matilda. Near Lincoln in 1140 Stephen chivalrously threw away the advantage of deployment on high terrain to descend pell-mell to a plain to meet Matilda's forces. The result was Stephen's defeat and capture. Had Matilda skillfully used this opportunity, she could have ruled England thereafter in fact as well as in name. But she alienated many barons by her autocratic behavior and while in London forfeited the support of the suspicious citizens by equally haughty behavior and the levy of a heavy tax. These independent burgesses soon rose up, expelled Matilda, and received Stephen's wife along with William of Ypres and his mercenaries. Matilda fled to Winchester. Swiftly Stephen's forces proceeded there where they routed her army; she barely escaped the capture which befell her brother Robert. By late 1141 Robert was released in return for Stephen, who now renewed the fight with more popular support than he had before Matilda's disastrous rule. In 1142 only a midnight escape of Matilda over ice and snow from Oxford Castle enabled her to slip out of Stephen's hands. By 1145 Stephen controlled most of England. Robert of Gloucester, the principal royalist leader, died in 1147 and the Angevin cause reached its lowest ebb. Down to 1153 Stephen ruled an almost tranquil kingdom. It was Henry Plantagenet who caused the renewal of fighting.

Between 1141 and 1145 Henry's father Count Geoffrey of Anjou had championed Matilda's cause in Normandy and had successfully subdued this region. Until 1150 when Henry became of age Geoffrey ruled Normandy and then handed it over to his son. From this powerful springboard, Henry was at last in a position to challenge Stephen. But before he did so, death and luck added two other rich possessions to his duchy. In 1151 his father died from a fever contracted after a foolish swim in an icy pool; Henry succeeded him as count of Anjou. In 1152 he married Eleanor of Aquitaine, who had just been freed from her marriage to Louis VII of France. The royal couple had been completely unsuited to each other; the warm-blooded woman from the Midi found Louis VII too monkish, and he found her flirtations unbearable. When Eleanor produced no male heir, Louis prevailed upon the pope to nullify the marriage upon the grounds that they were so related as to break church law. Immediately the young Henry snatched up Eleanor and thereby added to his holdings the duchy of Aquitaine. The unimaginative Louis VII had lost lands more than double the area of the royal domain and Henry had almost completed the formation of the Angevin Empire; he lacked only England. In 1153 he invaded England and skirmished inconclusively with Stephen for about ten months. Meanwhile Matilda had died and Stephen lost his son Eustace whom he had looked to as his successor. The death of Eustace removed the chief incentive of Stephen to continue the struggle. Tired and discouraged, he permitted the church to arrange a truce and a meeting for the conclusion of peace. In November 1153 the Treaty of Winchester was concluded. According to its provisions Stephen was permitted to rule England but recognized that upon his death Henry would succeed him. In less than a year, on 25 October 1154, Stephen died and Henry came from Normandy to acquire his kingdom. Twenty gloomy years of history had concluded the Norman period; they were to be followed by one of the most creative periods in English government during the Middle Ages.

IX

The Feudalization of England

THE Norman Conquest of England amounted to a revolution in English society. Anglo-Saxon institutions and law, though remarkably strong after 1066 and preserved by the Conqueror and his successors, nevertheless underwent striking transformation between 1066 and 1087. In effect the period to 1135 revolves around the remodeling of Anglo-Saxon institutions by the Norman kings to meet their concept of strong and efficient government. To attain this end they worked through the medium of the only political system they knew—feudalism. Before we can hope to understand, therefore, how English institutions were molded by Norman feudalism we must acquaint ourselves with Norman feudal government on the Continent.

A succession of outstandingly strong Carolingians in the eighth century ending with Charlemagne in 814 had erected a vast Frankish Empire too large to be maintained by the agrarian economy upon which it depended; even if relatively peaceful conditions had continued, internal weakness would have caused the collapse of the Empire. But in the last years of Charlemagne's life, attack from without had begun; the ninth and tenth centuries were to witness constant fighting by the Carolingians against Viking, Saracen, and Magyar. Within the borders the successors of Louis the Pious were so preoccupied with civil war that they seldom came to the aid of their regional subordinates, the counts and dukes, who were saddled with the defense against the fierce fighters from without. Partition succeeded partition in the Empire until central authority had evaporated. With each partition, be it in Germany with its duchies or France with its numerous counties, the Carolingians lost all contact and effective control over the officers, who usurped the Carolingian powers and forged miniature states of their own. Thus were formed such German duchies as Saxony, Franconia, Bavaria, and Lotharingia, and such French duchies and counties as Toulouse, Aquitaine, Anjou, Flanders, and Champagne. The sole protectors of the local populace, the rulers of these states were regarded henceforth as the real rulers. The governments they built were small replicas of the Carolingian which Charlemagne and his predecessors had erected upon military and political principles that we call feudal.

In Germany and most of France the dukes and counts of these local areas were so successful in their defense that hardly any territory was lost to the foreign invaders. Only in northern France in that area between Flanders, Brittany, the Channel, and the Île de France (French royal domain) did the Vikings or Northmen (thus Normans) secure a beachhead. Failing in their attempt to establish themselves in Burgundy or around Paris, a large group of Normans settled under their leader Rollo in the territory that was to be called Normandy and made their headquarters at Rouen. From here they could not be dislodged. Finally in 911 the Carolingian ruler of France, Charles the Simple, recognized the *fait accompli* and concluded peace with Rollo at Saint-Clair-sur-Epte. Charles recognized Norman possession of the lands between the Somme and Brittany and in return Rollo became the vassal of Charles. Actually Charles had secured a powerful ally and gave nothing away that he had not already lost. The Normans, still heathens and barbarians, soon exhibited their gift of adapting themselves to foreign cultures. Within a short time they became Christians, intermarried with the natives, accepted Frankish culture and institutions, and adopted the French language. A hundred years later they had lost practically all identity.

It is pointless to continue any political account of the Normans. It suffices to note that the 150-odd years between 911 and 1066 resembled the history of the other French feudal states. The dukes tried constantly to widen their borders at the expense of such neighbors as Flanders, Blois, Maine, and Anjou. A strong duke's rule was accompanied by internal order and relatively efficient functioning of government. A weak duke or disputed succession led to the military and political anarchy typical of western Europe in the tenth and eleventh centuries. It was only luck and the support of his lord, the Capetian king, that enabled William, the bastard son of Duke Robert the Devil, to defeat the feudal faction of nobles who supported his cousin. After many strenuous campaigns William literally destroyed his enemies, beheading them, razing their castles, and confiscating their lands. By 1066 he had so restored order that he could boast of being ruler of the most efficiently run feudal state of western Europe; only the counts of Flanders could challenge his achievement.

It is with the Norman use of Frankish institutions that we are most concerned. For the Carolingian mayors of the palace and rulers such as Charles Martel, Pepin, and Charlemagne, the problem of providing for the services of government was acute. Their kingdom, almost landlocked and completely dependent upon the resources of land, forced them to devise some method of obtaining service from land rather than from money. Their solution was the development of the feudal system. In the first place they made use of a custom long ingrained in the Germanic peoples. As we have seen, the Germans knew of a highly personalized and honorable relation between noble men, that is, lord and man. For protection, military glory and adventure, and booty, the German aristocrats customarily became the companions or men of distinguished war leaders and owed to them their ultimate loyalty and service. Until the eighth century the vassals, as these military retainers came to be styled, apparently received no land that entailed the performance of specific service. And yet we know that the Carolingians filled up the military and administrative positions with royal vassals and rapidly expanded the system until all men of consequence were their vassals. Then in the eighth century, beginning probably with Charles Martel, the Carolingians began to grant their vassals estates of land in return for a specialized type of military service—heavily armed warriors (knights) mounted on large warchargers (the *destrier*). Because their maintenance was far costlier than that of simple footsoldiers, knights were provided with large estates of land. Originally termed benefices (*beneficia*), these lands were later called fiefs (*feoda*).

In the eighth century, then, vassalage was united with fief-holding and a real feudalism had developed. Of the two elements, vassalage was the more essential; before a man could receive a fief he had to be a nobleman in the vassalage of a lord. Erected primarily to provide knight service, feudalism was soon put to other uses. Over their administrative or political subdivisions of the kingdom–the marches and the counties–the Carolingians had placed lieutenants with administrative, judicial, financial, and military powers. To pay them the Carolingians awarded large fiefs. So it was that feudalism came to provide the ruler with the essential military and political services. Soon all levels of government were permeated by feudalism and the royal vassals in turn granted out fiefs to their vassals. The Carolingian Empire had become a feudal structure; after its disintegration it was the model for the states founded by the dukes and counts. Meanwhile the principles of feudal tenure were perfected and when the Normans settled in France they could observe a highly developed military and political system at work in neighboring Flanders and Anjou. The Normans appropriated this system and worked it into the most efficient government of western Europe. Norman feudalism was fundamentally like the feudal system of other states but by 1066 it had developed some peculiar traits.

All men of the aristocratic class who obtained fiefs from the Norman dukes first had to become their men or vassals. To do this the future vassal had to perform homage (*homagium*) and swear fealty (*fidelitas*) to the lord. Although a vassal did not necessarily have to receive a fief, remaining at times simply a household knight completely maintained by his lord, most vassals generally obtained estates of land with all the appurtenances and rights attached thereto. These included economic dependents to work the land, buildings, implements, and various financial and judicial perquisites such as the right to hold a seignorial court and enjoy the profits of justice. In addition, some fiefs brought with them the exercise of public authority. The fief (*feodum*) provided the income necessary to support the vassal and his family and to enable him to render the services required by the lord.

The vassal was invested with the fief by the lord who handed over possession, marking such transfer by the giving of some symbolic object such as a piece of turf, stick, or knife. It is important to note here that the vassal did not receive ownership of the land; he received only possession regulated by a variety of conditions. He enjoyed possession only so long as he fulfilled his feudal obligations. One must distinguish fiefs from those scattered pieces of land owned by men who owed no service for it; such land was called allodial. For some time fiefs were not considered heritable and were thought of as reverting to the lord upon the death of a vassal. Only after the vassal's heir had done homage to the lord could he receive investiture of the fief. Later, however, all fiefs came to be governed by heritable tenure. Though absent from Roman and Germanic law, the principle of primogeniture, which demanded that the fief must pass intact to the eldest son, came to dominate feudal inheritance. This rule, essential for the efficient functioning of feudalism, mitigated against struggle for succession and made one man responsible for the service owed by the fief. When public powers and an office went along with the fief, it meant that one man would control them. Later women were permitted to do homage and to receive investiture of fiefs, but that was after feudal law had become more refined and the essential military character of feudalism blunted. The Normans were never sympathetic towards the custom of parage that prevailed in some parts of Europe; by this custom the fief could be divided equally among younger children as co-heirs and one of them would do homage and assume responsibility for the obligations of the fief. Deprived of any chance to attain land in Normandy, younger noble sons had to look elsewhere for opportunities. This situation helps to explain the adventures of the Hauteville family in southern Italy and Sicily, as well as the enthusiasm of the Normans who followed William the Conqueror to England.

We have talked of homage, vassalage, and fiefs. Now we must inquire into the obligations and relations entailed. Both lord and man accepted mutual obligations. Should the lord fail to protect his vassal, attack him, plot against his life, attempt to reduce him to servitude, or commit adultery with his wife, this was cause for desertion of the lord. In turn the vassal had to conduct himself suitably towards the lord and render the services called for by his fief. Either, failing to fulfil his responsibilities, was guilty of perfidy and the feudal contract was broken. Throughout western Europe the vernacular literature praised these noble relations governing lord and man. But let us proceed to the specific obligations of the vassal. His essential duty was the performance of knight service. The amount of knight service varied from fief to fief but each vassal was generally required to serve personally and to supply a certain number of other knights. Smaller fiefs usually carried lighter obligations than larger ones but, with the Normans, the assessment of knight service was an arbitrary matter depending upon bargains struck between lord and man. The Normans customarily owed five knights or multiples of five to the dukes. A popular number owed was ten knights, which formed a constabulary. That the number of knights supplied had no relation to the amount or value of land held, and that knight service was introduced by William the Conqueror to England, has been ably demonstrated by John Horace Round and Charles Homer Haskins. How the vassals provided their quota of knights did not concern the dukes. At first the vassals maintained most of them in their establishments and completely provided for them. These were the household knights. Such an arrangement, however, proved cumbersome and awkward for the vassal, and the household knight constantly aspired to hold land so that his social status would be improved. Eventually the vassals resorted to enfeoffing land to knights who were their vassals and who were obliged to perform a stipulated amount of knight service. They, in turn, if they so desired, could enfeoff some of their land for military service. The vassals had to serve in the field at their own cost for forty days per year. If circumstances required a longer campaign, vassals extended their service only if they so desired and received extra compensation from their lord.

There were other than military obligations owed by vassals for their fiefs. According to feudal custom of northern France, lords collected pecuniary contributions upon three well-defined occasions. These contributions, called aids, could be demanded when the lord's eldest son was knighted, upon the marriage of his eldest daughter, and when the lord was captured and had to be ransomed. Gradually custom dictated the amounts that could be demanded. In addition to the aids, the vassals were expected to extend hospitality to the lord and his household. This meant feeding and lodging the lordly establishment for one night a year; later this service was commuted into a money payment. Whenever summoned, the vassal had to perform suit to court. Sometimes he might merely help his lord celebrate a festive occasion such as Christmas, a marriage, or a knighting. At other times he would be asked to give advice and consent upon matters affecting the lord such as war, peace, and alliances. Possibly he might be asked to consent to an assessment not provided for by feudal custom. The vassal could attend court in a judicial capacity where he and his fellow vassals would settle disputes among themselves or between themselves and the lord. It was here that every vassal received judgment by his peers; the feudal law declared by the court settled the case. This was feudal justice and should not be confused with seignorial justice. The latter was a right of almost any vassal and involved holding a manorial court for the peasants on the land. The custom was local and differed from region to region. Originally granted to vassals by the kings and great princes, seignorial justice came to be accepted as a matter of course.

Another set of relations between lord and vassal was determined by a group of customs called the feudal incidents. When a vassal died his fief did not descend to the eldest son merely upon the performance of homage. The son had to pay a sort of inheritance tax, styled relief. Often this relief was assessed arbitrarily but pressure brought to bear on the lord led to the assessment's being limited in amount and based on the rank of the vassal and the value of his fief. Should a vassal die leaving no suitable heirs, the fief escheated, that is, reverted to the lord, who could dispose of it as he wished. Because he frequently regranted the fief to the highest bidder, this feudal incident was greatly valued. When a vassal died leaving a young son, the lord acted as the guardian of this minor until he was old enough to become a knight and fulfil his feudal obligations. The incident of wardship permitted the lord to enjoy the revenues from the fief until the heir took over. The incident of marriage pertained to those occasions when a vassal had only a female heir. During the vassal's life or after his death, the lord's permission had to be obtained for marriage. When the vassal died, the lord became guardian and married the heiress off to the most suitable man with the highest bid. Not able to fulfil the knightly duties required by a fief, a woman could not become a vassal and hold a fief during the early Middle Ages; her husband did homage and received investiture of the fief. Later such stringent rules became more flexible and women came to do homage and hold fiefs. The last of the incidents was forfeiture. When a vassal failed in his feudal obligations, the lord confiscated his fief. Perhaps the vassal might meekly accept this action but, if there was any possibility of successful resistance, he would counter the forfeiture with a formal act of defiance, arguing that the lord had failed in his obligations. In any event the vassal was known as a feudal felon and only success in war could reverse his status. Less serious differences between lord and vassal could be settled by the time-honored technique of trial by combat.

So far we have limited our examination of Norman feudal tenure to those fiefs requiring knight service. There were, however, other feudal tenures known to the Normans which called for varying services less than knight service. In this category were fiefs granted for the service of castle-guard. Rather than providing service in the field these fiefs supplied a stipulated number of knights to defend the lord's castle for a specified time. A grouping of fiefs around a castle to provide guard for the whole year was called a *castellaria*. Then, too, there were fiefs held under the tenure of serjeanty that required minor and varied services. Such fiefs might oblige the holder to provide auxiliary fighters, or horses, or arms, or to fulfil administrative functions. Lastly we come to the tenure of free alms or *frankalmoin*. Many ecclesiastical establishments were granted fiefs in return for spiritual services such as praying for the health of the donor's soul. It should be understood, however, that they also could, and did, hold fiefs requiring knight service or castle-guard; until the investiture struggle abbots and bishops did homage, received investiture of fiefs, and fulfilled in person their military duties. When the Hildebrandine reform movement forced such ecclesiastics to retire from the business of fighting, a compromise was reached. The prelate could still do homage and be invested with the fief but he had to provide the military service through subinfeudation of land to knights. All other obligations were rendered except that, quite obviously, the incidents of relief, marriage, and wardship were not applicable. The lord, however, recouped his loss of these financial perquisites by administering church fiefs and enjoying their revenues in the interval between the death of a prelate and the installation of his successor. No lord was ever overzealous in finding or approving of a successor; in this connection the actions of William Rufus and John are infamous.

Although in the eleventh century the custom of liege homage was not deeply rooted, it certainly was by the twelfth century. For some time it had been possible for a vassal to hold a number of fiefs, each from a different lord. If all was peaceful, this was a good arrangement; but what did the vassal do if his lords fought among themselves? When a vassal had held only one fief, naturally his paramount loyalty was to his lord; the multiple holding of fiefs, however, complicated this rule. The problem was resolved by grading the homage. A vassal customarily did liege homage to the most powerful of the lords, to the lord who had granted him the richest fief, or to the lord from whom he had held land longest. To this liege lord the vassal owed his first loyalty. To the other lords he owed but simple homage and served them only if such service did not conflict with his obligations to the liege lord. Later even liege homage came to be graded, but that need not concern us here.

We have so far concentrated solely on describing the Norman form of feudalism. Before proceeding it should be emphasized that feudalism was not the destructive political force it so often is labeled. Actually the only system that could provide essential political and military services when Europe was gripped by an agrarian economy, it proved exceedingly useful and constructive when limited to an area small enough for the prince to maintain the highly personalized relations inherent in feudalism. The Carolingian Empire was too vast for any political or military system to be successful but in such small states as Normandy, Flanders, and Anjou feudalism proved an effective political device for forging highly efficient government and maintaining a strong centralized rule. But precisely how did the feudal prince adapt feudalism to the business of governing?

To examine Norman feudal institutions in the eleventh century is to understand better how much the Norman dukes had modeled their government upon those of such neighboring states as Flanders and Anjou. Because Normandy was a conquered territory the dukes could even improve upon the models by choosing what was best and then standardizing the institutions more than was possible for other rulers. As in Flanders, it is the tight control William the Conqueror and some of his predecessors maintained over the government and their vassals that explains their strong and efficient government. Like all great feudal lords, the dukes granted along with many of their fiefs the exercise of some public justice. Such justice should not be confused with the seignorial justice wielded over the peasants or with the feudal justice that concerned only members of the feudal aristocracy. Nor should it be confused with the customs of the duchy (*consuetudines comitatus*), granted by the dukes, which included the right to collect certain tolls, exercise varied market privileges, and exploit nonjudicial sources of income. We learn of public justice from a document of the late eleventh century which tells us that the dukes customarily enjoyed a monopoly over the following category of crimes: assault to and from the ducal court, crimes committed while on military service and just before and after it, violations against pilgrims and the ducal coinage. On the other hand, the duke shared with his barons jurisdiction over the following offenses: housebreaking, arson, rape, and seizure of sureties. The penalty for these crimes was death or mutilation. In granting out public justice, called pleas of the sword, the dukes were sparing; over all the recipients they kept a vigilant surveillance to guard against usurpation of more rights or malhandling of the ones received.

A far different matter was ecclesiastical justice, which should be thoroughly understood because it underlay the Conqueror's extensive reform of the English secular and spiritual courts. The bishop's court had jurisdiction over the enforcement of the truce of God and over offenses perpetrated in churches and churchyards and on the way to and from church. Fines came to the bishop from criminous and delinquent clerks, members of clerks' households, and men living in the bishop's enclosure. From nonecclesiastics the bishop collected fines for adultery, incest, desertion, divination, attacks on priests and monks, and the burning of church buildings. Fines also came from the ordeal and from anyone excommunicated for not submitting to justice. The ecclesiastics holding fiefs from secular lords, however, were subject to their feudal courts. Ecclesiastical justice and rights to the profits of justice varied from region to region but ultimately all stemmed from the dukes and their right to grant them. Constantly the dukes interfered in church courts. They enforced church enactments on reform such as celibacy. The dukes controlled and presided over ecclesiastical councils, appointed and deposed bishops and abbots, gave approval for the excommunication of their vassals, and stipulated that papal legates could not be accepted unless ducal consent had been obtained. In control over bishops and abbots, the Norman dukes far surpassed other princes. The dukes were the special protectors of abbeys and thereby crowded out the *avoués*. Always the bishops were under the authority of the ducal *vicomte*. Even with the truce of God the dukes cooperated so closely that they absorbed it into their own peace. It was really ducal peace that guaranteed the Norman countryside. The dukes controlled feuds, assaults and ambushes, and jousts. No one could destroy property while reclaiming land nor could loss of land be inflicted except in the proper ducal or baronial court. All castles and fortified points had to be handed over to the dukes on demand; they could garrison them if occasion so warranted. No castles could be built without ducal license. The peace offered by the truce of God was slight in comparison to that offered by the dukes.

In the realm of ducal finances we find that by the eleventh century the revenues controlled were numerous and efficiently administered. There were rents from domains and forests; revenues from mills, salt-pans, fishing rights; monopoly over all big fish caught, over wrecks, and over treasure-trove. In the towns the dukes held much land and enjoyed profits from tolls, markets, fairs, and coinage, as well as the profits from justice already noted. It is hard to determine from the evidence available what kind of financial machinery the dukes had in the eleventh century for collecting these incomes. It would appear that administrative districts called either *vicomtés* or *prévôtés* were organized into financial units and that for each unit the *vicomtes* or *prévôts* had to account for a yearly farm; from these revenues they made fixed and special payments, being credited with these amounts in the accounting. Apparently the annual farms were rendered to the ducal *camera*, still a part of the household as it was in eleventh-century England. By comparison Norman finance was much more advanced than that of the Capetian and Angevin rulers. Only the financial system of the Flemish counts was superior.

The ducal authority was wielded locally by the *vicomtes* or *prévôts*, whose administration covered a *vicomté* or a *prévôté*. They were not just officers in charge of the ducal lands but had wide public authority devolved upon them from the dukes. Their functions and powers closely resembled those of the Anglo-Saxon sheriffs. The *vicomte* commanded the local troops, guarded ducal castles, maintained order, proclaimed ducal enactments, collected the farm, administered ducal justice, helped enforce the truce of God, attended the ducal court where he witnessed charters and helped judge disputes, carried out inquests, and enacted court sentences. There were also officials of ducal forests who protected the hunting rights of the dukes.

We come now to the ducal household. By William the Conqueror's reign there is the usual collection of officers that served the great feudal princes—a chamberlain, seneschal, butler, constable, and marshal. Besides administering to the ducal family's spiritual care the chapel staff also formed the secretariat, carrying out many of the functions of the chancery, which did not exist prior to 1066. No ducal seal was used before the Conquest. As ill defined as the Anglo-Saxon witenagemot, the duke's court, composed of bishops, counts and other great feudal lords, *vicomtes*, and the household officers, met only irregularly and was always dominated by the dukes. All sorts of business came before it including witnessing of charters, counsel on matters of war and peace, and judicial affairs. The disputes on record dealt with baronial misdemeanors, conflict of secular and spiritual jurisdiction, and differences over possession of land. To obtain evidence the *curia* used the inquest system and secured information under oath, ordeal, or battle. Its members were sent out to implement court sentences, as, for example, to partition lands. In judicial disputes the men acting most frequently as judges were those best versed in law and procedure—the bishops and the *vicomtes*.

To summarize this description of Norman government it may be said that by 1066 Normandy was completely feudalized and completely controlled by the duke, who vigilantly limited his vassals in their exercise of military and civil powers through a well-organized system of local administration. Officials on all levels did his bidding; be it through *curia ducis* or the church, the duke's will prevailed. Though neither on the local nor on the central level did Norman administration quite attain the stage of development shown by Anglo-Saxon institutions, the point is that what the Norman dukes had, they administered vigorously. This vigor was to amalgamate Norman and English institutions and transform both into more effective organs of government in the eleventh and twelfth centuries.

Such, then, was the Norman feudal government of 1066. Guided by its principles, the Norman rulers were to revamp much of what they found in the Anglo-Saxon institutions. But again the Normans were to exhibit their uncanny ability to adopt new institutions and improve upon them. Generally they preserved rather than destroyed. The most radical change was the introduction of feudalism into England, an area that had known no real feudalism prior to the Conquest; it was feudalized to a greater degree than even Normandy because the Conqueror began with a clean slate. He molded feudalism into a political and military system compatible with his conception of strong government. On both the central and the local level there was a fusion of Anglo-Saxon and Norman institutions rather than abrupt substitution. The Normans had a household with domestic and public functions; so too did the Anglo-Saxons. The Norman feudal council or *curia ducis* was not unlike the witenagemot. In England as in Normandy a chamber received the princely revenues and an accounting was made regularly. At neither place was there a chancery but the writing offices staffed by chapel clerks approximated this department. The Anglo-Saxon writ and seal were quickly adopted by the Normans. Locally, the Norman *vicomtés* administered by the *vicomtes* were similar to the shires and the sheriffs. The Normans had no hundreds but instead had officers who held the ducal castles and administered the territory spread around. In their towns the Normans had urban centers much more advanced in government and bourgeois liberties than the Anglo-Saxon boroughs. The principal differences between the seignorial systems were terminology and the lack of slaves on Norman manors. In matters of finance the Norman rulers found in the Danegeld a far more efficient tax than the arbitrary *tailles* they levied upon their feudal and nonfeudal subjects. They eagerly pounced upon this tax and added to it the feudal aids, incidents, profits of justice, and other such sources of income. Anglo-Saxon seignorial custom the new Norman lords retained, supplementing it with Norman custom. With feudal custom, they introduced a completely new body of law. The Anglo-Saxon law of the public courts was retained, modified only when necessary to serve feudal concepts of government and to bring the English church into line with the canons of the church and the recent Hildebrandine reforms. For the period between 1066 and 1154 no better expression than "Anglo-Norman" could be used to characterize the institutions of the Norman rulers.

X

Central Administration: Kingship and *Curia Regis*

I. KINGSHIP

WE HAVE seen that Anglo-Saxon kingship primarily involved an examination of the Germanic traditions, practices, and history that combined to produce a leader imbued with powers setting him above other leaders. When William conquered England, his ducal powers were firmly established; he had only to decide which of them to retain and to unite with Anglo-Saxon royal prerogatives. That he and his successors chose and blended skillfully accounts for one of the salient features of Norman England—strong monarchy. When powerful enough, the Anglo-Saxon kings would endure few limitations imposed by the witenagemot. Even more absolute were the Norman kings, who ruled as autocrats. They took all the power feudal custom gave them, and much more. Feudal theory on advice and consent of vassals there might be, but it counted for little with the first three Normans. The lip service paid to a variety of sanctions, rights, and customs that made men into kings should not beguile us into believing that these hardy rulers put much stock in them. Besides full exercise of the strong ducal feudal prerogatives and absolutist usages received by way of the Carolingians from imperial Rome, the Norman kings based their right to rule on the time-honored principles of royal blood, election, divine sanction, designation, and personal ability.

Without the blood of the ruling family in him, no man had any royal claim except through success in arms. By the eleventh century blood had to be reinforced by right of inheritance and primogeniture. Under the feudal system experience had demonstrated that the only effective method of succession was for the eldest son to succeed his father and take over intact powers and possessions. This was done whenever possible but in England circumstances dictated in such a way that primogeniture did not have an opportunity to operate until Henry II. As William the Conqueror's eldest son, Robert Curthose became duke of Normandy in 1087. England, despite the Conqueror's claim that it was his by right, actually was his by conquest; accordingly he bestowed it upon his next eldest son, William Rufus. Robert and Rufus, however, if given the chance would have set aside feudal custom and their father's will. William Rufus died without heirs and Robert Curthose's claim to England as eldest of the family was immediately swept aside by Henry I, who, being on the spot, coerced and cajoled himself to the throne. This accomplished, he held it by force and deprived Robert of Normandy in 1106. As Henry's eldest son, William was to inherit England and Normandy but his death in the disaster of the White Ship again set aside custom. With no male heirs Henry worked for the acceptance of his daughter Matilda, who was never to know real rule. Stephen's only claim was descent from the daughter of the Conqueror and the appeal of a man over a woman as ruler. Death took his son Eustace, but even if Eustace had lived, his father did not have the power to enforce primogeniture. Success in arms and civil war fatigue combined to make Matilda's son Henry king.

Lack of male heirs or practical politics forced the Norman kings to designate their successors. On the Conqueror's deathbed he named Rufus as royal successor although he did not deny the right of approval by the baronage. Before William's untimely death Henry I formally designated him as heir and at Salisbury in 1116 demanded that the great council do homage and swear fealty to William. Three times Henry designated Matilda as his successor and on each occasion secured an oath of fealty from the baronage and its promise of support. After the birth of Matilda's son Henry in 1133 Henry I designated him as heir and secured a baronial oath of fealty. Henry of Huntingdon tells us that Stephen designated Eustace as his heir but seems to have been unsuccessful in securing his recognition in 1152. The technique of designation, whether or not there was a male heir, was a useful device for identifying the successor with the royal power and for preparing acceptance by the barons.

Although we speak of election, it is more accurate to use the expression approval. Whatever the records may say, the Conqueror was not elected. He was accepted by a segment of the defeated Anglo-Saxon aristocracy that came out of London to make its peace; it came to approve what ill fortune in arms forced it to accept. In the case of William Rufus, he crossed the Channel as soon as his father's last breath had been drawn, made the royal will known to Archbishop Lanfranc, and was then crowned king at Westminster. The baronage did not formally approve him but neither did it withhold approval by supporting the claim of Robert. The barons seem to have taken their cue from the archbishop, who, despite William's notoriety, apparently reasoned that the Conqueror's will should be respected. Henry I always claimed that he had been elected and he was, if a handful of partisan barons can be qualified as the great council speaking for all the barons. This it obviously was not. Under pressure from Henry the few barons remaining at Winchester after William's death did what they were told. Three times the baronage approved Matilda as Henry's successor and during the civil war a part of it accepted and approved her as queen, but no real election occurred; Matilda never attained enough power to have herself crowned queen. Stephen secured his crown by negotiating with various English barons to whom he made important concessions. At no time in the

Norman period did election occur; if the Normans themselves or later successors and writers spoke of election, it was to camouflage acts quite to the contrary. Election of the king in medieval England was never more than a useful fiction.

Another fiction but one generally subscribed to was that a man was king by grace of God (*Dei gratia*). No ruler was considered a king until after his coronation. Before the ceremony he was a feudal prince; after it he had acquired certain regalian qualities. Once anointed, the king underwent a metamorphosis by virtue of the divine power received. No longer was he an ordinary layman; he was now the vicar of God and as such held powers superior to all other mortals. No man could be a lawful king without being crowned. All the Normans were, and they skillfully used the ceremony to demonstrate their superior status and authority. To help remind their subjects of this divinely given power the Normans symbolized it throughout the year by wearing their crown amidst regal splendor and ceremony in the presence of the great council. Thrice a year, at Easter, Whitsuntide, and Christmas, the kings presented themselves in all their regal glory and paraphernalia. Here solemn pomp and festivity were blended. After the litany *Christus vincit, Christus regnat, Christus imperat* was chanted and other ceremonial functions were performed, the king and barons made merry over food and drink. Another attribute associated with royalty and claimed by many of its members was a thaumaturgical power. The first to claim this power was Henry I. During the twelfth century his successors claimed greater such powers until, with the canonization of Edward the Confessor in 1161, they could point to descent from a saint. Not unlike modern rulers who have utilized all sorts and shades of emotions, beliefs, and superstitions to magnify their persons, the Normans well understood the value of these techniques to create in their people a sense of awe and reverence.

Through coronation a king acquired divine powers and received the cloak of legality but at the same ceremony he also admitted the vague and theoretical limitations that medieval men commonly supposed distinguished kings from tyrants. Like their Anglo-Saxon predecessors the Norman kings swore a coronation oath and thereby undertook certain obligations to their subjects in return for obedience. At his coronation the Conqueror swore the oath of his English predecessors and promised to treat the English according to the same justice as the Normans; furthermore, he enjoined that good peace would be observed in the realm. No sooner had William Rufus arrived in England than he promised Lanfranc to govern justly, equitably, and mercifully, and to defend the church and follow his good counsel. Thereupon he was crowned. Later in his reign Rufus swore again on two occasions to govern his realm well. But these promises like all his others were forgotten once their immediate purpose had been achieved. Though vague and unkept they were not without value; they found their way into a tradition and custom that assumed both rights of the governed and royal obligations.

Such custom became more explicit with the disputed successions of Henry I and Stephen when both had to bargain with the baronage and make more specific concessions for recognition. It was then that these promises were put into "charters of liberties." Whether or not they upheld these charters the kings had for the first time admitted in writing that they were under law and would govern according to it. For such formal promises the subjects swore oaths of fealty, thereby creating mutual obligations of king and subject. To gain immediate and wide support of the barons, Henry issued a coronation charter after his crowning at Westminster.[1] His chief purpose in issuing the charter was to convince the barons and church that he would reform the abuses of his brother Rufus; as such it was good propaganda. All unjust exactions and abuses against church and realm were forsworn and the good laws of the Confessor and Conqueror were restored; debts to Rufus were forgotten and peace and good coinage were to be given the realm. But what loomed largest in the charter were Henry's promises to exact only the customary feudal services and dues owed by vassal to lord. When crowned at Winchester, Stephen imitated Henry I in issuing a charter that confirmed the laws and liberties of the Confessor and Conqueror. Popular tradition has it that he soon made more specific concessions—cessation of church and forest abuses committed by Henry and abolition of the Danegeld. In April 1136 Stephen felt it necessary to bid for further support by issuing another charter. Although most of the concessions guaranteed privileges of the church, Stephen agreed to deforest lands taken over by Henry and to maintain just laws and customary judicial procedure. Here, then, were three charters stating what the king would and would not do; but neither Henry nor Stephen fulfilled their promises. Henry's charter was but a cleverly devised document to create a broad enthusiasm for his kingship, and Stephen's smaller replicas were meant to accomplish the same result. Henry was soon too powerful to bother about keeping his word and Stephen, too weak. For the moment the charters led to no tangible gain. The charter of Henry was destined, however, not to be wasted. Men throughout England had become acquainted with it through hearing it read at the county court. During the twelfth century memory of it was retained and Henry II diplomatically confirmed it after his coronation. In the early thirteenth century it provided precedent and political platform for the baronial struggle against John. Though the kings of the eleventh and twelfth centuries were generally powerful enough to play loosely with their "scraps of parchment," their thirteenth- and fourteenth-century successors were to be so plagued by these early statements of royal duty as to be forced to abide by them.

In the last analysis the Norman kings were masters almost without limitation. They did only that which led to strong government, that which was expedient and politically practical. That sometimes their ideas of government happened to coincide with what we would call constitutional precepts

[1] SM, no. 23.

was purely accidental. Bothered by no scruples they obligated themselves to their subjects merely when it served their purpose and then but temporarily. Only the historical change that occurs with time forced later kings to take coronation oaths and promises seriously. England's urgent need was strong rule and this the Normans provided; constitutional refinement could come after these energetic men had rejuvenated English institutions and forged a government that was to be the best of twelfth-century Europe. The royal personality dominated all institutional development in the first century of English history after 1066.

2. THE KING'S GREAT COUNCIL

The Anglo-Saxon witenagemot was composed of those great men who were related to the king, those who possessed large estates of land, the principal ecclesiastics, and a small, select group of officers who formed the royal entourage or household. Indefinite in composition and function, the witenagemot was consulted only when the kings thought it advisable. The king had no obligation to summon his witenagemot, and the chief men were under no definite obligation to attend. After 1066, although some chroniclers still referred to the *witan*, it came to be known as the *curia regis* or *magnum concilium*. This Norman court, as we shall see, performed many functions of the witenagemot but Norman feudalism made of it a totally different institution. Where the men of the witenagemot owed membership to their exalted rank in church and state, the members of the Norman court attended because of their feudal obligation of suit to court. The Norman court was a feudal court of the royal vassals or tenants-in-chief who composed the baronage. With the witenagemot there was slight obligation to attend whereas with the Norman court obligation alone explains the composition and summons to attend. For their fiefs the royal vassals had to render the feudal service of suit to court; although the king's obligation to summon his vassals for this service was not too clearly defined, he customarily summoned them to court when fundamental matters of law, state, war, and church were involved. Apart from feudal obligation it was the royal prerogative to summon any person to court; thus nonfeudal personnel were to be found at various courts.

As for the composition of the *curia regis*, the official records, chiefly the charters, and the chronicles show that in addition to the king and his wife and sons the courts consisted of the archbishops, bishops, abbots, earls, barons, and principal officers of the royal household.[2] Also there were always minor functionaries from the household providing secretarial assistance plus a few subvassals who for certain reasons accompanied the barons to court. Collectively such a gathering was considered a court of the king's tenants-in-chief (barons). Unlike the Saxon prelates who, as the chief church officers, attended the witenagemot, the ecclesiastics now attended from feudal obliga-

[2] SM, no. 27.

tion. All held great fiefs from the kings and were obliged to render feudal service. Membership was not limited to those barons holding English fiefs but included also those holding fiefs in Normandy; frequently the barons held fiefs on both sides of the Channel. Actually the *curia regis* was but the *curia ducis* become a royal court. Some Saxons can be found in the courts immediately after the Conquest but by 1087 the membership was exclusively Norman. Household officers such as the chancellor, chamberlain, marshal, and constable attended to provide their specialized knowledge and assistance; they too, however, were royal vassals and owed suit to court. During the Norman period all barons had the right to attend court and often they graced the courts summoned to celebrate the great festivals or some other event such as a knighting or marriage. Normally, though, the lesser barons did not attend the ordinary sessions. According to *Domesday Book* the king had about five hundred tenants-in-chief of which 170 were great barons. These names dominated the courts but never did more than seventy-five attend; the average attendance was fifty. Some of the greatest barons as well as those with talents needed by the king were in the most constant attendance, but even with them the composition varied from court to court. Certainly one of the largest assemblies of the Norman period was that held by the Conqueror on the Plain of Salisbury in August 1086. There a majority of the barons, great and small, plus their vassals, swore an oath of fealty to William as their paramount lord. An exceptional assemblage, it was one of few attended by a large number of lesser barons who in no respect can be considered members of the court.

We do not yet know why some names constantly appear at the courts and why the composition fluctuated. Usually a large number of barons attended the great courts held at the crown-wearings and feast celebrations; every royal vassal had the right to attend these courts and did so in accordance with traditional custom. For these assemblies summonses were seldom issued. There were, however, exceptions. When Robert Mowbray, who had revolted against William Rufus, failed to attend the Easter court of 1095 because he feared a trial, William stated that Robert would be declared a feudal felon unless he responded to the royal summons and presented himself at the Pentecost court. The Norman kings convoked a considerable number of other courts to handle pressing business for which summonses had to be issued. There is evidence of such summonses from all the kings but the best comes from *The Anglo-Saxon Chronicle* describing the *curia regis* of February 1123: "the king sent his writs over all England, and ordered his bishops and abbots and thegns [barons] all to come and meet him for his council meeting on Candlemas Day at Gloucester, and they did so. When they were assembled there, the king ordered them to elect an archbishop of Canterbury." We have enough evidence to conclude that some barons were summoned by name and these more often than the rest of the baronage. The royal summons helps to explain why some barons formed the nucleus of the *curia regis* and why a small fraction of the total baronage composed these courts. It is evident that the minor barons were summoned only under exceptional circumstances. The key to composition of the *curia regis* was feudal obligation tempered always by royal prerogative and practical necessity.

The witenagemot had never assembled with any marked regularity. Under the Normans this was changed. Following the custom of their duchy, the kings always celebrated the great festivals of Easter, Whitsuntide, and Christmas with their court. On these occasions they wore their crowns and surrounded themselves with all regalian pomp. Generally mass would be conducted by one of the archbishops, who would then place the crown on the royal head. After the ceremonial functions and the inevitable feasting, matters of state would be discussed. These three annual courts were supplemented when necessary by courts assembled at the royal will. Other events calling for the assembling of the feudal court were marriages of members of the royal family and the knighting of the king's sons. For all these festive occasions we find the largest number of barons in attendance. To add to the pomp and gaiety the barons often brought along their vassals. To these we may add envoys, officials, visiting church dignitaries such as papal legates, and guests of feudal states on the Continent.

It is no longer correct to say, as did Liebermann, that the powers and functions of the Norman *curia regis* were inferior to those of the witenagemot. They were simply better defined in that the autocratic Norman kings had their will 95 percent of the time and but used the court as a sounding board for public opinion. What vague powers the witenagemot had, the Norman *curia* had also but rarely wielded; Norman government was almost exclusively a royal affair. In the discussion that follows it will be evident that the Norman kings, like their predecessors, used their court only when expedient. As supreme feudal lords of England, the kings freely disposed of their land, enfeoffing as much or little as they desired. Often members of the court were witnesses to charters, which must be understood as providing written evidence for a previous oral donation of an estate of land or privilege. We also know that occasionally members of the court witnessed the oral transactions and at such times the records say that the court gave its advice. Again, however, the court served only as a body of witnesses to give formal sanction to a royal act that could be and often was carried out solely by the king. In fact, members of the court seem to have been present at only the most important concessions. Appointments were seldom made with the advice of the court. Earls were created out of hand; bishops and archbishops were often nominated without baronial advice, although the baronage did exert some influence on some of the nominations of William Rufus, Henry I, and Stephen. The appointment and dismissal of royal officers such as the sheriffs was purely a matter of the royal will. It is useless to argue that the kings took the court into confidence on matters of royal private concern.

The kings appear to have arranged marriages and other such familial matters as they saw fit and to have discussed such decisions with the court only as a gesture of taking the barons into their confidence. For example, in 1121 Henry I talked over his second marriage with the court, but he ignored it when arranging for Matilda's second marriage in 1131 to Geoffrey Plantagenet, count of Anjou.

We now come to the more public functions. When the kings felt the need of backing for their relations with the papacy or with foreign powers, they would look for approval to the court. We find, for example, that William Rufus with the support of his court denied the bishop of Durham right of appeal to the papal court. Henry I's settlement of the investiture struggle with the papacy in 1107 was approved by the court. In 1116 it backed Henry's resistance to a papal legation. Henry I wrote to the pope that the barons would sanction no detriment to the crown, even though their action might be against his personal will. In all these instances there was no royal obligation to consult the barons; they were consulted and their approval was used for purposes of propaganda—a technique employed to create an impression of strong and wide support. We have some evidence for assuming that there was much consultation on minor administrative affairs especially the conduct of war in the field and the garrisoning of castles and towns. As with foreign affairs so with legislation the kings secured assent when they thought it desirable, but as much legislation was enacted without as with curial assent. Henry I's coronation charter states that the Conqueror amended some of the Confessor's laws with the counsel of his barons. True, when the Conqueror separated lay and ecclesiastical courts in the 1070's it was done with the advice of his court; on the other hand he introduced trial by combat without consulting the court.[3] Some time between 1108 and 1111 Henry I enacted laws regulating the holding of hundred and shire courts, and at another time he legislated on coinage; in neither case was baronial counsel obtained.[4] What little evidence we possess on this problem tends to suggest that the kings legislated more commonly without the court; as yet the royal will was all-important.

The court's control over taxation was limited to the customary feudal aids. In 1110, for example, it assented to an aid for the marriage of Matilda to Henry V of Germany. The court had no control over nonfeudal taxation and all Danegelds were authorized by the kings alone. In matters of law the *curia regis* was first of all a feudal court governed by Norman feudal custom and procedure. The Norman court therefore had a jurisdiction and custom unknown to the witenagemot. By piecing together records of the pleas and stray bits from the chroniclers we secure a reasonably good idea of judicial business at the royal court. It was as a vassal of the Conqueror that Bishop Odo of Bayeux was tried for infidelity to his feudal lord. In 1075 Earl Roger

[3] SM, nos. 16, 17.
[4] SM, no. 24.

of Hereford was sentenced to imprisonment for life, the penalty prescribed by Norman custom for feudal revolt. In 1096 Geoffrey Bagnard appeared before the court and accused William of Eu of participating in the revolt of 1095 against William Rufus; the Norman trial by combat was used to decide the case and, according to *The Anglo-Saxon Chronicle,* Geoffrey "fought it out with him, and overcame him in trial by battle, and when he was overcome, the king ordered his eyes to be put out and that afterwards he should be castrated." These are but a few of the cases of high treason tried by the court during the Norman period. It should be noted that the Norman penalty of mutilation, probably introduced by the Conqueror, was the sentence.

The trial in 1088 of William, bishop of Durham, for feudal revolt against William Rufus is an especially good example of the informality and lack of clearly defined regulations that characterized the procedure. When the trial opened, the bishop immediately presented his case, not waiting for the usual formal accusation. His chief argument rested on the contention that as a bishop no feudal court could try him. Arguing for the king, Lanfranc insisted that his lands had been seized or forfeited as fiefs and that he was being tried as a vassal. William Rufus then interrupted to suggest that the bishop answer the accusation. Both the bishop's pledges agreed that they were sworn to preserve the safe conduct of the bishop so that he could answer the accusation. Again the bishop pleaded his special status but was followed by Hugh de Beaumont making the formal accusation. Still the bishop refused to answer. At this point the court got out of order; insults and arguments were shouted by all present. Finally it was decided to adjourn the court temporarily so that those judging could decide whether to continue as a feudal court or to accept the bishop's claim that he could be tried only by canon law. After long delay it was decided that the trial should continue according to feudal custom. The bishop now contested this decision, demanding the opportunity to consult with the bishops who sat in the court. Lanfranc refused such counsel because the bishops were judges. The king also refused the request and the bishop consulted for a while with his own followers. Returning to the court, he refused the judgment saying that he could not be judged by a lay and feudal court. Lanfranc overruled him and the bishop then asked permission to make a personal appeal to Rome. Again the court adjourned to decide on his request. When it reconvened, on behalf of the king and court, Hugh de Beaumont made known the court's judgment. The bishop was told that because he had not answered the accusation and because he had appealed to Rome the court had declared his fief to be forfeited.

In a nonfeudal capacity the Norman court continued to function much as did the witenagemot. It was a court of the first instance and tried cases of the great men which customarily fell in the category of civil disputes. At times, however, other disputes would be adjudicated as, for example, differences between great prelates. Much reliance, especially in the Norman period, was put upon the evidence of Anglo-Saxon charters and the testimony of Saxons who stated the custom of English land law. When in 1070 Bishop Wulfstan of Worcester proved his better right to various lands claimed by Thomas, archbishop of York, it was done by written evidence. A point needful of emphasis and not to be forgotten is that the most important and most clearly defined obligations of the *curia regis* were its feudal and nonfeudal jurisdiction. Feudal custom obliged the king to summon his vassals to judge their peers and they were obliged to render suit to court. This body of great men was also the only logical court to adjudicate nonfeudal differences between men of high standing.

In regard to functions there yet remains the contention of Liebermann that the *curia regis* "as a corporate body . . . felt itself as the guardian of English liberties and as the successor of the witan." Such a view is extremely unrealistic. The *curia regis* did not elect the king and so did not, as Liebermann asserted, become associated in the minds of the people with the coronation charters granted. The small group of partisan barons around Henry I when he issued the Coronation Charter had no part in his confirming the laws of Edward the Confessor; he was but following the precedent of his father, who had realistically conceived the fiction that he ruled as the successor of the Confessor and according to English custom. Neither Normans nor Saxons thought of the *curia regis* as the successor to the witenagemot, the corporate guardian of English liberty. To attribute such a concept to the barons or to the people is but a fanciful exercise in theory. It credits men of the early twelfth century with a sophistication and understanding of political theory quite foreign to this crude age. When the *curia regis* concurred with the policies of Henry I towards the papacy, it guarded no "national interest" but merely supported a long tradition of independence common to both the English and the Norman church.

The *curia regis* had some independence and initiative but our evidence is too scant to push this conclusion very far. As royal vassals the barons could take their differences to court and they could accuse vassals of treasonable action against the king. The king, however, had the sole right to determine when to proceed or when to refuse the cases. Only on rare occasions did the barons flout the royal will in judicial decisions. This they did in 1095 in the trial of Anselm, archbishop of Canterbury, when William Rufus accused him of disloyalty. Coerced into submission, the bishops sided with William and withdrew their obedience to Anselm. When the barons, according to Eadmer, were asked to do likewise they replied: "He is our archbishop: he has to govern religion in this land, and in this respect we, who are Christians, cannot deny the authority of his office while we live here, especially as no stain of office is attached to him to compel us to act otherwise in regard to him." Then, "smothering his anger, the king bore with this answer, taking care to refrain from contradicting their argument openly, lest they should take too great offense." William had to dismiss his charges. Occasionally the *curia regis* suggested a course of action as, for example, in 1093 when it asked that prayers be offered to seek divine guidance in the selection of a worthy archbishop of Canterbury. This suggestion was made to William Rufus, who "showed some indignation" but nevertheless "assented thereto." When Henry I secretly arranged for the marriage of Matilda to Count Geoffrey of Anjou the *curia regis* protested, arguing that Henry had promised to consult the barons on the marriage of his daughter and that this action nullified their oath of fealty to Matilda. There are cases of royal and baronial give-and-take in the court and certainly on some occasions the royal decision must have been altered. Although the king did not have to take the advice or receive the consent of the *curia regis*, he could not entirely ignore baronial opinion on all the great issues and disassociate the barons from a part in the formulation of royal policy. The successful kings consulted with the barons on important matters and did not consistently oppose the baronial will. No Norman king was so powerful that he could long play the tyrant. We can attribute no list of definite functions and rights to the *curia regis*; most of the Norman governing was done alone or along with the approval of a court that was as yet basically a rubber stamp. But some independence there was and, like the Saxon kings, the Normans had to make concessions to the opinion of the powerful. Highly autocratic as they were, the Norman kings were not absolute.

3. THE KING'S SMALL COUNCIL

In our discussion of the great council or *curia regis* we limited our investigation to the composition, functions, and rights of those great assemblies of royal vassals or barons summoned to the traditional festivals and feasts and to the special meetings where they consulted formally with the king on urgent and important matters of state. The expression *curia* or *curia regis* had, however, a much wider meaning. *Curia* could signify a place such as the royal residence or palace; it could also include those persons constantly about the king serving him in his household. *Curia regis* referred to a fairly permanent court or council of men who were constantly about the royal person helping him in the routine business of government. In fact, the core of the great council was the small *curia regis* or council that was equal to all governmental demands except those of the greatest import. Then the king generally reinforced his small council with the barons and thereby created a great council. As we shall see, it is extremely difficult and hazardous to draw a distinction between great and small council; if any can be made, it is on the basis of size and a rough definition of business. We thus have a great council at the traditional gatherings and on those occasions when personal summonses were issued to the major barons along with general summonses to the minor barons in order to secure their approval or advice on other than routine questions. Otherwise when we meet the term *curia regis* it means the small permanent council that dealt daily with normal administration.

The composition of the small council had a greater constancy and permanency than that of the great council. The regular members were of the household—the chancellor, chamberlain, seneschal, butler, constable, and minor assistants and clerics. Though sometimes great barons, more often these officers were lesser barons who held their offices through professional competency and royal favor. It was the household that provided the professional skill to help direct central administration. Not of the household but a principal member of the court was the justiciar. Less regular in attendance were curial administrators of minor baronial rank who were outside the household proper. Few of these men had titles, that of minister being the most specific of which we have record. Often they served at court on the small council and the rest of the time represented the king and his small council in varied administrative tasks in the field. Besides these more professional men a few prelates and barons were always in attendance, some of whom seem favored over the rest for their counsel to the king. Any of the group just mentioned could come from Normandy or England and could serve the king on both sides of the Channel. In the reign of Henry I the chroniclers emphasize that Henry relied heavily on the counsel of such great barons as Count Robert of Meulan, Earl Hugh of Chester, and Roger Bigod. Faces changed, however, for while moving around his possessions the king took counsel from the hard core of his council plus certain barons in the area. Though the small council varied in composition, collectively its members formed a permanent group which was always at hand to help guide the royal government. As such it was the antecedent of the king's council that evolved during the reigns of Henry III and Edward I, but men did not as yet consider it different from the great council; none of its members except the chief officers had any titles, and none took a special councillor's oath.

What, if any, were the special duties or rights of the small council? The answer is none. It dealt with the same business as the great council; theoretically there was no difference. What seems to be certain is that the king used the small council for all governmental business except that of the utmost gravity. Counsel was given daily as was approval to all sorts of royal acts. William Rufus was frequently charged with taking bad advice from sycophants and unscrupulous men in his council. Members of the small council were the principal witnesses of royal charters; only the most formal charters were witnessed by the great council. The council oversaw much of the royal administration such as finance and the relations with local officers in the shires, hundreds, and boroughs. Certainly more litigation came before the small than the great council, which was concerned with only the greatest disputes. When a member of the court was sent out to adjudicate disputes in the counties, the small council did not act as a court. It did, however, when cases came before it at Westminster or while the king was on the move. In the latter case the hard core of the council would be reinforced by prelates and barons of the locality. Numerous records of such cases have been preserved. In 1085 while in Normandy the Conqueror, along with two abbots, some barons, and his butler, decided a civil dispute between a baron and an abbot. The following year William disposed of a civil plea while going through Wiltshire. The court that adjudicated this case was larger than the normal small council and seems to have been what Adams would call a "reinforced small council." It included the king and his two sons, two archbishops, eight bishops, eighteen barons, and two household officials; it was almost a great council.

In legislation, as previously noted, the king enacted laws with or without council and with either great or small council. Among the laws Henry I enacted or modified with the advice of the small council were ancient customs pertaining to wreck, measures, counterfeiters, and inferior money; reforms in the currency; renovation in the system of rendering account to the exchequer; and substitution of liability for murder fines to the hundred from the agrarian communities. In Normandy legislation on the truce of God was enacted in the small council.

4. CONCLUSIONS

Norman central administration continued much of the old English; the parallels between them are numerous. The Norman kings retained the useful features of the Anglo-Saxon government and invigorated the old institutions by importing efficient Norman practices. In spite of the continuity and similarities it is wrong to conclude that the Norman kings and courts consciously thought of themselves as the continuators or repositories of the old Anglo-Saxon way of life. When the Normans adopted some of the English institutions they were but doing what they had done two centuries before with Frankish institutions—they preserved the best features and then typically developed them into a state of high efficiency. The Norman kings did all that the English kings had done, and much more. As the feudal lords of all England and of all the great men they exercised a far tighter control over concessions, rights, and men. In theory they abided by the customs and ceremonies of English kingship but this was a political façade to cover up a royal power autocratic and almost unlimited. The strong Norman kingship is the dominant force from 1066 to 1135 and overshadows all other institutions. To this ambitious and ruthless royal drive the Anglo-Norman institutions owed their development.

The duplication or overlapping of functions found with the great and small councils well illustrates the lack of distinction in the earlier Middle Ages between courts or departments. Both great and small councils did anything demanded of them. The only lines we can draw between them are based on size and the import of the business at hand. Except when the kings required a large sampling of opinion, approval for an extraordinary measure, or a court to adjudicate a serious dispute between great lords or rights appertaining to the royal prerogative, the small council sufficed. With its more professional and experienced members it was better equipped to govern; it was the permanent core of the great council. The idea that either of these courts could limit the royal will had not yet been conceived. When the kings went to the great council to get approval for some enterprise it was only to create an impression of strong baronial support. None of the Norman kings flouted baronial opinion all the time, yet never would they admit a restrictive power of the great council. Kingship was at its strongest under the Normans. Subsequent history was to be the story of steadily more powerful courts which eventually came to limit the royal power.

XI

Central Administration: Justiciar, Household, Chancery, Exchequer, and the Royal Income

1. THE JUSTICIAR

EVEN if the Norman kings had not been masters of both England and Normandy they, like their continental contemporaries, would have been forced upon occasion to delegate some or all of their authority. The need to divide their time between the two possessions entailed delegating authority more frequently and paying closer attention to the persons empowered to govern in the royal name. All the Normans except Stephen spent much time in Normandy; Henry I was in the duchy for half his reign. Both William the Conqueror and Henry I delegated special duties to the queens or their sons; generally they were authorized to preside over trials. Trusted vassals or officers described variously as regent, custodian, and prefect were delegated wider authority and during the royal absence in Normandy were empowered to govern in the king's name. Without doubt these royal lieutenants were vice-regents or vice-royals. In 1067 when the Conqueror visited Normandy he left the governing of England to Bishop Odo of Bayeux and his Norman steward, William fitz Osbern. Occasionally other great men such as Lanfranc received similar powers. When the Conqueror was in England, however, no one acted as a vice-regent. The supervision of trials, and certain administrative affairs that could not be attended to personally, William delegated to one of his trusted barons. It was in such a role that Geoffrey of Coutances acted when he represented William in 1075 at Penenden as presiding officer of a court that adjudicated a dispute between the archbishop of Canterbury and Bishop Odo of Bayeux.[1]

Under William Rufus the temporary vice-royalty developed into a more permanent and well-defined office. The men appointed came to hold it not only when William was in Normandy but also when he was in England. Actually William spent most of his reign in England but nonetheless seemed to feel the need to delegate much of his work to a lieutenant. Endowed with real ability only in fighting, William concentrated on that, entrusting a large share of the administration to skilled professionals. At the outset he turned over such work to his uncle Bishop Odo of Bayeux and Bishop William of Durham, who were both entitled justiciars by later chroniclers. Their par-

[1] SM, nos. 19A, B, C.

ticipation in a subsequent revolt, however, led William never to put trust again in a great baron. He surrounded himself with men of secondary baronial rank or of humble and obscure background. Such a man was the infamous Ranulf Flambard. He never carried more than the official rank of royal chaplain but he is undoubtedly the first real justiciar (*justiciarius*), as these vice-royals came to be styled. Of a humble Norman family Flambard became a clerk and received training as a minor official at the ducal court of Caen where the treasury was also located. After holding a few minor ecclesiastical offices he became chaplain to the Conqueror and clerk to the chancellor (1083–1085); then he passed into the service of William Rufus. Under Rufus, as Eadmer says, Flambard became the executor of the royal will. He was not, as some historians have argued, the treasurer, nor was he responsible for first applying the feudal aids and incidents to England, but he did streamline the royal administration, transforming it into a ruthlessly efficient organization that drained dry all possible sources of revenue. Flambard developed strong feudal institutions into even more efficient ones, making them work overtime for the royal benefit. Typically, the documents describing his hand in the royal government are almost exclusively orders or directions to the royal officers. To soothe baronial resentment at the high-handed methods and exactions of Flambard, Henry I imprisoned him in the Tower. He soon escaped and, in the royal grace again by 1101, peacefully administered the bishopric of Durham for the next twenty-five years. Here, again, he used his singular administrative ability to develop the bishopric's resources. Undoubtedly Henry often wished that he could have retained Flambard; had Flambard's reputation been less unsavory, he certainly would have.

Fortunately Henry discovered a man the equal of Flambard and in most respects more scrupulous; this was Roger, bishop of Salisbury, the first who can definitely be called justiciar of England. This remarkable man began his career much as Flambard had. He had been a poor priest at Caen who endeared himself to Henry I by the rapidity with which he could dispose of the divine services. Before 1100 Henry had rewarded such merit by making Roger his chaplain and household steward. Once Henry was king, Roger's efficient service was rewarded first by an appointment as chancellor and then by the bishopric of Salisbury; around 1107 or 1108 he was named justiciar and held that office until removed by Stephen in 1139. Entitled *justiciarius* by the chroniclers, Roger was further described as *secundus a rege*. As chancellor and then justiciar Roger remodeled much of the Norman administration. He expanded the jurisdiction and improved the procedure of the *curia regis* in matters of justice. Under his surveillance the famous exchequer became a definite financial department. Simeon of Durham believed that Roger made most of the decisions for the royal government and when we see his tremendous prestige and influence in arranging ecclesiastical appointments, extending the strong arm of royal justice, and organizing the royal revenues, we must admit that Roger was a sort of medieval prime minister but a minister immeasurably more powerful because his only responsibility was to his lord the king.

Like any practical politician Roger employed men with backgrounds similar to his who owed their position and advancement to his patronage. With Roger we first observe a professional household or curial staff composed of men of humble origin whom the chroniclers contemptuously write off as being raised from the dust. Though the barons may have disliked this development, it pleased Henry, who saw his improved administration net him a constantly larger income. Roger provided also for his relatives. For his nephew Alexander he secured the bishopric of Lincoln. Another nephew Nigel became bishop of Ely in 1133. In 1130 Nigel had become a key officer in the Norman treasury and with Stephen's reign he became treasurer of the exchequer. Roger's son, Roger the Poor, held the chancellorship during the first years of Stephen's reign. Under Henry II Richard fitz Nigel became treasurer and wrote that incomparable treatise on medieval finance, *The Dialogue of the Exchequer*. Roger, then, concentrated around him a dedicated group of civil servants who continued his fine tradition in the Angevin period.

As second in command the justiciar created departments, directed their administration, and molded royal policy. At no time was he a member of the household or the curial departments. He might reside for long periods in the household and even revise its operations, but never did he receive its livery. Though ordinarily the presiding officer at the exchequer, he was more than a financial officer or baron of the exchequer. He was the chief royal justice (*capitalis justiciarius*) and directed the procedure at the royal court as well as the missions of the itinerant justices who became prominent under Henry I; he was not, however, merely a justice. He was the royal mediator with spiritual and lay powers; he did whatever was required by the king. The justiciar made the royal court more malleable and elastic and thereby began that long and fruitful process by which central institutions developed from the court whenever the press of government demanded them. Our last remarks are in the nature of a warning. It was not until Henry II's reign that the justiciar was the sole royal officer to be styled *justiciarius* of all England. Previously the various justices all carried the title of *justiciarius* and some officers of the court were even called chief justices. At times, therefore, it is well-nigh impossible to distinguish between ordinary judges and the royal lieutenant, but a difference there was and one should never make the mistake of regarding the royal justiciar as simply a judge concerned only with the law.

2. THE ROYAL HOUSEHOLD

Royal life in the Norman period was highly ambulatory. There was no capital, just a series of favorite residences generally located near royal forests.

The king with his court traveled almost constantly in England and Normandy dividing his time between royal estates and those of his vassals. With the king were all the accoutrements for living and governing—clothes, food, drink, parchment, chests of money, and a staff sufficient to minister to the royal domestic needs and to state business. Sometimes the great council was with the king and always there was a small council in attendance, but closest to the royal person was his household staff, which, of course, helped compose the great and small councils. There is no value in debating whether the Norman household owed more to ducal or to Anglo-Saxon antecedents. All households of this period were similar to the classic Carolingian organization, which seems to have sired most of the subsequent feudal households. The Norman household was probably of Anglo-Norman origin. Certainly the names of the officers and their more specialized functions were derived from the ducal household. The plurality of some of the offices appears, however, to have come from the Anglo-Saxon organization. At any rate both Anglo-Saxon and ducal households accomplished the same basic functions and little alteration of Anglo-Saxon practices occurred immediately after 1066. By then a staff whose primary purpose had been domestic administration had acquired also the work of public administration.

For a minute description of the household officers, of some of their functions, and of their maintenance we have that peculiar document on the *Establishment of the Royal Household* composed about 1135.[2] Most officers may be rapidly disposed of because they had no public administrative or constitutional consequence. First in this category were the master butler, stewards, and constables. The steward, sometimes called *dapifer* in England, was comparable to the Norman seneschal in the duchy but never headed the household or gave birth, as some have thought, to the later justiciar. The office of steward frequently had two holders, both great barons. Their duties were chiefly ceremonial, such as placing the dishes before the king at banquets. As great barons the stewards could be influential but the office itself never developed into a key administrative post. As for the butler, his functions never brought him into the stream of administrative work; he always remained a domestic official. The constables introduced by the Normans were unlike the old *stallers;* their military duties were very circumscribed, being limited to the business of supply. They also saw to the royal sport by supervising the care of horses, hounds, hawks, and the necessary personnel such as the huntsmen, houndsmen, and foresters. Next in rank were the marshals and the master of the writing office. Subordinates of the constables, the marshals came from less important families. Their chief work was ushering. They preserved order in the king's hall and recorded expenditures of the household officers on tallies. By the time of Henry I there was a chief marshal assisted by four undermarshals. The master of the writing office (actually a chancery), who assisted the chancellor, was concerned with

[2] SM, no. 29.

supervising the clerks. Last in rank were the minor functionaries and menial servants who assisted the principal members of the household. All the officers we have noted were chiefly concerned with domestic affairs; let us now turn to those officials whose domestic work made them great state officers and put them in charge of departments that eventually were to separate from the household and become independent.

3. THE CHANCERY

There is still debate whether in 1066 either the Norman or the Anglo-Saxon household knew an official styled chancellor, a name derived from *cancelli* which signified a screen behind which secretarial work of the household was conducted. We have previously concluded that in all but name both establishments had such an officer. When the increase of administration required the organization of a secretariat it was only natural that the chaplain of the court along with his clerical assistants should be entrusted with this function. To these literate members of the household the ruler gave the custody of the great seal which authenticated the documents they drew up. Officially the first chancellor was the Norman chaplain Herfast, first mentioned in the year 1068. At first the chancellors were drawn from the lower ranks of the ecclesiastics, though most were eventually promoted to a bishopric. By the reign of William II the chancellors were selected from among the more important men and under Henry I they were taken from bishops. So powerful an individual as Roger of Salisbury was chancellor prior to holding the justiciarship. By this time the chancellor was the principal household officer with the best opportunity for preferment. As under the Confessor his greatest trust was custodianship of the great seal. He headed the staff of the royal chapel, which served also as the writing office (*scriptorium*). When not caring for the royal family's spiritual needs, the clerks drew up the documents issued under the great seal; some may have devoted all their time to secretarial work. The immediate supervisor of this staff was the master of the writing office, who also guarded the seal most of the time. By the reign of Henry I this officer had attained rank next to the great household officers and could normally expect to become a bishop. Later this office was to become the vice-chancellorship. The chancery personnel of the household were advantageously placed for preferment; the most humble clerk could reasonably hope to climb to the top rung of the household, and then the ecclesiastical, ladder. A perceptive clerk such as Bernard, Henry I's scribe, could use his strategic position to acquire valuable land as he advanced upward.

The operating procedure of the household chancery was as yet extremely primitive and highly informal. When obliged to issue a document the king stated his intent to the chancellor, who then instructed the master of the staff to produce the suitable document. When this was done the chancellor appended the great seal to it in the presence of royal witnesses whose names were listed at the end of the text.[3] Though the witnesses sometimes affixed their crosses to the document, customarily they did not. The witnesses, selected predominantly from the household, were supplemented by whatever barons happened to be at court. Throughout the reign of the Conqueror the Anglo-Saxon secretarial procedure looms large; some of its practices became a permanent part of the Norman chancery methods. For a time many charters continued to be composed in Anglo-Saxon rather than in Latin. Occasionally the grantee would still produce the necessary charter to be authenticated by the great seal. There was practically no difference between the solemn Norman charters and the ones preceding them until 1070 when a change is perceptible. The Norman clerks started to employ the writ (*breve*) for routine business and to reserve the charter for the most important transactions. Even the writ, as we have seen, was a Saxon innovation; the Normans simply developed it into a more efficient document. As in Saxon days the simple writ contained only minimal information plus a short list of witnesses and the name of the place it was issued. There developed, however, a combination of the writ and charter which we call the writ-charter. It contained more information than the simple writ and was an improvement over the old charter; under the Angevins it was to develop into the letters close and patent which practically put an end to the old charter.

By the end of the Norman period the chancery was the strongest department of the household with a tradition and operating procedure of its own. As yet a part of the household, it was not to go out of it until the thirteenth century. Already discernible were the initiative and flexibility that combined to make it a marvel of feudal administration in western Europe under Henry II and his sons and a fundamental step in the development of the common law system. Through the chancery the king officially made known his will and exercised his prerogative; it was the royal mouthpiece through which much of the administration was funneled.

4. THE EXCHEQUER

From the Saxon kings the Conqueror inherited a relatively advanced financial system. The household chamber had evolved into more than a domestic treasury and storage room for precious documents and possessions; it received most of the royal revenue from the entire realm, collected and rendered by the sheriffs of the shires, each of whom was apparently responsible for a fixed annual farm. This expansion of the chamber plus its highly itinerant nature had caused the Confessor to establish a storehouse or sedentary treasury at Winchester to hold surplus valuables and money. To this organization the Conqueror brought a financial system revolving around the ducal *camera*, which was similar to the Saxon chamber though less developed. The advance in financial administration that occurred during

[3] SM. no. 27.

the next seventy years resulted from invigoration of the Saxon system by Norman innovators.

Without overly concerning ourselves with chronology, which is extremely indefinite for this period, let us examine the advances in administration made during the reigns of William II and Henry I. As under the Saxon kings the household chamber continued as a bedchamber (*camera regis*) where the king slept and kept his clothes in a wardrobe (*garderoba*). This establishment was managed by a master chamberlain represented by two rotating chamberlains assisted by menial servants who served the royal domestic needs. But there was another part of the chamber, the chamber of the court (*camera curie*), which was the royal privy purse or financial department of the household; it was the true financial heir of the Saxon and Norman *camera* handling both domestic and state finance. Headed by the master chamberlain and administered by several chamberlains, this part of the chamber received payments and made disbursements for any royal needs.[4] As in the late Saxon period it also had a financial adjunct—the treasury at Winchester—which for a time was the core of royal finance. Perhaps early in Henry I's reign the treasury became more than a storehouse with a few custodians and took on the administration of the king's revenue. It is uncertain whether the treasury and its personnel were considered a part of the chamber staff; it would seem not. The chamber nevertheless seems to have supplied the staff, which consisted of a treasurer and assistants chosen from clerics because of the complexity of the work. This staff lived at Winchester and drew its support from manors in Hampshire. The master chamberlain had no jurisdiction over them; only when they temporarily resided in the household would they draw its livery. The work of this staff now included that of the old Saxon and Norman chamber. It received most of the royal income, disbursed it, maintained accounts that were periodically audited by specially designated barons, and supplied the chamber with most of its money. From the chamber had sprung an almost independent financial department that superseded it in carrying the brunt of financial administration.

The Winchester treasury, however, did not long retain its dominance in finance. Liebermann has with excellent reason suggested that the treasury was a pre-exchequer treasury-court and thus the parent of the exchequer, another financial department that absorbed the treasury and was independent of the chamber. Except for name and method of financial computation, the exchequer resembled the treasury. All that was required for the exchequer was a regular financial board or court to supervise the staff and audit the accounts plus a checkered cloth on a table—the abacus—for the purpose of accounting. Although the term "exchequer" (*scaccarium*) does not appear until 1110, Liebermann feels that a treasury supervised by a board—the barons of the exchequer—and using the checkered cloth for accounting existed as early as the reign of William II. Be that as it may, it is certain that

[4] SM, no. 29.

the early reign of Henry I saw the origin of the exchequer, a department that has retained its financial supremacy to the present.

Because our information on the exchequer is not complete until the Angevin period, for the present we can only describe its principal characteristics. It was located in London where it and its permanent staff remained no matter where the king went. The staff of the Winchester treasury melted away and it declined into a local storehouse managed by the sheriff of Hampshire. The exchequer treasury located at London became the realm's storehouse and formed one of the two divisions of the exchequer—the exchequer of receipt (lower exchequer). Meanwhile the justiciar Roger of Salisbury reorganized the staff and procedure. He selected all key officials from the chamber, thus maintaining the close relation that had existed between chamber and Winchester treasury. In fact some of these officials who composed the auditing board (*barones de scaccario*) served the king in other official capacities. They might sit on the *curia regis* in the capacity of judges or advisers, or they could be delegated to other administrative tasks. Throughout the year the exchequer functioned with a staff composed of the treasurer, two chamberlains, and some subordinates; this was known as the lower exchequer. On Easter and Michaelmas the staff was augmented by key officers of the court and household to form the barons of the exchequer, who then audited the accounts of the sheriffs for the counties. The sheriffs paid their revenues into the lower exchequer but accounted for their receipts and expenses at the upper exchequer before the barons. Most of the revenue went to the exchequer, which met the royal obligations. Though the chamber still collected some revenue, most of its money for domestic operation and the king's privy purse was supplied by the exchequer. As already noted in the chapter on the Norman sources, the record of all receipts from the sheriffs and other accountants as well as the disbursements made on behalf of the king's business was kept on the Pipe Rolls which began some time during Henry I's reign; the first extant one dates from 1130 but obviously it was preceded by others.[5]

Not to be neglected in a discussion of the exchequer was its system of account—the checkered cloth—whence the exchequer derived its name. The necessity for a swift as well as visual method of computation was acute in an age when few men were literate and when Arabic numerals and the zero were not used in western Europe. Anyone who has attempted to solve the simplest arithmetical problems with Roman numerals knows how futile it can be. Wooden sticks (tallies) with notches cut along the edges to represent sums of money served well as receipts and continued in use through the twelfth century, but they did not help the barons or sheriffs do their arithmetic. They resorted to the abacus, which consisted basically of columns divided by vertical lines. Each column represented a decimal stage, that is, units of tens, hundreds, thousands, and so on. In the appropriate column

[5] SM, no. 25.

would be put a number of counters to represent the sum of money. When no counter was placed in a column it was an indication of "zero." Today a similar arrangement in the form of a frame of wires with beads on them introduces a young child to his addition and subtraction. The English abacus or exchequer was nothing other than the Chinese *swanpan* in the form of a checkered cloth on a table. The principle of the abacus was imported from the Continent. By the end of the tenth century Gerbert, later Pope Sylvester II, had learned about the abacus from the Arabs in Spain and had referred to it in one of his treatises. Later other scholars wrote on the principles of the abacus. During the eleventh century it was much discussed in Lorraine, a center for mathematical study. In the early twelfth century at the cathedral school of Laon two treatises on the abacus were written by Ralph of Laon and Adelard of Bath. As Haskins and Poole have shown, there were lively cultural and theological ties between England and these areas from the time of the Confessor. It was inevitable, then, for the abacus to reach England and to be employed by the royal officials for keeping their accounts. Although Poole seems to think that knowledge of the abacus came in the early twelfth century from Laon by way of Adelard and other English scholars who studied there, Haskins has produced evidence suggesting that the abacus was already known in the last quarter of the eleventh century and may have been introduced by a learned scholar of Lorraine, Robert by name, who became bishop of Hereford in 1079.

Though not our chief concern it should be noted that at the time the Winchester treasury controlled the royal revenue a similar situation existed in Normandy at Rouen where a treasury and its staff received the revenues from Norman counties (*vicomtés*) and disbursed them for the king. Later when the English exchequer superseded the treasury, the same development occurred in Normandy. By 1130 we have evidence of a Norman exchequer functioning in the same manner as the English, and probably the men who were barons of the English exchequer served also as barons of the Norman exchequer and helped the king supervise its operation. It had, however, a permanent staff.

In both England and Normandy, then, an expanding government stimulated by the growing money economy required the primitive and basically domestic machinery of the chamber to spawn the treasury, which in turn yielded to the more efficient and sophisticated exchequer.

5. THE ROYAL INCOME

In an age when money was not yet plentiful and when a ruler's income depended upon how much he could extract from his land and collect by virtue of his miscellaneous prerogative rights, the Norman kings were notorious for their greed and the skill with which they satisfied it. They explored all possible avenues leading to increased revenue and had no qualms about how they obtained it. Making allowance for the bias of *The Anglo-*

Saxon Chronicle from which we derive much contemporary opinion, we must largely accept its judgment; the success of the dukes in squeezing money out of their duchy indicates that they came to England not without an unsavory reputation in such matters. It was the Saxon chronicler's opinion that the "king and chief men loved gain much and over-much–gold and silver–and did not care how sinfully it was obtained provided it came to them. The king sold his land on very hard terms–as hard as he could . . . and did not care how sinfully the reeves had got it from poor men, nor how many unlawful things they did." We may confidently assert that the Conqueror and his vassals brought to England considerable pecuniary skill and applied it with vigor to an already efficient financial organization.

The principal financial innovation of the Normans in England came from the introduction of feudalism. It brought to the king a new set of revenues unknown to his Saxon predecessors–the feudal aids and incidents. Contemporary evidence shows the kings to have exploited these new revenues to the fullest. Ranulf Flambard, the minister of William Rufus, so unscrupulously pushed his royal lord's claim to these rights that Henry I, upon becoming king, had to remove him; Henry promised in the Coronation Charter to take aids and customs only according to feudal custom. Subsequent Pipe Rolls show, however, that he customarily exacted more from the aids and incidents than feudal custom allotted him.[6] Particularly exploited were the incidents of forfeiture, escheat and marriage, and the regalian rights over church land. From the fiefs of land granted to their vassals the kings secured most of their military service. Each fief provided a quota of knights, castle-guard, or serjeant's service. It has been estimated that the Conqueror could put five thousand knights in the field. The royal vassals were also expected to contribute to the fortification of royal castles, to repair bridges, and to maintain roads. Such obligations were nothing other than the old Saxon *trimoda necessitas*. Besides these public services there were varied administrative functions which the vassals performed locally for the king.

Closely allied to feudal service was the Saxon *fyrd* or the Norman *arrière-ban*. This was the principle that able-bodied freemen were liable to military service, whether or not vassals of the king. In numerous instances this custom was enforced. In the rebellion against the Conqueror in 1075 the land *fyrd* was called out by some sheriffs. In 1094, although they never fought in Normandy, thousands of Englishmen were mustered to go overseas with William Rufus. Under Stephen in 1138 the *fyrd* of northern counties was used to augment the feudal levy fighting against the Scottish king. At times the Saxon *fyrd* was used. In 1071, for example, the Conqueror used it against rebels of Ely; William Rufus employed it in the Norman expedition of 1091. A naval force levied upon the principle of the *fyrd* prevented Earls Edwin and Morcas from escaping England in 1071. Since the late tenth century mercenaries had been used in western Europe and the Conqueror

[6] SM, no. 25.

had employed some in his expeditionary force. Not until Henry I, however, when the reviving money economy largely made it possible to finance them by the substitution of money payments for knight service, were they used in any significant numbers. Formerly fined for failure to provide knight service, by Henry's reign vassals could make a money payment (scutage—shield money) in place of knight service when mutually satisfactory to king and vassals. In 1100 on lands held in fief by the church a scutage was taken in lieu of quotas of knight service; later, scutages were taken from lay vassals.[7] Under Stephen the scutage was levied at the rate of a mark or pound on the knight's fee.

Other income came to the kings by virtue of their extensive prerogative powers. Whether by right of inheritance from the Carolingians or through usurpation and arbitrary exaction, all the rulers of Europe at this time claimed profits from tolls and coinage, rents from forests, and the proceeds from treasure-trove and wreckage of the sea. All came to demand nonfeudal aids or taxes. When in need of money, they arbitrarily assessed an aid upon their vassals. There is evidence that William Rufus and, early in his reign, Henry I levied nonfeudal aids to help finance Norman campaigns. In 1096, for example, William demanded 10,000 marks for a campaign; other evidence suggests that he was constantly assessing the church fiefs with these aids. Our first good witness to this form of taxation is provided by the Pipe Roll of 1130. Here there are entries referring to *dona* (gifts) paid by the church and *auxilia* (aids) paid by boroughs.[8] The latter aid was subsequently called a tallage and was no different from the *taille* assessed on French towns and *Bede* assessed on German towns; nor was it different from the tallage assessed arbitrarily by lords upon their peasants. Throughout western Europe the ruler assessed his feudal vassals and towns and took what he could get from them.

Another tax that emerged primarily out of the royal prerogative was the Saxon Danegeld. Though there is evidence that the Normans may have inherited some such tax from the Frankish kings, it was in no way comparable to the geld assessed on hides and carucates of land in England. This tax the Conqueror enthusiastically embraced, developing it into an even more profitable income. Although under the Confessor the Danegeld had not been collected annually the Conqueror and his sons received it yearly down to 1130. The chroniclers refer to it as an annual tax and are corroborated by the *Leges Henrici*.[9] Traditionally assessed at the rate of two shillings a fiscal hide, by 1084 it had mounted to six shillings. The famous inquest made in 1086 which resulted in *Domesday Book* seems to have been connected with the geld. Scholars still disagree as to the primary purpose of this

[7] SM, nos. 25, 27D.
[8] SM, no. 25.
[9] SM, no. 26.

magnificent record. Some say that it was to ascertain the feudal service due the Conqueror; others, that it was to provide a description of the new realm; and still others, that it was to be a guide for reassessment of the geld on a uniform basis in order to replace the rather arbitrary and artificial assessment by fiscal hides. No readjustment of the geld seems to have been made, yet undoubtedly the Conqueror contemplated a fiscal use for this record because it provided him with information on the value of all land held by him and of him from 1066 to 1086. If lands had risen or fallen in value such information would obviously prove of value to the king for tax assessment. Throughout the reign of Henry I the geld was ordinarily assessed at its traditional amount of two shillings the hide. For us the importance of the Danegeld is that it is the first example of direct taxation on land since the fall of the Roman Empire in the West.

The profits from justice also stemmed from the royal prerogative and constantly increased as the royal justice expanded its jurisdiction. In fact, the expansion of the king's justice in the period of its early development can be explained satisfactorily largely by the royal need for money. Any case tried in the royal court netted the king a sizable fee, and all the profits from those actions that fell under the category of the king's pleas went into the royal hand. Closely associated with judicial profits were a series of miscellaneous revenues. When the slayer of a Norman was not apprehended, a murder fine (*murdrum*) of 46 marks was assessed on the whole hundred.[10] Any breach of the laws of the royal forests resulted in a severe fine or composition. If for any reason a man incurred the royal displeasure, he was amerced or fined and had to pay dearly to get back into the royal grace. These payments were of all kinds. The Pipe Rolls list money, gilt spurs, land, horses, hounds, hawks, falcons, chickens, grain, herrings, lampreys, pepper, and cumin. Special fines (agreements) were made with the king to arrange an advantageous marriage or guardianship.[11] After Stephen's reign many charters came to be inspected and confirmed by the king to forestall forgery. Whenever the king or chancellor examined a charter, a fee was charged. It was customary for the chief ministers to buy their offices. Geoffrey, the chancellor of Henry I, paid £3006 13s. 4*d*. for this profitable office. We may rest assured that his investment soon brought Geoffrey a handsome profit from the fees charged when sealing documents and from the other perquisites attached to the office. Sheriffs also bought their offices and offered huge bribes to obtain the royal privilege or favor. Special incomes came from the Jews, who paid heavily for the royal protection. They were tallaged at will and, periodically it seemed, the kings confiscated most of their possessions. Whenever one of their community was charged with a

[10] SM, no. 18.
[11] SM, no. 25.

misdemeanor or with murder committed against a gentile, the whole community would be assessed a staggering fine. In 1130 the Jews of London paid a fine of £2000 because of the accusation that one of them had slain an infirm man.[12]

The largest part of the Norman royal income came from the county farms, which represented the totals of profits, rents, and rights derived from the royal domain, that is, the lands held directly by the king in each county. The sheriff was responsible for the management of the royal estates and for guarding the rights. Twice a year, as we have seen, he rendered account of the county farm (*firma comitatus*) at the exchequer. The custom of the sheriff's paying in a lump sum for all the profits and rights connected with royal land existed before 1066 but only became regularized throughout all the shires under the Normans. For example, the infamous Geoffrey de Mandeville, who held a plurality of counties under Stephen, rendered account of £300 for London and Middlesex, £300 for Essex, and £60 for Hertfordshire. Much of the estate administration was left to subordinates or was farmed out to men who paid for the privilege. Included in the farm were profits from hundred courts when they were annexed to a royal manor plus the royal rights and revenues coming from boroughs located on royal land. These revenues included aids levied on boroughs as well as profits from justice and indirect taxation. By the reign of Henry I, however, some of the more prominent boroughs had paid lump sums to the king in order that they might collect their own taxes and render account directly to the exchequer. In 1130 the burgesses of Lincoln paid Henry 200 marks of silver and 4 of gold so that they could pay the farm of the borough (*firma burgi*) directly to him and thus by-pass the sheriff. The ordinary pleas heard in the county courts were yet included in the farm of the county.

It should be noted that there were miscellaneous incomes derived from the pleas of the crown, forfeitures, and all sorts of scattered rights, which the sheriffs collected and rendered to the exchequer; on the Pipe Rolls they were listed apart from the farm. When one totals up all the incomes listed in the Pipe Roll of 1130 due to the king they come to roughly £66,000.[13] No financial system of western Europe could boast as large a sum. The anarchy that followed Henry I's death caused a general decline in the efficiency of the central administration. Neither Stephen nor Matilda proved capable of the strong direction exerted by their predecessors, and when Roger of Salisbury and his relatives were removed from office, the nerve center of the efficient structure of Henry I was destroyed. Despite this retrogression, some of the administrative machinery continued to function; in those counties not touched by war, the sheriffs collected the royal income and rendered ac-

[12] SM, no. 25.
[13] SM, no. 25.

count for it. The speed with which Henry II rehabilitated the financial structure indicates how well the Norman kings had constructed it. Norman initiative and imagination had developed a financial system organized around an exchequer that put its hands firmly upon every income that came to the king by virtue of his prerogative and in his role as feudal overlord of England and greatest landholder. The efficient functioning of this system depended, however, upon a strong king; strong indeed were the first three Normans.

XII

Local Administration: Counties, Hundreds, Manors, and Boroughs

THE efficiently organized central administration of the Normans is proof of their genius as organizers, but this endowment is even more apparent in the strong local institutions that continued their existence after the Conquest. The greatest contribution of the Normans was in the close surveillance established by the central administration upon local organs of government. Experienced in the art of forcing their will on local turbulent elements in their duchy, the Norman rulers were prepared for the task of reducing their new realm into a pattern of orderly local government closely controlled from the top.

1. THE COUNTY AND SHERIFF

The largest and most important division of local government was the shire, which the Normans retained but called a *comitatus* or county because comparable areas in Normandy (*vicomtés* administered by *vicomtes*) had gone under this name. Within the thirty-odd counties of Norman England were the smaller divisions of hundred, manor, and borough. The administrators of the counties were the sheriffs, who like the viscounts were delegated royal powers. The Conquest had destroyed all vestiges of the political power of the Saxon earls, who by 1076 were no more. There were some Norman earls but they were not comparable to their predecessors; most bore the title by virtue of their feudal status as counts in Normandy. Vast public powers were wielded by only a few, such as the earls placed over palatinates along the Welsh and Scottish borders which served as buffer military lands comparable to the frontier marches of the old Carolingian Empire. Along the Welsh frontier were the palatine earldoms of Herefordshire, Shropshire, and Cheshire. To the north was the County Palatine of Durham, controlled by the bishops. These areas were granted to close relatives of the Conqueror or to great Norman barons who, within their jurisdiction, had all the regalian rights of a king and governed like one. This power was their reward for the defense they provided against the Welsh and Scots. Here the sheriff had no authority; the earls were accountable only to the king from whom they held their earldoms in fief. Except for Durham, however, the earldoms did not long exist. By the early twelfth century all the earls had forfeited their lands because of feudal revolt and henceforth sheriffs administered the regions as counties. Thus the sheriff continued, as he had since the late tenth century, to be the key officer of the county.

The Anglo-Saxon sheriff, it will be remembered, was generally a prominent landholder in the shire that he headed but the office was not heritable and the kings could appoint and dismiss sheriffs at will. The Anglo-Saxon shrievalty was not a feudal office as was that of the Norman viscount. Under the Normans the office remained nonfeudal although there was danger that it might lose this quality. Within five years of the Conquest all sheriffs were Norman and were customarily prominent barons holding the most land in the county. With such power they easily retained control over the English and restrained the Norman nobles from revolt. The Conqueror appointed men close to him, men whom he believed he could implicitly trust. At no period in English history was the sheriff as powerful as under William I and William II. Such power, however, could and did become dangerous for the royal authority when sheriffs remained in office for an extended period and when they passed their office down to their eldest son. This practice smacked of feudalism, reminding one of those feudal offices on the Continent that the French lawyer has termed *fiefs de l'office*. By 1100 most shrievalties had become hereditary. In six counties son succeeded father. In Gloucestershire six members of a family held the office in succession. In Worcestershire and Devonshire an even longer descent in one family can be traced. Conflict with royal authority occurred when these powerful sheriffs ceased using their influence to govern for the king and instead led feudal revolts against him, just as the *châtelains* and *prévôts* did weekly in feudal states such as the Île de France, Burgundy, and Anjou. Some revolt broke out against the Conqueror and it increased under his son. At this point we can discern an attempt by the king to strip such men of their power.

Under William Rufus a new class of men began to receive shrievalties. They were men drawn from simple knights at the bottom of the feudal hierarchy or men who had served in the royal household in a clerical or financial capacity and could be trusted by the king because they owed all to the royal favor. Such a group of curial men and knights looms large by Henry I's reign, a group of new men whom the chronicler Ordericus Vitalis refers to as having been raised out of the dust. A new civil servant was thus resorted to in order to escape the drift towards feudal offices and the anarchy they produced. Before 1100 at least two sheriffs were appointed who were completely landless and owed all to the king. One of these was Hugh of Buckland, who was sent out from the royal court; under Rufus he headed three counties and in 1110, eight. At the same time five other such men administered nine other counties. In 1130 two men who had served in the court, Aubrey de Vere and Richard Basset, together controlled eleven counties. Such centralization was not permanent, however, because if continued it could have led to the large Anglo-Saxon earldoms that flourished under the

Confessor. It seems to have been an expedient resorted to by William II and Henry I while they rid themselves of the old sheriffs and cast about for loyal successors. Soon most counties were headed by a sheriff who almost invariably came from the court, the local civil service, or the knightly rank. Such men loyally upheld their royal benefactors and in the case of curial officials were transplanting the influence of the central institutions to local government. Often these men continued to advise the king and so helped to establish a stronger bridgehead between him and the small political communities.

Unfortunately the feudal anarchy that followed with Stephen and Matilda undid this reform. In the pattern of feudal administration on the Continent, some of the sheriffs became more powerful than Stephen and Matilda; the shrievalty temporarily became a heritable fief held by powerful barons whose military support was thus rewarded. Such was Geoffrey de Mandeville, whose bloody career has been reconstructed for us by John Horace Round. At one time he controlled the shrievalties of London, Middlesex, Essex, and Hertfordshire, holding them as heritable fiefs. He, of course, guarded all the castles such as the Tower of London. He frequently changed sides, serving the one who bribed him the most richly. Not until Henry II was the power of the sheriff curtailed and the office filled with new men whose first interest was in serving the king.

Meanwhile William Rufus and Henry I devised other controls over the sheriff. For a while the sheriffs had been the only local representatives of royal justice but under Rufus we find in some counties resident justices who were empowered to hold the king's pleas. Such justices can be traced back to the ministry of Ranulf Flambard. Resident justices also arose in Normandy at this time. The *Laws of Henry I* refers to a resident justice and in 1102 a document informs us that a justice in Suffolk and Norfolk presided with the sheriff over a royal plea.[1] Undoubtedly such men also had administrative duties and were well located for checking against maladministration of the sheriff. We continue to meet these justices in the early years of Stephen's reign and then they were supplanted by the itinerant justices, who provided more efficient control. Just how did these justices impinge upon the sheriff? Already under the Conqueror powerful barons who were close to the king as advisers and who were most prominent in the *curia regis* would be occasionally commissioned to hear a case or a group of cases at the county court.[2] We have evidence of such judicial commissions sitting at Edmundsbury in 1076 and 1079. These judicial delegations continued under Rufus and were supplemented by itinerant justices who, in lieu of the sheriffs, were empowered to hear the crown pleas, that is, those cases reserved for the royal justice. In 1096 a judicial commission had a circuit including Devon and Cornwall for the purpose of holding royal pleas (*ad investiganda regalia*

[1] SM, no. 26.
[2] SM, nos. 19, 20.

placita). With Henry I well-defined judicial circuits were established and for each, itinerant justices presided over those cases listed under royal pleas; the sheriff's only function was to produce the proper people and preserve order at the county court. We may be sure that both Ranulf Flambard and Roger of Salisbury used itinerant justices to carve down the judicial power of the sheriff. These justices communicated royal commands to the counties and through careful observation during their travels could report back to the king how well the sheriffs were executing their duties and the trend of local opinion. In addition to their fiscal and administrative duties, evidence of which comes from the Angevin period, there is no reason to doubt that the justices were securing all sorts of information from local men summoned to the county court. Armed with this information the kings could better check the activities of their sheriffs. The itinerant justices proved to be the best check of shrieval power as well as a bridge between king and local government. Selected from prelates and barons who were prominent in household or court the itinerant justices were emanations of the royal court and its authority. They connected the king to all parts of his realm.

The last restraint put upon the sheriffs was the exchequer with its system of financial account. Once the exchequer knew the exact amount of the yearly farm plus the other profits of justice and revenues that accrued annually, it became difficult for the sheriff to pocket any for himself. Both taxpayer and king thus benefited from the scrupulous accounting held at Michaelmas and Easter. The sheriffs now had to make up any difference from their own income and were fined for financial misfeasance. The judicial, administrative, and financial controls placed over the sheriff were only in their formative stage but they saved England from falling under the authority of unscrupulous feudal officers who flouted princely authority as they extorted contributions from the local populace.

The functions of the sheriff were those of his Saxon predecessors plus many others added by the Normans. As the permanent judicial representative of the king he presided over the county court and there held the royal pleas until relieved of them by the itinerant justices; he continued, however, to preside over the nonroyal pleas. He also presided over the hundred courts or was represented by a subordinate. At these courts he was responsible for securing the attendance of those who were members and those who were summoned for judicial or other business.[3] He had the task of empaneling juries of local men to supply information for the king or to ascertain judicial facts. He had to enforce the decisions of the royal courts. In effect, the sheriff was a type of police officer; he had to maintain order, proclaim the king's peace, help in the hue and cry, and make arrests. As the chief military officer he was commander of the county levy or the *fyrd* (*arrière-ban*). He provided guards to protect royal possessions or the king himself while in the county. He had to round up beasts of burden to provide transportation

[3] SM, no. 26.

for the king. Sometimes the sheriff was custodian of the royal castle, had to look to its repair, and had to insure its defense by exacting the feudal service of castle-guard or by hiring mercenary men-at-arms and crossbowmen. In an administrative capacity he carried out the orders of royal writs as, for example, protecting certain persons and their lands, confiscating lands, acting as guardian, and placing persons in possession of royal land, incomes, or privileges granted to them. As a financial officer he supervised the management of all royal land so that it netted the highest revenue possible. He collected the farm of the county, a set annual income derived from the royal estates and profits from county and hundred court. In addition, he collected profits from the special pleas of the crown, a murder fine paid by hundreds, the Danegeld, and sums owed by individuals and communities, running from amercements to the farm of a borough. When boroughs collected and paid their own taxes, the sheriff lost this duty. Many of these revenues never saw the exchequer because they were disbursed on the spot on behalf of the king as a result of permanent or special order. Yearly the sheriff paid fixed sums such as alms and charities and salaries to royal officials. Under special order there was no end to the various disbursements. The sheriff also had to provide hospitality, maintenance, and transportation for royal messengers, officers, and very important personages. What remained after these expenses went to the exchequer.[4]

As long as the sheriff fulfilled these obligations to the royal satisfaction there was little royal interference. It was only when the royal revenue was short or when the sheriff committed extortions against royal lands and rights that he was fined, punished, or dismissed. We must remember that the king appointed loyal sheriffs and controlled them by exchequer and itinerant justices merely to protect his own interests; a sheriff faithful to the king could indulge in all sorts of maladministration that bled the county populace. Though richly rewarded with lands for their services, the sheriffs derived their largest income from what they extorted from the people over and above the farm and other payments. This was a perquisite of the office and was taken for granted; it is why so many men were willing to pay dearly for the office. Against the greed and exactions of the sheriffs there was little recourse. These crude and rough lieutenants only mirrored the sternness of the Norman rulers, whose first interest was power and wealth. Not unless the sheriffs joined in feudal revolt, misused royal property, or misappropriated royal revenue did the ax fall. The populace outside the clergy and feudal aristocracy was still considered a type of possession like land or cattle to be exploited; and this the sheriffs did in sundry ways. In 1130, for example, the Pipe Rolls record that Restold, sheriff of Oxfordshire, owed the exchequer £116, which he extorted from villeins and burgesses living on crown land. He was to be punished not for the extortion but because he had been caught extorting and had not turned the ill-gotten money over to the king.

[4] SM, no. 25.

It is no wonder that such towns as London and Lincoln were willing to pay huge sums for the right to collect their taxes and render account directly to the exchequer.[5]

Despite the abuses inherent in the shrievalty, it was the most efficient system of local administration devised by a prince of western Europe; it contributed immeasurably to the strength and wealth of the Norman house and to the law and order that ordinarily prevailed in the realm. In Normandy the feudal *vicomte* under Henry I was an efficient local administrator, as was also his counterpart in Flanders—the *châtelain*. Their replacement, however, at the end of the twelfth century by nonfeudal bailiffs (*baillis*) modeled after the sheriff proves that salaried officers appointed and dismissed at will were more efficient and amenable to the prince's authority. But such an officer could not be used until a state's administrative system was highly organized and based in larger part upon a money economy.

2. THE HUNDRED

Under the Anglo-Saxons the hundred had developed into a key local organ of government administered by a subordinate of the sheriff—the hundred reeve. The Norman invigoration of the county and introduction of feudalism into England lessened the importance of the hundred. Much of its business was absorbed by the county court, and feudal lords were to secure jurisdiction over hundredal justice and thus incorporate the court into their judicial system. The *Laws of Henry I* asserts that some of the hundred courts did not have enough judgment finders to render decisions.[6] The paucity of evidence for the reigns of William I and William II suggests that many of the hundred courts had ceased functioning. Without doubt the absorption of hundreds into feudal franchises was the chief cause for this decline. Henry I, however, ordained that hundred courts should meet as in the time of Edward the Confessor and that the landed class should attend as in Saxon times.[7] We may conclude, therefore, that courts were again held monthly and that the main service was still preservation of the peace. Here criminal justice of minor import was adjudicated and here twice a year all men of the hundred assembled so that the peasants could be placed in tithing groups to help preserve the peace. At such occasions the sheriff seems to have presided. Petty civil cases also came before the hundred court, although most civil justice was handled by the county court.

The hundred retained fiscal importance because it was still the basic unit for the assessment of the Danegeld and failure to pay the geld resulted in a fine levied at the court. As a local unit of the county the hundred owed an annual farm, collected by the hundred reeve, who was an undersheriff performing functions delegated to him. It is difficult to distingush the hundred

[5] SM, no. 25.
[6] SM, no. 26.
[7] SM, no. 24.

reeves from other reeves whose chief function seems to have been tax collecting. Both were indiscriminately called *ministri regis* or *ministri vicecomitis*. Evidence from Devonshire shows the hundred reeve collecting the farm and, despite the little evidence pointing to other functions, we may assume that he presided over the ordinary hundred court and performed minor administrative tasks.

3. THE MANOR

Except for a few boroughs Anglo-Saxon England had been composed of agrarian communities termed manors (*maneria*). The Norman Conquest did not change this economic pattern, only strengthened it. Under feudalism classes were sharply differentiated and came to be more clearly defined. During the Norman period the great mass of the population (c. 1,500,000) were peasants living on manors possessed by the king, the feudal aristocracy, and the church; only a small part of the population were burgesses living in boroughs. The manor was not a political but an economic unit for the exploitation of the land and consisted of a community composed of the lord of the manor and a group of peasants cooperating in the cultivation of the land. A manor could comprise a small fief but generally a fief consisted of a number of manors concentrated in one hundred, in several hundreds, or in various counties. The great fiefs could comprise a number of hundreds, a fact that explains why the hundred's importance decreased.

There is still sharp debate over the status of the peasants—how many were free and what they could do with their freedom. Most scholars agree that the Conquest ended slavery but downgraded the freedom of the ordinary inhabitant of the countryside. One school of historians, however, argues that a substantial number of peasants retained a considerable degree of freedom and mobility. Admittedly many, according to custom, were defined as legally free but how much could such freedom mean in the face of restrictions imposed by an economy fundamentally one of nature? Economic necessity dictated that few peasants could ever use their legal freedom; most were bound to the soil and seldom had access to a free court for their own legal difficulties. When mentioned in the manorial records, the peasant appears predominantly as a simple cultivator of the soil governed by a strict economic routine. But this subject, however fundamental, is subsidiary to our main concern—the place of the manor in local administration.

The feudal lords of the manors had jurisdiction over a variety of courts. All lords, from the greatest to the pettiest without vassals, held manorial courts for their economic dependents, the peasants. The lord's reeve generally presided over a court which declared the manor's custom. Such jurisdiction was considered valuable because of the profits of justice; few were the peasants who could obtain their day in a public court. In the manorial court, held fortnightly and commonly called the halimote, were tried petty disputes between peasants and offenses such as trespass on manorial woods, meadow, and pasture, or failure to perform ban and week services. The court consisted of peasants, who declared the law and, under the supervision of the reeve, enforced the decisions. From manor to manor the custom varied, although there was a tendency for manorial custom of the large fiefs to become standardized. According to feudal law all lords who had vassals had the right and obligation to hold a feudal court that declared feudal custom. Such a court was based upon the principle that vassals could have their complaints or disputes settled by their feudal peers, the lord's vassals in his court. This was the famous feudal custom of judgment by peers. These courts were limited to the feudal aristocracy and adjudicated cases involving feudal land tenure and services owed to the lord. Henry I's ordinance on the courts stipulated that differences between vassals of the king should be settled in the *curia regis*, those between vassals of a baron should be tried in his feudal court, and those between vassals of different lords should be adjudicated in the county court.[8]

Feudal justice obviously took business away from the public courts, business they would have handled in the Anglo-Saxon period. But the most serious inroads were made by franchisal justice, which was the exercise of public justice. We have seen that in the Anglo-Saxon period almost every lord came to receive a portion of public justice and that the great lords obtained the exercise of a justice almost as high as the king's. It has even been argued that some Saxon lords controlled hundredal justice. Such rights or franchises were granted by royal charter. The Conquest merely quickened the transfer of public justice into private hands. Although on the Continent feudal lords generally usurped the rights of public justice, the Norman dukes had permitted little of this, being strong enough to grant such franchises only to those whom they wished to reward. In England, however, the Norman kings were much more prone to transfer certain categories of their justice to the royal vassals. More lords were now granted control of hundreds and with such power generally went the jurisdictional rights of sac and soc, toll and team, and infangenetheof. Some royal charters released tenants of ecclesiastical lords from attending county and hundred courts. None of these rights so conferred seem to have applied to criminal jurisdiction with the exception of infangenetheof, which empowered the lord to hang a thief caught stealing on his lands.

Some lords had acquired the right of holding courts in order to place all men of the hundred in tithing groups. This view of frankpledge, as it was called, was not, however, granted by royal charter but seems to have arisen by virtue of prescriptive right. At first some lords held the view of frankpledge and, when the kings did not interfere, such a right eventually came to be considered as strong as those conferred by royal grant. In 1290 Edward

[8] SM, no. 24.

I admitted this right if the lord could show that his predecessors had taken the view of frankpledge as far back as Richard I's coronation in 1189. A common right of lords was the enforcement of the assize of ale, a law to insure that the ale was of good quality and sold at a fair price. For violating this law an elaborate system of fines was devised. *Domesday Book* tells us that at Chester in 1086 the penalty for brewing bad ale was the cucking-stool. All these judicial rights were jealously guarded by lords because they were a good source of profit. One reason Earl Roger revolted in 1075 was that the sheriff tried cases on his lands which should have been in Roger's jurisdiction. This incident proves that with powerful sheriffs guarding the royal rights there was not much opportunity for private lords to usurp royal justice. The sheriffs derived enough profit from justice so that their interests dovetailed with those of the king.

Administratively the relation of manor to hundred was complicated. If each hundred had been composed of nicely defined manorial units, the administrative chain of command would have been simple. Only occasionally, however, were manor and agrarian village community coincident. Most communities were split up among lords who held lands and rights splintered into numerous villages and hundreds. One village could have several or half a dozen lords. Thus public obligations in the hundred were imposed customarily upon the agrarian village rather than upon the manor. It was the reeve, priest, and four good men of the village who had to attend hundred and shire court for legal and administrative purposes. The Norman inquest system, about which we will have more to say later, secured all sorts of information from village juries. When the great inquest of 1086 was made, the king's officers derived much of their information from village juries consisting of the priest, reeve, and six villeins.[9] When the hue and cry was raised it was the responsibility of all the village to apprehend the criminal and keep him in custody; for failure in this and for all sorts of infractions, the village was fined. For concealment of crime, for hunting in the royal forest or catching the royal fish, for damaging royal property, and for receiving men not in tithing, stiff fines were levied on all inhabitants; never was it a matter of individual liability. It was the same with financial assessments; the village as a whole was assessed and then the impost was apportioned. The communal activity of the village should not be overemphasized but certain judicial, financial, and administrative obligations were imposed upon the village by lord or group of lords and the inhabitants collectively had to perform these public duties. The agrarian village was fundamentally an economic grouping exploited by the lords who controlled it. Rarely was it a legal unit, and never should it be viewed as a political division of the hundred. It was but an economic concentration of land, men, and rights upon which king, royal official, and lord imposed obligations and taxes.

[9] SM, no. 21.

4. THE BOROUGH

Briefly, the early Anglo-Saxon borough may be said to have been scarcely differentiated from the countryside or from the administrative organization of the hundred. Most boroughs had developed into prominent military and administrative centers of hundred and shire, but beyond the soldiers and royal officials few of the inhabitants could be separated by occupation from those tillers of the soil living on manors. The prominent residents of boroughs, such as the thegns, were primarily landholders. For purposes of administration and taxation the borough was a part of the territorial system of county and hundred. Borough courts were almost exclusively a part of the public court system. No burgesses enjoyed a special status except some living in a few boroughs that had received royal favors. Only at ports and other strategically located boroughs did there exist before 1066 the burgess privileges and the borough organization that characterized urban areas by the end of Henry I's reign.

England like western Europe had been affected by the revival of trade and commerce in the eleventh century. Certain well-situated boroughs, like the Cinque Ports on the Channel or London, Rochester, Bristol, Lincoln, and York, had developed as trading centers with burgesses dealing in mercantile occupations. These burgesses because of their different life with its quickened pace, mobility, and necessary economic freedom had acquired from the Saxon kings or by prescriptive usage certain elementary bourgeois privileges, but in the form only of economic and legal rights. With the Conquest, however, these privileges were acquired by the great mass of boroughs, new boroughs were founded, and boroughs that had obtained the elementary privileges forged ahead to win the political privileges we associate with urban self-government.

Long familiar with urban developments on the Continent, which were advanced over those of England, the Norman lords applied some of these lessons to their new possessions. Many of them founded new towns (*villes neuves*) with elementary bourgeois privileges patterned after Norman towns; this was especially true in the west and north country. The Norman lords along the Welsh border modeled their new boroughs after the little Norman town of Breteuil. On the evidence of *Domesday Book*, Earl Hugh of Chester, who founded the town of Rhuddlan around a new castle that he had constructed after 1066, granted the privileges of Breteuil to the men who lived in the area next to the castle.[10] Our information on the boroughs of Cardiff and Tewkesbury founded by the earls of Gloucester is quite complete. All inhabitants enjoyed burgage tenure, that is, the right of paying a fixed annual rent for the land and tenements held from the earls. With certain restrictions each burgess was free to alienate his land and house. Freedom of sale and devise extended to movable

[10] SM, no. 22.

property. No burgess was liable for heriot or relief; each was free to marry. Burgesses could be tried only in the borough. Tolls were limited in amount and none of the ordinary manorial restrictions held in the borough. Such privileges are typical of the whole west country.

To the north similar foundations were made, the most notable being that of Newcastle-upon-Tyne by Henry I.[11] In the charter of foundation are all the standard elementary privileges, many inspired by the charter Henry had granted previously to the Norman town of Verneuil. Here the burgess had freedom of mobility, freedom of alienation, and burgage tenure. Burgess privileges were heritable by son. Any peasant living for a year and a day in Newcastle undetected by his lord automatically became free. No manorial restrictions or customs existed in the town. Except for pleas of the crown all cases involving burgesses were tried at the borough court. Compurgation was the method of trial except when a merchant was accused of treason; he then had to undergo trial by combat. No military service could be required except for urban defense. There was a limitation of forfeiture and men not of Newcastle could be distrained in and out of town without official authority. Burgesses of Newcastle had a monopoly on the sale and purchase of goods. Official tolls were established and all merchandise brought by ship had to be sold on land with the exception of salt and herring. These customs of Newcastle became the model for dozens of other boroughs founded in northern England and Scotland.

Meanwhile the larger and older established boroughs such as London, York, Lincoln, Norwich, Northampton, and Winchester were informally acquiring the same privileges. When we read of them it is of established customs which Henry I or Henry II are confirming. Thus whether by charter or by informal acquisition, boroughs in the Norman period were all attaining the legal and economic rights necessary for their rapidly increasing population of free bourgeois. Such a step was, however, only the first on a long path towards greater freedom and privileges. It is to be noted that none of these boroughs had obtained political authority; all were still administered by the sheriff or his lieutenant, the portreeve, who wielded judicial, financial, military, and administrative powers. The next step in the Norman period was for the larger boroughs to become self-governing communes.

Just what influence proved decisive in the evolution from elementary legal and economic to advanced political liberties is debatable. Undoubtedly the great communes of Flanders and northeastern France must have exerted some influence on the English boroughs. The brisk commercial intercourse made it easy for the English burgess to observe the advantages of urban self-government. Such communes as Saint Omer, Bruges, Ghent, Cambrai, and Beauvais may well have served as models. But the continental influence ought not to be overemphasized inasmuch as communes and towns with elementary liberties sprang up simultaneously throughout western Europe

[11] SM, no. 28D.

with no demonstrable influence exerted by one on another in numerous cases. Towns and then communes developed in response to the European phenomena of the revival of trade, the return to a money economy, and the increasing legal, economic, and political requirements of the bourgeoisie. One thing is certain: by the early twelfth century the burgesses of the large boroughs were securing a training for political responsibility as they engaged in collective mercantile pursuits, gained confidence in their newly won freedom, and organized associations for the benefit of their economic and social welfare. Though there had existed in Saxon England certain social and religious guilds or associations and though peace (*frith*) guilds had sprung up at some boroughs such as London, Gross definitely established that these guilds were not the economic merchant guilds that one finds after the Conquest. The merchant guilds can be found under the Conqueror; they may have been inspired by continental merchant guilds, which were considerably older. By the early twelfth century the merchant guilds of Oxford, Beverley, York, Leicester, Winchester, and Lincoln were well entrenched and wielded a heavy influence upon borough affairs. These guilds were organized by the most prominent merchants of a borough to regulate local trade; the ultimate goal was complete local monopoly of trade. They constructed guild houses where they held meetings to elect officers and to conduct business. As with all such organizations the social needs of the members were fulfilled by banquets and convivial sessions. Most of the guilds also provided for the care of ill members, guarded widows and minors left behind by a dead member, and, when necessary, provided decent burial for unfortunate members. All such activites developed the communal and political consciousness of the members. While still under the political control of the king these guilds with their merchants, inevitably the leading citizens, took a major part in the direction of the social, economic, and political life of the borough.

There is a striking analogy between the organization of the merchant guild and the borough governments that developed in the twelfth century. Both had their aldermen and leaders or mayors. Though such places as London and Norwich had no merchant guilds in this period, it seems certain that the merchant guild must have been a key institution in the evolution towards self-government. Already controlling the economic life of the borough, the guild members were the logical men to work for political rights; it is they who negotiated with the king. We have seen that burgesses were exempt from pleading outside their borough. They were freed from attendance at shire and hundred courts and were authorized to establish courts of their own to adjudicate legal disputes. Here minor civil and criminal justice was dispensed At the borough courts the law that governed them was different from the customs of hundred, shire, manorial, and feudal court. Here evolved a custom eminently suited to the new economic and legal requirements of the middle class. Developing out of commercial give-and-take, trial and error, and practical and rational business necessity, this new law, law merchant as it was called, gave the burgess swift and efficient justice and spared him the indignities of the anachronistic custom found in other courts. Though these courts were presided over by the portreeve, the suitors who declared the law and handed down decisions were invariably the leading citizens of the borough—members of the guild merchant. As Stephenson has pointed out, "the gild merchant and the burgess community were practically identified in many localities." We may conclude that it was the guild merchant which came to direct urban affairs and represent the community in its relations with the king and his officers. An instrument of communal activity when the boroughs were ruled by royal officials, the guild took the lead in the fight for political freedom.

Like the counties, boroughs on the royal domain owed the king an annual farm called the *firma burgi* consisting of land rents, dues and tolls, profits from mills and mints, and sundry other revenues. This farm was collected and rendered by the sheriff or the portreeve. Because of the extortion involved, the leading boroughs were willing to pay the king a sizable sum to escape the financial supervision of the sheriff and his functionaries; to bypass these unscrupulous middlemen was worth any price. When boroughs secured the right to collect the farm and render it to the exchequer or to the sheriff, who merely carried it to Westminster, they were described as rendering the *firma burgi*. Probably in 1130 London received a charter from Henry I permitting its citizens to farm the town of London and county of Middlesex for £300 annually.[12] In the same year the Pipe Roll records payment of 200 marks of silver and 4 of gold by the burgesses of Lincoln to hold the borough directly from the king and render a yearly farm of £140; they continued to do this under Stephen.[13] *Domesday Book* proves that similar bargains were struck with lesser places such as the Cinque Ports. Such a privilege was a definite advance towards self-government. The borough privilege *firma burgi*, however, does not seem to have bestowed the status of self-government despite the affirmative argument of Tait. Such an arrangement meant that the burgesses promised to collect and pay a fixed annual sum to cover the farm, but the sheriff or portreeve still received it. All urban revenues outside the farm were still the sheriff's responsibility; his subordinate presided over the borough court and fulfilled all the other administrative tasks connected with the community.

True urban self-government was not attained until a borough had its own elected town council and officials who assumed all the duties of the sheriff and dealt directly with the king. The only town that seems to have achieved this political independence in the Norman period was London. Possessing but elementary privileges and governed by the sheriff, London continued under this system until 1130 when Henry I granted it a charter of communal liberties. This was the charter that granted London the privilege of rendering its own farm. Henceforth the sheriff was to be elected by the burgesses; thus

[12] SM, no. 28B.
[13] SM, no. 25.

London was the first to have an elected magistracy—the essential privilege for self-government. We may also infer that from about this period the town council of aldermen was elected. The charter also provided for exemption from arbitrary taxation; for trials restricted to London, even royal pleas, which were to be presided over by an elected justice; for exemption from trial by battle and guarantee of compurgation; and for the holding of a weekly municipal court governed by law merchant.[14] London remained self-governing until Henry II destroyed these privileges to punish London for its support of Stephen. Not until 1191 did London again acquire the status of commune.

The Norman period, therefore, saw the creation of scores of boroughs and the evolution of all towards elementary bourgeois privileges. The greatest boroughs attained some political rights such as rendering their annual farm. Only London attained the status of an independent self-governing borough dealing directly with the crown. But no matter the degree of political independence attained, the borough had escaped from the territorial administration of the hundred and county. Its inhabitants had separated themselves from the peasantry and the feudal aristocracy and had initiated the movement that would make the third estate one of the two most powerful economic and political groups in England.

[14] SM, no. 28B.

XIII

Anglo-Norman Law

I. THE COALESCENCE OF ANGLO-NORMAN LAW

THE strength, resiliency, and capacity for growth imparted to English institutions by the Conquest was no less marked in the realm of law. Maitland has called the Conquest a catastrophe that determined the future history of the law. For a number of reasons, however, the legal changes caused by the new rule developed slowly and did not manifest themselves until a considerable time after 1066. Our knowledge of Norman law between 911 and the Conquest is remarkably obscure. This 150-year period occurred just after the fall of the Carolingian Empire when its institutions had collapsed and its capitularies had ceased to be enacted. What law the Normans had was borrowed from the Frankish custom they found in Normandy and neighboring feudal states; it was characteristically feudal. This law was not recorded and we know of it only from meager scraps of evidence such as stray charters and a short statement of ducal rights. Not until that late twelfth-century legal compilation, the *Très ancien coutumier*, do we have a description of Norman custom.

The written law of the Norman duchy was crude when compared to the magnificent corpus of Anglo-Saxon dooms. Like the Anglo-Saxon legal procedure, the Norman was typically Germanic. In trial by battle, however, the Normans had a mode of proof that one never finds listed along with ordeal and compurgation in England. Perhaps Norman criminal law was more highly developed because we hear less of money compositions and more of punishment. This may be explained by the stern and brutal measures that the dukes had to employ to reduce anarchy in their duchy. The Norman ecclesiastical jurisprudence, early in touch with the civil and canon law revival of Italy, was clearly superior to the English and was successful in marking a distinction between the legal jurisdiction of church and state. Although all Norman peace was the duke's, the concept of ducal peace had originally been taken from the truce and peace of God, which came to the duchy from southern France; we never hear of the truce of God in Anglo-Saxon or Norman England. Besides having no written law to bring with them, the Normans also had no jurisprudence. Such a gap is not surprising in view of the but recent revival of Roman law in Italy and the neglect of professional study of law throughout western Europe. In Abbots Herlwin and Lanfranc of the monastery of Bec, however, the Normans possessed two men famous for their knowledge of law. Herlwin had gained a practical legal knowledge from the observation of trials and so profound a mastery of the law that he was constantly called upon to express his opinion on temporal cases. Lanfranc had acquired a mastery over Roman and canon law at Pavia before coming to Bec where he learned of Norman custom. When he went to England with the Conqueror he so soon mastered Anglo-Saxon law that he could discourse skillfully upon the most complicated points of law.

With but a few exceptions the Normans came to England lagging far behind English legal development. From the outset English law had the advantage because it was written. Naturally such an advantage did not result in the speedy absorption of Norman custom; in fact Norman custom did not early show any perceptible influence except in the skein of feudal relations that took hold of England. The Norman period is one of slow legal transition. By the reign of Henry II the legal language had completed this transition; Anglo-Saxon had gradually disappeared as the written language of the court and, under the influence of the prominent ecclesiastics who helped staff the central administration, had been supplanted by Latin. The Normans so controlled the government and dominated the courts that their French tongue came to be the language of pleading in the court.

For a time it looked as though England might know two laws—English and Norman—with the concept of the personality of the law prevailing. In this case the Norman would have had his law and the Englishman his. At first the Conqueror seems to have favored a dual legal system. The chronicler Ordericus Vitalis relates how in 1074 the Saxon earl Waltheof and Earl Roger of Hereford were tried by the *curia regis* for treason. Roger was tried under Norman law and was sentenced to forfeiture of his lands and perpetual imprisonment. Waltheof was tried by English law and was condemned to death. As had happened earlier on the Continent, however, the personality of the law rapidly succumbed before the territoriality of the law. It was too late for a dual system, as well as too impractical. Moreover, if William hoped to perpetuate the fiction that he ruled as the legal successor of the Confessor, he would, according to English law, have to favor this custom. Soon the distinctions that separated the two laws began to be blotted out; by Henry I's reign the process was almost completed.

To illustrate how the two laws meshed let us take the case of land law. Those Saxons who fought with Harold and who resisted the Normans were considered liable for punishment under the crime of revolting against a lawful lord; their land was forfeited and granted to Norman lords. As they appropriated the Saxon estates, the Normans retained what English law was useful to them and added to it the beneficial parts of Norman law. Taxes like the Danegeld were retained and other old Saxon judicial and financial prerogatives were exercised. With a large body of English custom remaining in force, the courts had need of English testimony, which only the natives could supply. Naturally the Normans and English mingled in court when pleas were entertained. About 1075 in the county court of Kent at Penenden Heath, Geoffrey, bishop of Coutances, representing the king, presided over a trial in which Lanfranc, archbishop of Canterbury, brought suit for the recovery of lands and rights claimed by Bishop Odo of Bayeux. In the course of the three-day trial Lanfranc recovered many manors and rights, and the ancient customs of Kent were defined. The man who clarified the old English land law was the Saxon Aethelric, bishop of Chichester, "a very aged man and one very learned in the laws of the land" (*vir antiquissimus et legum terrae sapientissimus*). By express command of the Conqueror he had been summoned to declare the law. To cite one more case we find that about 1077 Geoffrey presided over a royal court at which the Saxon men Eadric, steersman of the Confessor's ship; Kineward, former sheriff of Worcestershire; Siward of Shropshire; and Thurkill of Warwickshire declared that anciently the bishop of Worcester held sac and soc over certain lands; after their statements the abbot of Evesham no longer contested this right.

While such evidence proves the survival of English law after 1066, proof of its strength comes from those law books of the Norman period which explain English custom to the Normans. The value of these records has already been summarized in the chapter on the Norman sources; here we need only to comment on what these books say about the law. In general they describe a legal period in which a still strong English law collides with Norman feudal custom. This conflict and adjustment in the law was both the reason for the composition of these law books and the cause of their obscurity and ill-arranged content. No one was sure just what the law was but, as these books indicate, men wanted to describe the law with reasonable certainty. The complicated legal cobwebs created by the Conquest were not academic matters; they were of fundamental importance for the Norman lords. When a crime was committed or adjudication over land was necessary, there immediately arose the questions of who had the right of doing justice, who would enjoy the profits of justice, and how large would be the fines. Before such problems could be resolved there had to be considered in the case of a crime where it was committed, what kind of offense it was, what the status and tenurial relations of both offender and victims were, and numerous other points. Under Anglo-Saxon law these matters were quite precisely regulated; feudalism and its custom scattered much of the old to the winds. There were no certain answers to the jurisdictional and legal entanglements that cropped up on all sides. For some time the Norman lords settled the complications in their favor, interpreting law in their favor and usurping whatever rights they could. It was fortunate that England had the strong Norman kings who eventually were able to alleviate this legal chaos and rechart Anglo-Norman law on an orderly course.

In this uncertain transitional period we have seen that English law formed the great part of law after 1066. To this firm foundation, however, the Normans made some substantive and procedural contributions. Much of the change resulted simply from a new meaning and use given to old customs and institutions. Subsequent discussion of Norman legislation and administrative orders will explain how change occurred; for now, it is enough to say that original Norman importations consisted of feudalism with its law and strong tradition of private jurisdiction, the separation of spiritual and lay courts, trial by battle, the murder fine (*murdrum*), and the Frankish inquest. Feudalism we have discussed, and the other contributions except the inquest fall under the heading of legislation. Before describing the inquest it is well to remark that some scholars still argue for a possible English origin. They find it in the law of Ethelred the Redeless enacted at Wantage in 997. As we have previously seen, this doom was designed to curb lawlessness in the northern Danelaw. At regularly held wapentake courts the twelve leading thegns and the reeve were, upon oath, to indicate all men they suspected of wrongdoing. The accused men were then tried. Such an institution resembles a jury of accusation but there is no evidence that it was used outside northern England or that it long operated. The Conqueror definitely introduced the Frankish inquest system, which was to be the germ of the famous grand and petty juries.

The Frankish inquest (*inquisitio*) was derived from the royal prerogative. It did not come from the customary court procedure, from ordeal and compurgation, or from any of the Germanic law that covered northern Europe in the early Middle Ages. It developed from a royal initiative working outside the customary law that resulted in a more efficient justice in royal courts as well as in an administrative device that maintained and protected royal rights throughout the realm. It has now been established that the inquest was derived from the Roman emperors of the third and fourth centuries, who used their imperial authority to buttress their disintegrating powers and rights in the provinces. To insure that the imperial treasury (*fiscus*) received the revenues it was entitled to, as well as to curb the maladministration and usurpation of imperial authority by provincial officers, Diocletian periodically sent out from his court trusted officers to tour the provinces. Operating under imperial instructions these investigators (*agentes in rebus*) checked on the collection of taxes, remedied the abuse of power by local officers, listened to complaints, and asked the local populace for certain information desired by the emperor. Thus Diocletian and his successors established a liaison with local government and managed through these imperial itinerant "eyes and ears" to maintain a close supervision of provincial government. With the fall of the Empire in the West many of its institutions were preserved by the Germanic kings; among the prerogative rights adopted by the Frankish kings was this imperial inquest system, which operated on the principle that whatever information was needed to maintain a strong and efficient government must be given under oath to royal agents.

Our evidence is too meager to allow us to say much about the inquest under the Merovingians; we only know that occasionally curial agents called inquisitors (*inquisitores*) were sent out to secure information under oath and check on abuses of power. Under Charlemagne this institution was given new vigor with the enactment of the capitulary creating the *missi dominici* in 802. The Empire was divided into regions called *missatica* to which were sent a team of trusted imperial agents (*missi dominici*) consisting of a high ecclesiastic and a powerful lord, such as a count. Armed with precise instructions and much royal authority, they traveled through a region securing all sorts of information by asking specific questions from men sworn to tell what they knew. In addition they countered local abuse of power and presided over certain justice reserved to the emperor. An effective instrument for holding the Empire together and unifying custom and institutions, the inquest declined under Charlemagne's weak successors and almost disappeared in the second half of the ninth century. Again anarchy swept over western Europe and when from amidst the ruins we pick out the feudal states that took over the Carolingian Empire we can still see exercised some of the old prerogatives, among them the sworn inquest. But throughout France and Germany it was an anemic affair. The Normans adopted it from the Franks and evidence points to its use before and after 1066. It seems likely, however, that if the Conquest had not transplanted it to England it would have eventually disappeared from history; it did disappear on the Continent, submerged by the resurgence of Roman and canon law and their procedure.

As soon as England was conquered the sworn inquest loomed large in royal government and justice. It functioned along the same lines as in Normandy. In the duchy the viscounts and justices sent out from court were empowered to hold sworn inquests at local courts to obtain information for central administration and to settle judicial disputes over land. Some time between 1070 and 1079 Richard, viscount of Avranches, held a sworn inquest at Caen by order of the Conqueror. In 1133 Henry I had his officers put certain questions to men living on the lands of the bishop of Bayeux to ascertain how much knight service was owed. Later under Geoffrey Plantagenet justices were sent out from the ducal court on definite circuits to try certain causes. To settle the numerous disputes over the possession of land, men of the locality would be summoned before these justices and swear under oath who had the better right of possession. In England we have seen that *Domesday Book* was compiled as a result of the great inquest of 1086 when royal officers were sent out on seven circuits and, at the county courts, asked for the information demanded by the Conqueror from men sworn to tell all that they knew about the land, its appurtenances, and its value. From the verdicts of such juries eventually came the great survey. As an example of the inquest's judicial use, let us look at a case in 1082 which already bears a faint resemblance to jury trial for civil causes. The Conqueror directed three of his great barons and advisers, the bishop of Coutances, the count of Mortain, and Lanfranc, to summon the courts of several counties to hear a plea between the abbot of Ely and certain lords. Those English who knew what lands and rights were possessed by the abbey of Ely in the Confessor's day were to declare the facts under oath. This verdict of the jury (note that it was not a judgment) was the basis upon which the three justices decided what lands and rights the abbot of Ely still rightfully possessed.[1] Here the sworn inquest was used to determine one question—possession. There are other instances of such judicial use from the Norman period but the inquest used in lawsuits does not become common until Henry II's reign. Under the Norman kings the inquest was introduced and applied to problems of government and justice; it remained for the Angevins to develop it into the grand and petty juries. By its transplantation it had been saved. Its counterpart in Normandy, after that territory fell under French rule, was to disappear and be superseded by Roman legal procedure.

The Norman Conquest coincided with the renaissance of Roman law in Italy and the beginning of an attempt to compile and systematize into an intelligible form the vast corpus of canon law. At Pavia in the first half of the eleventh century there grew up a law school whose teachers and students knew the Institutes of Justinian. In the last quarter of the century the *Digest* again becomes known; in 1076 it was cited at a Tuscan court. By 1100 the renowned law school of Bologna was flourishing; Irnerius was numbered among its great teachers. Men from all over Europe flocked to Bologna and other Italian schools. It was at Pavia that Lanfranc had studied before going to Normandy. At Bologna between 1139 and 1142 Gratian composed his *Decretum*, a work that became the most authoritative text on canon law. By the time of King Stephen the principles of Roman and canon law were familiar to men scattered about western Europe; the Conquest linked England to this development. Gaining momentum slowly, the Roman and canon law began to show marked influence during Stephen's reign. Though certain legal books such as the *Laws of Henry I* and some chroniclers prior to the second quarter of the twelfth century quoted or referred to Roman and canon law maxims, such citations were but taken from stray quotations found in the ordinary stock of books read by an educated cleric around the beginning of the twelfth century. Lanfranc's contact with Roman and canon law was more direct. At Pavia he had studied some Roman, canon, and Lombard law and had become a renowned lawyer. After coming to Normandy he opened a school at Avranches; it seems certain that here and later at the abbey of Bec he taught some Roman and canon law. His letters show that as archbishop of Canterbury he often cited canons and decretals. In his capacity as chief adviser to the Conqueror, undoubtedly he slipped various Roman and canon law principles into the Norman law and government. His student

[1] SM, no. 20A and B.

Ivo of Chartres was steeped in Roman and canon law and was responsible for drawing up the agreement that settled the investiture struggle in 1106 between Henry I and Anselm.

Records of trials from William Rufus and Henry I show ecclesiastics familiar enough with the canon law to plead its privileges and bring books on canon law to the courts. More frequent became demands for trial by canonical court and appeal to the papal court. The decisive impetus to the study of Roman law, however, was provided by the Italian Vacarius, a skilled lawyer brought to England by Archbishop Theobald of Canterbury to help in his struggle with Stephen and his brother Henry, bishop of Winchester, who had secretly arranged to become papal legate. It was Vacarius who first taught Roman law in England. He taught in Theobald's household and then at Oxford where the first stir of the great university had only begun. His influence was so important that his patron's opponent, Stephen, attempted to muffle him. In 1149 he wrote the first textbook on Roman law produced on English soil. Drawing largely from the *Code* and *Digest* it became the standard text on Roman law, a book (*Liber Pauperum*) prepared for those poor students who could not afford the Roman texts. Meanwhile the study of Roman and canon law spread throughout the realm and at Oxford a strong school of law was established. By the time Henry II succeeded to the crown a large number of educated men knew their Roman and canon law and were available to help this juridically inclined king launch the remarkable legal reforms of his reign.

We have so far talked only of English and Norman custom that coalesced to form the Anglo-Norman law. Some legislation was required, however, for the introduction of Norman custom into England, for the preservation of English custom, for the enforcement of new legal principles and institutions, and for an increased emphasis upon some of the old institutions or a remodeling of them. Though legislation helped to accomplish all these things there exists remarkably little that one may term legislation from the Norman kings. Despite their extraordinary talents for strong government, the four Norman kings were not great legislators. The most significant law of the Conqueror was his ordinance separating ecclesiastical courts from secular courts. Bishops and archdeacons were ordered to absent themselves from the public courts and no cause or offense falling under ecclesiastical law was to be tried in a secular court.[2] The chronicler Eadmer relates that William still retained a firm grip over the English church by insisting that all church legislation enacted by the archbishop of Canterbury and council of bishops must secure his approval and that none of his barons or ministers could be excommunicated or accused by a bishop without his permission. Another ordinance early in William's reign established trial by combat as a mode of proof. When accused of theft or homicide by a Frenchman, an Englishman had a choice

[2] SM, no. 17.

between battle and ordeal. An Englishman, accusing a Frenchman, could demand battle. If the Englishman did not ask for battle the Frenchman could then clear himself with oath-helpers according to Norman law. Should poor health prevent either from accepting battle, then a champion could be used.[3] Such an ordinance tended to favor the Frenchman who had known battle, but basically the new procedure was surprisingly impartial.

The rest of William's legislation is contained in an unofficial compilation summarizing various decrees that have not been preserved for us. The following are the most important. The laws of the Confessor were confirmed. Hundred and county courts were to assemble as always. Capital punishment was abolished. All freemen were to be in frankpledge and to swear fealty to William. Special rules were provided for guaranteeing and securing sales. Men were not to be sold overseas. Special penalties were introduced for the murder of Normans who had come to England with the Conqueror. To protect his followers from assassination, William stated that when any Norman or stranger was secretly murdered and the murderer was not produced in court the whole hundred would be liable for payment of a murder fine (*murdrum*). If the slayer was not surrendered in seven days, an assessment of 46 marks was made on the hundred in which the crime occurred. Unless proved differently all men so slain were considered Norman.[4] The process of submitting proof that the victim was of English descent was called presentment of Englishry and remained a part of English law to 1340.

Under the Conqueror's successors there was even less legislation. In 1093 William Rufus, lying sick upon what he feared was to be his deathbed, hoped to atone for his manifold sins by granting a charter of liberties to his subjects. All that we know about the charter is that good laws were to be maintained, debts to the king were written off, and captives were freed. Immediately upon recovery Rufus ignored the charter. Henry I in his Coronation Charter made more specific concessions. He confirmed the laws of the Confessor as amended by his father. He abolished the feudal abuses of Rufus and promised to forego the heavy exactions made by his brother against the church.[5] Other evidence tells us that most of these promises were broken. Beyond this charter all that is extant is a writ of 1109–1111 ordering that hundred courts should be held as they were under the Confessor. This writ also defined more clearly the relations of feudal and public courts.[6] From various chroniclers we learn that Henry restored capital punishment, enacted harsh measures against counterfeiters, and established uniform measures and weights. For the reign of Stephen all that exists are his two charters of liberties. The first confirmed the good laws of Henry I; the second, more specific, redressed maladministration of sheriffs, buttressed established legal

[3] SM, no. 16.
[4] SM, no. 18.
[5] SM, no. 23.
[6] SM, no. 24.

procedure, and granted extensive rights to the church. One of these rights was that the church should be "free"; this vague promise contributed to the bad relations between church and state under Henry II.

The laws we have summarized above are all we have for a period of ninety years; obviously they comprise but a very small portion of Anglo-Norman law, which consisted essentially of English custom infused somewhat with Norman. Lack of legislation in an age that witnessed rapid progress in the administration of justice seems paradoxical until one understands that the Norman rulers did most of their governing through administrative instructions given orally or in writ to the royal officers and justices. By virtue of their royal prerogative these strong Normans constantly ordered the initiation of new institutions and procedures which eventually transformed the English legal system. The royal prerogative led to the formation of a royal justice so much more rational and expeditious than that meted out in the feudal and old public courts that it was eventually to sweep them out of existence. Only royal courts could employ the sworn inquest and only the power of a king could command the survey that produced *Domesday Book* or could initiate the administrative machinery that created the exchequer and its Pipe Rolls. By means of formal and informal administrative interference in justice, finance, war, and politics the Normans forged their efficient government.

2. THE COURTS AND THEIR JURISDICTION

So slight were the distinctions made in the Middle Ages between legislative, judicial, and executive functions, and so foreign was the concept of departmentalization with defined duties, that it is impossible to avoid some repetition when studying English medieval institutions. The clearest case of such nonspecialization was the *curia regis;* it possessed legislative, executive, and judicial powers. Here, according to feudal law, as we have noted, were tried all the vassals of the king who owed suit to court and had as their feudal right trial by their peers. The court could be small or large but it was the highest feudal tribunal of the land where the criminal and civil causes of the greatest men were tried. But the *curia regis* was more than a feudal court; it was as in the Anglo-Saxon period a court of last resort in cases of default of justice. If the justice at hundred or county court was not adequate, a man could appeal to the king's high court, which, in this capacity, acted as a nonfeudal court, as an ultimate public court. There were also occasions when upon default of justice in an inferior feudal court the case would be brought to the royal court. A distinguishing feature of the *curia regis* was its lack of rigid legal procedure. In a period of sharp conflict between the laws many cases could be settled only by drawing upon an assortment of law; a decision could be governed by a combination of English,

Norman, and feudal legal principles. Consequently the royal court had a jurisprudence that was flexible, expeditious, and reinforced upon occasion by Roman and canon law principles. The law of this court was, as Maitland so aptly described it, "equity rather than strict law." Initiated and rationalized by the royal prerogative this legal flexibility added a vast new jurisdiction to the royal court, a jurisdiction that by Henry II's time dwarfed the traditional legal scope of the *curia regis*.

Like their English predecessors, of whom they considered themselves the lawful successors, the Norman kings had wrapped up their prerogative authority with all sorts of vague powers that surpassed customary or feudal rights. The Normans, like the English kings, believed themselves empowered and obliged to take whatever action was necessary to preserve the peace, protect the weak, and maintain good justice. The exceptional strength and ability of the Normans let them exercise their prerogative much more actively; no part of the government escaped interference. We have seen that the English kings concerned themselves with certain criminal cases such as breach of the king's special peace, housebreaking, ambush, and neglect of military service. These cases are placed in a more serious category than ordinary crimes such as theft because they are considered injuries to the king or breaches against his prerogative right; they came to be called pleas of the crown. Such offenses belong solely to the king's justice and he enjoys all the profits. In the *Laws of Henry I*, which is the next evidence we have on these pleas, the number is greatly increased. Thirty-seven offenses are listed, including a considerable number of infractions of royal fiscal rights. We find breach of the king's peace, treason and breach of fealty, murder, counterfeiting, robbery, rape, breach of surety, default of justice, contempt of royal writs, Danegeld, treasure-trove, shipwreck, and neglect of military service.[7] In the growth of this list we may be certain that although the king's concern for law and order was a cause, another interest was need of money; to increase his income the king only needed to use his prerogative and throw his jurisdiction over another offense.

To complement the prerogative in expanding royal justice there was the traditional concept found early in Germanic custom that law is intimately connected with the peace and that whoever breaks the peace breaks the law and so becomes an outlaw. As we have noted, all freemen had a peace but the king had the greatest and in the course of time his peace was extended to snuff out other peaces. Under the Confessor the king's peace covered designated times, persons, and places; a crime committed against these peaces was a crime against the king. The peace of the Norman kings was rapidly expanded by means of the appeal (*appellum*), which was an accusation of crime made by the offended individual. The Norman justices began to permit the wronged person, called the appellor, not only to appeal the person

[7] SM, no. 26.

suspected of the crime but also to appeal him of breaking the king's peace. The accused person (appellee) was not permitted to deny breaking the king's peace although the offense he committed had in no way infracted the royal peace. By the creation of this fiction, practically any offense could be interpreted as breach of the king's peace and so brought before the royal court.

The last judicial concept that enforced royal justice was that of felony (*felonia*), a word that came from the Latin *fallere* ("to deceive"). The concept of felony, as brought to England by the Normans, referred to the feudal crime of betraying or committing treachery against one's lord. Such a crime was punishable by death and resulted in the forfeiture of all goods and lands to the lord. Any crime that did not break the feudal contract or faith, no matter how serious, was not a felony. When the *Laws of Henry I* was composed there was still this distinction; soon thereafter it began to blur and felony took on a broader meaning. One finds the appellor accusing the appellee not only of breaking the king's peace but of committing a felony. It shortly became necessary to include the word "felony" in the appeal or it was not admitted. Whether or not the appellee had committed a felony, he was not permitted to deny it. Again royal greed seems to be the best explanation for the expansion of the concept of felony. Any crime called a felony meant that if the appellee was found guilty his possessions escheated to the king. The more crimes called felonies, the greater the income, and so the list of felonies continued to grow throughout the twelfth century. The fortuitous yet conscious combination of the royal prerogative with the concepts of the king's peace and felony gave royal justice a flexibility that enabled the royal court to spread its jurisdiction over all sorts of places and men and over almost any type of offense. Alone, these fictions and powers might have failed; they succeeded because the king sold a better brand of justice than competing courts could offer.

In expanding his justice the king created a problem, that of expeditiously handling the cases that now crowded his court. A small *curia regis* was always about the king and continually dispensed justice. But there were inconveniences in having a single court. Because it had many functions and could not dispense justice daily, cases could pile up alarmingly. In that the royal court was itinerant, it was often difficult to get a case before it; in any event much travel, delay, and expense were involved. Such drawbacks caused the Norman kings to extend the exercise of royal justice beyond the court itself. We have referred to the Norman practice of delegating certain members of the court as royal justices to preside over causes held in local courts. Under the first two Norman kings the sheriffs acted as royal justices and dealt locally with pleas of the crown. When the sheriffs acted in this capacity the county courts over which they presided became royal courts. During the reign of William Rufus his minister Ranulf Flambard, in an attempt to exert closer supervision over royal financial rights and to augment the profits of justice, created royal resident justices who were empowered to try pleas of the crown. By Henry I's reign they were well established in England and Normandy. The *Laws of Henry I* states that the resident justices had the right to try theft, robbery, arson, and other such royal pleas. In his charter to London Henry I permitted the men of that borough to elect a justice who could hold pleas of the crown.[8] Resident justices declined during Stephen's reign and were supplanted by the more efficient itinerant justices.

Already under the Conqueror and Rufus there had been experimentation in the form of sending out from the court to a county or group of counties a judicial commission with powers to try all pleas of the crown. Again Ranulf Flambard seems to have been identified with this development because in 1095 and 1096 his name appeared on such judicial commissions. It is Roger of Salisbury, however, who must be credited with the real organization of itinerant justices assigned to judicial circuits. In 1116 a justice held royal pleas for Huntingdon. About the same time itinerant justices visited Devon and Cornwall. The Pipe Roll of 1130 shows that in 1129 and 1130 justices sent out from the court tried royal pleas in almost all the counties; among the pleas held were those of breach of the peace, treasure-trove, counterfeiting, and forest infractions. *The Anglo-Saxon Chronicle* was aghast at the number of criminals the justice Ralph Basset disposed of in 1124 while holding pleas in Leicestershire. He "hanged there more thieves than ever had been hanged before; that was in all forty-four men in that little time: and six men were blinded and castrated." Though it was only with Henry II that the full potential of the itinerant justices was seen, their annual trips to the counties relieved the *curia regis* of much routine judicial work, enabling it to concentrate on the more important and complicated pleas. As we have emphasized, the itinerant justices spread the influence of the royal court throughout the realm and enabled it and the king to keep local officers such as the sheriffs under control. These justices sent out from the court provided the essential link between local and central government that was to be one of the main strengths of English government.

The jurisdiction of the *curia regis* was further enlarged by the exchequer, which under Henry I developed into a permanent financial board of account and into a royal court for adjudicating causes pertaining to the king's revenue. Well before 1130 Roger of Salisbury organized the judicial duties of the exchequer. The barons of the exchequer who comprised the court were also members of the *curia regis*; in effect, then, this financial court was the *curia regis* sitting as a court to hear financial cases. By 1135 the exchequer court had developed a tradition and its own peculiar legal procedure. Its justice was so swift and efficient that sheriffs and royal debtors treated it with great deference. The fines were stiff that it assessed upon the sheriffs and those who failed in their financial obligations towards the king. By the end

[8] SM, nos. 26, 28B.

of the Norman period the kings had succeeded in establishing the royal court's supremacy over all other courts, public and private. Its law came to stand above all other custom and was the common law that was already at work binding the realm together.

We turn now from the royal court and its branches to the inferior courts with their local jurisdictions. The first of these are what may be called communal courts. The largest and the one with the highest jurisdiction was the county court; its competence extended to all kinds of cases. Here were tried criminal cases, pleas of the crown, land disputes between tenants of different lords, and actions for wrongs and debts. It could even declare outlawry against a defendant who failed to appear in court. Until the spread of the royal court's jurisdiction, it was the most important court of the realm. When the Norman kings came to empower sheriffs, resident justices, and itinerant justices to hold royal pleas, they did so at the county courts. If the sworn inquest was used, the court became a royal court. There was thus established a close tie between the county court and courts held by the itinerant justices. The courts of the itinerant justices, however, developed a different jurisdiction and procedure and became associated with the royal central courts. This brought about a distinct separation from the county court resulting in the decline of its jurisdiction. Before the growing royal justice usurped much of the competence of the county court, it as well as the hundred court was a tribunal of general jurisdiction; the modern system of courts with lesser jurisdictions running up to the great courts with general jurisdictions was as yet unknown. The difference between the courts depended upon the status of the suitors. To the county court came the important landowners while to the hundred court came the lesser. According to the *Laws of Henry I* the suitors of the county court were barons who assembled twice a year to judge cases under the presidency of the sheriff.[9] Here men of the county were judged by their peers. On occasions when the opinion of the judges was split, the majority opinion prevailed.

All the counties were divided, as we have seen, into hundreds or wapentakes, each with its court. The court met once a month, presided over by a reeve or the hundred-man who was the deputy of the sheriff. The suitors, who also acted as the judges, were minor feudal lords or landholders. The jurisdiction of the hundred court, like that of the county court, was general; even civil cases were handled until the administration of the frankpledge system caused a distinction between the court sessions that dealt with criminal pleas. Eventually the hundred court lost jurisdiction over pleas of land and became a court dealing principally with cases of debt and trespass.

The other courts with local jurisdictions in the Norman period were what we call private or franchisal courts. Under the system of Anglo-Saxon land tenure England had seen most landholders receive from the crown the right

[9] SM, no. 26.

to exercise a certain amount of public justice. On the Continent during the same period the political anarchy and feudal system had pushed the process much farther. Where the territorial prince was weak the rights of public justice were usurped and exercised in the vassal's court. Where the prince was powerful, as in Flanders and Normandy, such jurisdiction could be exercised only by virtue of comital or ducal grant. The introduction of feudalism with its strong emphasis upon the exercise of public powers accompanying the possession of fiefs definitely stimulated the exercise of public justice by the feudal lords who received fiefs from the Conqueror. There is no need to repeat what we have already said in the chapter on local administration; we know that numerous hundred courts fell under the jurisdiction of great feudal lords and that most of them exercised by royal grant the public justice previously held by the Anglo-Saxon thegn. It suffices to remark that when a lord held franchisal justice he exercised it at his principal manor house in the halimote where by feudal and seignorial right he already held feudal and manorial courts. To the feudal courts came his vassals to be tried by feudal custom. At this court land disputes were settled, forfeiture and feudal treason declared, escheated lands returned to the lord, wardships and marriages arranged, homage done, and grants of fiefs witnessed. To the manorial court came the unfree tenants or peasants to be tried for petty crimes, disputes over land, and violations committed against the agrarian routine of the manorial community. The peasants presided over by the lord's reeve were the judges and declared the custom of the manor. With the manorial as with the feudal court the lord acquired the right to hold it upon the basis of the feudal principle that the lord could exercise judicial rights over his tenants, feudal and nonfeudal.

When a lord, therefore, had by royal franchise obtained control over public justice, he would normally hold this public court at his manor and there render justice to the men within the jurisdiction of this court. Its law was that of the hundred and county; here feudal and seignorial custom did not hold and in it only freemen could bring their pleas. Most franchisal courts dispensed justice no higher than that of the hundred court. The chief jurisdiction that the Normans added to sac and soc, toll and team, infangenetheof and utfangenetheof, was the right to view of frankpledge. There were also some grants of freedom from suit to hundred and county court. Only the great palatinates, such as Chester and Durham, received franchises permitting their lords to exercise justice as high as that of the king. When royal justice began its rapid expansion in the twelfth century the lesser franchises could not withstand the competition and were gradually wiped out.

The last of the franchisal courts were those of the boroughs. From the early eleventh century some of the largest boroughs had been holding courts that adjudicated differences between the burgesses or between burgess and foreign merchant. Such a court dealt with disputes occasioned by commercial transactions and arrived at decisions governed by law merchant, a law that, with local variations, developed throughout western Europe between the tenth and twelfth centuries by trial and error to meet more expeditiously the legal requirements of the new merchant class. By 1066 some of the English boroughs had through prescriptive right special courts with special privileges and customs distinguishing them from other local units of government. For the ordinary public justice, however, burgesses were subject like other freemen to the jurisdiction of hundred and county court. With the stimulation of the Conquest legal privileges of boroughs were extended until by the reign of Henry I his charter to London tells us that the Londoners were freed from hundredal and county jurisdiction. Some of the liberties, we may be certain, had long existed and were but confirmed. It was granted, for example, that the local merchant court called the husting should meet weekly and that henceforth no penalty would be levied upon the defendant or plaintiff who used the wrong formula (*miskenning*) in a judicial process. Sanction was also given for another borough court, the folkmoot, to meet thrice a year for extraordinary business such as election of borough officials and watch and fire prevention. Henry swore to support the citizens in all claims to lands, pledges, and debts in and out of London. Land disputes were to be adjudicated in accordance with borough law; all debtors who failed to pay their obligations had to stand trial in London.

These judicial privileges so far are not startling; the concessions that follow contain the radical innovation. Besides electing their own sheriff Londoners were permitted to elect a justice who, to the exclusion of all royal officers and justices, would record all royal pleas and try them. No Londoner could be tried outside London, nor did he have to stand trial by battle or to make his proof other than by oaths accepted in London. By this franchise London got a public court to add to its municipal court; its competence was equal to that of any royal court sitting under a royal justice to hear pleas of the crown.[10]

We have no evidence of other similar grants but they certainly existed because the twelfth century was the great age of English urban development. Franchisal courts flourished until confronted with a more efficient royal justice dispensed in the royal common law courts; they then began to surrender their jurisdiction and to be absorbed. While reserving a full discussion for later, we at least ought briefly to mention here the franchisal courts called fair courts (pie powder courts) held by lords, ecclesiastical establishments, or boroughs possessing the royal right to hold a fair. The term "pie powder" was derived from the French *pied poudré* or the Latin *pede pulverosi*, which referred to the dusty-footed itinerant merchants attending the fairs. Held during the fair such a court was generally presided over by the representative of the lord or institution holding the fair; the

[10] SM, no. 28B.

judges were merchants who, as in borough courts, declared the law merchant. Our earliest evidence for such courts comes from the Norman period; the Conqueror and Rufus granted the privilege of holding them to the church of Saint Mary of Thorney and to the bishop of Winchester for the fair of Saint Giles. Henry I granted a court to the bishop of Norwich. In 1110 he made a grant to the abbey of Ramsey establishing the famous fair of Saint Ives "with sac and soc and infangthef, just as any fair has in England . . . and all, while going and remaining there and going thence, shall have my firm peace."

3. PROCESS AND PROCEDURE

Process and procedure in the royal and public courts were little changed by the Conquest. In addition to the frankpledge system, trial by battle, and the sworn inquest the most significant Norman contribution was the enforcement of an already mature system of process and procedure. Again the Normans adopted and strengthened rather than destroying and replacing. Despite the boasts that the Conqueror and his sons oft made about their good law and order, Anglo-Norman society at best was rough and disorderly. In western Europe the strong rulers had only just begun to bring order out of the post-Carolingian chaos and to restrict the violence of a crude society. Anglo-Saxon England had made remarkable progress towards a state of affairs where men increasingly obeyed a law made and enforced by the king. Not unnaturally the Conquest caused a return to violence, flouting of the law, and bitter hatred of the conquered for the new masters. Only harsh measures by a stern family of rulers headed England again in the direction of a well-governed and relatively peaceful society.

To cope with local order the Normans developed a policing and security system called the institution of frankpledge. The name does not appear until the second decade of the twelfth century but the institution seems to have existed since the Conqueror's reign. Derived from the Norman-French *franc plege* (free pledge), a translation of the Latin *plegium liberale*, the term stemmed from the fact that those in frankpledge were legally considered freemen. This concept was soon broadened to include all villeins. It is difficult to decide whether this institution was an Anglo-Saxon or a Norman creation. Though the frankpledge suretyship does not appear in the records until a half-century after the Conquest, this is no proof that it was Norman. Gneist, Waitz, and Stubbs have argued for a Norman origin; scholars such as Vinogradoff, Maitland, and Liebermann have argued to the contrary. Among the various Anglo-Saxon precedents that have been suggested are the guild-brethren such as the frith-guild of London, the tithing, and the *borh* (suretyship). For the frith-guild there is no evidence. The connection between the tithing and frankpledge is closer because both involved collective police functions by local groups; the tithing did not, however, involve the suretyship that is found with the frankpledge. We have seen that the *borh* originally consisted of a lord's providing surety for his tenants but that in the late Anglo-Saxon period lords sloughed off this irksome duty and pushed it upon their men, who assumed a collective suretyship for the members of the tithing group to which they belonged. There can rightfully be seen, then, in these two separate institutions of the tithing and *borh* the ingredients of the Norman frankpledge system—a tithing group of ten performing police duties under the direction of a headman and an association to effect suretyship for its members. All that was needed was for the Anglo-Saxon collective *borh* with its suretyship obligation to be assumed by tithing and to be made compulsory. We can credit the Normans with meshing the two between 1066 and 1100 and thereby adapting two English institutions to their own needs. It was the legislation of the Conqueror that forced most men into a frankpledge group with police and surety responsibilities and connected these groups with the hundredal organization.[11]

Examining the frankpledge system as it existed at the end of Henry I's reign, we find that, at the age of twelve, men became members of a frankpledge group and swore allegiance to the crown. Those immune were vagabonds and foreigners, for whom a local community could not be responsible, and the feudal aristocracy, who were regarded as the custodians of the peace requiring no surety. Other groups not included were clerics, women, individuals mentally and physically handicapped, and domestic servants and functionaries under the personal pledge (mainprise) of a lord. The frankpledge system pertained chiefly to the villeins. In the Norman period the tithing consisted of ten and, depending upon population, there could be any number of tithings to a manor or hundred. Frequently tithings were named after the chief pledge or head of the tithing to whom members owed obedience. Failure to obey resulted in amercement of the group.

The tithing had three functions. First, it served as a pledge for the appearance of its members in court and accompanied those who had to appear in court, sometimes even to Westminster. Custody was frequently an obligation because there were no prisons. For failure to produce delinquent members the whole tithing was amerced. Secondly, the tithing had to pursue and capture thieves. Probably the tithing helped to apprehend men outside its membership for when the hue and cry was raised all the residents of the community were expected to join in pursuit. Often a whole community would be fined for failure to participate in the hue and cry. Lastly, the tithing had court duties. It served as a pledge for prosecution of a member's case, paid court fines if the case turned out badly, and produced evidence. Generally the head tithingman was one of the older and more substantial men of the community who was elected for a year's term when view of frankpledge was taken.

[11] SM. no. 18.

To insure that this local policing and security system remained in force and operated efficiently required central supervision. In the reign of Henry I it was the practice to hold each year two special sessions of the hundred court, at which time the sheriff or his deputy came around to inspect the groups. On these occasions depleted tithings were brought up to strength and all men were brought into tithings. This was called the view of frankpledge, known later in the Angevin period as the sheriff's tourn and, in eastern England, as the leet. The tithing in which a man was placed depended upon where vacancies existed and where the man lived. The ceremony consisted of administering an oath of fealty to the king and an oath that the new member would neither be a thief nor consent to theft; thereupon the man was enrolled on the tithing list. It is likely that as early as Henry I's reign some lords were granted the right to take the view of frankpledge in their private courts, thus adding this right to the exercise of public justice. When a lord held this privilege he was said to have a court leet. Leet originally designated hundredal divisions in East Anglia but was eventually applied to a private court with the right of holding view of frankpledge. Generally lords who held hundredal justice received this right and were entitled to exclude the sheriff from their court. As developed by the Normans, the frankpledge system was the most efficient police system of western Europe and lent itself later to other experiments made by the English kings in local government. It was one of the numerous institutions created by the crown that was to prove most useful in developing local self-sufficiency and skill in government.

Through the combined efforts of the frankpledge tithings and such officers as the sheriff and the hundred-man most individuals summoned to royal and public courts were produced; if they failed to appear after five summonses, they were outlawed and their possessions confiscated. Once the process was completed the court procedure began. To initiate a case in court in the Anglo-Saxon period we have shown how it was necessary for the plaintiff to accuse the defendant of an offense in the presence of good witnesses. Such procedure continued in the Norman period but in addition we note that important suits were also initiated by royal writs, which, though similar to the Anglo-Saxon writs, were in Latin and were executive orders. The royal writ was not in itself an instrument for initiating litigation but was a royal command purchased by the plaintiff and ordering the person accused to surrender certain lands, possessions, or money. When the command was ignored litigation followed by virtue of the fact that a royal command had not been obeyed, making the wrong of withholding land or other possessions triable in the royal court. As the power of royal justice increased, this concept of the royal writ was replaced by the view that the royal writ could be purchased to initiate litigation; when this occurred in the reign of Henry II, the royal writ became the principal instrument responsible for the expansion of the common law in the second half of the twelfth century.

With but few exceptions the Norman pleading, proof, and trial were like the Anglo-Saxon. In all respects the procedure was highly archaic. There was scarcely a hint of a trial where reasoning from evidence led to the truth of the facts under question. To begin, the plaintiff made his accusation according to prescribed form and his complaint was backed up by a group of witnesses (a *secta*) composed of friends or relatives who simply testified to its genuineness and lent a certain conviction to the complaint. Only the presentation of circumstantial evidence could transform the complaint, supported by the testimony of a *secta*, into proof. Next, the defendant made his defense by swearing an oath of innocence. It was then decided by what proof the issue should be judged. Occasionally the principals could choose the proof but customarily it was determined by a medial judgment of the court. Generally the defendant had to undergo the proof to establish his guilt or innocence. Two of the proofs were compurgation and ordeal; a third was that of witnesses who were comparable to the *secta* in that they were produced by the defendant or plaintiff to swear that they believed his story in court. If the proof was by witnesses, after each principal had told the court his version and his *secta* had supported him, the court decided the case in favor of the one whose number of witnesses was larger and whose testimony was more uniform, or occasionally in favor of the one whose witnesses were more credible. The facts of the testimony were not evaluated. A fourth mode of proof was battle, which resembled the ordeal because it depended not only on military skill but also on God, who supposedly gave the victory to the innocent. Such a proof was particularly perilous for those unskilled in the manly art of medieval self-defense; the powerful bully could accrue a substantial fortune in lands and goods by selecting and accusing those weaker than he. Infants, women, and the aged could appoint champions; later this provision was extended to male litigants physically unfit. Trial by battle survived until the nineteenth century (1819) although even under Henry II it declined in the face of a more reasonable form of proof initiated in the royal courts. When a proof had been undergone, the court then made its decision according to the law and it was executed by the sheriff and his subordinates.

It should be noted that the court concentrated on determining the mode of proof and who should undergo it, and on insuring that the correct procedure was followed. In a superstitious age when miracles were expected and when God was believed to intervene on the side of the innocent, these proofs seemed eminently satisfactory. It was still too early to expect that illiterate and passionate men would submit their disputes to a court and permit its members to hand down a decision based on evidence and reason. Only in the medial judgment or award of proof do we perceive a slight tendency in the direction of reason. In a dispute between Bishop Wulfstan of Worcester and Abbot Walter of Evesham in 1077 the *curia regis* awarded the proof to the bishop because he had witnesses and the abbot had none.[12] In another case during the Conqueror's reign between Bishop Gundulf of Rochester, and Picot, sheriff of Cambridgeshire, the royal court checked the procedure used. The record tells that a county court under intimidation awarded certain lands to Picot which were claimed by Gundulf. The bishop of Bayeux, who presided, distrusted the finding of the county court and forced it to swear again to its award. Later a monk intimately connected with the lands went to the bishop of Bayeux and told him the true facts about the rightful possession. The bishop then secured a confession of perjury from one of the twelve on the county court. At London before a *curia regis* the twelve were tried and convicted of perjury. Gundulf received the lands while the twelve and the whole county were amerced for £300. Such sleuthing was exceptional in the Norman period; we must wait until Henry II for any substantial application of reason to judicial procedure.

[12] SM, no. 19.

XIV

The Norman Church and State

IN ANGLO-SAXON England the church played a principal part in the unification of the kingdom and in the development of central and local institutions. So much, in fact, was the church a part of secular government that it has until this point been unnecessary to speak of the church as an institution separate from the state. There were no separate ecclesiastical councils, no legislation by the church alone, no special spiritual courts, and no logical organization or chain of command. Together church and state governed secular and spiritual society and exhibited a cooperation rare for the Middle Ages. In central and local government the bishop was a stalwart nearly as important as the earl and sheriff. The Norman Conquest resulted in fundamental changes in this scheme because it introduced church custom and tradition of the Continent that contrasted sharply with English practice.

1. THE CONTINENTAL BACKGROUND

Until the eleventh century the church on the Continent did not differ greatly from the English church. In the early Christian era the primitive church tended to withdraw from secular society but by the time of the emperors Constantine and Theodosius it entered actively into secular life. Under such church fathers as Ambrose, Saint Augustine, and Gregory the Great, the church chided western emperors for unchristian acts and, at the same time, threw its growing prestige behind all secular efforts to unify and strengthen government in the West. Gregory the Great as bishop of Rome was not only spiritual head of the West but also a sort of political ruler over the chaos that was Europe. In the dark period between the fourth and eleventh centuries when church and state united for survival it was generally the secular ruler, the man of war and strength, who assumed direction of church and state. The degenerate papacy when not appointed and controlled by Roman nobles was under the protection of the Carolingian emperors. It will be remembered that Charlemagne legislated for church and state in his capitularies, pushed the reform of the church by improving spiritual education, and personally selected the bishops and abbots. Such a royal theocracy was hardly different from what existed in England.

It was the feudalization of the continental church in the ninth and tenth centuries that resulted in a new church-state relation and caused friction between secular and spiritual authority. When the Carolingians and later the counts, dukes, and lesser lords granted fiefs of land to bishops and abbots in return for feudal service and conferred upon them the exercise of public power, secular control over church immeasurably increased. To guarantee that those who held the fiefs would faithfully perform the military and public obligations, secular lords insisted on making the ecclesiastical appointments. The appointee did homage and swore fealty for his lands and then the lord invested him with the spiritual office. Both in appointment and in investiture the lord had usurped a traditional church prerogative. Amidst the turbulence of the ninth and tenth centuries, however, the church had no alternative but to go along with this feudalization. Some of the most efficient rulers and warriors of the West were bishops as, for example, the bishop of Paris, who valiantly beat back the Viking attack on his town. However necessary the absorption of the church and its personnel in the post-Carolingian period, with the gradual return to political stability and economic recovery in the eleventh century the church was able to take stock of its position. Sparked by the Cluniac monastic reform and a series of strong popes beginning with Pope Leo IX (1049), the church began its great struggle to secure independence from secular government. The goals of the reforming church were never completely attained in the Middle Ages but in the eleventh century there occurred a determined onslaught on lay appointment and investiture, purchase of ecclesiastical benefices (simony), and clerical marriage which enabled ecclesiastics to pass on their offices to offspring just as did lay feudal lords. Amidst such a reform atmosphere the Norman Conquest was launched.

The policy of the Norman dukes had been to support the reform of clerical morals and to improve the level of the clergy and church organization. By 1066, however, the papacy had not yet made its influence felt on the question of lay appointment and investiture, and even with the papacy of Gregory VII the Norman rulers ignored papal pressure. The matter of moral and competent clerks was altogether different from that of ducal control over bishops and abbots. The Norman church was dominated by the authoritarian dukes, who appointed, deposed, and invested the prelates; tried them as vassals according to feudal law; and demanded knight service from them. With such a tradition of secular control over the territorial church behind him it is not surprising that the Conqueror initiated no reform that would loosen his tight-fisted grip over the English prelates. Throughout his reign the Conqueror adopted an attitude towards the church that set the tone for his successors. He pushed the spread of religious fervor and supported all spiritual and moral reform of the church, but here he stopped. As an almost absolute ruler he could brook no papal interference in the selection and investiture of prelates who comprised a part of his strong government. Likewise papal interference in English church organization and appeals to the papal court were forbidden or discouraged. William remained master of the English and Norman church and fought any papal act that might be a dangerous precedent.

As we have seen, William had little difficulty in securing papal sanction and support for the Conquest, partly because Pope Alexander II and his court regarded the invasion as a sort of holy war that would bring the English church into line with the organization of the continental church. Though William subsequently fulfilled many of the papal hopes for reform, it is yet debatable as to how much reforming the English church required. Until recently most historians argued that it had sunk to an abysmally low level in organization, morals, and intelligence and that only the renovation pushed by William and Archbishop Lanfranc saved the English church from total degeneracy. In part these claims are justified. The pope exercised little control over the church prior to 1066. Legislation, justice, and appointments were under secular control and Peter's pence, a tax of a penny on every hearth collected and sent to Rome since the early tenth century, had not been paid for a considerable time. Some prelates were guilty of simony and of holding offices in plurality. Some were illiterate and did not know the church ritual; few were celibate and most fought in person as did secular lords. In addition there were irregularities in diocesan organization. Over this church in 1066 presided Archbishop Stigand of Canterbury, who had secured his position illegally and was no man to push reform. True enough, certain of these abuses such as secular control of justice and poor diocesan organization were not found on the Continent, but the other evils were every bit as flagrant on the Continent and the papacy had made little progress in their eradication. When in the last quarter of the eleventh century the continental church showed signs of real reform, so too did the English church. The English church of the ninth and tenth centuries was hardly less degenerate than its counterpart and reform would have come to it also in the eleventh and twelfth centuries; the Norman Conquest but sped up the process.

The man responsible for initiating and administering William's reforms was his confidant, Lanfranc, who was elevated to the archbishopric of Canterbury in 1070. Having already dealt fully with Lanfranc's remarkable background and career we need here only to explain his attitude towards reform. His views were not too divergent from William's and to the end they amicably cooperated in matters of ecclesiastical policy. We may doubt that Lanfranc desired to push reform any farther than William did; he was above all a moderate and practical statesman who backed only what he thought could be enforced. Intelligent, well-educated, and of a cosmopolitan background, Lanfranc was no idealist. Practical reform by a reforming papacy he would support, but on vital matters he surrendered no more than did William; he had no desire to sacrifice small gains or even his own career merely to support a papacy concerning whose spiritual character he had no illusions. He had lived too close to the eleventh-century popes to believe that any possessed morals and spiritual qualities elevated enough to entitle them to unquestioned and tame obedience. Lanfranc's achievements never won him canonization.

2. WILLIAM I AND CHURCH REFORM

The reforms of William were directed principally at the secular church. To accomplish his objectives he had first to staff the English church with Normans sympathetic to his program. The first step was the deposition of Archbishop Stigand in 1070 by a church council held at Winchester; his successor was Lanfranc. William and Lanfranc next tackled the fifteen English bishoprics. At the same council of Winchester various English bishops were charged with irregular behavior and deposed. Bishop Leofwine of Lichfield, for example, was a married man with sons; he resigned and retired to a monastery. More English prelates were subsequently removed until by 1080 deposition or death had disposed of all but one—the venerated Wulfstan of Worcester, who retained an eminence in church and state until his death. The replacements were Normans and Lotharingians and continued to be for the remainder of the Norman period. In order to make himself the sovereign ecclesiastic in England and to introduce a logical chain of command Lanfranc next took issue with the archbishop of York, who traditionally had governed the northern church independently of Canterbury. In a church council held at Winchester in 1072 the primacy of Lanfranc was established. Previously the archbishop of York had made an oral profession of obedience to Lanfranc, but now the council ruled that he would be subordinate to Canterbury, that he and his bishops must attend councils summoned by his superior, and that by custom the archbishop of York owed an oath of obedience to the archbishop of Canterbury.

Having won the battle for primacy Lanfranc turned to the renovation of ecclesiastical administration. Authorized and backed by the Conqueror he convoked a series of church councils which enacted legislation. In this connection it should be observed that William still retained control over these assemblies, that he presided over some of them, and that they included numerous lay barons. Such a scheme was hardly different from the old witenagemot when it legislated for the church. Sometimes it is impossible to distinguish such an assembly from the royal court. At any rate councils of 1072, 1075, and 1076 reordered diocesan organization. To bring English diocesan government into line with continental, where since the late imperial period bishops had their headquarters at the chief town of the *civitas*, Lanfranc secured legislation transferring various English diocesan centers from villages to towns. It was thus that the sees of Lichfield, Selsey, and Sherbourne were moved to the urban centers of Chester, Chichester, and Salisbury. Subsequent transfers continued until by 1087 the rural cathedral was a relic of the past. In the lower ecclesiastical ranks Lanfranc secured enactments regulating parochial organization. Within his diocese the bishop was to be supreme and was to hold a synod twice a year to enact diocesan legislation. At these times he would appoint the archdeacons and other ecclesiastical officers of the diocese. All diocesan clergy were forbidden to participate in judgments involving life and limb. No priests or monks were permitted to go from one diocese to another without their bishop's approval, and even with his approval they could not serve another parish. Such rules fostered greater clerical stability and recognized as well the feudal custom that parishes were considered under the control of the lay lords whose lands they occupied, and that the lord had the right to appoint his priest. Under this feudal custom inequities arose but Lanfranc was not ready to challenge this valued right.

The most significant conciliar legislation was that of 1076 which enacted that henceforth there should be separate spiritual courts throughout the realm.[1] It complemented an ordinance issued by the Conqueror about 1072 separating ecclesiastical from secular justice. Before 1066 both secular and spiritual justice had been rendered at hundred and shire court under a customary law that manifested slight canon law influence. The enactment of 1076 ordered that no bishop or archdeacon was to preside over cases of an ecclesiastical nature in the hundred court and that no spiritual plea should be tried in a public court. Those connected with spiritual pleas were to be summoned to a court presided over by the bishop or his subordinate, where sentence would be governed by canon and episcopal law. He who thrice ignored the bishop's summons was to be excommunicated and the sheriff was to enforce attendance. By Henry I's reign the ordinance had been extended to county courts. Henceforth all clerics were tried in spiritual courts as well as all laymen who were accused of moral infractions. This separation of spiritual and secular jurisdiction, while bringing the English church into conformity with continental usage, raised for William and Lanfranc more serious problems. A fertile and elastic ecclesiastic jurisdiction now expanded the meaning of spiritual plea to cover a multitude of evils. It encroached constantly on civil jurisdiction and reserved for its tribunals clerks who had committed murder and robbery. We also detect church courts beginning to claim jurisdiction over all causes arising out of the marriage contract. The public and royal courts lost their jurisdiction over the clergy and over a large number of offenses; now two laws held in the realm. The creation of spiritual courts was soon to accomplish what the Conqueror never dreamed of; it facilitated papal interference in the English church and fertilized the bitter church-state disputes between Anselm and Henry I, and Becket and Henry II.

The other subject that looms large in the conciliar legislation pushed by Lanfranc is clerical morality. A wide range of subjects was covered. Simony was forbidden; so too were divination and the use of spells. On the matter of clerical celibacy Lanfranc desired reform but realized that he could not

[1] SM, no. 17.

enact radical measures in the face of centuries of clerical marriage. His moderate legislation typifies his sensible attitude towards all reform. In 1076 he introduced measures that would henceforth make clerical marriage impossible. The council enacted that no canon or priest should have, take, or keep a wife and that bishops should not ordain any candidate for the priesthood or diaconate without receiving an oath of celibacy. But this legislation looked forward, not backward. All priests with wives were permitted to keep them. About all that Lanfranc had established was the principle of clerical celibacy; its practice on all levels would be long incoming. In the reign of William and his two sons clerical morals were not to be boasted about. Robert of Limesey, made bishop of Coventry in 1085, had a shocking reputation. Under William Rufus degradation of the church was scandalous. Most guilty of all was the royal chaplain Ranulf Flambard. In 1091 Herbert Losinga bought the see of Thetford for a huge sum of money. Under Henry I simony was prominent and celibacy was a habit shunned by high and low. Roger of Salisbury lived with his mistress. Bishop Nigel of Ely was married and was the father of Richard fitz Nigel; he installed as sacrist of his cathedral a married clerk. These few examples should make us question whether the Normans saved the English church from moral degradation.

Of reform other than administrative and moral, we have little to say. From an abbey himself, Lanfranc naturally was interested in reorganizing English monasteries to conform with continental practice; his *Consuetudines* is a collection of continental usages to serve as a guide for English houses. As with the secular church there was quite vigorous moral and organizational reform; numerous old English houses took on new life under the direction of Norman abbots imported from Bec and other distinguished monasteries. Beyond such internal reform Lanfranc did not press his authority; he generally chose the abbots but always subject to the approval of William, who frequently took a personal hand, as when he corresponded with John, abbot of Fécamp, to inquire about the qualifications of Ordericus Vitalis for the abbacy of Westminster. The appointment and investiture of abbots was a prerogative in which William would tolerate no interference.

When one enters into the no man's land of church-state relations he leaves behind that area where compromise and cooperation were possible. Where it was English and Norman church against papal spiritual and political pretensions, the Conqueror followed a monolithic line. No ground was surrendered that would weaken his authoritarian control over church and state; through him passed and upon him depended all church-state transactions. Any pope who advocated more than spiritual reform was *persona non grata*. At the peak of Gregory VII's fight to eradicate lay appointment and investiture, and even after he had humbled Henry IV, emperor of the Holy Roman Empire, William ignored Gregory's pleas and warnings. When feudalization of church lands favored the interest of secular lord, Gregory bitterly opposed it; when it worked in reverse, he welcomed the role of feudal lord. This was the position he had attained when the rulers of Norman Italy, Hungary, and Spain took their kingdoms in fief from him. Pushing this role wherever he thought there was a chance, Gregory demanded in 1080 that William do homage to him and hold England as a papal fief. He argued that William was indebted to the papacy on two counts: a pope had backed him as English king and a papal *curia* had awarded him the crown. William's reply was immediate and to the point: "I have not consented to pay fealty, nor will I now, because I never promised it, nor do I find that my predecessors ever paid it to your predecessors." All that William promised was that Peter's pence should again be paid.

As head of the English church William controlled all communication and relations with the papacy. No pope could be recognized without his approval, no papal letters or legates could be received without his consent, no bishops could go to Rome without his authorization. With the fall of Gregory from power William headed an independent church that for a while recognized no pope. Throughout his reign he operated on the assumption that the archbishop of Canterbury with the aid of the bishops was competent to govern the English church with no outside influence. The prelates were under William's benevolent scrutiny and could not excommunicate or implead any royal barons without his approval. Though not sympathetic to such highhanded procedure, Gregory never attempted to fight William on any of these issues; he was satisfied enough with the devoutness of William and with Lanfranc's reform to let sleeping dogs lie. As Gregory wrote to the bishop of Oléran in 1081, William did "not comport himself as devoutly as we might hope" but nevertheless in matters of reform "he has shown himself more worthy of approbation and honour than other kings."

The church-state conflict that even today remains unsolved in many respects originated partly from the feudalization of the church. By virtue of the fact that all bishops and abbots held a large portion of their land from the king they became his tenants-in-chief and owed to him the customary feudal obligations. About forty bishops and abbots owed feudal service to the Conqueror. Throughout western Europe between the ninth and eleventh centuries before the advent of papal power, the revival of canon law, and the beginning of writings theorizing on the supremacy of church over state, few prelates had any qualms about serving their feudal lord before their pope. Once, however, the popes began to exercise the plenitude of their theoretical powers and, through systematization and expansion of the canon law, to define the obligation and allegiance of prelates, a bitter struggle exploded between pope and ruler and between prelate and ruler. No matter what the choice involved—appointment and investiture, homage and fealty, lay or spiritual justice, performance of military service, or obedience to royal or papal prerogative—prelates were bound to offend and to be uncertain of the grounds for their action.

While all medieval men were agreed that the guidance and care of human spiritual life was tremendously important and that no temporal action should be committed to deprive man of his heavenly reward, the state also had a good case; there must be some temporal actions if there was to be political order. Churchmen must be acceptable to the king because of him they held rich lands and for him performed feudal services; upon the bishops, the king long had to rely for his advisers and administrators. None could be suitable who served pope first and worked for a program whose goal was the reduction of royal power. With this arrangement most prelates agreed; they valued their rich fiefs and their political pre-eminence. Under the team of the Conqueror and Lanfranc few churchmen challenged this scheme of church-state relations. Both men were devout and energetic enough in church reform to blunt any drive for freedom of the church. And too, the full force of the investiture conflict did not reach England until the late eleventh century. The only challenge of royal authority was the claim of some prelates to ecclesiastical privilege. Bishop Odo of Bayeux protested against his imprisonment for revolt against the Conqueror but Lanfranc justified it on the basis that Odo was seized and tried as a baron and not as an ecclesiastic. The unsuccessful revolt of Bishop William of Durham against William Rufus in 1088 resulted in the confiscation of his lands. The bishop protested that these lands were part of his bishopric and that he could be tried only in a spiritual court. His plea was overruled; his lands were confiscated as a fief and he was tried as a royal vassal by the *curia regis*.

The struggle of church and state became serious only with the succession of William Rufus. A greedy and unreasonable man, he lacked the moderation of his father. Early in his reign the death of Lanfranc deprived him of that prelate's sensible counsel. In every respect he was anathema to the church. His personal life was most immoral and he committed every known outrage against the church. Working through Flambard he despoiled the church by increasing feudal burdens, by prolonging vacancies and appropriating revenues for years on end (right of *regale*), by farming out church lands to the highest bidder, and by appropriating the personal property of a deceased bishop (right of *jus spolii*) rather than permitting its distribution for charitable purposes. He blocked ecclesiastical communication with the papacy and hedged or failed to recognize the popes. Only when he lay close to death in 1093 did he consent to appoint an archbishop of Canterbury to fill a four-year vacancy. His choice fell upon the renowned theologian Anselm of Aosta, the prior of Bec. A choice quickly repented of upon William's recovery, it placed at the head of the English church a man more scholar than statesman, a man unfamiliar with English church structure, and one completely in sympathy with the reforming papacy. The curtain was now raised for the drama of the investiture struggle in England.

3. THE INVESTITURE STRUGGLE

Having reluctantly accepted this lay appointment, Anselm did homage and fealty for the lands of Canterbury and then was invested by Rufus with the pastoral office. Anselm thereby did initially all that was counter to the papal program he supported. Then the struggle began. Rufus refused to restore lands that he had usurped at Lanfranc's death and he refused Anselm permission to receive the pallium (archbishop's cloak) personally from the pope. The matter was debated before a royal council of barons and prelates held at Rockingham in 1095; there Anselm got so little support from the overawed bishops that he consented to receive the pallium from a papal legate. After this rupture Anselm continued to needle Rufus. He put pressure on him to recognize Urban II as pope and still pleaded for the chance to go to Rome. Outraged, Rufus summoned him before the great council to be tried for disloyalty. Anselm countered that he could be tried only by the pope. Rufus urged that he be deprived of his office and expelled from the realm; the fearful bishops would have agreed but the barons refused to find him guilty. Foiled here, Rufus now attempted to gain papal support against Anselm; he recognized Urban II and then asked Urban's legate to depose Anselm. The legate refused and Rufus found himself completely outmaneuvered. He was still saddled with the obstreperous archbishop, whom he could no longer even accuse of recognizing a pope not royally sanctioned. For two years the trouble smoldered only to flame up in 1097. Rufus ordered Anselm to appear before a great council to explain why the feudal contingent of Canterbury supplied for a Norman campaign was ill trained and equipped. Anselm refused to appear and asked permission to talk over his troubles with the pope. Denied the royal license, Anselm defied Rufus and stole away to visit the pope. He thus forfeited Canterbury and remained an exile on the Continent until Henry I's reign. No papal threat, not even excommunication, forced Rufus to restore Anselm and lose the revenues from Canterbury.

The coming of Henry I to the throne brought some improvement to church-state relations. His coronation promise not to sell churches, or to farm them, or to levy unjust exactions upon them, was never kept. He did, however, fill up the vacant bishoprics and abbeys and was reasonable enough to realize that he must negotiate for the return of Anselm. It was to be no easy task because Anselm had been royally feted throughout western Europe as a celebrated scholar and defender of church right; his attendance in 1099 at a council in Rome strengthened his conviction against lay investiture and the performance of homage to lay lords. Invited back to England by Henry, Anselm arrived in 1100 prepared to push Gregorian reforms. Met with a demand to do homage in order to receive back his lands, Anselm refused point-blank. After several embassies to the pope failed to solve the deadlock, Anselm returned to exile in 1103. Negotiation continued, however, in a moderate and sensible vein until 1105, when the pope pronounced excommunication against those English bishops who received investiture of their offices from Henry; Anselm then threatened Henry with the same sentence. Such a threat to his prestige caused Henry to seek an interview with Anselm in Normandy. Though no settlement was reached at their meeting, the two continued to hammer away at their differences with the help of the pope and the famous canonist Bishop Ivo of Chartres, a skillful compromiser. In his writings he advocated that kings could not confer the spiritual office upon a bishop but that they did have the right to invest him with his temporal powers and possessions (the *regalia*).

Finally, in 1106 a settlement of the investiture struggle was reached between Henry and Anselm at Bec in Normandy and was confirmed by a council held in London in 1107. According to the chronicler Eadmer and the Constitutions of Clarendon (1164) Henry surrendered his right of spiritual investiture of ring and staff and agreed to free ecclesiastical elections. In fact, however, Henry insisted that elections be held at the royal court and under his supervision. Homage must be rendered for the lay holdings before spiritual investiture occurred. Beyond the right won for spiritual investiture, the church attained nothing; all the abbots and bishops continued to be royal vassals responsible for feudal service and, in practice, freedom of election was meaningless. Anselm fully realized that the appointments remained a matter of royal will; the church nominated and elected only those men who it knew would be completely acceptable to the king. The type of man so elevated remained unchanged; his spiritual achievements were always secondary to his skill as a royal officer or administrator. A bishopric was but a reward for royal service which generally continued and was henceforth paid for by the church. Before his appointment as bishop of Salisbury Roger had loyally served Henry and he went on to become chancellor and justiciar. Before becoming bishop of London Richard of Belmeis had been sheriff of Shropshire; like Roger, he produced successors who perpetuated the administrative-ecclesiastical tradition. However small the church gains in the English compromise of 1107, fifteen years later the popes could win no more with the German emperor Henry V and were willing to use this compromise as the basis for the settlement of the investiture struggle at the Concordat of Worms (1122).

The other outstanding problems of Henry's reign were the right of ecclesiastical appeal to the papal court and the recognition of papal legates. None of the Normans had permitted the appeal of cases, lay or spiritual, beyond the king's or archbishop's court because they feared that they would lose their role of ultimate arbiter of justice, and that royal law would have to compete with a strong law from outside. William, bishop of Durham, had appealed his case in 1088 to the pope but nothing had come of it; not until Henry's reign do we have much evidence of appeal to Rome and then Henry permitted it only with spiritual causes. Although Henry occasionally allowed English bishops to attend councils on the Continent, he seldom recognized the powers of papal legates sent to England. Such papal representatives with *ad hoc* powers had come to England as early as Offa's reign and frequented England under the Confessor, but the new powers given them by Gregory VII caused strong royal reaction against their coming to England. Armed with papal authority to concern themselves with all church matters, they could theoretically supervise ecclesiastical taxes, direct reform, preside over councils, and hear cases appealed to the pope. As his legates they took precedence over all English churchmen, even the archbishop of Canterbury. Time and again Henry forbade the entry of papal legates into England; finally the pope agreed that no one should act as a legate in England unless Henry asked for one. Eventually a more workable arrangement was reached in 1126 during another dispute over precedence between York and Canterbury. To insure the authority of Canterbury Henry and the pope agreed to have a permanent legate in England who should be the archbishop of Canterbury. Until the thirteenth century this agreement was in force and England was guaranteed an English legate.

A tactful, well-balanced individual, Henry I sensed the necessity of limited cooperation with the church; his few concessions secured a *modus vivendi*. But there was no further reform or retreat; Henry simply restored church-state relations to what they had been under his father. The church was not free. Like the Conqueror, Henry ordered the church and condoned some abuses even his father would have opposed; he sold offices to the highest bidder, prolonged vacancies, and promoted all sorts of uncelibate clerks. The church had yet to win a significant victory.

It was primarily due to church support marshaled by his brother Bishop Henry of Winchester that Stephen won the throne in 1135. To retain the church's backing Stephen surrendered more to it than his predecessors had. In his two charters of 1135 and 1136 he confirmed all the promises Henry had made in 1100 plus adding a few of his own. He swore not to practice simony and to give bishops full jurisdiction over the clergy. He promised that the church should be free. None of these promises did he keep. He countenanced simony, prolonged vacancies, condoned seizure of church property, imprisoned Roger of Salisbury, restricted episcopal jurisdiction over clergy, and forbade appeals to Rome. Originally the church's protector, he eventually was regarded as a tyrant by ecclesiastics. But civil war so weakened Stephen's position that he could not make his authority stick. Under his grant of freedom the church took liberties previously unknown. Papal power greatly increased. The pope came to be acknowledged as the supreme authority in spiritual affairs. In spiritual justice he was regarded as the final arbiter and lawgiver. To him the English clergy drew close during the time of strife between Stephen and Matilda. As a papal legate, Henry of Winchester helped the advance of papal power. He encouraged appeals to the papal court; for 1151 we have record of three such appeals made from a church council. The anarchy of civil war also increased the use of excommunication because it was one of the few weapons left to protect the life and property of the clergy.

When Stephen died in 1154 a combination of his weakness and civil war had made the English church the freest in its history. There were held some free elections of bishops and abbots which the popes began to confirm. Some abbeys and churches had attained papal bulls that placed them under immediate authority of the pope. Independent church councils were held; ecclesiastical jurisdiction became stronger and better organized with provision made for appeal to the papal court. As for communication, English clergy frequently crossed the Channel, and papal letters and bulls freely entered the realm. Twenty years of anarchy had given the church what it could not win from the two Williams and Henry in seventy years. Not until Henry VIII would the church lose what it had gained under Stephen. But close at hand was a man who would fight bitterly to restore relations to their pre-1135 status—Henry Plantagenet, who, coming from his possessions in Normandy, Maine, and Anjou, was ill disposed towards freedom of the church. In the household of Archbishop Theobald of Canterbury, however, was a clever clerk named Thomas Becket who, by his martyrdom, was to administer to Henry II one of his few defeats.

BIBLIOGRAPHY

The history of Norman England has been covered recently in a number of books. The most erudite is D. C. Douglas, *William the Conqueror: The Norman Impact upon England* (Berkeley, 1964), a work most sympathetic to the Normans as are two other of his books on broader themes: *The Norman Achievement* (London, 1969) and *The Norman Fate, 1100–1154* (London, 1976). William I is portrayed much less sympathetically by Frank Barlow, *William I and the Norman Conquest* (London, 1965). Other good surveys are H. R. Loyn, *The Norman Conquest* (London, 1965) and R. A. Brown, *The Normans and the Norman Conquest* (London, 1968). William Rufus and Henry I have been the subjects of articles but no books. There are two studies, however, of Stephen: R. H. C. Davis, *King Stephen* (London, 1967) and H. A. Cronne, *The Reign of Stephen* (London, 1970). John Le Patourel in *The Norman Empire* (Oxford, 1977) studies the Normans in England and Normandy.

Much of what we know about Norman England comes from *Domesday Book* which has been extensively studied. As fundamental for the study of this great record as F. W. Maitland's *Domesday Book and Beyond*, cited previously, is J. H. Round's *Feudal England* (London, 1895). V. H. Galbraith has revised Round's conclusions in *The Making of Domesday Book* (Oxford, 1961) and *Domesday Book: Its Place in Administrative History* (Oxford, 1974). See also R. W. Finn, *The Domesday Inquest and the Making of Domesday Book* (London, 1961).

Research on Norman feudalism must begin with J. H. Round's essay in *Feudal England* whose conclusions are supported by F. M. Stenton in *The First Century of English Feudalism*, 2d ed. (Oxford, 1961) that is considered the best study on the subject. Carl Stephenson concurs with the position of Round and Stenton in his *Mediaeval Institutions*, cited previously, as does also R. A. Brown, *Origins of English Feudalism* (London, 1973). The views of these scholars that feudalism was imported by the Normans has been questioned by C. W. Hollister, *Anglo-Saxon Military Institutions* (Oxford, 1962) and *The Military Organization of Norman England* (Oxford, 1965). Studies on special aspects of feudalism are H. M. Chew, *The English Ecclesiastical Tenants-in-Chief and Knight Service* (Oxford, 1932), E. G. Kimball, *Serjeanty Tenure in Medieval England* (New Haven, 1936), Sidney Painter, *Studies in the History of the English Feudal Barony* (Baltimore, 1943), I. J. Sanders, *Feudal Military Service in England: A Study of the Constitutional and Military Powers of the Barones in Medieval England* (Oxford, 1956), and Bryce Lyon, *From Fief to Indenture: The Transition from Feudal to Non-Feudal Contract in Western Europe* (Cambridge, Mass., 1957). For the nature of feudal institutions in Normandy and elsewhere on the Continent see C. H. Haskins, *Norman Institutions* (Cambridge, Mass., 1918), F. L. Ganshof, *Feudalism* (London, 1952), and Marc Bloch, *Feudal Society* (Chicago, 1961).

Some of the books cited for Anglo-Saxon society also deal with Norman social structure and manorialism. In addition see Vinogradoff, *English Society in the Eleventh Century* (Oxford, 1908), H. M. Cam, *Liberties and Communities in*

Medieval England (Cambridge, 1944), A. L. Poole, *Obligations of Society in the Twelfth and Thirteenth Centuries* (Oxford, 1946), R. W. Finn, *The Norman Conquest and Its Effects on the Economy, 1066–1086* (London, 1971), and L. C. Latham, *The Manor*, Historical Association Helps, No. 8 (London, 1931).

The most stimulating but debatable book on Norman central institutions is H. G. Richardson and G. O. Sayles, *The Governance of Mediaeval England from the Conquest to Magna Carta* (Edinburgh, 1963) which challenges the interpretations of such as Stubbs, Round, and Maitland. A good survey remains G. B. Adams, *The Origin of the English Constitution*, new ed. (New Haven, 1920). An excellent article on the entourage of the Norman kings is G. H. White, "The Household of the Norman Kings," *Transactions of the Royal Historical Society*, XXX (1948), 127–155. The first of the great justiciars has interested E. J. Kealey, *Roger of Salisbury, Viceroy of England* (Berkeley, 1972). For a comparison of Norman-Angevin and Capetian government see Charles Petit-Dutaillis, *The Feudal Monarchy in France and England from the Tenth to the Thirteenth Century* (London, 1936). Cf. C. W. Hollister and J. W. Baldwin, "The Rise of Administrative Kingship: Henry I and Philip Augustus," *American Historical Review*, LXXXIII (1978), 867–905. For the exchequer and taxation see R. L. Poole, *The Exchequer in the Twelfth Century* (Oxford, 1912), Charles Johnson, *The Course of the Exchequer by Richard, Son of Nigel (Dialogue of the Exchequer)* (London, 1950), G. H. White, "Financial Administration under Henry I," *Transactions of the Royal Historical Society*, VIII (1925), 56–78, and R. S. Hoyt, *The Royal Demesne in English Constitutional History, 1066–1272* (Ithaca, N.Y., 1951). For a comparison of early English financial institutions with those of the continental states see Bryce Lyon and A. E. Verhulst, *Medieval Finance: A Comparison of Financial Institutions in Northwestern Europe* (Providence, R.I., 1967).

Besides the works of Morris and Cam cited previously the following pertain to local administration in the Norman and subsequent periods: W. A. Morris, *The Frankpledge System* (Cambridge, Mass., 1910), Gaillard Lapsley, *The County Palatine of Durham* (Cambridge, Mass., 1900), J. W. Alexander, "New Evidence on the Palatinate of Chester," *English Historical Review*, LXXXV (1970), 715–729, and H. M. Jewell, *English Local Administration in the Middle Ages* (London, 1972).

Good for study of the Norman council and its legal jurisdiction and procedure is G. B. Adams, *Council and Courts in Anglo-Norman England* (New Haven, 1926). The most detailed study of the council but needing revision particularly for the Norman period is J. F. Baldwin, *The King's Council in England* (Oxford, 1913). Also in need of revision is M. M. Bigelow, *History of Procedure in England from the Norman Conquest; the Norman Period 1066–1204* (London, 1880), one of the few works on the subject. For developments in criminal law during the Norman period and later see Julius Goebel, *Felony and Misdemeanor: A Study in the History of English Criminal Procedure* (New York, 1937). A new edition and translation of the laws of Henry I is L. J. Downer, *Leges Henrici Primi* (Oxford, 1972). For the development of the writ see R. C. van Caenegem, *Royal Writs in England from the Conquest to Glanvill* (London, 1959). A book that disagrees with the conclusions of Van Caenegem but that also provides a superb account of Norman-Angevin legal development is D. M. Stenton, *English Justice between the Norman Conquest and the Great Charter* (Philadelphia,

1964). See also G. W. Keeton, *The Norman Conquest and the Common Law* (London, 1967), Alison Reppy, *The Ordinance of William the Conqueror, 1072: Its Implication in the Law of Succession* (New York, 1954).

An old standard work on the relations of the Norman state and church is Felix Makower, *Constitutional History and Constitution of the Church of England* (London, 1895). A reliable survey of the secular church is Martin Brett, *The English Church under Henry I* (London, 1975). Perhaps the best study of the investiture struggle is Z. N. Brooke, *The English Church and Papacy, from the Conquest to the Reign of King John* (Cambridge, 1931). This book should be read in the light of what has been written by N. F. Cantor, *Church, Kingship, and Lay Investiture in England, 1089–1135* (Princeton, 1958). For some of the leading churchmen see A. J. Macdonald, *Lanfranc*, 2d ed. (London, 1944), Margaret Gibson, *Lanfranc of Bec* (Oxford, 1978), and Donald Nicholl, *Thurstan, Archbishop of York (1114–1140)* (York, 1964).

Part Three

HENRY II AND HIS SONS

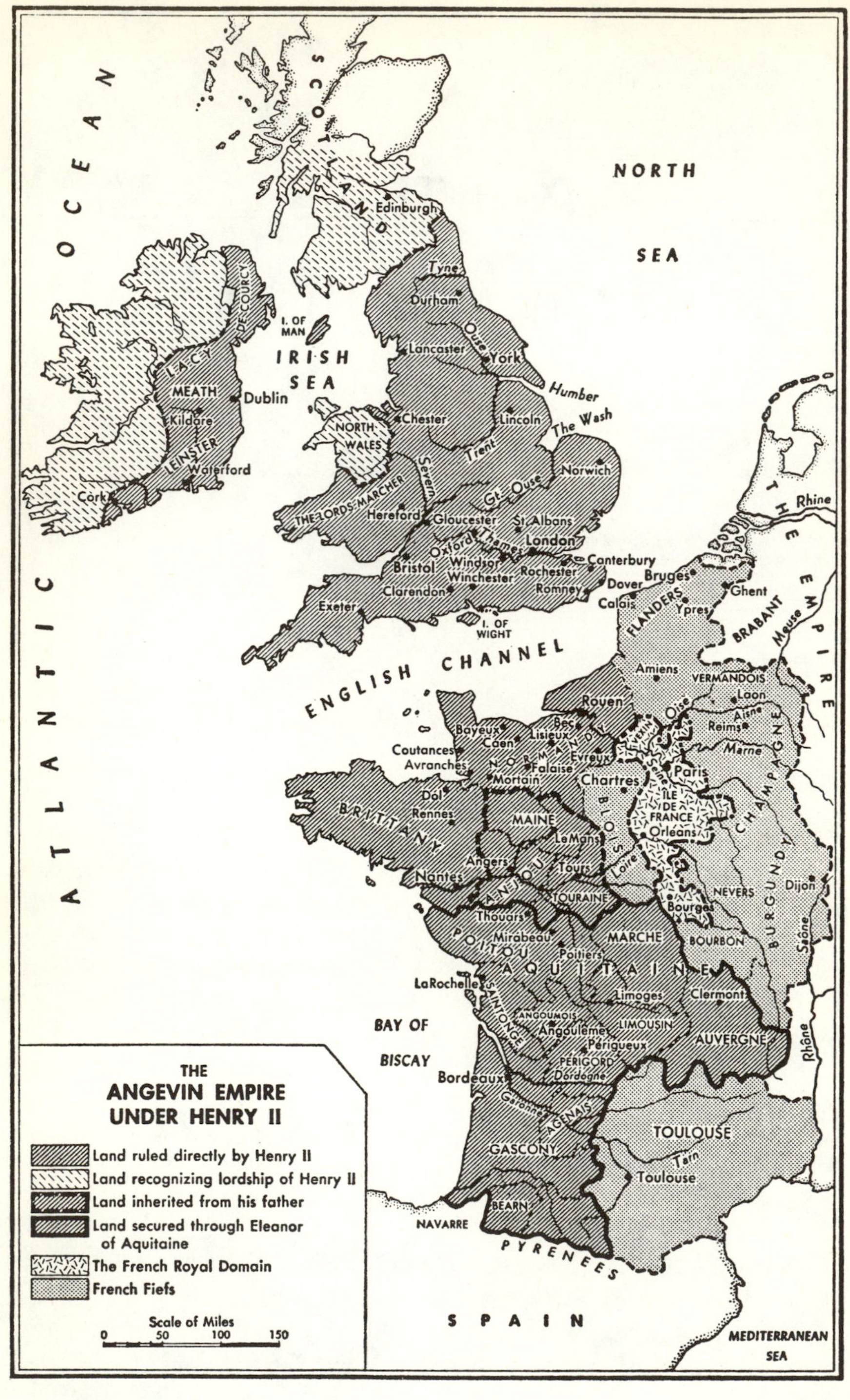
THE
ANGEVIN EMPIRE
UNDER HENRY II
Land ruled directly by Henry II
Land recognizing lordship of Henry II
Land inherited from his father
Land secured through Eleanor of Aquitaine
The French Royal Domain
French Fiefs
Scale of Miles
0 50 100 150
ATLANTIC OCEAN
NORTH SEA
IRISH SEA
ENGLISH CHANNEL
BAY OF BISCAY
MEDITERRANEAN SEA
SCOTLAND
Edinburgh
Tyne
Durham
Ouse
York
Lancaster
Humber
Lincoln
The Wash
Chester
NORTH WALES
Trent
Severn
Norwich
THE LORDS MARCHER
Hereford
Gloucester
Gt. Ouse
St. Albans
Oxford
Thames
London
Bristol
Windsor
Rochester
Canterbury
Winchester
Clarendon
Romney
Dover
Exeter
I. OF WIGHT
I. OF MAN
DE COURCY
LACY
MEATH
Dublin
Kildare
LEINSTER
Waterford
Cork
Calais
Bruges
Ghent
FLANDERS
Ypres
BRABANT
Meuse
THE EMPIRE
Rhine
Amiens
VERMANDOIS
Laon
Aisne
Reims
Marne
Rouen
Oise
Bayeux
Caen
Lisieux
Bec
Evreux
NORMANDY
VEXIN
Coutances
Avranches
Falaise
Mortain
Paris
Seine
Chartres
ILE DE FRANCE
Orléans
CHAMPAGNE
Dol
Rennes
BRITTANY
MAINE
Le Mans
BLOIS
Angers
ANJOU
Tours
Loire
Nantes
TOURAINE
NEVERS
BURGUNDY
Dijon
Bourges
Saône
Thouars
Mirabeau
POITOU
MARCHE
BOURBON
Poitiers
AQUITAINE
La Rochelle
SAINTONGE
Limoges
Clermont
ANGOUMOIS
Angoulême
LIMOUSIN
AUVERGNE
Périgueux
PÉRIGORD
Dordogne
Rhône
Bordeaux
Garonne
AGENAIS
TOULOUSE
GASCONY
Tarn
Toulouse
BEARN
NAVARRE
PYRENEES
SPAIN

XV

The Angevin Sources

THE Norman kings were the first to realize the value of orderly records and consequently surpassed contemporary rulers in the accuracy and quantity of official records. After establishing order out of the disorder inherited from Stephen, Henry II returned to the Norman tradition of recordkeeping which reached its fruition with his son John. Increasingly records were enrolled for preservation and, as the business and complexity of royal government grew, new records were devised to keep the king and his officers abreast of affairs. There are few occasions, at least for constitutional history, when royal records are lacking and narrative records must be used to fill the gap. As in the Norman period, the chronicles and biographies supply color and intimate facts about the royal court and its life.

I. NONNARRATIVE SOURCES

A. Records of the Chancery

Pre-eminent among the Angevin records are those royal enactments, ordinances, and directives that defy neat classification. Sometimes in the form of a writ, other times in the form of an assize, they were issued in whatever form was most expedient. Dealing primarily with royal administration these various documents, however issued, were essentially legislative acts, the most important of which were the assizes, whose acts concerning justice and local jurisdiction, such as the Assize of Clarendon (1166) and of Northampton (1176). Some assizes, the Assize of Arms (1181) and the Assize of the Forest (1184), provided for a national militia and for administration of the king's forests.[1] When we deal with Angevin legislation there will be opportunity to explain the derivation of the word "assize" and to differentiate it from other enactments; at the moment it suffices to indicate that a variety of legislative assizes were issued between 1154 and 1216. Of a similar but less formal nature were the royal constitutions such as those of Clarendon (1164) and the ordinances such as those of 1188 that provided for the Saladin tithe.[2] Even less formalized were the administrative instruc-

[1] SM, nos. 31, 32, 34, 35.
[2] SM, nos. 30, 38.

tions given by the kings or their justiciars to the officers, particularly the itinerant justices on the eve of a circuit (*iter*). There was the commission of 1170 given by Henry II to a group of itinerant barons authorizing them to inquire into the abuses of sheriffs. This commission set in motion the Inquest of Sheriffs, which entailed replies to the questions of the barons that resulted in the wholesale removal of sheriffs. In 1166 Henry commissioned his sheriffs to hold inquests on the amount of knight service owed to him by tenants-in-chief. From this inquest came the valuable returns of the tenants (*Cartae Baronum*) which provide the best evidence on Angevin feudalism. These and other records of a financial nature are presented in two later compilations called the *Red* and *Black Books of the Exchequer*. In 1194 the justiciar Hubert Walter handed the itinerant justices a set of instructions, the so-called Articles for the General Eyre, which minutely defined the jurisdiction of the justices and probably formally created local peace officers called coroners.[3]

Although the documents above were drafted by the chancery staff, they do not fall under the standard classification of chancery records as do the following. The Angevin kings carried on considerable correspondence with the great princes and ecclesiastics of England and the Continent. The letters and other documents such as treaties, bulls, and privileges that resulted from such correspondence are a mine of information on the issues separating Henry II from his adversaries the French kings as well as from his wife Eleanor and his headstrong sons. Most useful are the collections of correspondence between Henry II and Archbishop Thomas Becket and between John and Pope Innocent III; they provide our best information on the great struggle between church and state and on some of the events leading up to Magna Carta. Though having no special connection with the chancery, the letters of that eminent scholar John of Salisbury provide a good commentary on the bitter dispute in the twelfth century over appeals from English courts to the papal court.

As always the charters are one of the principal chancery records; many originals are extant, some found in the royal archives and others in the private archives of the recipients such as ecclesiastical establishments and great feudal families. Lacking the originals, one can frequently find copies in the cartularies kept by most of the leading churches and monasteries. Of these charters the first that come to mind are Magna Carta and the affiliated charters and drafts that led up to it. The routine charters continued to make donations of land and privileges to the church and royal vassals, thus providing a picture of the social and feudal structure of twelfth-century England. As the towns grew in importance with the reviving money economy, Henry and his successors increased their charters of privileges to these urban centers; from them we learn of local urban government and of the

[3] SM, nos. 36, 40A.

financial relations between king and town.[4] These royal charters are supplemented by royal and private wills, indispensable for reconstructing the landed holdings of a feudal family or church. As under the Normans the writ continued as the work horse of central administration, serving as the principal instrument for making known the royal will in feudal, military, political, financial, and legal matters.

The innovation in chancery records, however, was the introduction of the enrollment system. The Norman kings, as we have seen, had begun to enroll annually on Pipe Rolls all the revenue due them from the counties. Long before the twelfth century the church had copied all the acts and charters pertinent to ecclesiastical establishments upon cartularies which were folio books of parchment. Sometimes a cartulary contained all the charters but usually it was selective, recording only acts considered essential for the lands and privileges of a monastery or acts that dealt with certain lands or particular matters such as public privileges of government received from a king. By the twelfth century secular princes also had their cartularies and some had developed a system of registering acts and charters according to subject matter; one register, for example, would contain acts relative to homages and another, records of donations made to vassals. By the late twelfth century there was consequently good precedent for the preservation and classification of records. In the reign of John the chancery under Hubert Walter began to enroll all the documents issuing from it to insure adequate record of royal transactions passing through that department; this practice also provided the recipients of royal documents records to fall back upon should the original be lost. The great chancery enrollments that began at the end of the twelfth century were arranged chronologically; all documents irrespective of subject matter or importance were recorded. With but few gaps these enrollments continued to the end of the Middle Ages, providing a documentation on central government unrivaled by any other medieval state. In 1199 the Charter Rolls began; here were copied the charters that conveyed the richest and most solemn royal concessions such as royal liberties, immunities, privileges, and possessions to great persons and the church. They were always witnessed by members of the court, and the chancellor appended the great seal to them.

By John's reign the press and variety of government business forced the chancery to develop other types of records. For public matters affecting administrative areas or a number of people, the letters patent were devised. These were documents written upon an open sheet of parchment with the great seal pendant (hanging) at the bottom. Generally they were addressed to the royal officers, whose responsibility it was to implement the royal order, and to all those affected by the order. Letters patent were used for treaties, diplomatic negotiations, correspondence, appointments, grants,

[4] SM, nos. 39, 43, 44.

and confirmations. Eventually the clumsier and longer charter was almost superseded by this more practical chancery product. By 1201 letters patent were enrolled and the Patent Rolls provide some of the richest evidence on English constitutional history in the thirteenth and fourteenth centuries. Eventually the Patent Rolls were classified according to subject matter or to the area they concerned; we thus find the Norman, Gascon, German, Roman, Welsh, Scottish, and Treaty Rolls. Along with the letters patent developed the third great chancery record—the letters close. Drafted to meet a miscellany of business, they concerned the individual and dealt with matters pertaining only to him—royal mandates, letters, acceptances of homage, and payment of wages. Written on a small sheet of parchment the letters close were rolled into a cylinder and sealed by the small seal. By 1204 they were enrolled on the Close Rolls.[5] These, then, were the three great series of enrollments that have provided a major part of our evidence on royal government to the end of the Middle Ages.

We can rapidly dispose of the remaining chancery records. Evolving out of the letters close in the early thirteenth century were the writs of *liberate* consisting of orders by the king or his officials to officers of the exchequer for the payment of money to royal creditors. These orders for payment were enrolled on the Liberate Rolls. Since the Conquest it was customary for men who desired a royal favor such as land, a lucrative marriage, or a profitable office to offer the king a sum of money or some other like consideration. These offers or fines, as they were termed, may have been enrolled as early as Henry II's reign; there is record of such enrollment for 1194–1195. With John, the Fine Rolls become an annual enrollment. Because such payments were made into the exchequer, the chancery had to inform that department what debts should be collected. For this purpose the chancery began to enroll all these bargains on a roll which would be sent to the exchequer; in turn it transferred the appropriate information to the Pipe Roll. These new enrollments were called Originalia Rolls and are extant from 1195–1196. The last chancery enrollment to arise in this period was the Memoranda Rolls. Whenever the collection of a royal debt was complicated, involving financial problems that required the expert advice of the exchequer, all necessary data and advice were noted and enrolled for future reference. Enrollment began in 1196 but did not become regular until 1199. These are the principal chancery records, which, we should remember, must frequently be supplemented with other nonroyal records such as ecclesiastical cartularies and registers, manorial account and court rolls, and borough records which become numerous in the early thirteenth century.

B. Financial Records

Under Henry I that marvelous financial record the Pipe Roll had come into existence, only to disappear after one year (1130) and not to reappear

[5] SM, no. 41.

until after the debacle of Stephen and Matilda. With the second year of Henry II's reign the Pipe Rolls recommence and continue yearly with but few gaps to the end of the fifteenth century. They present the most complete picture of royal finance for the Angevin period.[6] They are, nonetheless, supplemented by other financial records demanded by the expanding royal revenue. The Norman exchequer, as we have noted, began to function almost as early as the English. There are, however, no Pipe Rolls or Great Rolls of the Norman Exchequer extant until Henry II; there are then a few for his reign as well as for the reigns of Richard I and John. To maintain record of the income received from sources other than those recorded in the Pipe Rolls, the exchequer began to keep Receipt Rolls. These rolls are referred to by that famous financial treatise *The Dialogue of the Exchequer*; there is a fragment surviving from 1185 and then the rolls are preserved somewhat regularly after 1194. For the year 1185 there exists the *Rotulus de Dominabus* (Ladies' Roll), which resulted from an inquest of Henry II to determine the crown rights over wardships, reliefs, and other incomes due from widows, orphans, minors, and heiresses of tenants-in-chief.

The last two records to be included with the exchequer documents are so classified, not because they deal primarily with financial matters, but because they were stored in the treasury. The *Cartae Antiquae*, for example, were charters granted to the church and private individuals who then secured the enrollment of these documents at the exchequer for safekeeping. Such a practice provided a duplicate which, in case of judicial dispute, could be referred to without the original's having to be produced. Thanks to this practice, developed some time during Henry II's reign, we are in possession of charters that stem back to Ethelbert of Kent. In 1195 begins that marvelous collection of records called the Feet of Fines which recorded conveyances of property, or final concords as they were styled. In a typical agreement reached on the conveyance of land, two parties would decide to have the record drafted in triplicate rather than in duplicate. Drawn up in the form of a chirograph the three copies were cut apart; each party received a copy, and the third, the bottom copy, was given to the treasurer, who was to guard the record "in perpetuity." For six centuries the Feet of Fines thus continued to be drawn up. These records were extremely valuable for court procedure because they contributed to the use of evidence in trials and provided an orderly record on the possession of land.

Two other financial records, the Mise and the Prest Rolls, grew out of the royal household rather than the exchequer. They recorded the amounts of money paid to the royal household by the exchequer. The Mise Rolls contain minute accounts of the daily expenses of the household and court and thus afford an intimate picture of the king and his associates as they traveled about the realm. Until 1216 we have only a fragment of a roll for

[6] SM, no. 37.

Richard's reign and two rolls for John's.[7] The Prest Rolls consist of annual accounts of payments made by the exchequer to officers of the household and other servants for advances and accommodations on their wages or for the performance of special duties. Only two survive from John's reign.

C. Legal Records

The Angevin propensity for keeping records is also borne out by the new legal records of the period. Where prior to Henry II and his sons our evidence for judicial proceedings in the royal court is mostly due to chance survival of stray documents, thereafter our information on royal justice comes from a group of legal records called Plea Rolls that may be classified according to the type of royal court before which a plea was heard. Unlike the Chancery Rolls, which were membranes of parchment sewn end to end to form a large roll for storage purposes, the Plea Rolls consisted of membranes sewn together at the top, one upon another, so that consequently they did not form a long continuous roll. No extant Plea Rolls exist for Henry II's reign but references in other documents to legal records and to his intensive legal reforms argue strongly for the existence of such records. Though the first Plea Rolls for the cases heard before the itinerant justices date only from 1195–1196, it is likely that these Eyre Rolls, as they are classified, may have existed as early as 1166, the year of Henry II's reorganization of the judicial circuits.[8] Subsequently Henry required that the itinerant justices keep record of all judicial fines arising from the pleas held on their eyres so that they could be collected by the sheriffs and rendered to the exchequer; in this way the Eyre Rolls came to be kept.

It is most difficult to distinguish between pleas heard in the presence of the king and his justices and those heard in the presence of a group of royal justices designated for this purpose by the king. Both types of pleas, though actually held in the *curia regis*, came to be classified separately. From 1178 when a group of five royal justices had been empowered to hear pleas at Westminster in the king's absence, it seems probable that record of such judicial proceedings must have been made; our earliest example, however, does not come until 1194. Such records are called Common Bench Rolls or *de banco* rolls and are thereafter extant. The record of pleas heard before the king and his justices are called the King's Bench Rolls or the *coram rege* rolls; they begin in 1200, when a number of justices regularly followed the king about. The fourth valuable legal record developing in this period was the Rolls of the Great Assize. About 1179 Henry II inaugurated the grand assize enabling certain civil causes to be settled by jury rather than by battle. All the writs issued to persons permitting them to obtain jury trial were recorded on rolls kept in the chancery; with the writ were included the particulars of the case. Although of lesser importance the Rolls of the Forest

[7] SM, no. 42.
[8] SM, no. 40B.

Pleas begin during John's reign and offer a good commentary on the extent and organization of the royal forest as well as on the type of infractions committed against forest law.

D. Treatises on Royal Government

The maturity of Angevin government and the knowledge and sophistication of some of the royal officers is seen in a few of the works composed to describe the organization of royal government. These treatises could logically be discussed along with the financial and legal records, but inasmuch as they have broader interests, it has seemed better to deal with them separately. As an excellent supplement to what is learned about the exchequer from the Pipe Rolls, *The Dialogue of the Exchequer* by Richard fitz Nigel, the great-nephew of Bishop Roger of Salisbury, describes all the operations and the staff that performed them. As the illegitimate son of Nigel, who was the nephew of Roger and eventually bishop of Ely and treasurer under Henry I, Richard came from a distinguished family of civil servants. He was educated at the monastery of Ely and, as his writing shows, received a sound liberal education, probably as good as could be obtained in twelfth-century England. Soon after Henry II's accession to power Richard entered the royal service. His father purchased the treasurership for him in 1158, a post he held until his death in 1196. Meanwhile, receiving rapid ecclesiastical preferment, he became bishop of London in 1189. He seems also to have been a trusted royal councillor who often served as an itinerant justice and a judge of the court of the common pleas. He was, in fact, a typical practical-minded administrator not interested in theory but only in getting things done efficiently. Although trained in Latin grammar and literature, exposed to scholastic ideas, and greatly experienced in law, he wrote in a simple, almost pedestrian style, with little thought of getting enmeshed in political philosophy or theology. Completed some time before 1179, the *Dialogue* was meant to serve as a manual for those who staffed the exchequer. The literary form is that of a dialogue between an important exchequer official and a subordinate desiring firsthand instruction. The treatise is divided into two parts. The first describes the structure and functions of the exchequer—the staff and its work, the Pipe Rolls and writs, the system of account on the chessboard (*scaccarium*), and the tallies and system of weighing. The second part explains exchequer procedure—all the sources of royal revenue and its collection, how accounts were rendered by royal officers and debtors, and how these men were treated at the exchequer. One of the most unique handbooks on government in the Middle Ages, the *Dialogue* should be read by whoever hopes to gain an insight into English medieval finance and administration.

What Richard fitz Nigel did for financial administration, Ranulf Glanville, in his *Treatise on the Laws and Customs of England*, did for law.[9]

[9] SM, no. 33.

Like Richard, Glanville was a professional civil servant, working himself up the ladder. His first prominent position was the shrievalty of Yorkshire in 1163. In 1174 he captured the Scottish king in battle and thereafter received rapid promotion. From sheriff, envoy, and royal judge, he became the justiciar of England in 1180, a post held until 1190 when he died while serving with Richard I on the Third Crusade. Though some scholars doubt whether he wrote this law book, attributing it rather to Hubert Walter or to a group of justices, the weight of the evidence supports Glanville. Completed in 1189, it is again a practical treatise by a royal servant who writes from his rich experience as sheriff, judge, and justiciar. Glanville had only a smattering of Roman law, probably having read the Institutes. The new jurisprudence of the twelfth century but led him to cast his book in a more logical form and to make a distinction between criminal and civil cases and between possessory and proprietary actions. His chief theme is the royal court and the justice it dispensed, for it was this court and its affiliates along with the judicial writs and assizes that were forging the English common law in the twelfth and thirteenth centuries. An extremely popular book because of its lucidity, it soon spawned numerous copies; as late as the middle of the thirteenth century lawyers were still using it and bringing it up to date. That such a book could be written during Henry II's reign demonstrates how far advanced were the legal system and thinking of that age in England. Both Germany and France had to wait another seventy-five years before they possessed comparable law books.

Where the two above treatises were practical manuals composed by experienced royal servants, the *Policraticus*, which sheds light on the church-state struggle of the twelfth century, was written by the famous theologian and scholar John of Salisbury (d. 1180), who had studied with the most renowned masters at continental universities, had served in the household of three archbishops of Canterbury, and had ended his career as bishop of Chartres. The *Policraticus* (*The Statesman's Book*) was completed in 1159–1160 while John was a secretary of Archbishop Theobald. Concentrating on the nature of secular government, it is the first real treatise on political philosophy in the Middle Ages. As one might imagine, John argued that a prince must rule his state according to Christian dogma. So long as the church and its rights were sovereign, it followed that secular society would be well ordered and governed according to divine plan. But when religion was attacked and when the ruler did not obey the church, troubles began. The ruler then forfeited his prerogative as a political vicar of God and must be removed. John went so far as to argue that to remove an evil ruler assassination could be justified as done according to divine will. To summarize this work in detail is impossible, but it should be emphasized that John was almost exclusively concerned with the spiritual controls over princes rather than with the problem of proper balance between ruler and the governed, or with the practical limits of authority a ruler could wield on behalf of his people. Despite its religious and theoretical tone, this work provides a good view of church-state relations, written as it was by a servant of the church and on the eve of the bitter dispute between Henry II and Thomas Becket.

2. NARRATIVE SOURCES

We cannot here delve into the numerous Angevin biographies, sermons, and other miscellaneous sources except to remark that some, such as the ten biographies written on Thomas Becket, provide valuable facts and observations on the principal historical actors of the age. Our concern is with the chroniclers, and then of necessity with only the leading chroniclers and historians. As in the Norman period most historical compositions were done by monks and canons. The most illustrious such writer for Henry II's reign was the Augustinian canon William of Newburgh, who completed his *English History* about 1198. Though much of this work deals with earlier English history, it still is one of our best accounts of contemporary events. More than a chronicler, William selected his facts, arranging them in a logical pattern rather than merely listing events. He was one of the first critical historians and rejected a good deal of early English history as mere fabrication and myth. Ill informed on much of what he wrote about for Henry II's reign, and ignorant of a lot more, William treated what he did include with a rare moderation and objectivity. His account of Thomas Becket is particularly sane and impartial, and in Chapter XXVI of Book III he provides our best sketch of Henry II as a king.

A tendency of the age was for historical works to be composed increasingly by clerks who had not seen the inside of a monastery. They had imbibed the best education available in western Europe and then had entered the royal civil service, working their way up the administrative ladder to a key position and eventually to a rich ecclesiastical office. Upon these widely traveled, experienced, urbane, and secularized men the kings had to rely for the staffing of the central administration. From them came the type of history worthy of the dynamic twelfth and early thirteenth centuries. Such a historian was the anonymous author (often erroneously named Benedict of Peterborough) of *The Deeds of Henry II and Richard*. Written some time before 1193 it is a full account of Henry's reign after 1172 and in it are numerous royal records, a fact that points to the author's possible service in the royal government. Another historian, Roger of Hoveden, was definitely connected with the government. A clerk and justice, he associated with prominent men and included in his history copies of royal documents he had handled. In his *Chronicle* Roger used much material from *The Deeds* and continued that history down to 1201; from 1192 to 1201, therefore, his account is original and contemporary. The other work written by a clerk is the *Outlines of History* by Ralph of Diceto. He may never have served the king, but from his vantage point as archdeacon of Middlesex and dean of Saint Paul's he was in close touch with the royal government. His history, also fortified with documents and letters, is an original account for the period 1172 to 1201, and from 1188 on is contemporary. To round out these histories of Henry's reign is the *Chronicle* of Robert of Torigni, a Norman monk who was prior of Bec and abbot of Mont-Saint-Michel. It affords an independent account between 1150 and 1186 and is most useful for the policies of Henry II on the Continent.

Although some of the works discussed above encompassed the reign of Richard I, they may be supplemented by *The Deeds of Richard I* (original from 1189 to 1192) of the Winchester monk Richard of Devizes and by the Norman-French metrical composition, *The History of William Marshal,* which describes the famous knight William Marshal, companion and servant of Henry II and his sons. The latter provides a valuable commentary on feudal society and its ideals along with intimate details on the services rendered by a faithful vassal to his lords. With but few exceptions the chief historians of John's reign are again monks. Some time before the end of the first quarter of the thirteenth century an anonymous "minstrel" of Béthune completed *The History of the Dukes of Normandy and the Kings of England.* Up to 1199 it is but an abridgment of William of Jumièges. The part from 1199 to 1216, however, seems to have been written by an eyewitness to the events and consequently is useful for John's reign. A number of continental chronicles help to supplement the English works. Turning to the monkish accounts there is the *English Chronicle* by the Cistercian Ralph of Coggeshall, which appears to be original for the years 1187 to 1223. The monk Walter of Coventry, writing long after John's death, probably between 1293 and 1307, has left behind his *Memorials.* His account of John's reign and particularly of the years 1212–1216 is one of the best because it was derived from a chronicle of the monastery of Barnwell which had minutely recorded the events of these critical years. Our principal account of John's reign comes, however, from *The Flowers of History* by Roger of Wendover, who until recently was accepted as the definitive authority on John. Even though he has now been proven unreliable on certain points, we must yet rely on him for the events leading up to Magna Carta. A monk of Saint Albans, he undoubtedly saw much of John and knew a considerable amount about this turbulent character. Using Hoveden and Diceto down to 1200, Roger thereafter becomes independent and remains so to 1235, the end of his history.

Wendover's successor as historiographer at Saint Albans was Matthew Paris, who is considered the greatest English medieval historian. Though much of his historical writing covers the period from 1216 to 1259 and though he wrote all his history during Henry III's reign, his work is of value also for the reign of John. The foremost achievement of Matthew was the *Greater Chronicle* (from creation to 1259), of which the part to 1235 was based primarily on a work of John de Cella, abbot of Saint Albans, and on the history of Wendover. Matthew revised both, however, and continued them independently down to 1259. This section is especially valuable because of the insertion of charters, writs, and papal bulls. Later he abridged this history into the *English History* to cover the period from 1066 to 1253; it is in some respects an improvement, for numerous biased and highly subjective passages have been deleted or revised so as to present the material more objectively. Matthew's other works relevant for English political and constitutional history are the *Flowers of History*, a revision of the *Greater Chronicle* from creation to 1066 plus certain revisions of the later part, and his *Life of Langton*. In addition he wrote on the history of Saint Albans and its abbots. Matthew probably ranks as the major English medieval historian because he expressed public opinion more accurately and completely than any others of his craft. When too often he is given to criticism and to unhistorical judgments based on bias and local sentiment, it is nevertheless done in a brisk and direct style that gets across the subject matter. Like other historians of his age, he also used too little discretion in what he chose to include. On the other hand, despite the multiplicity of inconsequential minutiae, he generally recorded and commented upon the key historical news, a thing others often neglected. Well located on a principal highway but twenty miles to the north of London, Matthew was in close touch with events at the hub of the kingdom and knew the king and many of his officials quite well. If one looks to Matthew for critical historical thinking he will be disappointed, but Matthew is such an improvement over both his predecessors and his successors that he is one of the few in the Middle Ages whom one may justly label a historian.

XVI

Angevin England, 1154–1216

IN THE following story of Henry II and his sons it will be noted that only casual attention is given to the struggle of Henry and John against the church and to the conflict between John and the barons. These events, so essential for the understanding of English institutions, must be dealt with in chapters apart; they will here be mentioned only in so far as they clarify the flow of political and military history.

1. THE REIGN OF HENRY II (1154–1189)

There is no more apt description of a ruler's accession to the throne than the assertion of Gerald of Wales that when Henry II was crowned king on 19 December 1154 he was smiled upon by the "admirable favor of fortune." Endowed with a strong physique and robust health he was also singularly intelligent and possessed a good princely education. Keen for the chase yet equally intrigued by legal intricacies, good literature, and the sophisticated talk of cultured companions, this man, who spoke, wrote, and read Latin and French, feverishly concentrated on the business at hand, whether it was war, diplomacy, or hawking. Probably the greatest of English medieval kings, he left the deepest imprint upon medieval institutions. All Angevin history is little more than a commentary upon the magnificent achievements of Henry II. A few years before falling heir to England Henry had acquired in rapid succession some of the richest lands of France. In 1150 he succeeded his father Geoffrey Plantagenet, count of Anjou, as duke of Normandy. Upon the death of Geoffrey in 1151 he received the county of Anjou. In 1152 after the dull and pious Louis VII of France had secured the papal annulment of his marriage to Eleanor, duchess of Aquitaine, Henry swiftly courted and married her, thereby acquiring most of southwestern France. This, then, was the nucleus of the Angevin Empire, this the core from which the Empire expanded after Henry's position was consolidated in England.

Within six months after his coronation Henry brought order to war-torn England. The Flemish mercenaries of Stephen were expelled, the English supporters of Stephen were quashed, and all adulterine castles were leveled or turned over to royal officers. Those desirous of making their peace and willing to pay dearly enough to buy it were taken into the royal grace; even some former administrators of Stephen found a place in Henry's government. The transfer of royal power was abetted, moreover, by the passing away of the feudal barons who had fought in the civil war; only a few lived on under Henry. In general Henry wisely refrained from vindictive measures and pardoned all who had been opponents of his mother Matilda. By 1155 with every branch of his government operating efficiently Henry could turn to other than domestic problems.

Like his Norman predecessors Henry was fundamentally a French prince who considered his continental possessions of paramount importance; twenty-one of his thirty-four years as king were spent on the Continent. But England provided a base of operations and rich resources, and consequently Henry strove to maintain peace in his kingdom and to stabilize its frontiers and guarantee their security. The Welsh and Scots had taken advantage of royal weakness during the civil war to encroach upon English territory. The Scottish kings had pushed their border in some places sixty miles south of the old Berwick-Carlisle castle line. The Welsh had occupied considerable territory in the west marches. To these inroads Henry immediately addressed himself. In 1157 when he was at Chester poised for an attack against the prince of North Wales the Scottish problem was temporarily solved. Weakened by bitter feuding in his kingdom the young king Malcolm IV felt it wise to make peace with Henry. Going to Chester Malcolm did homage to Henry and, with his brother William, surrendered such northern English fiefs as the honor of Carlisle and the earldom of Northumberland and agreed to hold other Scottish lands in fief. This settlement pacified the northern frontier until 1173. Henry then proceeded west along the coast to Rhuddlan and by this show of force persuaded Prince Owain Gwynedd to submit. Owain did homage, delivered over hostages for good behavior, and surrendered the English territory he had occupied. Henry next turned to South Wales and by the end of 1158 had forced its prince to surrender all the Norman lands and to conclude peace. Wales troubled Henry no more. For Scotland a final settlement came out of the revolt of 1173–1174 staged against Henry by his sons. The Scottish king William the Lion joined the insurgents and invaded northern England. He was, however, as unfortunate as the other rebels. Henry's forces commanded by the sheriff of Yorkshire captured him at Alnwick Castle and Henry then drove a hard bargain. By the Treaty of Falaise in 1174 William had to take Scotland in fief and to surrender five of his strongest castles to Henry as guarantee of future good behavior. Henry also gained the right to receive the homage of the Scottish nobles without any reservation of loyalty to the Scottish king. By these ignominious terms the status of William had become that of an English earl. Thus it was that Henry brought peace, swiftly and cheaply, to his island kingdom.

Though the archaic land of Ireland would seem to have no bearing upon the security of England, a succession of fortuitous events finally caused

Henry to show his power there. As early as 1155 he had formulated a vague plan for an Irish expedition which, sanctioned by the pope, was to have the respectable disguise of a crusade. Welsh, Scottish, church, and continental affairs, however, intervened, forcing temporary postponement of this venture. Meanwhile internal Irish troubles combined to force a subsequent English intervention. Ireland had sunk far since the glorious days of Irish missionary activity and cultural achievement in the early Middle Ages. Peripheral to the mainstream of western European history it had become backwash territory, socially and politically organized on an antiquated tribal system that fostered anarchy in the seven kingdoms into which the island was divided. The Norwegian conquests of the ninth century seemingly had no impact; they merely contributed to the anarchy. The Irish church with its peculiarly loose organization further accentuated decentralization and was in serious need of reform. Since 1066 it had looked to Canterbury for advice and for some of its clergy. By the middle of the twelfth century the orthodox influence was so great that a synod adopted a system of church government modeled after that of the western church. This decision bound Ireland closer to England; the reformed church, in order to prosper, required English political and spiritual support. Soon thereafter political turmoil paved the way for entry of the English. In 1166 one Dermot MacMurrough, king of Leinster and a powerful ruler, was unseated by rebellion and fled to England. There, failing initially to secure help from Henry, he enlisted aid from the Welsh and English barons in the western marches, chief of whom was Richard fitz Gilbert, earl of Pembroke. As on previous occasions these Norman lords ruthlessly exploited their opportunity; they conquered the coastal area and by 1171 had discredited the Irish rulers. But Henry's vassals had been too successful. Just as they were in a position to carve out independent Norman states, Henry thought it propitious to show his hand. He landed in October 1171 and after a brief march through the land persuaded the Irish kings, the Welsh, and the Norman lords to submit and do homage for their kingdoms and lands. In addition, Henry required knight service from the Normans and secured for the royal domain extensive land and towns such as Dublin. This done, Henry returned to England and in 1172 the pope confirmed his lordship over Ireland.

Henry had spent a relatively short time in pacifying the English borders and taming the Irish but he was to find that his work on the Continent was never to end. There the variegated pattern of possessions comprising the territory that historians have called the Angevin Empire offered no easy political solution. Each region—Normandy, Maine, Touraine, Anjou, Poitou, and Aquitaine—had its own customs and political tradition and, as Henry clearly saw, no great centralization or administrative conformity could be obtained. He could only aim at forcing acknowledgment of his lordship and obedience to his imperious will. But even this limited objective was continually obstructed by local particularism and by interference from the French kings fearful of the overmighty English vassal who possessed land and wealth far greater than that of the Île de France. Almost to the end of his reign Henry outmaneuvered opposition or conspiracy, seldom having recourse to war; diplomacy and marriage were his favorite weapons.

Early in 1156 Henry was able to leave England in order to take stock of his French possessions. Soon after landing in France he did homage to Louis VII for his fiefs and then toured his lands receiving homage and supervising administrative detail. During the course of his labors Henry cleverly contrived to block the pretensions of his younger brothers, Geoffrey and William, to French land. William never secured any and Geoffrey, who possessed some castles and the county of Nantes at the mouth of the Loire River, was deprived of these. Acquisition of Nantes gave Henry's county of Anjou access to the sea. In 1158 Henry initiated negotiations with Louis VII for the return of the Norman Vexin, which Louis had occupied during the English civil war. A marriage pact was concluded engaging Henry's three-year-old son, Henry, to Louis' daughter, Margaret, six months of age; her dowry was to be the Vexin. Though the two kings were soon at odds over the county of Toulouse, which both claimed by virtue of having been or being duke of Aquitaine, little serious fighting occurred. Rather than set a poor example for his vassals by attacking Louis, who had occupied the town of Toulouse, Henry retired, leaving the question of Toulouse to be settled later. He then secured papal authorization for the marriage of his son to Margaret and persuaded Louis to give his permission. In 1160 the marriage was celebrated and Henry got his prize—the Vexin.

Except for intermittent skirmishing between Henry and Louis from 1166 to 1171 the period to 1173 was characterized by peace on the Continent. During this interlude Henry worked to provide his sons with suitable possessions. His eldest son, the Young Henry, was to inherit England, Normandy, and Anjou; his second son, Richard, was to get Aquitaine; John and Geoffrey were to be married off to suitable heiresses. The Young Henry was early associated with his father in governing and in 1170 was crowned king of England, an act performed to secure a peaceful succession. Richard became duke of Aquitaine in 1167. In 1169 he and the Young Henry, yet only boys, did homage to Louis VII for their fiefs. In 1166 Henry arranged for Geoffrey to marry Constance, the heiress of the county of Brittany. He still had to provide for his favorite, the baby John. Finally, in 1173 Henry found him an heiress—Alice, heiress to the counties of Maurienne and Savoy located in the French Alps. Never was Henry more powerful than in 1173; he was recognized as the richest and greatest prince of western Europe. He had not only preserved the integrity of his English and French possessions but reinforced them along the borders by strategic acquisitions. The Vexin had been added to Normandy; acquired as fiefs were the county of Berry, adjoining Poitou and Touraine, and that of Auvergne, adjoining La Marche and the Limousin. Even the count of Toulouse had been forced to perform homage for his county. Most of France, including the richest part, belonged to Henry. Besides these tangible gains he won also the more intangible diplomatic successes. He retained the counts of Flanders as military allies through a sizable money fief and subsidiary pecuniary considerations. By marrying his eldest daughter Matilda to Henry the Lion, duke of Saxony and Bavaria, he founded the Angevin-Guelf coalition that lasted almost to the end of John's reign. He married his daughters Eleanor and Joan to the kings of Castile and Sicily, respectively. He even fished in the troubled waters of Italy, granting financial support to the Lombard communes in their struggle against the Hohenstaufen emperor Frederick I. Such a network of alliances expanded Henry's sphere of influence and completely encircled his unfortunate overlord Louis VII.

Feudal fortunes fluctuated rapidly, however, and within the year Henry was faced by a formidable revolt from his sons and some barons backed by Louis VII. The immediate cause was the marriage agreement made for John. Count Humbert of Savoy insisted that John must possess suitable land before Alice and her dowry would be his. When Henry decided to give three Angevin castles to John, the Young Henry, still without a castle, and Geoffrey, within whose appanage the castles lay, were outraged. Richard joined in their discontent and the three, encouraged by their mother Eleanor, raised the standard of revolt. Both sides acted swiftly. Henry captured and imprisoned Eleanor and mobilized a large force of mercenaries. Supported by Louis VII and his vassals the Young Henry fomented revolt in Normandy, Anjou, Brittany, Gascony, and England; the king of Scotland and the counts of Flanders and Blois promised considerable military assistance. Henry II's recovery was phenomenal; a motley feudal coalition was to discover the amazing power of an efficiently centralized royal government. In quick succession he smothered revolt in Brittany, Normandy, and Anjou. The justiciar and his lieutenants did an equally thorough job in England. First a group of English rebel barons supported by an invading force of Flemish mercenaries was routed and its leaders were imprisoned. Then the sheriff of Yorkshire, with a northern levy, defeated and captured the Scottish king. Finally in the summer of 1174 Henry himself struck the last blow. Louis VII, the Flemish count, the Young Henry, and other feudal lords had laid siege to Rouen, but the appearance of Henry at the head of his mercenaries was all that was needed to break their spirit. Louis quickly sued for peace and with the Treaty of Montlouis in 1175 the family feud was ended. With all the rebels, Henry was lenient. Suitable land and revenues were provided for the three sons, and the count of Flanders was again received as a loyal ally. As for John, now eight, his betrothed had died and so Henry richly provided for him with castles and lands in England, Normandy, and Anjou. To the royal favorite again went the greatest share.

For the next ten years Henry ruled supreme; scarcely a ripple of discontent broke the calm and efficiency of the Angevin Empire. The befuddled old

Louis VII was pushed around at will until he graciously died in 1180. His successor Philip Augustus was but a lad, loyally protected for the next few years by his great vassal. The Young Henry pouted and complained of nothing to do and suddenly died, perhaps of boredom, in 1183. Though a grievous loss to Henry the death of his son was not catastrophic. Self-indulgent and egotistical, the Young Henry, like Stephen, would have failed dismally as king. Though Richard now became the heir he would not play the role, despite the urging of Henry that he associate himself in the royal government. Richard preferred the more dangerous and exciting military exercise of crushing petty feudal revolt in Aquitaine. Like William Rufus, his predecessor of a century before, Richard had no taste for the business of routine government. Henry, still bent on lavishing upon John more authority and land than a mere lad could handle, made him king of Ireland and in 1185 sent him to govern the island. His unsuccessful reign ended after a year because in 1186 Geoffrey, count of Brittany, died; John, now second in royal succession, was entitled to more impressive titles and lands. But for other than the fortunes of Geoffrey and John was the year 1186 notable. Henry II, aging rapidly, was in no mood or condition to face the opposition that two ungrateful sons and Philip Augustus were preparing for him. Having mastered his vassals in the royal domain Philip Augustus was now ready to launch a campaign to destroy the Angevin Empire. Throughout 1186 Philip accused the royal vassal of sundry actions unbecoming a vassal and inflamed the suspicious Richard against his father, even suggesting that Henry had seduced Philip's half sister Alice to whom Richard was promised in marriage. In 1187 Philip invaded Touraine and Henry secured a truce only at the price of handing over two castles; this was the first land lost by Henry since 1154.

The last two years of the old king's life witnessed unmitigated defeat. There was no longer any trust between Henry and Richard, and the cancer of suspicion grew alarmingly under the proddings of the shrewd Philip. He spurred revolt throughout the Angevin Empire and secretly wooed John into conspiracy. Not even the fall of Jesusalem in late 1187 or the meeting of Philip and Henry in 1188 where they kissed and vowed to recover the Holy City from the infidel could stem the unfolding of the last tragic moments for Henry. With Richard convinced that new outbursts of revolt in Aquitaine were fomented by his father to forestall his going on a crusade, Philip took advantage of this break to conquer Berry, Auvergne, some of Touraine, and Vendôme, all of which he kept. Late in 1188 when the three met to conclude a truce Philip, by prearrangement with Richard, demanded that the latter be given possession of Anjou, Maine, and Touraine, or, as an alternative, marry Alice immediately and be recognized as heir to all the Empire. With his refusal Henry sealed the entente of Philip and Richard. In Henry's presence Richard knelt before Philip and did homage for all the French fiefs, an act that initiated the final blow against Henry. Supported now only by his bastard son Geoffrey and a few barons and mercenaries,

Henry lost on all fronts. Quickly Anjou, Touraine, and Maine fell. Fleeing from Le Mans, Henry should have headed for the security of his Norman castles but against the advice of Geoffrey the worn-out and sick man turned to his old land of Anjou hoping to win Chinon. His pursuers then relentlessly cut off retreat, boxing him up at Colombières not far from Tours; here the dying Henry made his humble submission. He did homage to Philip, recognized Richard as sole heir, consented to the marriage of Richard and Alice, promised to surrender Auvergne and Berry to Philip and to pay him a war indemnity, and agreed that such towns as Le Mans and Tours were to be held by Philip until all the peace terms were fulfilled. Henry then departed but not before demanding to see a list of the conspirators; heading the list was John. Carried back to Chinon Henry lingered for a week and finally breathed his last in the arms of his one faithful son—Geoffrey the Bastard. Henry's reign had been brilliant except for the last three years and these could have been avoided if he had tried to understand the thoughts and passions of his high-spirited brood. A blind trust in them and a favoritism for John, the worst of the lot, spelled ruin for a man who otherwise was overly realistic about men and their motives. If Henry had any other political defect it was his failure to comprehend that he could not deal with Philip Augustus as he had with his father. It should be emphasized, however, that these defects as well as most of the political and military events of his reign pale before the strides made in law and administration under his guidance.

2. THE REIGN OF RICHARD I (1189–1199)

It is not surprising that most schoolboys have difficulty in remembering Henry II and his reign but never forget Richard the Lion Hearted. Whereas Richard did all that a boy dreams of doing and was what a boy dreams of being, Henry accomplished what only those who understand superb statesmanship and legal ability can appreciate. Henry was a businesslike ruler; Richard, a chivalrous adventurer. Probably equal to his father in intelligence, and definitely his superior as a fighter and in those qualities of generosity and comradeship, Richard failed to appreciate the responsibilities of rule and, like William Rufus, left that boresome task to clerks and humdrum men. He was exclusively a French prince caring not for England but for its money. He visited England twice for a total of six months, on both occasions to secure money for his wars. It is a tribute to Henry's work that English government functioned for ten years almost as efficiently in the royal absence as in its presence.

Richard's first thought was to free himself for the crusade he had sworn against the Turk Saladin. In return for some territory in Auvergne and Berry and payment of a large war indemnity Philip Augustus recognized Richard as Henry's heir. The two then agreed to go on the crusade together. To his father's loyal adherents Richard granted an easy pardon, even rewarding some such as the famous knight William Marshal with land and titles. It was more difficult to satisfy his relatives. He gave the archbishopric of York to Geoffrey the Bastard. To his traitorous brother John he gave not only the county of Mortain in Normandy but also six counties and five castles in England, in addition to the hand of Isabel, heiress of the rich earldom of Gloucester. This irrational generosity was to be regretted almost within the year. As for his nephew, Arthur of Brittany, the son left behind by Henry's third son Geoffrey, Richard permitted him for the moment to remain a ward of his Breton relatives. According to feudal primogeniture Arthur had the best claim as Richard's successor as long as Richard had no heirs, and Richard seems to have recognized him as such early in his reign. The last item of business before departure on the crusade was to provide for the governing of England in his absence. After his coronation at Westminster in September Richard dealt with this matter. Unfamiliar with England, her traditions, and her institutions, he handled this administrative problem clumsily. He removed most of his father's team, including Ranulf Glanville, the trusted justiciar, and replaced them with his friends, most of whom paid dearly for their positions; Richard was bound to raise money for his crusade. To neutralize the power of the justiciarship Richard gave it to two men—Hugh de Puiset, bishop of Durham, and William Longchamp, a favorite servant who had worked himself up the civil service ladder. This done and having sold all the offices and privileges he could, Richard took his money back to France and prepared for his holy expedition.

Though the military exploits of Richard while on the Third Crusade constitute the basis of his fame they are peripheral to the central theme of English history and shall be treated cursorily. His capture of Acre (1191) and his other military successes against the Turkish leader Saladin proved his high military capacity, though he failed in winning the main objective—Jerusalem. Dissension among the crusading leaders, disagreement with the Europeans of the Latin States, and strong infidel resistance weakened the military effectiveness of the crusaders; Richard was ultimately content to conclude an agreement permitting Christians to make pilgrimages to the Holy City. What merits attention are the nonmilitary events of 1191–1192. Richard and Philip Augustus, traveling together on the crusade, agreed at Messina in Sicily to settle the matter of Richard's marriage to Alice. Richard sought a solution because his mother Eleanor had found a new bride for him—Berengaria, the daughter of the king of Navarre—and was bringing her to Sicily. For 10,000 marks and Richard's consent to hold each French fief separately and to render homage and the necessary services for each Philip freed Richard from his engagement to Alice. By forcing these terms on Richard, Philip strengthened his position as lord and defined more clearly the status of his feudal relations with each of Richard's fiefs. He thereby maneuvered himself into a position from which he could constantly harass Richard with feudal demands or complaints. As soon as Acre fell Philip feigned ill health as an excuse to desert the crusade and return home where there was more remunerative work to be done. Despite his oath to Richard that he would not tamper with his lands, Philip approached John and the two began conspiring to deprive Richard of all that he possessed. Informed of this treachery Richard at last embarked for home in the autumn of 1192 after having concluded his settlement with Saladin. Fearing to pass through France where Philip and John were lying in wait for him he sailed up the Adriatic with the intention of slipping disguised through Germany and then taking boat for England. Unfortunately he was detected in Austria and clamped into prison by Duke Leopold, who had come to hate him as a result of crusading differences. Early in 1193 Leopold was forced to hand over his prisoner to his lord the emperor Henry VI, who, being Hohenstaufen, was naturally eager to get his hands on an ally of his Guelf opponents. Henry VI held all the high cards and played them masterfully. Cognizant that Philip and John would pay a high price to get possession of Richard he so cleverly stressed this eventuality that the royal captive agreed to pay a ransom of 150,000 marks, do homage for England, and work for a Guelf-Hohenstaufen *rapprochement*. Finally the first installment was paid and in early 1194 Richard was liberated at Mainz and departed for England.

During his absence the routine government had functioned smoothly but at the top echelon of administration struggles for power had created bitter divisions. However capable as a justiciar and however loyal to Richard, William Longchamp had been a poor selection. The feudal aristocracy resented this upstart of humble origin, who fanned hatred by his own insatiable ambition, greed for riches, and ignorance of English custom. First he contrived to remove that proud aristocrat Bishop Hugh of Durham from a share in the justiciarship. Already chancellor, he then became sole justiciar and soon obtained appointment as papal legate. After capturing these high offices William proceeded to alienate a majority of the barons by his extravagant living and conceited behavior. This discontent played into the hands of John, who posed as the leader against the unpopular royal minister. In 1191 John and the malcontents took up arms, and civil war was avoided only by the arrival of Walter of Coutances, archbishop of Rouen. Sent by Richard to settle the differences between John and William, Walter was armed with powers to take any necessary action. From 1191 to 1194 he was the real ruler. William remained justiciar and might have continued in power had he not outraged public opinion by mistreating Geoffrey the Bastard upon his arrival in England to assume his duties as archbishop of York. On the pretense that Geoffrey failed to swear fealty to Richard, William sent men to seize him and, when the archbishop took sanctuary, they dragged him out of the church. Immediately Geoffrey became a martyr, the church protested, and John found the opportunity to mount his own star. William was removed from office and henceforth had no power. Philip Augustus now drew John into a conspiracy against Richard on the promise that he would be recognized as lord of all the French fiefs. Philip began to attack and occupy English territory while John worked to foment revolt in England. This he could not do in the face of loyal opposition by Walter of Coutances. Early in 1194 when Philip heard of Richard's release he sent John this message: "Look to yourself, the devil is loosed." John fled to France and soon Richard landed in a kingdom loyal but chafing under the heavy taxes levied to pay the ransom. Richard punished the conspirators, although pardoning John, and then extorted more money from his subjects to finance his revenge against Philip Augustus. In May of 1194 he was ready to cross the Channel and, after replacing Walter of Coutances as justiciar with the able Hubert Walter, departed for Normandy, never to see England again.

Richard was more than a match for his crafty opponent. During the next five years he repeatedly defeated him in battle, on one occasion almost capturing him, and retook all the land lost in his absence. Looking to the defense of his possessions he initiated the construction of castles strategically located along the frontiers. Most imposing was the Château Gaillard (Saucy Castle) high above the Seine at Les Andelys in Normandy. Built on a limestone cliff and modeled after the castles of Syria, it anticipated the later concentric castles and was the military marvel of the West. It was begun in 1197 and completed in a year. At its completion Richard is said to have proudly exclaimed: "Is not this a fine saucy baby of mine, this child of a year old?" In 1199 Richard led an expedition into Limoges to subdue a feudal revolt of two powerful vassals. While he was besieging the castle of the lord of Chalûs an arrow found his shoulder, the wound became infected, and within ten days he was dead. Contrary to traditional accounts he did not die while foolishly seeking treasure at Chalûs. His death deprived England of the only man who was a match for the wily Philip Augustus. He left behind a glorious military reputation but little else, not even any heirs.

3. THE REIGN OF JOHN (1199–1216)

Just before his death Richard, realizing that it would be better to leave his possessions to a man rather than to a boy, designated his brother John as successor instead of his young nephew Arthur. But designation did not of itself lead to approval. Although feudal law gave Arthur the better claim, the English and Norman baronage, led by Queen Eleanor, the archbishop of Canterbury, and William Marshal, rallied to John, preferring rule by a mature man. The nobles of Maine, Touraine, and Brittany did homage to Arthur while Eleanor received the homage of the Aquitanian vassals. John, quickly installed as king of England and duke of Normandy, then turned to acquiring the rest of his possessions. Aquitaine was his through his mother but, with Philip Augustus again at his usual occupation of dividing the Angevin family and then ruling, the other lands came less easily. Philip Augustus had acknowledged Arthur as heir of the Angevin Empire, garrisoned some of Arthur's castles, and, acting as guardian, carted him off to Paris for safekeeping. Warfare began but it was desultory; John was not the leader that

Richard was and at the moment Philip could not give campaigning his full attention. He was occupied with a bitter struggle against Pope Innocent III, who had blocked divorce from his queen Ingeborg. Soon John and Philip settled their differences by the Treaty of Le Goulet (May 1200). John was recognized as sole heir and Arthur was to hold Brittany in fief from him. For this recognition Philip's price was the Norman Vexin (except Château Gaillard) and the county of Évreux. Philip's feudal rights over the Angevin fiefs had been further tightened but John had done amazingly well in securing his father's legacy practically intact.

Like so many youngest sons John grew up spoiled, pampered, and undisciplined; these faults, combined with the other Angevin vices, made John's reputation one of the blackest of English kings'. John, contrary to some other unsuccessful medieval kings, was endowed with a good mind and exceptional administrative ability. He thoroughly understood the English government, repeatedly innovated efficient administrative reform, conceived broad political and military policy, and at times brilliantly implemented it. These attributes were nullified unfortunately by lack of sustained drive, inconstancy, periodic laziness, inability to command wide respect and loyalty, and unfortunate utterances that contributed to poor public relations with church and vassalage. John lacked moral character and by his greedy, cruel, and vulgar behavior canceled in a moment what he had accomplished over the course of years through the expenditure of much time and money. In his defense, however, it should be recognized that the problems of the Angevin Empire had taxed the exceptionally able Henry II; not John's deficiencies alone, but time and fortune spelled his ruin.

John's troubles, largely of his own making, began immediately. Securing annulment in 1200 of a childless marriage to Isabel of Gloucester he then journeyed through his French possessions towards Portugal with the intention of marrying one of its princesses; he got no farther than one of his vassal's fiefs—the county of Angoulême. Here he saw and became enamored of the count's daughter, Isabelle, and married her with the father's consent. But there was an obstacle to this marriage. Isabelle was betrothed to a neighboring lord, Hugh the Brown, count of La Marche and one of John's vassals. Suddenly deprived of succession to Angoulême, embarrassed by his royal lord, and brushed aside without a penny's compensation, Hugh was furious. He appealed to John's overlord Philip Augustus to help him get feudal justice. Here was the wedge Philip had long waited for and as quickly as he could—the spring of 1202—he cited John to stand trial in the feudal court of Paris for the accusations brought against him by Hugh. John repeatedly ignored the summons, as Philip knew he would. In April, therefore, Philip proclaimed his royal vassal a traitor and pronounced the forfeiture of all his fiefs; this judgment was acted upon by the invasion of John's lands. Lacking strong support from his vassals, John made no spirited defense. But one lucky incident did occur which if utilized correctly would have saved John his empire. Arthur, who had been reinvested by Philip with the Angevin fiefs, except Normandy and Aquitaine, had his forces in the field and had bottled up Eleanor of Aquitaine in the summer of 1202 in the castle of Mirabeau in Poitou. When Arthur was about to take the castle, John in one of his rare fits of action marched the eighty miles from Le Mans to Mirabeau in forty-eight hours, surprised the besiegers in the early morning, and captured Arthur and two hundred of his chief supporters. With such a haul John could have dictated harsh terms but again he fell back into idleness and treated his prisoners so badly that he incurred universal hatred. Many languished to death in miserable captivity and for others John demanded exorbitant ransoms. As for Arthur, although mystery still surrounds his death, most of the evidence suggests that John was responsible for it in the spring of 1203. One story has John murdering Arthur with his own hands one night while drunk, and then dumping him into the Seine. However accomplished, Arthur's death cost John all support in the Loire area and by 1204 Anjou, Maine, and Touraine were lost. Normandy fell next, though with its castles it could have stood if given any support. John seemed paralyzed. Castle after castle fell, even Château Gaillard in March of 1204. The Norman barons then surrendered town after town until by summer Normandy was lost. In 1205 Philip occupied Poitiers, the capital of Poitou, and in 1206 Brittany was his. Only Aquitaine remained to John. For the Angevin house it was a colossal tragedy but in the end it was for England's good. Eventually the French kings would have won these lands and therefore it was well they were lost early. The barons now had to decide which fiefs to hold, their French or their English; upon this decision they became either French or English. Henceforth the English kings devoted most of their time to England, and its inhabitants expended their energy primarily upon insular projects. Severed politically from Normandy and the northern fiefs the English entered upon that stage of development that was to differentiate their institutions from others of western Europe. It was at this point that the residents of England began to consider themselves different from the French; they were becoming Englishmen.

After four years on the Continent John returned to England and except for a few months remained there until his death. The last eleven years of his reign were filled with three overriding preoccupations—his fight with Pope Innocent III, his preparations and grand strategy to win back the lost Angevin inheritance, and the struggle with his barons that culminated in Magna Carta. John had not been in England long when in 1205 that able Angevin administrator Hubert Walter, archbishop of Canterbury, died. As previously, there were two principal parties who thought they had the better right to elect or influence the election of the archbishop—the monks of Christ Church, Canterbury, and John, whose predecessors had usually secured the election of their candidate. Ignoring John's injunction that they should elect John de Gray, bishop of Norwich, the monks secretly elected their subprior. When informed, John was furious and forced the monks also to elect Gray. Innocent III thus found himself faced with two candidates. In 1206 he quashed both elections as being illegal and suggested a compromise candidate, Stephen Langton, an able and well-educated Englishman serving at the papal *curia*. In 1207 Innocent consecrated Stephen as archbishop and, by flouting the royal will in this matter and usurping a right considered the royal prerogative, initiated a bitter struggle with John. Each had reasons and precedents to bolster his stand and neither would compromise. Supported by the baronage, who feared papal interference, John successfully defied the strongest medieval pope for eight years. In 1207 Innocent placed an interdict on England and in 1208 John confiscated all the possessions of the clergy who observed it. In 1209 John was excommunicated but continued to thrive. Growing more embittered at the church he drove most of the clergy into exile and took their possessions into his own hands; in addition he demanded huge amounts of money from all ecclesiastical establishments. Not until 1213 did John feel a need to negotiate a settlement, prompted undoubtedly by the news that Philip Augustus planned to invade England and that this expedition would be blessed by the pope as a crusade. Innocent's intention was to depose John, who, faced by such formidable opposition, agreed to a settlement with Pandulf, the papal legate. John promised to accept Stephen Langton, to reinstate the exiled clergy, to compensate the church for its losses, to take England and Ireland in fief from the pope and do homage for them, and to pay an annual tribute to the Holy See. However complete John's defeat might seem, one must realize that he avoided the French invasion, which was blocked by Innocent, and that he secured in the pope an ally who was to support him loyally in his struggle with the baronage.

After his defeat by Philip Augustus John was often on the point of leading an expedition to Poitou or Normandy to win back his lands but always it was postponed. Until 1214 his military efforts consisted of an Irish expedition in 1210, so successful that he was able to impose a tight control over the island and to introduce the English administrative system. Other shows of force kept the Scots and Welsh in line and preserved the bond of lordship imposed upon them by Henry II. John's consuming desire, however, was the humiliation of Philip Augustus, an objective he had plotted towards for years. By means of money fiefs, subsidies, and good war pay he had erected a strong continental military coalition in the Low Countries, the Rhineland, Normandy, and Poitou. His diplomatic agents were at work throughout western Europe spinning a web around Philip. John and the Guelf emperor of Germany, Otto IV, were working together on a plan to crush their French enemy. Early in 1214 the preparations were complete. John was to strike at Philip from the southwest of France; Otto IV, heading a force composed of Germans and English allies from the Low Countries, was to strike from the northeast. Until July all went well for John and he reoccupied Poitou; then, faced by a French army under Philip's son, Louis, and uncertain of the loyalty of his forces, he retreated to La Rochelle. Meanwhile with his army Otto marched towards Paris from Flanders. On 27 July 1214 Otto fought a decisive battle against Philip Augustus at Bouvines. Otto's army was completely routed. Otto fled from the battlefield but such men as the counts of Flanders and Boulogne and John's half brother, Earl William of Salisbury, were captured. John purchased a truce from Philip, now the greatest ruler of Europe. A dismal failure, John returned in October to a hostile kingdom.

The unsavory character of John had never bred devotion or loyalty in the rank and file of his vassals, but generally a distrust; they felt his insatiable greed for money knew no bounds. Militarily he had never triumphed and to gain prestige a medieval ruler had to excel in war. John's administrative ability, though superb, led him to develop Angevin government into a despotism and himself into an arbitrary ruler who flouted the feudal custom that governed the relations with his vassals. A decade of residence in England had imprinted John's despotic nature deeply upon English politics. It was but natural that pent-up disaffection should erupt upon the return of a king defeated and bankrupt. Minor explosions had given warning of the events of 1214 and 1215. In 1212 the army John had collected for invasion of France had to be disbanded because reports of treason warned him that he could not rely on his barons; the rumors of defection and foul play heightened John's natural suspicion. Again ready to strike in 1213 he was blocked by his barons, first on the pretext that they could not follow an excommunicated king and secondly on the argument that their feudal tenure did not oblige them to fight overseas. John planned to take vengeance on the ringleaders who were organizing a program of resistance. At meetings of the barons and in their negotiations with John, Stephen Langton assumed a leading role. He was at Saint Albans (4 August 1213) where it was proclaimed at a great council that the laws of Henry I should be enjoyed. Later at a meeting of discontented barons at Saint Paul's in London he read the Coronation Charter of Henry I; the barons declared that they would fight for its provisions. Only the most strenuous efforts of Langton prevented John from fighting the northern barons in late 1213. When John sailed for Poitou in early 1214 the conflict was postponed, only to gain momentum upon his return.

The baronial party consisted principally of northern and eastern men, many of them young lords who lacked the experience and restraint of some of the older barons, like William Marshal, who remained loyal to John. Some of the opposition were reckless and deceitful and inspired no confidence in their political program. When John demanded a scutage from those who had not fought on the Continent he met almost complete refusal; and so the struggle began. The aim of the barons was to force John to put his seal to a document that would stipulate in specific terms the laws and customs by which he would govern; they wanted, in reality, to turn the clock back to the days of Henry I. John's plan was to dodge such a commitment and to secure the support of the church; in March 1215 he took the cross, thereby becoming a crusader protected by the pope. About the same time the barons had assembled under arms at Stamford. At this stage events crescendoed rapidly to a climax. The barons renounced their homage and declared war. John answered by building up his mercenary force. Twice in May John agreed to meet most of the baronial demands but the barons wanted his complete humiliation and surrender. Apparently Langton and William Marshal spent most of May and early June hammering out an agreement that would be acceptable to both the barons and John. Finally on 15 June 1215 the barons and John met at Runnymede meadow along the Thames between Windsor and Staines. There John put his seal to a rough draft called the Articles of the Barons, which was then revised and put into polished form. On 19 June the revised document, Magna Carta, was issued under the great seal, with both John and the barons swearing to uphold its provisions.

Although the charter was to be read in every county court and although John seemed initially inclined to keep peace, the hotheaded baronial leaders were bent on destroying him. Civil war soon raged in England. John called upon the spiritual weapons of his protector Innocent III, who excommunicated the barons. They appealed to Louis, the son of Philip Augustus, to join them in the fight against John; his reward was to be the crown. Aroused from the lethargy that had gripped him since his return from Poitou John organized the coastal defenses and with his loyal barons and mercenaries showed a flash of the drive he had displayed at Mirabeau Castle. Within three months he and his experienced army reduced the north and east of England where the barons were strongest and hemmed them in at London. At this point Louis decided to aid the barons and safely crossed the Channel in May 1216. Unhappily for John a severe storm had destroyed the fleet assembled to prevent the landing of Louis. The cause of the barons was strengthened by Louis; some of the royal castles were surrendered and some of John's supporters deserted. Although Louis and the barons soon took southeastern England, in the central region where John had retired the royal strength was considerable and from here he prepared a counteroffensive. In early autumn he was on the march but by October he was suffering from a severe case of dysentery caused by tremendous exertion, poor diet, and much drinking. He was, however, still capable of tremendous action and work, riding as much as forty to fifty miles a day and then tending to business in the evening. While he was campaigning in Lincolnshire his illness was aggravated by news that his baggage train with all the household possessions, including all the royal paraphernalia and much treasure, had been lost in quicksand while crossing the estuary of the Nene River. This news was received on the twelfth of October. During the next four days he headed for Newark, arriving on the sixteenth. By now he had to be borne on a litter and could advance no farther. He died October the eighteenth after having made a will providing for the protection of his young son Henry, who was to inherit the kingdom; he was buried near the shrine of his patron Saint Wulfstan at Worcester. So ended a man who, though as capable as his father Henry II, was as much a failure as Henry was a success.

XVII

Central Administration

I. KINGSHIP

UNDER the three Angevins—Henry II, Richard I, and John—kingship attained a power unequaled until the reign of Henry VIII. By ingeniously reinforcing and expanding the strength and scope of Norman feudal autocracy these Angevins produced an absolutism that defied the conventional limitations of feudalism. The powers that John wielded, if seen by his grandfather Henry I, would have aroused the delight and envy of the tough old Norman. The Angevins retained the time-honored buttresses to royalty; they ruled by grace of God, royal blood, conquest, and descent from Edward the Confessor. Though none were given to wearing the crown, and did so only at the great court functions, Richard and John accentuated royal pomp. Richard used the plural "we" when granting charters and John was the first to style himself king of England (*Rex Angliae*) instead of simply king of the English (*Rex Anglorum*). Henry II and his sons encouraged the belief in royal thaumaturgical power and in 1161 Henry prevailed upon the pope to canonize Edward the Confessor; henceforth the English kings could claim descent from a saint. By the middle of the twelfth century scholastic and legal learning had so progressed as to add other arguments favoring strong kingship. To print indelibly upon the royal mind the high responsibilities of Christian rule, clerical writers steeply elevated royalty. Set by God above all other men and granted extraordinary power with which to govern, the prince was all the more accountable for his actions to God. He who failed to rule according to divine law became a medieval tyrant. The revived study of Roman law showed itself in the arguments of lawyers upgrading royalty in order to exalt its authority as the giver of law and justice. As church and lawyer strengthened their hold on medieval society they heightened the concept of royal power. The famous lawyer of Henry II, Ranulf Glanville, though fully steeped in feudal theory, quoted the famous maxim of Justinian's Institutes: "What is pleasing to the prince has the force of law." In his *Dialogue of the Exchequer* Richard fitz Nigel stated that royal deeds were to be judged or condemned not by mortal men but by God. Not long after such statements neither Richard nor John felt it necessary to issue coronation charters; John obviously considered himself a ruler whose will knew few traditional limitations.

Although such theory and pomp strengthened royal authority it was nevertheless brute power based upon the king's position as lord of all England that constructed the bridge to autocracy. With no man above him the king was accountable only to himself. This first lordship of England (*dominium*) carried with it a jurisdiction which, though born of feudalism with its homage and fief-holding, under the Angevins overstepped the traditional feudal bounds to royal action. The ingenuity with which the Angevins nourished their jurisdictional powers took them far along the road to absolutism and brought innovations in their tenure of power totally foreign to the concepts of such a strong feudal lord as Henry I. Only the royal word or writ was needed to expand the scope and power of jurisdiction. But this is not the place to describe in detail the mushrooming of the royal jurisdiction and prerogative; it suffices to note that no matter what the feudal custom or theory the royal will got its way. It seised and disseised, by order it decided litigation, and throughout all administration and relations with subjects it forced decisions favorable to the king. Because rule was highly personal and familiar the royal will was all the more prominent. Almost always on eyre the king snooped into the corners of England and decided the matters at hand. If advice was needed it was secured from those intimate or familiar with the king—the *familiares* (the royal councillors). Angevin kingship was entirely different from Norman kingship; the only reason it broke down was that it became too efficient and autocratic in the hands of John, who lacked the personality, the magnetism, and the military ability to control the barons whose one thought was for a return to the days when kings were limited by feudal custom implemented by the vassals. Had Henry II been succeeded by two more like himself the events of John's reign might have been prevented and the constitutional development of the thirteenth century might not have occurred. And perhaps Edward I might have gained repute as the king who developed absolutism to the high level attained in France by his contemporary Philip IV. English institutions, it is certain, were not so efficacious that they could lead only to constitutional monarchy.

2. CURIA REGIS: THE GREAT COUNCIL

However negligible the real limitations to their power, none of the Angevin autocrats except John consistently thwarted and ignored the collective sentiment of the barons, which found expression in the *curia regis*, the great feudal council of tenants-in-chief. This council of the royal barons, although still called *curia* or *concilium* upon occasion, now came to receive a more precise terminology such as *magna curia* or *magnum concilium* to differentiate it from the small *curia regis*. Occasionally the chroniclers called it a *colloquium*, a fact indicating that men of the Angevin period considered the meeting of the royal council and king a discussion of affairs of the realm.

Though at times the records show decisions taken at these meetings arrived at by common counsel (*commune consilium*), we are not warranted in calling this assembly the common council of the realm. As for the sessions of the great council the Angevins still convened it to help celebrate Christmas, Easter, and Whitsuntide, as well as the coronations. These festive gatherings, however, became more irregular and infrequent; the Angevins preferred to convoke special great councils to consider issues pertinent to the whole realm.

As in the Norman period the great council was composed of all the royal vassals, that is, the baronage. Theoretically any royal vassal had the feudal right to attend but in practice only the greater barons consistently did so. On rare occasions perhaps all royal vassals were summoned, but generally the famous councils were a highly selective group. At the Council of Clarendon in 1164 a total of only fifty bishops, earls, and barons were present.[1] At Richard I's coronation sixty barons were present. Such evidence supports the statement of Magna Carta that a great council consisted of the two archbishops, the bishops, abbots, earls, and greater barons. But even with this body there was no consistency in attendance. What can be said is that those barons familiar with and useful to the king attended regularly; the rest, sporadically. Of the lesser barons only those attended, and then but occasionally, whose services or competence benefited the king; the others seldom came to a great council because their large number made consultation with the king too unwieldy. Only if he needed broad support or strong expression of opinion did the king reinforce the customary sessions. When the great council tried Thomas Becket in 1164 Henry II considered the trial of an archbishop of Canterbury so serious that he summoned numerous lesser barons to convey the impression that a feudal court representative of the realm was handing down the judgment. Magna Carta specified in writing what seemed a general rule; the lesser vassals were to receive a general, but not an individual, summons.[2]

Looking closely at the personnel attending the Angevin great councils we find lesser barons as well as vassals of royal barons present at the festive ceremonies and the feudal convocations for war, extraordinary occasions to which the minor feudal aristocracy lent glamor or fighting strength. The feudal levy summoned in 1177 to assemble at Winchester for a Norman campaign was just such an occasion. In the ranks of the ecclesiastical barons the bishops composed a large segment of the Angevin great councils while attendance of the abbots fell off and became irregular. Magna Carta did not stipulate that abbots were to be summoned by *name*. Archdeacons, deans, and priors also attended, not, however, by virtue of feudal tenure but because of their value as advisers to the bishops or the king. Such men were present, for example, at the famous arbitration of Henry II in 1177 regarding a dispute

[1] SM, no. 30.
[2] SM, no. 44.

between the kings of Castile and Navarre. On this occasion their knowledge of Roman and canon law would be of value. At times the Angevins, particularly John, summoned by writ ordinary clerics and laymen to lend their particular administrative skill to problems before the great council. Perhaps the most interesting experiment in combining the session of a feudal great council with groups of nonfeudal royal tenants occurred in 1213. John first ordered the sheriffs to send the reeve and four men of each agrarian community of the royal domain to meet with him for assessing the losses of the church during the interdict. Then later in November he used the same procedure in conjunction with the great council. He ordered the sheriffs to have the barons and four good knights of each county meet him at Oxford for a discussion of weighty matters.[3] Unfortunately we have no evidence for the Oxford assembly and scholarly opinion holds that it did not meet. This technique was, however, to be used later in the century when parliaments were convened by Henry III and Edward I.

We come now to the matter of the summons to a great council. Although there is no official evidence of summonses until John's reign, for the reigns of Henry II and Richard the chroniclers amply testify to the royal custom of summoning the greater barons by individual writ. Benedict of Peterborough informs us that in 1170 when the Young Henry was crowned, Henry II sent writs to the bishops, abbots, earls, and barons. The first extant writ of such a summons is of the year 1205.[4] Then in 1215 Magna Carta made this standard procedure; henceforth individual writs under the royal seal summoned these men to the great council. The lesser barons never received individual summonses; but they must have been informed about councils in some manner for, according to feudal custom, they had the right to know about them. Magna Carta clarified this point by stipulating that all tenants of the king should receive a general summons proclaimed by sheriffs and royal officers at county courts and such other places as markets.[5] Ultimately the composition of every great council was governed by the reason for its convening. For great festivals and ceremonies, swelled by numerous lesser barons and nonfeudal tenants, it would reach its greatest size. For matters of war it would be predominantly of lay barons; for ecclesiastical matters touching upon papal relations, taxation, and clerical election, predominantly of ecclesiastical barons. On one occasion when the archbishop of Canterbury appealed to the great council for a crusade the ordinary populace came to hear the plea.

The business of an Angevin great council was little different from that of its Norman predecessor. It concerned itself with anything the king presented to it. Like the Norman council and the Anglo-Saxon witenagemot the Angevin council had no specific rights and only helped to govern when the king so willed. The king himself, if so inclined, could initiate and settle affairs of

[3] SM, no. 41E.
[4] SM, no. 41A.
[5] SM, no. 44.

state in the absence of his great council. At no period in the Middle Ages did the royal will and independence attain greater height. However powerful the Angevins, even John realized that it was a diplomatic and even necessary action to consult upon occasion with the great council. The records most frequently speak of the council as a consultative body giving counsel. At one time it deals with the welfare of the realm; at another, with the business of the realm. Some of the concerns broached by Henry II were the establishment of peace in 1154, the destruction of adulterine castles, and the re-establishment of the administration and custom of Henry I's reign. In 1162 the great council was consulted about unsatisfactory fiscal and church affairs, in 1170 about the malversations of sheriffs, and in 1176 and 1179 about judicial reform. The Constitutions of Clarendon setting forth church right were presented to the great council for discussion.[6] Henry II met with the council on foreign and military affairs regarding Scotland, Ireland, Wales, and his continental fiefs. Under John it offered advice on the terms of peace to be negotiated with Pope Innocent III and it was partially on the basis of this counsel that peace was concluded in 1213.

The great council was still the highest court of the realm despite the judicial innovations of Henry II, which decreased its volume of legal business. Primarily it entertained only important causes. To cite but a few of the most illustrious cases there was the charge heard in 1164 that the constable, Henry of Essex, had committed treason in the Welsh campaign of 1157 by dropping the royal standard and spreading the word that Henry II was dead. Robert de Montfort accused him, challenged him to combat, defeated him, and thus proved his guilt. In the same year Thomas Becket, archbishop of Canterbury, was accused of various acts against the king and was found by the great council to be at the royal mercy for all his possessions. In 1194 the great council entertained the charges brought against John for treasonable action against Richard. Though the Angevins legislated with the advice of the great council when they so desired, more legislation was accomplished by king and small council and by administrative decree. Some of the legislation in which the great council had a part were the Assizes of Clarendon and Northampton introducing legal reform, the Assize of Arms invigorating the old *fyrd*, and assizes of Richard and John in 1197 and 1205 setting up standards for weights, measures, and money.[7] Customary taxes were not considered a matter for discussion. Feudal taxes came regularly, scutages were taken without consultation, and the Danegeld was collected until 1162 as though derived solely by right of the royal prerogative. With the new forms of taxation that developed in the Angevin period the kings felt more compulsion to obtain advice and consent. In 1166 Henry discussed with his great council in Normandy how best to provide a grant of money for the defense of the Holy Land. It was decided to assess each person at the rate of 6*d*. per

[6] SM, no. 30.
[7] SM, nos. 31, 32, 34.

every pound's worth of chattels. In 1188 Henry secured the assent of his barons of Maine, Anjou, Touraine, and England for levying the famous Saladin tithe—a tax levied at the rate of a tenth on movable goods.[8] In 1193–1194 the great council debated how best to raise the money needed to ransom Richard. Cases of John's obtaining a grant from the great council occurred in 1204, when the rate of the scutage was raised, and in 1207, when a tax of a thirteenth was levied on personal property.[9]

Little can be said of the elective right of the great council. Henry II required no election because he had a strong heritable claim, had arranged with Stephen for the succession, and previously had received the baronial fealty. Henry II had the Young Henry recognized and crowned to provide for a peaceful succession and upon the Young Henry's death in 1183 Richard became heir as the eldest son. John's claim was clouded by Arthur's but no election occurred. His recognition in England was pushed through by such leading magnates as William Marshal and Hubert Walter as well as by the queen mother Eleanor. In the election of prelates and in the appointment of royal offices the council had no part. Rarely would the king sound out the council on a suitable candidate. For affairs of state and government policy the kings charted their own course with the help of a few intimate councillors. They seldom consulted with their council about treaties, marriages, donations of land, and diplomatic and ecclesiastical relations.

The one occasion when the great council took initiative was during the absence of Richard in 1191. It deposed the unpopular justiciar William Longchamp and selected in his place Walter of Coutances, it recognized John as Richard's heir, and it approved of communal government in London. Seldom did the great council oppose or block the royal will. Many years were to pass before this could be done. In the trial of Becket in 1164 the whole council cowered before the impassioned Henry, and Becket was lost. In 1198 the great council spearheaded by the bishops of Lincoln and Salisbury actually succeeded in resisting the justiciar's demand for a heavy and unprecedented tax for the Norman war but to little avail for this block was circumvented by another tax which resembled the old Danegeld. If Richard had been present there certainly would have been no successful opposition. Time and again John beat down resistance to his heavy and frequent taxation, until finally the scutage of 1214 released a pent-up hatred that was utterly to defeat him.

It may be said of the position of the great council in the scheme of Angevin government that its functions and rights were little more defined than under the Normans. Its work was yet indefinite, unspecialized, and performed only when demanded by the king. Angevin government functioned with or without the great council. Almost invariably, however, the Angevins had recourse to the council in times of emergency when strong baronial support

[8] SM, no. 38.
[9] SM, no. 41c.

was required against the church or for military projects against France. As in the past none of the three kings could consistently ignore the feelings of the greatest landlords of the realm. The barons as such had a weighty vested interest in the affairs of the realm and could hinder the royal projects by refusing to participate in war and to grant supply. If pushed far enough the royal vassals could renounce their homage and revolt; this they did in 1215 and administered a stinging defeat to John. But however little defined was the status of the great council, the fact that it was called upon for advice and consent established a precedent for the time in the thirteenth and early fourteenth centuries when its constitutional role in medieval government would be recognized.

3. CURIA REGIS: THE SMALL COUNCIL

Absolutistic by nature and in practice the Angevins preferred to do much of their governing through the small council, which in composition and function remained basically as it was under the Normans. Those most intimate with the king dominated the membership; constantly the records mention the justiciar, chancellor, and household officials such as the chamberlains, constables, and chaplains. Also included were royal relatives and certain great barons whose services were especially valued. Heavily domestic and official in composition the small council was nevertheless regarded as a feudal court equal in power to the great council. Distinction between great and small council is often impossible but in general the evidence depicts the small council as a permanent advisory body close to the royal presence and composed of a small group of men who consistently attend. Most permanent were the great central officers and household staff plus a few distinguished lay and ecclesiastical barons. Less permanent were those barons and skilled officers who reinforced the council because their competence was required or because they lived in the vicinity where the king chanced to be doing his work. It is accurate to say that the small council was comprised of those at hand. The most striking Angevin development was the king's reliance upon men of obscure and humble origin, men skilled in reading and writing Latin and trained in Roman and canon law. This is the period when the intelligent cleric comes into his own and proves his superiority over the rough and illiterate feudal baron. John, especially, employed foreigners and intimates of humble origin in his small council. At times he and also Henry relied upon them for advice to the exclusion of the other members of the council.

Constantly with the king on his peregrinations, the small council was foremost an advisory body, a forum for the discussion of any affair. When Becket was tried before the great council in 1164 Henry conferred privately with the small council at various stages of the trial. William Longchamp, upon accepting the justiciarship in 1191, swore that he would do nothing without the advice of the small council. Under John the letters patent and close testify to the large volume of business conducted by the small council. With all three Angevins the small council was most active when they were engaged on the Continent. Another function of the small council was that of a court which, like the great council, handled feudal jurisdiction but in addition served as a court *coram rege* where nonfeudal royal pleas were heard. In this latter capacity only the most difficult cases were reserved for it whereas in the former capacity it sat for routine feudal justice, the great causes being heard by the great council. As a court the small council was quite small. In 1155, for example, it consisted of the king's brother, the chancellor, the two justiciars, the steward, the constable, the royal physician, and a man called Ralph de Sigillo. By John's reign the familiar and domestic element prevails in the documents recording legal business. In legislation the small council probably had a more active role than the great council. There was legal talk about the difference between royal acts approved by small and great council, the theory being that laws enacted by king and small council were valid only for the royal life whereas those enacted with great council were valid in perpetuity. But such legal theorizing had no reality because administrative decrees and temporary ordinances had as much force as laws by king and great council. It is a commonplace that the majority of the legal innovations were accomplished by Henry II through administrative decree or word of mouth after consultation with those about him. After consultation with the small council many of the assizes were issued; upon its advice Henry established the court of common pleas in 1178; and John often legislated with it. We may conclude that the laws, however instituted, were equally valid and effective, and that the small council did not only all that was done by the great council but, because of its proximity and professionalism, much more. There was, however, a distinction made by contemporaries between the two. The small curial group was hand-picked and not representative of the baronage as was the great council; consequently, the baronage never considered the acts of the small body as having the authority of acts of the larger. This sentiment was expressed by Magna Carta when it asserted that scutages and aids could be levied only with the approval of the great council.[10] In the last analysis the king decided whether his business could be expedited better by great or small council. Upon the small council fell the burden of government, leaving to the great council only the paramount political, military, financial, legal, and administrative issues.

4. THE JUSTICIAR

Fundamental for our understanding of Angevin central administration is the small council's role as the intimate circle through which the government was funneled and directed. Doing all that the king willed and becoming increasingly competent in its work the small council in the Angevin period saw its component parts develop into highly specialized and competent or-

[10] SM, no. 44.

gans, becoming in some cases, such as with the exchequer and chancery, separate departments. It is our task in this and the following sections to examine the work of these central offices and departments—the justiciar, household staff, and chancery—in essence, the core of the small council. We have previously seen in the Norman period how long royal absence from England and expanding duties of kingship gave rise to the justiciarship, which under Roger of Salisbury became the greatest office of the realm. Roger was removed in 1139 by Stephen and the office remained vacant until the reign of Henry II. As soon as royal authority was restored he reintroduced the office and it retained pre-eminence into the early years of Henry III's reign. This period, during which a line of great justiciars raised the office to the apogee of its power and was responsible in large part for the rapid progress in law and administration, has been justly called the "Age of the Justiciars." Empowered by the kings with executive discretion, justiciars left a profound imprint upon administration, law, and finance.

Henry II apparently preferred to split the authority of the justiciar between two men; from 1155 to 1168 two prominent barons, Earl Robert of Leicester and Richard de Lucy, shared the office. Robert of Leicester seems, however, to have been superior in authority because he consistently acted as vice-regent during Henry's absences and took a leading part in the great councils such as those of Clarendon and Northampton. He helped to prepare the Constitutions of Clarendon, was a key royal negotiator with Thomas Becket, and pronounced the sentence of the Council of Northampton upon Becket. At Robert's death in 1168 Richard de Lucy became sole justiciar and continued so until retirement in 1178. He too was a key participant in the Becket affair, successfully defeated the rebellion of 1174, and served as vice-regent. The office remained vacant for a year and then Henry appointed Ranulf Glanville, who retained it until Henry's death. This first great Angevin justiciar came up through the ranks of the civil service, attaining his first important office, the shrievalty of Yorkshire, in 1163. As sheriff of Lancashire in 1174 he defeated the Scottish invaders and captured their king in battle. Hereafter the royal eyes were upon him. He held in quick succession such offices as justice in eyre, envoy to Flanders, justice of the king's bench, and then justiciar in 1180. By this year most of the fruitful reforms of Henry II had been inaugurated but Glanville's vigorous administration in the realm of justice and finance insured their remarkable success. Schooled in all aspects of government he used his practical hand to iron out wrinkles and build up a well-oiled administrative team of loyal and experienced officers. His tenure was abruptly ended by Richard and he died in 1190 while on the crusade with Richard, who had taken him along for safekeeping.

Richard returned to the practice of divided authority and appointed to the office Hugh de Puiset, bishop of Durham, and the chancellor, William Longchamp. Quickly William reduced Hugh's power to insignificance and in his capacity of chancellor put the great seal to acts of government arbitrarily authored by himself; he even went so far as to authenticate royal acts with his private seal. Richard faced such independence in 1191 by secretly empowering Walter of Coutances to assume the justiciarship if conditions warranted. They soon did and Walter, assuming the office, exercised it to 1193. Trained in the tradition of Henry II he handled the government for Richard as Glanville had for his father. He ended his tenure amidst financial preparations for paying Richard's ransom and was succeeded by the greatest medieval justiciar—Hubert Walter, a gifted administrator who served all three Angevins. He owed his career to Glanville, whom he served as a clerk. Under such patronage Walter developed rapidly, attaining before Henry II's death a place as baron of the exchequer and justice of the small council. Under Richard he became bishop of Salisbury, went on the Third Crusade, and then, returning to England in 1193 in order to help collect the ransom, was elected archbishop of Canterbury and appointed justiciar. He held this office until his resignation in 1198; thereafter he served as chancellor until 1205. Not only did Hubert successfully govern England during Richard's absence and keep him supplied with money and men for the campaign against Philip Augustus but he also introduced eminently successful financial and judicial innovations. In 1194 and 1198 he secured a new tax on land called the carucage, the first land tax since the abolishment of the Danegeld in 1162. In some justly famous instructions to itinerant justices for the eyre of 1195 he expanded the scope of their judicial and administrative powers and may possibly have created a new local peace officer called the coroner.[11] His overall supervision of the government surely must have prepared the way for the effective growth of the chancery during John's reign.

In 1198 Hubert Walter was succeeded as justiciar by Geoffrey fitz Peter, earl of Essex, who had also learned the art of Angevin government under Henry II and had served Richard in various capacities. Though not possessed of the innovating genius of Hubert, Geoffrey presided over a well-ordered administration until his death in 1213. After 1204, it should be noted, he did not have the independence of action possessed by Hubert; John resided in England and took perverse delight in the detail of government. Unfortunately, Geoffrey's moderation and reputation for honesty did not neutralize John's callousness, and yet John so respected his power that he dared not remove him. According to a chronicler, when Geoffrey died in 1213 John heaved a sigh of relief and exclaimed that now for the first time he was both lord and king. He appointed as Geoffrey's successor one of his Poitevin favorites, Peter des Roches, bishop of Winchester. A stranger to the Henrician tradition and to English custom he introduced practices that strengthened the administrative power of such household departments as the chamber and wardrobe and in so doing prepared the way for the decline of the justiciarship. An evaluation of his work must be postponed until Henry III's

[11] SM, no. 40A.

reign because the years from 1213 to 1216 were too abnormal to permit a just estimate of Peter's achievements. There was to be one more powerful justiciar in Henry III's reign and then the office disappeared, probably because the English kings henceforth worked full time at being kings of England and because they preferred to govern through the intimate and highly competent wardrobe staff.

5. THE HOUSEHOLD

A. The Chancery

Although the justiciar enjoyed an executive discretion over the royal household he was never a member of this domestic department that provided the majority of the small council's members. With the household always accompanying him, the king naturally relied upon its staff for advice more than upon other men. The constant service rendered to the king eventually caused some of the offices to become specialized and to break away from the household. Those offices which never lost their domesticity, such as the steward and butler, do not concern us. Likewise we shall ignore the functions of the constable and marshal except for noting that they had minor obligations in the exchequer. Our chief concern is with those officers whose financial and secretarial duties were fundamental for royal administration. We refer to those officers who labored in the chancery, chamber, and wardrobe.

Well launched by the Normans, the chancery developed under the Angevins as the most efficient secretariat of western Europe. Under Henry II administrative specialization had not progressed to where it pushed the chancery out of the household. None of the three chancellors of Henry—Thomas Becket, Geoffrey Ridel, or Geoffrey the Bastard—resided much in the household but they and their staff were considered members. The chancellors, though ranked under the justiciar, were nonetheless so important that seldom did they perform their functions in person, delegating instead numerous duties to subordinates. The vice-chancellor guarded the great seal and usually represented the chancellor at the exchequer sessions; the master of the *scriptorium* supervised the chancery clerks while they labored in the chancery and exchequer. Henry's chancery is remembered principally for its improved organization and development of new records. In addition to the formal charter and brief writ, there were emerging from the latter the letters patent and close with their specialized forms, the writs of *liberate* and *computate*. These short and efficient documents, which enabled the chancery to cope with the expanding and variegated business thrust upon it by the Angevins, prepared the way for enrollments of the chancery records under John. The other occupation of the chancery was custody of the great seal and its use to authenticate royal documents. Generally its care was in the hands of the master of the writing office while a duplicate of it used for exchequer business was guarded by the vice-chancellor.

The crowning achievement of the chancery—the enrolling of its records—came in John's reign. Undoubtedly Hubert Walter, with his wide experience in administration, saw the need for a duplication and orderly preservation of records. He must have noted and applied to the chancery the procedure of enrollment—the copying of royal documents on membranes of parchment sewn end to end—used for financial records as early as Henry I's reign to facilitate the business of the exchequer. Even before enrollment began, the chancery for the sake of recordkeeping had been forced to make duplicates of its writs (*contrabrevia*), which were filed. In 1200 enrollment began with the Charter Rolls, followed within two years by the Close and Patent Rolls. Thereafter as need arose new enrollments were begun. The royal administration, supplied now with a complete record of its business and able immediately to check on any of its actions, was greatly improved. This clerical innovation, moreover, necessitated additional chancery personnel and the organization of an archives, all of which tended to make the chancery more sedentary and contributed to its becoming an independent department under Henry III. With the loss of its mobility no longer could chancery or chancellor be always with the still extremely itinerant kings.

B. The Chamber

The principal business of the chamber and its subordinate department, the wardrobe, was finance, a subject to be examined in a later chapter on Angevin finance and taxation. There were certain functions of the chamber, however, closely related to the work of the chancery. As the chancery became less domestic and ceased traveling with the king, other machinery was needed for initiating royal administration. By virtue of its proximity and trained staff the chamber was now developed into a second secretarial office with its own seal for authenticating the documents it issued. It came to guard a second seal, the small seal (*parvum* or *privatum sigillum*), which subsequently became known as the privy seal. Since the time of the Carolingians, princes had wrestled with the problem of having seals located strategically enough to permit methodical and regular administration. The Carolingians had a duplicate made of their great seal, the German emperors had a seal for the various regions of the Empire, and the French kings had seals for the different fields of government such as law and finance. Delisle has suggested that Henry II used a signet seal to expedite administration when the great seal was not with him and that when Richard departed on the crusade he took with him the great seal leaving behind with the chancellor a small seal to authenticate the royal documents. Already, as we have seen, a duplicate of the great seal was kept in the exchequer to facilitate its procedure. By the reign of John the small or privy seal definitely was used to authorize royal acts of the chancery. This second seal, kept by the chamber, was always present to authenticate the royal will. It was used for chamber business, for initiating action in the small council, and in the absence of the great seal for validating writs and letters authorizing issuance of documents under the great seal. The small seal had now come to move the great seal. This new obligation of the chamber caused an increase in its clerks but they formed no separate staff; they were yet nominally under the chancellor's supervision because he still figured as a household officer in charge of royal seals and writing.

C. The Wardrobe

Until the reign of John the wardrobe was no more than a place of safe deposit for the money, treasure, and other valuables received by the chamber. As early as Henry's reign, however, it was directed by a wardrober, who headed a small staff, and increasingly the records speak of the wardrobe and its personnel, which saw to the storage and transport of all the domestic treasure and royal paraphernalia. During John's reign the wardrobe came to be used also as a deposit place for documents until by 1213 it was not only an archive but also an office where royal documents were drawn up. As Tout has so well expressed it, "the chamber was now assailed for the second time by that insidious process of bifurcation of which mediaeval institutional history is so full." Although it is possible that the Mise and Prest Rolls—those records noting payments by the exchequer to the household departments—could have been drawn up in the wardrobe, there is not enough evidence to warrant such a conclusion. What these and other records do show is a clear distinction by 1215 between chancery and wardrobe rolls and an increased staff to handle the additional secretarial and financial duties. One meets all sorts of humble functionaries such as clerks and ushers and carterers, but most significant is the clerk of the wardrobe, who must have supervised the drafting and preservation of wardrobe records after 1213 and who soon became the head (keeper or treasurer) of the wardrobe. At the end of John's reign the wardrobe was fulfilling the same functions as its parent the chamber. Perhaps there was still a subordination of the wardrobe to the chamber but, if so, it is difficult to perceive and emphasizes clearly that lack of medieval "system or symmetry." Departments were created and staffs increased to meet new administrative demands, but their parents continued performing the same functions; of proper authority, specialization, and chain of command there was yet none in England.

XVIII

Angevin Finance and Military Administration

I. THE EXCHEQUER

MUCH has already been said about the origin and work of the Norman exchequer. We have seen that it began functioning early in Henry I's reign and that it owed its organization and amazing efficiency primarily to that great justiciar Roger of Salisbury. Apparently the treasury, the lower exchequer, came from the Anglo-Saxon treasury while the court of accounting, the upper exchequer, was a Norman innovation. Owing chiefly to the paucity of the Norman evidence—there is but one Pipe Roll and a few references in miscellaneous writs, charters, and chronicles—little has been written about the organization and staff of the exchequer prior to the Angevins. With their advent examination becomes possible because of the copiousness of the records, which include Richard fitz Nigel's *Dialogue of the Exchequer*, an almost continuous series of Pipe Rolls, and many new legal, financial, and chancery records.

Before examining the exchequer there is need for a few introductory observations. The upper exchequer, it should be understood, was composed of some members of the small council who met to regulate the royal finances; it was actually the small council acting in a financial capacity. Early in Henry II's reign the accounting sessions at Easter and Michaelmas were regarded as occasions when the small council dealt with money matters in contrast to others when it dealt with justice, politics, and war. Gradually, however, as the membership became regularized and professionalized the exchequer became a financial department conducting its business at a particular place. This was its status by 1172 when it settled down at Westminster with but occasional sessions elsewhere. As for the treasury and its staff, it functioned throughout the year guarding, receiving, and disbursing money from its permanent quarters, which, as under the Normans and Saxons, were at Winchester. For the Easter and Michaelmas sessions it sent a staff to Westminster to cooperate with the upper exchequer and to transport the money back to Winchester after the sessions. All that was needed for a session of the exchequer was an ordinary room for the upper exchequer to meet in and examine the accountants, a small adjoining chamber to which the members—the barons of the exchequer—could retire to discuss weighty matters in private, and a third room for the lower exchequer where the money was received and stored during the accounting.

Let us now examine the organization of the two divisions of the exchequer. The treasury part, called the lower exchequer by the *Dialogue*, was known in the official records as the treasury of receipt or the exchequer of receipt. The supervision of the lower exchequer resided with the treasurer and two chamberlains of the upper exchequer represented by deputies. The chief deputy, who was the clerk of the treasurer, directed the work of the lower exchequer and, in addition, sealed the bags of money received from the accountants, made notations of the amount received with the name of the accountant and the purpose of payment, and inscribed the appropriate sum on the tallies of receipt which the accountants received. The other top officials were the knights of the two chamberlains, whose principal duties were carrying a set of keys for the money chests, weighing the money after it was counted, paying out money, and directing the cutting of tallies. These three officers—the chief deputy and the two knights—were responsible for the rest of the staff and for transporting the money between Westminster and Winchester. Other staff members were of less exalted rank and performed the work. Especially busy was the tally-cutter, who cut a tally for each payment made into the lower exchequer which served as a receipt and was then produced at the upper exchequer as evidence of payment. At the Easter term when the sheriff paid a portion of the farm he received a memoranda tally, and later, when an assay of his money was made, a combustion tally indicating the deduction made from his payment because of the percentage of bad money shown in the assay. At the Michaelmas session these tallies were matched against the countertallies and at the end of the accounting all would be destroyed and a new tally given to the sheriff which recorded the final state of his account. So important were these tallies to the accountants that the exchequer sessions were called "at the tallies." The custom of giving tallies as receipts continued until 1834 even though in Henry II's reign the lower exchequer began to keep a written record of its receipts known as the Receipt Rolls which recorded all the payments from each county.

Two other key servants of the lower exchequer were the pesour (weigher or silverer) and the meltor (fusor), who conducted the assay of the coins to insure that the royal receipt of money was in good coin. During the early Norman period much of the royal farm had been paid in kind but by Henry I's reign payment in kind had been commuted for money. Though this change was effected principally by the growing money economy, the king was quick to see its advantages. Being less ambulatory and no longer traveling constantly about his realm, he could not eat up the royal farm stored in barns. He also found receipt in money more valuable; he needed money to pay the wages of a growing civil service and mercenary troops. Under the old system of payment in kind the royal revenue suffered because the worst beast—the "Tantony pig"—was considered the equivalent of the best beast.

When the exchequer began to receive payment in money it devised tests to guarantee that the king received coin meeting the standards of the royal money. At first money was simply paid by tale (*ad numerum*), with the lower exchequer only checking to insure that 240*d.* were paid on every pound. Then the system of payment by weight was introduced. A sheriff's pound—240*d.*—would be put on one side of a scales and a royal pound on the other. If the scales failed to balance the sheriff had to add the number of pennies required to balance it and pay the same number of pennies for every pound of the farm rendered. Another check was the system of payment *ad scalam* whereby the sheriff would pay so many extra pennies per pound. Generally the scale was 6*d.* per pound.

Under Henry II payments blanch became prevalent. According to this system all money coming from farms had to be paid either in tested bullion or in specie which must be reduced to that condition before it was admitted at the exchequer. Although the *Dialogue* does not state definitely whether the royal standard was pure silver or a silver alloy, evidence points to the latter. The assay that determined good money was conducted by the weigher and meltor. First 44*s.* of the sheriff's money were sealed in a bag at the lower exchequer and taken to the upper exchequer where they were placed on a table and weighed against a good exchequer pound. If 240*d.* of the sheriff's pound balanced that of the exchequer then the sheriff returned to the lower exchequer for the assay. An assay fee of 2*s.* was first paid by the sheriff and then came the test made by the assayer and weigher in the presence of the sheriff and two other witnesses. Two hundred and forty of the sheriff's pennies were thrown into a melting pot, reduced to a molten state, and had the dross (scum or waste) carefully skimmed off by the assayer. Then devoid of impurities the bullion was placed in a vessel, taken again to the upper exchequer and weighed against the standard pound. The sheriff then compensated for any loss in weight by adding the number of pennies required to balance the good pound. He had to add that number for every pound owed. Some of the medieval records called this quaint procedure the trial of the Pyx. To do all this work there were menial servants—four tellers, a watchman, and an usher.

We come now to the nerve center of the Angevin financial system—the upper exchequer. In the diagram on page 260, we see that the specialized court of the exchequer—a part of the small council sitting in a financial capacity—consisted of the barons of the exchequer grouped about a central table at which the royal accountants were examined. The exchequer (*scaccarium*), as we have previously seen, was a large table, five by ten feet, covered with a black cloth divided by white lines into columns a foot wide. On these columns, indicating pounds, shillings, and pence, counters were placed to calculate the money owed and paid. Upon this large abacus were concentrated the minds and eyes of all present. Occasionally the more money-conscious kings such as Henry II and John attended the sessions, but ordinarily the

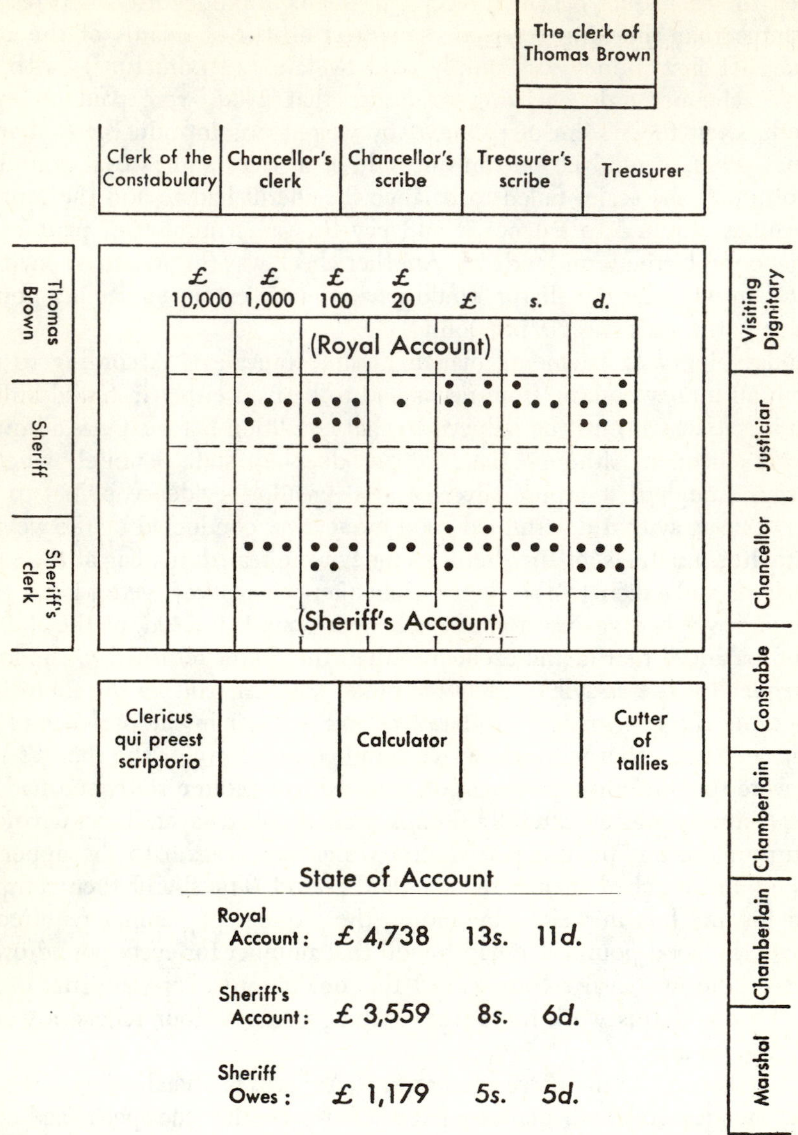

Diagram of the Exchequer Table. Adapted from Charles Johnson, *The Course of the Exchequer by Richard, Son of Nigel* (London, 1950), p. xlii.

procedure was supervised by their representatives. Though during the Angevin period these men customarily performed their functions, as the duties increased they, too, came to delegate their work to subordinates. At the head of the table sat the justiciar who, when present, was the head of the exchequer court and its proceedings and issued all necessary writs on his own authority. On his right sometimes sat a high-ranking dignitary whose presence had been ordered by the king, possibly to serve as a royal observer. On his left sat the chancellor. He guarded the exchequer seal and was responsible for the Chancellor's Roll (duplicate of Pipe Roll) and for the sealing of all documents. Usually his staff performed all these functions and he was often absent, being represented by a subordinate, even in the Angevin period. Like the justiciar, the chancellor was too active and important to be burdened with administrative red tape; if he attended it was only to provide proper liaison between exchequer and chancery. To the left but not at the table sat four more officers: the constable or, in his absence, a clerk who supervised payment of wages to soldiers and servants connected with the royal hawks and hounds; the two chamberlains, whose functions, though undefined, consisted in helping the treasurer and providing general supervision; and the marshal, who took custody of all vouchers (tallies, writs, etc.) presented by the accountants, guarded the countertallies, and observed their matching with the tallies of the accountants. The marshal also administered oaths, delivered writs of summons, and had custody of those arrested for default of payment.

On the right side of the table first came the treasurer, who, in the Angevin period, was the key officer because he usually conducted the proceedings. He received the accounts, orally examined the accountants, and dictated what entries were required in the Pipe Roll. These had to be absolutely accurate in that changes could be made only with the consent of the king and exchequer barons. As with the chancellor the treasurer's actual work was performed by assistants. Beside the treasurer sat his scribe (later called clerk of the pipe or pell), who made the proper entries. Next came the chancellor's scribe, who compiled the Chancellor's Roll and drew up writs of payment (*liberate*), allowance, discharge, and summons. Next to him sat the chancellor's clerk, who was charged with the most important work. He verified the accounts as they were presented and demanded evidence for every sum owed to the king or paid on behalf of the king by the accountant. He checked to insure that all writs of summons were responded to and that the Pipe and Chancellor's Rolls corresponded. He checked even on the actions of the treasurer. He was the deputy of the chancellor in his absence and finally, when the chancellor ceased attending the meetings, became the most important member of the exchequer. Eventually he became known as the chancellor of the exchequer and by Henry III's reign guarded the exchequer seal and headed the exchequer, a role he has held to the present. Last on this side of the table was the constable's clerk, who frequently deputized for the constable and carried about the counterwrits so as to verify the writs that might be produced by accountants during the session. On the left side of the table sat three other functionaries: the tally-cutter, who cut the needed tallies for the accountants, adjusted previous ones for the final account, and checked countertallies against all tallies produced; the calculator, who moved the counters about over the exchequer board; and the master of the writing office (chancery), called the *clericus qui preest scriptorio*, who, when present, supervised all the chancery scribes but was generally kept busy at the chancery.

The end of the table opposite the justiciar was reserved for those rendering accounts. The principal accountants were the sheriffs. In the Angevin period there were also the bailiffs of honors; the reeves of towns; custodians of temporalities of vacant bishoprics, abbeys, and escheated fiefs; and other miscellaneous debtors called to account. The principal accountants would be helped by a clerk, who did the necessary reading and writing. If they desired, they could produce witnesses to substantiate various parts of their accounts such as payments or services rendered on behalf of the king.

For approximately twenty years, between 1160 and 1180, Henry II was represented by a special deputy, named Thomas Brown. Though called the king's almoner he is better described as minister without portfolio. According to the *Dialogue* he kept a third roll which was his sole responsibility and was said to contain "laws of the realm and secrets of the king." Thomas appears to have been the ultimate check on the exchequer staff, responsible only to Henry for all that he observed and wrote on his roll. Some historians see in him the predecessor of the later King's Remembrancer. Apparently everyone stood in awe of Master Thomas because he was reported to be without equal in Europe for his knowledge of statecraft and finance. He jealously guarded all rights pertaining to the royal prerogative and set the tone for severe accounting sessions. From the stray bits of evidence available it appears that Thomas was born in England and belonged to a family of royal clerks serving Henry I. After brief royal employment around 1137, Thomas turned up in the Norman kingdom of Sicily in 1143 where he first served in the chancery. He probably secured employment there through the help of various English ecclesiastics who had gone to Sicily to serve Roger II in ecclesiastical and governmental capacities. Thomas soon advanced from clerk and served on the royal *curia* in the capacity of judge. He became also a collector of revenue and thus associated with the famous customs system (*diwan*) of Roger II. Apparently Roger's successor forced Thomas to leave Sicily, for in 1158 he returned to England and in 1160, after refusing offers from other princes, accepted employment with Henry II. Undoubtedly the administration of Henry II profited from the skills Thomas learned at the Sicilian court. The case of Thomas suggests that the relations of England and Sicily were quite intimate and that perhaps there was an exchange of administrative knowledge in the twelfth century.

We are now ready to observe a session of the exchequer. All members and accountants, it should be understood, were notified of the session well in advance and were expected to be present. The principal duty of the exchequer court was to conduct semiannual audits of the accounts of all royal debtors. All accounts were examined to determine the exact sums due to the king after allowance was made for previously authorized expenditures and services. Prior to the sessions the staff had to have all its information meticulously assembled and compiled on the Pipe Roll. Some of the staff, therefore, were occupied long in advance preparing all the necessary writs of summons as well as those which authorized any service or payment or change in the royal income. Every detail had to be collected and entered correctly in the Pipe Roll. Every source of income had to be anticipated and the facts assembled to determine whether the king received his due. With such things as budgets and a national system of governmental finance yet unknown, payments were made twice a year into the exchequer because the kings had to make certain they had adequate funds. At the Easter session, which was much more perfunctory than the Michaelmas one, the sheriff rendered account of half of the county yearly farm, stating orally what allowances were due him without having to produce the writs and tallies to substantiate this statement. At the Michaelmas term a full accounting was demanded. The other half of the farm was paid minus what allowances the sheriff had to his credit. At this session the sheriff had to present writs and tallies to substantiate all payments and allowances. Both at Easter and at Michaelmas the sheriff paid or, as it was termed, proffered half of the farm in cash; at Easter this act was followed by a view of the account and at Michaelmas by a completion (*summa*) of the account.

Assuming now that all preparations are complete and that the necessary participants are present we are ready for the "game of the exchequer." The treasurer opens the session by calling out the name of the accountant and asking whether he is ready to account. Upon an affirmative answer the machinery is set in motion. The accountant is asked to answer for the first item on the Pipe Roll. Pipe and Chancellor's Rolls are checked to verify previous entries; tallies, writs, warrants, and money are produced to satisfy the court; and the calculator makes the first move of the counters in the appropriate columns. This process is repeated for each entry under the rubric of the accountant's county. Farthest from him the calculator places the counters representing the money owed and nearest him, the amount rendered; and so he moves the counters until the accounting is completed. As the amounts demanded and rendered mount, the columns marked *d.*, *s.*, £, £20, £100, £1,000, and £10,000 get counters so arranged as to indicate the increase in the account rendered. The accompanying diagram illustrates how the position of the counters indicated the state of the account at any particular moment.

To understand these accounts better it is well to examine a typical Pipe Roll.[1] Therein were all the counties, listed separately, and other sources of revenue for which accounts were rendered. First appeared a rubric bearing

[1] SM, no. 37.

the name of the county. On the next line was the name of the accountant and opposite this entry the words *In thesauro* followed by a blank space. When the accounting was completed the total amount paid would be entered here. Next came the items for which account must be rendered with all the information listed down to the last penny. First appeared the fixed alms of the county paid yearly by the sheriff. Then came fixed tithes, fixed disbursements, and royal lands granted away. Last in this group of items came the casual disbursements out of the royal farm plus expenses incurred while performing legal duties in the county. When these were satisfactorily accounted for the sheriff was examined on purprestures and escheats. Fines were levied for every illegal enclosure or seizure of royal land (purpresture) and the sheriff had to collect and pay them into the exchequer. Also he was responsible for managing fiefs which had escheated to the crown and for rendering the incomes received. Then followed the pleas and conventions, the first being general judicial fines or amercements and the latter, oblations (lump sum payments) for a special royal favor. Next came the Danegeld (until it was ended in 1162), and the *murdrum* fines. Finally, the sheriff rendered account for sums owed by various individuals. When these items were accounted for, the court determined the final state of the farm of the county and made the appropriate entries. After the words *In thesauro* was now entered the sum received by the exchequer and at the end of all the entries of the county would be entered a last appropriate notation. If the sheriff had rendered account of what he owed he was said to be quit (*et quietus est*); if he still owed money he was said to owe so much (*et debet*); if he had paid more than the required amount he was said to have a surplus (*et habet de superplusagio*).

However thorough the above accounting system might appear it should not be assumed that the exchequer received all the royal income or that the Pipe Rolls provided a complete record of the total annual income. In the Angevin period it became, as we shall see, more and more common to pay money directly into the royal domestic treasury—the chamber or its subordinate department, the wardrobe. The exchequer was thus by-passed and although the appropriate entries were often made to note these payments and to give credit to the sheriffs, we must assume that numerous such transactions occurred with no mention in the Pipe Roll. Moreover, sources of revenue outside the farm of the county were developing from the new wealth produced by the evolving money economy and revenues were paid into the exchequer; such receipts were not recorded in the Pipe Roll, although eventually this type of income was entered upon the Receipt Roll. Despite some of its obvious shortcomings, however, the English exchequer was the most efficient treasury of medieval Europe. No system of the German emperors was comparable, nor of the French kings until the reign of Saint Louis. In the other principalities finance remained in the household until the late fourteenth and fifteenth centuries. We may say that the exchequer, though still the small council tending to financial affairs, had become a department of state finance with a relatively permanent and skilled staff which had its own procedure and customs (*lex scaccarii*). It definitely had gone out of the household and by the end of John's reign was a department so specialized and independent, and staffed so largely with deputies, that it had gone out of the small council.

A word should be said about the exchequer of the duchy of Normandy, which, it will be recalled, developed at approximately the same time as the English exchequer. Nothing is known about it during Stephen's reign and little more from the Angevin period because, unfortunately, the Great Rolls of the Norman Exchequer are extant for only a few years of the three kings and cease in the year 1204 when John lost Normandy. From these rolls, however, it can be seen that the organization and routine of the Norman exchequer were basically like that of the English. At a court held at Caen the *vicomtes* of the duchy's *vicomtés* rendered account of the farms just as did the sheriffs. It is interesting to note that when Philip Augustus acquired Normandy he continued to use the Norman exchequer. Some scholars have suggested that it provided the model for the efficient reforms made in his central financial administration.

2. THE CHAMBER AND WARDROBE

In the Norman period we left the chamber in a state of flux. Primarily a domestic treasury or privy purse of the household, it had expanded in cooperation with the Winchester treasury to handle public finance as well. Then in Henry I's reign it gave birth to the exchequer and seemed to revert to its first role of domestic treasury, getting funds in lump sums from the exchequer. Under the Angevins, however, it recaptured much of its prominence. As a part of the household it was close to the king and served as his personal treasury, financing whatever he or his family required. It was indeed domestic but, as in the Norman period, the kings made no rigid distinction between domestic and public finance and used the chamber whenever needed for finances of the realm. One may say that the king used whatever treasury was most convenient to handle the business at hand. Ultimately all the money was his to do with what he wished. By its ambulatory nature the chamber was often found convenient for other than personal needs especially when the king was traveling, visiting on the Continent, or engaged in war. From necessity and expediency the exchequer supplied the chamber with large amounts of money; frequently money was even paid directly into the chamber, a procedure especially sensible when the king was traveling through the realm and could tap a source immediately at hand to replenish his supply without transporting a great amount of money with him. The kings seem to have ordered certain royal manors to pay their incomes into the chamber and by-pass the exchequer; this method anticipated the chamber manors that Edward II created in the early fourteenth century.

The administrative work of the chamber demanded a well-trained staff; it expanded greatly during the later years of Henry II's reign. Besides two or three chamberlains, generally knights, there was a professional staff of clerks (*clerici camerarii*) who carried out the necessary reading, writing, and administrative functions. Here skilled clerks cut their teeth on royal administration and went on to mount the ladder of preferment; one of these was Walter of Coutances, who began as a chamber clerk and later became archbishop of Rouen and justiciar of England. The chamber became the training school of the Angevin civil service sending its personnel to chancery, exchequer, high church position, and royal court.

The chamber is best observed at work during John's reign, particularly after the loss of Normandy when John was traveling most of the time. By 1207 the evidence suggests that the sedentary exchequer could not meet the financial demands of John. The problem of transporting the money to supply the chamber became most difficult and often John was delayed while waiting to be replenished with exchequer money. When the daily chamber disbursements grew too large to be met by the Winchester treasury, John diverted money slated for the exchequer into the chamber. He also provided that castles such as Bristol, Corfe, Nottingham, and Exeter should serve as provincial treasuries; they received their money from the exchequer and supplied John's chamber as he passed in their vicinity. Eventually they paid out money by order of writ just as the exchequer did. This development again emphasizes graphically the lack of distinction between things public and private, as well as the king's disregard for doing anything according to custom if innovation served his purpose better.

The most remarkable development in the chamber was its changing relation to the wardrobe. In addition to becoming a key department of administration and a secretariat the wardrobe sloughed off its traditional function of chamber treasury. This change was most prominent under John. Because the wardrobe stored the chamber money it was but natural that it came to disburse money; beginning in 1213 the Mise and Prest Rolls show the wardrobe as "the financial department of the chamber." The Mise Rolls show it disbursing money for royal domestic needs, for military and naval supply, and for wages.[2] It became a key department in John's preparations for retaking the lost Angevin possessions. Always by the royal side, it was instantly responsive to any royal action requiring money. It paid out money fiefs, pensions, salaries, bribes, gifts, bonuses, and subsidies, all used to forge the continental coalition. Along with the chamber it became a sort of war office and quartermaster department and from its staff were selected clerks to undertake

[2] SM, no. 42.

secret and important diplomatic functions. Such activity caused the wardrobe to burgeon. By the end of John's reign it had become the key household organ of finance and administration.

3. ANGEVIN TAXATION

The efficiency of the Angevin financial machinery was matched by the ingenuity employed to tap the resources of the realm. The revenues were ordinary and extraordinary. The ordinary income that came semiannually into the exchequer and its affiliate the chamber was employed for routine government expense. The revenues comprising this income were the same as under the Normans—the farms of the counties, amercements levied by the royal justices, the farms of the boroughs, the feudal incidents, the revenues from vacant bishoprics and abbeys, and fines offered to obtain royal favors. In addition the royal prerogative brought to the king profits from the goods of felons, shipwreck, treasure-trove, profits of coinage, and tolls and dues. The Danegeld, the land tax, was levied quite regularly until 1162 when abandoned for more efficient taxes. One historian has estimated that these revenues netted John slightly under 40,000 marks yearly.

During the twelfth century the customary (ordinary) revenue was found to be insufficient, owing principally to the inflationary rise that began in that century and continued on through the thirteenth. The costs of an expanded and increasingly complex government mounted, and the rash of far-flung and protracted wars ate up the royal revenue almost as soon as the exchequer received it. Then, too, the financial machinery was not adequate for prompt collection of the revenue. Debts appearing year after year in the Pipe Rolls were whittled down only bit by bit. It is no wonder then that the Angevins cast about for new methods of raising money.

Some relief came in the extraordinary revenues. The three feudal aids were levied for the purposes of marriage, knighting, and ransoms; whenever such an occasion arose the Angevins took all the traffic would bear. Since Henry I's reign when royal vassals willingly began to commute knight service for money at the rate of 2 marks per knight's fee, scutages had been collected. Frequent scutages were levied by the Angevins for their wars; their policy was to increase the number of knights' fees liable for payment, increase the rate, and by hook or crook increase the occasions when a scutage could be taken. For this purpose was held the famous Inquest of Knight Service in 1166.[3] It may be remembered that the amount of knight service owed by each royal fief had been set by the Conqueror and upon the basis of this service scutage had been assessed. Henry II, however, realized that most royal tenants had enfeoffed land to knights since the Conqueror's day and consequently numbered as vassals more knights than those for which they paid scutage. If, for example, a baron owed the service of fifteen knights, scu-

[3] SM, no. 36.

tage would be levied only on this number even though he had enfeoffed land to ten additional knights. He paid no scutage to the king for the extra knights but was entitled to pocket the scutage he collected from them. This explains why in the inquest Henry asked each baron how many knights he owed to the king (the *servitium debitum*), how many knights had been enfeoffed before Henry I's death (the old enfeoffment), and how many had been enfeoffed since (the new enfeoffment). Whenever the old or new enfeoffment exceeded the quota owed, Henry argued that he could levy scutage on the higher number. This he did in the scutage of 1168, which netted him 6000 marks, but so great was the opposition that he ceased attempting to collect the increased amount. Richard levied several scutages but preferred a system of fines to help defray the mounting costs of putting a feudal army on the field. Instead of levying a scutage at a fixed rate Richard collected a lump sum from each vassal which was greater than the scutage. His justification was that he deserved more pecuniary compensation because when a baron chose not to fight he deprived the king not only of knight service but also of a commander in the field. When the fine was paid the royal vassal was exempted from service and authorized to collect a scutage from his vassals as reimbursement. John was enamored of scutages and levied seven between 1199 and 1206, and at least four others in the period down to 1214. He frequently increased the rate, sometimes to two and a half marks and sometimes to three marks. This latter rate was applied to the ill-fated scutage of 1214. Another of John's tricks was to levy scutages when he had no intention of fighting.

We have already met the tallage begun under the Normans. It should be remembered that this tax was arbitrarily levied by the king when necessity required and that his ultimate right to levy it rested upon the royal prerogative. Under Henry I and in the early years of Henry II the tallage was generally called an aid (*auxilium*) or gift (*donum*), but towards the latter part of his reign the term "tallage" (*tallagium*) was used. Under Henry II and his successors tallage was levied on the royal domain, that is, all the manors, towns, and boroughs held by the king plus all the fiefs that had escheated to the crown. The chief burden fell upon the boroughs. Religious houses were also assessed on the basis that they provided no military service. Though the tallage was a tax used to supplement the royal income, frequently it was levied along with a scutage. In that the tallage was levied on the royal domain no consent was required from the great council and the only consistent opposition came from the ecclesiastical establishments. Some historians have argued that Henry II realized the monetary potentialities of the tallage and therefore in 1162 abandoned the Danegeld in its favor. It is true that Henry favored this form of extraordinary taxation. It was not uniformly assessed but each borough, agrarian community, and religious house bargained separately with royal justices sent out for this purpose. After much haggling a round sum would be agreed upon; the taxable unit would then assess the tax, collect it, and generally turn it over to the sheriff. The justices were directed to cover definite circuits of counties and to contact within each county all the taxable units of the royal domain.[4] It is interesting to note that for certain taxes this individual negotiation continued into the thirteenth century, until finally the kings saw the expediency of collective negotiation at a parliament. Throughout the reigns of the three Angevins the tallage was a lucrative revenue, producing at times as much as £5000.

Under Richard the old Danegeld was revamped and revived. Technically considered an aid, it was a land tax assessed upon the carucate (plowland) and hide. The carucage, as it came to be known, was first levied in 1194 to help pay Richard's ransom. Upon this occasion it was levied on the basis of the Domesday assessment, that is, the carucates and hides assessed were fiscal rather than real units. The next carucage levied was in 1198 and this time the taxable unit was a carucate reckoned at one hundred acres. The manner of assessment is important because it was retained in the thirteenth century for the levying of parliamentary taxes. Into each county the king sent two commissioners—a knight and a clerk. These were supplemented by two knights from each hundred elected by a county court convened apparently by the sheriff. Then the reeve and four men of each agrarian community and the bailiffs of barons holding land in the community swore to the number of carucates on their lands before the two commissioners and two knights. After rolls were drawn up recording the number of carucates the two knights and bailiff of each hundred collected the money and turned it over to the sheriff, who rendered it to the exchequer. John levied but one carucage, that of the year 1200, at the rate of 3s. per carucate.

The chief Angevin tax innovation, which again emphasizes the change wrought by the money economy, was a percentage on the total value of an individual's movable or personal property. With new forms of movable wealth constantly sprouting up, new techniques had to be devised to tap them. The first such tax was levied in 1166 by Henry II to raise a religious subsidy for defense of the Holy Land. A levy of 6*d.* per pound (a fraction of a fortieth) was authorized but apparently never collected. The first tax collected was the Saladin tithe of 1188. Though ecclesiastical assessors levied the tax it was approved by the great council and assessed at the rate of a tenth of the total value of the income and personal property of all men who did not swear to take the cross. Any man suspected of making a fraudulent return had his property value fixed by a jury of four to six men selected from his parish.[5] The importance of this tax was that it served as a precedent for subsequent lay taxes of John which in turn became precedents for later parliamentary taxation.

This fractional tax on personal property was not levied as a secular impost until 1194. At that time a fourth of the value of movable property was col-

[4] SM, no. 37A and B.

[5] SM, no. 38.

lected to help pay Richard's ransom; this portion netted far more than the other assessments levied for the same purpose. A fourth was, however, uncommonly high. In 1203 a like tax consisting of a seventh of the value of personal property was levied by John as a fine upon the English barons who he claimed had inadequately supported him in his defense of Normandy. His reasoning stemmed from rationalization, not logic, because the clergy also were obliged to pay the tax. The most significant tax of this sort, levied in 1207, consisted of a thirteenth upon the personal property of both laity and clergy.[6] Though it was rammed through the great council the clergy bitterly opposed it; the archbishop of York refused to pay and was driven from England. Our interest in it lies in the method of assessment, which harked back to the plan of 1188 when each individual swore before justices to the total worth of his movable wealth. John's feeling seemed to be that a person put under special oath was more likely to report his true wealth than a jury, which, though under oath, would not be as familiar with each individual's assets. Special justices were sent to each county where they split up and covered every unit. For each agrarian community the bailiffs of the feudal tenants swore to the value of their lord's personal property; the other men made their oaths in person. A roll in duplicate recorded all the information; the justices returned one to the exchequer, and the sheriff retained the other. After a new set of justices checked on the accuracy of the assessment the sheriffs were ordered to collect the tax; John's hope was to collect it in two weeks but actually it took about three months. Those failing to pay the tax or swearing falsely were promptly fined, disseised, or imprisoned. The total raised was £60,000. This was the only such tax John levied; his income from confiscated church property up until 1213 obviated the necessity for much extraordinary taxation, and during his last three years of rule he was in no position to levy or collect such a tax. The tax of 1207 is especially notable because it epitomized the transition from feudal to nonfeudal taxation. Contrary to the aid or scutage, it was levied for no specific purpose and was, therefore, an arbitrary tax, which strongly hinted that the royal right of taxation was unlimited. The personal property of all classes was taxed and the basis of assessment was national. The agrarian community was the unit of taxation assessed by royal commissioners who secured their information from those living in the community. It was a practice not overlooked by Henry III or Edward I.

The rest of the royal income may be lumped under the rubric of miscellaneous. As royal justice expanded, profits grew. The Angevins were harsh with their amercements and disseisins and realized enormous sums from men who had to pay dearly for the royal grace or the return of their land. Every conceivable sort of composition was made with men who desired to buy land, a marriage, wardships, farms, and offices.[7] The sale of offices by Richard

[6] SM, no. 41c.
[7] SM, no. 37c.

and John attained scandalous proportions; practically anything was for sale. The profits from fees taken for the royal writ and inspection and confirmation of charters were very lucrative. But the kings, however unscrupulous and arbitrary in fleecing their subjects, constantly had to seek still other means of supplying their insatiable need for cash. All the kings taxed and fined the Jews on any pretext because they were under the special protection of the king and must comply with his whims. By Richard's reign a special exchequer was operating to handle Jewish finances. In 1187 Henry II seized a fourth of their property for the crusade and Richard bled them for his ransom. Although John conferred their privileges for 4000 marks he almost destroyed them by fines and tallages. When the tallage of 1210 was levied the story is told how John condemned a Jew of Bristol to have a molar tooth jerked out each day until he paid 10,000 marks. After suffering the loss of seven teeth he capitulated. Like all their medieval brethren, the Angevins resorted to borrowing, not only from the Jews but from affluent Christian merchant bankers. The English merchant banker William Cade loaned large sums to Henry II. Richard and John borrowed heavily from Flemish and Italian merchants and even negotiated loans with the Knights Templars and Hospitallers. Despite the lack of a budget and an overall systematic plan of taxation, the Angevin financial administration was the most advanced of Europe and had begun the transition from a basically feudal system of taxation to a nonfeudal system.

4. THE SINEWS OF WAR

The Norman military organization was essentially feudal; it relied upon the feudal levy, which supplied about five thousand knights. During the Norman period the knight was at his apogee. When necessary, however, the Normans supplemented knight service with mercenaries and utilized the *fyrd*. This situation changed rapidly under the Angevins, and Stenton, who has thoroughly studied English feudalism from 1066 to 1166, has concluded that the latter date marks a decline in the traditional feudal system. Be that as it may, feudalism still provided the large part of the Angevin armies. What bears observing are those developments initiated by the Angevins in a strong drive to supplement a feudal army no longer equal to the military demands. The Inquest of Knight Service ordered by Henry II in 1166 had a military as well as a financial purpose. He desired a recent and accurate record of the number of knights that could be put into the field by his royal vassals; one estimate puts the number at six thousand.[8] In 1212 a similar inquest was made by John. Traditionally it had been the feudal custom that for his fief a vassal had to provide knight service in the field for forty days. Beyond this time pay would be received. Under the Angevins the custom

[8] SM, no. 36.

broke down. By Richard's reign the knights who fought in Normandy were paid daily wages for all service and received remuneration for damages suffered to horses and equipment. To show how far the money economy had infiltrated feudalism there is the case of 1198 when Richard demanded a grant to maintain three hundred knights in Normandy for a year at wages of 3s. per day. It had become too expensive to provide unremunerated knight service by the late twelfth century. Armor was more elaborate and costly and the campaigns lasted longer and were waged over wider areas. Another attempt to combat this inflationary tendency was the demand for reduced contingents from the royal vassals. To keep an army in the field for longer periods Richard experimented with summoning only a third of the knight service owed to him at one time. It was common for those tenants burdened with the services of but one knight or a fraction of a knight's fee to combine their resources to put one knight in the field for a specified amount of time. The feudal summons was still accomplished by the royal writ which ordered the sheriffs to collect the royal vassals with their vassals and then to assemble them all at a designated mobilization point.

It was characteristic of the Angevins to use their increased financial resources to adapt feudal custom to money. To supplement the old feudal levy they granted annual cash incomes called money fiefs in return for a specified amount of military service. Such a custom was already common under Henry II, who had granted the counts of Flanders a money fief of 400*m.* in return for the service of five hundred knights. This practice was skillfully used by John to build up a vast continental army for the campaign of 1214. It will be remembered that one form of feudal tenure had provided castle-guard; with the Angevins most of this service was commuted for money and the custodians of the royal castles—sheriffs or special castellans—used hired men-at-arms and crossbowmen. The serjeants who owed less than knight service became for all practical purposes royal stipendiaries.

Whatever the form of service required by feudal tenure it was all supplemented now by mercenaries, who could be hired in greater numbers as the royal financial resources increased. Such professionals were often not as reliable as the vassals but war was their occupation and they generally proved to be more skilled warriors, willing to fight the year around. The Angevins thus secured an army that could be kept in the field for long periods. Though many men were knights the majority were footsoldiers and therefore less expensive to maintain. The prominence of the footsoldier indicates the dominance of feudal cavalry to be not so complete as it had once been. Henry II quelled the revolt of 1173–1174, it may be remembered, primarily with mercenaries, and he always had a band ready for his continental campaigns. Richard increased their use and became very fond of some of his skilled and loyal mercenary captains such as the famous Mercadier. John eventually had to rely almost solely on mercenaries. They fought in the field for him, guarded his castles, and even became sheriffs. Many were granted rich possessions, were married to feudal heiresses, and were well launched on respectable feudal careers. However much has been written about mercenary disloyalty little is found under the three Angevins. Their good pay was a powerful incentive for loyalty and such captains as Mercadier, Falkes de Bréauté, William Casingham, and Philip Marc were completely loyal and rendered far greater service to their royal master than did the feudal barons. Their only hope of advancement was based on the nexus of royal favor, trust, and good pay. In another hundred years money would be almost the sole nexus of military service.

Though the *fyrd* had been retained it was in need of rejuvenation. Under Henry II the able-bodied freemen with their weapons had been levied only during the revolt of 1173–1174 and had rendered good service under the sheriffs. Under John the *fyrd* was used occasionally to provide coastal defense for the Channel area. It never figured prominently as a fighting force, however, until the whole system was revamped by Edward I in 1285. This military reform, it should be noted, stemmed back to Henry II's Assize of Arms enacted in 1181, which had as its goal the strengthening of the principle that every able-bodied freeman was liable to provide weapons according to the worth of his chattels and to serve the king at his own expense when summoned by the sheriff of his county. Royal justices were sent out to ascertain those who had incomes of fourteen and ten marks. Those with the higher income had to possess the equipment of a knight; those with the lower, to maintain less expensive armor and arms. The burgesses of the towns were similarly required to maintain arms and armor and to fight at the royal summons. All swore to fight for the defense of the realm and those who failed to abide by the assize could be disseised of their possessions.[9] However logical an arrangement it did not catch fire until a century later. Feudal thinking was still too strong to admit the concept that the royal subjects owed military service solely on the basis of their allegiance to the crown.

It is evident by now that the sheriff was a key official in the Angevin military administration. He summoned and helped to assemble the feudal host, he frequently was a royal castellan, and of course he served as a commander in the field. He was also responsible for calling out and leading the county *fyrd*. He was the local royal quartermaster. He paid wages, secured equipment and food, and arranged for ships to transport contingents overseas. Any service that was required generally fell to the sheriff. Those like Glanville, who were successful, immediately caught the royal eye and advanced swiftly. John could not have survived as long as he did without the brutal and efficient mercenary sheriffs behind him. They commanded his armies, guarded his towns and castles, provided him with a bodyguard, and kept the royal subjects cowed.

[9] SM, no. 34.

XIX

Local Administration: Counties and Boroughs

A DETAILED discussion of local administrative history under the Angevins would be redundant, for in general it was but a continuation of the Norman. There was, however, some real change and innovation. Two definite trends can be seen between 1154 and 1216. In one the local officers lost much authority and independence. The central government spread out its tentacles by means of itinerant justices and curial commissioners who constantly usurped what had been the traditional work of the sheriff and his deputies. But this trend, rather than smothering local administration, had the opposite effect. The royal officers, largely dependent upon the local populace for the execution of judicial, financial, and administrative functions, inaugurated in the nonofficial class an interest and participation in government which imparted to this class a valuable political consciousness and experience. Centralization progressed, therefore, at the expense of local offices and traditional circumscriptions such as the hundred, but not at the expense of the local populace. The second trend that occurred was for the boroughs, after slow progress under Henry II, to acquire the privileges of self-government and so to escape further the administrative organization of the county and its officers.

I. COUNTIES AND SHERIFFS

There is no need to examine the hundred and manor in much detail; under the Angevins they declined in administrative and judicial importance, and what functions they still performed were the same as under the Normans. View of frankpledge was held at the hundred, which continued to retain a minor civil and criminal jurisdiction. And the *murdrum* fine was still assessed on the hundred. But the history of the hundred court as well as that of the franchisal was to lose ground to royal justice. The traditional manorial court continued as before but it, too, lost some jurisdiction in the twelfth century when peasants began to get their freedom through the commutation of labor services and other means as the money economy drove wedges here and there into the manorial system. Under the Angevins, therefore, our interest necessarily centers on the county and the sheriff.

The county and its court remained the local circumscription through which the king primarily worked, and the sheriff continued as the principal local royal officer, although becoming steadily the one who carried out the instructions of curial justices rather than the one who received the royal order and then implemented it. The policy of the three Angevins was basically that of Henry I. They continued to hem in the sheriff's freedom of action and appointed men of humble origin whose loyalty could be depended upon and who, until the last three years of John's reign, were predominantly English. The itinerant justices were the principal means of subordinating the sheriff. They had the authority to force the sheriffs to serve judicial writs and to do their bidding, be it to empanel juries or to convene the county court. The itinerant justices could easily check upon maladministration. This was the object of the Inquest of Sheriffs in 1170 when Henry II ordered justices to investigate financial irregularities of the sheriffs. After Henry had studied the report of this investigation he removed wholesale most of the sheriffs and replaced them with trusted men who had served at the royal court in an administrative capacity. Although in 1194 a similar investigation was contemplated by the government of Richard it never took place. But it was from this year on that sheriffs were prohibited from serving as royal justices in their counties. And then, later, Chapter XXIV of Magna Carta enjoined that they could not hear the pleas of the crown. By 1216 the sheriffs' judicial powers had been reduced to presiding over county courts that handled local and ordinary litigation.

Despite the shackling of his authority the sheriff remained the principal cog in local government; moved and controlled from above he transmitted motion and control to his county. He supervised his deputies, the reeves of hundreds, and the bailiffs of towns. Responsible for local order, he directed the efficient operation of the frankpledge system, guarded prisoners, insured the appearance of men for trial in the local courts as well as those of the itinerant justices, and heard indictments made in the courts over which he presided. He also received royal orders to publicize and execute. Consequently, he tended to administrative routine and the collection of the royal revenue. He was the king's tax collector, responsible for all royal income except for towns and individuals which arranged to pay their taxes and personal obligations directly to the exchequer. In addition to the farm of the county and the profits of justice he usually was liable for collecting the extraordinary taxes such as the tallages, carucages, and fractions. The Angevin sheriff, by no means the powerful administrator of Norman days, was a still indispensable local officer and was to remain so until the late thirteenth and early fourteenth centuries.

2. THE BOROUGH

The Norman age was the great creative period of towns. Not only were they founded by the scores but under the impetus of an active money economy they acquired most of the economic, social, and legal liberties essential to a mobile, mercantile middle class. Few boroughs, however, attained the status of self-governing municipalities as had the great communes in Flanders and Italy. Some large enough had secured the privilege of rendering account of their farms (*firma burgi*) directly to the exchequer, thereby freeing themselves from the sheriff's authority in this sensitive matter. But only London had received a charter from Henry I that in most respects made it self-governing. Although in 1141 the citizens of London had formed a sworn association—known on the Continent as swearing a commune—to preserve its political rights, within the year Stephen and Matilda had between them deprived London of its communal status and not until fifty years later was it to be regained. When Henry II became king he further punished London, this time for its pro-Stephen sympathies, by increasing the farm to over £500 and retaining strict control over the sheriffs who administered the Middlesex-London area. Henry was conservative in his feeling towards communal government and in his reign no progress was made towards urban self-government. About all one can say is that he favored the foundation of new towns and did not block the extension of elementary bourgeois liberties. Some of the large boroughs, though retaining the privilege *firma burgi*, had yet to attain their ultimate goal of freedom from the financial and judicial organization of the county. It was under Richard and John that the boroughs began to acquire this coveted freedom.

To explain the winning of communal status by the English boroughs in the late twelfth and thirteenth centuries two theories have been advanced. One holds that the continental communes of northeastern France and Flanders exerted so decisive an influence on the boroughs that when they secured the privilege of electing their mayor and town council of aldermen they were copying the example of the continental communes with their *maires* and *échevins*. The other explanation contends that municipal incorporation was the final stage of a long evolution towards self-government in which the principal drives were social and economic. In this evolution the fight for political privilege was led by the most prosperous and influential citizens, who almost always were the principal members of the guild merchant, an economic association through which these men discussed matters of common interest and negotiated with royal officers and king. When they finally attained their coveted goal, they but acted naturally in electing men of their own guild and class to the mayorship and the council of aldermen, which, as an executive body, served in an administrative, legislative, and judicial capacity. Throughout Europe the same process was unfolding. To explain the emergence of the commune in England by pointing to certain great continental communes as stimulants and models is not in general as convincing as to explain it on the basis of social and economic drives. The latter argument, however, depends at best upon evidence sparse and limited to a few boroughs.

Our best evidence is for London. Chafing under royal officers since Stephen's reign the leading Londoners took advantage of Richard's absence in 1190 as well as of the domestic discord between William Longchamp and his opponents—the bishop of Durham, John, and Walter of Coutances—to recover their political privileges of fifty years earlier. Anxious to get its support Longchamp granted London the right to elect its own sheriffs and to render its farm of £300 direct to the exchequer. As the breach between Longchamp and John widened, London moved again to better its position. In 1191 its inhabitants swore a commune and forced from John and Walter of Coutances recognition as a self-governing municipality.[1] By 1193 the records tell us that London had a constitution and that it elected a mayor and a council of aldermen. When Richard returned in 1194 he confirmed the liberties of London and reduced its farm in return for the sum of 1500*m*. The first charter of communal liberties did not come, however, until 1199 when John granted one in return for 3000 marks. There was for a time much popular agitation over the manner in which the mayor and aldermen managed municipal affairs, but after the outbreak of disturbances in 1201 and 1206 this governing body became firmly entrenched. The only other change to the London constitution occurred just prior to Magna Carta. Courting the loyalty of the Londoners against the barons, John permitted them the right to discard the rule of life tenure for the mayoralty and to elect a mayor annually. By 1215, then, London had become a recognized self-governing municipality whose rights were guaranteed by royal charter. The mayor and aldermen, though elected magistrates, were not, as we shall see, elected by all the citizens; the candidates for office came from a select clique of the leading merchants of London.[2] Communal government in early thirteenth-century England was, as on the Continent, oligarchical.

After London our clearest evidence on borough government under John comes from Northampton and Ipswich. Though not until 1215 can we safely say that Northampton had received John's permission to elect a mayor or a council composed of twelve of the most discreet men of the town, there is strong presumption that they exercised this right as early as 1200; in that year John granted Northampton a charter which served as the model for a charter given to Ipswich that same year definitely granting it the right to elect its magistracy. Though Gloucester, Lincoln, and Shrewsbury also received grants modeled after Northampton's charter the Ipswich charter provides the fullest account of early thirteenth-century borough politics.[3] Upon receiving their charter the burgesses of Ipswich assembled in a churchyard and chose two good men as bailiffs or reeves. They then elected four coroners to keep the pleas of the crown, two of them being the bailiffs. At the same meeting it was agreed that twelve good men should be elected to a

[1] SM, no. 39C.
[2] SM, no. 39D, E, and F.
[3] SM, no. 39A.

town council, which should be charged with the governance. The burgesses assembled for this election the following Sunday. The bailiffs and coroners selected four good men from each parish who then selected the councilmen and included among them the bailiffs and coroners. This done, the twelve councilmen had the burgesses swear that they would obey their new governing body. Other meetings were subsequently convened for the selection of more officers. To collect the taxes and pay the borough farm four leading citizens were chosen to assist the two bailiffs. Two beadles, also men of means, were appointed to make attachments and distresses and to carry out commands of the council. When later it was decided to have a common seal for the borough it, along with the charter, was turned over to the custody of the two bailiffs and one coroner. Finally, one of the council was chosen alderman of the guild merchant with four other councilmen as his associates; they were to administer the guild affairs. They then proclaimed to all the people of Ipswich that they should appear before them on an appointed day to enroll themselves in the guild and to pay their fees.[4]

From this graphic account of borough organization we can see that a royal charter inaugurated a town government with a seal. The government was in the hands of a group who wielded judicial, executive, and financial powers. The oligarchic nature of the government is evident; a limited group of influential men held all the offices and were selected by a small group of the leading citizens. The majority of the burgesses merely approved previous actions by this oligarchy. Eight of the twelve councilmen held fourteen offices in the borough and guild. In effect, the borough community was the equivalent of the guild merchant; both were governed by the same officers, all leading merchants of the guild. All burgesses who wished to enjoy the borough liberties had to be guild members in good standing. We could have no better example of the oligarchic complexion of borough government in the thirteenth century or of the dynamic role of the guild merchant in first securing and then controlling self-government. This was the pattern followed by numerous boroughs which attained the privilege of self-government during the course of the thirteenth century. Of democracy we find none. Nevertheless the boroughs were now becoming political entities represented by a magistracy with which the kings must deal just as they dealt with the barons and knights of the shires. For some time yet the king would deal with each borough individually on matters of taxation and other borough services. Eventually he was to realize that it would be more efficient to deal collectively with them just as he did with the baronage and clergy. Then the boroughs would send men to a central assembly to discuss with the king his demands and business. When this point was reached parliament was in the making.

[4] SM, no. 39B.

XX

Angevin Legal Innovation

HENRY II is the true founder of the great English common law. His reign is pre-eminent in English history for its legal progress, and only the judicial and legislative innovation of Edward I bears comparison. Much of what Henry did had antecedents dating back to his grandfather Henry I but it was the new twists and imagination that Henry applied to these antecedents that made him a great legal innovator. He built upon the old and sturdy custom and procedure he found about him. Employing the strong central authority and royal prerogative he took the reins and directed and molded until by 1189 his legal system was recognized as the most perfect of western Europe. As with the Normans, it must be emphasized that most of the change was attained without legislation. In Henry's long reign we count only eight enactments that can be justly entitled legislation. Henry and his ministers wrought change informally by word of mouth or by a brief royal writ. For the most part we must write the history of law under Henry II with our eyes glued upon him and his ministers; from them came the administrative orders which effected change in organization of the courts, rise of new judicial procedure, increase in judicial writs, and constant but subtle change in the law.

It would almost seem that the gods smiled upon Henry's judicial work. Thanks to the rise of the universities, the revival of Roman and canon law, the growing money economy, and the wide-ranging contacts afforded by the Angevin Empire, Henry, well-educated and cultured, was able to surround himself with men who could help him develop good and strong law in England. It is not coincidence that we find constantly about Henry such figures as Glanville, Richard fitz Nigel, Becket, Richard of Ilchester, John of Oxford, Geoffrey Ridel, Roger Hoveden, Walter Map, and Hubert Walter. He drew upon some of the best minds of Europe to help in his tasks and the results achieved prove that he selected wisely. It is altogether fitting that the date of English legal memory established by Edward I should go back to the coronation of Richard I (1189). The great English legal system had been founded, its records had begun to be kept, and it had been described for the first time in a textbook by Glanville; it had come of age. One ought to bear in mind, however, that Henry, in spite of sincerely desiring good justice in his realm, had other motives for its institution. The spread of good royal justice was a sure and rapid means of adding to the royal pocketbook. Royal justice was a commodity that must be purchased; it was, as Maitland has so aptly expressed it, indeed royal in the twelfth century.

I. THE ROYAL COURTS

Any court held in the royal presence or in the royal name was a royal court (*curia regis*). The chief modification of the royal court under the Angevins was the increase in the number of courts that acted in the king's name. The amount of litigation that new, efficient, and speedy royal justice brought to the royal court was too much for one central tribunal to handle; at the end of Henry's reign the *curia regis* had spawned three royal courts. At the top of the pyramid remained the great council, which, as always, heard the causes between the most powerful men as well as matters that concerned the king. It was an extraordinary tribunal for extraordinary cases. It will be remembered that in the dispute between Henry and Becket the latter was tried before the great council at Northampton. The assembled prelates and barons had the function of finding judgment, which was pronounced by the justiciar. In 1163 Henry and his great council heard a dispute between the abbot of Saint Albans and the bishop of Lincoln. Upon this occasion Henry surprised the court with his knowledge of charters. He examined the Saint Albans charter and stated that the Anglo-Saxon landbooks without seals were nevertheless valid because they had been confirmed by a sealed charter of Henry I. Proof of the wide renown of Henry II's justice in Europe came in 1177 when he was asked to arbitrate the dispute between the kings of Navarre and Castile. This dispute was handled like an ordinary plea before the great council and it handed down a judgment in accustomed habit. For settling such pleas the great council was the obvious tribunal.

There was, however, slight difference between these cases and the numerous ones heard by the small council, presided over by the king or his justiciar. Generally this court disposed of most pleas that came before the royal court, only those being reserved for the great council that required the weighty judgment of the baronage of the realm. Both Henry and John participated frequently in the judicial sessions of the small council, which were numerous because it was a court that operated regularly throughout the year. At such times the court was said to be held in the presence of the king (*coram ipso rege*) and eventually it came to be known as the court of the king's bench (*coram rege*). The pleas in which the kings participated were numerous. One took place in 1157 before Henry, the two archbishops, three bishops, the chancellor, the two justiciars, and a few barons. The court sat at the chapter house of the monks of Colchester and Henry frequently retired to a side room to discuss in private certain points of law with his councillors, or to have an audience with one of the litigants. Little formal procedure is evident. Some members of the court had previously espoused the litigants, and Richard de Lucy, the justiciar, acted as an advocate for the abbot of Colchester, who was his brother. During the session members of the court consulted with the abbot. John often forbade his small council to hear a case unless he was present; under him justice was swift and frequent but it suffered often from his arbitrary and unscrupulous methods. He respected neither custom nor procedure and seemed to settle each plea upon the basis of his own whim. His law was virtually prerogative law.

Generally under Henry and the justiciars of Richard it was a great boon to get a case heard before the skilled personnel of the small council; men followed the king and council all over England, Wales, Ireland, and the continental possessions to obtain a hearing. Though this court had its merits it also had the faults of being occupied with all sorts of royal business and being highly itinerant. Often litigants would find that their cases were postponed repeatedly because the king and council were occupied with urgent affairs of state, or that they would have to travel to the far corners of Europe to find the king and his court. This was the situation confronting Richard de Anesty in 1158 when he claimed certain lands against Mabel de Francheville, whom he accused of illegal possession because of illegitimacy. Before the king and his court could hear the case the question of illegitimacy had to be settled by an ecclesiastical court. Richard had to send to Normandy for a royal writ permitting this question to be heard by the court of the archbishop of Canterbury. Eventually the case was appealed to the papal court and finally settled in Richard's behalf. This litigation was extremely slow, being adjourned from place to place and time to time. For other royal writs Richard had to send to Norway and had to travel to Gascony and France. Finally, upon Henry's return from his continental stay, during which he had waged war and concluded treaties, Richard got his case before the royal court. Still, the hearing was adjourned from week to week as Richard followed Henry around England and into Wales and back. At last Henry authorized two justices to hear the case and Richard was awarded a favorable judgment. Five years had passed since he had initiated his plea and he had spent £188 8*s.* 8*d.* on trips, messengers, legal advice, board, room, witnesses, and miscellaneous items; in addition he had given 100 marks of silver to the king and 1 of gold to the queen. It was alleged in 1194 that a certain Simon Grim had pleaded his suit for seven years in different courts. In 1213 a litigant referred to a plea to which his father was a party during Henry II's reign and which had dragged on for eleven years. Despite extenuating circumstances for such cases, they illustrate that the small court was overtaxed with legal business and that some relief had to be found.

Since Henry I's reign the small council sitting in a financial capacity as the barons of the exchequer had disposed of judicial as well as financial business. The judicial pleas heard were those touching the royal revenue. Under Henry

II the judicial functions of the exchequer increased; we hear of cases being decided that had no connection with royal finance. In fact the court of the upper exchequer became known as a royal court where pleas could be heard just as before the small council in its judicial capacity. In the thirteenth century this was to result in the separation of the judicial from the financial court. In Henry II's reign, however, the exchequer court (for financial or nonfinancial cases) was considered separate from the small council and was, therefore, the first of the great common law courts to split off from the royal court. The exchequer court, however, did not relieve the bottleneck of litigation because it was composed of basically the same group of men as the small council. About the year 1178 Henry acted to ease this situation; he ordered that five men whom he would designate—two clerks and three laymen—were to sit permanently as a *curia regis*—customarily at Westminster—to hear all suits of the realm. Only cases of the highest importance or those involving thorny legal issues were to be reserved for the king and his small council. Here, then, Henry established a small central court to render justice throughout the year at a permanent location. It was composed of the chief royal advisers, such as Glanville and Richard of Ilchester, and repeatedly included the justiciar, treasurer, and two or three bishops. Frequently it was augmented by other justices, sometimes as many as twelve, but they were outside the core and did not regularly attend. Upon occasion the new court convened away from Westminster whereas the exchequer court seldom did. At times it is difficult to distinguish between this court and that of the exchequer in that the justices were often the same for both. Each was, however, a separate court with a separate seal.

By the end of Henry's reign there was, then, a permanent central court at Westminster consisting of a group of legal experts before whom any freeman could bring his plea. But the line between the small council and the permanent court at Westminster was as yet blurred. During the royal absence the permanent court heard most of the royal pleas although the small council in a judicial capacity (the king's bench) had a reserve of justice over the great and complicated causes. When the king was at Westminster he and his small council would hear the pleas; at such times the small council actually fused with the permanent court and the judges could be the same as those who staffed the court in the king's absence. We have here in the permanent court the origin of what later in the thirteenth century was called the court of the common pleas. Despite the fact that in the royal absence this permanent court conducted most of the judicial business and heard pleas of all types, be they between two freemen (common pleas) or be they pleas affecting the king, it was not as yet distinguished from the small council. Neither court had separate plea rolls such as the later *coram rege* and *de banco* rolls and both were simply called the *curia regis*. The innovation of the permanent central court was, however, a tremendous boon and speeded up justice. Theoretically a court for any freeman, it did not in practice ordinarily entertain pleas of humble freemen, even the knights of the counties. The expense and effort of bringing a plea to the court were yet too costly for the rank and file; for many years it would remain a court which could be afforded only by the greater feudal lords. Although it helped greatly to ease the judicial burden of the king and small council it was not adequate for keeping abreast of the litigation that poured into the royal courts in the Angevin period. Still other royal courts had to be provided if Henry and his circle of legal experts hoped to match their highly popular judicial innovations in procedure with an equally good court system and to make the royal justice readily available to all freemen.

Henry II and his sons met these demands by incorporating the itinerant justices into their judicial system. We have seen how Henry I sent out the itinerant justices sporadically to try certain royal pleas at the county courts and how they began to supplant the sheriffs and resident justices as royal judges on the local level; he did not, however, organize the itinerant justices by circuit and send them out annually on their judicial journeys (eyres or *iters*). Though still performing their judicial visitations in some areas during Stephen's reign the itinerant justices almost disappeared from the legal panorama and had to be revitalized by Henry II, who had become familiar with such an institution in Anjou and Normandy. He immediately began sending out itinerant justices with the view of organizing the counties into judicial circuits and making the eyres systematic. From the outset the records speak of the justiciar, chancellor, and constable holding pleas on circuit. Various articles of the Assize of Clarendon in 1166 were enforced by itinerant justices; in 1168 a group of four of Henry's most trusted advisers at court went out into most of the counties; in 1175 England was apparently divided into three circuits with two justices covering the northern and eastern counties, two the southern and western, and the king and his court traveling about trying cases in the rest of England. After the enactment of the Assize of Northampton in 1176 eighteen justices were sent out from court on six circuits to execute various legal provisions.[1] In 1179 twenty-one justices were used on four circuits. We may safely say that the year 1176 marks the beginning of annual visitations of itinerant justices to the counties which were organized into judicial circuits.

Again Henry II had improved upon a judicial custom of his grandfather and in so doing had created the last great subdivision of the royal court. He had now successfully brought the justice of the royal court to every corner of the realm where all freemen could take whatever litigation fell under the rubric of royal pleas. The court of the itinerant justices, though a *curia regis*, was slightly inferior to the king and small council, the permanent court at Westminster, and the court of the exchequer. While each of these courts was a principal royal court (*capitalis curia regis*), only two of them could

[1] SM, nos. 31, 32.

hear practically every royal plea, though, of course, the king and his court could hear all royal pleas. Under the Angevins the itinerant justices were authorized to try only those royal pleas, both civil and criminal, stipulated in the royal instructions given to them prior to departure on their eyres. Generally, but not always, the itinerant justices were from the permanent curial staff and, in any case, the curial element always loomed large. All the great officers at some time or other were sent out on circuit. From the standpoint both of the counties and of the central administration such a system had much to recommend it. The local populace obtained a hearing of their pleas before the most skilled men of law in the realm, men who also staffed any one of the other three parts of the *curia regis*. The itinerant justices brought the king's justice down to a local level and spread it throughout the realm, thus making royal justice common to the kingdom. So it was that a strong foundation was laid for the common law, a legal liaison was inaugurated between court and county, and local public and feudal justice gradually yielded to the more efficient, swift, and reasonable justice of the king.

Beyond their judicial duties the itinerant justices also served in a useful administrative and financial capacity, thus further bridging the gap between local and central administration. Under the Normans they provided the best check upon malpractices of the sheriff; under the Angevins their control over the sheriff increased. They became the eyes and ears of the king. In the tradition of the Norman commissioners and the Carolingian *missi dominici* they conducted a variety of royal inquests to ascertain the royal legal, fiscal, and proprietary rights. In the eyres of Henry II that were solely fiscal, the justices secured financial information through the inquest system; questions demanding specific information were directed to juries empaneled from local communities. By centralizing local justice in the itinerant justices, the Angevins could enforce a variety of fiscal claims. After 1166 the itinerant justices amerced all tithings which neglected their frankpledge obligations of producing members who had failed in their duties and had absconded. Agrarian communities whose members were not all in tithings were fined. The *murdrum* fine was levied upon hundreds. Both hundred and agrarian community were amerced when not responding to the hue and cry or when failing to appeal all suspected criminals. County courts were amerced for false judgments. Indeed, by the reigns of Richard and John the Pipe Rolls are filled with amercements. And finally, the itinerant justices transmitted royal orders to county and hundred. For this flow of information in both directions no better device could have been found; from the Angevin period the itinerant justices rather than the sheriffs provided the principal link between court and county and so facilitated the spread and uniformity of royal administration and justice.

Before turning to the other courts of Angevin England let us briefly summarize the above remarks. At the end of John's reign there was hardly more than one royal court despite the legal bifurcation we have witnessed. Each division had a certain specialization, and yet in many cases pleas entertained by the great or small council could also be heard in the other divisions. It is still too early—with the exception of the court of the exchequer—to talk of separate royal courts with special categories of legal jurisdiction and with their own plea rolls. The exchequer court was a distinct common law court which concerned itself with financial litigation not heard by the other divisions; it had its own tradition and a curial group which constituted the barons of the exchequer. As for the other divisions, all we can say is that they were evolving rapidly into distinct courts. The great council heard the greatest causes. The king and his small council heard all the ordinary pleas when convenient and from this court later evolved that of the king's bench with its *coram rege* rolls which heard cases between the king and his subjects. In the royal absence the permanent court at Westminster heard all pleas to which the king was not a party except the most important and complicated ones; from it was to grow the court of the common pleas with its *de banco* rolls. The itinerant justices heard only certain authorized royal pleas; before long they would be empowered to hear all pleas on their general eyres or assizes and these would be recorded on the Assize Rolls.

2. THE PUBLIC COURTS

We now come to the public courts outside the *curia regis* system. The principal tribunal was that of the county. In the Norman period under its presiding officer, the sheriff, it had, with the exception of those pleas reserved for the king and his court, jurisdiction over royal justice, civil litigation, and various criminal offenses; it was the most active court of the land outside of the royal court. Though under the Angevins it remained the highest local court, it followed the decline of the sheriff as Angevin administrative, judicial, and financial change replaced local authority. This decline, like that of the sheriff, was in terms of independence and authority rather than in functions. Actually the county court became more active in response to the growing governmental demands placed upon the local inhabitants. In the realm of justice the county court rapidly became a forum where the members of the court periodically assembled to cooperate with the itinerant justices in fulfilling the instructions of their eyres. Here the new Angevin judicial procedure impelled the members to serve on indicting juries for criminals and on recognition juries to settle civil disputes. By the end of the twelfth century these sessions were important occasions. Some weeks before the justices began their eyres a writ of general summons was sent to each sheriff ordering him to summon all the prelates, barons, knights, and freeholders of the county, as well as four men and the reeve of each agrarian community, twelve men from each borough, and all others who had a reason to appear before the justices. Upon the arrival of the justices their writ of authority was first read, followed by the list of their judicial business—the type of pleas to be heard. Thereafter all local officers from the sheriff on down were at the command of the justices and were at court to implement judicial business. Having disposed of the preliminaries, the justices got down to business. They ordered the empaneling of juries to indict all men suspected of criminal offenses and tried such appellees by the customary ordeal. For civil cases juries were empaneled to settle disputes over land. Beyond this legal work the justices performed other administrative tasks: securing information from the court members, assessing fines, and transmitting royal orders. The county court was a periodic clearing house for royal business and information.

As royal procedure grew in efficiency and royal justice expanded in jurisdiction, these county assemblies under the itinerant justices increasingly dispensed justice at the expense of the customary county court under the sheriff. By the thirteenth century most of its civil and criminal jurisdiction had been lost to the itinerant justices and courts of common law; it retained only the pettiest types of pleas adjudicated by time-honored procedure and customary law. The decline of the hundred court followed that of the county court. Under the Normans, as we have noted, the hundred court lost most of its jurisdiction, and by the thirteenth century, under the presidency of the sheriff's deputy—the hundred reeve—it adjudicated only the most minor civil disputes. As a criminal court the regular monthly hundred sessions ceased to function. Only when the sheriff visited the hundred twice a year on his tourn for the purpose of taking the view of frankpledge was criminal justice on the agenda. Petty criminal offenses were then adjudicated by the sheriff and suitors. These sessions were considered separate from the ordinary hundred court and, as such, criminal justice was said to be dispensed at the court of the sheriff's tourn.

The franchisal courts, which under the Normans had increased in number and had frequently acquired hundredal jurisdiction, shared the fate of the other public courts except that their decline was less precipitate because the feudal lords who enjoyed franchisal courts jealously fought to hold on to their traditional jurisdictions and perquisites. Even Edward I was not able to rout such courts.

Like all freemen, the burgesses of the boroughs were affected by the growing royal justice. Under the Normans these urban inhabitants had won numerous judicial privileges. Not only had they secured the right to hold courts for adjudicating commercial disputes under law merchant, but they had also secured the privilege of being tried for criminal and civil offenses only within the borough and at its court. To preside at these courts came the sheriff or his deputy; both royal and nonroyal pleas were held. When London secured the right to elect its own sheriff it thereby excluded outside interference in its judicial affairs. But not for long, because by the Angevin period the itinerant justices were including the boroughs in their visitations along with the county court. These judges could not be excluded and the boroughs felt the full influence of the common law as it was administered in the central royal courts. Despite the continuance of burghal courts governed by customary and merchant law, where royal pleas were involved the burgesses were as much subjected to royal jurisdiction as were men of the countryside. It is interesting to note that in their local courts the burgesses clung to archaic custom and procedure long after it had disappeared from the county and hundred courts. Progressive economically and socially, and manifesting a high degree of reason in their business transactions, the burgesses were nevertheless strongly imbued with urban particularism and clung blindly to outmoded custom merely because it was local and particular.

3. THE FEUDAL AND MANORIAL COURTS

Only a few words need be said about the nonpublic courts—the feudal and manorial. One word—decline—best characterizes their history in the Angevin period. Though feudal courts were the great bastions of strength for the barons, they could not withstand economic and legal progress. As the money economy chipped away at things feudal there was less need for feudal justice; fewer disputes arose over failure to perform knight service or other feudal obligations. As the climate of opinion became less feudal men worried less about feudal rights. Also suit to court was bothersome; some vassals had to travel considerable distances to their lord's court and if they had a number of lords such an obligation was onerous. The fact was that feudal courts were less needed. The increase of royal jurisdiction did to them what it had done to the public courts. Royal jurisdiction was extended to cover all disputes over possession of land as well as over right to land. All major criminal offenses were royal pleas. A lord lost jurisdiction over civil justice by virtue of the writ *praecipe* (command or precept) if he did not immediately obey the royal order to restore disputed land to the plaintiff (customarily a vassal) who had secured such a writ.[2] Although Magna Carta provided that this writ should be discarded, other writs replaced it so that no lord could hold his feudal jurisdiction intact against the king's justice. Lastly it should be emphasized that the more rational, efficient, and rapid justice secured in the royal court was much preferred to the slow and crude procedure of the feudal court. By virtue of its popularity alone royal justice could have vanquished its competitor; whatever its cost, litigants believed it a bargain compared to what they had known.

The peasants who were unfree were outside the pale of the royal courts. As always they were tried in the manorial court of their lord. This court was composed of the peasants presided over by the manorial reeve or the lord; into it came the litigants to plead their cases and to be judged according to manorial custom. Against this entrenched system only the money economy

[2] SM, no. 33F.

could make an inroad. As the boroughs grew and spread, they provided islands of freedom to which the peasant could escape and, if he lived there undetected for a year and a day, could become free. In some areas of England where land reclamation was in progress, lords and ecclesiastical establishments lured peasants to participate in clearing the land by promises of freedoms like those enjoyed by burgesses. In the twelfth century exchange of money became so customary that the commutation of labor services began. The peasant, by paying an annual rent for his parcel of land, sloughed off all his manorial services and was henceforth responsible only for paying a rent. Actually then, he became free and could leave the land if he desired to sell or alienate it; the lord's only interest was the rent. As the commutation of labor services quickened its pace more villeins escaped the manorial regime and consequently its court. As freemen, they could get justice in the royal court or in the more humble public courts. By John's reign, royal justice through the common law courts was so strong, so widespread, and so popular that it either had smothered or was soon to smother its competitors.

4. CIVIL PROCEDURE

However fundamental for the growth of the English common law, the system of royal jurisdiction developed by the Angevins must take a place second to the procedural innovations. Herein lie the originality of the common law system and the reason why the royal courts so quickly snuffed out rival competition. The success of this procedure stemmed from two royal legal instruments—the writ and the jury. In our discussion of the royal writ we have described it as a brief royal order directing a royal officer or administrative body to perform a certain command. We have also emphasized the importance of the Norman-Angevin writ in contributing to the efficient administration. Short and flexible, it was open to all types of uses and a word to the chancellor by king or justiciar could result in a writ ordering new administrative, financial, or judicial procedure. For any need or emergency a new writ could be manufactured immediately. It was one of the achievements of the Angevins to realize the almost unfathomable legal possibilities of the writ. Through it they inaugurated new civil trial procedure and constantly marked off pleas that could be tried only in the royal courts.

Since the Normans, the kings had upon occasion heeded the complaints of plaintiffs by issuing writs that ordered the adversaries to settle their dispute in a royal court or that directed pleas to be handled by the proper sheriff or feudal lord. Customarily these writs descibed the nature of the complaint and instructed the royal court, sheriff, or feudal lord to see that right was done. As this custom grew, so too did the chancery staff, which took over the task of writing out writs and which, to save time, used certain writs as models and made up blank forms to expedite the quick issuance of any number of different writs. At this point the writs began to be classified according to subject matter and recipient. Under the general classification of original writs—those used to originate pleas at royal courts—there branched out different categories. Those issued by the chancery as a matter of routine were called writs of course (*brevia de cursu*); they were classified still further on the basis of the legal instructions. Further delineation came with writs introduced to settle disputes over possession and proprietary right in land. We thus meet the possessory writs or assizes as distinguished from the writ of right for proprietary actions.[3] Meanwhile new writs were manufactured to enable an endless number of pleas to get into the royal courts. Royal justice was for sale, available to any freeman who desired to buy the writ tailored to his legal need. As the subtle distinction between possession and proprietary right developed and was recognized by lawyers, there emerged a further classification of writs initiating litigation to settle proprietary actions—the writs of entry. The roots of these writs can be found in the writ *praecipe*, which under Henry II ordered an individual (generally the lord) holding land demanded by a plaintiff to surrender it or to appear at a royal court to have the dispute over right settled. All writs of entry were similarly phrased and suggested that a tenant's right had some flaw. It was always declared in these writs that the tenant's entry into the land was by a means which gave him no good legal claim to proprietary right. For the present it is enough to have noted the beginning of a dichotomy of writs, those dealing with possession and those with proprietary right. We shall have occasion to speak further of these writs in a moment when we investigate their introduction into the Angevin legal procedure.

The jury, like the writ, was of Norman vintage. Under the Normans, as a sworn jury of men who were expected to know certain facts, it was a means of obtaining information under oath. We have seen that it became a part of Norman administration, that it was used to obtain the information for compiling *Domesday Book*, and that soon after the Conquest juries of men helped to settle disputes over possession of land and jurisdictional rights. The latter use was, however, only occasional; in general the time-honored Anglo-Norman procedure was followed. Henry II continued the administrative use of the jury and showed his legal imagination by making it a regular means for settling civil disputes. Men of a community presumably familiar with the facts of a certain case were summoned to court and ordered to declare under oath the facts as they knew them. This institution is known as the jury of recognition. To such a jury practically any question might be put—who should possess a certain piece of land, who should hold this court, and who should exercise these rights. We must distinguish the jury of recognition from other similar institutions with which it has frequently been identified. The jurors or recognitors of the twelfth century by no means had their origin in the Anglo-Saxon doomsmen who deemed the dooms in the

[3] SM, no. 33.

public courts nor did they form a court which delivered a judgment. The recognitors were assembled for only one purpose—to recognize or declare the truth regarding a specific question put to them. Moreover, they were not witnesses collected by the litigants and then put to a sworn oath that supported the sworn statement of the litigant. The recognitors were empaneled by a royal officer and ordered to tell under oath whatever was the truth. Obviously such an oath differed from that of the compurgators who swore to a litigant's oath.

One more matter must be mentioned before we can discuss the use of the writ and jury—the connotation of the term "assize." Originally assize (*assisa*) meant simply the sitting of a court or of a council. Later it came to denote the decisions taken and enactments passed at such an assembly. We hear of the Assizes of Clarendon and Northampton and of the Assize of Arms and numerous other assizes of beer, weights, and measures. Many of Henry II's enactments dealt with new procedure to be used in trials to determine possession and proprietary right. Consequently when writs were devised to implement the legal enactments promulgated at royal councils, they took the name of assize. We thus hear of possessory writs being called possessory assizes. Under the Angevins assize had a variety of meanings; it could refer to enactments by king and great council, by king and small council, by justiciar with either of the councils; it could refer to administrative and judicial instructions given by king or justiciar to the itinerant justices prior to their eyres; and it could refer to the judicial writs.

Whereas under the Normans trial by jury for civil cases was exceptional, under Henry II and his successors it became the normal mode of trial. The jury of recognition was first employed to settle disputes arising out of conflicting claims of church and state. By the twelfth century church courts were claiming jurisdiction over all land held by the tenure of free alms. Trouble arose when there was a question as to whether land was held in free alms or by feudal tenure. Neither the church nor secular courts were in a position to settle this question; it must be done by a third body. One provision of the Constitutions of Clarendon issued in 1164 by Henry II declared that by ancient custom this question should be answered by a jury in the royal court. It stated that a jury of twelve men was to be empaneled from the countryside and under oath asked whether (*utrum*) the land was held in alms or lay fee.[4] Here began the assize *utrum*, the first of the four petty assizes or writs.

The other three assizes (writs) dealt with possession. Apparently at the Council of Clarendon in 1166 Henry issued his next important assize, that of novel disseisin (recent dispossession). Unfortunately the original enactment has not come down to us; our information about it comes from chronicles and the thirteenth-century lawyer Bracton, who said that Henry and

[4] SM, nos. 30, 33c.

his council spent many wakeful nights over this radical new legal procedure. The principle of the assize was that no freeman could be disseised (dispossessed) of his land unjustly and without judgment. Any person who claimed to be so disseised could obtain remedy by purchasing the writ of novel disseisin. In the presence of royal justices a jury was summoned and under oath asked whether the plaintiff had been disseised.[5] If the jury gave a verdict favorable to the plaintiff his land was to be restored. Keeping in mind that this assize did not concern proprietary right but only possession, we may say that it provided a swift remedy for settling contested possession and that it put the royal protection over all freemen's seisin. So eminently reasonable and satisfactory was this assize that the barons made certain it was guaranteed by Magna Carta. In the Angevin period the disseisin had to be recent or the plaintiff could have no remedy. During Henry II's reign the question put to the jury was whether disseisin had occurred since the last royal crossing to Normandy. In 1194 the Plea Rolls state that the limiting date for legal action was the first coronation of Richard I in 1189. In the thirteenth century longer periods were granted until finally in the later Middle Ages and Tudor era the period was lengthened to centuries and made the question of possession academic. Actually the question then settled was one of proprietary right.

The second possessory assize was initiated at the Council of Northampton in 1176; this was the assize of mort d'ancestor (*assisa de morte antecessoris*, meaning assize of the death of ancestor). According to this assize if a man died in possession of a heritable tenement, his heir was to secure possession of the land against the claim of any man even if it could be established that a better proprietary right existed. The question put to a jury in a royal court was who possessed this land on the day when he who died was alive and dead. If the verdict was given for the dead man then his heir got possession. This assize was a frontal assault upon feudal justice because often the defendant in such a plea was the lord of the dead man and had seised the land. When a writ mort d'ancestor was purchased, such a legal issue could no longer be settled in the lord's court.[6]

The third possessory assize was that of darrein presentment (*assisa de ultima presentatione*, meaning assize of last presentment). This was devised to facilitate the settlement of disputes over the advowson (protection) of churches. According to this assize if a church was vacant (with no priest or proper churchmen) and its advowson (generally meaning the right to appoint to the office) was disputed by two men, a jury was to be summoned and asked under oath who presented the last priest. Therefore, without raising the question of right of presentment the assize acted on the principle that the individual who presented last should also present this time. Probably this assize was enacted after 1179, the year when the Lateran Council of

[5] SM, no. 33B.
[6] SM, no. 33A.

the church provided that if a church remained vacant for several months the proper bishop should make the appointment. The assize provided a quick remedy so that one or the other of the secular litigants could make the appointment before the bishop.[7]

These, then, were the four petty assizes—*utrum*, novel disseisin, mort d'ancestor, and darrein presentment—of which the last three were the possessory assizes or writs. With all four the sworn inquest is applied to civil procedure; a jury under oath answers a question which provides the verdict. This procedure, followed only in a royal court, could be secured by any freeman who purchased the suitable writ.

We have concentrated thus far on procedure introduced to settle dispute over possession; the matter of proprietary right has not been introduced because until now it would only have confused our understanding of possession. If one desired to be pedantic he could maintain that in the twelfth century there was only one real proprietary or allodial holder in England: the king, who owned all the land of the realm. All others held land immediately or indirectly of him and therefore only held possession. Theoretically plausible, this view is unrealistic because more than possession was involved. Behind the possessions involved with the three petty assizes there was a more fundamental question of proprietary right or ownership. Under any of the three possessory assizes a man might be awarded possession even though he might have less right to the land or presentment than his unsuccessful opponent. For example, the successful litigant or his father may have unlawfully seized possession of land which the other litigant and his family may have possessed by grant since the days of the Conqueror. The possessory writs do not settle this question, and the example illustrates that behind possession there was a more fundamental possession that we would call proprietary right or ownership. The distinction is subtle and the relation between possession and ownership relative, but the law and lawyer recognized it and there was legal procedure developed to settle dispute over ownership.

The customary trial in a proprietary suit was judicial combat. The plaintiff must offer battle, or wage it through a champion. It was a crude, barbarous, uncertain, and frequently unjust means of settling so fundamental an issue, and during the course of the twelfth century with the renaissance in law it was brought under attack. As background for comprehending the great innovation made in this procedure, the following points must be thoroughly understood. Trial by combat to determine proprietary right was the preserve of the feudal courts and the king could interfere only when justice was not done. Henry II changed all this. Glanville tells us that Henry enforced the rule that no freeman had to answer for his land without the king's writ. No matter where the suit, a royal writ had to be purchased in order to initiate proprietary action. Generally this was done by a writ of right (*breve de*

[7] SM, no. 33D.

recto), which commanded the feudal lord to do right to the plaintiff and warned that if right was not done the sheriff would settle the dispute.[8] The writ of right guaranteeing that no man could be deprived of his land without a judgment proved to be a fertile precedent for what later was called due process of law. Henry also began to interfere with such disputes more arbitrarily by means of a new writ called *praecipe* (precept or command). This writ was directed to the sheriff ordering him to instruct the holder of the land to return the disputed land to the plaintiff.[9] If it was not done the defendant would be summoned to the royal court where the case would be settled. This royal procedure was felt to be so serious a breach in feudal custom that the barons inserted a provision in Magna Carta eliminating the writ *praecipe*. The fact remains, however, that Henry II had made a successful assault on feudal jurisdiction over proprietary disputes and was prepared to initiate procedure that eventually administered a fatal blow to feudal justice.

Around 1179 Henry instituted the grand assize, a legal enactment considered the most fundamental in the history of the common law. Glanville singled it out as pre-eminent among Henry's reforms and called it a royal boon (*regale beneficium*) to the tenant of land. Under this assize the defendant (tenant) could decline the trial of uncertain and dangerous judicial combat and have the dispute settled by a jury in a royal court. If he took this course and purchased the writ, then four knights of his community were chosen to elect a jury of twelve knights who were required under oath to say which litigant had the better right to the land in question. It was not strange that Glanville considered the grand assize a great boon to the tenant, because he as the possessor was favored. Although the plaintiff must offer battle, the tenant could refuse and have the dispute settled by the verdict of a jury in the royal court. So reasonable and sensible was this procedure that it immediately became popular and feudal justice precipitately declined. As early as Richard I's time a *Curia Regis* Roll records that in one year there were 135 proprietary suits settled by the grand assize.

Unlike the possessory assizes the grand assize was not a summary action. With it, all sorts of delays or essoins were permitted, causing a case to drag on interminably. This situation frequently compelled the litigants to purchase a license from the royal court permitting them to conclude a settlement out of court or, to use the proper legal phrase, a final concord. By the middle of Henry's reign such procedure was customary; it hastened as permanent and as legally valid a settlement as was possible to obtain from a jury's verdict. The assize of novel disseisin, however, could not be handled in this way because it involved a breach of the king's peace. The agreement was first drawn up in the form of a chirograph with each party getting a copy. By 1195 a third copy was made at the foot of the other two. The three were cut

[8] SM, no. 33E.
[9] SM, no. 33F.

apart in zigzag lines and the foot was placed in the treasury archives to serve as a future record. In this way developed the Feet of Fines. Though peripheral to our discussion, we should remark that this system of fines came to be applied to the conveyance of land, that is, when land passed from one owner to another through livery of seisin (delivery of possession). This transaction had been traditionally accomplished by an oral ceremony in the presence of witnesses or by a charter, but men now began to see the advantages of the fine. It was a legal document made in a royal court and preserved in the royal archives. It was the most secure method by which land could be transferred. By John's reign all variety of legal subtleties were employed by those transferring land to get the conveyance accomplished by means of a final concord in the royal court.

The five assizes just discussed provided the foundation for the English law of property; from them has in large part evolved this highly complex law. They established the principle that the royal courts could restore seisin to any freeman disseised without lawful judgment. Also enforced was the principle that, no matter in what court, trial by combat did not have to be accepted by the tenant in possession until a writ of right had been obtained which guaranteed a judgment for proprietary disputes. The grand assize even went so far as to encourage the settlement of proprietary disputes in the royal court. The assizes guaranteed the supremacy of the royal courts and of jury procedure and blazed the trail to trial by jury in other civil actions. Until the advent of the grand assize the original writs initiating the possessory assizes made mandatory the assize jury of recognition. With the grand assize, the defendant had a choice—jury or combat. It was the voluntary and flexible character of the grand assize that made it so popular and led to the submission of all sorts of litigation to the verdict of a jury. With the other assizes, an assize jury was summoned concurrently with the defendant and before he had pleaded; with the grand assize, the jury was not empaneled until the two litigants had pleaded and the defendant had chosen jury trial. The defendant's right to choose jury trial hastened the day when both litigants would voluntarily accept it. This legal evolution led Maitland to declare that "in course of time the jury, which has its roots in the fertile ground of consent, will grow at the expense of the assize, which has sprung up from the stony soil of ordinance." Throughout the Middle Ages old-fashioned modes of trial persisted. Compurgation remained until 1837 and combat until 1819, but both were reduced to insignificant proportions by the rational procedure of trial by jury before skilled judges in the royal courts.

5. CRIMINAL PROCEDURE

At the beginning of Henry II's reign traditional Norman criminal procedure was in full sway. A criminal of the feudal aristocracy was brought to justice by the appeal (personal accusation) of the plaintiff, who offered to prove his appeal by judicial combat, which frequently ended in the death of one of the combatants. When the vanquished survived, he was often horribly mutilated and then had to pay the penalty of his crime—hanging, severe corporal punishment, or exile and confiscation of his goods. Trial by combat, though waged by the feudal aristocracy, was more generally waged by approvers, individuals who had turned king's evidence and were released on the promise that they would appeal and fight the accused. Trial by ordeal was the more common form ordered by the courts. Either mode—by ordeal or by combat—was archaic and quite incapable of providing a just settlement. Moreover, it was difficult to appeal a man and reach that legal point where the accused was tried; delays and technical flaws so hindered the path of justice that commonly appellors dropped their charges. About all one can say for the two modes of criminal trial is that the king got his judicial profits whether the accused was found guilty or innocent. If he was found guilty, the king got the condemned man's chattels; if he was found innocent, the unsuccessful plaintiff was heavily amerced for false accusation. It was soon apparent to Henry that if he was to have law and order in his realm a more efficient method for apprehending and trying criminals must be found. His solution was the presentment or grand jury.

The presentment jury was an Angevin innovation. We first hear of juries used to indict people in 1159 and 1164.[10] First for Normandy and then for England Henry declared that church courts should employ such a jury. He insisted that no man should be tried in church courts merely on the basis of unsworn private accusations of wrongdoing. He who accused must do so publicly and under oath or else the accusation must come from a jury of twelve men of the community summoned by the sheriff. This judicial procedure, forced upon the reluctant prelates, shows that Henry was casting about for a more just and efficient method of appeal. Then in 1166 the Assize of Clarendon clearly formulated the institution of the grand jury. Issued with the consent of the great council, this assize introduced an investigation into all crime committed since Henry's coronation. In each county twelve men of every hundred and four men of each township (agrarian community) were summoned to the county court to declare on oath before the sheriff or before the itinerant justices the names of all those reputed to be guilty of murder, larceny, or harboring criminals. The sheriff was empowered to make all necessary arrests and was to receive the cooperation of sheriffs in other counties. Jails were even to be provided for the secure custody of those accused. Issued just before a general eyre of the itinerant justices, the Assize of Clarendon contained the instructions which were to guide the work of the justices.[11] It remained in force and was strengthened in 1176 by the Assize of Northampton. This assize, also issued just prior to an eyre, placed

[10] SM, no. 30.
[11] SM, no. 31.

forgery and arson on the list of crimes to be presented by grand juries.[12] A useful feature of this system was that the work of the grand jury could be increased whenever the king and his ministers saw fit. As the Assize of Northampton enlarged the scope of the grand jury's indicting powers, so too did later edicts. The articles of the general eyre in 1194 increased and more explicitly defined the functions and power of the itinerant justices.[13] An edict issued by the justiciar Hubert Walter in 1195 resulted in further perfection of the grand jury system. It emphasized the obligation of local men to cooperate in the hue and cry in order to capture criminals and it ordered that all men above the age of fifteen must take an oath before duly appointed knights to keep the peace. These knights seem to have been the ancestors of the later justices of the peace.

After the grand jury had brought in its indictment, the accused stood his trial before the itinerant justices at the county court. The trial was *not by jury* but by the ordeal of cold water. If a man failed at the ordeal, the Assize of Clarendon provided that he lost a foot and must leave the realm. The Assize of Northampton added that he who failed should also lose his right hand.[14] Apparently many failed at the ordeal because the Pipe Rolls record numerous cases in which the sheriff accounted for the chattels of those banished from the realm. Henry, having no illusions about the luck and irrationality of ordeal, inserted a clause in the Assize of Clarendon which forced men of bad reputation to abjure the realm even if they had successfully undergone the ordeal. Under these circumstances the grand jury virtually had the power of banishment over a man whom it presented. Already distrusted as a mode of trial in 1166, the ordeal survived in England until 1215 when the Fourth Lateran Council ordered the clergy not to participate in trials involving bloodshed; by this withdrawal of the church sanction, ordeal, which rested upon superstition and the supernatural, lost its *raison d'être*. This decree forced the royal government to seek other criminal trial procedure. Since the early thirteenth century some men accused of crime had been permitted, upon payment of a small fee, to have their cases decided by a jury. There is, for example, the case in the eyre rolls of Bedfordshire for 1202 of a man who, accused of wounding and killing, paid a mark for having the privilege of a jury decide his guilt or innocence. This custom became more popular and certainly provided a precedent for criminal jury trial in the reign of Henry III.

Another development contributing to trial by jury was the introduction of exceptions (*exceptiones*) into criminal cases. From the late twelfth century, lawyers were pleading exceptions that were not direct denials of the accusation. Defendants were able to purchase an exception from the king which gave them opportunity to secure a jury's verdict. The earliest excep-

12 SM, no. 32.
13 SM, no. 40A.
14 SM, nos. 31, 32.

tion was the writ of spite and hate (*de odio et atia*). The defendant would assert and then submit to the verdict of a jury that he had been maliciously accused of a crime out of spite and hate. He did not deny his guilt but raised another question of law which was determined by a jury. If the jury returned a verdict favorable to the accused then the case would be dropped and the plaintiff fined for a false appeal; if unfavorable, the accused still had the opportunity of denying the charge and undergoing trial by combat or ordeal. This development in the pleading of exceptions contributed to familiarizing men with jury trial and hastened the day when the accused would have the right of submitting immediately the whole question of guilt to the verdict of a jury. Early in Henry III's reign the writ *de odio et atia*, which Magna Carta had provided to be issued freely as a writ of course, became obsolete. It came to be employed primarily to secure the temporary release from prison of a man accused of homicide; if an inquest found that he had been accused out of spite and hatred he would obtain temporary release. Though the rise of the petty criminal jury really lies in the thirteenth and fourteenth centuries, the use of jury trial under the circumstances noted above, as well as the use of juries for indicting, trying civil cases, and securing information for the royal government, fertilized the ground for the growth of this great English institution.

Brief reference ought to be made to Angevin criminal punishment, which generally followed the Anglo-Norman custom of an eye for an eye and a tooth for a tooth. Hanging and mutilation plus forfeiture of goods and exile were the usual punishments. When a man was apprehended in a criminal act, justice could be summary; we hear of numerous men hanged on the spot. As for enlightenment regarding these crude punishments, all one can say is that royal courts were less inclined to inflict capital punishment and that criminal cases were frequently settled out of court, thus sparing the accused hanging or mutilation. But the whole criminal system of detection, process, and procedure was still primitive and unequal to providing what we would call law and order. As in the American West and other frontier areas, men and the times were cruel and rude and the process of civilization was slow.

6. THE CORONERS

By now it is evident that much legal preparation occurred in the counties prior to the visitation of the itinerant justices. The correct summonses and writs had to be issued, records had to be compiled listing the cases and their details so that they could be promptly placed before the justices, men and chattels had to be seized and attached, witnesses had to be secured, and indictments and investigation of crime had to be made. This work fell principally upon the sheriff, his subordinates, and the suitors of the local courts. Many of the details were attended to at the view of frankpledge. With the enormous increase of royal pleas and the regularization of the eyres under Henry II local machinery was not equal to the heavy burden. The Angevins therefore instituted the coroners, local officers who were to conduct all necessary criminal investigations prior to the arrival of the itinerant justices. Coroners appear in the records for the first time in the Articles of Eyre of 1194.[15] Maitland argued that the coroner dates from this year, while Gross contended that this officer was created some time in Henry II's reign because the regularity of the eyre system demanded such a local office to facilitate the efficient functioning of trials and the grand jury. The latter view is perhaps the more accurate; chapter twenty of the Articles of Eyre of 1194 no doubt refers to an institution created by Henry II.

In any event four knights from each county, who had to be residents of the county and to possess sufficient land, were to be elected by the court and swear under oath to the sheriff to fulfil their duties. They were elected for life and received no pay. Their chief function was to bring criminals to justice. They were to hold inquests on bodies of those supposed to have died either by violence or by accident and of those who died in prison. They also held inquests on bodily injury, rape, prison break, and other crime. Chattels of the accused were to be evaluated and guarded until after the trial; if the accused was found guilty his possessions went to the king. The coroners also attached the accused persons, those present at the scene of violent death, finders of dead bodies, and occasionally two or four of the neighbors. These individuals were then summoned to appear before the itinerant justices. In addition the coroners received criminal appeals, recorded all outlawries of the county, and made a record of their investigations. These records resulted in the Coroners' Rolls, which are extant from the year 1264. Not only did the coroner expedite royal justice done to criminals, but he served as an additional check upon the sheriff and aided him in some of his work. The coroner tried certain minor criminal cases and presided with the sheriff over jury trials for petty civil cases. At times he presided over the hundred court and held the view of frankpledge. He also performed a variety of other local administrative tasks for the king. Thus, by the thirteenth century, Angevin ingenuity had created another useful officer who carried out the royal will but who was elected by and served local men. The coroner provided another link in the chain between king and local government.

7. CONCLUSIONS

The foundation of the English legal system was laid by Henry II. During his reign men such as Glanville and Richard fitz Nigel were speaking of an English common law or custom. By extending the royal court system throughout England and by improving the old public and feudal justice, the Angevins put local custom and procedure to rout. Any freeman could purchase a variety of judicial writs which gave him access to the royal court. By means of the possessory assizes Henry popularized and regularized jury

[15] SM, no. 40A.

trial. By the grand assize he gave the defendant the opportunity to have the fundamental question of proprietary right determined by a jury, a choice that broke ground for jury trial for civil cases. By the writ of right Henry insisted that proprietary actions be settled by proper judicial judgment; the writ *praecipe* was a more forceful extension of this principle. In the category of criminal justice Henry constantly spread his jurisdiction over all the serious crimes and saw to it that criminal accusation became more common and systematic by the introduction of the grand jury. Within a few years after John's death, the petty criminal jury had taken form. That the barons sanctioned most of the Angevin legal innovation is evident from their having it guaranteed by Magna Carta.

Administratively and financially these judicial changes were beneficial to the Angevins. The profits from justice showed a handsome gain, and control over local administration was immeasurably tightened. The itinerant justices proved to be a most effective instrument of liaison with the county and of restraint over the sheriff. They performed a long list of administrative and financial duties outlined in their instructions for the eyres. Constantly ordered to secure information from local communities for purposes of justice, finance, and administration, they interrogated the men of county, hundred, and agrarian community who were summoned to tell under oath all that they knew in response to the questions. These local men, by cooperating together on juries of trial and presentment, apprehending criminals, collecting and helping to assess taxes, fulfilling offices created by royal order, doing all that the central administration willed, were participating in local government and through this experience attained a knowledge of politics and administration that would serve them well when later they were assembled in parliaments to discuss weighty matters of state with the king and his council. Under the Angevins self-government at the king's command had begun.

XXI

Angevin Church and State

I. THOMAS BECKET AND HENRY II

THE compromise of Henry I and Anselm over the investiture struggle calmed the troubled waters of church-state relations throughout the rest of Henry I's reign. Over the weak Stephen, however, the church won numerous victories, of which the most notable was the recognition of its freedom. Armed with this vague but powerful concession, the church made inroads against the royal authority that no strong king could countenance. One of Henry II's first objectives was to turn the clock back to the time of his grandfather. This policy is reflected in the brief charter of liberties granted at his coronation; it totally ignored the concessions made by Stephen and granted to the church only those liberties held under Henry I. That Henry II meant to follow in the path of the strong Normans is immediately clear. He accused a bishop of infringing upon the royal authority by procuring a papal bull to settle a dispute with an abbot. He so discouraged appeals to the papal court that as early as 1156 the pope complained to Archbishop Theobald of Canterbury that appeals were smothered in England. Obviously Henry intended to restrict the jurisdiction of the spiritual courts and to exert a tighter control over the administration of justice for the clergy.

That Henry's objectives were practical and legitimate, few historians will deny. But he and his sons had to fight a church that had attained its greatest power in the second half of the twelfth and early thirteenth centuries. Under the two able and dynamic popes Alexander III (1159–1181) and Innocent III (1198–1216) the church forged ahead in an effort to win in practice what it preached in theory—the supremacy of the pope and church over secular princes and secular matters. The struggle that ensued in England had its counterparts throughout western Europe. In England church courts legitimately handled causes of marriage, incest, and testament, but the church lawyers constantly increased spiritual jurisdiction by liberally interpreting any question of contract as a breach of faith and thus a case for their courts. When Henry II came to the throne, church courts were claiming jurisdiction over litigation concerning lay fees and debts. Rural deans and archdeacons were unscrupulously accusing laymen without sufficient evidence and frequently ignored even canon law. A man of Scarborough was blackmailed by a rural dean who threatened to accuse the man's wife of adultery although there was no evidence. The clergy could be tried and punished only in church courts, a custom that had created a scandalous situation by the time of Henry II. Because sentences of bloodshed could not be handed out, imprisonment was the most severe penalty a guilty clerk could receive, and even it was infrequent for prisons were too expensive to maintain. Generally the sentence was penance or at most degradation. Clerks without scruples were undeterred by such light punishment and literally committed murder, rape, and robbery. This immunity from punishment lured disreputable men into the church who could lead a life of crime with impunity. The chronicler William of Newburgh asserted in 1163 that over a hundred murders had been committed by clerks since Henry II's accession. With the assistance of his close supporter and minister, Thomas Becket, Henry planned to block the pretensions and abuses of the church. But, as he had done with his sons, Henry misjudged the character of Becket and made one of the few miscalculations of his reign.

Numerous biographies of Becket have been written and from all emerges the conclusion that he was a domineering, energetic, and able man whose drive towards success and power was hampered by few scruples or principles. He was indeed remarkably successful. Born in 1118, Becket was of bourgeois origin. He was the son of a Rouen merchant who settled in London and who eventually became a sheriff. Besides learning about business from a rich and prominent uncle, Becket received excellent training at the priory of Merton and at a London grammar school. But he was primarily a man of action and his formal education stopped here. He never acquired proficiency in the Latin tongue. Through a friend of good social standing he was introduced to Archbishop Theobald and was taken into his household. There he was entrusted with important work and sent on delicate missions to Rome. As his knowledge and horizons broadened, so too did his affluence. All sorts of benefices were lavished on him. He took minor holy orders and advanced up the ecclesiastical ladder. In 1154 he became archdeacon of Canterbury, a lucrative position that involved supervising all legal matters. Becket committed the usual malpractices and was often censured by the archbishop for failure to do his work. Although the church had supported him for the chancellorship in the hope that he could advance its cause at court, Becket completely forgot his old ecclesiastical patrons, busied himself in war and politics, and supported polices of Henry II against the church. Thinking that such a devoted servant would be useful to head the church of England, Henry nominated Becket as archbishop of Canterbury upon Theobald's death in 1162. Thus a man who had not yet become a priest was elected to this high office, but to Becket's credit it should be noted that he was reluctant to assume it. By resigning the chancellorship and devoting his energy and talents exclusively to the service of the church, Becket confounded his royal supporter as he had his church patrons. Though Becket's ability cannot be denied, his sincerity might well be questioned. He was vain, pompous, and ambitious; he overplayed every role. Inconsistencies or past loyalties bothered him not a whit. His goal was to be completely successful in any office or task. Actor that he was, he undoubtedly welcomed martyrdom.

In 1163 began the struggle between Henry II and Becket—two obstinate and spirited men. Becket went out of his way to antagonize Henry. He successfully thwarted Henry's effort to have the sheriff's aid (a type of slush fund) paid directly into the exchequer. He forbade certain political marriages arranged by Henry for members of his family. He excommunicated a tenant-in-chief without the royal consent. He permitted a series of nasty crimes perpetrated by clerks to go unpunished despite Henry's request that justice be done. The chronicler William of Newburgh admits that Becket and the bishops brought on their struggle with Henry because "they were more intent upon defending the liberties and rights of the clergy than on correcting and restraining their vices." To remedy such injustice Henry called a council at Westminster in October of 1163 and there stated that he had the right to punish criminous clerks who had been tried and found guilty in a church court. Under the prodding of Becket, all bishops save one refused to give their consent, and Becket and Henry parted with bitter words. Becket's success was, however, short-lived. Some of the bishops under the leadership of Gilbert Foliot, bishop of Hereford and bitter enemy of Becket, switched their support to Henry because they realized the legitimacy of his position. Becket then appealed to Pope Alexander III for support. But Alexander was in no position to alienate Henry. He was in a desperate struggle with the German emperor Frederick Barbarossa and needed the support of the powerful Angevin. After much temporizing, Alexander advised Becket that on this point it would be best for him to submit. Forsaken by the pope, Becket promised at the end of 1163 to agree to Henry's proposal.

It was now Henry's turn to overplay his hand. Had he been content to let the matter rest at this point the two men might have found a *modus vivendi*. Unfortunately, he was determined to set down in writing the customs that had governed church-state relations during the reign of Henry I. At a council which met at a favorite hunting lodge of his in January 1164, Henry issued the Constitutions of Clarendon.[1] Most of the provisions, which purported to be the customs of Norman kings, need only brief mention. No vassal or officer of Henry was to be excommunicated, or have his land put under interdict, without the royal consent. The prelates and clergy were not to leave the realm without Henry's permission. Appeals to the papal court were severely restricted; it was provided that church disputes were to go no further than the archbishop of Canterbury's court without the royal consent. Henry asserted his feudal right to enjoy the revenues

[1] SM, no. 30.

from vacant ecclesiastical benefices and insured his control over elections by insisting that the electoral bodies assemble in the royal chapel and elect a man suitable to the king. The man was to do homage and swear fealty to the king before receiving spiritual investiture of his office. Minor provisions dealt with legal relations between spiritual and secular courts. The clause over which Becket and Henry primarily clashed was the third. It specified that clerks accused of crime were to be turned over to a church court for trial after being interrogated by royal justices. There, in the presence of a royal justice whose purpose was to witness the proceedings, the clerk was to be tried and, if found guilty, turned over to the royal court for sentencing and punishment. Obviously this guaranteed that criminous clerks would receive their due, even to hanging and mutilation. Becket immediately protested against what he termed "double punishment" and quoted from Jerome that "God judges not twice for the same offense." For this legal point Henry was relying upon expert canon law advice and was on firmer ground than Becket, who interpreted the law as he thought it should be. Henry's proposal agreed with general European practice and church law. And yet despite its legality, Henry's stand alienated the prelates, who were not prone to swear to uphold written law. Becket did not put his seal to the document, but he finally agreed to it and the bishops fell in line. For the moment Henry tasted victory.

Through his desire for legal and written preciseness, Henry lost the support of Alexander III, who stated that he could not approve the Constitutions because some provisions were counter to canon law. Becket at once repented his action, reversed his stand, inflicted penance upon himself, and even tried to flee from England. In October at the Council of Northampton came the final break. Here a case involving a dispute over land between Becket and John the Marshal was heard. The trial had previously been scheduled at Westminster but Becket had excused himself because of illness. Now present, he was condemned for contempt of court and fined. Henry, bent upon destroying his enemy, also demanded that Becket account for certain sums handled while he was chancellor. Becket pleaded that he had been summoned only for the dispute with the Marshal and therefore did not have to account for the money, and he clasped a cross to him invoking the protection of the church against the royal wrath. He also argued that the bishops could not sit in judgment upon him. Henry ignored these protests and ordered the justiciar to pronounce sentence. Becket would not listen to it; he abruptly left the court and that night secretly embarked for France.

Becket remained in France for six years. His exile caused no great stir in England and Henry remained undisputed victor. On the international level, however, it became a *cause célèbre*. Louis VII of France tried to embarrass Henry by becoming Becket's protector and attempting to mediate no less than twelve times. Though sympathetic to Becket, Pope Alexander III did not permit him to make any rash move. He entertained representatives of both Becket and Henry at his court. As the years passed Becket became more vindictive and threatened all sorts of ecclesiastical penalties. His self-righteousness and stubbornness, and his refusal to negotiate sensibly with Henry, even alienated some of his supporters. Becket's fury reached its height in 1170 when Henry had his designated successor, the Young Henry, crowned king by the archbishop of York. Coronation had always been a prerogative of the archbishop of Canterbury and this fresh affront to Becket made his past disputes with Henry seem insignificant. In the matter of coronation the pope supported Becket, and an interdict was being threatened against England when suddenly in July 1170 Henry and Becket met in France and reconciled their differences. Actually no real settlement was attempted; the Constitutions of Clarendon were not even mentioned and it is difficult to determine the reasons for the *rapprochement*. It would seem that Becket desired to get back to England in order to take action against the bishops who had supported Henry. He immediately published sentences of suspension against certain bishops and returned to England where he was shunned by all royal officials. On Christmas Day from the pulpit of Canterbury he publicly castigated and excommunicated his enemies. In Normandy, Henry received reports of Becket's conduct and, in a towering rage, asked why he could not be rid of him. Four knights of the household took him at his word; they went to England and murdered Becket while he was conducting mass in the cathedral.

This rash act undid in a few moments what Henry had laboriously accomplished in sixteen years. All Christendom looked upon Becket as a martyr. In 1173 the pope made him a saint and there subsequently arose the cult of Saint Thomas. To escape the ire of the church, Henry conducted an Irish campaign in 1171 and skillfully negotiated for peace with the pope. In 1172 he met papal legates at Avranches in Normandy and settled his differences with the church. He swore that he had not commanded Becket's death, he promised to go on a crusade, and he agreed to restore all ecclesiastical possessions to Canterbury. Most important, he agreed not to block appeals to the papal court and to drop the customs governing church-state relations introduced in his reign. Henry suffered severe defeat on certain points. In granting freedom of appeal, he lost some of his control over ecclesiastical affairs. Appeals became more numerous; clergy could leave the realm without license and so receive instructions from Rome more easily; papal bulls no longer required the royal consent for entry. The pope now obtained greater control over the church and expanded the effectiveness of the canon law. On the matter of criminous clerks, Henry also met defeat. Hereafter a clerk arraigned in a royal court could claim benefit of clergy and be turned over to a church court for trial and sentence. Benefit of clergy remained until the nineteenth century. For his part, Henry kept control over church elections and retained most of his other prerogatives, such as vacant church incomes and the right of deciding in his courts whether land was lay fee or alms.

To the end of his reign Henry maintained amicable relations with the church and even won back some of his lost prestige. He skillfully controlled the elections of all prelates and in 1184 settled a quarrel over the election of an archbishop of Canterbury. The Pipe Rolls indicate that he managed to keep church offices vacant for long periods in order to enjoy their revenues. He made strong objections to the visits of foreign papal legates and closely restricted their activity. The later years of his reign are most important, however, for new developments in papal and crusading taxation. Even while Becket lived, Henry compromised somewhat on papal levies. In 1165 he allowed Peter's pence to be collected, and in 1166 he agreed that a tax of 6*d*. could be collected on each pound of personal property to provide military forces for the Holy Land. In 1188 Henry and the great council authorized the tax of a tenth on movable property for a crusade against Saladin; this tax became a notable precedent for future royal taxation in the thirteenth century.[2]

2. RICHARD I AND THE CHURCH

Richard I was appreciated by the church for his exploits as a crusader but was as heartily disliked as his father for his overbearing attitude towards the clergy and their rights. His arbitrary action against the church in Normandy caused Innocent III to place the duchy under interdict. In England Richard constantly asserted his will in church matters. At the outset of his reign he forced the canons of York to elect as archbishop his illegitimate brother Geoffrey, but by 1196 he had quarreled with Geoffrey and forbidden him to administer his diocese. For his trusted servant Hubert Walter he secured the archbishopric of Canterbury and later his appointment as papal legate. In 1196 when Hubert, acting in his capacity as justiciar, set fire to the church of Saint Mary-le-Bow to smoke out a London agitator, William fitz Osbert, and nine associates, there was great protest against such violation of sanctuary. But Richard protected Hubert until 1198 when he resigned his justiciarship under pressure from Innocent III.

Richard's most serious altercation with the church arose over the question of taxation. In 1197 Hubert Walter proposed to the great council that it provide Richard a force of three hundred knights to serve in Normandy for a year. His proposal was defeated through the protests of two bishops. That famous champion of the church Hugh of Lincoln argued that the church owed military service only in England and that it was not obliged to pay for service abroad; he was supported by Herbert of Salisbury. These two bishops led the first successful opposition to payment of a royal tax. In 1198 when the church fought Richard's carucage, he retaliated by depriving it of the

[2] SM, no. 38.

protection of royal courts; to buy back their protection it had to pay more than the carucage would have cost.

3. JOHN AND INNOCENT III

In John the church could find nothing to wax enthusiastic about. Though it had disliked the attitude of Henry and Richard, at least it did not consider them frivolous and irreligious, as it did John. Nevertheless, Hubert Walter entered John's service as chancellor and no bitter issue came between John and the church until the death of Hubert in 1205. Hubert was a restraining influence upon John and formed a bridge between church and state. Only on the question of taxation was there any altercation. The archbishop of York refused to pay a carucage levied in 1201, and John seized his lands. The Cistercians claimed immunity from taxation, refused to pay a fine, and were finally deprived for a time of the protection of the royal courts. In 1207 there was again opposition to a tax, but this time John gained his thirteenth on personal property and the church had to pay either the tax or a fine. Those prelates who refused to pay had their goods seized and were banished from the realm.

What sparked John's battle with the church and Innocent III was the election of Hubert Walter's successor as archbishop of Canterbury. Three parties had a vested interest in the election: the monks of Christ Church Canterbury, who canonically had the right to elect; the bishops of the metropolitan, who still claimed a right to elect; and John, who, if tradition were followed, could count on having his nominee elected. To forestall a quick election and to gain time to push his loyal friend John de Gray, bishop of Norwich, John postponed the election for six months; he hoped for the support of the bishops. To block this plan, the monks of Canterbury secretly elected their subprior Reginald and sent him to Rome to be confirmed. When John heard of this action he was furious and so cowed the monks that they denied having held an election and proceeded to elect John de Gray as archbishop. The net result was that Innocent III ruled both elections irregular. In 1206, upon his recommendation, the monks elected Stephen Langton, an Englishman well trained in the schools of Paris and recently made a cardinal priest at Rome. Innocent consecrated Stephen in 1207, but he did not go to England until 1213 because John would not confirm his election. John appropriated all the possessions and revenues of Canterbury and drove most of the monks into exile. About this same time Geoffrey, archbishop of York, was also exiled because of his opposition to the tax of the thirteenth, and the possessions of York likewise fell to John. Innocent replied with an interdict that became effective in March 1208; it meant the suspension of all ecclesiastical services in England for the next six years.

Through death or flight all the bishoprics save that of John de Gray and

Peter des Roches of Winchester were vacant, and when John de Gray went to Ireland in 1209 only Peter remained. Still, John was willing to negotiate, and it was only after point-blank refusal of the pope and Stephen to compromise, and after the threat of excommunication, that John's attitude hardened. After his excommunication in October 1209 he systematically began to appropriate church revenue. He ordered that the property of all secular and regular clergy who refused to celebrate divine services was to be confiscated, and he began to plunder the wealth of the church. The exchequer records note some of the sums that John extorted. Despite his arbitrary action and the distress caused by the interdict, John had general support; until 1212 it appeared as though he was the victor. Never was he more popular with his subjects, especially the barons, who were relieved of taxation while John lived off the church. It is paradoxical that John attained his greatest success when he defied the most capable and powerful of the medieval popes.

During 1209, 1210, and 1211 negotiations were initiated by both sides but they always broke down on some technicality or oath. In 1211 the papal legates Pandulf and Durand were empowered to lift John's excommunication if he would make certain amends, but John considered them too high. In 1212 the tide suddenly turned in favor of Innocent III. To begin with, the Welsh princes broke into revolt, and when John assembled a host to subdue them, he discovered at Nottingham that some of the barons were plotting against him. He abruptly disbanded the army, seized some barons as hostages for baronial good behavior, and outlawed two barons for treason. John now realized that his firm grip over England was slipping. In November, therefore, he sent emissaries to feel out the pope for a solution. It was decided that John should accept the terms offered him in 1211, and if he had not complied with them by June of 1213 Innocent would pronounce deposition. Soon John received more alarming news. At a council held at Soissons, Philip Augustus of France had announced his plan to invade England. Faced by baronial revolt, deposition, and invasion, John decided to surrender. In May he and Pandulf reached a settlement. John promised to recognize Stephen Langton as archbishop, to restore the exiled prelates, and to repay the church for all losses suffered during the dispute. Four barons acted as pledges for these promises. John then handed over Ireland and England to Innocent and received them back as fiefs upon the performance of homage and fealty. John agreed to pay an annual tribute of 1000 marks to the pope and, in addition, 700 and 300 annually for England and Ireland. This feudal arrangement, which bound England to the papacy for a century, has often been condemned by historians, yet it does not appear to have been considered outrageous at the time. It should be remembered that during the revolt of 1173 Henry II acknowledged the feudal supremacy of the pope, and that Richard did homage to the emperor Henry VI. And, too, Innocent III had similar feudal relations with other European princes. John considered it prudent to win the support of the great pope in the struggle against the barons and France. And Innocent did not fail John; he supported John no matter how arbitrarily he behaved in the next three years.

John's other relations with the church were linked to his struggle with the barons. Immediately after making his peace with the pope, John summoned an army to undertake the invasion of Poitou; the barons refused service on the pretext that John was still under sentence of excommunication. John received absolution from Langton in June and promised to defend the church, to confirm the good laws of his predecessors, to judge all men according to legal procedure and customs, and to restore the rights of all individuals and the church before the next Easter. Still the barons refused their service, and at a great council held at Saint Albans protested against evil officers and laws of John and referred to the Coronation Charter of Henry I as a standard of justice. Upon this rebuff John assembled an army to move against the baronial leaders as rebels. But Langton dissuaded him from such action, arguing that it was a violation of his promise to give freemen a legal judgment, and threatening to place the sentence of excommunication upon John and his adherents. Langton was now moving rapidly to the fore as leader of a baronial reform party, and at a subsequent meeting of the barons held at Saint Paul's in August he produced a copy of Henry I's famous charter and indicated that it contained the liberties promised by John at his absolution.

But if in Langton the barons had acquired a consummate leader, John had secured the support of Innocent and, towards the end of 1214, further cemented his relations with the pope by abandoning his control over ecclesiastical elections. This action was a repudiation of a cardinal Norman-Angevin policy, but John was in no position to continue this precedent. Whereas he had previously notified the chapters of vacant cathedrals and monasteries to fill the vacancies and, by charter, had granted the right of free election to various ecclesiastical houses, now he issued a charter to all religious establishments granting them the right of free election. He retained the right of assenting to elections, but he promised not to obstruct free elections or force elections to occur at the royal chapel. He also retained his right to the income from ecclesiastical offices while vacant.[3] Although old abuses continued, John had put himself on written record and his promises became a part of the custom of the realm until Henry VIII.

4. CONCLUSIONS

Had Henry II and John been opposed only by the English church, they would have been wholly victorious. But the international character of the church involved them with forces outside England. Without the support of the popes, neither Becket nor Langton could have stood up to the Angevins. It was the martyrdom of Becket that aroused the feelings of western Chris-

[3] SM, no. 43.

tendom against Henry II and forced him to renounce the most important provisions of the Constitutions of Clarendon. With John, a clever pope so skillfully combined the threat of deposition with the hint of backing the barons and of supporting Philip Augustus' invasion of England that John could do nothing but capitulate. With both Henry and John, an unhappy combination of events caused their downfall. Still, the victory for the church was not decisive. The Angevins established their right to tax the movable property of the church. Numerous provisions of the Constitutions of Clarendon remained in force. And though John was defeated in his fight to control elections, he retained the right of assenting to them.

With more tact and restraint John might have avoided the storm that was about to strike, but his wrathful seizure of church possessions and revenues and his banishment of the prelates united the clergy with the discontented lay baronage. Although in Langton the church provided a leader for the rebels, paradoxically his master Innocent III supported John to the end, a loyalty that brought John only more baronial resistance. The English church eventually broke with the papacy and supported the more popular cause which ended in Magna Carta. In this struggle Stephen Langton had a more acute understanding of the issues than Innocent III. He became more than a churchman interested only in protecting the liberties of the church; he became a statesman concerned with the just and legal treatment of clergy and layman. To him a legal trial in court was as important for a baron as for a churchman. It was in the fight for Magna Carta that Stephen Langton was to acquire stature.

XXII

Magna Carta and the Defeat of Angevin Absolutism

THE one historical document and event familiar to nearly everyone living in areas governed by the Anglo-American legal and political system is Magna Carta and its concession by King John on 19 June 1215 at Runnymede on the Thames. In the minds of most it is considered the progenitor of constitutional government. In both written and spoken word Magna Carta is writ large whenever the subject at hand is constitutionalism of the Anglo-American variety. Magna Carta is cited in scholarly monograph and note, in college and secondary school text, in newspaper editorial and slick brochure, in learned legal argument, and in political oratory commemorating great national events. Rare is he who escapes acquaintance with Magna Carta. To understand the reasons for its prominence, we must first understand the document itself and the scholarly opinions concerning it.

1. OPINIONS ON MAGNA CARTA

Between 1215 and the end of the Middle Ages Magna Carta acquired three roles. It was cited as legal precedent in the pleadings and sentences of the common law courts; it was adopted by the barons as part of their political program in the numerous struggles to curb the royal prerogative; and it came to be confirmed by the kings at the opening of parliaments. Most royal subjects thought of Magna Carta as a written document expressing certain fundamental laws by which the king should govern. But medieval men seldom wrote about or theorized upon Magna Carta, and in the period of Tudor absolutism it was indeed almost forgotten. During the Civil Wars of the seventeenth century Magna Carta was rediscovered and given the luster it yet retains. Confronted with the exalted Stuart ideas on divine right and royal prerogative, the common law lawyers and parliamentarians marshaled out Magna Carta and gave to it an interpretation that is still widely current among lawyers and political scientists. According to the great justice Sir Edward Coke and others, Magna Carta had saved England from the rule of tyrants, had consecrated basic civil and political rights, and had germinated

English constitutional government. More specifically, they declared that it put the king under law, limited his actions by the collective will of the nation, provided that there would be no taxation without parliamentary consent, and guaranteed in ringing terms that all men of England should have due process of the law and trial by jury. Such interpretation was inaccurate; it was based upon what the common law lawyers and parliamentarians wanted to find in Magna Carta rather than on what it actually said. In effect, these men so modernized and so transformed Magna Carta to make it work for them in the seventeenth century that it became a document quite unlike that of 1215. Because of this historical distortion, however, Magna Carta became a potent weapon in the struggle for constitutional government.

Imprinted with the great authority of Coke, this view of Magna Carta prevailed in the eighteenth century. The renowned lawyer Blackstone considered Magna Carta the principal bulwark of English liberties. The elder William Pitt referred to it as the "Bible of the Constitution." This opinion was held by most Anglo-American historians and lawyers until the end of the nineteenth century. It was but natural in view of the strong liberal-romantic movement that engulfed England during the nineteenth century. Such historians as Hallam, Green, Creasy, and Stubbs underlined what Coke had said and in their glorification of Anglo-Saxon democracy became even more sentimental. According to Stubbs "the demands of the barons were no selfish exaction of privilege for themselves. . . . They maintain and secure the right of the whole people as against themselves as well as against their master; clause by clause, the rights of the commons are provided for as well as the rights of the nobles. . . . The Great Charter is the first great public act of the nation after it has realized its own identity." This authoritative pronouncement was echoed by English and American scholars until the 1890's when finally there began a reaction against what one historian called the "Myth of Magna Carta." With more records now available for study, historians, trained in the so-called "scientific school of history" of the later nineteenth century, which taught objectivity and reliance upon what documents actually said, began a new interpretation of Magna Carta. Revised opinion, as enunciated by such scholars as Petit-Dutaillis, Jenks, and McKechnie, held that Magna Carta was a document of feudal reaction and a block in the road towards progress. The barons were characterized as a narrow, selfish, and untalented lot desirous of turning the clock back to the days of Henry I and of securing privileges that would benefit only themselves; never should they be regarded as the champions of political liberty, the founders of parliament, or the defenders of the rights of all Englishmen. This new interpretation of Magna Carta, though more scholarly and supported by more evidence, was little more correct than the interpretation it had supplanted; the truth lies somewhere between the two.

2. THE REASONS FOR MAGNA CARTA

Having already noted the political events of John's reign and the steps leading up to Magna Carta, we ought now to concentrate upon the causes that led to the baronial outburst of 1215. They may be broadly categorized as feudal grievances, judicial and fiscal complaints, and fear of royal tyranny. Since the Norman Conquest the most influential segment of English society —the feudal aristocracy—had been governed by feudal custom in its relations with the kings. Feudalism provided a military, political, social, and economic frame of reference by which the kings and their vassals were bound to act. A combination of homage, fealty, and fief-holding set up between the lord king and his vassals solemn mutual obligations which came to be reasonably well defined in the course of the early twelfth century. The feudal aristocracy was content with this traditional feudal custom, but unfortunately the strong-willed and ambitious Angevins were not. They regarded the custom as an obstruction to strong centralized government and did all in their power to eradicate most of it and to remodel the rest so as to increase the royal administrative, judicial, fiscal, and military power at the expense of their vassals.

We shall spell out only the salient features of the Angevin fight against the old feudal system. During his reign, Henry II had attempted to raise the *servitium debitum*, or knight service owed to him by his vassals, in order to increase the scutage that he could collect when vassals desired to commute their military service. Richard, especially after the beginning of his continental campaigns against Philip Augustus in 1195, made almost yearly demands for service overseas for extended periods of time or, in lieu of it, scutages or other subsidies. For the first time the barons began resisting military service outside England. Under John, however, there was no abatement. He constantly demanded military service or scutages for his disastrous campaigns between 1201 and 1204, and during 1214. These demands coupled with total military failure stiffened baronial resistance against service overseas and payment of scutage and taxes for unsuccessful and unpopular campaigns. We have seen that John's defeat at Bouvines plus his demand of a scutage upon return to England sparked the baronial revolt.

The Angevins had also increased their demands with respect to the feudal aids and incidents. Both Henry II and Richard were guilty of all manner of infractions such as mulcting their vassals of reliefs that were too high and arranging marriages and wardships profitable to the crown. Their actions, however, did not get completely out of bounds, although Richard came close in his insatiable greed for money to finance the crusade, to pay his huge ransom, and to fight his enemy Philip Augustus. Perhaps it was only Richard's absence from England that kept tempers from the boiling point. With John, the Angevin greed for money made a mockery of feudal custom and of the king as a feudal lord. The Pipe Rolls and chancery enrollments record the tremendous reliefs he charged, the unjust marriages he forced upon widows and heiresses, and the unfair arrangements he made for exercising the right to wardships. To escape unpalatable marriages or unprofitable wardship arrangements, vassals paid exorbitant fines. If they did not pay, their daughters were frequently married to foreign favorites or mercenaries of John from Poitou and Touraine, and the wardships were sold to the highest bidder, who then customarily drained the feudal resources dry. John levied scutages almost annually, whether or not a campaign was conducted, and ruthlessly increased the rate. No feudal custom, no obligation, not even homage itself, meant anything to John when pecuniary advantage was involved. Confronted with a lord who refused to govern by the only law they knew, the majority of the barons became discontented and revolted when the moment was opportune. It was a feudal revolt, justified by the feudal custom that when the lord would not honor his obligations to his vassals they were legally entitled to force their feudal right by arms. Their goal was to force John to grant them in writing a carefully defined list of his feudal obligations, and to swear to govern by them.

In the realm of common law the grievances of the feudal aristocracy were less justified. Even the barons would not deny that Henry II's legal reforms were efficient and beneficial. Too many of them had benefited under the new royal judicial procedure in the common law courts to want to turn the clock back to Norman days. Honestly and objectively administered, the Angevin judicial system could have escaped attack. But John selfishly used his father's innovations to augment his power and wealth. Although there was a superabundance of litigation in the royal courts during John's reign, the central theme of baronial discontent was paradoxically default of justice. Too frequently, litigants came to the royal court and received no justice; law and judgment of the court were set aside for the will of John. Without reference to the law, John handed down arbitrary justice. Moreover, he denied the royal courts to numerous causes and parties, and he sold his justice at exorbitant prices to others. John took over a marvelously efficient judicial system and then employed it to his own advantage. The barons did not dislike the Angevin judicial system, but they came to fear it as a system upon which John could impose his capricious sense of justice; if John were to continue unrestricted, he would become a tyrant against whom there would be no protection of land and right. The barons, therefore, urgently felt that they must impose legal restrictions upon him. They attempted to put into practice what John of Salisbury and other writers on political authority advocated in theory—a true and lawful ruler must be under the law and must govern according to it. A prince who was unrestrained by law and who was above it was a tyrant. When the barons finally compelled John by force of arms to govern by existing law, they were but following the commonplace tradition of feudal custom and medieval political thought.

No matter how honestly John might have administered the royal courts, there would have been some complaint. By constantly placing more pleas under royal justice and by devising new writs that diverted causes into the royal courts, the Angevins made sharp inroads into the jurisdiction of feudal courts and the profits of justice. Many of these innovations were so popular that the barons did not want to throw them out, but only worked to restrict royal encroachment upon justice that properly belonged to the baronial feudal courts. As we have seen, it was Angevin policy to use men of humble lay and ecclesiastical rank for many of the highest administrative and judicial positions because they owed their careers to royal favor and were therefore loyal to the crown. There was, however, intense baronial feeling against trial in royal courts before men who were not their peers, men who were in fact often their social inferiors. The barons naturally resented trial before such men and demanded trial by their feudal peers (*judicium parium*) according to feudal custom.

Another principal cause of baronial resentment was the increasingly arbitrary methods used by the Angevins to provide for their fiscal needs. Henry II, though staying within his feudal right in the levying of customary and extraordinary aids, stretched this right to the breaking point. He had some justification because the crown required more than customary feudal revenue to finance its expanding governmental responsibilities. But increased taxation is never popular, and discontent spread when the Saladin tithe opened up the resources of movable property to taxation not only for ecclesiastical but for secular use. Richard revived the old land tax in the form of the carucage and he, as well as John, called for high scutages upon the slightest pretext. John relied also upon taxation of movable property and, like Richard, imposed taxation upon possessions of the church for which the prelates claimed immunity.

Baronial hatred of John can best be summed up as fear of an Angevin absolutism which John had cunningly developed to the point where the established feudal order could have been snuffed out. At this point, when whatever pleased John had the force of law, the barons understood the dreadful possibilities. They and other elements of the realm already had witnessed a preview of such tyranny. John had shown that he neither tolerated nor trusted the conventional feudal ties of homage and fealty; he demanded far more leverage over his vassals. He forced upon many barons special oaths of fealty which, if broken, resulted in forfeiture of possessions. To insure loyalty and good behavior from others, he exacted hostages and land as pledges. He arbitrarily seised the land of numerous barons. For John, feudal bonds were not sufficient; his hold upon royal subjects must rest upon the weapons of the tyrant—fear, blackmail, brutal punishment, and death.

John's arbitrary and illegal destruction of the baron William de Braiose has often been cited to illustrate how the royal hand struck. In 1207, suddenly and for no reason, John turned against William, a former favorite, and disseised him of his extensive lands in the west country along the Welsh border. Declared a traitor, William and his family fled to Ireland. Unfortunately, in 1210 John captured William's wife and son, imprisoned them in Windsor Castle, and left them to starve to death. This is but one grim case of how John moved against and in his own inimitable manner cruelly destroyed those with whom he differed. Faced with such cases of wanton cruelty, the barons saw the necessity of uniting and of forcing upon John basic human decency and accepted law. They felt compelled to curb John's arbitrary will which epitomized their grievances—the flouting of feudal custom, increased and arbitrary taxation, the decline of their feudal jurisdiction, the lack of customary law and judgment in the royal courts, and the resort to force and fear to obtain the royal desires.

Discontent with John was not confined to the barons. For eight years the church had felt John's wrath and had suffered from his financial exactions and highhanded behavior. One who bore the brunt of John's vindictiveness—Stephen Langton—united church and baronage in opposition to John, led in hammering out the provisions of Magna Carta, and by virtue of his integrity and moderation not only made Magna Carta into a reasonable document of reform but acted as mediator between John and the barons and did all in his power to urge peace and a *modus vivendi*. His failure to attain peace was not owing to any shortcoming on his part. He had to fight the opposition of Innocent III, as well as an uncompromising John and baronage who intended to fight out their differences. John had also alienated the burgesses by his high taxes and by the oppressive and illegal local administrations of the sheriffs and bailiffs. To them, as to the baronage and clergy, it appeared that John had appropriated the efficient machinery of local and central administration to use it for extortion and bad government. Though the barons were the principal agitators, they were strongly supported by the lesser feudal aristocracy, the church, and numerous townsmen. As for the unfree—the villeins—they counted for nothing in the early thirteenth century.

3. THE CONTENT OF MAGNA CARTA

We may well begin analysis of the charter by disposing of the clauses relating to the church, to the burgesses of the towns, and to miscellaneous matters.[1] They are few in number and serve to emphasize that the principal recipients of the charter's concessions—the feudal aristocracy—concentrated upon rectifying feudal, judicial, and administrative grievances. Chapter I granted to the church its freedom, liberties, and right to free elections. Phrased vaguely, it conceded nothing but what had already been conceded by previous kings and by John himself, who had promised the right of free elections in his charter of 1214. Chapter XXII promised limitation of amercement to the clergy and provided that a clerk's ecclesiastical benefice was exempt from any fine. Chapter XLII provided that men should be free to

[1] For the subsequent discussion of Magna Carta see SM, no. 44.

leave and return to the realm. This included all freemen, but it was particularly welcomed by the clergy, who had been prohibited by the Constitutions of Clarendon from leaving the realm without the royal license. This freedom so eased the way for the papacy to encroach upon the royal prerogative that this chapter was omitted upon reissue of the charter in 1216. These were the only concessions won by the church.

Even less in number were the tangible gains of the burgesses. They likewise obtained freedom of travel (Chapters XLI and XLII) but they had never suffered from this restriction. Chapter XLI also freed the merchants from evil and excessive tolls. Chapter XIII, in providing that London as well as other boroughs and towns should enjoy the privileges and liberties obtained previously, but confirmed charters of liberties and privileges acquired through prescriptive use. These were the concessions made to the middle class. None represented any significant gain in privilege or freedom and one gets the impression that these chapters were included as a sop to the burgesses, especially to those of London who had thrown in their lot with the barons.

The next five chapters dealt with economic matters of benefit to both barons and lesser freemen. Chapter IX stated that in cases of debts owed to the crown the personal property of the debtor must be exhausted before he could be deprived of his lands, and that all his lands had to be attached before his sureties could be forced to pay his debt. Chapter X ordered that when a man had borrowed from the Jews and had died before the loan was repaid, no interest was to be charged while the heir was a minor. Furthermore, John agreed that if he acquired the debt he would demand no interest. Chapter XI pertained also to debts owed to Jews. If the debtor should die before repayment of a loan, the Jews could collect nothing until the widow's dower lands were freed from her husband's debt and until the debtor's minor children had been satisfactorily provided for. Chapter XXXIII may be interpreted as an aid to the navigation of inland waters because it ordered removal of all fish weirs so that they would not obstruct the passage of vessels. Chapter XXXV established a uniformity of weights and measures throughout the realm.

We now come to one of the two central themes of the charter—the reform of feudal grievances, a problem to which twenty chapters were devoted. Chapters II and III assured the levying of just reliefs and forbade the king to exact relief from a fief over which he had enjoyed wardship. Chapter XLIII governed the relief to be paid by the heir of a man who had held from a tenant-in-chief whose fief had escheated to the crown. John had exacted exorbitant reliefs from such subvassals but it was now provided that the heir should pay the king only the relief customarily paid to his lord. Chapters IV and V stipulated the responsibilities of guardians, with strict injunctions against the fief's being wasted by the guardian to increase his profits. Chapter XXXVII recognized that where a man held from the king by the tenures of fee-farm, socage, or burgage, and by the tenure of knight service from another lord, the claim to wardship lay with the superior tenure of knight service and the king had no right to it. Chapter XLIV forbade John to usurp wardship over ecclesiastical establishments founded by barons. In Chapter LIII John promised to restore all wardships that he had illegally usurped over both lay lands and church foundations. Chapters VI–VIII dealt with the incident of marriage. To forestall the marrying off of heirs and heiresses to foreign favorites or to the highest bidder, it was stated that the king could not arrange any disparaging or forced marriages. Furthermore, widows were under no compulsion to remarry and were entitled to receive without hindrance or fine their lawful dower and marriage portion.

Feudal aids and scutages next came under review. Chapter XII ordered that henceforth, except for the three customary feudal aids, no extraordinary aid or scutage could be levied except by the common counsel of the realm, that is, by the consent of the great council. To insure an orderly procedure for the assembling of the great council Chapter XIV stipulated that the archbishops, bishops, abbots, earls, and greater barons should receive individual summonses, and the lesser barons, general summonses through the sheriffs and local bailiffs. Chapter XV regulated the aids that the barons could collect from their vassals. John promised to grant no licenses for the levying of any aid except the three customary ones, and these were to be reasonably assessed. These three chapters, especially Chapter XII, have often been construed to mean that no taxation could be imposed without the consent of parliament. This is not at all the case. The great council was not a parliament; it was a royal feudal court exercising a traditional feudal right—the consent to extraordinary feudal taxes. The barons represented no one but themselves and spoke only for themselves. When the great council consented to the levying of a scutage, it meant only that the barons agreed that a campaign was warranted and that therefore scutage could be collected from those who preferred not to provide knight service. But no baron was bound by the great council's consent to a scutage; he could always supply his quota of knights. Chapters XVI and XXIX, regarding the obligation of military service, stipulated that royal vassals should be required to render only their customary quota of knight service and that none could be compelled to pay money in lieu of castle-guard if he wished to perform it. The last three feudal provisions of the charter extended further protection and security to the baronage. Chapter XXVI regulated the procedure to be followed in attaching the personal property of royal vassals who were also royal debtors. When such a vassal died leaving behind a debt, royal officers could evaluate his personal goods and then attach them to the value of the debt. Chapter XXVII prohibited John or any lord from seizing the land and goods of a vassal who died intestate. The deceased vassal's inheritance was to be distributed by his relatives and friends under the supervision of a bishop's court. Finally, in Chapter XXXII, John promised that the confiscated land of felons would be held for only a year and a day and would then be returned to the lord from whom the convicted felon had held. Feudal custom gave the land of a felon to his lord and the chattels to the lord holding the court. John had encroached on the lord's rights and now partially redressed this wrong.

To the subject of justice was devoted the next largest group of chapters—eighteen. Chapter XVII asserted that common pleas—the cases in which the king had no interest—were no longer to follow the king and the royal court about but were to be heard at a fixed place. This rendered royal justice more accessible and cheaper in addition to drawing a clearer distinction between the king's bench (the court *coram rege*) and the bench set apart for common pleas in 1178. Although this latter bench had been established to hear ordinary pleas at Westminster, its justices were prohibited from leaving the royal court, so that in practice the common pleas still followed Henry II around. This was not true under Richard, who was absent from England most of the time, and during John's reign this court ceased following the king about and established itself at Westminster. Even before Magna Carta it was considered an abuse to try common pleas elsewhere; therefore Chapter XVII merely confirmed a judicial custom that had evolved gradually since 1178. The barons were so well satisfied with the assize system developed by Henry II that they devoted two chapters to strengthening and regulating the procedure. Chapter XVIII stated that the three petty assizes—novel disseisin, mort d'ancestor, and darrein presentment—should be held in the county where the disputed land lay and that these assizes should be heard before itinerant justices who, with four knights of the county, should hold them four times a year. The effect was to speed up litigation and make it more accessible by removing the need of taking assizes before one of the other royal courts. A companion chapter, Chapter XIX, provided that there should be a sufficient number of suitors or recognitors at the county court so that if all the assizes scheduled could not be heard in one day, they could be heard on subsequent days. Moreover, if there were enough suitors only a certain number of them would have to attend court each day.

Chapter XXIV ruled that no sheriff, coroner, or other local officer was eligible to hold the royal pleas. It would seem, therefore, that only the royal justices could hold such pleas and that the barons condemned local administration of justice in favor of justices delegated by the court. It was another blow at the sheriff, whose long record of ruthless administration had earned him the reputation of a local tyrant. Chapters XXXIV and XXXVI dealt with royal writs. The former stated that the writ *praecipe* should not be issued to anyone if the feudal lord in whose court a dispute over right to land ordinarily would be heard should lose this jurisdiction to the royal courts. Some historians have agreed that this was a reactionary provision intended to abolish the writ in proprietary causes and thereby to undo some of the progressive Angevin legal innovation. But apparently the barons did not want to destroy the writ *praecipe;* they only wanted to guarantee that they would not lose their feudal justice by virtue of some technical complaint made in cases which they had the feudal right and competence to hear. The latter chapter ordered that in the future the writ *de odio et atia* should be issued without cost and should never be denied. The provision indicates that this writ, intended to protect from battle men unjustly appealed, had become extremely popular with the baronage.

Judgment, one of the prime objectives of the barons, was the subject of the next group of chapters. Chapter XXXIX, the most famous chapter of Magna Carta, stated that "no freeman shall be captured or imprisoned or disseised or outlawed or exiled or in any way destroyed, nor will we go against him or send against him, except by the lawful judgment of his peers or by the law of the land." This chapter has been commonly interpreted as guaranteeing trial by jury to all Englishmen, as prohibiting arbitrary imprisonment, and as granting to all men equal justice under the law, that is, due process of law. In reality, the chapter meant that legal judgment must precede execution, that John must not proceed arbitrarily against men but must bring actions against them in the royal court in accordance with existing legal procedure. As for trial by peers, the barons were primarily thinking in terms of trial by their baronial peers, but quite likely the clause also meant that all freemen should be tried by their social equals. The expression "law of the land" seems to mean royal, feudal, and local custom; no matter how and where judgments were made they must be made according to accepted law and precede punitive measures. Thus interpreted, Chapter XXXIX benefited only the freemen, meaning principally the feudal aristocracy. By asserting that legal judgment rather than brute force and royal whim should settle causes, the chapter had in it the germ of "due process of law." It did not, however, guarantee trial by jury for criminal justice because such trial did not begin until after trial by ordeal had been abolished by the Fourth Lateran Council in 1215. The criminal petty jury arose during Henry III's reign but it went through many changes before it became anything like our modern petty jury. Not until Edward III's reign was it completely separated from the grand jury so that it achieved real impartiality. As McKechnie has written, it is "an unpardonable anachronism" to introduce trial by jury into Magna Carta. Chapter XL, a corollary to its famous predecessor, added the praiseworthy guarantee that John would not sell, deny, or defer right or justice to anyone. Along with these two chapters may be read Chapters LII and LV, which enforced upon John the return of all lands, castles, franchises, and rights seized by him without legal judgment, as well as the remission of all fines and amercements imposed unjustly and against the law of the land. Any difficulty that arose over restoration and remission was to be settled by a judgment of the twenty-five barons organized to enforce the terms of Magna Carta upon John.

Chapters LVI and LVII redressed the wrongs of Welshmen unjustly dispossessed by Henry II, Richard, and John. Chapter LIX promised that the outstanding differences with the Scottish king would be settled in the same manner as were disputes with John's barons. Chapters XXXVIII and LIV concerned appeals. No royal officer could accuse a man without the use of credible witnesses. This ruled out arbitrary accusation and meant that a man could not be compelled to defend a civil action brought unsupported by witnesses nor could he be forced to undergo the ordeal without indictment. In the same vein Chapter LIV ordered that no one could be arrested or imprisoned upon the appeal of a woman except for the death of her husband. Severe and arbitrary amercements of John had been a bitter grievance, and they were redressed by Chapters XX and XXI, which stipulated that amercements for barons and other freemen were to be proportionate to the gravity of the offense and were to be assessed by a jury of neighbors. No man—feudal aristocrat, burgess, or villein—was to be so heavily amerced as to deprive him of his livelihood. The inclusion of the villein in this clause has often been interpreted as baronial solicitude for the villein. But this is a too liberal and humanitarian view; villeins were included because they were items of baronial property and amercing them too severely would lessen the wealth of the barons.

The last group of chapters concentrated upon reform of administrative abuses. Chapter XXV forbade any increase in the customary farms of the counties. Chapters XXIII, XXVIII, XXX, and XXXI dealt with limitations of royal work and purveyance. Henceforth no man or community could be forced to make bridges (to facilitate royal hunting) unless they had done so by custom. All royal officers were forbidden to take grain or chattels, horses, carts, or wood for repair of royal castles without payment or without the free consent of the men affected. Chapter XL enjoined that only men who knew and would obey the laws of England should be appointed officers; this obviously was directed against John's use of alien favorites. In fact, certain hated foreign favorites from Poitou and Touraine were designated by name in Chapter L and ordered removed from office. Chapter LI ordered that when peace had been restored John should remove from the kingdom all alien knights and mercenaries. Chapters XLIV, XLVII, and XLVIII were an attempt to force John to disafforest lands afforested in his reign, to reform evil forest customs and administration, and to cut down on the oppressive forest justice that had been extended to include land and men not within a royal forest area. A disgusting feature of John's government, as we have seen, was to demand special oaths of fealty and hostages to insure loyalty from his barons; he had applied a practice used in time of war to normal periods of peace and had shown his utter distrust for the feudal bond of homage. Chapter XLIX stopped this practice; it forced John to restore all hostages and charters demanded from men as sureties for their peace and faithful service. Chapter LVIII, drafted with the same intent, provided that John should immediately surrender the son of Prince Llewelyn of Wales, other Welsh hostages, and charters of fealty which had been demanded as security for peace.

Such were the first fifty-eight chapters of Magna Carta with their reforms, prohibitions, injunctions, and promises. The last four chapters concentrated on putting Magna Carta into effect. Chapter LX obliged John to concede to the vassals of the barons all the benefits guaranteed to them. Unfortunately, many commentators have given this chapter too democratic an interpretation. Some have concluded that it applied to all freemen; others, that it affected all the people. This is an exaggerated conception. Obviously the barons intended the provision to extend only to the subvassals of John or to the lesser feudal aristocracy. There is, moreover, no need to praise the barons for a beneficent interest in their vassals; the extension of Magna Carta's concessions to them was a politic course because it helped to secure badly needed allies in the struggle against John. Chapters LXII and LXIII forced John to remit all ill will and hatred that had arisen between him and the barons; he was, in effect, bound by oath to grant amnesty to all his opponents. It was then recorded that all the provisions were sworn to by John and the barons, and that in the presence of witnesses John put his seal to the charter. Chapter LXI contained the key provisions for enforcing Magna Carta; it was the security clause which provided that the barons should choose among themselves twenty-five barons to represent them and to enforce the concessions. Four of these barons were to report all infringements of John to the committee of twenty-five, which should do all in its power to correct the transgressions peaceably. If John gave no satisfaction within forty days, the twenty-five, together with all the other barons, were entitled to take up arms and force John to honor his obligations. This was in accordance with traditional feudal custom.

4. THE VALUE OF MAGNA CARTA

Before attempting to evaluate the significance of Magna Carta for English constitutional history we must be certain of its meaning in 1215 and we must be aware of its defects. Magna Carta was fundamentally a feudal document intended to benefit the most powerful element in English society—the barons and their vassals. Although other freemen—ordinary freeholders and burgesses—necessarily benefited from numerous clauses, chiefly those dealing with judicial, administrative, and economic matters, it is unrealistic to hold that they did so because of conscious baronial solicitude. Freemen were included simply because they had access to the royal courts and were touched directly by royal administration. Still, their inclusion did not mean that the masses of Englishmen profited from Magna Carta; the masses were villeins totally untouched by the events of 1215. Magna Carta was not a national document; it was a feudal document aimed at the restoration of government according to established feudal usages. By no means was it a liberal, democratic expression of the rights of the common man. Magna Carta did not, it must be emphasized, create parliament; it only regularized the summoning of a great council. It did not establish the principle that there could be no taxation without consent and representation; it merely stated that the baronial great council must give its consent to extraordinary feudal aids and scutages. It did not guarantee trial by jury, nor did it embrace such other more modern legal principles as *habeas corpus*, equality before the law, or due process of law as it now functions. To be sure, these and other cherished judicial rights developed in the Middle Ages, but during the three centuries after Magna Carta.

Although there was provision to make John govern in accordance with the laws and customs enunciated by Magna Carta, there was no adequate enforcement. Magna Carta did not initiate effective limited monarchy. The expedient of the twenty-five barons and ultimate resort to arms was clumsy and but legalized the right to rebel. This method did not prevent the king from misgovernment; it merely punished him for it. The sixty-first chapter devised no constitutional machinery for controlling the king. The barons also failed to delineate the powers and functions of a great council when summoned. Its role, except in taxation, was left too vague. We may well conclude, therefore, that the liberal-romantic-democratic interpretation of the seventeenth, eighteenth, and nineteenth centuries is far from accurate and contains many grievous errors.

We have noted the reaction against the old liberal views which came with the turn of the twentieth century. The school of historians identified with the "new view" of Magna Carta harshly attacked the motives and actions of the barons and pictured them as self-seeking, incompetent, narrow, feudal reactionaries who wanted to live in the past, preferably in the good old days of Henry I. Their goal was to destroy the advances made by efficient Angevin government. There is much truth in this critical view. Many of the barons were incapable, hotheaded, and devoid of any political program; they merely wanted revenge against John and, as subsequent events proved, meant to destroy him. The more enlightened, such as Stephen Langton and William Marshal, seldom thought in other than feudal terms, and consequently the ultimate product was a feudal document which restated and confirmed much of the past. But why criticize men of 1215 for not thinking in terms of the eighteenth-century enlightenment or nineteenth-century liberalism? The climate of opinion was feudal; within that framework they thought and acted.

What is evident from an analysis of the chapters is that the barons had a high regard for much of the Angevin judicial and administrative system; they kept it and strengthened it. Moreover, close scrutiny of Magna Carta reveals that despite their shortcomings the barons produced and forced upon John a useful group of concessions. In general the provisions were moderate and reasonable, phrased simply and clearly. One is impressed by the extreme practicality of the barons for the reform at hand. Here were presented real remedies for wrongs rather than theoretical arguments. Though a merit of the charter was the preciseness with which it defined the rights of John, thus eradicating uncertainty on many points of contention, some chapters were phrased broadly enough so that others besides the feudal aristocracy could benefit. That the barons were successful in compelling a king to grant them a written charter of rights proved valuable in subsequent efforts to limit royal power. John's capitulation proved that kings could be brought to terms. Although there is evidence that contemporaries looked with great favor upon particular redresses secured by various clauses, the importance of Magna Carta was due chiefly to its enunciation of the fundamental principle that there was a body of law above the king; in the words of Pollock and Maitland it said "that the king is, and shall be below the law." Here was spelled out the belief that the king was not absolute but was under the law of the land.

The manner in which Magna Carta was obtained set a precedent. Previously barons had opposed the king individually or in small groups, with the result that they were seldom successful. With Magna Carta a large segment of the baronage united for the first time in a common concern and won a victory. This was only the beginning of such national groupings to oppose the crown. Although, for the present, only the baronage showed through group interest and affiliation a collective consciousness, eventually the knights and burgesses followed suit and established the House of Commons as the chief limitation upon royal power. In devising the council of twenty-five, Magna Carta initiated baronial endeavor to win a constant share in the government. Though this struggle continued to the end of the Middle Ages, it was not the source of limited monarchy; that came rather with parliamentary control over the king.

From what we know about Magna Carta as of 1215, it is obvious that historically the twentieth-century interpretation is more accurate than that of the seventeenth, eighteenth, and nineteenth centuries. But the dramatic circumstances under which Magna Carta was won contributed to the subsequent belief that it was the palladium of English liberties. Such a view is of course based upon sentiment and imagination, and yet it is this view or myth that has made Magna Carta revered as the fountain of liberty in the Anglo-American world and has made it the battle cry of those who in later generations fought for liberty, democracy, and constitutional government. The misinterpretation and eulogizing of Magna Carta in the seventeenth, eighteenth, and nineteenth centuries has had a tremendous influence on constitutional and legal progress in both England and America. Believing firmly in the fictions woven into the "Myth of Magna Carta," politicians, statesmen, liberal agitators, lawyers, and judges have used them constantly in their struggle for democratic government, civil liberties, and legal procedure. Through the inaccurate interpretations, inadvertent or intentional, of Coke and the common law lawyers and parliamentarians in their struggle against the Stuarts, of Blackstone and the American Revolutionary Fathers of the eighteenth century, and of the nineteenth-century historians and jurisprudents, Magna Carta has been transformed into a document of liberty and, as such, has contributed far more to the cause of constitutionalism than it would have if left untouched. Two charters thus emerge for those who have studied Magna Carta—the real charter and the fictitious charter. Both have served their purpose.

BIBLIOGRAPHY

Some of the finest evaluations of the Angevin kings are in William Stubbs, *Historical Introductions to the Rolls Series* (London, 1902). We finally have a much needed modern study of Henry II in W. L. Warren, *Henry II* (London, 1973). There are also two recent books on Richard I: John Gillingham, *The Life and Times of Richard I* (London, 1973) and James Brundage, *Richard Lion Heart* (New York, 1974). Sidney Painter's *The Reign of King John* (Baltimore, 1949) is a fine study of John and of the baronial families. Cf. W. L. Warren, *King John* (London, 1961).

For the autocratic policies of the Angevins and their relation to Magna Carta see J. E. A. Jolliffe, *Angevin Kingship,* 2d ed. (London, 1963), Richardson and Sayles, *The Governance of Mediaeval England* (Edinburgh, 1963), and Margaret Howell, *Regalian Rights in Medieval England* (London, 1962). For the Angevin justiciarship see F. J. West, *The Justiciarship in England, 1066–1232* (Cambridge, 1966), C. R. Cheney, *Hubert Walter* (London, 1967), C. R. Young, *Hubert Walter, Lord of Canterbury and Lord of England* (Durham, N.C., 1968), and G. V. Scammell, *Hugh de Puiset, Bishop of Durham* (Cambridge, 1956). An excellent biography of William Marshal, companion and adviser of three Angevins, is Sidney Painter, *William Marshal* (Baltimore, 1933). A good picture of administration in Normandy is given by F. M. Powicke, *The Loss of Normandy* (Manchester, 1913) and by John Le Patourel, "The Plantagenet Dominions," *History,* I (1965), 289–308. Besides the studies on financial administration cited previously see S. K. Mitchell, *Studies in Taxation under John and Henry III* (New Haven, 1914).

Concerning the development of the common law is the excellent edition and translation of G. D. G. Hall, *The Treatise on the Laws and Customs of the Realm of England Commonly Called Glanvill* (Edinburgh, 1965). For the relation between feudal justice and the possessory assizes see the revisionary but difficult book by S. F. C. Milsom, *The Legal Framework of English Feudalism* (Cambridge, 1976). D. W. Sutherland traces the development of the most important possessory assize in *The Assize of Novel Disseisin* (Oxford, 1973). For the courts see R. V. Turner, *The King and His Courts, the Role of John and Henry III in the Administration of Justice, 1199–1240* (Ithaca, N.Y., 1968). The writing on law is discussed by T. F. T. Plucknett, *Early English Legal Literature* (Cambridge, 1958). See also J. P. Dawson, *A History of Lay Judges* (Cambridge, Mass., 1960) and R. B. Pugh, *Itinerant Justices in English History* (Exeter, 1967).

The relations of church and state under the Angevins are analyzed by F. W. Maitland in *Roman Canon Law in the Church of England* (London, 1898)and by C. R. Cheney, *From Becket to Langton. English Church Government, 1170–1216* (Manchester, 1956). The best study of Becket is David Knowles, *Archbishop Thomas Becket: A Character Study* (London, 1949) and the more recent *Thomas Becket* (London, 1970). Other good studies pertinent to the conflict of Henry II and Becket are Beryl Smalley, *The Becket Conflict and the Schools: A Study of Intellectuals in Politics* (Oxford, 1973), Avrom Saltman,

Theobald, Archbishop of Canterbury (London, 1956), and J. W. Alexander, "The Becket Controversy in Recent Historiography," *Journal of British Studies*, IX (1970), 1–26. For a picture of Gilbert Foliot, that important bishop and bitter opponent of Becket, see Adrian Morey and C. N. L. Brooke, *Gilbert Foliot and His Letters* (Cambridge, 1965) and *The Letters and Charters of Gilbert Foliot* (Cambridge, 1967). For the role of Innocent III in the investiture struggle with John see C. R. Cheney, *Pope Innocent III and England* (Stuttgart, 1976).

Of the two excellent studies of Magna Carta that by W. S. McKechnie, *Magna Carta*, 2d ed. (Glasgow, 1914) examines Magna Carta from a legal point of view while that of J. C. Holt, *Magna Carta* (Cambridge, 1965) looks at the document from a historical point of view. Other good but shorter works are: H. M. Cam, *Magna Carta, Event or Document* (London, 1965), S. E. Thorne et al., *The Great Charter: Four Essays on Magna Carta and the History of Our Liberty* (New York, 1965), *Magna Carta*, A. E. Dick Howard, ed. (Charlottesville, Va., 1964), H. E. Malden, *Magna Carta Commemoration Essays* (London, 1917), and V. H. Galbraith, "Runnymede Revisited," *Proceedings of the American Philosophical Society*, CX (1966), 307–317. For Stephen Langton's part in Magna Carta see F. M. Powicke, *Stephen Langton* (Oxford, 1928). B. C. Keeney furnishes the background for understanding the legal clauses of Magna Carta in *Judgment by Peers* (Cambridge, Mass., 1949). For the role of the barons see J. C. Holt, *The Northerners: A Study in the Reign of King John* (Oxford, 1961). The reissues of Magna Carta and its subsequent influence have interested Faith Thompson, *The First Century of Magna Carta: Why it Persisted as a Document* (Minneapolis, 1925) and *Magna Carta: Its Role in the Making of the English Constitution, 1300–1629* (Minneapolis, 1948). Cf. Herbert Butterfield, *Magna Carta in the Historiography of the Sixteenth and Seventeenth Centuries* (Reading, 1969).

Part Four

HENRY III AND EDWARD I

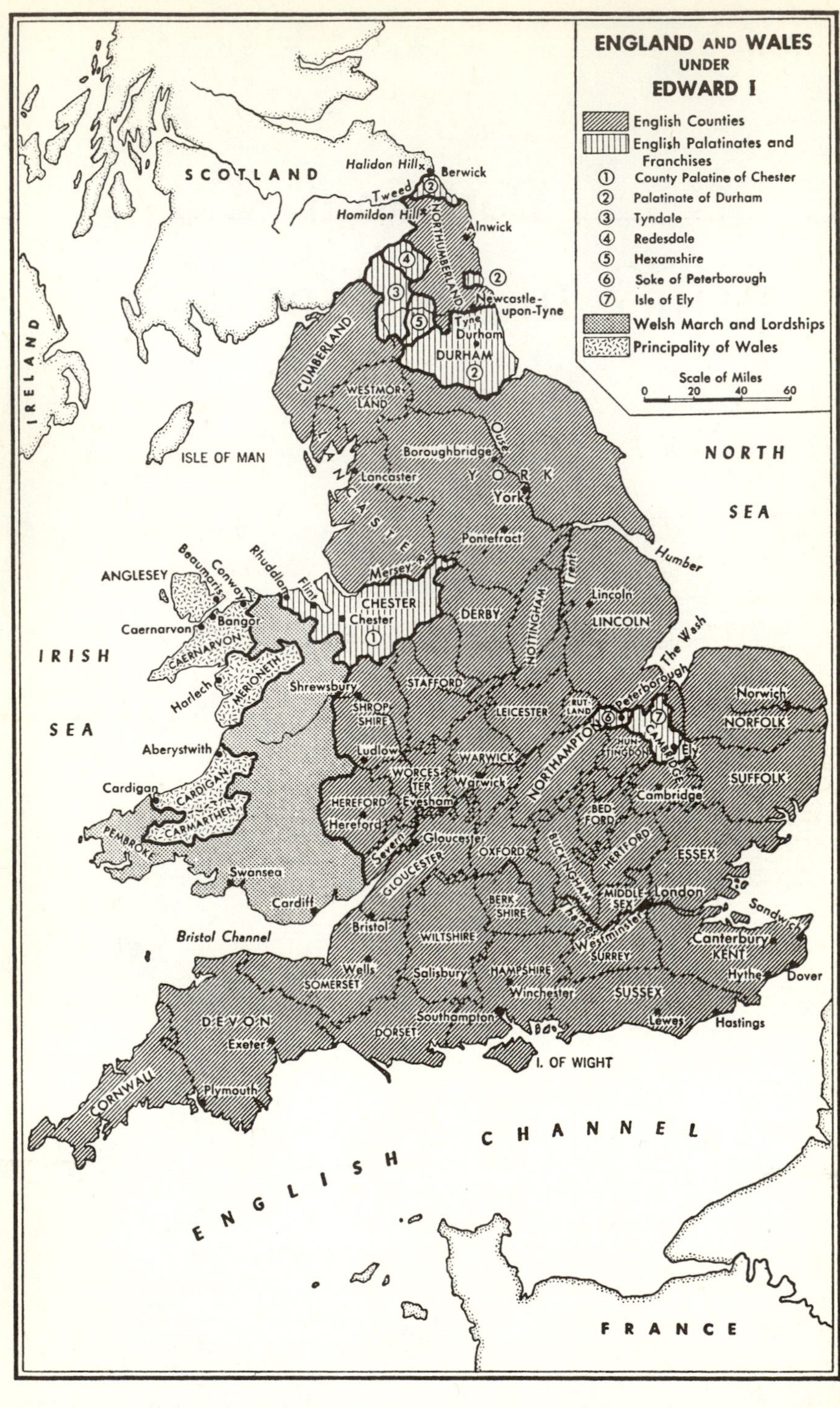
ENGLAND AND WALES UNDER EDWARD I
English Counties
English Palatinates and Franchises
① County Palatine of Chester
② Palatinate of Durham
③ Tyndale
④ Redesdale
⑤ Hexamshire
⑥ Soke of Peterborough
⑦ Isle of Ely
Welsh March and Lordships
Principality of Wales
Scale of Miles
0 20 40 60
SCOTLAND
IRELAND
ISLE OF MAN
NORTH SEA
IRISH SEA
ENGLISH CHANNEL
FRANCE
Halidon Hill
Berwick
Tweed
Homildon Hill
NORTHUMBERLAND
Alnwick
Newcastle-upon-Tyne
Tyne
Durham
DURHAM
CUMBERLAND
WESTMORLAND
Boroughbridge
Ouse
YORK
York
Lancaster
LANCASTER
Pontefract
Humber
ANGLESEY
Beaumaris
Conway
Rhuddlan
Flint
Mersey
CHESTER
Chester
Bangor
Caernarvon
CAERNARVON
DERBY
NOTTINGHAM
Trent
Lincoln
LINCOLN
The Wash
Harlech
MERIONETH
Shrewsbury
STAFFORD
SHROPSHIRE
LEICESTER
RUTLAND
Peterborough
Norwich
NORFOLK
Aberystwith
Ludlow
WARWICK
Warwick
NORTHAMPTON
HUNTINGDON
CAMBRIDGE
Ely
SUFFOLK
Cardigan
CARDIGAN
CARMARTHEN
PEMBROKE
HEREFORD
Hereford
WORCESTER
Evesham
Cambridge
BEDFORD
Severn
Gloucester
GLOUCESTER
OXFORD
BUCKINGHAM
HERTFORD
ESSEX
Swansea
Cardiff
BERKSHIRE
Thames
MIDDLESEX
London
Sandwich
Bristol
Bristol Channel
WILTSHIRE
Westminster
SURREY
Canterbury
KENT
Wells
SOMERSET
Salisbury
HAMPSHIRE
Winchester
SUSSEX
Hythe
Dover
DEVON
Exeter
Southampton
DORSET
Lewes
Hastings
I. OF WIGHT
CORNWALL
Plymouth

XXIII

The Thirteenth-Century Sources

DESPITE the long weak-willed rule of Henry III the thirteenth century saw no slack in zeal of the royal government to maintain orderly record of its transactions. It is no exaggeration to say that the reign of Edward I marks the golden age of English medieval records. Long experience plus the increasing scope and complexity of government largely explain the richness of thirteenth-century documentation. There was, however, another influence; Henry III and Edward I strove to personalize their government by means of loyal household officials. These professional civil servants—be they the infamous Poitevins and Savoyards or native English—constantly improved Angevin recordkeeping and experimented with new records in an effort to put governmental machinery at the royal fingertip. Throughout the thirteenth century the personnel of such household departments as the wardrobe lurk prominently behind the massive documentation that is the delight of the constitutional historian. Only to plug up an occasional chink or to provide color and background must one fall back upon the narrative sources.

I. NONNARRATIVE SOURCES

A. Records of the Chancery

For clarification and convenience thirteenth-century royal records are usually classified under departmental rubrics. However useful this device, it is at best arbitrary. For example, numerous records, though issuing from the chancery, came to be statutes and might very well have as their intent the regulation of taxation; such a document defies classification. Also, it reminds us of the lack of division in royal departments and of their interdependence. Treasury and chancery records were constantly overlapping. In this category, for example, were the so-called Scutage Rolls. Issued by the chancery after every military campaign to list all men who owed a money payment in lieu of service, they were transmitted to the custody of the exchequer so that it could collect the scutage. The web of medieval government defied all attempts to introduce strict departmentalization and method in the keeping of records.

Most celebrated but difficult to classify is Magna Carta with its reissues and confirmations. During the course of the thirteenth century the Great Charter assumed the form of a statute; and yet it was originally a charter issued by the chancery. It was reissued in 1216 and 1217 with important changes, and Henry III, upon attaining his majority in 1225, again reissued it with minor changes. It was the charter of 1225 that became the Magna Carta of subsequent ages. This in turn was confirmed upon certain occasions by Henry III and Edward I. Along with the reissue of 1217 was published the Charter of the Forest, which customarily was confirmed along with Magna Carta. Like its elder brother, it became statute law and defined the rules applying to land reserved for the royal park and forest.[1] Though dealing primarily with financial matters, the Fine, Memoranda, and Originalia Rolls issued from the chancery; all continued to be primary records in the thirteenth century.

As under the Angevins, the great trinity of chancery records remained the charters and the letters patent and close.[2] All continued to be enrolled. The letters patent and close became so copious that separate enrollments were made of various categories pertaining to certain business or areas of the kingdom. Early in the reign of Henry III the writs of *liberate* ceased to be enrolled on the Close Rolls and received their own enrollment. They give an excellent account of financial administration, particularly on the role of the wardrobe. Other documents likewise became separately enrolled. Letters patent and close dealing with Gascony, Germany, Scotland, Wales, and the papacy were enrolled as the Gascon, German, Scottish, Welsh, and Roman Rolls. Important treaties and negotiations formed the Treaty Rolls. Finally, there were the royal letters and minor miscellaneous documents which emanated from the chancery. These documents throw light on the great thirteenth-century constitutional issues between king and baronage but are more important for the story they tell of royal administration and foreign relations.

B. Financial Records

Throughout the thirteenth century the Pipe Rolls remain the principal guide to finance but increasingly other records supplement them. Under Henry II, as we have noted, the Receipt Rolls began to record revenue coming to the king from sources other than the farm of a county. These rolls increase in bulk and are joined by the Issue Rolls, which noted all payments and obligations of the exchequer. Writs warranting issues from the exchequer were being carefully preserved in files at the time of Henry II. They soon came to be enrolled and are extant almost *in toto* beginning with the fourth regnal year of Henry III. They provide a fine account of the financial relations of the wardrobe and chamber with the exchequer. In the opinion of some scholars the Issue Rolls supplant the Pipe Rolls as the chief record for central finance. These three principal records furnish our main account of

[1] SM, no. 45.
[2] SM, no. 46.

the exchequer. For particular aspects of finance, however, we can rely on various other records. In the thirteenth century officers other than the sheriffs, such as keepers of the royal domain, escheators, clerks, and commissioners, came to keep account of their receipts and expenses. Their records are useful for royal administration on the local level.

Under John we witnessed the origin of the Mise and Prest Rolls. These household accounts remained skimpy and sporadic until 1224. For that year and the three following there is a Wardrobe Account that has consolidated the information formerly preserved by the Mise and Prest Rolls. Thereafter there is, almost without exception, a Wardrobe Account extant for each year. As the wardrobe became one of the great financial departments the accounts grow in bulk and richness of detail. In this connection it should be understood that in the thirteenth century the wardrobe became a subsidiary treasury which received money directly from royal debtors as well as periodic lump sum payments from the exchequer. Because all the money was ultimately the exchequer's it was necessary for the wardrobe to render yearly a comprehensive statement of its finances to the exchequer. These statements were the Wardrobe Accounts tendered by the keeper and controller of the wardrobe. They were composed from subsidiary daily records upon which were jotted down the expenses of the household and its officers, and advance payments made by the exchequer to the wardrobe. Originally in the form of rolls, from 1289 onwards they were compiled in book form bound substantially in rough leather covers. Neatly arranged and provided with references, they were beautifully and carefully written by the wardrobe clerks. They testify to the administrative power of the household and clearly indicate why the barons fought the royal policy of supervising their realm through the household personnel.

It is impossible to summarize the many wardrobe documents but two merit description—the bills of the wardrobe and the wardrobe debentures. The bill was a small strip of parchment authenticated by the personal seal of the keeper of the wardrobe and it warranted payment by the wardrobe. The wardrobe debenture was a special type of wardrobe bill; it recorded a wardrobe debt, such as military wages. It was called a debenture because it always began with the Latin phrase *debetur in garderoba regis*, which recognized an obligation of the wardrobe. The recipient generally presented the debenture to the exchequer, which paid the debt. Both these records became prominent only with Edward I.

We should note, finally, the records of taxation. The receipts from the lay subsidies granted to Henry III were not entered on the Pipe Rolls but were kept on separate records by special tax commissioners. It is impossible here to describe in detail the method of assessment and collection but the three principal categories of records can be noted. First there were the rolls that contained the local assessment of the subsidy or tax. Secondly, a county roll summarized for the exchequer these local assessments. And lastly, there were the accounts of the chief tax collectors which comprised the final audit and account.

C. Legal Records

The principal Angevin legal records continued on in the thirteenth century. The most marked change in the Plea Rolls—those of the court of the exchequer, *curia regis, coram rege, de banco,* and assizes of justices in eyre—is their increasing bulk.[3] Along with the Plea Rolls should be lumped the original writs which, as we have seen, enabled those who so desired to bring their case into a royal court. Under Henry III and Edward I dozens of new writs were fabricated as the royal courts increased their jurisdiction and popularity and invited growing numbers of men to seek their justice. A register of original writs compiled towards the end of Henry III's life records the wholesale growth of these judicial writs. The prominence of the coroner as a local police officer is evidenced by the steady stream of Coroners' Rolls that begins under Henry III. All these records, which comprise the core of our legal evidence, are supplemented by numerous miscellaneous documents. The Patent and Close Rolls, for example, contain royal commissions ordered to hear special cases, including sometimes those of novel disseisin.

Probably the single most useful record produced since *Domesday Book* was compiled by a special royal commission. In 1274–1275 Edward I ordered an inquest held by commissioners in every hundred of England to determine the royal rights of jurisdiction. The commissioners put their questions to juries empaneled from the hundred and copied the answers down on rolls. These bundles of rolls were then reassembled and consolidated in a master record known as the Hundred Rolls. From this compilation comes our clearest description not only of the local rights of royal and private justice but of local administration and society in the thirteenth century. All sorts of commissions were authorized to obtain information for the royal government but we shall here mention only one other record so produced—the inquisition *post mortem* which dates back to Henry II and continues on to the reign of Charles II. This record came from the inquests held on the death of any tenant of the king. In the counties where the tenant held land, officers called escheators were ordered to summon a jury to inquire under oath what lands the tenant held, by what rents or services they were held, and the name and age of the next heir, in order that the king would know what rights of escheat, wardship, and perquisites were due him. These inquisitions generally spared the heirs and widows of the deceased litigation to obtain their lands and rights. In addition to being accepted as evidence in court, the inquisitions provide a most detailed description of the possessions of royal tenants-in-chief.

Without doubt the most novel type of legal record developing in the thirteenth century was the Year Book. However and by whom composed, the

[3] SM, no. 54.

Year Book appeared first during the reign of Edward I as an unofficial compilation of reports of the principal and most interesting cases pleaded in the various courts at Westminster. Perhaps interested spectators from the legal profession jotted down these law reports for future reference and study and eventually they were compiled annually in books which served as a basic part of the legal literature studied by members of the legal profession and those aspiring to it. Or perhaps the Year Books were officially compiled later in the Middle Ages. The important thing to note is that they were reports of cases and helped the lawyer to learn the various legal principles that applied in the royal courts. The Year Books appear some time in the 1280's and continue almost yearly to the end of the Middle Ages. Not only did the cases reported in the Year Books form a sort of vast legal handbook, but they also came to be cited as precedents by judge and lawyer.

During the thirteenth century Magna Carta became accepted as enacted law. This first statute was soon joined by others. The first set of laws to bear the title of statute were the Provisions of Merton issued by the king along with his great council in 1236. These were joined by two others during Henry III's reign. With the great spurt of legislation under Edward I a whole series of statutes were enacted. Such law was regarded as permanent and as having been promulgated by king with the counsel or consent of his great council and intimate councillors. Of a less permanent and solemn nature were the ordinances issued by king and small council.[4] Ordinances, issued generally without the advice of the great council, are difficult to distinguish from statutes. Any clear-cut distinction in the thirteenth century is impossible; the difference is too minute and what might originally have been enacted as an ordinance often became a statute. Not until the fourteenth century can we begin to separate with surety an ordinance from a statute.

Though we have been solely occupied with the records of the royal courts we should not forget the sources which have come down from the local county, feudal, and manorial courts.[5] These court records fill in details on local nonroyal custom. Also of value are the deeds preserved by the religious houses, manors, and great honors, as well as the records of wills guarded by the church. From these we learn much about the land law in the thirteenth century.

Let us now turn to the considerable body of legal literature produced by the ambitious members of a dynamic young law profession that was just beginning to take form. The time had come when lawyer and judge were learned and sophisticated enough to see the need for going beyond the mere study of cases, precedents, and statutes and for producing a literature that would give a rational description and interpretation of English law. It is this period that Maitland has so aptly labeled "the age of Bracton." The renowned English medieval judge, whose work has been called the "crown and flower

[4] SM, no. 52.
[5] SM, no. 52.

of English medieval jurisprudence," Henry de Bracton was typical of most medieval justices. He began his career as a clerk to a justice and then in 1245 jumped to justice in eyre; until his death in 1268 he took the county assizes. Between 1248 and 1257 he was a justice of the king's bench and a member of the royal circle that witnessed charters and gave legal counsel. Besides his official position he held a number of church livings. Maitland was certain that Bracton was both the author of the celebrated treatise entitled *Concerning the Laws and Customs of England* (*De Legibus et Consuetudinibus Regni Angliae*) and the compiler of a most useful *Notebook* containing some two thousand cases selected from those in the royal courts to which he added explanatory comments. Recently this conclusion has been questioned. It has been suggested that the treatise was begun as early as the 1220's, was added to and revised, and shortly after 1256 was abridged into the *De Legibus* as we know it. It is also proposed that the prime mover behind the *De Legibus* was the justice William of Raleigh who encouraged his law clerks to compile the *Notebook* for their legal edification and the *De Legibus* for the instruction both of themselves and other members of the legal profession. Best known among these clerks was Bracton. If this argument is valid Bracton could not have been the sole author but only a collaborator because the work was begun too early. Since this argument is debatable, it must still be assumed that Bracton was the author. The question of authorship, however, does not alter the content of this treatise whose theme is the English law digested from litigation in the royal courts. What made this work a milestone in legal literature was more than a knowledge of cases; it was Bracton's command of Roman law and legal literature that gave him an overall concept of a law book and an understanding of the method by which law and its principles should be explained. And yet his familiarity with Roman law did not influence him to attempt the molding of English law after the Roman; it but helped him to produce a rational and well-organized book. Any man who reiterated that the ruler should be under God and law because the law makes the king was certainly no advocate of Roman absolutism. The great merit of Bracton was that he accurately stated the best and approved practice of the royal courts.

Bracton's treatise found quick acceptance and numerous copies were made. It became the foundation and model for the legal literature written during Edward I's reign. It was, as we say, boiled down into handy texts. A chief justice of the king's bench—Gilbert Thornton—made an epitome of it. Two works appeared around 1290 which were little more than paraphrases of Bracton. One was the legal treatise called *Fleta*, authored perhaps by an individual of this name, and the other was the so-called *Britton*. This latter work, written in French possibly by the judge John le Breton, is more sound than *Fleta* and explains the law through the device of having it come from the royal mouth. The last principal treatise, entitled the *Summae* (abstracts), is on legal procedure and was written by the justice Ralph de Hengham.

Along with other short legal tracts it helped the lawyer to master the growing complexities of procedure in the royal courts. The only other legal works worthy of mention are the books of precedents, such as the *Brevia Placitata* and *Casus Placitorum,* drawn up for the use of pleaders in the king's courts, and guides to precedents and procedure in manorial courts, such as the tract *La court de baron* drawn up about 1268.

D. The Records of Parliament

Though it may be somewhat arbitrary to take and set apart as parliamentary documents a category of records produced by the chancery, such action may be justified by the fact that they dealt exclusively with parliamentary business and became divorced from the chancery as the parliament developed into a powerful and recognized institution during the fourteenth century. The cardinal records are the *Rotuli Parliamentorum* (Parliament Rolls), which consist of petitions to the king, the council, parliament, the chancellor, and other officers of the state. The rolls also contained answers and decisions given to the petitions as well as all the transactions occurring during a parliamentary session. The earliest parliament roll is of the year 1283; thereafter as parliaments were summoned more frequently rolls appear with regularity. Composed originally in Latin, they came to be written in French during the fourteenth century. For the next two centuries the Parliament Rolls are the key records because they record the history of the greatest institution developed by medieval England.[6] Of lesser status are the parliamentary writs of summons. Each time a parliament was summoned the king instructed the chancery to issue writs requesting the attendance of the great lords. These writs were drawn up individually in the form of letters close. The lesser nobility were summoned by a general writ in the form of letters patent. The sheriffs received letters patent directing them to send to parliament two knights from each county and two burgesses from each borough. These records help to indicate the purpose and frequency of thirteenth-century parliaments and to describe their composition.[7]

2. NARRATIVE SOURCES

The biographies, letters, and sermons of the thirteenth century can be rapidly summarized. None have much relevance for constitutional development except the correspondence and sermons of that great bishop of Lincoln, Robert Grosseteste (1235–1253). A strong defender of ecclesiastical rights and immunities, Grosseteste expressed himself adamantly on the relations of church and state, especially on clerical taxation and the jurisdiction of spiritual courts. In his sermons he attacked the holding of secular office by ecclesiastics and advanced the view that the church was the true media-

[6] SM, no. 51D.
[7] SM, no. 49.

tor between God and king. Like many of his educated spiritual brethren who wrote so-called "mirrors of the princes," Grosseteste composed a small tract on kingship in which he set forth the qualities, virtues, and maxims that made for good rulers.

The greatest of the historians and chroniclers of the thirteenth century was Matthew Paris. The others, though useful, bear little comparison. Again, with but a few notable exceptions, these writers came from the monasteries rather than from the secular clerks and royal officials as was the case under the Angevins. A prime exception is the alderman Arnold fitz Thedmar, who wrote *The Chronicles of the Mayors and Sheriffs of London,* a main source for the baronial wars, openly royalist in its sympathies. This chronicle is valuable not only for general history but also for the relations of London and the crown. Among monastic houses producing historical works, the old Benedictine foundations were pre-eminent. The *English Chronicle* of the Cistercian abbot Ralph of Coggeshall stands out but is of value for the thirteenth century only from 1216 to 1223. The chronicle of Roger of Wendover composed at Saint Albans carries history down to 1235. Also produced at the same abbey was the *Chronica* ascribed to William Rishanger. The part from 1259 to 1272 was undoubtedly written during Edward I's life but the remaining part from 1272 to 1306 was done later by a continuator. This work contains much official material relating to Scottish affairs.

Among the historical compositions coming from the Bury Saint Edmunds and Norwich group the best is that of Bartholomew Cotton, who arranged a composite Norwich chronicle extending from 1066 to 1298. For the years 1263–1279 and 1285–1298 this *English History* is an independent and original account based upon numerous official records, a large number of which are reproduced in the text. Walter of Hemingburgh, a canon of Gisburn priory in Yorkshire, composed a usable chronicle; and Nicholas Trevet, a man familiar with Edward I's court, an annalistic work. More interesting for our purposes, however, are the *Annals* of the monastic houses of Dunstable, Osney, Waverley, and Burton. Those of Burton contain an important group of documents presenting the baronial program of reform in the fateful days of 1258; among them is one of the texts of the famous Provisions of Oxford.

XXIV

England Under Henry III and Edward I, 1216–1307

ALTHOUGH the reign of Henry III was the third longest in English history it was one of the sorriest and most barren in the annals of the English people. For the monarchy it was a story of consistent failure in war and politics. It began and ended in disillusionment. This political environment hinged to uncertainty, lack of direction, and civil strife keynotes the reign of this highly moral but weak and useless king. Although out of the fires of the baronial wars was to come a new concept of orderly opposition to the crown, not until the reign of Henry's able son Edward I was England again to travel at the brisk tempo of constitutional advance that characterized her in the Norman-Angevin twelfth century.

I. HENRY III (1216–1272)

While John's death in October 1216 removed the principal obstacle to baronial resistance it did not stop the basic constitutional struggle; in fact it introduced a new crisis. For the first time since the Norman Conquest England was faced with an heir to the crown who was only a boy, a circumstance that involved a minority. To many, this foreboded a continuance of anarchy. Due to fortune, however, the reins of state fell to a capable and respected administrator. In a simple coronation ceremony on 28 October 1216 Henry was made king. The faithful baronial supporters then worked rapidly to form a government that could preserve the nine-year-old's position against the baronial rebels and their French ally Louis. The more moderate barons of the opposition facilitated the task by laying down their arms and uniting with the royalist party to make the old William Marshal, earl of Pembroke, *rector regis et regni*. There could not have been a better choice for a protector. Loyal servant and companion of three preceding kings, William was the most powerful baron of the realm. He was as respected for his integrity and common sense as he was famous for his military prowess. Around him rallied the new government including the old professional administrators like Hubert de Burgh and the rough foreign mercenary captains like Falkes de Bréauté. Sensible in ignoring the fact that Magna Carta had been repudiated by Innocent III and John, William Marshal used it to secure greater support. He, with the papal legate Gualo, reissued it in November after deleting Chapters XII, XIV, and LXI, which were superfluous with a minor under baronial control.

Having bid for and secured popular support for the legitimist cause, William Marshal next tackled his most acute problem—the defeat of the rebel barons and the expulsion of the French. He was fighting now alongside experienced captains against a group whose reason for opposition had been removed, and he made quick work of his task. Systematically, rebel castles were reduced and the enemy harassed in the field. The decisive engagement came in May 1217. Hastening to relieve the siege of Lincoln Castle, the Marshal surprised the rebels and captured three hundred knights, a number representing half of the rebel army. Still Louis continued the fight hoping that his plea for French reinforcements would turn the tide. His hopes were dashed in August when a French fleet crossing the Channel was intercepted by Hubert de Burgh and defeated. Louis was now forced to accept peace, which was concluded by the Treaty of Kingston on 12 September. Receiving full indemnity for his military expenditures, Louis renounced his claim to the throne and left for France. Soon, under the pressure of the new pope Honorius III, the rebel barons recognized Henry. To acknowledge Henry's good faith and intentions the Marshal reissued Magna Carta. The young Henry in the midst of his joy forgot that military victory was responsible for his success and attributed it to papal efforts; unfortunately for the unhappy monarch he never changed this opinion. Instead, he became a malleable tool in the hands of a series of popes who thought only of employing English resources to further papal struggles on the Continent.

The successful regency of William Marshal came to an end in May 1219 as he lay dying. His last act was to provide for a new agency arrangement. To the papal legate Pandulf went the personal protection of the young king. John's old Poitevin friend Peter des Roches, bishop of Winchester, remained the royal tutor; Hubert de Burgh became justiciar. When Pandulf left England two years later Peter and Hubert divided the authority. But Hubert so surpassed Peter in power and support that the justiciar soon had a monopoly over the government and retained it until his fall in 1232. Hubert ruled as the last of the great justiciars and did an able job of restoring royal authority. First he quelled local disorder and made secure the royal castles. Local barons were deprived of custodianship and even the rough and greedy mercenary captains were thrown out of castle and realm. Royal lands and revenues were resumed, and the various departments of state such as the exchequer and law courts were restored to their normal jurisdiction and operation. But, as with most forceful administrators, Hubert's feet of clay were his ruthless and highhanded methods. Also he had quite naturally secured along the way a long list of lands, revenues, offices, and perquisites that amounted to tremendous personal wealth. By these acts he had made baronial enemies who but waited an opportunity to turn the inexperienced Henry against him.

The impractical Henry needed little encouragement. For some time he had itched to wield the royal power and looked upon Hubert as the chief obstacle. As soon as he could, in January 1227, he declared himself of full age before the council and so entered his majority. He could now use the great seal, and he began to issue documents and to take stock of his position. Prodded by Poitevin friends and jealous barons Henry soon found all sorts of faults with his justiciar. First a series of campaigns against the Welsh prince Llewelyn was a dismal failure. Between 1228 and 1231 the Welsh carried all before them and won back marcher land. Peter des Roches, just back from the Continent, was quick to point his finger at the cause of failure—Hubert de Burgh. The real cause of Hubert's fall was the futile Breton campaign of 1230. In 1229 Henry and a large force had been foiled in their departure from Portsmouth and Henry blamed Hubert, whom he accused of obstructing the expedition. In the following year Henry led an army to Brittany, but it accomplished nothing. Lack of supplies, sickness, and incompetent leadership contributed to utter disaster. Henry now meant Hubert to be the scapegoat. In his suspicions that Hubert had halfheartedly supported his military venture Henry was correct, but Hubert's opposition to French wars was a policy justified time and again by subsequent English fiascos. Hubert's fall came in 1232. Distrusted by Henry, hated by Peter des Roches and the Poitevins, and unpopular with the barons and clergy, whom he had frequently treated harshly, he was completely isolated. A riot against unpopular clerics inspired by English exasperation with papal interference sealed Hubert's fate. A loyal son of the church, Henry chose to add this incident to the growing list of offenses of his justiciar. Hubert was deprived of his offices and of some of his lands and was forced by July into melancholy retirement. He died in 1243. Henry was now free to rule as well as to reign. His personal government dates from 1232.

At this point it will be useful to characterize Henry and to describe the dominant influences that swayed his rule. The son of a fitful man and a passionate mother, Henry had not the benefit of a well-ordered youth or of long association with his parents. His tutors, chief of whom was Peter des Roches, gave him a fair education and a real appreciation for French culture, but they were ambitious and unscrupulous adventurers who exerted no good influence over the young boy. Protected by the church, Henry could never convince himself that he had properly repaid his debt. He was a devout and sincere believer who was unfortunately too liberal with English money for papal projects. Of a much higher moral character than any of his predecessors, Henry nevertheless lacked the medieval requisites of a successful leader. He was no judge of character or efficiency and could always be depended upon to make unpopular appointments. Repeatedly his military campaigns were debacles. He could not command the confidence of his subjects. Easily influenced, he was guilty of favoritism to undeserving men. Autocratic in the Angevin tradition, he lacked the drive and common sense to translate his willful tendencies into effective action. He lacked also the intelligence and capacity of John. Had Henry been but wise enough to continue to surround himself with men of the caliber of William Marshal and Langton, he would have had the leisure to satisfy the cultural tastes which were his one achievement and interest. He was a far cry from his great contemporary Saint Louis of France. It would have been better to remember him as the patron of culture and the builder of churches than as a dismal political failure for fifty-seven years.

Three circumstances help to explain the violence of Henry's reign: the abuses of his foreign favorites and relatives, his subservience to the papacy, and his political and military failures abroad. From his father Henry inherited foreign servants and mercenaries who suffered temporary eclipse until 1232 but returned thereafter in full force. In 1232 Peter des Roches and his nephew Peter de Rivaux assumed prominent positions at court; they were soon followed by other Poitevins. Henry's mother Isabelle of Angoulême burdened him with a pack of parasitical half brothers from Poitou. Shortly after John had died Isabelle had returned to her first lover, Hugh the Brown of Lusignan, count of La Marche. By him she had four sons, who came to England and received every conceivable favor from lands and offices to ecclesiastical preferment. In 1236 Henry married Eleanor of Provence, the sister-in-law of Saint Louis. With her came a train of Provençals and Savoyards who swelled the host of parasites. Henry's Savoyard uncles, though possessed of ability, used it mostly for their own interests; they lacked proper appreciation of English law and institutions. These were the men who dominated household and court and soon became the focal point of bitter baronial attack. To Englishmen these foreigners epitomized the troubles of the realm.

Equally detested were the legates and nuncios that had swarmed over England since John's capitulation to the papacy. During Henry's minority these men helped to govern England and so established themselves that it was simple to exploit the English for their own and the papal interest. When the popes became embroiled in their bitter struggle against the Hohenstaufen they and their servants regarded England as a financial reservoir. The popes by-passed the English clergy and provided for vacant benefices themselves, usually appointing Italians many of whom never saw the white cliffs of Dover. Poorly paid underlings did the work. Needing larger sums of money the papacy stepped up its demands for contributions and taxes. Henry continually pressurized the clergy to contribute gifts to his holy father the pope and he fully cooperated in the collection of the hated papal subsidies, which went mainly for war and diplomacy. By 1244 the English church and the English people had had enough of papal encroachment on their traditional rights and from then on violently opposed all foreign interference.

On top of these troubles came the military disasters of Henry. Never was he able to demand the recognition of English lordship from the Scottish kings that had been won by his grandfather Henry II. The desultory Welsh campaigns were always inconclusive until Edward assumed actual direction of the government after 1265. But these failures paled before the continental ones. Here Henry showed utter incompetence and lack of leadership. First he allowed himself to be persuaded by the Poitevins to attempt the reconquest of his father's lost French lands and next he was deluded by the papacy into committing English dynastic prestige and money to the papal struggle against the Hohenstaufen in Sicily and Italy.

After John's defeat in Poitou and at Bouvines there was a period of uneasy truce. Henry, when he attained majority, intended to break it and to restore the Angevin prestige. There was, too, the strong possibility that English inactivity would invite French intervention in the duchy of Aquitaine, a situation that appeared imminent after the French expeditions against the Albigensian heretics of Toulouse had resulted in bringing that land under royal rule and putting the French next to English Aquitaine. In any event, as subsequent history was to show, there could be no real peace between France and England until every inch of French soil was controlled by France. Henry felt bound to oppose further French infiltration. The aim of his first expedition of 1230–1231 was the conquest of Poitou. Cooperating with the duke of Brittany, Henry landed on the Breton coast. After a fruitless march through Poitou he returned to Brittany, became ill, and then went home. The so-called Breton war dissolved in a truce of 1234 leaving Henry the poorer in reputation and money. His next serious attempt against Poitou was undertaken in 1242 when he struck from Gascony only to suffer a stunning defeat at Taillebourg. His prestige sank even lower. He abandoned Poitou and contented himself with holding the fiery nobles of Gascony and Aquitaine under his rule, a position he could maintain only because of the peaceable and moral character of Saint Louis, who scrupulously recognized the English legal and feudal right to southwestern France. Such a *modus vivendi* could not be other than precarious. Theoretically Henry still held all the old titles of his father and made claims to the old Angevin Empire while discontented nobles of the southwest schemed for French rule. Finally the two kings conferred at length and concluded the Treaty of Paris in 1258. Henry renounced all claim to the lands lost in France and did homage and fealty for Gascony and Aquitaine, which Louis promised to leave alone.

Meanwhile Henry was being drawn into papal schemes. After the death of the brilliant Hohenstaufen Frederick II in 1250 the papacy swore to rid itself forever of German power in Sicily and southern Italy. It cast about for possible candidates for the throne of Sicily and campaigned for funds to raise an army to fight various Hohenstaufen claimants. Henry proved the most pliable ruler approached. In 1254 he concluded an agreement whereby he accepted the Sicilian crown on behalf of his second son Edmund. This in itself was not too foolish, but Henry's promise to pay the papal military debts of 135,000 marks certainly was. For his subjects it meant increased taxation to fight an imperial war in which there was no interest. Papal debts continued to mount, papal financial demands increased, and when Henry could not meet his commitments he was threatened with excommunication. Such was the situation in 1257 when the barons united to halt any further foolishness.

Spurred on by a hard winter that brought widespread famine, the barons decided to oppose royal policy and in fact to control it. For years there had been sporadic quarrels and constitutional crises over who should dominate the small royal council. Considering themselves the natural feudal advisers the great barons believed that Henry should rely on them for his counsel; for his part Henry chose to use his prerogative to surround himself with professional English and foreign administrators who gave him complete loyalty. The balance of power changed frequently and now, finally, the barons meant to control king and council. In addition there had been long-standing differences over lay taxation. As the ordinary feudal revenues declined in value while the expenses of royal government mounted, there was more frequent recourse to extraordinary taxation. The barons believed that the king should live "of his own" and resolved to control royal expenditure so that the royal need for extraordinary taxes would disappear. This hope was as futile as were Henry's foreign adventures. The last three years of Henry's subservience to the papacy proved to be the spark that ignited the great constitutional crisis of 1258–1265.

For the moment we will deal but cursorily with the constitutional innovations of this crucial period and concentrate on the outcome of the dispute. In 1258 faced with bankruptcy Henry summoned to Oxford a great council or parliament of his barons and demanded a generous tax for his foreign enterprise. The barons, infuriated, responded to his demand with a program of their own. Appearing in full armor before Henry, they retorted that they would hear no more of the Sicilian business or of taxation until they had presented their grievances and until a committee had been appointed by king and barons to draw up a program of reform. This program was subsequently presented as the Provisions of Oxford. The document listed a long series of grievances (*gravamina*) and offered proposals for reform which amounted fundamentally to placing a baronial executive council over Henry that would control policy and the great departments of state such as the exchequer and chancery. The household was deprived of much of its administration and many of its foreign and native personnel were dismissed. Henry had to agree to these reforms. In reality an oligarchy had been substituted for an autocracy. For the next two years Henry reigned while an executive council of twelve barons ruled.

The baronial government was little more successful than Henry in attaining financial stability and administrative efficiency. At the outset the barons worked in harmony and vigorously attacked the evils of central and local government. But soon this spirit waned and they began working for their narrow feudal interests and vying for power. A situation like that of 1215–

1216 reappeared. Some barons returned to the royal fold; others supported the two powerful leaders Simon de Montfort, earl of Leicester, and Richard of Clare, earl of Gloucester, who were jockeying for power and were quarreling over how far investigation should go into baronial franchises. De Montfort and his party carried the day and investigation proceeded. In October 1259 the Provisions of Westminster were issued; they published and confirmed all baronial reform and decisions taken since the Provisions of Oxford but merely glossed over the bitter baronial difference that caused a split in 1260. Gloucester and his adherents defected and gave Henry's son Edward the opportunity to form a royal party that attracted the more moderate barons. A quick end to baronial government seemed imminent. In 1261 after the pope relieved Henry from his promise to abide by the Provisions of Oxford, Henry abolished them by royal ordinance, and the baronial council ceased to operate. Suddenly in 1262 there was a resurgence of spirit in the De Montfort party. Gloucester had died, and his son had joined the reform party. Civil war now appeared the only way to settle the dispute, but at this point De Montfort and Henry agreed to submit their differences to the arbitration of Saint Louis. Though he had the greatest reputation for fairness in western Christendom and was compared to Solomon, there was little doubt as to where his sympathies lay. No medieval king could do other than defend the prerogative and the dignity of royalty. In 1264 his decision was handed down in the Mise of Amiens. It completely vindicated Henry and freed him from obedience to the Provisions, which, it stated, ran directly against the holy and royal rights of kingship. De Montfort's answer was war. That same year at Lewes on the Downs of southeastern England he defeated a royalist army led by Henry, his brother Richard of Cornwall, and Edward. The three royalist leaders were captured and peace was concluded immediately by the Mise of Lewes. Until his death the following year De Montfort was the real ruler of England.

This remarkable person was a Frenchman, the son of the Simon de Montfort who had led the Albigensian Crusade in the early part of the century and had become master of the county of Toulouse. Having English connections through his grandmother, he had come to England in 1230 to establish his claim to the rich earldom of Leicester. Thereafter he was an English baron and for many years was close to Henry III. In 1238 Simon married Henry's sister Eleanor. Soon Henry and Simon quarreled and the newly married couple went to the Continent. Apparently back in the royal grace by 1248 Simon was made the royal lieutenant in Gascony and held this thankless administrative post until dismissed in 1253. During his tenure of office lack of royal support as well as a growing apprehension of Henry's incompetence turned Simon towards the reform party. Shoddy government disgusted him and he disliked Henry. By 1257 he was the accepted head of the discontented barons and was primarily responsible for drafting the Provisions of Oxford. However impossible his task and however narrow and feudal his outlook at times, he was an inspired and sincere proponent of reform and efficient government; no matter what his means they were devoted to attaining good and just government.

In accordance with the Mise of Lewes, Simon's first act was to reconstitute a baronial council. This time he limited its membership to nine and completely dominated it; he and the nine ruled England. Simon was shrewd enough, however, to perceive that his government must have a broader base than his baronial party and he began bidding for the support of the knights of the shires and the burgesses of the boroughs. In the same year of his victory he summoned four knights from every county to a parliament at London in order to secure their approval for his new government. Then in 1265 at his second parliament came real innovation. In addition to his baronial supporters he summoned two knights from each county and two burgesses from each borough to discuss matters of government and taxation. Simon had no idea of founding a new representative national assembly; he intended only to broaden the base of his support and to secure the adherence of the new moneyed and propertied classes. And yet in pushing aside the old feudal concept of reform and attempting to enlist all the powerful classes behind him, he became, almost unconsciously, a supporter of the representative principle.

The De Montfortian political experiment was short-lived. It was too foreign to an eight-hundred-year tradition of kingship and depended ultimately upon baronial cooperation. When Simon antagonized the young earl of Gloucester a crack appeared which became widened when Edward escaped from captivity. Edward was joined by Gloucester and together they raised the royal standard. This time the battle went against Simon and he and the baronial cause perished on the field of Evesham in August 1265. Baronial diehards held out, however, and not until 1266 was the struggle ended. On 31 October the Dictum of Kenilworth defined the terms of settlement between the king and the adherents of De Montfort. Dominant throughout is the spirit of moderation and amnesty. After declaring that the king would rule according to the law and give good and reliable government to his men the document stipulated that all the rebels could recover their lost lands, and also the royal grace, upon payment of the land's market value. With hostilities ended the government turned to the grievances that had inspired the strife between 1258 and 1266. In 1267 was enacted the Statute of Marlborough, which incorporated the major reforms of the Provisions of Oxford and Westminster. Though Henry had been victorious and had been restored, he and his advisers realized that concessions had to be made if peace was to continue. Henry went into a sort of semiretirement and turned the direction of government over to Edward. By 1270 England was so well ordered that Edward went to the Holy Land on a crusade and was still there when his father died in 1272. That the energy and power of Edward were recognized is testified to by the peaceful succession; he did not touch English soil until 1274, yet there was not the slightest attempt at revolt.

2. EDWARD I (1272–1307)

To make an objective assessment of Edward I's character is difficult. For too long and to too many students he has been praised as the English Justinian, the Hammer of the Scots, the crusader, and a man of the highest moral integrity who always kept his word. Like all forceful and dominant figures Edward and his virtues have been unduly magnified. That he was one of the three ablest medieval kings and that his political achievements were numerous is historically true but he was not an exceptional genius towering above his age and anticipating the constitutional developments of later ages. He may stand apart but he was, like most men, a product of his age. When Edward succeeded to the throne at the age of thirty-two he had a thorough training in the art of ruling. He had shown himself to be a consummate political leader and a competent general; to him was due the peace of his father's last years. If we can trust the chroniclers, Edward looked the king. Tall and sinewy of build he was endowed with all the physical stamina and coordination demanded of a successful king. He loved the manly pursuits of war, tournament, hawking, and hunting; he excelled on horse and with the sword. His father would have given much to have been similarly endowed! Reared in a court with cultural tastes Edward appreciated learning, art, and theology, even though he never had the leisure or inclination to bestow much of his patronage upon them. His interests were practical and his achievements were recorded in great statutes, court records, parliament rolls, and strong castles. His weaknesses were few. If he was inclined to stammering, his speech was still emphatic and clear. If he had a tendency to dream and to be slothful—characteristics inherited from Henry—it was offset by a strong sense of purpose, dynamic energy, good powers of concentration, and a sense of order and efficiency. Given occasionally to the family trait of violent temper, Edward was in general a most reasonable man.

Compared to his three predecessors Edward was a towering figure, surpassed only by his great-grandfather Henry II. But as with most of his medieval brethren the tasks of kingship did not enthral him. His happiest moments were spent with horse, hawk, and dog. Though much of what Edward did was progressive, he hesitated to part with the past. The age of crusading had long since passed and feudalism was cracking up but Edward still dreamed of a grand Mediterranean crusade and strove to bolster the decaying feudal structure. His frame of reference was seldom in advance of his age, but rather lagged behind it when one reflects that his was the century of Dante, Roger Bacon, and Thomas Aquinas. Indeed, Edward was a weak replica of Saint Louis of France; he was devout, generous, good-intentioned, and hard-working. But he was too human to achieve the level of

Louis' life. He slipped too frequently and became vindictive, unjust, and enraged. He was too often influenced by the means rather than the end. He was proud, emotional, and given to living for the day or for a specific objective rather than for the glory of God. Perhaps it was England's good fortune to have the more human, practical, and warlike king.

Edward's reign looms so large in terms of legal and constitutional history that we will reserve these aspects until later and concentrate now upon his political and military accomplishments. Strong and good government, locally and centrally, was a prime Edwardian goal. That it was attained is reflected in the time and energy he could devote to Welsh, Scottish, and continental affairs. Though continually occupied with the French problem he was the first king since Henry II to concentrate on expanding the borders of the island kingdom. He dealt first with Wales, which had remained an independent collection of principalities under its Celtic princes throughout the Anglo-Saxon and Norman-Angevin period. In general the system of Welsh marches had proved an effective defense against the rough and turbulent Welshmen. During Henry III's reign, however, the marcher lords had neglected their defense and had become too highhanded in their dealings with the crown. Meanwhile the princes of North Wales had methodically increased their power in Wales. In 1267 England formally recognized the gains of Prince Llewelyn. He became Henry's vassal and was in turn acknowledged as the virtual ruler of all Wales. When Edward became king, Llewelyn refused to do homage and ruled Wales as an independent state. Having waged inconclusive war against the Welsh as Henry's lieutenant, Edward knew the strength of Llewelyn and determined to bring him under control and to reduce the lawlessness in the west country.

By 1277 Edward was prepared to launch his first Welsh campaign. Benefiting from the war experiences of the marcher lords and mobilizing men chiefly from the west country familiar with Welsh tactics and terrain, he led a large army into North Wales. He pushed Llewelyn back into rough and hilly terrain until he had surrounded and starved him out of the stronghold of Snowdon. Llewelyn was forced to restore to marcher lords the lands which he had seized and to do homage for the reduced principality of North Wales. Immediately Edward worked to Anglicize the lands restored, substituting English law and local administration wherever it was feasible. For the next five years there was an uneasy peace as the Welsh of the ceded territory smarted under the foreign English administration. In 1282 they revolted and called upon Llewelyn to deliver them. Edward then led a second Welsh campaign, which lasted for two years. During its course Llewelyn was killed and all Wales reduced. To protect his conquest Edward built at strategic points his famous concentric castles such as Caernarvon, Beaumaris, and Rhuddlan. Around them he planned fortified towns where English merchants went to live. These garrison towns were the centers of English rule and abetted the propagation of English culture. To cap his military conquest

Edward provided for the civil administration of Wales by the Statute of Wales in 1284. Wales was united to the English realm and organized into counties with English law, except for certain local peculiarities. The counties were arranged in two districts, each administered by a central or chief justice. The central courts of Westminster had no jurisdiction over the two justices and their courts. The old marcher lands remained apart from the innovation, enjoying such ancient immunities as their own courts and customs. Gradually English law and administration penetrated the entire Welsh country but it was not wholly integrated until the reign of Henry VIII.

Still one more expedition had to be waged to crush the Welsh who chafed under strong rule and the maladministration of the marcher lords. In 1294 a last revolt broke out all over Wales and it took almost a year of fighting before Edward subdued it. Henceforth there were no serious disturbances and Wales began the long and peaceful evolution towards complete union with England. Though still strong in local custom, culture, speech, and pride, the Welsh have become a more integral segment of the English nation than the Irish or the Scots. A by-product of the Welsh campaigns was an introduction to the Welsh longbow, which in English hands became the most fearsome weapon of western Europe in the fourteenth century. It but took a Welsh arrow to pierce a stout oak door near Edward's head to convince him that the longbow should become a weapon of his men.

The next military adventure of Edward was on the northern frontier where he intervened in the affairs of the Scottish kingdom. Until 1290 peace had governed the relations between the English and Scottish kings; Edward even ignored the English claim to lordship. Then arose suddenly the occasion for intervention and Edward cynically exploited it. In 1286 while riding in the darkness, the last member of the Scottish house, Alexander III, went over a cliff to his death. The only heir was his granddaughter Margaret, called the Maid of Norway. The Scottish nobles recognized her and then concurred with Edward's plan of marrying her to his eldest son Edward. But the impractical scheme was dashed to pieces in 1290 when the Maid perished in a storm on the high seas. There then arose a disputed succession with at least a dozen claimants. Of the royal collateral lines three men—John Balliol, Robert Bruce, and John Hastings—had the best claims. Scottish rules of succession were so tangled that it was difficult to establish the best claim; each man secured supporters, and civil war seemed imminent. Here was an opportunity made to order for Edward. Suddenly remembering his claim to act as overlord he summoned the Scottish nobles to meet him at Norham and there told them that it was his right to choose the king. For this intervention Edward could rely upon some nebulous historical and feudal precedent which, however, was so slight and so little recognized by the Scots that it was extremely dubious. But Edward was strong and the three contenders recognized his claim and swore to abide by his decision. Edward thereupon appointed a commisison to investigate the claims and, while awaiting the report, administered the Scottish kingdom. In 1292 he followed the advice of the commission, named Balliol king, and received from him homage and fealty for the fief of Scotland. This award was no doubt legally correct but it ignored the powerful Bruce support. Balliol became an English puppet and Edward's foot was in the door.

Edward's next act was to make his lordship effective. He interfered in administration, entertained legal appeals, and in 1294 upon the outbreak of his war with Philip IV of France demanded troops from Balliol. The latter might have obeyed had not Scottish feeling run so high that he lost control. A committee of Scottish nobles assumed the real governance and declared all Scottish lands held by the English forfeited. It compelled Balliol to conclude an alliance with France in 1295, thus beginning the long Franco-Scottish entente, and in 1296 it led an expedition into northern England. Edward, on the eve of a French expedition, swiftly reversed his plans and conducted a lightning campaign into Scotland. The fortress of Berwick was taken and sacked and its defenders were slaughtered. In quick succession Perth, Stirling, and Edinburgh yielded, and Scottish resistance melted. Within five months Balliol surrendered his crown, Scotland was subdued, and English government was introduced; three commissioners ruled Scotland in Edward's name.

As with Wales Edward's initial success was not conclusive. The Scots resisted the unpopular and callous English administration and numerous nobles refused to swear fealty to Edward. Periodic outbursts occurred until 1297 when all the Scots burst into rebellion under the popular leader William Wallace. The rising was ignited when Wallace killed an unpopular official. At first all the successes were Scottish. Backed by intense patriotism and fighting on his own terrain, Wallace outmaneuvered the English captains who commanded during Edward's absence in France. The decisive engagement was fought at Stirling Bridge in September 1297. There the earl of Surrey's army was slaughtered and most of Scotland was evacuated. Only a line along the River Tweed was held. For the moment Wallace became the ruler of an independent Scotland.

To deal with the rebellion Edward concluded a truce with Philip IV of France, hurried back to England, and mobilized a new army to invade Scotland. By late 1297 he was ready to strike and in 1298 was operating in Scotland. The action was ruthless; no quarter was given on either side. Experience and organization were with Edward and he finally forced Wallace to give battle at Falkirk. Here Edward skillfully employed his cavalry and longbowmen. He used the longbow to cut up the solid formations of Scottish spearmen and then sent his knights through the gaps. Once the Scottish formations were broken fighting was hopeless; the footsoldiers were cut down by the knights and Falkirk ended as one of the great English victories. Scotland was reoccupied and Wallace and his men became fugitives. Edward's victory, however, bore small returns. Scottish resistance was still unbroken and he had to conduct ceaseless operations against Scottish guerrillas. Yearly the aging king led expeditions north until in 1305 Wallace was captured and executed. For a short time all resistance ceased. But within a year rebellion again shook Scotland, led this time by Robert Bruce, a grandson of the claimant of 1290. Throughout 1306 Edward prevailed but in 1307 Bruce won some successes. Then the old king marched north on his last expedition. Despite his sickly condition he prepared for operations at Carlisle Castle. From there he headed north but died on 7 July at Burgh-upon-Sands on the Solway just south of the Scottish border. To his incompetent son Edward of Caernarvon was bequeathed the unfinished Scottish business. It was not the fate of Scotland to be united to the English crown by conquest.

What energy remained to Edward after his island exertions was devoted to shoring up English defenses in southwestern France. The Peace of Paris had temporarily solved Anglo-French relations but under a less pacific monarch than Saint Louis it was only natural for the French to return to their traditional pastime—expulsion of the English from French soil. Peace was renewed at Edward's succession when he did homage for his French fiefs and received certain lands which had been promised in 1258 but had never been ceded over. For the next thirteen years the *status quo* remained. Meanwhile Edward prepared for less peaceful times by improving the administration of Aquitaine and Gascony and by building fortresses along the French frontier. This work was done mostly during his residence in Gascony in 1273–1274 and 1286–1289. He conducted numerous inquests to ascertain his rights and what was needed in the way of reform. In 1274, for example, he defined the feudal obligations of his Gascon vassals and compiled a survey of tenures and customs comparable to the Hundred Rolls. In 1289 he issued the great ordinances that revamped administration throughout Aquitaine and Gascony. Duties were defined for the highest officers—the seneschal of Gascony and the constable of Bordeaux—on down to the humblest servants. The royal rights were protected, justice was improved and speeded up, and the system of direct and indirect taxation (such as the customs of Bordeaux) was made more efficient. Annual statements of Edward's financial position were submitted. It has been estimated that Edward constructed some 140 towns (*bastides*) which served the dual purpose of fortresses against the French and centers of rural economic exploitation. These foundations, something like the *villes neuves* of the eleventh and twelfth centuries and the Welsh fortified towns of the thirteenth, served as outposts of English administration and culture. Finally Edward turned to stimulating the economic relations with England which led to increasing the volume of the Gascon wine trade.

Edward's labor was not wasted because in 1285 there came to the French throne one of its three ablest occupants—Philip IV. His life's ambition, like that of his famous predecessor Philip Augustus, was the formation and unification of a greater France. The great obstacle to this goal was the rich

English possessions, which he meant to occupy. Like Philip Augustus, he used his right as feudal overlord to intervene in Edward's lands and played upon an incipient French nationalism to turn the fiery men of Gascony and Béarn against English rule. Philip made little headway, however, until 1293. Then maritime rivalry between French and English sailors broke out into fighting in the Channel and in 1294 a combined English-Gascon fleet defeated a French fleet. Taking advantage of the fact that Gascons had been involved, Philip persuaded Edward to surrender temporarily a part of Gascony as a guarantee that French losses would be compensated. Once his forces occupied this land Philip confiscated all Gascony. Edward's only recourse was war, which dragged on inconclusively until 1303. The Welsh and Scottish exertions absorbed too much English strength to permit sending an expeditionary force that could drive Philip out. Expeditions of 1294 and 1296 were too minor to be fruitful. In 1297, however, Edward planned a double-edged campaign, one force to strike from Gascony under his lieutenants and another led by himself to invade France from the land of his ally, Count Guy de Dampierre of Flanders. But the whole effort was unsuccessful. English barons refused to serve overseas or pay taxes to support an expedition. Edward and his army were needed in Scotland. In Flanders, the Flemish and English could not get along and fought in the streets of Ghent. After a few months neither Edward nor Philip could see much to be gained from a Flemish campaign and in October 1297 they concluded a truce; Count Guy was left to the tender mercy of Philip. The truce also included operations in southwestern France. It was renewed annually until a treaty of peace was concluded at Paris in 1303. According to its terms Gascony was restored to Edward by a distraught Philip whose army had just been slaughtered by the Flemish at Courtrai. For the moment Philip had all that he could do to defend northeastern France.

When one tallies up Edward's military exploits he finds that the Welsh conquest was a conspicuous success, that the continental operations preserved the conditions imposed by the Treaty of Paris in 1258, and that the Scottish adventure was premature and could not have been successful even if Edward had been followed by three rulers like himself. For his military exploits Edward has achieved a notable place in the political annals of English history. But, like Henry II, Edward forged his real achievements in the fields of administration and law. Edward's great statutes and experiments in representative assemblies, however dull by comparison with his military campaigns and diplomatic intrigue, were to be his enduring contributions to English history.

XXV

Central Administration

THE student of English medieval institutions not only must envisage the core of central government as composed of king, council, and household but must also realize that the functions and power of each constantly expanded and contracted. Ultimately, it was the crown that retreated most, losing its effective power to a transformed and augmented council that became the sovereign authority in the realm. Until John's reign there had been constant growth of royal power with but few setbacks. Kingly retreat began in the thirteenth century. It was not that the king had a less exalted view of his prerogative, but that political, social, and economic forces of the age made Angevin autocracy unworkable. The theme, in fact, of thirteenth-century constitutional history is the struggle between the king and the larger community of his subjects for a share in or a control over the organs of central government. King, council, and household, with such subordinate departments as the exchequer, chancery, wardrobe, and chamber, were all a focal point in the contest for power between king and barons.

I. THE KING

Loss of royal prestige brought about by John, Magna Carta, and the minority of Henry III limited the prerogative of kingship. Until papal declaration of Henry's majority in 1224, and even until the beginning of his personal government in 1232, a council of natural advisers—the barons—guarded the destiny of central government. When Henry III became actual ruler in 1232, he ended the sixteen-year arrangement of subservience of crown to baronage and asserted all the traditional Angevin prerogatives. He intended to dominate the departments of central administration as had his father and grandfather. History was to prove that Henry lacked the capacity for this task and that his belief in thinking he could restore kingship to the heights it had reached under Henry II was anachronistic. The decline in power of Henry III and Edward I is chiefly attributable to lack of money. Had they been able to live principally "of their own," that is, from their customary incomes, then they could have governed as independent autocrats. But this was impossible. The royal resources shrank in value as new forms of wealth developed and fell into the hands of a new class of royal subjects. To the new sources of money Henry and Edward had to go, and each time they did so they compromised the royal independence. These remarks must be borne in mind as we turn now to the royal powers.

The long list of prerogatives that Henry claimed was but that body of right held by his predecessors; there was no novelty in his assertion of them. Recalling that Henry was unable to restore all the powers to this list, we shall examine the principal developments affecting the royal prerogative in the thirteenth century. Though kingship had been hereditary under the Norman-Angevins, heritable right had been set aside. A rough and practical age conveniently forgot about custom and precedent whenever it was expedient to do so; Matilda was passed over by the barons for Stephen and the mature John was supported over the boy Arthur. Just prior to crowning John, Hubert Walter declared that no man could claim the crown by heritable right but that election was necessary. When the boy Henry succeeded John, therefore, it marked a distinct advance for heritable right. From here on kingship was viewed as hereditary; the principle of inheritance applied to the English kingship for almost two hundred years. It is significant that Henry III's son Edward reigned before he became king in 1272.

Though the coronation oaths of Henry III and Edward I are not extant, we are certain that they followed the traditional form. They swore to protect and respect the church, to keep the peace, to give good justice, to govern by just custom and law, and to abolish unjust laws. A French version of Edward's oath states that he will uphold the customs and laws of the realm made and chosen by the people. But what did this mean? It is apocryphal that a writ could run against the king and force him to appear in court as a defendant; the law had no force against the king. Both the legal records and Bracton state that the king cannot be sued or punished by the law. It follows, therefore, that the king can do no wrong. Should he do wrong, then the only course is to petition the royal conscience and humbly beseech redress. Indeed, the law does not run against the king; it is above him. Time and again Bracton and others reiterated that the king was above all men but below God and law; inasmuch as the law made a king, he was bound to obey it. A ruler who did not obey the law was a tyrant, and yet for breaking the law he was punishable only by God. The only real restriction was the king's moral obligation. In an age of faith both the king and his subjects believed that divine wrath would fall upon him if he ignored his high moral trust. No king would dare to flout his mission on earth as God's appointed civil governor.

Such was the theory of kingship. But Henry III was to demonstrate that theory evaporated before necessity. A king could not be a failure in the eyes of the realm nor could he administer bad government without some sort of reckoning. A successful king stayed at least within the law if not within the spirit of responsiveness to the will of the realm; Henry did neither, and so caused the barons to think that they could bridle him. They attempted it in

1258 without success. Their goal was the same in 1297 when Edward I was forced by financial distress to agree to baronial demands. Like efforts were repeated in the next two centuries, all with little success. In the Middle Ages the king was still a person whom the law could not coerce. Control over the king was achieved only in a later age when he came to be indirectly coerced through his officials, who were held legally liable for all the acts of royal government. The one method for coercing the king in the thirteenth century was that resorted to by the royal vassals in 1215—feudal revolt, justified by the custom that if the lord failed in his obligations the vassal would have recourse to renouncement of allegiance and to revolt. Such redress did not prove satisfactory; it governed only the action of royal vassals and stopped short of deposition.

As a lawgiver and fount of justice the king theoretically was as absolute as in the twelfth century; in fact some historians have argued that Edward I was the equal of Henry II. They base this view on the famous line from Justinian's Institutes, *quod principi placuit legis habet vigorem*, found in a document of Edward's chancery. It is now generally accepted that this phrase had no absolutistic connotations for Edward; a scribe inserted it in a preamble as a rhetorical flourish and Edward undoubtedly was not familiar with it. From the comments of English lawyers we may be certain that whatever pleased the king did not necessarily become law. Bracton showed clearly that this phrase did not apply to Henry III. He argued that if the law makes the king and the king rules by it then his will is limited. Notwithstanding the laws made by king without the consent of the great council and the new judicial remedies (writs) developed by king and advisers, the tradition of cooperation and consent was not left behind. The great statutes of Henry III and Edward I were enacted by king and council. Edward was forced to agree that no new judicial writs could be made without the assent of the great council. By 1285 statutory consent was even necessary to modify old established writs. Law and remedy-making were no longer simple administrative affairs as in the twelfth century but were a matter of legislation by king and great council, or its successor, parliament.

2. THE JUSTICIAR

We have noted that the last great Angevin justiciar, Hubert Walter, resigned in 1198. This date initiated the decline of that office. Under John there was less need for such an officer. John loved the business of governing; he tended to administrative detail, concentrated powers in his own hands, and became his own chief minister. After the loss of Normandy in 1204 there was little royal absenteeism in England and therefore no need for the justiciar as a vice-regent. Hubert Walter's successor, Geoffrey fitz Peter, earl of Essex, though a capable administrator, did not wield the power of Hubert. Just before his death in 1213 his sympathies lay with the baronial cause.

John's Poitevin favorite, Peter des Roches, then became justiciar. Though most efficient and clever, he was too unscrupulous, and he compromised himself for some years because of his intimate ties with John. During the civil war the office had no opportunity to function normally, and with John's death there was no official place for Peter. He became the tutor and personal guardian of Henry III, and Hubert de Burgh became the justiciar for the next sixteen years.

Hubert de Burgh was the last effective justiciar. His power stemmed in part from the minority of Henry, which necessitated a strong vice-regent. We have seen how he relegated Peter des Roches to obscurity and became, after William Marshal's death, the most powerful figure in the realm. Formerly a sheriff and a capable administrator of Richard and John, Hubert did an efficient job of restoring the government. Instrumental in negotiating peace with Louis of France and the barons, he rapidly pacified the realm. He revived and continued the Angevin administrative system. In 1217 the exchequer was already operating and soon the rest of the central and local administration had resumed as normal a functioning as a minority permitted. Hubert's fall was caused by his haughty behavior towards the barons, by his financial peculations, by Henry III's desire to become the real ruler, and by the jealousy and desire for revenge on the part of Peter des Roches and the Poitevin gang. After returning to England in 1231 Peter des Roches moved swiftly to destroy Hubert. With his capacity for intrigue and his influence over Henry he secured Hubert's dismissal on 29 July 1232. A supporter of Peter, Stephen de Segrave, received the office, but he was dismissed in 1234. The office then lapsed until 1258–1261 when the barons attempted unsuccessfully to revive it. In reality, the office of justiciar ceased its existence with Hubert and became but a monument to the stern and strong administration of the Norman-Angevins.

3. THE SMALL COUNCIL

The great council (*curia regis*) has been treated until now as an organ of central administration. It was, to be sure, concerned with central government for the rest of the medieval period, but less intimately so during the course of the thirteenth century as it turned away from the king and his executive departments to become the core of a new national assembly—parliament. A detailed study of the great council will come in a subsequent chapter on parliament; for the moment we shall deal only with those organs of government intimately connected with the king.

The Angevin small council (*curia regis*) was composed of a few trusted barons, justices, principal officers, and professional servants from the household departments. Though certain men were always in attendance there was as yet no standard size or definite membership. The king took counsel from whom he desired but showed a tendency by John's reign to confide more in the household officers. The important point is that the king constantly took advice from a small council whose functions remained unspecialized. It did all the king commanded and could do anything done by the great council. Only for the most fundamental matters of the realm did the kings feel constrained to consult the great council. The reign of Henry III inaugurated a new phase in the development of the small council; at his death the small council had differentiated itself from the large and had become an organ which, though accomplishing any task desired by the king, rendered counsel and specialized service not done by great council or such departments as the chancery and exchequer. The foundation of the privy council had been laid.

During Henry's minority from 1216 to 1224 a council governed England. It is difficult to determine, however, what kind of council it was. The suggestion that the barons appointed a standing council of regency consisting of William Marshal, Peter des Roches, and the papal legate is not borne out by evidence; all that can be said is that these three were most prominent. Almost as frequent in attendance were old supporters of John such as Hubert de Burgh. The membership and number constantly varied as different subjects were discussed and as the great barons were consulted on weightier affairs of the realm. There was an active council, and to meet the needs of a minority there was a quickening and adaptation of the *consilium*. But there was not a clearly delineated small council with regularized attendance. There was as yet no privy council. Upon this active but formless council Henry depended until his personal rule began in 1232. He relied upon it for counsel, but less frequently so as Hubert de Burgh in his capacity as justiciar tended to make more decisions by himself, a step that led the barons to accuse Hubert of making himself the only councillor.

Until 1232 the small council had, in general, represented baronial opinion. Afterwards this was not the case. Henry assumed the prerogative of appointing and dismissing his councillors and took counsel from whomever he chose. The rest of his reign witnessed a constant struggle over control of the small council. The barons countered the assertion of royal prerogative with the argument that they were the king's natural and feudal councillors and should be represented in the small council. Henry's policy of securing the services of a competent group of professional civil servants was probably justified; he but erred tactically in choosing them largely from the greedy and grasping foreign gang of Poitevins and Savoyards. The barons were outraged at the nepotism shown to these professional foreigners, who came to be called the "evil counsellors" of Henry. In the battles that ensued there was constant cry for reform in household and court, but the real baronial objective was control of the small council. Only during crises did actual reform in finance or administrative procedure occur.

Between 1232 and 1234 Poitevins such as Peter des Roches and Peter de Rivaux were ascendant in the small council. Working from their important household offices, they made the council into an essentially household affair; they excluded the barons and maneuvered them out of traditional political strongholds. Baronial retaliation was bitter and rapid. The Poitevin councillors were accused of perjury to an oath sworn "to furnish the king faithful counsel." This is the first reference we have to a councillor's oath. In 1234 under attack from the barons in a great council the Poitevins fell. Strongly supported by the clergy led by Edmund Rich, the new archbishop of Canterbury, the barons presented a long list of grievances on 9 April and demanded the dismissal of bad advisers; the archbishop threatened to excommunicate Henry if he did not act. On 10 April, so a chronicler tells us, Henry "dismissed his iniquitous counsellors, and recalled to his following the natural men of the realm, submitting to the counsel of his prelates." Henry was forced to receive as councillors nine men acceptable to the barons. This and subsequent changes in the council were accomplished with the utmost informality; it was said only that a man was admitted or removed. Here and in other ways the yet unfixed and informal character of the small council is underlined.

Another conciliar crisis arose in 1237 over the restoration of Stephen Segrave and other unpopular advisers. Uncowed by a baronial demonstration against foreigners in the spring of 1236 which had driven him to the Tower of London, Henry persevered in governing through foreign and domestic favorites of the household. In an extraordinary great council in January 1237 Henry asked for an aid and was met with the answer that no money would be granted until the present councillors were dismissed and replaced by natural (baronial) ones. Henry capitulated because of financial necessity and consented to the appointment of twelve suitable men, headed by the Savoyard William of Valence. Though a foreigner, William was acceptable and was designated as *consiliarius regis principalis* along with such baronial stalwarts as the earls of Warenne and Ferrers. According to Matthew Paris they swore to give faithful counsel and the king swore to accept it. For the first time members of the small council are described as appointed and sworn. The ineffectiveness of such control was evident within the year. After the great council adjourned Henry returned to his old tricks and most of the familiar household faces soon reappeared. In 1239 Stephen Segrave was described as a *praecipuus consiliarius* who held "the reins of the royal council." The clerk John Mansel, the son of a simple English priest, worked up the rungs of the official ladder until he became one of the most influential councillors and also the most infamous. Records speak of him as "the special and familiar counsellor" who was "moderator at the royal counsels." He was called the wealthiest clerk in the world and was believed to possess three hundred benefices.

The barons chafed under royal control of the council until 1244 when another test of strength occurred. The expenditure of large sums on the disastrous Poitevin expedition of 1243 necessitated calling a great council for the supply of funds. After deliberation, the barons agreed that they would do nothing without the assent of all the great council. Thereupon a joint committee of twelve representing the prelates, earls, and barons drew up a comprehensive reply. If we can trust Matthew Paris, they presented a scheme for the reform of the council. According to a draft of the plan included by Paris it was proposed that the great council should choose four of the most capable nobles to be on the royal council and to be sworn to execute just royal government. Two of the four could be the chancellor and justiciar, and at least two should personally attend the king at all times. They could be removed from office only by the consent of the great council. These proposals, though constituting the first comprehensive baronial program to control king and council since Magna Carta, and though known by the rank and file of the baronage, were never formally approved by the great council or presented to Henry. Nevertheless enough pressure was put upon Henry for him to name four councillors meeting with baronial approval. Though not a real concession, this compromise conciliated the baronage and neutralized their reform scheme.

Until 1257–1258 the barons were virtually unrepresented in the small council. There are occasional references to a few barons in council as, for example, in 1250 and 1256, but Henry's practice and theory was to determine royal policy in small councils of councillors "whom we have ordained." The Sicilian affair of 1257, however, ended Henry's domination of the council and inaugurated eight years of constitutional crisis fired by struggle of king and barons for conciliar control. In a clerical convocation of 1257 the clergy refused Henry a grant of money until he accepted a plan of reform which dealt largely with the swearing of a councillor's oath. The chroniclers state that an oath was taken by the members of the council as well as by the barons of the exchequer, the justices, and less exalted local officers. Fortunately the text of this oath has been preserved and provides for the first time the form of an official oath which was the basis for future oath-forms. This oath probably was used for the rest of Henry's reign; it appeared also in the reign of Edward I. The legal writer Fleta quoted the oath almost verbatim. Towards the end of Edward's reign part of the oath was elaborated and revised to form the councillor's oath of 1307. The oath of 1257 stated essentially that councillors should give good and loyal counsel, guard the integrity of the royal domain, dispense rapid and impartial justice according to the laws and customs of the realm, and receive no bribes or rewards for services. Any councillor found breaking these oaths was to be excluded from the council and was to lose his land, rents, and income for one year.[1] Though the oath did not settle the problem of conciliar control, it established the practice that whoever sat in the small council was obliged to swear a prescribed oath, infraction of which was punishable. Hereafter we are on firmer

[1] SM, no. 53A.

ground in defining the small council and can safely say that it consisted of those men who had taken the councillor's oath.

Within the year the whole realm was shaken by the constitutional crisis inaugurated by the Provisions of Oxford. Though general reform of royal administration was the theme of the Provisions, the main baronial objective was control of the small council and royal government. There was no novelty in the proposal that councillors and key officials should be selected by the great council and be responsible to it, yet for the first time the barons gained, at least temporarily, complete control of royal administration. In May 1258 Henry was forced to agree to the appointment of a baronial committee of twenty-four—twelve named by himself and twelve by the barons—to reform the realm. In June a great council of barons acting on the proposals of the committee made the following demands of Henry: in all matters of state he should be advised by an executive council of fifteen responsible to the barons, and he should accept a justiciar, chancellor, and treasurer nominated by the great council and responsible to the executive council. To insure regular consultation with the great council it was also provided that there should be three annual meetings with the small council, along with an additional council of twelve named by the baronage, "on behalf of the whole community of the land, to consider common needs." To elect the council of fifteen, the committee of twenty-four designated four barons from its members—two royal and two baronial.[2] By 6 July the fifteen had been named and sworn (*ceo sunt ceus ke sunt jurez del counseil le rei*) and had begun their duties. With nine baronial adherents the council of fifteen gained control over Henry. Besides delivering good counsel it was to amend, redress, and reform all matters of state. On 7 August Henry proclaimed the council's authority and swore to abide by its counsel and decisions.

Until 1260 it can be said that this predominantly baronial council governed the realm with or without the king. The royal executive power was wielded by the council in the king's name. For eighteen months the council was effective in its control over the chief state and household offices and over local administration. Necessary reform and redress of grievances were undertaken. All documents of the chancery initiating executive action were noted as authorized by council. In the autumn of 1259 the Provisions of Westminster laid down specific instructions governing the functions of the treasurer, chancellor, and revived office of justiciar; the exchequer was the target of extensive reform.[3]

At this time Henry went abroad and the council provided the sole government at home. But there was confusion and division of authority because too often the council of fifteen consulted and cooperated with the advisory watchdog council of twelve. There developed a conflict of interests and an overlapping of functions. To distinguish between the councils is sometimes

[2] SM, no. 47A and B.
[3] SM, no. 47C.

difficult. In December 1260 the baronial tenure of power collapsed; the council of fifteen disappeared and was supplanted by the old royal council. In 1261 with the sanction of the pope, Henry repudiated the Provisions of Oxford and again assumed unrestricted authority; the Oxford experiment for the moment lay dormant.

With the De Montfortian victory in 1264 the barons made one more serious effort to organize and control the council. In a great council held at Lewes in June 1264 it was stated that Henry was to act by a council of nine nominated by three electors chosen by the barons. Three of the nine councillors were to be in constant attendance with the king; vacancies were to be filled by nomination of the three electors. We know that Simon de Montfort and two of his close associates comprised the electorate, which nominated a completely pro-Montfortian council. Unfortunately little is known about its authority and work; we can only surmise that De Montfort governed through the council and obtained its sanction until his death in 1265. Because of the unsettled political and military conditions the council met irregularly and infrequently. From time to time a stray record indicates that it was conceived as an executive body separate from the great council and as an indispensable department of state. Certainly this council of nine was an improvement over the complicated conciliar machinery instituted by the Provisions of Oxford. In it resided the executive power, distinct from other interlocking committees and councils.

The fall of De Montfort and his party marked the end of baronial experiments to control the council. But the events of 1257 and the succeeding years were not without effect. Although composition of the council was again determined by the king, the idea of a sworn council, separate from great council, was so deeply ingrained that it was henceforth an essential part of central administration. Another lesson learned by the king was that he should choose his councillors from the barons and natives of England rather than from foreign favorites. In general throughout the rest of Henry's reign there was a distinct council of sworn councillors composed largely of barons. This body in effect directed government between 1270 and 1272 when Henry was aged and sick, and when Edward was on his crusade. The trials of Henry's long reign had transformed an undefined council (*consilium*) into a sworn responsible council, the membership of which was determined by the councillor's oath appearing for the first time in 1257.

Though there were no striking innovations in the small council under Edward I, it became further entrenched as a distinct and permanent executive organ of central government. Stubbs drew attention to this fact long ago when he said that Edward "seems to have accepted the institution of a council as part of the general system of government, and whatever had been the stages of its growth, to have given it definiteness and consistency." Under Edward the problem of what made and composed a council was settled. The swearing of the councillor's oath became a regular practice, indicating a definite membership and specific duties. The documents often refer to an act as witnessed *cum juratis de consilio ipsius domini regis*. By 1307, as already noted, a more precise oath had evolved from that of 1257; the councillor's oath had become established custom.[4] Those councillors referred to as "ordained and retained" were principally officers of the royal court and household. At the head of every list appeared the chancellor and treasurer; they often summoned and presided over the council. Next came officers from the household, customarily from the wardrobe. There were then justices, barons of the exchequer, chancery clerks, and a few minor functionaries, as well as some doctors of canon and civil law, and some messengers and envoys. Edward, like his father, preferred to use skilled professionals and clerks from his household but was generally blocked by the barons, who fought the elevation of professionals to the council. The barons did not deny that competent officers were required in the royal administration but saw no need for making them councillors. Whenever the king had his way the number of professionals increased and was augmented by prominent representatives of Italian banking firms and by minor ecclesiastics. The barons were represented predominantly by earls and bishops. We seldom meet the same faces from council to council. Only the most trusted and intimate councillors such as the chancellor, treasurer, and a few household clerks attended regularly. Others attended when their special skills and knowledge were required. In regard to the composition of the council we can merely conclude that it was a heterogeneous body of sworn councillors numbering several scores, chosen because of their political and military prestige or because of their special talents.

Let us turn now to the work of the small council as an organ of state. It was, we must remember, an omnicompetent body that could do whatever the king asked of it. It was therefore an administrative, financial, and judicial body. In one week it might act in all capacities. It maintained close relations with the chancery, exchequer, and courts of the common law such as those of the king's bench and common pleas. Until the reigns of Henry III and Edward I it is frequently impossible to distinguish between the council and these other organs to which it helped give birth.

The essential duty of the council was to give advice whenever the king asked for it. This function overshadowed the administrative work until the reign of Edward I. Then the evidence portrays the council as making administrative decisions. From 1297 authorizations appear for the issue of chancery writs "by council." More and more decisions were made in the royal absence. The council dealt with financial matters, particularly those that the barons of the exchequer did not feel competent to settle. As a judicial body, the council dispensed various types of justice. It could sit as a feudal court and decide causes between royal vassals. It could sit as a common law court and

[4] SM, no. 53B.

adjudicate great civil or criminal cases in accordance with the common law and its procedure. It was also a court of equity which independently or with the king dispensed justice or handed down remedies unattainable in local public, feudal, or common law courts. When necessary the council supervised the work of the chancery. The council or certain delegated members negotiated with foreign powers and concluded treaties and agreements. It sat on occasion as a council of war, advising on tactics, strategy, recruitment, and supply. Fundamentally the thirteenth-century small council did all that was done by its eleventh- and twelfth-century predecessors. But less often did it do the work of chancery, exchequer, and common law court as it emerged ever more prominently as a central executive department that had become the nerve center of royal government.[5]

4. THE CHANCERY

By the reign of John the chancery had advanced to a stage where it was no longer an undifferentiated part of the household. It had established a separate identity under a great officer of state; it had its own personnel; it drew up and enrolled most of the royal documents; it had custody of the great seal and could authenticate documents; and it had a routine peculiar to itself. But it had not yet become an independent department like the exchequer; it was still close to the king and within the purview of the household. Thus it continued down to the death of the chancellor Ralph Neville in 1244. Neville had risen from simple chancery clerk to vice-chancellor, and then in 1226 the great council selected him to succeed Richard Marsh as chancellor. Though Neville owed his appointment to the barons and had obtained the bishopric of Chichester in 1222, there is no evidence that he was a baronial man. He seems to have remained fundamentally a royal clerk in outlook. Even after the assumption of all royal power by Henry III in 1232 Neville remained chancellor and cooperated with the king. Between 1238 and 1242 he lost custody of the great seal but retained the chancellorship until his death. To this point the chancery remained almost as it was under John. The staff was predominantly that of clerks and serjeants of the king's chapel and the chancellor and his staff secured their income from the fees of the great seal. Almost all orders received by the chancellor to issue documents under the great seal were oral. Repeatedly the warrants for the documents are described as given *per ipsum regem*. The chancellor must have been in attendance at the court almost daily and been accounted a member of the household.

After 1244 the close relation of chancery to household was relaxed; we can perceive a decided trend for the chancery to go out of court, that is, to become a separate department. Perhaps one influence working for the separation of chancery from household was use of the privy seal after 1230 to au-

[5] SM, no. 54E.

thorize the issuance of documents under the great seal. Though the privy seal was not used often for this purpose it pointed to the day when the chancellor and great seal would be separated from the king for long periods and when all warrants received would be under the privy seal. As the great seal became less personal to the king it became ever more the seal of England moved by the privy seal. Inevitably this led to the chancery's going out of court and increasing the scope of its administration. Another development causing departmentalization was the growing feeling among the baronage that the chancellor should be a state officer accountable to the whole community of the realm, as well as a medium through which pressure could be exerted upon the king. The fact that no chancellor was appointed from 1244 to 1258, his duties being delegated to various household officials, demonstrated to the barons the danger that the chancellor and his staff could be absorbed by the personal government of the king. A key demand in the Provisions of Oxford was the appointment of a chancellor. Another cause for separation of the chancery may well have been the establishment in 1244 of the hanaper department to receive and account for all the profits customarily received by the chancellor. This new department derived its name from the practice of keeping writs and answers to them in a hamper (*in hanaperio*). Henceforth a keeper of the hanaper received all fees of the great seal, paid the chancery expenses, and presented an account of his receipts and expenditures. The result was that the chancery staff and the chancellor, after one was appointed in 1258, became salaried officials. This step, the payment of annual salaries, differentiated the chancellor and his clerks of the chancery from the clerks of the household. As early as 1244 a record speaks of separate quarters for the chancery staff, and in 1260 while Henry III was in France some of the chancery staff remained in England *in officio cancellarie* dealing with routine business. Soon, increased use of the privy seal by the wardrobe would enable the chancery to conduct most of its business out of court.

We have seen that the baronial demands of 1258 included the appointment of a chancellor. This was done and the new chancellor then swore to seal writs dealing only with routine affairs; any important or extraordinary document must be authorized by the council. In addition, the chancellor was accountable to the council and barons for his conduct in office and was to hold the chancellorship for but one year. Though this arrangement was short-lived, it indicates that the chancellor and his staff were coming to be regarded as a department of state accountable to the barons, the natural representatives of the realm. After the baronial defeat in 1265, though a chancellor continued to function, his department temporarily ceased its journey out of court. During most of Edward's reign the chancellorship under Robert Burnell (1274–1292) renewed its close relation with the wardrobe. The two seemed almost interchangeable. Frequently, the wardrobe kept the great seal and issued documents under it. When the king went abroad, taking Burnell and the wardrobe staff with him, some of the chancery remained behind to handle domestic matters. As the wardrobe reached the summit of its power under Edward I, the chancery definitely became subordinated. A key wardrobe official, John Benstead, often kept both privy and great seals, and the overworked wardrobe constantly pressed chancery clerks into its service. Even though the privy seal came to be employed more frequently to warrant documents under the great seal, there does not appear to have been any bureaucratic rivalry or tendency for the chancery to leave the court. Practically the only difference between chancery and wardrobe was that the former was still regarded as the necessary department to draw up and issue documents dealing with great affairs of state as well as judicial writs required to initiate proceedings in the common law courts. This close rapport of chancery and wardrobe continued until 1292, the year of Burnell's death. Edward so trusted Burnell that he dispensed with the hanaper system and permitted the chancellor and his clerks to enjoy the profits from the fees.

After 1292 the chancery once more began to move away from the wardrobe and this time its course was not to be diverted. Burnell's successor, John Langton, was deprived of the chancery profits and given an annual salary of £500. The quarters of the chancery were moved outside the court, and the privy seal loomed ever more prominently as an instrument for authorizing chancery action. Then, too, the press of business, just as earlier with the common law courts, contributed to making the chancery a distinct department of state located permanently at Westminster. Expediency and convenience, dictated by the mushrooming judicial writs, by the swelling stream of petitions for grace and favor, and by the mass of rolls and documents, were soon to make the chancery a sedentary department like the exchequer located at Westminster. The final differentiation of chancery from household was not to come until the reigns of Edward II and Edward III, but the last years of Edward I saw a trend in this direction. The increasing press and complexity of government forced the kings to depersonalize and departmentalize the chancery as their predecessors had the exchequer and courts of common law. By Edward III's reign the chancery was primarily a department of central administration rather than a secretariat and record-keeping bureau. The stage was set for the chancellor and his staff to head a new prerogative court of equitable justice—the high court of chancery.

5. THE ROYAL HOUSEHOLD

We have seen that the Norman-Angevin household gave birth to the principal organs of central administration. It supplied key members of the small council, it produced the exchequer out of the chamber, and it nurtured the chancery, which became entirely independent in the fourteenth century. The household, as the center of administrative initiative, reached its peak of efficiency under John, who employed the overlapping subdepartments of chamber and wardrobe to accomplish a large share of his financial, secretarial, and administrative business. Though for a time the minority of Henry stunted the activity of the household, in 1232 it again became the vital center of royal government. We must envisage Henry's struggle to revive household government as a return to traditional Norman-Angevin administration; in attempting to control the varied facets of government through his household Henry was doing only what Henry II or John had done. The barons fought household administration throughout the century, not because they did not believe in it and desired to substitute something better, but because they wanted to have an important share in the appointment of household officers and in household policy. On each occasion that the barons obtained a voice in the household they carried out no significant reform; they merely removed foreigners and favorites who had executed unpopular royal policy. What the barons wanted in regard to the household was what they fought to win with the small council—control. The reigns of Henry III and Edward I are characterized on the one hand by the royal attempt to concentrate administrative activity in the household staffed by royal appointees, while, on the other, the barons fought constantly to install representatives from their class and thereby influence and control royal government.

We have long ceased to be interested in the various household officers whose domestic functions did not draw them into public service. It suffices to remark that they remained members of the household but came to exercise predominantly honorary services. For hunting and war the marshals and constable still rendered valuable services. From the Household Ordinance of 1279 we learn that a multitude of minor functionaries performed the routine services required by a household as yet fundamentally itinerant.[6] One innovation noticeable in the household of Henry III, and even more so in that of Edward, was the addition of a permanent military bodyguard of selected knights and bannerets; this guard accompanied the king on his travels and served as a small elite permanent army and general staff that helped to mobilize and command the army in time of war. As part of the household these knights and bannerets were completely maintained and paid yearly salaries or fees. Edward normally maintained about twenty bannerets and forty knights. We are not primarily concerned, however, with such nonpolitical functions of the household; we must concentrate on the wardrobe, which dominated all household activity in the thirteenth century.

We shall reserve until later a discussion of the wardrobe as a financial department of the household and focus at the moment on its less important nonfinancial functions. By the end of John's reign the wardrobe was doing all that its elder brother the chamber did; in practice they were equals. But in theory and in the administrative chain of command the chamber seems

[6] SM, no. 52c.

to have exerted a jurisdiction over the wardrobe until 1232. From then until the fourteenth century the wardrobe was the center of household government. Its elevation was due principally to Peter des Roches, chief councillor from 1232 to 1234, and his nephew Peter de Rivaux. Their goal was a restoration of the personalized government of John. Within a few months Rivaux secured life appointments to the following positions: he became custodian of the wardrobe, chamber, and treasury of the household; keeper of the privy seal; royal chamberlain of London; and royal buyer at all fairs and markets. To these offices he added scores of local ones. In complete control of the household, Rivaux was now in a position to unify and control all royal government. It was through the wardrobe that he chose to funnel the royal will; he was chiefly responsible for making it the most powerful household department. This status was in no way altered by the dismissal of both Peters in 1234. Though there was much talk of reform in the household between 1258 and 1265, the barons, beyond attempting to make the wardrobe more dependent upon the exchequer, did no more than push suitable baronial men for the household offices. This was but an interlude; wardrobe and household emerged tied more closely than before to the royal will.

The reign of Edward I has been accurately regarded "as witnessing the zenith of the Angevin conception of administration centered on the household." As with Henry I and Henry II, the household seemed the most efficient organ of administration to a dynamic and energetic king. Moving about with the king, it carried out the royal orders directly and with a minimum of bureaucratic red tape. It was the center of business; its officers were key members of the small council; it supervised royal finance, mobilized and supplied armies, carried out diplomatic missions, and provided the higher personnel of chancery, exchequer, and common law courts. Upon these intimate servants—the *familiares*—most of whom were of humble origin and came to the fore solely because of their ability, Edward felt that he could rely. They were skilled professionals, owing all to royal favor. The household, and in particular the wardrobe, was the training school for a force of civil servants. Nearly all the key officers came from the household. In this category were five of Edward's six chancellors, three of his treasurers, and Walter Langton, the last of his treasurers (1295–1307), who became the leading councillor. It would appear that almost all the greatest Edwardian ministers had at one time been a clerk in the wardrobe where they learned the royal will and the techniques of personalized government. Only towards the end of his reign when in financial straits did Edward have to defend this system against baronial attack.

We have a fine account of wardrobe organization in the Household Ordinance of 1279, the first such record since *The Constitution of the King's Household* in the first year of Stephen's reign. The ordinance summed up the regulations and procedures of the household as they existed in the latter part of Henry III's reign and in the early years of Edward's.[7] Throughout, the wardrobe is portrayed as the key organ of administration. Though the stewards were still theoretically the lay heads of the household, their position had become purely honorary. The clerical keeper of the wardrobe was the real head and consulted daily with the other subdepartment heads on matters of administration and finance. Below him were two officers, the controller and cofferer, whose functions were mainly financial. Next was the staff that accomplished the routine work—the clerks, ushers, and subushers. Outside the wardrobe proper were the marshals who maintained order and supervised the routine of the household, a staff that provided for transportation, and twenty serjeants-at-arms who formed a household bodyguard. All members of the household were furnished to some extent with food and clothing and received a yearly salary or benefice. Because the clerks were often out of court on financial, diplomatic, and military missions, they were granted special allowances to cover their expenses. Under Edward the wardrobe had various storehouses in London and Westminster and the personnel assigned there were completely maintained.

Occasionally friction and rivalry arose among the wardrobe, exchequer, and chancery, although under Edward there was a surprising amount of cooperation despite the wardrobe's performing numerous duties that would seem to fall properly within the purview of chancery or exchequer. Even in the late thirteenth century specialization and departmentalization were so little practiced that duplication, bifurcation, and overlapping did not concern the king or administration. Functions were assigned to whatever department seemed at the moment best able to fulfil them. Under Edward the wardrobe business was as broad as the king's executive powers. Flexible, mobile, and constantly with the king, the wardrobe was the most sensitive of central organs. Royal government was still essentially household and the king took care to channel his will through the wardrobe.

We have already commented upon the intimate connection between wardrobe and chancery, and we shall soon discuss the relationship of wardrobe to exchequer, but let us pause briefly to examine the wardrobe and its custody of the privy seal. Since the reign of John frequent absences of the chancellor from court and an increasing load of business had made it imperative to supplement the great seal with another seal of authorization. As soon as possible Henry III acquired a privy seal; there is evidence that he was using one by 1230. When Peter de Rivaux controlled the household he was given custody of the privy seal. He was the first keeper of the privy seal and thereafter it was generally under the custody of the keeper of the wardrobe. Because its primary function was to warrant issuance of documents under the great seal, it was little used until the chancery definitely began to move out of court in the 1290's. It was used, however, when king and

[7] SM, no. 52c.

chancellor were separated, and the wardrobe by virtue of its custody of the privy seal became a sort of second chancery. During the baronial crisis when the barons exercised control over the chancellor, Henry III employed the privy seal to authenticate all sorts of documents. Under the privy seal he repudiated the Provisions of Oxford. Henry seems to have contemplated substituting the privy for the great seal because, kept by the wardrobe, it was less exposed to baronial influence.

The end of hostilities stopped great use of the privy seal and it did not again become prominent until the late years of Edward I. After 1292, the year of Burnell's death, the privy seal came to the fore in administration. Not only did it warrant issuance of chancery writs and exchequer payments, but original writs also came to be issued under it. The privy seal therefore became an instrument for regular administration as well as for the various royal personal and diplomatic correspondence. At times convenience alone decided whether the chancery and great seal or wardrobe and privy seal should issue a document. Generally the wardrobe secretariat issued warrants under the privy seal to chancery and exchequer, a role that increased as the chancery definitely went out of court. The privy seal, customarily about the king's person, initiated the royal will by warranting the use of the great seal.

6. CONCLUSIONS

Central administration as developed by the middle years of Edward I's reign continued essentially unchanged down to 1297. Under the drive and energy of Edward the administration functioned smoothly with a minimum of friction between council, chancery, exchequer, and wardrobe. All these departments were staffed by officers and subordinates predominantly of the royal choice. Any overlapping, conflict, or duplication of work was subordinated to the underlying principle that it was all the king's work. Despite the century-long baronial attempt to have a voice in government by means of controlling appointments to council and household positions, Edward took counsel from whomever he so desired and appointed and dismissed royal ministers at will; the "sworn councillors" were of his own choosing. Though the barons fought this old Angevin practice, they seldom met success. Edward's curialist professionals completely dominated central administration; rarely did the natural (baronial) councillors secure much influence at court.

There was no recrudescence of baronial opposition to royal administration until 1297 when the Scottish and French wars caused Edward to press ruthlessly upon the barons and community of the realm for funds and service. For the first time in his reign Edward, like his father, was forced to make some concessions to the barons. But as in Henry's reign the barons did not attack the system of royal administration. They made, in fact, slight gain in placing their own men in council and wardrobe; central government remained bureaucratic. The Confirmation of the Charters granted by Edward on 5 November 1297 left administrative practice untouched. The importance of this concession lies in its acknowledgment that for all extraordinary taxation the king must get the consent of great council or parliament. Its sole effect on royal administration was to limit the financial discretion and independence of the king.[8]

A continual need for money forced Edward to convene succeeding parliaments for supply. When the royal need for money showed no signs of abating, baronial resentment smoldered and finally flared up in the parliament of 1300 so that Edward was forced to assuage baronial feeling by granting the so-called *Articuli Super Cartas* (Articles on the Charters). This document, composed of twenty articles, was a supplement to the Confirmation of the Charters. The clauses dealing primarily with central administration concerned purveyance, the use of the privy seal, the chancery, and justices of the king's bench. The articles on purveyance, which restricted the abuses of royal officers including those of the household, aimed not to eliminate purveyance by the wardrobe but to secure proper authorization for it under the great or privy seal; the wardrobe continued the unpopular custom of purveyance. Limitation was placed upon the use of the privy seal but not for the purposes of general administration. The sixth clause stated that "henceforth no writ touching the common law shall be issued under the small seal." The baronial objective, therefore, was not to prohibit the use of the privy seal in its proper administrative sphere but to ward off the wardrobe from attaining an influence and jurisdiction over the common law courts. Judicial writs were considered to be only within the scope of chancery and great seal. The barons felt that judicial use of the privy seal might thwart the course of common law justice by facilitating royal interference. As for the chancery and justices of the king's bench, it was provided that they should remain with the king and itinerate with him so that there would always be men expert in the law to dispatch judicial business. Though some scholars have held that the barons intended the chancery to serve as a continual check on the wardrobe, the evidence does not substantially bear out this view. If the chancery had been staffed by baronial men such a view would appear to be correct. But the chancery and the king's bench were filled with royal appointees who had the same function as the wardrobe staff —execution of the royal will. In no way could the presence of chancery and king's bench weaken the royal independence. Administratively their presence was inconvenient, as Edward realized in 1306 while preparing to go on his last Scottish expedition. To dispatch normal government business and to facilitate royal justice the chancery and king's bench were left behind at Westminster.

In practice a century of struggle between the royal prerogative and the baronial natural councillors had caused slight diminution in royal power and

[8] SM, no. 51A.

central administration. In 1307 central government was basically the king's just as it had been in the twelfth century. Perhaps the barons believed central government organized around chancery and exchequer to be more constitutional and amenable to baronial will because of their long tradition and peculiar organization and procedure. The exchequer had long ago gone out of court and the chancery was soon to follow, a circumstance that seemed to make them more independent of the king and responsive to the realm. But this interpretation of baronial political thinking is too modern. As yet the barons showed no signs of consciously regarding the chancery and exchequer as state departments of the realm opposed to the personalized administrative household. And even if they had, no control could have been wielded unless chancery and exchequer were staffed by baronial nominees. Effective control over the king and his government was not to come via baronial men sitting in royal council and household. It was to come, even as the barons began to perceive, through control of the king's purse strings, control held by a national assembly of barons supplemented increasingly by representatives of the men from town and county.

XXVI

Innovation in Finance and Taxation

FINANCIAL administration and taxation in the thirteenth century are primarily the story of modification and innovation in the central organs of finance to keep abreast of rising income and expenditures and to tap the new forms of wealth developing in the realm. Financial innovation reflected the transition from a feudal and manorial society to a nonfeudal society based largely on a money economy. In the history of taxation the thirteenth century is the most significant of the Middle Ages. The customary feudal and land taxes became antiquated and were superseded by impositions levied upon the new liquid and mobile wealth of England. It can be said that the origin of modern taxation began in the thirteenth century.

1. THE EXCHEQUER

There were two central financial departments that received and disbursed the royal money—the exchequer and the wardrobe. Under Henry II and his sons the exchequer had attained the peak of its power and had become the most efficiently organized financial system of western Europe. But no organization, however well established, could long function effectively under the shadow of civil war, a long minority, and lack of strong direction. Though William Marshal and Hubert de Burgh had gone far towards re-establishing the semiannual sessions of accounting, too many county farms were in arrears and too few sheriffs were honest in the rendering of their accounts to produce the needed revenue. Hubert tried sporadically to rectify these shortcomings but no major reform came until the so-called Poitevin regime of 1232–1234 when Peter de Rivaux combined all the principal financial offices in his hand and began an extensive overhauling which continued down to 1258. Whether the work was carried out by Poitevin, Savoyard, or Englishman, a unity was achieved between 1232 and 1258. It is wrong to regard the Poitevin regime, or that of any other royal favorites, as an attempt by Henry to scuttle the exchequer or other Angevin administrative machinery. Perhaps inefficiency, civil war, and spendthrift propensities have obscured Henry's part in financial reform but, we must emphasize, he has not been given due credit for attempting to restore and perfect Angevin financial administration;

this was his goal no matter how much personal weakness and inefficiency hindered its attainment.

The year 1232–1233 saw a buzz of activity at the exchequer. All accountable officials were summoned before Peter de Rivaux, the treasurer of the exchequer, to explain their arrears and to tell why local revenues were not being collected. Severe pressure was put upon the recalcitrant debtors and numerous conferences were held with the king and small council to settle the backlog of money problems. The principal financial records such as the Pipe and Memoranda Rolls attest this activity and monotonously record the phrase *debet respondere* (he should give or offer) following debtor after debtor. Immediately the records were kept more meticulously and early in 1234 Peter laid plans for a thoroughgoing investigation and reform of finances in the counties. Is it any wonder that the barons violently disliked this Poitevin upstart and tumbled him from power before his project got under way? His fall, though interrupting this work, did not end it; in 1236, 1250, 1253, and 1257–1258 he held various offices and exerted influence on continuing financial reform.

For two years after Peter's overthrow as treasurer the exchequer functioned without change. In 1236 it again became the object of reform. Undoubtedly Peter's return to England and temporary restoration to the royal council had some connection with this renewed activity. Innovation now centered about the sheriffs and the farms of the counties. Although numerous sheriffs had been replaced between 1232 and 1234, there was now in 1237 wholesale dismissal and replacement, and reduction in the shrieval powers. Henceforth the lands of the royal domain were kept directly in the king's hands. Two keepers were appointed to administer the royal domain with the goal of increasing its annual income. There remained to the sheriff from the old farm of the county merely the revenues from county and hundred court, frankpledge, and various minor payments such as the sheriff's aid. The sheriff became strictly accountable for this part of the farm and the details of his debts were enrolled on a new record called the *Particule Proficui* (itemized profits). The sheriff was even placed on an allowance to cover the expenses of his office. Shorn of a large part of the county revenue and reduced to strict accounting, the old Norman-Angevin shrievalty was now but a withered plum. The reduced financial power of the sheriff symbolizes the gradual decline of that once powerful stalwart of local administration.

Meanwhile the exchequer at Westminster was undergoing extensive change; it became highly professionalized under deputies of the barons of the exchequer, who seldom attended its meetings. We now meet professional barons of the exchequer in place of such officials as the justiciar and chancellor, who went out of the exchequer. Even under John the chancellor seldom had time to attend exchequer meetings and deputized his clerk, who checked the Pipe Roll and supervised the copying of the Chancellor's Roll, as his representative. This clerk was soon appointed directly by the king and during the 1230's became the most important official. He was known as chancellor of the exchequer and headed that department, a role he still performs. As the chancellor of the exchequer now concerned himself solely with policy and executive business, his former duty of checking the records fell to two royal clerks called remembrancers, who developed great competency in exchequer routine. The remembrancers also assumed the work of the treasurer of the exchequer, who, as he became a grander personage more remote from the daily business, surrendered direction of the exchequer to the chancellor of the exchequer. What had in the twelfth century been a part-time responsibility of great officials of the royal council became in the thirteenth century the full time occupation of skilled professionals.

The court of the exchequer also increased its jurisdiction in royal justice. As one of the central courts of common law there came before it all cases dealing with royal revenue. It adjudicated all financial pleas and investigated financial abuses of royal officers and infractions against royal financial rights. The exchequer, it must be borne in mind, was equally a financial and a judicial court. Its Plea Rolls bulk large in the thirteenth century as litigants increasingly realized that swift justice was obtainable at the exchequer.[1] When the sheriff was reduced to being one of numerous accountants, he relinquished what were termed foreign (*forinseca*) accounts, that is, accounts outside his responsibility. These consisted of the accounts of revenue rendered by escheators and by custodians of castles, honors, forests, and manors, and the accounts of the wardrobe, the customs, such possessions as Gascony, Ireland, and Wales, the profits obtained from vacant ecclesiastical benefices such as bishoprics, and the taxes upon land and movables. Eventually as each of these accounts came to be specially audited the staff of the exchequer had to be expanded.

Abreast with new auditing techniques and records went a program to streamline and lighten the burden of recordkeeping. After 1236 the exchequer resorted to issuing tallies to creditors in lieu of cash payment. The tally was generally so drawn up as to order a collector of some royal revenue to honor it and pay the specified sum to the creditor. The collector then turned the tally in to the exchequer and received proper credit against his account. Such tallies became negotiable. Rather than presenting them to a financial officer, a creditor could transfer them to a merchant-banker and receive his money. The latter would generally charge a commission and eventually turn the tally over to the proper accountant. This practice facilitated credit at many levels and obviated the need for creditors to go to Westminster to secure their money. Actually these tallies were "wooden money" and were a primitive form of the later bills of exchange. To handle the multifarious financial transactions and new forms of income received, the exchequer began to transfer certain categories of business from the Pipe Rolls to other rolls.

[1] SM, no. 54c.

Though some of the new enrollments can be traced back to Henry II and John, only in the 1230's did they become continuous and bulky. The chief records were the Receipt and Issue Rolls, the Liberate and Originalia Rolls, and the Exchequer of Plea Rolls. To relieve the Pipe Rolls of recording old debts to the crown, the Estreat (duplicate) Rolls were begun. On these rolls were customarily listed the fines and amercements imposed in the courts which were to be collected by the sheriffs and sent to the exchequer. Here was an up-to-date account of most of the outstanding debts. On the Pipe Rolls were entered only the total sums collected on these debts by the sheriffs. It seems that the professionals at the exchequer were continually experimenting with new methods to facilitate their work and pare down a red tape that could easily become suffocating. A number of experiments tested under Henry III matured under his son; perhaps if eight years of Henry's reign had not been blotted with civil disorder, many of the financial reforms attributed to Edward would be credited to his father.

During the baronial crisis of 1258–1265 the barons talked much about reforming the exchequer and making it responsible to the will of the realm. But, as with the other organs of central administration, they were less interested in reform than in control of the strategic offices. The inheritance of the exchequer from the civil wars was the virtual collapse of its financial machinery and the outright refusal of many accountants to collect the royal revenue and render it to the exchequer. In their desire to control the royal finances the barons insisted in the Provisions of Oxford that all revenues of the realm must be rendered to the exchequer.[2] If carried out, this reform would have modified the financial administration and, with baronial men staffing the exchequer, would have given the royal opposition considerable financial control. All that resulted was an increase in exchequer disbursements to the wardrobe, and even this system of feeding the wardrobe proved ineffective because the baronial council found it necessary to warrant the payment of some revenue direct to the wardrobe. The Provisions of Westminster in 1259 called for extensive exchequer reform by means of special commissions which were to investigate conditions in the exchequer and the exchequer of Jews (a special treasury handling the financial transactions of king and Jews), and to report fully at the next great council what reform was needed.[3] The only tangible result was the appointment of a commission including the justiciar, treasurer, and three barons to supervise the receipts and expenditures of certain revenues, such as those from wardships and escheats, so as to establish a reserve fund for the payment of royal debts. None of these innovations was lasting because of baronial lack of agreement on how far reform should go, and because war made the routine of government academic.

The aftermath of the civil war was heavy debt and inactivity between 1263

[2] SM, no. 47B.
[3] SM, no. 47C.

and 1268 when the exchequer scarcely functioned. Despite the ambitious work of reconstruction accomplished by the barons of the exchequer during a period of twenty years, recovery was slow; in 1280 the royal income did not yet equal that of the years just preceding 1258. Debts were still being recovered during Edward II's reign. Despite the orderly administration of Edward I his tremendous military efforts further strained the exchequer's resources and necessitated administrative renovation that permanently reduced the jurisdiction of the exchequer. But let us turn now to the details of the exchequer's rehabilitation.

First the barons of the exchequer attempted to untangle the skein that had become the Pipe Rolls. Though the recording of debts had been somewhat relieved by placing many on the Estreat Rolls, too many were still appearing on the Pipe Rolls. So many, in fact, during the early years of Edward's reign that no proper check could be kept. Finally in 1279 the largest and most difficult debts to collect were inscribed on a separate record, called the *Rotulus Pullorum* (roll of offshoots) because it was an offshoot of the Pipe Roll. The Statute of Rhuddlan in 1284 effected more revision of the accounting system. Another roll, the *Rotulus de Corporibus Comitatum* (roll of the farms of the counties), was begun and upon it was entered the old farm (still owing) of the counties plus all subsequent acquisitions of land by the king. After the old farms came the major debts in each county. When such lists became too long to use with any efficiency there arose a new roll—the exannual roll. Henceforth only the farms for which the sheriffs actually rendered account were placed on the Pipe Roll. As a result of the determined work of reconstruction and reform Edward's income almost reached that of Henry III just before the civil war; soon after 1272 all the sheriffs collected the county revenue and scrupulously rendered account for it.

Down to 1297 the exchequer operated on a level of efficiency almost equal to that of the earlier thirteenth century. Then suddenly its annual receipts fell to less than a fourth of the usual income and stayed there for the rest of Edward's reign. One cause for this decline was the increased use of sheriffs and other royal accountants to pay royal creditors directly from their revenues. This technique expedited matters by permitting payment on the spot and by-passing the risks and delays of transporting money to the exchequer. The military exigencies of the Welsh, Scottish, and French wars encouraged this practice because prompt payment of war wages and of supplies was the essence of the success of Edward's numerous campaigns. The second cause for the reduced exchequer income was the growth of the wardrobe as the key treasury of Edward I. It came to receive huge payments directly from such accountants as the sheriffs and to disburse tremendous sums in its capacity of treasury of war. Thirteenth-century financial history actually centers about the phenomenal rise of the wardrobe and its supersession of many traditional exchequer functions. This typical medieval development again proves that the English kings used and built up whatever departments expedited royal government.

2. THE WARDROBE

We have already seen that the nonfinancial functions of the thirteenth-century wardrobe were considerable, yet they are obscured by its financial role. Under John the wardrobe, though remaining subordinate to the chamber, had so developed that it did everything the chamber could do and at times their functions overlapped. The wardrobe had ceased being simply a storeroom for the chamber which in turn had expanded its work beyond the royal household; both chamber and wardrobe had joined the exchequer in public finance. Little is known about either of these household departments between 1216 and 1219 but by 1220 both were operating as they had under John and soon thereafter the wardrobe began to outpace its brother in the financial work accomplished.

Why the wardrobe should supersede the chamber as the principal household treasury is not wholly clear. Tout has suggested that the papal unification of curial financial administration may have had its influence because the pope responsible—Honorius III—was well known by Henry III and Peter de Rivaux. Tout also felt that the chamber was too rigid and antiquated to be adapted to the demands of thirteenth-century finance. Such suggestions are partially true but the key to the wardrobe's pre-eminence seems to be Peter de Rivaux, who, as the principal financial officer of the household in the early 1220's and between 1232 and 1234, became identified with the wardrobe rather than the chamber and decided to make it the nerve center of royal finance. Already in the 1220's significant change was afoot. Payments from the exchequer were increased and beginning in 1227 the yearly wardrobe accounts became regular. The wardrobe had become solely responsible for the household finances and had begun to take a major share in public finance. It paid all sorts of government expenses and, in the words of Tout, was "not only becoming upon occasion a second treasury, but a war office and admiralty as well." By 1234 the wardrobe's ascendancy as the household treasury headed by an officer called clerk, keeper, or treasurer was definitely established. Henceforth the chamber dropped into obscurity, not to emerge again as a prominent institution until the reign of Edward II.

More striking than the supersedure of the chamber as the household treasury was the wardrobe's expanded role in public finance. As the preferred department of Henry's favorite officers, whether foreign or English, the wardrobe was the instrument selected to centralize administration and place it under the personal direction of the king. The exchequer had been out of court too long to be flexible and responsive to the royal will. The wardrobe with its lack of tradition and procedure offered unlimited opportunity for innovation, especially in finance. The characteristics that best describe the wardrobe are malleability and mobility. It could be expanded and contracted to whatever size was necessary to accomplish the business at hand. And it was constantly at the service of the king, accompanying him wherever he went. Ultimately and in theory all the wardrobe's money came from the exchequer, but expediency and convenience caused Henry III and Edward I to employ the wardrobe to accomplish the active financial work. It paid most of the royal debts, it collected much of the royal revenue, and it secured credit and loans. For all these activities, however, it was accountable to the exchequer. The Wardrobe Books or accounts constitute the annual records submitted to the exchequer; along with such others as the Liberate Rolls they provide our best picture of wardrobe activity.

The financial resources of the wardrobe were augmented in three ways. As it moved about the royal possessions it collected revenues directly from the realm; it received regularly large sums of money from the exchequer; and it contracted loans with foreign and English merchants and bankers who were guaranteed future payment with interest at the exchequer or by future receipts from royal taxes such as the wool customs. The wardrobe also requisitioned enormous quantities of supplies, guaranteeing subsequent payment by sheriffs or exchequer. The mobility of the wardrobe made it the obvious department to do the "leg work" of the exchequer, and in its use to facilitate military finance its adaptability is particularly evident. It took a prominent role in all of Henry III's Gascon campaigns. In 1242–1243 and 1253–1254, for example, it went overseas and disbursed funds on the spot. It paid the wages; bought, requisitioned, and disbursed the sinews of war. To keep it supplied with money the Gascon revenues were diverted into it and huge sums were sent from England by the exchequer. The wardrobe also pledged the royal credit for loans payable later by the exchequer. The stationary exchequer remained at Westminster, collecting its ordinary revenues, paying the expenses of the realm, and keeping the wardrobe supplied with money. In fact, the prime function of the exchequer was to maintain the wardrobe at peak efficiency during war. It even purchased supplies and forwarded them to Gascony when the wardrobe's funds were inadequate. During peace the wardrobe staff contracted, but Henry III kept it occupied with a task previously executed under John—purchasing special supplies for household use. Wardrobe clerks traveled about, purchasing food, jewels, silks, and furs, and became heavily involved in purveyance and pre-emption.

There may be some truth in Tout's assertion that the barons tried to wield closer control over the king and his government by making the wardrobe totally dependent upon the exchequer during the crisis of 1258–1265, and perhaps temporarily the wardrobe lost its administrative supremacy, but its recovery was so rapid that under Edward I it reached its apogee. The barons had been unsuccessful in devising a permanent control over the wardrobe and, as previously noted, saw at the same time that it served a necessary administrative function. Though Tout has overdrawn his picture of Henry

III's and Edward I's resorting to the wardrobe to escape baronial control and surveillance, there is indeed some validity to the conclusion that the intimacy of the king with the wardrobe enabled him to exert his prerogative more freely than was possible through the exchequer and chancery, which were somewhat more responsible to the baronage and the community of the realm.

This opinion is supported by the pivotal importance of the wardrobe in Edward I's administrative scheme. If it became a second chancery it became also a first exchequer. A study of the pertinent financial records suggests that between 1295 and 1307 the exchequer practically abdicated the administration and distribution of the national revenue in favor of the wardrobe. But obviously the great military efforts of Edward do much to explain the high pitch of wardrobe activity. The writs of *liberate* suggest that the major portion of exchequer revenue was paid to the wardrobe and that it collected even more revenue directly from the realm. Occasionally wardrobe officers took over exchequer positions to facilitate cooperation between the two treasuries. Credit and loan devices were greatly extended. In lieu of paying for supplies, the wardrobe made out tally receipts which could be turned over to a sheriff or to the exchequer for payment. All sorts of loans were negotiated with Italian, Gascon, and English bankers. Within four years the Ricardi of Lucca loaned £54,000, and between 1286 and 1289 while the wardrobe was in Gascony it negotiated a total of £107,000 in loans. For the multitudinous services that could not be paid for on the spot, wardrobe debentures were devised. The recipient would receive a little strip of parchment, sealed with the personal seal of one of the wardrobe clerks, which recorded the name of the creditor and the nature of the debt. This debenture could be presented later at the wardrobe or exchequer for payment. The recipients of debentures could raise money on them by pawning them to bankers, who were authorized by pledges to sell the debenture at what profit they could make if the loan was not repaid by a specified date. But these financial expedients could not meet the tremendous military requirements of the Scottish and French wars. Arrears piled up alarmingly and the wardrobe fell so far behind in accounting for its receipts and expenditures to the exchequer that the latter lost financial control. The scope of the wardrobe's work was so great that it required depositories for its money and records. This led to the establishment of various storehouses, with the main ones located in the Tower of London and in the crypt of Westminster Abbey. The reputed richness of the treasures at Westminster led to a burglary in 1303 in which even some of the monks of the abbey were deeply implicated.

During the campaigns of Edward the wardrobe functioned almost like a war cabinet and general staff. The household bannerets and knights coalesced with the wardrobe and, as a sort of small standing army and officer corps, directed the recruiting and mobilizing of all forces except those of the feudal levy. These men, who acted as commanders, were supplemented by twenty to thirty mounted serjeants-at-arms, twenty-four archers, and a small force of infantry, all of whom performed duties resembling those of noncommissioned officers. Even the wardrobe clerks mustered and led their own forces. Ralph de Manton, cofferer of the wardrobe from 1297 to 1303, met his death on the battlefield in 1303 while fighting the Scots. For the Scottish campaign launched from Berwick and Carlaverock in 1299, the wardrobe presided over an expansion of household forces from 70 to 750. But fundamentally the wardrobe's main work in war was the finance of war wages and the matériel of war. It did all that is done in modern armies by the quartermaster departments and general staffs.

As an administrative department for the finance and direction of all extraordinary military and civil demands of the government, the wardrobe was the most efficient instrument yet devised by the English kings. It met the demands of Edward I as the exchequer had met those of Henry II. Its malleability, mobility, and constant proximity to the king chiefly explain why it was selected for this work. Untrammeled by custom and rigid procedure it could be adapted to practically any use. It was staffed principally by clerks whose sole loyalty was to the king, within whose power lay their advancement. Utterly devoted to him the wardrobe personnel constantly experimented with new administrative techniques in order to keep their department equal to its burdens. That these men were generally successful in satisfying their royal benefactor and master is proved by the large number who were promoted either to the great state offices or to the leading ecclesiastical positions of the realm. Both Henry III and Edward I favored governing through the wardrobe partly because they escaped the watchful eyes of the suspicious barons and also because the wardrobe accomplished their orders best and most rapidly. Had the chamber or exchequer or another department shown itself better equipped to accomplish the royal will, it would have been selected. Henry and Edward were like their Norman-Angevin predecessors; they governed through the departments that expressed the royal prerogative most effectively. That the wardrobe could and did do whatever Edward wanted is testified to by the Wardrobe Account of 1297, which records the activity of the wardrobe while Edward was in Flanders attempting to launch a campaign against Philip IV of France. Besides caring for the domestic needs of Edward and his household the wardrobe staff gave him counsel, formed his treasury, served as a general staff and quartermaster department, acted as an office of admiralty, and conducted diplomatic relations.

3. THE ROYAL INCOME

By John's reign the ordinary crown revenues had so declined that he resorted to all types of innovation, legal and illegal, to pay the expenses of a government that cost more to operate in an age saddled with inflation. The decline of feudalism and seignorialism had begun, with a resultant drop in the revenues these systems produced. As the money economy became more vigorous, creating new forms of wealth, taxes had to be contrived to tap them. Shrewd administrator that he was, John strove to squeeze more from his old taxes and to supplement them with new ones. So unpopular did his success make him that Magna Carta strictly limited his powers of extraordinary taxation. However bitter the relations engendered between king and crown, a radical transition in the form and base of the tax structure had to come. Perhaps increased scutages, too heavy aids, and such new taxes as the carucage and a percentage on movables were no solution, yet upon this shifting and troubled financial foundation Henry began his reign, and over the question of taxation occurred his bitterest disputes with the baronage.

In the battles that developed neither Henry nor the barons were prepared to make the compromises and concessions necessary. To be sure, Henry legitimately required more money and more extraordinary taxes to cover government expenditures, but his needs could have been scaled down considerably if he had been sensible in his relations with the papacy and the French kings and had not been a witless spendthrift with his foreign relatives and favorites as well as with his intellectual and artistic hobbies. On the other side, the barons should have been practical enough to see that the king could no longer live of his own and that despite their distaste for extraordinary taxes they were inevitable. But out of the struggle over taxation clouding all of Henry's reign and the last decade of Edward's there emerged new taxes that prevailed to the end of the Middle Ages and that provided much of the basis for modern taxation.

Before concentrating on the principal direct taxes it will be well to dispose of the miscellaneous sources of revenue and extraordinary methods used to obtain additional money. Anchored in the king's prerogative were the rights of pre-emption and purveyance. At any market or fair the king had the right of purchasing what goods he desired before all other buyers; this usually worked to his profit because he bought below the normal market price established by the law of supply and demand. All accountable officers of the exchequer, as well as the wardrobe staff and the special buyers of the royal household, had powers to purvey for their royal masters; in time of war the constables and marshal also exercised this power, which permitted them to requisition goods, food, or vehicles of transportation. In theory the items purveyed were to be paid for or restored, but in practice they seldom were, a circumstance that caused a great outcry against purveyance and attempts to regulate it.

Closely akin to such rights was the king's power to demand all sorts of free service from his subjects. All able-bodied freemen were liable to civil and military obligations to be rendered free of cost. When we subsequently describe local government we shall have occasion to see how the freemen of the communities were continually burdened with administrative tasks to be performed gratuitously. They had to attend court, provide police service, assess and collect taxes, and furnish information about their community whenever asked for it. Likewise, according to ancient English custom dating back to the Anglo-Saxon *fyrd*, every able-bodied freeman had to fight for the king, serving in the field without pay and providing weapons according to the worth of his chattels. In an ordinance for the preservation of the peace (1242) Henry III ordered that the land and chattels of all freemen be assessed and that such men should possess "arms according to their [respective] possessions in land and chattels."[4] Edicts of 1230 and 1252 were similar to the ordinance of 1242, which was further elaborated by Edward I's Statute of Winchester in 1285 setting up the system of commission of array. Royal commissioners sent out by the king were empowered to recruit from borough and county quotas of men for military service. They were to select so many archers, men-at-arms, sappers, miners, and other such personnel, and lead them to a place of mobilization. From the time of their selection to the time of their disbandment these men served without remuneration; the basis of their service was allegiance to the crown.[5] Remuneration began to be given towards the end of Edward's reign but it did not become a regular practice until the fourteenth century.

Throughout the thirteenth century, although the vigor of feudalism was fast waning, feudal service owed by virtue of fiefs held from the crown was demanded of the royal tenants-in-chief. The type of service most in demand was still military but as the expense of maintaining knights in the field necessitated the king's accepting reduced quotas, its importance declined. Also, as society became less rude and martial the feudal aristocracy became less accomplished in war and consequently less valuable to the king. Moreover, new military techniques were already combining to make the once proud knight a vestigial organ on the field of battle. The longbow and pike, and soon gunpowder, were to make him as ridiculous as Don Quixote. The core of all armies was to be the footsoldier paid and maintained by royal wages.

If, however, the military value of the feudal aristocracy declined slowly in the thirteenth century, it was counterbalanced by the new obligations imposed. Possessing the most land in each community, the feudal aristocrats had the greatest influence and prestige as well as the administrative experience that comes from estate management. As they shifted from being primarily fighters to landlords so, too, did their royal obligations. As the leading members of local communities these feudal aristocrats were burdened with the administration performed at their own expense and on their own time. Knighthood had, in fact, so lost its appeal that many young men did not aspire to it and by remaining squires (candidates for knighthood) hoped to escape not only knight service but the most onerous of the civil burdens of their community. So many eligible men were taking this course that the kings began to distrain them to take the order of knighthood. In 1224 Henry

[4] SM, no. 46H.

[5] SM, nos. 52E, 50B, C, and D, 46F and I.

III ordered the sheriffs to compel all men holding a knight's fee worth £20 yearly to take knighthood. Like orders continued to be issued by Henry, and Edward followed suit in 1278, 1282, 1292, and 1297.[6] The tendency of Edward's reign was, however, to increase the yearly value of the estate thus excusing many men who otherwise would have been distrained. The alternative to obeying the royal injunction was payment of a heavy fine, an action frequently resorted to rather than accepting the military, civil, and financial obligations of knighthood. In addition to military service the royal tenants-in-chief were still responsible for all the other miscellaneous feudal services, such as suit to court, as well as the pecuniary exactions of the aids and of relief. From the feudal incidents of escheat, wardship, and marriage the kings received valuable incomes which became progressively more valuable as feudalism became less political and military and more economic.

Throughout the thirteenth century one can trace an ascending line in royal borrowing from Italian societies of bankers, Bordeaux and English merchants, and the Jews. To meet pressing and immediate financial needs the kings had to contract loans at high interest which were repayable later by the exchequer or from a future tax or customs duty. There was always a certain amount of borrowing from the Jews, whose freedom from ecclesiastical penalties for usury permitted them to engage in moneylending and pawning activities. But their role as great moneylenders to kings has been exaggerated; the Jews provided much more money through the arbitrary fines and taxes indiscriminately imposed upon them.

The chief bankers of the English kings were the Italian merchants of Siena, Lucca, and Florence who established agents and branches in the principal towns of western Europe in the thirteenth century to facilitate their international banking and trading business. Their role as collectors of papal taxes and lenders to the papacy greatly expedited their international dominance in finance, and obviously mitigated the ecclesiastical penalties ordinarily incurred by this sinful occupation. John secured loans from such bankers, but not until Henry III and Edward I did the Italians begin to operate on a grand scale. For traveling expenses and diplomatic business all royal envoys were provided with letters of credit, which were honored by bankers and merchants from all over western Europe. Henry borrowed heavily from Italian bankers for his Sicilian project. He financed his Gascon expeditions by borrowing from Bordeaux, Poitevin, and Savoyard merchants. Bankers of Lucca acted as collectors of wool customs for Edward I between 1276 and 1292 because essentially most of the receipts went to them to repay the royal debts. Repeatedly Edward borrowed money pledged on a source of income or tax before it was due. In 1280 various bankers from Lucca and Flanders granted Edward a loan on the promise of receiving the tax of a fifteenth granted by parliament. Ten societies of bankers from Florence and

[6] SM, no. 50A.

Lucca received payment from receipts of the wool customs in 1294. And in 1304 the Frescobaldi of Florence were granted all wool customs received from foreign merchants. Ultimately, of course, it was the realm that underwrote these loans, and it was for this reason that the Italian bankers became so hated towards the end of the thirteenth century. Besides loans obtained from professional bankers both Henry and Edward occasionally negotiated loans with Low Country princes, with the pope, and with English bishops, monasteries, and boroughs. With the latter, however, the loans were forced and they could expect little profit. Often the loans ended up as gifts.

4. DIRECT TAXATION

We now come to the principal taxes. We have seen that the scutage was a payment in lieu of military service. Since the time of Henry I the king had been entitled to such a payment from royal vassals when they failed to supply their quota of knight service. The custom of taking scutage was well established by John's reign and was generally collected at the close of a campaign. Though John infuriated his barons by levying so many exorbitant and unwarranted scutages, this form of taxation continued; scutages were levied at frequent intervals down to 1258.[7] Between 1218 and 1258 at least twelve scutages were levied, all at varying rates on the knight's fee. Many scutages were also augmented by fines, paid by the tenants-in-chief, which were regarded as compensation to the king for the loss of men who ordinarily would serve as military commanders. The scutage retained its original character throughout the reign of Henry III and into that of Edward I. It was levied without much difficulty even while Henry III and the barons were struggling over the question of new and increased taxation. During the last few years of Henry's reign, however, there were no scutages, and only three were levied during Edward's reign. This ancient feudal impost was becoming obsolete and had ceased to be remunerative. With the decline of feudalism in the thirteenth century taxes dependent upon the feudal system inevitably depreciated in value. The kings summoned the feudal levy less frequently and when they did, they secured fewer knights than formerly. The cost of putting a fully armed knight into the field had become so great that quotas of knight service had to be reduced. This in turn reduced the number of knights' fees a royal tenant had to pay scutage on and consequently decreased the royal income. The rate per fee was raised, but this could not go on indefinitely in the face of feudal decline. Tied to a system rapidly becoming vestigial in the thirteenth century and tapping only the feudal class, the scutage disappeared. It emerged occasionally in the fourteenth century but after 1385 never appeared again.

Another form of direct taxation that was most remunerative during the reigns of the three Angevins was the tallage. First used by Henry II, it was

[7] SM, no. 46A.

assessed in round sums on boroughs and the royal domain. Tax agreements were struck through individual negotiation with each borough and community of the royal domain; no standard rate was applicable. With certain modifications the tallage remained a principal form of direct taxation during Henry III's reign. Tallages were levied fourteen times between 1217 and 1268, customarily to liquidate heavy royal debts.[8] Under Henry III as under Henry II, tallages were authorized by king and small council; they were authorized because, as the formulas read, the king caused them to be levied. The conventional phrase for authorization of a tallage would read like this: "Because we have tallaged the cities, boroughs, and our demesne generally throughout our realm of England." The clauses of Magna Carta forbidding extraordinary taxation apparently did not apply to the tallage. It was a tax levied by virtue of the royal prerogative. What also seems certain is that the tallage was not an aid (*auxilium*) because the boroughs and royal domain had no right to refuse payment of it. With an aid it was usually assumed that those liable to taxation had the right to refuse.

During the reign of Henry III the method of assessing tallages changed considerably. Teams of royal tax assessors visited the realm, which was divided into circuits of counties. At the beginning of Henry's reign the tax assessors were curial officials or great lords such as William Marshal, but by the end of his reign most were escheators familiar with local financial conditions. The sheriff was usually a member of the tax commission. As the group went to each county of its circuit, it could visit each borough and manor and negotiate with its representatives, or it could go to a central place and meet there with the local representatives. The latter method was preferred by the end of Henry's reign. The tallage under Henry II had been based upon a rough assessment of a man's wealth in both real and personal property, that is, his land, houses, goods, and revenues. Under Henry III the same method prevailed despite periodic attempts to adjust the tallage to the fluctuations in population and wealth. Unfortunately, we are poorly informed about the details of assessment and can only say that the tallage was based on the general wealth of a borough or a manor of the royal domain. In most cases tallages were collected according to the principle of the levy in common, which means that round sums were paid by individual units. Occasionally, however, the royal government introduced the principle of assessing the tax per capita. Each taxable individual then swore to the value of his real and personal property, and a more accurate estimate of a unit's taxable wealth was obtained. But this approach was bitterly opposed, especially by London, and the government had little success with it. Like all medieval taxes, the tallage tended to become stereotyped and to lose its value. It was paid only by units that had customarily paid it; no new manors or boroughs were added to the tallage lists. The tallage came to be a set, arbitrary sum that became ever less representative of the realm's wealth.

[8] SM, no. 46F.

By the close of Henry III's reign the tallage had almost ceased to be a regular part of the royal income. Only one tallage was levied by Edward I, one by Edward II, and one in 1332 by Edward III which was later countermanded. Never again was the tallage assessed. The cause of its decline seems to have been the royal desire to substitute a more remunerative tax in the form of a percentage on movable property. There was no sharp protest against the tallage by the royal subjects; the royal initiative principally explains its demise. We must, however, admit that arbitrary assessment and individual negotiation became less and less popular and increasingly difficult to apply during Henry III's reign. Both boroughs and communities of the royal domain preferred to negotiate collectively with the king and to transform an arbitrary system of taxation into a voluntary one. This transformation can be traced throughout the reign of Henry III. By the time of Edward I the principal form of direct taxation was the aid or percentage on movable property granted to the king by the community of the realm in great councils or in parliaments.

To our remarks on tallage should be added a few words concerning the special tallages levied upon the communities of Jews. This was the chosen method of taxing these unfortunate people, who were completely under the royal protection and at the royal mercy and who had to pay almost any figure demanded of them. Failure to supply the suggested figure could result in banishment and forfeiture of all property, in physical torture, or in lesser penalties. John cruelly exploited the Jews; a tallage in 1210 netted him £44,000. Henry III exacted at least eight exorbitant tallages and Edward I followed suit. For the Jews there was no consent or negotiation; there was but compulsion and dire necessity to pay.

Another Angevin tax, the carucage, introduced during Richard I's reign, was little used in the thirteenth century. It was a land tax, assessed originally on fiscal units called hides or carucates (names for plowland) and eventually upon areas of land. John levied the carucage but once, in 1200, and his son Henry III collected it upon only three occasions—in 1217, 1220, and 1224. The carucages of 1217 and 1220 are of special interest because of the methods employed to assess and collect the tax. In both cases the barons or great council gave consent and it was collected from both laity and clergy. For the carucage of 1217 a group of knights in each county was directed to assess and collect the tax. The sheriff assisted and enforced payment. The money was received by the sheriff and knights and then turned in to the exchequer. In the carucage of 1220 a serious attempt was made to evaluate the land taxed; wasteland, for example, was exempted.[9] This experiment is significant; it marks a step towards taxation on personal property which became the principal form of direct taxation during the rest of the Middle Ages and which ultimately superseded all other forms of direct taxation.

[9] SM, no. 46c.

The novelty of the carucage was that it was a national tax, not one limited to a particular class. In this respect the tax on personal property was like the carucage. Its basis was property and not tenure; no matter from whom they held land or by what tenure, men paid this tax into the royal treasury. Also like the carucage, the tax on personal property was considered one to which those taxed must give their consent. This consent was first given in the great council and later in parliament; in either case action was collective and resulted in creating a uniform tax proportional to the value of property.

Let us now examine the development of the tax on personal property. We have noted that feudal law provided for three fixed aids payable by vassals to their lord. Magna Carta confirmed this custom. The kings were therefore entitled to three fixed aids which they could collect whenever occasion warranted. The new tax did not come from these aids, but rather from the voluntary or gracious aids granted occasionally by royal vassals to the king in order to defray special expenses or debts. Such voluntary aids were granted to Henry II and to his two sons. On a number of occasions we have seen that the aids took the form of a tax on movables, that is, a certain percentage of personal property. In this tax category was the Saladin tithe of 1188, part of the ransom money raised for Richard I, and the famous thirteenth of John in 1207. What is significant about this tax is that a new assessment was made each time the tax was authorized. Consequently, as the wealth of the realm increased, so too did the tax. Even though the tax was nonfeudal, the feudal class had to pay it. Every man, regardless of his status, was liable for the tax if he possessed personal property. This type of property was held in large amounts by the middle class of the boroughs, the class that rapidly accrued wealth in the last three centuries of the Middle Ages, and with it, increased taxes. Resting heavily upon the wealth of the middle class and flexible enough to reflect its steady rise, the tax of a percentage on personal property became the standard tax, voted to king in parliament.

Throughout his reign Henry III supplemented his income derived from the more traditional ordinary and extraordinary revenues with the tax on personal property. In 1225 a great council consented to an aid of a fifteenth on personal property to finance war in Gascony. Though all men entitled to attend the great council were not present, they were bound by the decision, as were other classes of men. The tax was paid by all tenants-in-chief, men of the royal domain, burgesses of the boroughs and cities, clerical tenants-in-chief, and religious houses.[10] Henceforth the percentage, as the tax on personal property came to be called, was levied frequently and at varying rates. The personal property was assessed and the tax collected by empaneled local juries working closely with local officers such as the sheriff and with royal officials sent out from the court. In 1226 a sixteenth was levied upon church property, in 1232 and 1237 a fortieth and thirtieth were levied upon

[10] SM, no. 46D.

laity and clergy, in 1254 a tenth was imposed upon the clergy, and in 1270 lay and clerical tenants-in-chief paid a twentieth.[11] Such evidence indicates that by the end of Henry's reign the percentage and the men who paid it still varied.

Though Edward I levied a fifteenth and a thirtieth on temporal property in 1275 and 1283, not until the second half of his reign did he systematically exploit this tax and experiment to make it more efficient.[12] Seven taxes on movables were levied between 1290 and 1307—the fifteenth of 1290, a tenth and sixth in 1294, an eleventh and seventh in 1295, a twelfth and eighth in 1296, a ninth in 1297, a fifteenth in 1301, and a thirtieth and twentieth in 1306.[13] In 1290, 1297, and 1301 a plan of single rating was employed; all movable property of the realm was taxed at the same rate. This followed the precedent of the Angevins and Henry III. In 1294 someone in the royal government conceived the idea of separating urban from rural districts and assessing the personal property found in the former at a higher percentage.[14] This double system was employed that year and again in 1295, 1296, and 1306. Whenever there were two rates, such as a tenth and a sixth, the rural districts paid a tenth of the assessed value of personal property while the urban districts paid a sixth. Such a graduated rating was just and more remunerative not only because the burgesses possessed greater wealth but because much of it, uncollected from customers and debtors, was difficult for the assessors to uncover. Though it was some time before the double rating system prevailed, it was employed often by Edward II and was regularized under Edward III, when urban districts paid a tenth and rural, a fifteenth.

Another point to be emphasized with such taxation is that it had to receive consent, but the form of consent varied. During the critical and formative period of parliament there was no precise idea that consent to this tax was a function of parliament, consisting of barons, knights, and burgesses. The thirtieth of 1283 was granted in provincial assemblies of knights and clergy. Knights granted the tenth in 1294.[15] Barons and knights consented to the eighth of 1297. And, it should be emphasized, special meetings or convocations of the clergy were becoming the accepted means of raising taxes from the church. On the other hand, in 1275, 1295, 1296, and 1301 the taxes on movables were granted by full parliament. What seems clear is that during Edward I's reign consent to extraordinary taxation was essential but the form in which it was expressed was not yet defined. Full parliaments were at times convened to give consent to taxation but this was not yet considered mandatory, nor would it be until the reign of Edward III.

That the powerful interests of the realm insisted upon consent to taxation

[11] SM, no. 46G.
[12] SM, no. 49D.
[13] SM, no. 49E and F.
[14] SM, no. 49E.
[15] SM, no. 49D and E.

is proved by the famous incident of 1297. In that year, because of his heavy military commitments, Edward I was compelled for the fourth consecutive year to demand a tax on personal property. Such a demand repeated so often was without precedent; nevertheless an irregularly constituted assembly consisting of a few barons close to Edward gave their consent to an eighth and a fifth. Most of the barons, however, supported by the prelates opposed the tax and demonstrated against it in force. With Edward already en route for a campaign on the Continent, the government in England capitulated, summoning the barons and elected knights of the shire to discuss the matter. Led by the great barons, the assembly declared the former grant null and void and consented to a new one of a ninth in return for the royal confirmation of Magna Carta and the Charter of the Forest. Among the clauses added to the Confirmation of the Charters (*Confirmatio Cartarum*) one dealt solely with extraordinary taxation. The essential part reads: "And for us and our heirs we have also granted to the archbishops, abbots, priors, and other folk of Holy Church, and to the earls and barons and the whole community of the land, that on no account will we henceforth take from our kingdom such aids, taxes, prises, except by the common assent of the whole kingdom and for the common benefit of the same kingdom, saving the ancient aids and prises due and accustomed."[16] Fearful that the numerous extraordinary taxes granted under extreme pressure during the past four years might undermine the strong tradition of no extraordinary taxation without consent, the baronage forced Edward to confirm his adherence to this principle embodied in Magna Carta and to spell it out further by swearing that he would levy no tax without the consent of the taxed. This concession advanced constitutional government and the principle of no taxation without representation but did not yet mean parliamentary consent to taxation. The king is still not bound to parliament; he is bound only to get the assent of some body that speaks for the community of the taxed.

The percentage on personal property was the principal innovation in thirteenth-century taxation. Other older and accepted forms of taxation declined and no others experimented with proved as remunerative. One new fiscal device does, however, deserve a few remarks because it was resorted to again late in the fourteenth century. In 1222 a great council granted a poll tax at the rate of 3 marks per earl and 1 per baron, 1s. per knight, 1*d*. per free tenant, and 1*d*. per individual who had chattels worth half a mark. Included were tenants of the church and those residing in cities, boroughs, and on the royal domain. There was no opposition to this new tax but it did not net the government what was anticipated and was consequently not resorted to during the rest of the century. It was, however, a national tax and as such helped to prepare the way for national taxation.

In connection with the discussion of the percentage on personal property

[16] SM, no. 51A.

it was observed that the clergy were frequently made liable. The method used by the royal government to secure a clerical tax was, however, different from that employed for lay taxation. The great prelates—the archbishops and bishops—as tenants-in-chief of the king attended sessions of the great council and gave their consent to taxes for which they, like the other barons, were liable. This was not true for the rest of the clergy—the lower clergy. Taxes had to be obtained by different means. In 1226 when a sixteenth was levied upon the clergy, the pope ordered the clergy to make the grant and the archbishop of Canterbury wrote to all his bishops saying that the papal injunction should be obeyed. Thus it was necessary for the pope to intervene, for the archbishop and bishops to admonish in order to obtain this clerical grant.

Lacking any clerical organization to authorize a uniform tax, each bishop was held responsible for securing approval of his diocesan clergy. This procedure typifies clerical taxation in the thirteenth century. Clerical taxes were almost always obtained from diocesan synods or provincial convocations. Except for a period of experimentation under Edward I when representatives of the lower clergy were summoned to meet along with the barons and lay representatives in parliament, the clergy met in separate assemblies to vote royal supply. In 1254, for example, the bishops were directed to summon their clergy to diocesan synods to consider a grant. In 1280 the diocesan synods of the province of York gave their consent to a tenth. In the same period also developed the practice of convening provincial synods or convocations of the archbishoprics of Canterbury and York. By 1283 the procedure for sending proctors to provincial convocations was regularized. From then on each diocese was represented by two proctors for the clergy and one proctor for each cathedral and collegiate chapter. At these assemblies all sorts of business were discussed, including approval of royal taxes. Later we shall say more about these convocations and their relation to parliament; for now it is enough to have noted that a great council or parliament could authorize a tax but that the lower clergy did not feel bound by any such decision until they had met in their own assemblies and given their approval.

5. INDIRECT TAXATION

Indirect taxes in the form of customs had been collected by the English kings since the twelfth century, but they played no significant part in royal finance until the reign of Edward I. Those that had been levied were frequently nullified by exemptions to boroughs and fairs, or they were granted to local lords. For a time John levied a fifteenth on the value of exports and imports, but the practice soon ceased and nothing is heard about indirect taxation until 1266 when an *ad valorem* customs on foreign trade was imposed. We know nothing about the rate or how long the tax remained in force; there was, in effect, no organization of customs until the accession of Edward I. Previously when the kings desired to profit from foreign trade they had simply seized the merchandise and forced the merchants to ransom it. In 1275 when parliament granted Edward a tax on wool, it laid "the legal and historical foundation" of the customs system. The grant authorized a customs of half a mark on a sack of wool or on 300 woolfells (hides with wool), and one mark on a last (bundle of 200 hides) of leather; this customs was levied on all wool exports.[17] Under pressure of war in 1294 Edward received consent from the merchants to increase the customs; a sack of wool now paid five marks; 300 woolfells, three marks; and leather, ten marks. But within the year the remonstrance of parliament was so strong that the customs was reduced to three marks on the sack or on 300 woolfells, and five marks on leather. In 1297 Edward, desperately needing money, summarily seized the wool of all English merchants and secured what he could for it on the market. Such arbitrary action in the future was prohibited by the Confirmation of the Charters; the wool customs was reduced to the original rate established in 1275.

Edward's need of money was so compelling, however, that he resorted to a new stratagem in 1303. He negotiated with foreign merchants who dealt in exports and imports and agreed to grant them liberal trading privileges in return for increased rates on wool export; the figures set were 40*d.* per sack of wool or per 300 woolfells, and half a mark per last, in addition to the ancient customs of 1275.[18] This extraordinary maneuver infuriated the English merchants, who protested violently against this private agreement. Though the money came from alien merchants, ultimately the royal subjects paid for the increased customs because the import prices rose while the export prices declined. Within the year the English merchants assembled at York and proclaimed their refusal to abide by the agreement. The increase of 1303 was soon called the new customs to distinguish it from the ancient customs of 1275. It was regarded as an evil toll (maltote) whereas the one of 1275 was considered a legal toll. In addition to increasing export taxes on wool the new customs also regulated all other commodities imported and exported. Cloth paid 2*s.* 18*d.*, or 1*s.* on the piece; imported wine, in addition to an old customs, paid 2*s.* on the tun (cask); all other imports and exports paid 3*d.* per sterling pound's value. The duties on wine and miscellaneous goods were models for customs levied in 1373 called tunnage and poundage which served as the basis of indirect taxation for centuries. The English merchants continued to protest the maltote of 1303 and finally, in the Ordinances of 1311, Edward II was forced to declare the new customs on wool and leather illegal. Once more the ancient and legal customs of 1275 became the accepted rate for indirect taxation on wool.

[17] SM, no. 49B.
[18] SM, no. 51C.

6. CONCLUSIONS

In the history of royal financial administration and taxation the thirteenth century was one of innovation. It was an era of flux caused basically by the transition from a feudal and seignorial society to one nonfeudal and nonseignorial. As the money economy prevailed, as money increased in circulation, as liquid wealth gained and landed wealth decreased in value, and as every aspect of life quickened its pulse, new approaches to administration and taxation had to be instituted. The twelfth-century machinery of the exchequer, already antiquated, had to be streamlined to keep abreast of increased revenue and burdens; especially was this true of the exchequer's system of records. Bound as it was to Westminster and the realm, the exchequer proved too immobile to provide the kings with the quick financing needed for the French, Welsh, and Scottish wars. Prodded, therefore, by the royal finger, skilled professional servants of the household developed the wardrobe into a second treasury that on occasion almost superseded the exchequer in scope of financial administration. Mobile and constantly attendant upon the king, it received and disbursed revenue on the spot and became a great war treasury and quartermaster department. Such innovation was not received kindly by the barons, not because they opposed efficient administration, but because they desired to control administration and suspiciously regarded a household department as less easy to control than the exchequer or chancery. This changing relation between exchequer and wardrobe is typical of the bifurcation and duplication that characterized all the departments of English medieval government.

The modification in the tax structure was even more radical. With their foundations crumbling the old services and incomes derived from feudal and seignorial right no longer sufficed. The royal government had to devise new taxes for siphoning the realm's new wealth. The twelfth-century taxes that proved remunerative, such as the scutage, tallage, and carucage, were retained. But eventually, as they became inadequate, they were replaced by the percentage on personal property equipped to tap the new resources of the realm. This tax netted the king an income commensurate with the realm's wealth because each time it was authorized a new assessment of property was taken. To provide an annual and relatively stable income for which he would not repeatedly need to secure consent, Edward I introduced the customs on wool and dipped the royal hand into a resource that steadily increased. But with all these taxes the consent of the taxed was required, and this necessitated consultation with some group that could give its consent and speak for the community of the realm. Negotiation for taxation was the fertile ground which gave root to parliament.

XXVII

Local Government by Royal Command

LOCAL government under the Normans and Angevins had three principal phases. First, the Norman kings so feudalized England that the traditional public functions of shire and hundred were subverted and replaced to a large extent by feudal courts and obligations. Then, under the Angevins, feudalization ceased; it was consciously blocked, especially by Henry II, who saw the danger of permitting too much local government to be executed by royal feudatories. His great innovations in royal justice, his limitations placed over the sheriffs, and his use of itinerant justices and local men to check local maladministration did much to defeudalize local government and to bind it closer to central government. Henry II and his sons put the substantial landholders to work by ordering them to accomplish local tasks. These men reported on judicial proceedings to the central courts, served on judicial and administrative juries, performed police and guard duties, assessed and collected taxes, and did much other work for the king. As a result local government in 1216 was less feudal and more public, but public in the sense that it was more royal, more closely supervised by Westminster, and more administered by local men who acted under royal law and order.

The third phase concerned the boroughs. The economic revival that swept over England in the eleventh and twelfth centuries gave birth to trade, industry, burgesses, and towns. First came the borough as a privileged economic, social, and legal community. Then the borough acquired the right of self-government. By the early thirteenth century the boroughs that had attained self-government were political communities distinct from the organization of county and hundred; they dealt directly with the royal government. At this time, then, there were two local political communities with close ties to royal government—the rural political community consisting of the county and its various subdivisions, and the borough with its peculiar customs and rights. Our task is to examine how further change in the thirteenth century strengthened local self-government and prepared both county and borough to take their place in the national scheme of government through representation in parliament.

I. THE COUNTY

Though the thirteenth-century county was a unit composed of various political divisions and social classes—what the records called "an estate of the community of the shire"—it is best to study the "community of the county" by concentrating upon the sheriff and his tasks. Except in those counties where the shrievalty was hereditary and except for two periods following the Provisions of Oxford in 1258 and the *Articuli Super Cartas* in 1300, the sheriff was appointed in the exchequer by the treasurer; the term of appointment depended upon the royal pleasure. The baronial attempts in 1258 and 1300 to secure election of sheriffs in the county courts represent the feeling that royal favorites and incompetent men were appointed to the shrievalty and that the barons and local landholders suffered abuses from this system. Though election never proved satisfactory, generally from 1258 to 1307 landholders of the county were appointed sheriffs. This is indicative of the strong sentiment that if the sheriff had a stake in the county he would do a more competent and honest job of administration. Despite demand for limitation of tenure to one year, neither Henry III nor Edward I gave ear to it. A longer term of office made the sheriff a more efficient administrator; if limited to a year he would have to leave the office just as he had learned something about its many obligations. The thirteenth-century sheriff was generally a substantial landholder of the county he administered; consistently he was a knight who had been prominent in the local court and administration. The sheriff as well as other officials who shouldered the burden of local government often came from the prominent class of the county, a class distinguished by the lawyer Bracton and others as *busones* (chief persons).

The work of the sheriff and the county may be classified as administrative, financial, and judicial. In an administrative capacity it was the duty of the sheriff, assisted of course by local residents, to make arrests and to guard prisoners. Normally all criminals were taken by the traditional system of frankpledge and hue and cry and were then handed over to the sheriff when he came around on his tourn; ultimately, however, the sheriff was responsible for apprehending and imprisoning them. Whenever an individual was indicted by a jury, presented by a local officer, or appealed by a private person, the sheriff had to make an arrest (the medieval expression is "attach"). The formal accusations and presentments were customarily made in the hundred courts at the sheriff's tourn twice a year, although they could be made at the county court. The individuals arrested were then placed in the county prison, generally the sheriff's castle, to await local trial or trial by royal justices. Closely associated with arrest was distress. All manner of goods were distressed to force men to appear in court, or to make compensation for civil and criminal injuries. It was a common sight to see shrieval subordinates driving cattle to the castle pound.

The execution of royal writs consumed most of the sheriff's time. Early in the fourteenth century the sheriff of Bedfordshire received two thousand writs in seventeen months. The commonest writ dealt with litigation; it entailed that the sheriff secure the presence of litigants in the king's courts to settle disputes falling under the category of pleas of the crown. If litigants failed to comply with the summonses the sheriff would then be compelled to attach goods, perhaps to distrain, and in the last resort to seize the body of a stubborn litigant. Other writs commanded the sheriff to collect royal revenues, summon local troops, and conduct surveys of royal lands and rights.[1] Most of these writs had to be endorsed by the sheriff and returned to Westminster as evidence of fulfilling the tasks enjoined.

Writs constantly came to the sheriff ordering him to empanel juries; we repeatedly read of the sheriff getting together a body of jurors. The juries empaneled were judicial and administrative. One jury might be summoned to give indictments, another to give a verdict in a case of novel disseisin. Juries were empaneled to inquire into injuries against royal right and property. The famous inquest of 1274–1275, which produced the invaluable Hundred Rolls, is an example of the work of such juries. At other times juries had to assess property for purposes of taxation or to inquire into the age of an heir of a royal vassal. When the object of the jury was to investigate and to provide information, the sheriff remained an interested party and ultimately conveyed the findings to the king. But with judicial juries the sheriff's part ended once the jurors had been empaneled.

Another heavy responsibility fell to the sheriff when he was commanded to summon the military forces of the county. Traditionally, as we know, it was an obligation of all freemen to serve the king when summoned and to supply arms according to the worth of their chattels. In fact, since 1181 various royal ordinances had defined not only the military obligations of freemen but also those of villeins; residents of both countryside and borough were burdened with military service, which the sheriff was responsible for producing whenever summoned. The sheriff had to keep lists of men liable for service, conduct periodic inspections, procure supplies, keep royal strongholds repaired and garrisoned, and communicate royal orders to the king's vassals. Some of these obligations were similar to police functions; watch and ward was not only for defense but also for local security. And the military array of the county was at the sheriff's disposal for breaking up bands of thieves and quelling disorder; it was, in fact, the *posse comitatus*. The traditional system of military obligation and recruitment was reorganized in 1285 by the Statute of Winchester, which officially inaugurated the commission of array. Under this system royal commissioners sent out from the court were directed to secure quotas of different types of fighters from each county, assemble them, and lead them to a central mobilization point. The

[1] SM, no. 50.

men recruited were maintained and later paid royal wages.[2] It was this system that provided a large part of the Edwardian armies for the Welsh and Scottish wars. But even with the commission of array the sheriff and his subordinates were responsible for securing the county quotas. By the time the commissioners arrived the sheriffs had already procured most of the men and had at hand lists of men liable for service.

We now come to those tasks of the sheriff that were fiscal. As under the Normans and Angevins, the sheriff's principal financial responsibility was to render the county farm at the Easter and Michaelmas sessions of the exchequer. Before the money owed to the king could be paid into the exchequer, it had to be collected. Payments were received at the county court and at the sheriff's tourn and there was much door-to-door collection by shrieval subordinates—the bailiffs. The customary center of receipt and account was the sheriff's castle where a receiver supervised the collections and accounts. Here accounts were done on the abacus or counting board, and royal debtors were given tallies as receipts for payment. Although the customary payments of the county—the fixed renders—still loomed prominently among the sheriff's accounts, they gradually declined as feudal and seignorial profits sank. This loss was offset by the marked increase in profits from the county court. In 1258–1259 the sheriff of Essex collected £5 12*s.* 7*d.* from litigants for fines, fees, and amercements. And in 1264–1265 sixteen sessions of the county court of Kent produced £79 12*s.* 8½*d.* The sheriff also collected the profits of royal justice, that is, the fees for royal writs and the amercements from men found guilty of trespass or losing suits in the royal courts. Extracts from the royal court rolls—*estreats*—were filled with sums to be exacted by the sheriff. Men with enough money could still reach bargains with the king so as to escape royal justice or to purchase the royal mercy; and all these fines had to be collected by the sheriff. He was the indispensable local servant of the law courts, the exchequer, and the chancery.

A less regular but more remunerative income of the crown was the extraordinary taxes levied by the councils and parliaments. The sheriff had a part in the collection of the scutages, tallages, aids, and percentages either as a designated collector or as an auxiliary officer. He had to empanel assessors and insure that the payments authorized were collected. It must also be remembered that the sheriff had to guard such royal perquisites as treasure-trove and wreck and that he was an important purchasing and spending officer of the crown. He had to furnish supplies for domestic, military, and charitable purposes. He had to keep the royal table supplied with venison from the royal forest, send timber for repair of the royal palace or castle, and requisition and transport grain for use of the royal army. In this latter duty he was carrying out the royal prerogative of prise or purveyance. With proper royal authorization he could purvey whatever the king needed—food,

[2] SM, no. 52E.

transport, or services—regardless of the interested parties' desire and pay for them, if at all, at a later date. In 1252, for example, the sheriffs of ten counties were ordered to purvey and to send to Westminster 76 boars, 60 swans, 72 peacocks, 1700 partridges, 500 hares, 600 rabbits, 4200 fowls, 200 pheasants, 1600 larks, 700 geese, 60 bitterns (small herons), and 16,000 eggs. In 1267 requisitions on ten counties were so heavy that their sheriffs brought "nothing but writs" to the exchequer. Almost as unpopular as purveyance of supplies was the requisition of services for the construction and repair of royal buildings, roads, and bridges. The system of purveyance was resorted to so often and was so open to local extortion that it became one of the chief complaints of barons and parliament in the late thirteenth and fourteenth centuries.

A discussion of the sheriff's judicial functions is actually a study of the courts he held—the county court and the tourn. Though traditionally since the Anglo-Saxon period the county court had assembled twice a year, by the thirteenth century some courts met every six weeks and most convened monthly. By the reign of Edward I monthly meetings were the rule. In addition to the regular sessions there were special ones, ordained by the royal writ, for royal judicial and administrative business. Special sessions were ordered to meet the itinerant justices when they came to the counties on their eyres; the eyre was in practice a session of the county court. When special taxes were levied special courts were convened to assess and collect them. In 1220, for example, the sheriffs were ordered to assemble their county courts for the purpose of electing two knights to assess and collect a carucage.[3] The fifteenth of 1225 was collected in the same manner. We must also make a distinction between what was termed a great county court (*magnus comitatus*) and a full county court (*plenus comitatus*). The former consisted of the two courts that met every six months and that stemmed back to the Anglo-Saxon period; more suitors were obliged to attend these courts than the monthly sessions. The latter court was an open public session attended by men under customary obligation and was generally convened by royal writ to hear the king's proclamations, such as statutes, to attend to his business, to hear accusations of crime, and to witness the installation of local officers. Usually when the king ordered men to be selected or elected for some royal task it was done *in pleno comitatu;* in such a fashion were knights selected to represent their county at parliament. The regular sessions of the county court lasted but a day; the special ones could sit for an extended period.

The meeting place of the county court was determined by ancient custom though at times royal charter designated where the court would convene. It was useful to have a customary place of assembly because the suitors would know where to go and the traders could take advantage of the influx of

[3] SM, no. 46c.

people. Throughout the thirteenth century some county courts met out in the open. The Hundred Rolls tell us that Essex county court met in a green place in Chelmsford hundred. According to Bracton, however, the customary meeting place was the sheriff's castle located in the chief borough of the county. But in the latter part of the thirteenth century we hear frequently of specially erected shire halls or halls of pleas upon heaths and green places, and they gradually superseded the castle.

Attendance or suit to county court was a duty resting upon certain men, or to be more exact, upon certain lands of the county. Because of the burden of attendance numerous landholders purchased or secured exemption from suit to court. This practice makes it difficult to determine what men in the thirteenth century actually owed suit to regular sessions of the court. We are sure that not all freeholders were bound to attend and that only certain men received summonses through the sheriff. Perhaps feudal obligation accounted for suit to court in the eleventh and twelfth centuries but not completely in the thirteenth century. We must envisage the typical county court as a mixed body of knights, freeholders, and villeins. Customarily lords performed suit through their stewards and any freeman could perform it by attorney. We must agree with Maitland when he said that in general the regular county court "was formed of miscellaneous elements; there were tenants by military service and socage tenants, tenants-in-chief of the king and tenants of mesne lords, great and small men." What can be said is that the individuals who generally owed suit to regular sessions were the gentlemen—the great lords, knights, squires, and substantial freeholders—who had not secured exemption. When special sessions or full county courts were convened to hear royal pleas or perform royal business, the sheriffs were empowered to summon men who did not customarily attend. They summoned the great prelates (bishops and abbots), all laymen who held land by feudal tenure (earls, barons, and knights), free tenants, four law-worthy men and the reeve of each manor (agrarian community), and twelve law-worthy burgesses of each borough. When royal pleas were heard the presence of twelve men from each hundred was required in order to make presentments.

Contemporary descriptions of the county court at work are rare. One for Lincolnshire in 1226 does reveal a few intimate glimpses. When the sheriff was ready to begin the session, he summoned the suitors about him and took his seat to preside. The causes for the term were then called up and after they had been heard all day there still remained seven score. The sheriff presided and the suitors found the judgments, which dealt largely with the allotment of proof. The accepted proof of the county custom was still compurgation, ordeal, and the duel. Once the proof had been undergone the suitors handed down a sentence in accordance with the county law; the procedure was little different from the Anglo-Saxon where the doomsmen deemed the dooms. When the county court dealt with pleas of the crown proceedings were only preliminary. Occasionally, but not regularly, presentment juries indicted men to the sheriff and some crimes were still prosecuted by the old process of private accusation, known technically as appeal. Private appeal was, however, cumbersome because of the pledges required for prosecution and because of the numerous legal steps involved. Appeals of felony might be sued also in the county court and there still occurred presentment of Englishry. In addition to these legal transactions, upon rare occasion the king authorized the sheriff to try a criminal plea of the crown. The county court also pronounced outlawry against those who failed to appear in court for a criminal or civil case.

The civil jurisdiction of the county court had steadily lost ground before the royal courts in the twelfth century and by the thirteenth century was limited to personal actions in causes involving no more than 40s. Most civil actions were quite petty. There were pleas of trespass and debt, of unjust caption and detention of beasts; and some lords resorted to replevin (recovery) proceedings to collect rents. To expedite civil justice the sheriffs were empowered to preside over certain causes that exceeded 40s. Proceedings under the writ of right, for example, were instituted in the county court and ordinarily continued there unless the grand assize was invoked. Fugitive villeins and their goods could be claimed in the county court, and the sheriff was empowered to hear numerous complaints concerning nuisances and encroachments. These cases indicate the great extent of the civil jurisdiction of the county court even in the late thirteenth century. Convenient, held frequently, and simple in procedure, the county court appealed to the common folk.

As far back as the Norman Conquest and perhaps earlier, the sheriff had toured his county twice a year visiting every hundred where he was not excluded by royal franchises enjoyed by private lords. This was known as the sheriff's tourn, which on a small scale resembled the eyre of the itinerant justices. When the sheriff arrived at the hundred he was met by four men and the reeve of each agrarian community, who fulfilled the customary obligations. Four functions were accomplished on the sheriff's tourn: the sheriff and the coroners received indictments for pleas of the crown, the sheriff tried minor offenses that fell under his jurisdiction, steps were taken for the apprehension and custody of individuals accused of infracting royal law, and the frankpledge groups were investigated to see that each tithing was full and that all of age were in frankpledge. When the sheriff received criminal indictments two steps were involved. First each township (agrarian community) reported offenses to a jury of twelve freemen who formally presented all offenses of the hundred under various categories called articles of the tourn. The sheriff had no jurisdiction over the serious offenses; they were enrolled on the Coroners' Rolls and were held for trial by the itinerant justices. The sheriff's judicial power was wielded only over petty offenses such as encroachment on public land, brewing and baking contrary to government regulations, and use of dishonest weights and measures. Beyond these judicial proceedings the tourn served as a check upon local police organization and a means for the collection of customary revenue of the hundred.

Under the Angevins there arose local officers who began to exercise some of the sheriff's powers and to serve as a check upon him. At least since 1194 and perhaps since the latter part of Henry II's reign each county was served by two, three, or, more customarily, four coroners, who kept (investigated and recorded) pleas of the crown. Elected at the county court the coroners were county gentlemen like the sheriff; they were therefore men of some local repute, independent of the sheriff, and were his colleagues rather than his subordinates. They served for life or until no longer able to perform their demanding tasks. In cases where lords possessed extensive royal franchises, crime and violence on their land was investigated by their appointees, called "coroners of liberties." The chief role of the coroner was to keep a vigilant eye on the sheriff and to maintain a record of all crimes and actions that impinged upon royal law or right. An intriguing picture of the coroner at work is provided by the Coroners' Rolls, which began to be kept regularly and filled copiously during Henry III's reign. They show coroners present at the execution of thieves caught red-handed, at pronouncements of outlawry, at appeals of crime in the county court, and at the presentment of crimes. Whenever and wherever in the county there were violent, mysterious crimes and events the coroner had to proceed to the scene, hold an inquest, and report the findings on the Coroners' Rolls, thus providing the legal record upon which the royal judges acted at the eyres. Another obligation that weighed heavily upon the coroner was to deliver fugitives from sanctuary and to send them out of the realm. Customarily fugitives from justice were immune from arrest while in a church; there they would remain until arrival of the coroner, who would officially order them to abjure the realm by a specified date and at a stipulated seaport. The fugitive could return only if he received the royal pardon.

Another official colleague of the sheriff was the constable, whose chief task was the custody of royal castles in the county. Though the records tell of imprisonments and arrests by constables, it is clear that their major concern was with local military affairs; they were directly responsible for the defense, repair, and provisioning of the king's castles and were empowered to secure county recruits and supplies for the royal army. The other local officers who worked along with the sheriff were just coming into prominence towards the end of the thirteenth century. Called keepers of the peace (*custodes pacis*) they seemed to be appointed to help maintain county peace during periods of emergency such as civil war. They are first heard of during the hostilities between Henry III and the barons in 1264–1265 and were instructed to keep order. Into the fourteenth century these keepers of the peace were primarily local police captains who exercised their powers to keep violence and disorder at a minimum. In a way these men assisted the sheriff in keeping the peace and, like the coroners, served as a check upon his power.

Faintly discernible in their police duties, however, is one which was to make the keeper of the peace primarily responsible for the local administration of justice. In 1277, for example, when Edward I ordered the knights of the shire to elect a local knight as keeper of the peace it was stipulated that this knight would remain in the county and not serve on the projected Welsh campaign; he was to hold inquests into the keeping of the peace. Here we see the first step of a transformation that was to turn the keeper of the peace into the justice of the peace of the fourteenth century.

2. THE HUNDRED

Though each county of England had been subdivided into hundreds and wapentakes prior to the Conquest, subsequent feudalization of local government had deprived sheriffs of authority over numerous hundreds which fell under the control of feudal lords. It has been estimated that when Edward I became king there were 628 hundreds, of which 270 were royal and 358 private. That so many hundreds had become private was owing to royal charter, prescriptive right, and usurpation. It was to ascertain how and by what right lords had acquired such political authority that Edward I ordered his famous inquest of 1274–1275. Generally the Hundred Rolls supply the answers. The point to be emphasized with royal and private hundreds is that the sheriff had little or no authority in the latter. The degree of shrieval authority depended usually upon the terms of the royal charter. In some hundreds the sheriff and his officers had no right of entry; in others he could only make his tourns; and in still others he wielded more extensive power. The position of the sheriff became extremely confused when political and judicial rights in a hundred were divided among three or four lords; with each lord the relations of the sheriff would be different. But whatever the relations and powers of the sheriff in regard to private hundreds, he had certain responsibilities and had to make reports to the royal justices and the exchequer. He had to account for certain revenues owed to the king and to enforce the royal commands. For example, all royal rents and dues, all presentments of royal pleas at his tourn or at the private leets of the lords had to pass through the sheriff's hands. Though a few of the greatest liberties, as for example the boroughs, dealt directly with the royal administration, in general the sheriff was the middleman through whom administrative and judicial matters of private hundreds had to funnel.

Both king and lords were jealous of their political and judicial powers in the hundred. This jealousy stemmed fundamentally from their interests in the hundredal revenue called the "value," which consisted of the profits of the hundred court and of the perquisites and customary payments owed at specified times. In the greatest liberties the lords kept all the profits; in all others the king and local officials each received a share. The hundredal farms, whether from private or royal hundreds, represented a rough estimate of the annual income paid by the responsible officer, usually the bailiff, to the sheriff or to the lord, less the amount deducted for the bailiff's work. We may be certain that king and lord always got their due and that the bailiff always got considerably more than his fair share at the expense of the local residents. Private hundreds, we may conclude, spread the "value" out among more hands and opened more doors to extortion and corruption, but whether private or royal the hundred was controlled in the last resort by the king, whose writs held in all hundreds and whose ultimate sovereignty had to be respected.

Both royal and private hundreds were directly administered by bailiffs sworn to execute their office loyally on behalf of the king and sheriff and, in case of private hundred, on behalf of the lord. In royal hundreds the sheriff appointed the bailiff; in private hundreds the interested lords appointed him. As much as possible bailiffs were selected from solid and respectable landholders of the community; if they were clerks who could read and write, so much the better. To assist with the burden and routine the bailiff had a considerable staff composed of clerks, bedels, subbedels, serjeants, and messengers. The great protest of all hundreds was that there were too many of these obnoxious and greedy officers, who in our time would be the bureaucrats of political machines. The primary function of the bailiff's staff was execution of the administrative and fiscal orders of the sheriff. Though the number of agrarian villages varied in the hundreds it has been estimated that a bailiff had to administer the affairs of ten to twenty villages.

The chief responsibility of the bailiff was to preside over the hundred court, which by Edward I's time was meeting every three weeks. Custom and tradition dictated that the court was held at a particular village; the sessions were conducted under cover of some hall. To these courts came about forty or fifty men, both suitors and litigants. As with the county court, various lands were obligated to send suitors to court. When the sheriff made his tourn at the great hundred court held at Easter and Michaelmas, more suitors were required to attend. On these occasions the tenurial obligation was supplemented by the communal; each village had to send the reeve and four men, normally villeins, to represent it.

In the thirteenth century the hundred court continued the judicial decline begun in the Norman period. Royal and private courts had siphoned off most of its jurisdiction. A description of 1234 stated that the legal business of the ordinary hundred court consisted of pleas of battery and brawls not amounting to felony, of wounding and maiming beasts, and of debts collectable without royal writ. To such petty legal business can be added that of trespass. In addition to these judicial proceedings some hundred courts held regular inquiries into the keeping of the assizes of bread, ale, and measures; others witnessed presentments made by the village tithings. Here, too, occurred transfer of lands before witnesses and the proclamation of royal orders and statutes. Such jurisdiction was a far cry from that of the Anglo-Saxon period when the hundred was one of the principal public courts and entertained more causes than the shire court. In the thirteenth century only the sessions at Easter and Michaelmas when the sheriff made his tourn constituted really major hundred courts.

The hundred of the thirteenth century was still an essential link in police and military administration. Police and military obligations were barely distinguishable and were the responsibility of a high constable of the hundred. In 1242 Henry III ordered that for each agrarian village there should be two constables whose duty was to muster all men of their community liable for military service and to present them for periodic inspection held by the sheriff and two specially appointed knights from each hundred. The same enactment clearly states that this military force is also responsible for keeping the watch and participating in the hue and cry.[4] The posse of the hundred (*posse hundredi*) was a military and police organization which carried out its functions by virtue of the allegiance and obligations owed by all men to their lord the king. The high constable of each hundred kept a list of men liable for service and the equipment that they must supply. There was consequently a reasonably efficient military and police organization for village, hundred, and county, and it was this system that Edward I worked into the commission of array when he revamped the military organization of the realm by the Statute of Winchester in 1285.

3. THE FEUDAL UNITS OF THE COUNTY

Turning now from the public circumscriptions of local government—the county and hundred—we come to the feudal units of the counties which were controlled by the king, by his tenants-in-chief, or by subvassals. In each county, as we know, the king held extensive estates of land or manors which comprised the royal domain. The amount of royal land varied from county to county but a cursory examination of the pertinent thirteenth-century evidence, the Hundred Rolls, shows that the royal domain had markedly shrunk in the two hundred years since 1066. This decrease was caused by lavish grants, by sale, and by other agreements whereby the crown parted with its land.

In the thirteenth century, however, much land yet remained to the crown and was administered by the sheriffs until the middle of Henry III's reign. In 1242 the royal manors were taken away from the sheriffs and given to officers called escheators. By 1275 there were two escheators for the realm, one responsible for royal land north of the River Trent and the other for that south of the Trent. For each county there was a subescheator. The escheators occupied themselves solely with the management of royal land and land that came temporarily to the king or escheated to him permanently. Whenever a tenant-in-chief died it was the duty of the county escheator to

[4] SM, no. 46H.

occupy the fief of the deceased and to administer it until the heir acquired formal possession. If the heir was of lawful age and paid the stipulated relief, he received immediate possession; if he was a minor, the escheator managed the fief until he attained legal age or until the royal right of wardship was sold to some individual. If there were no legal heirs, the fief escheated to the crown and was administered by the escheator.

Administration of royal land was simple and routine; so, too, was that of the fiefs possessed by royal vassals. But there was considerable strife and complication over the judicial and public powers wielded by lords over their fiefs and the hundreds in which they were located. This had always been a point of contention between the kings and their barons but the whole question was exacerbated by Edward I when he initiated the *Quo Warranto* proceedings of 1274–1275 in order to ascertain how much royal judicial and political power was illegally held by his tenants-in-chief. The royal attitude was that if a lord could show warrant for the exercise of royal legal and political power, it should be retained; but when no warrant could be produced, it should be surrendered. We shall discuss the *Quo Warranto* proceedings later; our reference to them at this point is to emphasize that it was accepted custom, antedating the Conquest, for lords to exercise such rights.

There were a few great feudal lords with liberties (royal franchises) that gave them regalian powers. Such powers, for example, were enjoyed by the bishop of Durham, the earl of Chester, and some of the Welsh marcher lords. Almost as exalted were the powers possessed by the abbots of such abbeys as Glastonbury, Ramsey, and Bury Saint Edmunds. On these lands royal justice was dispensed but it was administered by nonroyal officials so that all the profits went to the lords. Less extensive but still lucrative judicial rights were ordinarily held by five or six leading lords in a county. The earl of Clare, for example, did not permit a sheriff on his lands; he executed all royal writs, exercised the right to hang thieves on his gallows, and enforced the royal assize of bread and ale. Legally and illegally the earl of Clare had withdrawn suitors from royal hundreds to his court. Below such a lord as the earl of Clare there were in each county many lesser lords with less exalted powers, each of whom held a court and invariably exercised some justice that was royal. These lords justifiably held seignorial (manorial) courts for their villeins and free tenants and here enforced local custom. Legally or illegally, however, they had added to this simple justice some of the king's, the most common of which was the enforcement of the assize of bread and ale and the view of frankpledge. Below these lords were others more humble who exercised only seignorial rights. By the end of the thirteenth century this right was little valued because so many peasants were obtaining freedom and, with it, the right to trial in royal and public courts.

Besides jurisdictional liberties, many lords enjoyed those we may call administrative. Some of the proud earls and abbots possessed gallows to hang thieves, prisons to guard criminals until trial, and the pillory and tumbril for punishment of petty crimes. Even more prized was the right to levy royal debts and to execute royal writs; this freed the lord from any interference by royal officers. Finally, there were the fiscal privileges, consisting mainly of the perquisites and profits from the court. In some cases lords did not hold public justice but participated in the profits from public courts and received a percentage from the sheriff. Numerous lords had the right to hold markets, and some, to hold fairs; both privileges netted lucrative fees. Fortunate indeed was the lord who possessed regalian power, or even the lord who possessed but a few rights. With all such royal franchises went the obligation of exercising good government for the king; if a lord failed in this responsibility his penalty was forfeiture of royal judicial and political power.

The century composed of the reigns of Henry III and Edward I witnessed a profound change in county and hundred. Both continued to decline as autonomous legal and political units and were lashed ever more firmly to the central government which continued to spread out the tentacles of its power. By 1307 local government had in fact become royal government carried on by officials of county and hundred appointed by the king or elected locally, and by juries of responsible residents. Local government was controlled by the local landed oligarchy of sheriff, coroner, bedel, subbedel, summoner, and juror. But ever behind and above such men was the king with his council, exchequer, central courts of common law, and itinerant justices who placed all local government under constant surveillance. Though both county and hundred lost in local autonomy, they were still essential links in the government of the realm because their residents provided, albeit by royal command, all the government there was except for that on the central level.

4. THE BOROUGH

Borough government was local like that of the county and hundred but it must be treated separately because it differed from rural organization and never became a regular unit of county administration in the Middle Ages. Borough government also differed widely from one borough to another. The municipal institutions of the borough were at various stages of development and were governed by local peculiarities. Variation in the institutions and chronological lags in development explain why borough government is so obscure and complicated. Stubbs almost pleaded ignorance of borough history and Maitland stated in one of his famous dicta that the history of the borough could not be written. This statement, though perhaps too strong, underlines the difficulty of studying municipal institutions.

We are little concerned with the social, economic, and legal privileges of the borough and need only to emphasize that the single element common to all boroughs of the thirteenth century was burgage tenure, which bestowed these special privileges upon the burgesses. We are interested rather in the relation of the borough to local and royal government and in the development of municipal self-government. The period when real self-government began and spread among the boroughs was during the reigns of Richard I and John. London, it will be remembered, became a commune in 1191, and John bestowed communal privileges on numerous boroughs such as Winchester, York, Bristol, and Ipswich. Borough self-government continued to expand under Henry III and Edward I although they granted fewer charters than their predecessors. This does not mean that their attitude towards self-government was like that of Henry II, but that they received fewer applications or demands from boroughs for what had been so coveted under the Angevins.

Though it is vain to look for any uniform type of municipal government, one feature is characteristic of all boroughs—government was customarily exclusive and oligarchic. Standards of wealth plus various social requirements limited all important offices to a small percentage of the citizens. The large and older boroughs tended to be more oligarchic, but in all the qualifications were such as to bar ordinary residents from office and even from the franchise. In some boroughs a burgess had to pay a certain amount in annual taxes to be qualified for the vote. In others he had to own so much land or at least the piece of land upon which he resided, or he had to be a member of the guild merchant or craft guild. And in yet others he had to fulfil all these qualifications. It is certainly safe to say that borough government was not democratic.

The amount of judicial and political independence held by the boroughs varied extensively. Some of the leading boroughs were almost independent of royal interference while others had to grant entry to all sorts of royal officials. But however self-governing, none became as powerful and independent as the great towns of Flanders, Italy, and Germany. The king's officers may not have interfered in the internal politics of some of the leading boroughs, but the royal sovereignty was completely respected. The greater boroughs of the thirteenth century secured the privilege of farming their revenues; that is, they were permitted to assess and collect dues and taxes owed to the king and to account for them directly at the exchequer. Most boroughs received the privilege of exempting their citizens from pleading outside the boroughs. For the settlement of minor criminal and civil actions the burgesses went to the borough court with its custom and procedure. Borough law was quite different from county and royal law. For example, borough law permitted land to be bequeathed by will whereas the common law rejected this action. On the other hand much borough law was archaic in substance and procedure, but the burgesses clung to it as a matter of local tradition. Most boroughs were exempt from attending the county and hundred courts and even appeared as distinct groups before the itinerant justices when they came to the county court on their eyres. On these occasions each borough had to send twelve burgesses to represent it and all burgesses involved in royal pleas had to appear as litigants before the royal justices. For military and police duties the boroughs also had a responsibility to the county. To preserve the peace the sheriff was empowered to enforce watch and ward in the boroughs and to forbid tournaments and events that might incite riot. All burgesses were liable for military service and were governed by the old Assize of Arms of Henry II and the new commission of array inaugurated by Edward I. All local details were handled by borough officers elected by the burgesses.

A municipal magistracy elected by the burgesses was the most essential of all the attributes of self-government. By 1216 more than a dozen boroughs had obtained this coveted right and during the thirteenth century the process of urban incorporation continued. A typical borough council generally consisted of a mayor, who not only represented the borough community but also served as a sort of administrative officer for the king, and twelve or twenty-four aldermen elected or selected by various methods depending upon the character of the municipal constitution. Most boroughs also had seals to legalize their acts and to symbolize their corporateness. Only the greatest boroughs such as London had the right to elect their own sheriffs and to exclude royal officers. Many boroughs, however, had the right to return royal writs, which meant that borough officials executed the royal orders and so signified their action when they returned the writ to the proper royal officers. Some twenty boroughs obtained this right from Henry III between 1252 and 1257.

These judicial and political rights were enjoyed in varying degree by all the important boroughs but, as we have noted, did not extend to all boroughs. Down to the reign of Edward I all urban communities regardless of size were called boroughs if they possessed the privilege of burgage tenure. Whether new or old, royal or seignorial, this was the case and no attempt was made to classify them. On several occasions, notably in 1275 and 1283, an effort was made to sort out the larger boroughs from the smaller.[5] Royal writs directed the sheriffs to send representatives from "boroughs" and from "merchant towns" to meet in parliament with the king. The latter apparently signified the small boroughs and those without advanced political privileges. But unfortunately this distinction did not continue to be made, and when the king wished to consult with representatives from urban communities, his writs indiscriminately ordered the boroughs to send representatives to meet with him. Consequently, the number of urban communities considered boroughs increased in the latter part of Edward I's reign. But the lack of distinction contributed to much confusion, especially with taxation. If a community was considered a borough its royal tax rate was higher than if it was taxed as a part of the county. It will be remembered that the tax of a percentage eventually came to be a tenth on boroughs and a fifteenth on the

[5] SM, no. 49A and D.

counties. Invariably, local and royal officials differed as to what communities should be placed on the list of boroughs. Ultimately, though not during Edward I's reign, the problem settled itself; the small boroughs and most of the seignorial boroughs were unable or unwilling to send representatives to national assemblies and to assume all the financial burdens involved. They considered parliamentary representation a reward incommensurate with the burdens entailed. In the fourteenth century the number of boroughs decreased; the small ones came to be taxed along with the county and, in the process, lost some of that urban exclusiveness that had set them apart from the countryside.

The problem of what constituted a borough was part of a larger problem of the thirteenth century. In its dealings with the boroughs the crown was undecided whether to treat them as independent bodies or as parts of the community of the county. For purposes of taxation it dealt separately with the greater boroughs but in other matters it was never certain whether to go directly to the boroughs and ignore county organization or to work through the latter. In 1265 when desiring to consult with their representatives, Simon de Montfort addressed his summons directly to certain boroughs; his plan was followed by Edward I in 1283 when he dealt directly with the boroughs and, in deliberation with their representatives, enacted the statute *De Mercatoribus* at Acton Burnell.[6] But ordinarily Edward I and his council found it more convenient to deal with the boroughs as parts of the counties, and therefore when consultation with the boroughs was desired writs for the election of representatives were customarily sent to the sheriffs, who saw to it that the boroughs elected two burgesses to represent them in parliament. This development partially explains why the burgesses and knights of the shire eventually coalesced into the estate of the commons.

5. LOCAL SELF-GOVERNMENT BY ROYAL COMMAND

Though the expression "self-government at the king's command" is a contradiction in terms, it is by now evident that local government on county, hundred, and borough level was largely carried on by the residents themselves. Outside the boroughs the country gentry were performing the tasks of local government and were, in effect, unpaid royal officials. The judicial services required by royal itinerant justices and by county and hundred courts touched virtually all freemen of the county. Many were suitors, jurors for grand and petty juries, or compurgators; almost all were called upon to act as sureties and witnesses. The police obligations fell upon all. Freemen and villeins were within frankpledge and were constantly responsible for the lawful behavior of the members of their tithing; the hue and cry was for all a weekly routine. Local men had to keep the peace and when the king went to war all freemen were liable to serve him with weapons according to the

[6] SM, nos. 48C, 49D.

worth of their chattels. The administrative duties were numerous. As jurors the local residents had to give the king answers to a variety of questions. What was the value of this estate, what royal buildings were in need of repair and how much would be the cost, what were the royal rights here, and what usurpation of royal power had occurred there? So the questions ran. When royal taxes were levied, local men assessed and collected them. All residents served as detectives who checked upon the royal officers. The sheriffs, hundred bailiffs, coroners, and all other officers were local men and checked upon each other. Except for the sheriffs, bailiffs, and their subordinates, none of these men were paid. They did all that they did because it was the king's command. Whatever they did was subject to the inspection of the royal council, the exchequer, the common law courts, and the gimlet-eyed itinerant justices. As the historian A. B. White has said, "The king's justices were umpires, but the people had to play the game." And Helen Cam has aptly stated: "Whichever line of local administration you follow you find the king at the end."

But on the other side of the coin was a picture of knights, squires, and freemen who for generation after generation had performed the king's work and had become experienced in its ways. They had become practical, hard-headed administrators and politicians who knew the business of government. When called to negotiate with the king in parliament and to represent the will of their community such men had the experience and tradition to bargain successfully and eventually to translate the expression "with the consent of the community of the realm" into a reality. Long and arduous labor for the king had paid off on the national level and had contributed to make parliament a success. In their development of local government by royal command the kings had unwittingly trained a class of men who ultimately cooperated with the baronage to limit royal authority and to transform England into a constitutional monarchy. This rapport between central and local government, which never developed in the leading states of the Continent, is one answer to why medieval England alone gave birth to successful constitutional government.

XXVIII

The Evolution of Parliament

OF THE ten centuries that separate the years 450 and 1485 two loom preeminent for the constitutional progress of medieval England. The twelfth century saw the rise of efficient central government and the foundation of the common law system. The thirteenth century witnessed the remarkable growth of the common law and, what truly dominated the history of this century, the formation of that institution called parliament, the supreme achievement of medieval England. However essential were the central and local organs of government and however admirable the common law and its principles, they were but subordinate and supporting elements—the flying buttresses and columns—of the great Gothic cathedral that was parliament. All medieval English institutions were bound to and supported this crowning edifice. Though the local and central institutions and the common law system enabled parliament to take root, their survival and efficiency, and in fact successful constitutional government, rested upon a strong and dynamic parliamentary system. Without the rise of parliament in the thirteenth century and its growth in the following two centuries the previous seven centuries of institutional and legal development would have been in vain. Without parliament England undoubtedly would have emerged from the Middle Ages like the principal states on the Continent, saddled with absolutism until the nineteenth century.

The English parliament and its later counterparts in western Europe have ever been the targets of criticism from the conservative right and the radical left. The critics of the right, generally the advocates of unlimited monarchy, dictatorship, or some form of strong-man rule, have charged that parliamentary government was inefficient, cumbersome, and wasteful. The critics of the left, notably the communists and affiliated political faiths, have bitterly denounced parliamentary government as the citadel of the wealthy bourgeois oppressor and as the chosen instrument to oppress the common man. Though on the Continent such attacks have brought down and continue to bring down parliamentary democracies, this has never been the fate of the English parliament. Amidst criticism, even during the darkest moments of England's history, it has continued to prosper. It stands as western Europe's oldest and most convincing evidence that parliamentary government guarantees the greatest amount of individual liberty. Parliament is a living testimony to that famous dictum of Lincoln that those people are the best governed who govern themselves. It has proved itself through the centuries and though Thomas Carlyle, if writing today, would win adherents to his cult of the great man in history, he would probably win fewer than he did in the nineteenth century when he described the House of Commons "as six hundred talking asses, set to make laws and to administer the concerns of the greatest empire the world had ever seen."

Our task in the following pages will be to inquire into the origin of parliament, into its composition, into its organization and functions, and into its nature. This inquiry, however, will be limited to the preliminary phases of parliamentary development because the thirteenth century was an age of experiment. Only in the fourteenth and fifteenth centuries did parliament mature and acquire those distinct features that characterize it today.

I. THE KING'S COUNCIL

Our study of central administration has shown that all the kings—Anglo-Saxon, Norman, and Angevin—had a court or council to assist them with the governance of their realm. Styled the *curia regis* since the Conquest, this royal court consisted of two parts, the great council and the small council. For the present our attention will be focused upon the latter, which, in the age of parliament's first growth, was the nucleus of every parliament. The small council, as we know, was a permanent council in constant session which did all that the king commanded. Into the reign of Henry III it consisted primarily of professional administrators and judges. They gave the king counsel and helped him to legislate, to tax, to dispense justice, and to administer the affairs of his realm. Being royal appointees, the men serving on the small council were devoutly loyal to the king and his concept of government.

Under Henry III the small council underwent two important changes. In the first place it became a definite body whose members took a specific councillor's oath; henceforth the small council was clearly differentiated from the great council. In the second place the barons repeatedly attacked Henry and his small council because they resented being governed by men who, for the most part, were foreign friends of Henry III. The barons had sporadic success in imposing their men upon Henry, notably between 1258 and 1265 when special baronial councils or committees were placed over him. This baronial experiment with conciliar control over the king—a throwback to Magna Carta—was a failure, and under Edward I the small council was again composed of men appointed by the king because of their special administrative capacity. Few times in the Middle Ages was the small council as efficient and powerful as under Edward I. With his small council he did practically all that needed doing, even at times in the fields of taxation and legislation.

Traditionally, as we know, the kings did almost as much governing with their small council as with the great council. Generally it is impossible to say what could and could not be done by the small council, although we may generalize somewhat and say that for the greatest matters of state the great council was consulted. Though a king like Henry II did whatever he desired in the absence of the great council, this was no longer true in the thirteenth century. Neither Henry III nor Edward I could make general laws for the whole realm by themselves or with only the advice of the small council. And though both Henry and Edward attempted by irregular means to extort money from their subjects, neither thought of levying extraordinary taxes without the consent of those taxed. This consent was customarily given by great councils assembled for such a purpose. With both legislation and taxation, however, the small council played a fundamental part; it gave counsel to the king on legislation and fiscal business and helped to formulate royal legislative and fiscal policy.

Throughout the thirteenth century the small council retained its judicial power unimpaired. It was the *curia regis* and as such could hear any plea of the land. For some of the greatest causes it was a court of the first instance and in this capacity could dispense common law or feudal custom. It could, because of its special position, dispense any kind of justice, and it was this feature that contributed to the extraordinary amount of judicial business. All sorts of men of varying status and from different courts petitioned the king and council for justice, a justice they seemed unable to obtain elsewhere. As the fountainhead of justice, the king could, if he chose, give justice of any sort; he did so through his small council. Only for the greatest causes would the busy king lend his presence. The council was, therefore, the dispenser of the highest justice of the realm, which was available to all freemen. By the time of Edward I petitions for justice and for redress of grievances poured in upon the council in such great numbers that a highly organized staff and procedure had to be developed in order to expedite the business. We shall reserve discussion of the details of this organization for later, but it is essential to emphasize that most of the petitions were received when the king had summoned a great council or an even larger body of the realm to meet in conjunction with him and the small council. In 1290 when the small council was so afforced 250 petitions were presented and on a similar occasion in 1305 at least 500 petitions were received.

For the moment enough has been said about the small council. What must be recapitulated is that in the second half of the thirteenth century the small council was predominantly a permanent small group of professional administrators and judges—from fifty to seventy men—who served the king in almost any capacity. It was an executive body that gave counsel and helped to formulate policy. It was a judicial body—the highest court of the land—that dispensed justice of any type. Invariably when the king desired or found it necessary to meet with more of his subjects in a great council or national assembly at Westminster the small council was present. We may even say that when parliament had developed, no parliament assembled without the small council. It was the core of every parliament; without it parliament could not have functioned.

2. THE GREAT COUNCIL

When on certain occasions the kings met with their small council afforced with other men of the realm from whom they wanted counsel or other service, the *curia regis* became a great council. We already know that it was theoretically a body of all the feudal tenants-in-chief (barons), who owed the duty of attendance and advice at their royal lord's court. It could be held as often or as seldom as the king willed, but customarily it convened on those solemn occasions of Christmas, Easter, and Whitsuntide. A great council could be summoned, however, whenever it was necessary. Theoretically each tenant-in-chief was to receive a special writ of summons to a great council but we know that in practice the Angevins never sent special summonses to each royal vassal. Only the greatest barons received individual writs; the lesser barons received a general summons through the sheriffs. As early as Henry II a distinction had arisen between the major and minor barons and the latter were already choosing not to attend sessions of the great council. For the small baron attendance was expensive and burdensome and was in no way remunerative for the effort and energy expended. The lesser barons customarily absented themselves and devoted their time to the management of their lands and to local politics. This suited the kings because it made the great council smaller and more manageable for consultation and, in any event, what really counted was the counsel and consent of the great barons.

The method of summoning major and minor barons to meetings of the great council was formalized by Chapter XIV of Magna Carta. The barons drafted a procedure whereby individual writs were to be sent to the greater barons and general summonses through sheriffs to the lesser barons. Actually a general summons was interpreted as permission for nonattendance and the great council subsequently included only the great barons plus the small council and whatever other officials and advisers were required for the business under consultation. From this time on membership in or attendance at the great council no longer rested upon feudal tenure but upon a special writ of summons which was, to a degree, dependent in the thirteenth century upon the royal will.

In the thirteenth century the great council was normally summoned for discussion of important matters of state when the kings needed to sample public opinion more widely and to obtain support for some enterprise from the great men of the community of the realm. Among the weighty affairs that required attention of the great council was extraordinary taxation. It will be remembered that Chapter XIV of Magna Carta provided for baronial consent to scutage and all taxes other than the customary feudal aids. When the king, therefore, intended to levy an extraordinary impost, he had to secure "the common counsel of the kingdom," to be given by the archbishops, bishops, abbots, earls, and greater barons. They were to be summoned to a specified place forty days before the council convened. There the business should "proceed according to the council of those who are present, although all those summoned may not come." In the thirteenth century, then, it was established custom of the realm that the king should consult with his great council for weighty business and for extraordinary taxation. The decisions taken at meetings of the great council were considered binding upon all because, as the natural advisers of the king, the members of the great council represented the realm and by their consent bound the community of the realm.

Such an arrangement might appear quite efficient but in practice it did not function satisfactorily. The custom of summoning the greater barons was not yet old or common enough so that all were called to every great council. Some who expected to attend were not summoned and others were summoned but sporadically. It would be some time before king and barons would agree as to who was a "greater baron." This inevitably aroused the feeling among some barons that the king was governing without his natural advisers and that he must be forced to abide by established custom. Even among the barons summoned regularly there was widespread discontent with the king; they felt that he was conducting too much government by the small council. The prolonged struggle between Henry III and the barons was the upshot of this discontent. The baronial experiments in the form of the Provisions of Oxford and Westminster represent an attempt to place the king under the control of his natural advisers by packing the small council with barons and by providing for periodic meetings of the great council. It will be recalled that the barons at Oxford demanded that the great council (the word "parliament" was used) be summoned three times a year to consider the "common needs of the kingdom."[1] Though the baronial experiment failed, it emphasized most forcibly a generally held opinion that the great council spoke for the community of the realm on all important issues and ought to be consulted. It was a lesson that not even the strong Edward I often forgot.

3. THE WORD "PARLIAMENT"

The English word "parliament" is an Anglicized form of the French noun *parlement* derived from the verb *parler* meaning "to talk." Parliament literally means a "talking together," a conference or meeting where there is talk, debate, or deliberation. The word is of special interest to us because of the

[1] SM, no. 47B.

eventual institutional meaning it assumed. Into the thirteenth century we have seen that the *curia regis* was known under other terms. Generally the great council was called the *magnum concilium* and the small council simply the *concilium*. Towards the end of the twelfth century one detects some variation in the terminology; the word *colloquium* was used frequently by chroniclers to describe sessions of the great and small council and continued to be so used in the thirteenth century. Meanwhile another term—*parliamentum*—was coming into use for describing meetings of the great council. The word has been traced back to Henry II's reign but it was first used in a record of the king's bench in 1236 referring to a great council as a royal court of law and by the chronicler Matthew Paris to describe such a meeting in 1239. Thereafter it appeared more frequently; the Provisions of Oxford used it and from 1275 on it often appears in the official records.[2]

The point to be made about parliament is that it does not yet signify a new institution. It was merely a word, perhaps considered more expressive, for describing meetings of both the great and the small council. We may conclude that in the thirteenth century it described any occasion when the king met with his great or small council and talked over affairs of state. Even by the end of Edward I's reign parliament had still not acquired the meaning associated with it today. We can concur with Maitland when he said, "As yet any meeting of the king's council that has been solemnly summoned for general business seems to be a parliament." And we may add that a parliament could accomplish any affair of state. In the form of the small council it could be a court—thus the expression "High Court of Parliament"—or it could be an executive body giving expert counsel on a variety of business. In the form of the great council it could be a High Court of Parliament or a body legislating and giving consent to taxation or discussing great matters of state such as war or a treaty of peace. But parliament in the late thirteenth century could be even more; from political and economic necessity the king was beginning to augment his great and small councils with men who represented the lesser aristocracy and freemen of the counties and the burgesses of the boroughs. The great transformation undergone by the king's council in the thirteenth century was the addition of the representative element. When in the course of the fourteenth century the representative element became a regular part of the king's council, these assemblies were called parliaments and came to be differentiated from the king's small council and from occasional meetings of the king with his barons in great councils.

4. THE REPRESENTATIVE ELEMENT OF PARLIAMENT

In the pages of Stubbs' monumental *Constitutional History of England* parliament is regarded as the means by which each class in the community of the realm was admitted to participation in the national government as

[2] SM, no. 49A.

soon as it was ready for this task and trust. Edward I, so Stubbs believed, was conscious of this role of parliament; he realized that the men comprising his local communities of counties and boroughs were ready to assume their rightful place in the government and so summoned them to his parliaments. Although it is dubious whether Edward I viewed parliament in this light or whether he looked upon his men of the counties and boroughs as prepared to assume a share in his government, it is true that the residents of county and borough had attained such a status in the community of the realm that Edward felt compelled to summon them to parliament.

From our examination of local government in the thirteenth century we have seen that a much-governed realm was governed largely by local men who did so at the royal command. This was particularly true with the knights and squires—"the gentry" of the counties. In the boroughs the burgesses who controlled the municipal offices gained invaluable experience in government and the game of politics. These men were learned in government by the time it was found expedient to summon them to national parliaments.

In this connection there is another development that we have discussed but not related to parliament. In doing the king's work locally these men also served as representatives of their communities. Long before the first representatives were summoned to parliament, representation was occurring locally. Particularly in the second half of the twelfth century knights and freemen assumed the role of local representatives. This, we know, resulted from the use of these men by Henry II and his successors for judicial, financial, and administrative matters. In the procedure of the sworn inquest they were repeatedly empaneled to give information to the king and to perform multitudinous tasks for him. Usually preferred for these juries were the substantial landholders, the knights, who were thought to represent the knowledge and opinion of their community which was bound by the answers and acts of the juries. In this capacity the representative character of the men is clearly evident. When they assessed and collected taxes, they represented the community; when serving on grand juries, they represented the opinion of their community about men suspected of crime; and when selected by the king to inform him of his rights and of encroachments upon royal right, they represented what was known by their community. Under sworn oath they were commanded to tell the facts which, it was understood, were known by the community. In that most of these juries reported to royal officials at the county court, it became an occasion when local communities of the county were represented in a wide range of business. The representative character of the county court was so marked in the late twelfth and thirteenth centuries that Stubbs considered it a small local parliament. When representatives of the counties were finally assembled in national parliaments, he regarded these as merely a concentration of local county parliaments.

The representative character of such county functions is evident but what about the boroughs? Though separated from much of the county organization they were still faced with occasions when certain men had to represent them. Locally, of course, the borough council was to a degree representative of all the burgesses, and it was frequently the council that negotiated with royal officers. We have seen that when the king tallaged boroughs, his officers negotiated with the councils, who, on behalf of the community, promised a set amount and then collected and paid it to the exchequer. The same technique was used later with the percentage on movables. In fact, the borough council represented the urban community in all dealings with the royal government. In the matter of royal justice all boroughs were obliged to send to the county court when the itinerant justices appeared on their eyres twelve burgesses who were to indict any burgesses suspected of breaking the royal law. Again these men were acting in a representative capacity by telling what was known or suspected.

By the year 1250 all the ingredients necessary for what became a parliament were present. There was the king's permanent small council, the great council, and knights and burgesses doing locally what they soon would be doing in parliament. Laws were made, taxation was approved, and justice was dispensed, but not yet in the form that characterized parliament. The great council approved of laws and taxation on behalf of the community of the realm, and both barons and lesser men of the realm petitioned the king and his council for justice. But in order to have what we understand as a parliament, all this work should be done in an assembly consisting of the king, of the small and great councils, and of elected representatives from the counties and boroughs. For some reason, whether it was the king's desire to expedite the process of government or to secure a more complete backing for his projects, whether it was his wish to learn more about his realm or to simplify the presentation of petitions, or whether it was his need of money, experimentation in adding representatives to the small and great councils occurred. By the end of Edward I's reign a parliament often included the knights of the counties and the burgesses of the boroughs. There had taken place what Stubbs called a concentration of local parliaments and what other historians have termed a concentration of juries.

Long before both knights and burgesses were summoned to parliament there had been consultation of the king with local representatives. As early as John's reign, and probably before, there was realization that it was more efficient in time and effort to concentrate men at one point and conduct pertinent business *en masse* rather than to transact it individually with the barons, the counties, and the boroughs. It was but logical that the kings should adopt this technique, which had been employed throughout the twelfth century by royal officers in the counties. An early example of such consultation occurred in 1204 when John summoned twelve men from each of the Cinque Ports to meet with royal officers "to talk about the king's affairs" and "to do the king's service as directed." In 1207 and 1208 writs summoned representatives from specified boroughs and ports to deal with problems of coinage and shipping. The most celebrated cases of John's reign came in 1213. In July John summoned the reeve and four lawful men from certain villages of the royal domain to assemble at Saint Albans and there to report on the losses and damage suffered by the church at the royal hands. Though this meeting apparently was not held, it indicates how men from all over the realm were being concentrated to do the royal business. The other case occurred in a summons of November. The sheriffs received writs directing them to "have four discreet knights of your county come thither to us . . . to speak with us concerning the affairs of our kingdom." The knights were to meet at Oxford with a great council of barons.[3] Though, again, it is doubtful whether this assembly convened, it is the first case in which all the counties would have been represented by knights meeting in conjunction with the great council.

For some time we hear no more about such summonses and then in 1227 occurred the first known concentration of elected knights in Henry III's reign. To help settle complaints about the manner in which sheriffs were holding the county and hundred courts, the king directed each sheriff to have elected in full county court four lawful and discreet knights who should meet with the king and his council at Westminster in order to discuss the complaints. This is clearly an example of men elected to represent and to speak out for their counties in a central assembly. The main purpose of the meeting seems to have been to secure information.[4] Though various such concentrations occurred after 1227, few included all counties or resulted from election. We must wait until 1254 for another example of the type we seek. Henry III was in Gascony and desperately required money. Failing to obtain it through normal methods, the regents in England resorted to calling an assembly at Westminster to which were summoned along with the great council two representative knights from each county and representative clergy from each diocese "to provide . . . what sort of an aid they will give us in so great an emergency." The writs directed the counties and dioceses to decide beforehand what they could grant and so to instruct their representatives, who would report to the small council.[5] Although little discussion of taxation occurred at this meeting because the amounts to be granted had been determined locally, there was still a concentration of elected knights of the counties appearing before the small council probably in conjunction with the great council.

The next real advance in bringing the representative element into parliament was during the baronial crisis following 1258. Apparently with the aim of courting popular support, both Henry III and Simon de Montfort sum-

[3] SM, no. 41E.
[4] SM, no. 46E.
[5] SM, no. 46J.

moned representatives in addition to the barons to discuss their problems. In 1261 Henry III ordered his sheriffs to have before him at Windsor three knights from each county "to deliberate on the common affairs of our kingdom . . . and to treat concerning peace between us and them [the barons]."[6] Interestingly, the insurgent barons had already summoned three knights from each county to meet with them at Saint Albans, and Henry seemingly was attempting to sabotage this meeting with one of his own. Its significance lies in the fact that Henry wished to discuss public affairs with representative knights who were not previously instructed by their counties what to say or do.

The next step came in 1264 after Simon de Montfort's victory at Lewes. In the name of Henry III he directed the sheriffs to have elected in each county four knights who were to meet with him and the barons at London "to deliberate . . . concerning our affairs and those of our kingdom."[7] This act emphasizes that the representative principle was advancing and places the progress of national representation upon the threshold of real parliaments. The few ingredients that were lacking were soon supplied; they came when De Montfort called his famous parliament for early 1265. Facing a decline of baronial support after Lewes, De Montfort apparently hoped to gain a wider base of support from the country gentry and borough middle class. He summoned to an assembly five earls and eighteen barons, two knights from each county, and two burgesses from each borough. The purpose of the meeting as stated in the writs was to establish "peace and tranquility" in the kingdom.[8] The advance in this assembly was, of course, the inclusion of representatives of the boroughs. Now all the constituent elements of a historical parliament were present: the barons, who eventually would form the House of Lords, and the knights and burgesses, who eventually would form the House of Commons. But with this estimate we must stop and not attribute any further significance to this "parliament." All we can admit is that Simon de Montfort employed constitutional forms to summon for the first time all the regular elements of a later parliament. We must not think of him as the "father of parliament" who consciously set out to form such a body. Like his predecessors and successors, he was experimenting with national assemblies that included representative elements and happened to be the first to summon the burgesses. His parliament proved to be a precedent but not until there had been much more experimentation. We must also realize that the representative elements included in the parliament met under the summons of a rebel with a revolutionary body of barons. As Stubbs has said, "It was not primarily and essentially a constitutional assembly." But in the first sixty years of the thirteenth century the groundwork had been laid for parliament. Edward I was to build upon it in the years that followed.

[6] SM, no. 48A.
[7] SM, no. 48B.
[8] SM, no. 48C.

5. THE TRANSITIONAL PERIOD OF PARLIAMENT

From the parliament of Simon de Montfort in 1265 to the well-known Model Parliament of 1295 parliament passed through a period of transition and experimentation. The king and his council, as yet wedded to no one method of holding parliaments, continued to experiment with various forms. No one could be certain about what form parliament would finally assume nor did anyone probably concern himself much about how parliament should be constituted; it was merely looked upon as an expedient and flexible device for assisting the king in some of the work of government. The different forms taken by parliament in this period prove how vague was its future shape. One historian has shown that out of a total of some seventy assemblies held between 1258 and 1300, all of which the records call parliaments, representatives of the counties and boroughs were summoned to only nine. To illustrate how parliaments varied after 1265 we must look at some in detail.

Immediately after Simon de Montfort's defeat at Evesham and barely two months after his parliament, Henry III summoned in May 1265 a parliament which consisted of the great council and two canons from cathedral chapters. In the two other parliaments of Henry III there is mention of only the great council.[9] We must conclude that Henry completely ignored the precedent of Simon de Montfort. In the first parliament of Edward I held in 1273 the three constituent elements of a later parliament were present—the great council, knights of the counties, and burgesses of the boroughs. These three elements were again included in a parliament of 1275 which granted the "ancient" wool customs.[10] But in another parliament of that year only the great council and knights were present, and they granted the king a fifteenth.

The year 1283 saw a number of parliaments, all differently constituted.[11] A parliament summoned for January 1283 was held in two parts. The barons who were fighting for Edward in Wales attended neither part. Four knights from each of the five northern counties and two burgesses from each of the boroughs were summoned to York. At the same time knights and burgesses from the rest of England were assembled at Northampton. Another peculiar feature of this parliament was the addition of representatives of the lower clergy; it seems likely that the parliament may have been split after the example of the clerical convocations that met at York and Canterbury. The purpose of this divided parliament was to raise money for the Welsh war. This parliament also shows that the royal government could do business with the representative element of the realm in the absence of the great council. A second parliament of September 1283 held at Shrewsbury along the Welsh border was also unique in its organization. The baronage was present as well

[9] SM, no. 48D.
[10] SM, no. 49B.
[11] SM, no. 49D.

as knights and burgesses from some of the boroughs. After attending to various matters, the parliament divided and the burgesses went to Acton Burnell where they discussed commercial matters and agreed to the statute *De Mercatoribus*. The barons, remaining at Shrewsbury, tried Prince David of Wales. This parliament demonstrates that Edward had no set idea on what should constitute a parliament but that he summoned the barons to perform one of their traditional obligations—judgment of a feudal peer—and that he included the merchants to deal with matters affecting only them. Each element dealt with its own business.

Down to 1295 the parliamentary pattern continued to vary. In one parliament of 1290 attended at first by only the great council, the famous statute *Quia Emptores* was enacted; but then a week later knights of the counties were added so as to bargain with them for a grant.[12] In 1294 another parliament included the great council and the knights; assembled for matters of taxation, it consented to a tenth.[13] Meanwhile the boroughs were dealt with separately by royal officials and agreed to a sixth. In the autumn of 1295 Edward sent out the summonses which were to result in the assembling of his Model Parliament of November. Although he had met with his great council earlier in the summer to dispatch some judicial business and to discuss his foreign problems, a combination of a Welsh revolt, the outbreak of war with Scotland, and hostilities with France compelled him to summon another parliament in the autumn so that he could explain his political and military problems and his great need of money. He determined to summon all the classes of his realm in order to secure a broad base of support and consent to a sizable tax. When assembled, the Model Parliament included all the great prelates: the two archbishops, eighteen bishops, sixty-seven abbots, and the heads of the religious orders of the Knights Hospitallers, the Knights Templars, and the Order of Sempringham. Lay barons included seven earls and forty-one greater barons. Here, then, were the prelates and barons who would in the future constitute the House of Lords. Provision was also made for representatives of the lower clergy. Along with their special writs of summons the bishops received instructions to cite beforehand (*praemunientes*) the deans or priors of their cathedral chapters, the archdeacons of their dioceses, a representative proctor from each chapter, and two representative proctors from the parish clergy of their dioceses. Summoned in addition were two knights from each of thirty-seven counties and two citizens or burgesses from each of 110 cities and boroughs. This parliament included a larger number of members than any other medieval parliament.[14]

The Model Parliament of Edward I is generally regarded as a landmark

[12] SM, no. 52F.
[13] SM, no. 49E.
[14] SM, no. 49F.

in the development of parliament. In one respect this view is justified; it was a "model" in that it contained all the elements included later in all parliaments. But we can attribute nothing more to it. Edward obviously did not regard it as a precedent or model for his future parliaments. Of the twenty other parliaments in his reign only twelve contained representatives of the counties or boroughs and only three followed the model of 1295. There is no reason to believe that Edward hoped to achieve a parliamentary form which would become a standard legislative institution or that he thought taxation could be approved only in such a parliament. The fact that the preamble of the writs contained the famous Roman legal maxim "what concerns all should be approved by all" (*quod omnes tangit omnibus approbetur*) does not mean that Edward acted on this principle. The phrase was undoubtedly the rhetorical device of some scribe and Edward probably saw it for the first time when he read the writs. That such an assembly could be convoked by an English king in 1295 is great in itself and requires no explanation of finely spun legal or political theory. It seemed the most expeditious method of securing what Edward wanted at the time—consent to a tax, which he received in the form of an eleventh from the barons and knights, a seventh from the burgesses, and a tenth from the clergy. The Model Parliament was, to be sure, a more complete application of the representative principle on a national level and, because it was in accord with the trend to add representatives to the great council, was remembered and became a precedent for the formation of parliaments in the fourteenth century.

Though the Model Parliament may be regarded as the culmination of the period of parliamentary origin, it is still too early to consider parliament a fully formed institution with a definite place in English government. Many developments were yet necessary to guarantee parliament a permanent place in history and to make it the institution that converted England into a limited monarchy. One development happened soon after 1295 and laid down one of the chief principles that was to guide the growth of parliament for the next two centuries. Despite the large grants received in 1295, Edward remained in serious financial trouble. The French and Scottish wars dragged on and he could not persuade the baronage or the knights and burgesses (the commons) to grant him enough supply. In addition, the clergy, urged and commanded by Pope Boniface VIII only to grant supply to the state with papal permission, were stoutly resisting further taxation. Blocked from obtaining supply through regular channels, Edward in desperation decided upon arbitrary means. In 1297, as we have seen, he forced an irregular assembly, which neither in summons nor in composition was a parliament, to grant him an aid. Consulting with a few barons, he secured their approval to collect an eighth from the barons and knights and a fifth from the burgesses. Before this aid could be collected, however, Edward embarked for Flanders to prosecute the French war, and the greater barons immediately forbade its collection. Prior to embarking, Edward had also seized wool about to be exported, giving tallies to the merchants and the promise of subsequent payment. Having failed in his negotiations for a grant from the clergy, he arbitrarily assessed a tax upon them, threatening outlawry and confiscation of their lands if it was not paid.

As soon as Edward had embarked, the most powerful elements of the realm rose up against his arbitrary measures and, under the leadership of the baronage, refused any money until he withdrew from his position and confirmed Magna Carta with the addition of certain other articles. Acting for his father, Prince Edward agreed to their demands. At Ghent on 5 November 1297 Edward I confirmed this agreement in an act known as the Confirmation of the Charters (*Confirmatio Cartarum*).[15] The essential part of Edward's confirmation was his promise to take no aids, tasks, or prises without the common assent of the realm. He also agreed that no new tax would be imposed upon wool without common consent. Skipping over the details and technicalities of this act, we may state that it ingrained as law for king and community of the realm the principle that no extraordinary and direct taxation could be collected without the common consent of the realm. And though as yet "common consent of the realm" did not mean a parliament consisting of the baronage and the representatives of counties and boroughs, it did mean that a parliament, whatever its composition, must give its assent to taxation. By the reign of Edward III this assent was always given by a parliament consisting of the representatives, and it continued to be so given. By forcing the king to summon parliament whenever he needed supply, the Confirmation of the Charters proclaimed that he could not act arbitrarily in the matter of taxation but must depend upon what his subjects chose to grant him. It guaranteed that the king would have to summon more parliaments, and this meant increased negotiation which could lead only to further curtailment of royal prerogative. In the fourteenth century bargaining and concessions for supply became the theme of parliamentary history. By securing control of the royal purse strings, the community of the realm discovered that it could limit the king.

6. CLERICAL REPRESENTATION

The clergy and their representative assemblies have been briefly referred to in connection with royal taxation. And it has been noted that the lower clergy customarily met in diocesan synods or in provincial convocations of York and Canterbury to grant supply to the king. We must now discuss how the representatives of the lower clergy came to assemble with the baronage and lay representative element in parliament.

Since William the Conqueror had separated church and state in the eleventh century, the English church had been developing a system of organization more compatible with that of the Continent. There had evolved before

[15] SM, no. 51A.

the thirteenth century two ecclesiastical assemblies to transact spiritual business. One was the diocesan synod consisting of the clergy of the diocese; the other was the provincial synod (convocation), one for York and one for Canterbury, attended by the bishops, some of the abbots, and the archdeacons. At these convocations the clergy dealt with ecclesiastical affairs as well as negotiating with the king on matters affecting church-state relations. It must be kept in mind that throughout the Middle Ages the church acted as an independent power and rival of the state and that sovereigns had to deal with it almost as they did with other sovereign states. When, for example, the clergy had grievances against the king, they were discussed and formulated in the synods and then presented to the king in parliament or in council by the prelates. With strong papal backing the church had established its right throughout Europe to grant taxes to the state through its own synods or convocations. The English church did this in the thirteenth century, and we have seen how the kings negotiated with such assemblies for clerical taxation. Quite probably the frequent negotiation between church and state and the increasing demands for church money contributed to the perfection of the convocation in the thirteenth century, converting it into a truly representative assembly.

In 1226 came the first step towards real representation of the lower clergy; proctors representing the cathedral chapters and monasteries were added to the traditional membership. In 1273 and 1277 representatives of the parochial clergy were added and then, between 1280 and 1283, in the provinces of both Canterbury and York the convocations assumed their final form, which was probably hastened by the increased pressure of Edward I for money. Henceforth all elements of the clergy were present or represented; the convocations had become completely representative. Both convocations generally met at the same time so that they could more readily expedite common problems. Each consisted of bishops, abbots, priors, deans of cathedral and collegiate churches, archdeacons, and heads of various religious orders, all attending in person. The parochial clergy were represented by two proctors from each diocese; each cathedral and collegiate chapter, by one proctor. Such were the convocations with which the king had to deal.

While the convocation was assuming its final form the kings were experimenting with other methods of transacting business with the church that were eventually to result in full church representation at the Model Parliament of 1295. As early as 1177 Henry II had summoned deans and archdeacons to a meeting of the great council; John had done likewise on several occasions. The first parliament summoned in 1265 after Simon de Montfort's defeat contained two canons from each cathedral chapter. To the split parliament of 1283 Edward I summoned knights, burgesses, and clerical representatives.[16] His model for this action seems to have been the church

[16] SM, no. 49D.

convocations, which had just attained their final form. It is interesting to speculate on what might have been the fate of parliament had Edward and his successors continued to summon and to deal with only provincial parliaments. It seems probable that parliament would have suffered the fate of the French estates general in the fourteenth century when it was broken down into provincial estates that were incapable of withstanding the royal power. France, as a result, became an absolute monarchy. In any event, after more than a century of experimentation in uniting the clerical element with the lay elements in great councils and parliaments, all elements were brought together in one body in the Model Parliament. For the moment, at least, the clergy had become a part of parliament—the prelates as greater barons and the lower clergy as representatives.

Why Edward I included clerical representatives in his parliament when he could deal with the church through its convocations will never be completely understood. The whole medieval spiritual and political tradition was against such a fusion and Edward, experienced in the stubborn and independent attitude of the church, must have known that the church would not willingly part with its independence. The only explanation seems to be that Edward thought it would be simpler to treat with all the estates of his realm at one time and in one body and hoped that he might possibly bring more pressure to bear upon the clergy when they were but one part of a parliament. Though this is not the place to discuss the future role of the clergy in parliament, we must point out that they did not regularly attend the rest of Edward's parliaments. Possibly because of the bitter struggle between Boniface VIII and Edward the lower clergy showed a marked reluctance to participate in parliament and appeared only at a few. They continued to attend parliament irregularly in the first thirty years of the fourteenth century. Thereafter we never hear of clerical representatives in parliament. They met in their convocations, frequently held at the same time as parliament, and voted supply to the king. Parliament henceforth was to contain only the baronage, the knights, and the burgesses. In similar national assemblies on the Continent the clergy, as the first estate, retained a prominent place until the end of the Ancien Régime. The withdrawal of the lower clergy from parliament helped to make possible the future fusion of knights and burgesses into the commons forming the House of Commons.

7. AN EDWARDIAN PARLIAMENT AT WORK

Down to this point we have limited our remarks to the various elements constituting a parliament under Edward I and to how they became a part of parliament. We can now gainfully inquire into what an Edwardian parliament did. Divesting ourselves of any preconceived view, gained perhaps by a knowledge of what a modern parliament does, we must think ourselves back to the days of Edward I when parliament was an embryonic institution just beginning to assume some of the functions performed by parliament today. Generally parliaments assembled at Westminster as they do now. The reason was that Westminster had been the principal residence of the English kings since before the Conquest; here was centered the great historical tradition and consciousness of England. For centuries the royal government with its various departments such as the exchequer and common law courts had been established here. Here was the Abbey Church where England's kings were crowned. The meeting place was the Great Hall constructed by William Rufus which stood beside the royal palace. This Norman structure was quite a contrast to the ensemble of neo-Gothic Houses of Parliament seen today along the Thames Embankment. But we must look into this old Norman hall if we would learn about an early parliament.

The parliament that we shall witness is that of 1305, the first for which there is adequate documentation. Some weeks before the parliament assembled in the spring, writs of summons had been sent throughout the realm, individual writs to the great spiritual and lay barons who composed the great council and general writs to every sheriff commanding him to have elected from his county two knights and two burgesses from each borough. A *praemunientes* clause had been attached to each bishop's writ ordering representative proctors of the lower clergy to be present. These were the elements summoned to meet with the king and his council, which was ordinarily afforced for such an occasion with the judges of the common law courts and lawyers and jurists skilled in Roman and canon law. The number of men attending this parliament totaled almost seven hundred. There were approximately 50 of the king's council, 200 spiritual and lay barons, 150 representatives of the clergy, 74 knights from the counties, and 200 burgesses from the boroughs.

But what was the occasion for this parliament? To everyone the announcement of a parliament meant that the king and his council, small and great, were ready to receive petitions and dispense justice. To the baronage the parliament meant that it would be asked for counsel regarding relations with Philip IV of France, the Scottish problem, and the king's dispute over the investiture of a new archbishop. Perhaps the baronage would be called upon to help enact new statutes proposed by the king and his small council and, most important, to consent to a grant of money. Although the knights and burgesses might find their journey to Westminster a change from local routine, probably few looked with enthusiasm upon their task. Though paid by their counties and boroughs for the expense of the trip, they viewed parliament with misgivings. Few had any illusions about their importance despite their local prominence in politics or their considerable wealth. Many would have to supply the king with information about local government, some would have to act as witnesses for petitions. All knew that they had been given full power of attorney (*plena potestas*) to speak for and to represent and bind their constituencies on whatever matters were presented. All knew that they would present petitions to king and council. What worried them most was what they knew from experience to be inevitable—a request for money.

It is now the first morning of Edward's parliament and all the pomp and traditional celebration of medieval England is in full progress. On a dais at the end of the Great Hall sits King Edward upon his throne. On his right is the archbishop of Canterbury and on his left the chancellor. Just below and to the front the members of the small council sit upon wool sacks brought in for their comfort from the wool staple close by. Near the council are the common law justices and experts in Roman and canon law whose legal advice will be needed for framing statutes. Outside this inner ring, and to the right of the throne, sit the spiritual barons together with archdeacons and deacons from the cathedral chapters. Probably to the left and in front of the throne stand the lay barons; behind them towards the rear of the hall, the knights; and then finally at the rear of the hall, the burgesses.

This assembled and solemn parliament was opened with a prayer by the bishop of London followed by a sermon of the archbishop of Canterbury whose text was fittingly: "How shall a court correct the ills of the whole realm, unless it shall first be itself corrected?" Next came an address by the chancellor outlining the purpose of the parliament. Weighty political and military matters must be discussed, petitions were to be presented and redressed, complaints were to be received, and, finally, the king's great undertaking caused such a heavy drain on his financial resources that a gracious aid was of the utmost urgency. His message delivered, the chancellor directed the members to deliberate on the business outlined and then to report back their decisions on supply to the small council. The assembly was then adjourned. Immediately the king and his council went into Saint Stephen's Chapel; the clergy, barons, and knights remained in the Great Hall to discuss the tax; and the burgesses departed to the neighboring Abbey Refectory to talk over their contribution. When a decision on the tax was reported to the small council, most of the members would then depart for home.

The main business of the parliament was accomplished by the small council in the council chamber. It was the core and essence of parliament; it drafted most of the statutes, gave counsel, directed administration, and, above all, dispensed justice. Perhaps when weighty domestic and foreign problems were discussed some barons of the great council would participate. Knights and burgesses would appear before the council with information desired by the king. Appointments to administrative posts would be made. And to the council would come delegations announcing their decisions on taxation. At this parliament the barons and knights granted a thirtieth and the burgesses a twentieth. Finally, petitions were presented, and petitioners appeared to prosecute their cases. A group of burgesses or knights might present a petition on behalf of their constituencies asking for a royal favor or for the redress of some local grievance such as the corrupting of juries or inefficient administration of royal officers. To this extent, then, did the knights and burgesses participate in the parliaments of Edward I.

Once the tax was granted, the members of parliament were again assembled, thanked for their gracious cooperation, and instructed to depart for their homes. Most of the barons and all the representatives left immediately but the small council remained behind, probably for another three or four weeks, transacting important business, mostly legal. The parliament of 1305 was still in session and would be until the council had dispatched its business. To this parliament were submitted five hundred petitions which the council had to handle. By a system of committees the petitions were sorted and dealt with in an appropriate manner. Most were transmitted to the officers and courts in whose domain lay the proper action. Actually the council acted on only the most important and difficult petitions; with the others it but initiated action. Rarely did a supplicant get a desired answer from the council. His final answer usually came much later and in a different court or department. But as the High Court of Parliament, a court above all other courts, the small council resolved difficult or doubtful judgments, provided remedies for new legal actions, and dispensed equity, that is, justice, when for some reason it could not be secured in any other royal or public court.

Such was a typical Edwardian parliament. From the evidence available it is obvious that the representative element did little. It presented some petitions, supplied information, and consented to taxation. As yet the representatives were unorganized and formed no House of Commons. They initiated no business and framed no statutes; upon occasion they did consent to legislation. Though their consent to taxes was necessary, they did not use this power to gain any control over the government or its policies. The "core and essence" of parliament was the small council, which initiated and transacted practically all the business. But despite the insignificant role of the representatives, they were elected by the counties and boroughs with power of attorney to act for and bind their constituencies; once they consented to a tax it had to be paid. They were experienced administrators and politicians who, when given the opportunity, knew how to strike the best bargain possible for county and borough. Eventually more frequent sessions of parliament and the coalescence of the knights and burgesses into the commons would increase the power of the representative element and transform it into the key ingredient of parliament.

8. THE NATURE OF PARLIAMENT

Enough evidence pertinent to parliament has now been examined to attempt some conclusions about its essential nature and the reasons for its origin. We must bear in mind, however, that the remarks which follow pertain to an institution just arising and still amoebic in form, composition, organization, and method of work. As yet nothing was constant. The rights and functions of parliament were undefined. The House of Commons and House of Lords were not formed. All we can hope to do with this incomplete institution is to formulate some reasonable observations. In doing this we must evaluate the principal scholarly opinions held on parliament.

Though many historians had studied parliament, not until the last quarter of the nineteenth century did they become highly scholarly and critical. The modern study of parliament began with the *Constitutional History of England* by William Stubbs, a work with which any discussion of parliament must commence. Briefly, Stubbs held that parliament was the means by which the various classes of the realm were admitted to participation in the government as soon as they were equal to the responsibility. Between 1215 and 1295 the realm became sufficiently united and its various classes sufficiently qualified for parliament to come into being. A significant advance was made in the parliament called by Simon de Montfort in 1265. Then after thirty years of experiment Edward I, fully determined to bring the realm into his government, summoned the Model Parliament of 1295 that prescribed the permanent form in which the classes would participate. It was an assembly of estates. To the baronage, now limited and defined by a system of individual summonses, were added representatives of the counties, boroughs, and lower clergy. Stubbs viewed the following two centuries as but a period when parliament developed more fully in accordance with Edward's master parliamentary plan of 1295.

Stubbs dominated the study of parliament until the last few years of the nineteenth century when various works began to appear suggesting major revisions. In 1900 a German historian, Ludwig Riess, wrote a book emphasizing the petitory function of parliament. He argued that the knights and burgesses were summoned in order to present petitions to the king and his council on behalf of the communities sending them. Somewhat earlier, however, Maitland had studied in detail the parliament of 1305 and had come to some conclusions that suggested the first radical change in the Stubbsian thesis. Upon Maitland's revision of Stubbs most subsequent research has turned. Describing first the parliamentary proceedings of 1305, Maitland emphasized that a full or general parliament was regarded as in full session until 6 April although all members except those of the small council had been dismissed on 21 March. This discovery led Maitland to conclude "that a session of the king's council is the core and essence of every *parliamentum*" and that parliamentary proceedings were predominantly legal. The real innovation of his argument, of course, was the major position assigned to the small council in parliament. Subsequently historians such as C. H. McIlwain, A. F. Pollard, H. G. Richardson, and G. O. Sayles elaborated upon the conclusions of Maitland, and his theory is still a prevailing one. According to Richardson and Sayles, parliament took definite form in 1258 with the Provisions of Oxford when regular sessions of the small council began for the dispensation of justice. They called only those sessions parliaments in which justice was dispensed; assemblies that discussed politics, voted supply, and enacted statutes were not, in their opinion, true parliaments. They did not regard parliament as anything more than a high court of justice until the reign of Edward III when the baronage captured control of the small council and, in cooperation with the knights and burgesses, converted the principal business of parliament into that of politics, legislation, and taxation.

The chief deviation from the "conciliar theory" has been that of Bertie Wilkinson and Maude V. Clarke. The latter in a series of learned articles held that the origin of parliament must not be sought in the small council but in the long medieval tradition of "representation and consent." She felt that an Edwardian parliament was founded upon the principle that the various classes of the realm were to participate in royal government and to cooperate in and share responsibility for the common endeavor. As for the principle of consent, she believed that it was a typical feudal custom that had been fused with the representative principle during the course of the thirteenth century. The view of Miss Clarke, quite similar to that of Stubbs, is weakened by the insertion of some dubious evidence, yet her ideas merit attention because they suggest that too narrow an interpretation of parliament's functions is incompatible with what the records tell us.

The theory advanced by Wilkinson somewhat resembles that of Miss Clarke because he argued that parliament was "the greatest of all expressions of the medieval tradition of government by consent and the co-operative state." He contends that long before the reign of Edward I there was a political tradition of cooperation between the kings and their subjects. For personal and routine government the kings relied upon the advice of the small council, but for the great political affairs they asked for the counsel and consent of the community of the realm, which was regarded as being expressed by the great council. With the reign of Edward I the community of the realm came to be represented not only by the barons but by the knights and burgesses. According to this interpretation, parliament and the small council were distinct institutions with different functions. The council had a place in the sessions of parliament, but the latter was not an enlarged session of the former as Maitland and his school had contended. Parliament was the appointed institution for achieving cooperation and consent when great political affairs had to be discussed between the king and the community of the realm. Obviously Wilkinson's thesis is poles apart from that of Maitland. Its weakness lies in its attempt to separate completely the functions of small council and parliament and in its limiting so narrowly the scope of conciliar business. But a valuable result of the Wilkinson research has been renewed attention to the political functions of parliament.

In contrast to Wilkinson, Maurice Powicke and T. F. T. Plucknett are inclined to take a more flexible and eclectic view of parliament. Neither looks upon it as an institution definite or fixed in the thirteenth century but rather as passing through a formative stage. Both agree that it developed around the council but part with Richardson and Sayles at this point. Powicke emphasizes that on occasion the small council assisted by the common law judges dealt with judicial business and that these meetings were called parliaments. When the king summoned the great council to meet with him, these assemblies were termed parliaments; often they did not coincide with the judicial sessions of the small council. Then there were those occasions when barons and the representative element of the realm were summoned to national assemblies; these, too, were regarded as parliaments. Powicke does not feel, therefore, that the transaction of judicial business should be the sole criterion of a parliament. He prefers to regard an Edwardian parliament as extremely malleable. In a variety of forms it dealt with justice, politics, and finance, and on all such occasions it was considered a parliament. Powicke emphasizes that Edward's reign was a crucial period for parliamentary development because in time and place the sessions of the small council, the great council, and the representative element began to coincide and to transact whatever business was on the agenda.

These are the principal theories on the functions of parliament. But there still remain the arguments advanced to explain why representatives from the counties and boroughs came to be summoned. Though Riess' view that they were brought to parliament to present petitions has some validity, it is weakened by the criticism of Wilkinson, who pointed out that it was customary procedure for the subjects to come to the council with their petitions rather than for the king to summon them to parliament for that purpose. Moreover, G. L. Haskins has shown that under Edward I the representatives introduced relatively few petitions for their communities or for groups or individuals. The petitory theory does not seem to account satisfactorily for the appearance of the representative element in parliament. More and more research is confirming the old belief, held by Henry Hallam, Rudolf Gneist, and to a degree by Stubbs, that Edward I was led to summon representatives to parliament principally by his need and desire to obtain their consent to taxation. They came with full power of attorney to act for county and borough and to bind them to decisions of parliament. We must acknowledge the fact that the earliest function of the representatives was consent to taxation, that this continued as the chief function, and that through the right of consent to taxation the representatives won control over the crown. The knights and burgesses—the core of the middle class—had become the moneyed element of the realm and the kings had to have their money to carry on the government. The royal need of money dominates the opening addresses of each parliament, and what most concerned the knights and burgesses was the amount that would be demanded of them by the king. The English kings valued the knights and burgesses primarily as a source of supply. Through experimentation, they came to see that taxes could be most efficiently secured by bringing these men to parliament.

We may conclude that a parliament under Edward I was flexible in function, composition, and organization. Of whatever it consisted, whether of simply the small council, the great council, both, or both afforced by the representatives, it did what the king desired. It dispensed justice, discussed politics, legislated, and consented to taxation. But however these functions were accomplished, all was done in parliament. The representatives, added mainly from financial consideration, did on occasion express public opinion of the realm on some great undertaking, present petitions, supply information, and approve statutes. The principal innovation of Edward I's reign was the addition of the representative element to parliament, a step of great significance for future constitutional development.

XXIX

The Age of Bracton

IF THE twelfth century was unique for the foundation of the common law system the thirteenth century was equally so for the judicial and legislative developments that insured the ultimate triumph of the peculiar system of English law. Except for the Tudor period, the common law system was little changed after the thirteenth century until the epoch of judicial reform in the nineteenth century. Despite the civil war and a series of unsettling constitutional experiments, Henry III's reign was remarkably fruitful in legal progress; at his death the principal medieval features of the common law system had been drawn. They had, in fact, been summarized by the illustrious judge Bracton in the first real legal commentary of the Middle Ages. This work is a testament to the busy legal century that separated Glanville from Bracton.

Even more important than the reign of Henry III was that of his son Edward I, so often called "the English Justinian." Edward's reign ended one phase in the development of the common law and inaugurated another. Living in an age of constructive legislation and of great lawgivers such as Frederick II of Sicily and Louis IX of France, Edward legislated for a realm that had just formed a great legal system. Imbued with a strong sense of orderliness, he promulgated statutes which systematized the tangled skein that had become the common law system. More legislation was enacted during a thirteen-year period of his reign than in any succeeding age. Not until the reign of William IV (1830–1837) does the legislation compare in amount to that accomplished under Edward I. The Edwardian statutes touched upon almost every point of law, both public and private. So well did they accomplish their objectives that criminal and civil law were basically untouched down to the nineteenth century. The lawyers of the eighteenth century had to be as familiar with Edward's statutes as with statutes and cases of their own day. So well did Edward build in civil law that the essential principles of land law today stem from two of his great statutes. Before studying in detail various aspects of the common law system we must first sketch in the principal lines of legal development during the reigns of Henry III and Edward I.

1. THE COMMON LAW

Though speculation about law and ideas of Roman jurisprudence appears in Bracton's *Laws and Customs of England* this is exceptional in the thirteenth century. The English lawyers were not interested in the philosophy of law and did little speculating on the difference between custom (*ius*) and law (*lex*). Generally no distinction was made between the two, although Bracton distinguished between what he called *consuetudo* (custom) and *lex*. As yet lawyers had not expressed any views on the relation between enacted and unenacted law, between custom and law. The assizes of Henry II, though enacted law, had filtered down into and become fused with the mass of unenacted law. In Edward I's reign some lawyers were just becoming aware of enacted laws (statutes) that could make and change law and that could be promulgated only by the king with the consent of a great council.

The phrase "common custom" (*ius commune*) had long been known to the canon law scholars but was seldom used in the secular courts until Edward I's day when the preferred phrase became "common law" (*lex communis*). By then common law was contrasted with statute law and royal prerogative. But such distinction, it should be noted, came only after there was considerable enacted law as well as law that had developed from prescriptive usage, from the experience of trial and error, or from some special charter or writ. Common law is traditional law, that "which has always been law and still is law." In this sense it was different from a statute or an ordinance. By the reign of Edward I common law also meant the law of temporal courts as distinguished from the ecclesiastical law of church courts which throughout the Middle Ages had jurisdiction over such temporal matters as marriage and testaments. The sense, however, in which we shall most often refer to common law is "general" as opposed to "local" or "special" law. The common law was the royal law, common or general throughout the realm. It was that law which contrasted with whatever law was particular, extraordinary, or special. Thus understood, common law was the royal law of the realm; it was a law that the laws of local, special, and ecclesiastical courts could never be.

2. THE COMMON LAW UNDER HENRY III

In 1216 there was little of what may be called enacted law; it may be said to have begun with Magna Carta, which came to be considered the first statute. In this connection it must be understood that there were four versions of Magna Carta: that of 1215, and succeeding ones of 1216, 1217, and 1225. The last, issued by Henry III upon attaining his majority, represents the final form and is the Magna Carta referred to in subsequent ages. In the development of public law Magna Carta was of utmost importance. It was regarded as a definite statement of the law as it existed under Henry II and as a concise formulation of the king's rights and limitations. In the minds of all, this practical charter meant that the reign of law should be supreme. As the ultimate standard of what a king could and could not do, Magna Carta was repeatedly used to limit the royal prerogative and was constantly confirmed. Henry III confirmed it in 1237 and Edward I in 1297.[1] Down to the fifteenth century it was confirmed at the opening of parliaments. Sir Edward Coke counted thirty-two confirmations during the Middle Ages. Often, however, to secure confirmation of what was regarded as the fundamental law of the land, the royal subjects had to pay the king their good money.

Throughout Henry III's long reign Magna Carta formed the principal body of statute law; it was added to but twice. First was the Statute of Merton in 1236 enacted by the king and great council. It attended to a variety of legal matters such as damages in actions of dower, redisseisin, and limitation of judicial writs. The most famous clause contained the declaration of the barons that they would not change the laws of England (*nolumus leges Angliae mutare*). This stand came in response to a request of the clergy asking that children born before marriage of the parents should be considered legitimate. The other statute of Henry's reign, the Statute of Marlborough, came in the year 1267. Enacted basically to settle the disputes of the civil war period, it consisted of certain concessions which Henry had been forced to give the barons in the Provisions of Westminster in 1259. It concentrated for the most part on redressing grievances of the lesser landholders. Matters such as wrongful distress, fraudulent conveyance, and false judgment dominate the clauses.

The body of statute law for Henry III's reign was supplemented, however, by numerous other measures that may be termed ordinances and that were administrative acts of the king and small council rather than legislation. The ordinances dealt with special and short-term matters, although some eventually found their way into statute law. Throughout the thirteenth century it is difficult to distinguish between ordinance and statute, and later compilers added to the confusion by mixing the ordinances with statutes and terming them such.

The lack of formal legislation under Henry III should not deceive us, however, into thinking that the common law was not growing. In the domain of land law it took tremendous strides, primarily at the hands of the judges in the royal courts who through writs devised legal remedies to meet new cases. The judges also presided over cases in which decisions plowed new legal furrows and set precedents for subsequent cases. The reign of Henry III was the golden age of judge-made law. By the invention of new remedies the judges, though professing merely to declaration of the law, were in effect making new law. Throughout Henry's reign the judges had a free hand in

[1] SM, no. 51A.

devising new remedies; they made law by their judicial writs just as Henry II had made the bulk of his by informal written and oral orders.

The judges of Henry III responsible for the rich development of the law were a group of learned men, primarily ecclesiastics, who were thoroughly grounded in canon and Roman law in addition to the common law. Almost without exception they were men with long experience in royal justice and administration, professionals who devoted much of their time to legal work. One of the foremost changes in this period was the separation of hearing and deciding cases from other government work. For all practical purposes this separation occurred in 1234 with the dismissal from office of Stephen Segrave, the last real justiciar. With him the justiciar as the principal royal executive officer and the chief presiding officer over the *curia regis* ended. The separation was not formalized until 1268 with the appointment of a "chief justiciar to hold pleas before the king." Henceforth a justiciar was a royal officer who dealt only with judicial work. There thus began a new line of principal justices who were simply presidents over a royal court. About the same time the presiding judge of the court of common pleas also came to be styled justiciar or chief justice. Judges were no longer statesmen or politicians but simply men learned in the law.

The new school of judges, then, were royal clerks and ecclesiastics. Such, for example, was Stephen Segrave, who, though condemned as a selfish and unscrupulous politician, was praised as an able judge. Almost all the common law judges, who customarily served first as chancery clerks, had studied canon and Roman law, and some, like Thomas of Marlborough, even traveled to Italy to attend the lectures of the famous jurist Azo. John of Lexington, a judge of the court of common pleas, was described as learned in both canon and Roman law. This knowledge was essential because the judges dealt constantly with foreign, commercial, and ecclesiastical matters that required a sound acquaintance with such law. It is doubtful whether men less learned in law could have handled the varied cases that poured into the law courts. Men broad in the law were needed to deal with the different types of men, transactions, and problems, and to define the relations of canon and Roman law to the common law. A practical working knowledge of the three laws was essential even for the conveyancers who drew up the legal documents, because the documents, to hold up in the courts, had to meet the rigid demands of the law.

Of the numerous judges who made legal reputations under Henry III we can discuss only the most famous. One was Martin of Pateshull, who had been a clerk under John and who was appointed to the bench of common pleas in 1217. He was concurrently archdeacon of Norfolk and dean of Saint Paul's. He was a master of Bracton, who informs us that Pateshull was one of the ablest judges of his day. One fellow judge asked to be relieved from going on a judicial circuit with him because he wore out colleagues by his incessant activity. He was one of the first professional judges to gain his reputation solely as a lawyer. William of Raleigh, with whom Bracton began the study of law, was a justice of the bench of common pleas by 1228. He had much to do with the Statute of Merton and is credited with having drafted some of the clauses.

We have already spoken of Bracton, the most famous lawyer of medieval England, and of his legal education, his busy life as a royal judge, and his legal writing. Of interest now is what Bracton tells us about thirteenth-century common law and what influence he wielded over it. His treatise underlines two permanent characteristics of the common law—the dependence of its procedure and practice upon the writ and upon decided cases. Bracton said that the law should go from precedent to precedent. He stimulated what we call case law. One decided case became the precedent for the decisions of similar cases. In the realm of adjective (procedural) law we learn from him about the various forms of action, the forms of relief, and the rules of court procedure. Despite the influence of Roman law on Bracton, when he discussed the relations of the king to law—what we would call constitutional law—he held that the royal powers should be exercised subject to law, which was enacted with the consent of the great council and which was the bridle of the royal power. The sum and substance of Bracton's view on king and law is contained in his famous dictum: "The king himself, however, ought not to be under man but under God and under the law, because the law makes the king." With the pleas of the crown Bracton tells how the royal courts are rapidly acquiring jurisdiction over all the serious offenses and stifling the justice of local and private courts. He reflects on the great advance in the principles of criminal liability. Take, for example, Bracton's stress on moral guilt. He held that homicide was not committed unless the will to injure was present. He contended that it was the will and intent which created the offense. This attitude reflects a radical break with the traditional system, which held a man responsible for his acts however remotely connected with intent and will. In the realm of civil law Bracton spoke freely about land law, property, and personal status.

The extent of Bracton's debt to Roman law is still being debated. If it was large, as some legal historians argue, then considerable Roman law found its way into English law because of Bracton's great prestige; if it was small, as other historians argue, then his treatise consisted for the most part of genuine English law. The latter view seems the more convincing and credits Bracton's familiarity with Roman law with making it possible for him to organize his legal material and to mold it into a reasonable and logical treatise. Maitland has said that Roman law stimulated Bracton and other lawyers "to think seriously and rationally of English law as a whole, to try to set it in order and represent it as an organized body of connected principles."

The influence of Bracton on the common law in succeeding centuries, though variable, has been significant. Bracton summed up the law as it had developed by the middle of the thirteenth century and passed it on to future generations of lawyers. He accomplished for the law in the thirteenth century what Blackstone accomplished for it in the eighteenth. For a century after its appearance, Bracton's great book dominated English legal thought and study. It was copied and recopied, condensed, and summed up. Then in the latter part of the fourteenth and fifteenth centuries Bracton's influence waned as English law became completely insular and its practitioners became ever more disinterested in the theory of law and ignorant of Roman law except for a few maxims. In the sixteenth century, however, Bracton's influence regained prominence and his work held a place of honor in the legal world of the seventeenth century. Both common law lawyers and parliamentarians used Bracton to demonstrate that the king was and should be under the law. Bracton was respected as an authority and cited in the common law courts. In both English law and constitutional history he has played a valuable role because he helped form the thought and tradition that successfully resisted absolutism.

The accomplishments of Bracton and his colleagues underline the great strides made by the practitioners of the common law since the days of Glanville. For a century they had labored in an environment of legal freedom; they had been almost unrestricted in the legal remedies and procedures they could initiate. They were not hampered by statutes or by a jealous lawmaking parliament. They were the legal pioneers of England, responsible for at least 90 percent of the law made in the reign of Henry III. Served by such lawyers, the royal courts rapidly became the regular courts for all important cases except those claimed by the church. The law of the royal courts continued to squeeze the life from the old local courts so that local law steadily gave way to common law. All favored the triumph of royal justice because its procedure was more summary, more rational, and more practical. Procedure, archaic, clumsy, and unprogressive, could not compete with a justice that was offering jury trial not only for civil but also for criminal cases.

3. THE COMMON LAW UNDER EDWARD I

The reign of Edward I marks a radical break in the method of making law. A superb organizer and administrator, Edward was appalled at the informal process by which law grew and frustrated by the confusion he found in the different branches of law. His most notable achievement was to legislate order into the enlarging labyrinth of the common law. Like the other major institutions such as parliament, the household departments, and the council, the common law system was transformed into a definite organization. We can, for example, clearly distinguish between the court of common pleas, the king's bench, and the small council. We can begin to say what cases are properly entertained in each court. Statutes are beginning to rigidify many points of law which the judges and lawyers, however clever, cannot circumvent or modify. It is becoming possible to separate an ordinance from a statute. The former is made only by the king in small council; the latter is enacted by the king in great council or parliament. The statute is a general and timeless law; the ordinance is a special and limited administrative order that always gives precedence to statutory law. Edward's reign is the great watershed in English legal history; all law prior to the great legal reforms of the nineteenth century stems from it.

The first result of Edward's vigorous legislation was to block the development of unenacted law and to slow up the growth of the common law. But it must be remarked that judge-made law had been losing momentum since the middle of the thirteenth century. Though the common law judges devised legal remedies through new writs, only the chancellor could issue them; he, of course, also devised and issued writs on his own. The barons tried to limit the writmaking power of the chancellor during the period of bitter conflict between them and Henry. They resented having a chancellor—a loyal friend and servant of the king—wield so much power because they realized that a new writ was a new law. They feared his power even more when Henry ruled without a chancellor and personally ordered the issuance of new writs. In this fear the barons were joined by the common law judges, not because they feared new judicial writs, but because they wanted to have exclusive control over their invention and had strong feelings against outsiders' tampering with their law and its procedure. The Provisions of Oxford specifically stated, therefore, that no new writs could be sealed without the consent of the king and his council (the barons). There was the belief, which continued to grow, that the law was almost complete and would suffer by further additions and modifications. Though ultimately this trend of thinking would limit the legal innovational power of the judges, they supported it and began to decide whether writs issued by the chancellor were innovations; if they believed they were, they refused to entertain them in their courts. Such a check upon legal innovation was so arbitrary that the Second Statute of Westminster in 1285 attempted a compromise. It was stated that when a new remedy was needed the clerks of the chancery should postpone issuance of a writ until after consultation in parliament with men learned in the law. But even this slight concession to innovation was opposed by the judges, who felt that their legal system was perfect and that they were the natural defenders of a law which only they could declare. Maitland has written: "Henceforth the common law was dammed and forced to flow in unnatural artificial channels. Thus was closed the cycle of original writs, the catalogue of forms of action to which nought but Statute could make addition."

The judges had abetted what became admitted principle under Edward I, that changes in the law could be made only with the consent of parliament. Henceforth any growth of the common law was by the fiction and evasion of the judges, who preferred circumlocutions to law consciously and continuously changed by themselves. Thus confined, the common law lost jurisdiction and elasticity. Large tracts of law such as merchant and maritime law were abandoned, and the power to give equity was completely surrendered to the king and his council, who soon gave it to the chancellor and his clerks.

The shift from judge-made to enacted law is reflected in the transformation taking place with the lawyers. Though learned and clever in the English law, they no longer have the breadth and depth of Bracton and his associates. The two law texts of Britton and Fleta are hardly more than brief summaries of Bracton's book and but note what changes Edward's statutes have wrought in the law. The lawyers have obviously become more specialized and provincial; no longer do they care about or study Roman law. They know little about derivative legal systems on the Continent. There will be no more influence wielded by the Roman law until the sixteenth century. This exclusiveness is also seen in the type of judges who work for Edward. More and more they are laymen; clerics are becoming the exception. It is generally felt that churchmen should not staff the common law courts, not only because of their sympathy to the canon and Roman law but also because they ought not to preside over courts wherein judgments ordering death and bloodshed are meted out.

The insularity of English law attained by the end of Edward I's reign had both negative and positive results. In losing a knowledge of Roman law the lawyers permitted the common law system to become a confusing puzzle of undefined principles. It became cumbersome and ill equipped to keep pace with the new demands made upon it by political, economic, and social change. Its course charted, the common law plodded on until it became archaic in the nineteenth century. Then the Industrial Revolution and the radical change it brought forced basic legal reform, reform with which the names of Bentham and Mill are associated. On the positive side it may be said that English law was saved from Roman law; thus England was spared an absolutism nurtured by the legal maxims of Roman law. In enunciating the doctrine that the king must rule by law and in winning the support of parliament for this principle, the common law insured the triumph of constitutionalism.

Another development of Edward I's reign was the emergence of a powerful and influential legal profession which supplied the royal judges and dominated the practice of law. The human element of the law became so organized and professionalized that men had to labor enormously in learning and practicing the law. The professional lawyer of Edward's day did nothing but practice law. He had no other occupation; he was neither a cleric nor a royal administrator. He made his living from the law by representing litigants and giving legal advice. This institutionalization of the profession was but another sign that the common law was breaking away from other legal disciplines and from other professions.

The legal profession that took form under Edward I consisted of two classes—pleaders and attorneys. Traditionally in England a litigant had been permitted the assistance of friends when pleading in court; there is definite evidence of such a practice beginning with the reign of Henry I. All litigants except those accused of a felony were allowed assistance. The chief advantage of having a pleader speak for an individual in court was that the pleader could disavow a mistake made by the litigant and thus avoid loss of a case through an error. The litigant who used a pleader had two chances of escaping error. In the thirteenth century it was customary to ask the litigant if he desired to abide by the statement of his pleader. Richard de Anesty in his famous case that dragged on for five years used a number of pleaders, including Glanville. Men who made a profession of being pleaders in the church courts frequently practiced their skill in the royal courts. The regulation of pleaders in the canon law courts seemingly influenced the organization of pleaders for the royal courts. By the middle of the thirteenth century the records speak of pleaders in the royal courts as a professional class; they had begun to wear their distinctive dress, the coif. In the earliest Year Books there is reference to the conduct of great causes by skilled pleaders, by a clique of such renowned men as Louther, King, Huntingdon, and Heyham. Regarded as learned men whose opinions on the law carried much authority, they seemed to dominate all the important litigation. Regulations were issued concerning the practice of the pleaders in the royal courts. In 1292 the king ordered his judges to provide a certain number of pleaders who were to have the exclusive right of practicing in the royal courts. These men were to have apprentices who were to train in the law. Some of the expert pleaders were retained by the king to plead his cases and were called servants or serjeants-at-law. In the fourteenth century they were to dominate the practice of law.

The other class of the legal profession was the attorneys. An attorney was an individual appointed (attorned) to stand in the principal's stead. The right of having an attorney was derived from the royal prerogative; the English kings were the first to empower men to represent them and to perform various tasks. By Glanville's day the right had been extended to those engaged in civil litigation in the royal courts. Before the attorney could appear, however, the principal had to go to the court and appoint him and receive authorization by royal writ. Generally litigants appointed attorneys when going abroad, on a crusade, or on the king's business. In the reign of Henry III the attorney was not a professional man; he could be any person empowered to act for another. A wife, for example, could represent her husband. Gradually men appeared who made a business of representing whoever would employ them. By Edward's day there was a professional class of attorneys. They were included in the regulation for pleaders in 1292, which in effect authorized certain pleaders and attorneys to appear in the royal courts. Earlier the municipal council of London in a move to exclude those unlearned in the law had ordained that only authorized pleaders and attorneys could practice in the civic courts. The royal directive of 1292 seems to have had the same objective. The men appointed secured a monopoly of practice. By this time pleaders and attorneys had definitely become separate legal practitioners and they exist as such in England today. The attorney represented his client and appeared in his place; the pleader spoke on behalf of his client, who was present in court or represented by his attorney.

Whereas Bracton and the lawyers of his day learned their law from Glanville and minor legal treatises, from cases enrolled on the Plea Rolls, and from experience, the lawyers of Edward I's reign learned their law principally from another type of legal literature—the Year Books. We have seen that the Year Books were law reports of cases and the discussions that took place in court. They included the arguments of the pleaders as well as the opinions of the judges. It appears that they were first compiled by men interested in studying the law—the apprentices. The Year Books supplemented the Plea Rolls and the textbooks as the principal means of learning the law. Students concentrated upon the cases reported. These reports became so well known, so widely used, and so authoritative that they could be cited in the courts. The common law had become case law. A case or a series of cases made a precedent that was accepted as law.

We must assume that for some time men who desired to learn the law served as apprentices to the judges and to the pleaders. This informal system worked well while clerics predominated. Learned men who could read and write, they did not require the assistance needed later by laymen. To provide for the new class of men entering the law during Edward I's reign guilds or fraternities sprang up which eventually became the Inns of Court—the famous English law schools. The necessity to receive royal authorization to practice in the courts may have stimulated the development of legal education in order to meet certain professional standards. Moreover, it seems likely that the men authorized to practice were also authorized to train apprentices, who, when they met the standards, were accepted for practice in the courts and could, in turn, train other apprentices. Young men seeking to learn the law naturally congregated about the central law courts at Westminster during term time and lived where the judges and lawyers lived. Here they became apprentices and learned the law from observing the masters in the courts and from study of the standard legal literature and cases. They got together informally at their lodgings to discuss the law and sometimes to have mock trials. There are references to such discussions in the 1290's, and in 1305 a Year Book tells us that one of the royal judges was baffled by a knotty case which had been manufactured by a group of students in order to settle a difficult legal problem. These students may have already been organizing themselves into legal guilds so that they could discuss the law and lodge together in a dwelling or a large hall. Organization stopped here under Edward I, but in these first steps can be discerned the origin of the Inns of Court—Lincoln's Inn, Gray's Inn, and the Inner and Middle Temple. These associations worked out a system of instruction and discipline and came to confer what in effect constituted law degrees. In the fourteenth century the Inns of Court were one of the great legal institutions associated with the common law system.

All the developments we have discussed testify to a remarkable advance in the common law under Edward I, but the crowning achievement of this consummate administrator was his legislation. Though we shall discuss some of his statutes in detail when we examine civil and criminal law it will be useful at this point to note the principal statutes and their content. The first great Statute of Edward was that of Westminster I in 1275. It dealt with every aspect of the law—civil, criminal, constitutional, and procedural. Its fifty-one clauses treat such matters as wardship, jury trial, limitations of actions, and essoin. In 1276 was enacted that peculiarly titled statute Rageman. Apparently the term "Rageman" was a nickname for the Hundred Rolls, derived from the ragged appearance of the returns resulting from the *Quo Warranto* proceedings of 1274–1275. These returns necessitated pleas to settle the jurisdiction held by franchise courts and the Statute Rageman was enacted to assign justices to hear these pleas. The Statute of Gloucester in 1278 dealt further with the *Quo Warranto* proceedings by fixing the competence of local and franchisal courts and giving landlords remedy against termors (lessees) who permitted the land to lie waste.[2] In 1279 came the Statute of Mortmain or *De Viris Religiosis*, which prohibited granting land to the church except under royal license.[3]

Four years intervened before the Statute Acton Burnell or *De Mercatoribus* was enacted in 1283. It made royal law of what had long been the custom in many boroughs, the registering of debts due to merchants for collection without the delay of litigation.[4] The statute most resembling modern statutes was that of Wales in 1284. It was a codification of the rules of English law so that this law could be introduced into the conquered land of Wales. This statute resembles some of the nineteenth-century codifying acts drawn up for introduction into lands of the British Empire. In the same year the Statute of Rhuddlan prohibited trial of common law cases in the exchequer court unless the king was directly interested in the litigation. The Statute of Westminster II followed in 1285 and probably ranks as the most important in the development of land law. Fifty clauses treat such legal matters as estates tail, mortmain, novel disseisin, *nisi prius*, and limitation of the issuance of writs. There were also two other statutes in 1285. That of Winchester improved the police system and reorganized the old assize of arms in the form of the commission of array; that of *Circumspecte Agatis* (act circumspectly) dealt with the proper spheres of lay and ecclesiastical jurisdiction.[5]

After a lapse of five years there came in 1290 the Statute of Westminster

[2] SM, no. 52A.
[3] SM, no. 52B.
[4] SM, no. 52D.
[5] SM, no. 52E.

III, sometimes called *Quia Emptores* (since purchasers). This statute ended subinfeudation by new rules set up for the alienation of land by feudal lords.[6] Seven years later in 1297 occurred the constitutional crisis that ended in the *Confirmatio Cartarum* and the approval of some new articles, chief of which dealt with the proper method of granting supply to the king. Closely associated with this famous confirmation was the *Articuli Super Cartas* (articles on the charters) of 1300, which again confirmed Magna Carta and the Charter of the Forest and included an enactment on the subject of conspiracy.[7] The last great statute of Edward was that of Carlisle in 1306–1307. It restricted the sending of money out of the realm by the church and so initiated a series of later statutes directed against anti-English practices of the church such as appeal of cases to the papal court and the appointment of foreigners to English benefices.

4. THE ROYAL COURTS

Of the local public, franchisal, and private courts we shall say little; they will be mentioned only when necessary to explain the common law court system in the thirteenth century. We will concentrate upon the central common law courts and the itinerant courts. In the middle of the thirteenth century the central royal courts were taking final form, a form and distinctness that was to last until they were absorbed by the Supreme Courts of Judicature in 1875. These courts were three—the king's bench, the court of common pleas, and the exchequer. During Henry III's reign the first two courts followed in the path of the exchequer and became separate courts. Until Henry III attained his majority in 1224 he could not hold a court *coram rege*. Under John the separation between the court of common pleas and king's bench had disappeared; one court tried all cases. But after 1224 when Henry III became of age the two divisions of the *curia regis* re-emerged. Men were ordered to have their pleas heard at the king's bench or at the court of common pleas, and each court had its own records—the *coram rege* and *de banco* rolls. We have seen that the disappearance of the justiciarship contributed to the separation of the courts; after 1268 when the office was no more, each of the three courts secured a chief justice.

Theoretically the king's bench was a common law court held before the king and his justices. Both John and Henry III held justice in person and their justices followed them about the realm. But such attention to legal detail could not continue; inasmuch as all justice flowed from the king, he abandoned the practice of sitting regularly in court and delegated justices to represent him. By the fourteenth century it was exceptional to find the king sitting on his bench. In matters of jurisdiction the king's bench was the central court for pleas of the crown. Criminal cases had to be initiated before

[6] SM, no. 52F.
[7] SM, no. 52H.

itinerant justices in the county where the crime was committed, but when the king's bench was in the county it served as a court of first instance. It could, by virtue of powers of general jurisdiction, remove any criminal case from the itinerant justices and dispose of the case itself. It had a large control over all royal officers such as the sheriff and would hear complaints against them. It could hear any civil case in which breach of the king's peace was involved. By the thirteenth century any use of force, however trivial, was interpreted as breach of the peace and could be brought before the king's bench.

The king's bench had jurisdiction in cases where the correctness of the decision of an inferior court was in doubt. This did not mean that a case could be appealed to the king's bench; there was no such thing as appeal. It meant that an error or errors had to be alleged in the case as judged in an inferior court and that the erroneous judgment must be upset in new proceedings. This was done through a writ of error, which removed the case to the higher court where the errors were presented by the plaintiff. The defendant was summoned by writ of *scire facias* (make to know) to hear the errors and the new case then determined whether the alleged errors were real errors. Finally, it should be noted that through fictitious legal means the king's bench stole much legal business from the court of common pleas. This is principally explained by the desire of the justices of the bench for more legal business; each case meant fees, from which the justices derived much of their living. Competition between the courts for legal business became very bitter with the result that jurisdiction became much less definite. The judges resorted to any subterfuge to attract cases into their courts.[8]

The court of common pleas was the central court with jurisdiction over all cases between private individuals. Private cases did not, as we have seen, follow the king about. They were heard at the court which, as prescribed by Magna Carta, sat permanently at Westminster. The court of common pleas had exclusive control over all cases except those of trespass in which the king's peace was involved and then it had a concurrent jurisdiction with the king's bench. It could supervise and correct the errors of older local public courts and it had exclusive jurisdiction over its own officials.[9]

The third central common court was the exchequer, which had become a distinct and separate department of state in the twelfth century. During most of the thirteenth century there was little difference between the financial and judicial functions of the exchequer, and it retained close relations with the *curia regis*. By the end of Edward I's reign, however, the judicial work was separated from the financial and the judicial part of the exchequer became closely connected with the other two common law courts. Various developments led to this separation of functions. The exchequer got its own

[8] SM, no. 54F.
[9] SM, no. 54A.

Plea Rolls in 1236–1237.[10] The ten "barons of the exchequer" ceased to denote high officers of the exchequer and meant instead officers with mixed judicial and administrative duties. By the early fourteenth century the importance of judicial functions caused the king to select barons of the exchequer from prominent exchequer clerks or from eminent lawyers of the common law courts. In Edward I's reign the exchequer got its own chief justice, called the chief baron, and by the end of his reign we may say that the court of exchequer had become a separate common law court distinct from the old financial department. This court was presided over by official barons, often professional lawyers, and had its own records and routine. The fiscal work of the exchequer was performed under the supervision of the lord treasurer and the chancellor of the exchequer; the judicial work was conducted by the chief barons and three or four other barons. The court of exchequer had jurisdiction over revenue cases and, through legal usurpation, over common law litigation that ordinarily should have been heard in the other two courts. But this latter jurisdiction was taken on primarily in the fourteenth century. In the thirteenth century revenue cases came to the exchequer by way of petition. If a subject thought he had a claim against the king, he would present a petition to the king and his council and the matter would be referred to the exchequer with the injunction to render justice. Where a question of general law was involved, the barons of the exchequer were told to associate themselves with the justices of the two other courts in order to be instructed on the point of common law involved. But this step was unnecessary as the exchequer became more proficient legally and was staffed by competent lawyers.

These, then, were the three central courts of the common law. They did not, however, exhaust the royal justice. If one could not get justice in them, he could go to the king's council or parliament.[11] Though in the thirteenth century a distinction had arisen between the small and great councils, the king did justice in either and men were not careful to note where justice was done. For example, errors of the inferior courts could be brought before the small or great council. Eventually only the great council—the future House of Lords—would be the ultimate court of error in parliament. But in Edward I's day the small council was also an ultimate court of appeal. It actually disposed of more cases than the great council and was as Maitland described it "a standing committee of the other." The development of the peculiar prerogative justice of the council that one finds in the court of the chancery and Star Chamber was only to take definite form in the fourteenth and fifteenth centuries. The judicial characteristics of the small council that gave rise to this justice may be seen, however, in the fact that the small council, as well as the large, could dispense any type of justice, not only

[10] SM, no. 54C.
[11] SM, no. 54G.

common law justice but also equitable justice, which was not bound by any corpus of law.

Below the central courts of Westminster were those of the itinerant justices, who had been commissioned to transact all types of royal justice in the counties on their judicial eyres since the reign of Henry II. The judicial commissions varied in scope. The broadest commission was to hear all pleas (*omnia placita*) in the counties. When the justices sent out from the king's central courts received such comprehensive commissions, they were known as justices in eyre. All legal business of a county pending in the king's courts was transferred to the court of the itinerant justices, and the litigants, rather than going to Westminster, appeared before them. With a general eyre the justices received instructions empowering them to secure information and to inquire into local maladministration; this information was secured from empaneled juries of hundred and county. The instructions or articles of the general eyre (*capitula itineris*) concentrated on crime and royal financial rights. Inquiries into robbery and murder were mixed with those into illegal profits of the sheriffs. For these eyres a full county court of all freeholders was convened. Here juries, judicial and administrative, furnished the information; here trials were conducted; here amercements were slapped upon county, hundred, and tithing for neglect of local police or government responsibilities. The general eyre was regarded as a burden and anticipated with trepidation. So "inquisitorial" and exacting were the inquiries and penalties that in 1237 the residents of Cornwall hid in the woods rather than face the itinerant justices. All complained that general eyres occurred too frequently. In Henry III's reign, therefore, they were held not oftener than every seven years, though of course the king could order them whenever he deemed it necessary. With taxes and information increasingly secured in national assemblies and with justice done more often by less comprehensive commissions, purely judicial in nature, the need for such broad judicial and administrative visitations lessened. By the reign of Edward I the general eyre had ceased.

In the thirteenth century three judicial commissions became prominent and whittled away the power of the general eyre. One was the commission of assize, which heard the three possessory assizes of novel disseisin, mort d'ancestor, and darrein presentment. It was composed of itinerant justices who were commissioned to go out and hear only possessory causes. These commissions had been popular in the latter part of the twelfth century, and it may be remembered that Magna Carta enjoined four such commissions yearly. In the reissue of 1217 the number was reduced to one a year and this became the practice in the thirteenth century. At first it had been customary to commission four knights of the county to hear these possessory assizes but under Henry III professional judges were also used. Generally one curial judge was sent out to associate with some of the county knights. By the end of the thirteenth century statute law provided that one of the justices must be of the king's bench or court of common pleas, or be a serjeant-at-law.

The Statute of Westminster II in 1285 added greatly to the duties of justices of assize. By this time many legal actions other than the assizes were tried by jury. When a case was ready for trial at Westminster a jury from the county in which the case had originated had to travel to Westminster to hear the case and to submit a verdict. This was a heavy burden for the litigants and jurors and slowed down the process of justice. It was for this reason that the statute of 1285 intervened and modified the system. It provided that all actions should be triable before the justices of assize. According to the procedure set down, the central court at Westminster where the case had been initiated would direct the sheriff to have the jurors at Westminster on a certain date unless before (*nisi prius*) that date justices of assize should arrive in his county. The same statute ordered the assizes to be conducted three times a year although in practice there were but two. In any event the justices of assize would normally arrive before the scheduled date of trial at Westminster and the case would be tried "at *nisi prius*." Customarily the justice delegated to hear cases *nisi prius* was from one of the central courts but, while acting in this capacity, he was simply a judge commissioned to take the assizes of a certain circuit. No matter in what court the assize had been initiated, the judge held the assize but did not represent any of the three courts. He presided over the assize but did not give judgment. The court in which the action began gave judgment after the judge had conducted the trial.

The second specialized commission to develop in the thirteenth century was that of gaol (jail) delivery. Found at the outset of the century it directed certain justices to deliver a certain gaol of all prisoners. Because men were generally imprisoned only if charged with homicide, the commission was no great burden. Though it could be given to a royal justice it went more frequently to local men of the county such as prominent knights. The advantage of this judicial commission was in relieving the pressure on inadequate prisons and in speeding the judicial process.

The third new commission, that of oyer and terminer (from the French words meaning "to hear" and "to settle"), developed after that of gaol delivery. It was issued sporadically during Edward I's reign and came into regular use when the general eyre ended. This commission was given to two or three royal justices or to great landholders of the counties. Men so empowered were authorized to hear and to determine all felonies and other crimes in the county. The commission was more comprehensive than that of gaol delivery because it empowered the justices to receive indictments against individuals not in jail. Both commissions, it must be understood, authorized the trial of criminal cases that were pleas of the crown. The whole procedure of indictment, pleading, and trial was conducted before the commissioners, and they passed judgment and sentence. These commissions were quite different from the commission of assize, which authorized the hearing of civil cases whose final judgment was handed down in one of the three central courts.

These three judicial commissions injected new vigor into the common law system by making royal justice more swift and by dispensing a greater amount locally where it was easily accessible to the residents. By the end of the thirteenth century the central courts were relieved of much litigation that was done locally, often under the supervision of local men. Gradually, however, these commissions were transferred almost completely into the hands of royal justices. Royal justice was dispensed locally by royal justices from Westminster.[12] This development promoted close rapport between central and local justice and prohibited local justice from splintering into provincial custom and procedure. A central control guaranteed one royal law common to the realm.

5. CIVIL PROCEDURE

The complicated legal detail that superimposed itself upon royal legal procedure in the thirteenth century is outside the scope of this book. We can but briefly summarize the salient features. The first procedural step in real property cases was the process. A defendant was summoned by the sheriff to appear at a particular court on a certain date. To insure appearance pledges were generally taken. If the defendant proved uncooperative, some of his chattels would be attached. If this action did not bring him into court, his land would be seized and awarded to the plaintiff. The award, however, was subject to a suit in right initiated by means of a writ of right. Such extreme action was seldom taken because the defendant usually answered the summons. Normally the case was delayed by endless essoins happily supplied by lawyers to the defendants. For actions on personal property much the same process held, except that it was extremely difficult to seize the chattels involved. With personal property cases numerous essoins were also permitted.

After the various steps in the process had run their course and the defendant had come to court, the civil pleading began. The defendant could answer the plaintiff's accusation with a simple denial as in Saxon and Norman times, although generally he answered with exceptions or supplementary statements that gave him much more room for legal maneuver. If the defendant answered the plaintiff's original declaration (count) with an admission of guilt, then judgment followed. But if he chose legal maneuver, a number of courses were open to him. He might answer the declaration with a demurrer, which meant that he would admit the facts of the declaration but deny that they were subject to any legal action. This raised a question of law which then had to be settled. If the demurrer was upheld, the case was

12 SM, no. 52G.

thrown out; if not, it would continue, subject most likely to other demurrers. The defendant could also reply with any number of pleas. He could, for example, deny that the court had any jurisdiction over the case. He could plead that he was a minor and not obliged to defend the suit until he attained legal age. He could plead an abatement which alleged that there was a legal defect in the writ or the plaintiff's declaration. A more complicated plea was to plead in bar, which meant that an answer was given on the merits. The defendant could answer with a traverse—a denial. To a traverse the plaintiff could demur or he could join issue with it. The defendant could also answer with a confession and avoidance, whereby he admitted the facts of the declaration but pleaded other facts that changed the legal situation of the case. To a confession and avoidance the plaintiff could reply with a traverse or with a confession and avoidance. The defendant could then plead a surrejoinder. To it the plaintiff could plead a rebutter and to it the defendant could plead a surrebutter. Finally the litigants would reach an issue of law or an issue of fact, which would then be decided by the justices and the jury. Though some of these pleadings were not fully developed until the fourteenth and fifteenth centuries, their principles were well understood in Edward's day. It is hardly necessary to say that they prolonged justice almost endlessly. Such freedom of tortuous pleading helps to explain why the common law became so cumbersome and why complaints are repeatedly heard in the fourteenth and fifteenth centuries that justice is unobtainable in the common law courts.

The next stage in civil procedure was the trial. By the reign of Edward I trial by jury had become the dominant form, though in certain cases the defendant could have trial by compurgation and battle. Originally introduced to cover only the possessory assizes, the assize *utrum*, and the grand assize (to determine ultimate ownership), jury trial was eventually extended to cover most civil cases; it was the simplest and most logical manner of getting justice. Twelve good and lawful men of the community—neighbors who were witnesses to the facts—were empaneled by the sheriff to be at court and, after listening to the pleading, to give the verdict. Once it had been given, the court judgment followed in accordance with the point of law involved. The judgment was then executed by the appropriate officers. After judgment had been handed down, the defendant could secure another trial by the allegation of error and take his case to a higher court. Or he could purchase a writ of attaint and sue the jury for giving a false verdict, an act considered semicriminal because the jurors were supposed to know the truth and were sworn to tell it; if they did not, they had perjured themselves. The writ of attaint first appeared in 1202 and by the end of the thirteenth century was applied to all actions concerning land. When such a writ was secured another jury, twice the size of the first, was empaneled to give a verdict on whether the original jury had perjured itself. If the verdict was "guilty," then those of the jury who had given a false answer were punished while the others were unpunished. The defendant also won his case.

6. CRIMINAL PROCEDURE

When criminal actions were involved the first step was the process of arrest. The local officers with the assistance of the local police organization, the tithing groups, would give the hue and cry and attempt to arrest the criminal. When an individual evaded arrest he became a fugitive from justice and was asked (exacted) by the county court to appear. Exacts were carried out at five county courts. If the fugitive still did not heed the summons the sentence of outlawry was pronounced and he could be slain on sight and his property forfeited to the crown.

In the case of criminals found with the guilt upon them, the procedure was most summary. The individual was arraigned before the court, condemned, and executed without being permitted to say a word in his defense. Maitland has said that this summary procedure in the thirteenth century was "ridding England of more malefactors than the king's courts can hang." Though the procedure of individual appeal remained in England down to 1819 it was frowned upon by the royal courts because of the motives from which the appellor often acted. The appellor was frequently an approver serving as the king's evidence. He was a person who confessed his guilt to a crime and then in return for a pardon appealed other criminals. Such appeal was open to flagrant abuses and came to be admitted by the courts only after the closest examination. Declining already in the thirteenth century, this procedure of appeal was decadent by the end of the Middle Ages.

The normal method of bringing criminal cases to trial in the thirteenth century was by indictment of a grand jury. Dating from the Assize of Clarendon enacted by Henry II, the grand jury had developed constantly in the ensuing years. The king and his justices broadened the original pleas of the crown until all criminal actions save the pettiest were triable in the royal courts and indictable by a grand jury. At both the general eyres and the sheriff's tourns presentments were made by representative juries from the hundred. The bailiff of the hundred selected two or four electors who in turn chose twelve men. From these fourteen or sixteen men a grand jury of twelve was constituted. The articles of the eyre were read to this jury and it was directed to indict all men known to have committed, or suspected of having committed, any of the offenses listed. The jurors could present from their own knowledge or from what they learned from other residents of the hundred. The presentments made by the grand jury did not constitute an assertion that the indicted person was guilty, only that he was suspected. The trial that followed tested the suspicion raised.

Once the suspected criminal was in court the pleading began. Unlike litigants in civil cases the criminal suspects were not permitted legal advice, a rule that held until the nineteenth century. They were compensated for this by being allowed a large number of technical pleas which nullified the indictment. The rule that a man must, at peril of his life, plead the right plea could not be fairly enforced against a suspect ignorant of the law. It became customary, therefore, to allow the suspect who had pleaded not guilty to urge any point he could offer in his defense. Even if convicted, he was allowed to introduce any argument or fact to show why sentence should not be passed. As a typical example, a suspect might plead that the indictment did not specify on which Feast of Saint Peter the crime had been committed. Many of these pleas were developed in the thirteenth century as the legal profession increased in skill; they formed the basis for the intricate legal stratagems employed by the clever criminal lawyers of today.

As with civil procedure, the trial followed the pleading. Criminal trial by ordeal had been outmoded by the judicial innovations of Henry II, and its death knell was sounded by the Fourth Lateran Council of 1215 when it forbade clergy to take part in the ordeal because it involved bloodshed. Trial by battle remained, but it had always been limited for the most part to the feudal class. It, too, declined in popularity as life became less martial and men less skilled in arms. Moreover, no man could be tried by battle when indicted by a grand jury because this made the crown the accuser and forced the indicted to accept the mode of trial approved by the royal courts. Trial by battle did not disappear, however, until 1819. Compurgation, though still in existence, had been discredited since the introduction of the grand jury and other criminal procedure by Henry II; it was seldom used.

Meanwhile men were becoming familiar with jury trial for civil cases, and it was becoming common for a man appealed of a crime to purchase the writ *de odio et atia* to have a jury determine whether he had been accused out of spite and hate. By the end of the twelfth century men indicted by the grand jury were also permitted to purchase this writ and, in effect, have a jury determine whether they had been maliciously indicted. Whether a man was appealed or indicted, if the jury found that the charges were motivated from spite and hate, the case was ended. In effect the writ *de odio et atia* gave the accused a type of trial by jury. This trial jury was called a petty jury (from the French *petit*, meaning "small") to distinguish it from the grand jury, which was customarily larger, consisting of at least twelve jurors and sometimes as many as twenty-four. By the early thirteenth century, therefore, the groundwork was laid for trial by jury.

The problem to be faced after 1215 was to find another form of trial for criminal cases. Frankly neither the law nor the lawyer knew what to do about the indicted men overflowing the inadequate jails. It seemed almost sacrilegious to sentence a man who had not undergone one of the traditional proofs. There was the feeling that mere human testimony and humans could not send a man to his death. In 1219 upon the eve of the first general eyre of Henry III's reign, the council had to make some provision for trial.

A writ of instructions addressed to the justices shows the indecision of the royal councillors. It began by admitting confusion in regard to proper trials for criminals. It then stated that for certain serious crimes the accused was to be held in prison; for other less serious crimes the accused was to be expelled from the realm; and for very light offenses the accused was to find pledges for good behavior. The writ concluded by instructing the justices to use their own discretion while on the eyre. Not a word was said about compelling those accused to undergo trial by jury.

Apparently such confusion lasted through most of the thirteenth century; various experiments were tried. As early as 1221 some of the royal justices accepted the verdict of an extremely strong and reliable jury and condemned the prisoner if found guilty even though he refused trial by jury. All concerned, however, still seemed reluctant to force a man to accept trial by jury because the jurors who composed the petty jury were the same as those of the grand jury. Concerning trial by jury Bracton straddled the fence, along with other justices. It was prevailing opinion that a man so tried had been prejudged and that no verdict other than guilty could be expected. Men resented having to abide by the decision of prejudiced indictors, prejudiced because thirteenth-century jurors, petty and grand, were regarded first as witnesses, as men who knew the facts. Should any juror be ignorant of the facts, he was expected to acquaint himself with them by any means possible. Under these conditions trial by jury could not be impartial. Still, it seemed the only solution and royal justices cast about for means of persuading the indicted to accept jury trial or, as the records say, to put themselves upon the country. For a while the expedient of locking a recalcitrant man in prison for a year and a day with scarcely anything to eat or drink was resorted to as a means of compulsion. Apparently it achieved some success for the legal records tell of many men putting themselves upon the country.

Trial procedure thus drifted until 1275. The Statute of Westminster I then enacted that "notorious felons openly of ill fame who will not put themselves on inquests for felonies with which they are charged before the justices at the king's suit, shall be put in strong and hard imprisonment (*en le prison forte et dure*)." So began the famous *peine forte et dure* (pressure hard and severe) which survived until abolished in 1772. Such felons were loaded with heavy chains and placed on the ground in the worst part of the prison; they were fed a little water one day and a little bread the next. We also learn that more iron or stones were put upon the individual to make his imprisonment more painful and to persuade him to accept trial by jury. Under such hideous conditions many men chose to die rather than to take their chances with trial by jury. They did not want their families to be deprived of property that was automatically forfeited to the crown upon conviction of serious crimes. When men died under hard and severe pressure they did so without having been convicted of crime in a court and the families therefore inherited the property. Such a severe alternative served to break down recalcitrants, however, and we hear of many more men putting themselves upon the country. Maitland has said that one should think of *peine forte et dure* "whenever one hears talk of trial by jury as of an obviously just institution. Our ancestors did not think so."

Meanwhile various innovations were slowly transforming the composition of the petty jury. During the period when it was merely the presentment jury sitting in a different capacity there were times when it was composed of the presentment jury plus men secured from four neighboring communities such as agrarian villages. When such a combination forms the petty jury, we then occasionally find that the verdict differs from the judgment found in the presentment. Towards the end of the thirteenth century the presentment jury was gradually augmented by jurors selected at random from the general region, that is, from the different hundreds of the county. The petty jury formed from such jurors became more representative and impartial but still retained its witness-bearing nature.

The next step in the evolution of the petty jury came at the turn of the century. It became the practice to form a special trial jury of twelve from members of the presentment jury and from one or more jurors selected from presentment juries of various other hundreds. Although there is some evidence that the accused came to have the right of challenging those members of the trial jury who had also been on the jury indicting him, no hard and fast rule about having men serve on both juries was enacted until 1352. In the Statute of Treasons it was stated that "no indictor shall be put in inquests upon the deliverance of a party indicted of trespass or felony if he be challenged for the same cause by him which is so indicted."[13] The petty jury finally came to be separated from the presentment jury and to be drawn from the country at large. But it took five centuries to remove all the means of influencing the jury and to render it impartial.

We shall say no more about the petty jury for the present except to note certain of its characteristics. Throughout most of the thirteenth century it was considered primarily a source of information rather than a body constituted to judge facts presented to it. The jurors were selected from the neighborhood in which the crime was perpetrated for they were considered better qualified to tell the truth about what happened. The jurors were a group sworn to tell what they knew about the case; they were not an impartial group listening to information supplied by other witnesses. Witnesses as we know them were nonexistent in the thirteenth century. The witness-bearing character of the petty jury explains why, into the fourteenth century, verdicts were interpreted as reflecting the opinion of "the country" or of the preponderant evidence. The petty jury was not regarded as a body that could know absolutely about the truth or falseness of a fact.

[13] SM, no. 62F.

After a man had been found guilty or innocent the judgment of the court followed. With criminal cases the law permitted more freedom to the judge in deciding upon the proper penalty because crime could not be measured in as precise penalties or terms as could civil wrongs. The execution of the judgment was by the responsible royal officers, generally the sheriff and his subordinates. Fines, imprisonment, banishment, infliction of wounding, and death were the common punishments. When the death sentence was handed down it was executed as rapidly as possible. The records telling of such a sentence frequently end with the phrase "Let him see a priest."

7. SPECIAL COURTS

Courts of special jurisdiction, both royal and nonroyal, can be treated to better advantage when we investigate the legal history of the fourteenth and fifteenth centuries. For the moment we shall but mention the principal ones. The borough courts with their special law merchant and royal legal franchises have already been noted. The boroughs to which numerous foreign merchants came for trade secured the right to hold courts for settling economic disputes between English and foreign merchants. These courts, called the courts merchant, developed their own law and procedure, which was, in a way, international because it dealt with commercial litigation that concerned merchants from all over Europe. There continued to be the special fair courts held by the lords and boroughs possessing such a right. They were called pie powder courts from an anglicized form of the French *pied poudré* (dusty foot) because they were frequented by merchants with dusty feet. The fair courts administered a special law merchant quite similar to that found in courts of fairs throughout western Europe. Royal courts of special jurisdiction were those of the constable and marshal, which had jurisdiction over the royal military forces and administered a martial law both savage and summary.

Outside the royal courts, the ecclesiastical system of courts was the most important. It was governed by a unified corpus of canon law that had a longer and prouder tradition than the English common law. Thanks to almost a thousand years of resistance by the church against usurpation of its independence the church courts enjoyed a high justice with a far-flung jurisdiction. In England the church courts had enjoyed such special status only since the Conquest, since William the Conqueror had separated lay and spiritual courts and had worked to model English ecclesiastical organization after that of the Continent. From the Conqueror's day on, crown and church had struggled to determine what rights properly belonged to each. The defeat of Henry II on the issue of benefit of clergy insured the English church considerable juridical independence and the opportunity to increase the competence of its courts over legal matters that could just as well have been adjudicated by secular courts.

The principal church court was that of the bishop for his diocese. Though the bishop often presided over the court, normally he delegated this task to his chancellor, who held what was called a consistory court. Frequently the bishop delegated authority to ecclesiastics called commissaries to hold his court in various parts of the diocese; these courts were known as commissary courts. By the thirteenth century when the diocese was subdivided into districts headed by archdeacons the courts of a bishop's diocese consisted of the consistory court and of local courts presided over by the archdeacons, who exercised jurisdiction over petty criminal cases and others governed by canon law. Since the canon law court system recognized judicial appeal, a case could be appealed from the archdeacon's court to the bishop's, then to the archbishop's, and finally to the papal *curia*. The court of the archbishop of Canterbury was known as the Arches because it convened in London in the church of Saint Mary-le-Bow, which had a spire supported by arches. This peculiar structural style caused the church to be called Saint Mary of the Arches. This court not only received appeals from the bishops' courts but was a court of original jurisdiction. It constantly encroached upon episcopal justice to secure more legal business. In addition to the court of Arches the archbishop held a court of audience at which he personally heard cases. There was also a prerogative court, whose jurisdiction was derived from the special prerogative powers of the archbishop. When a man holding land in two dioceses died, this court claimed the testamentary jurisdiction. Such was the court system of the archbishopric of Canterbury, and it was duplicated by that of the province of York.

The jurisdiction of the ecclesiastical courts was based upon the principle *ratione personae* and *ratione materiae*. Though the high legal claims of the church courts were never completely admitted by the crown and though eventually most of the jurisdiction was appropriated by the state, in the thirteenth century spiritual courts laid claim to three areas of justice. First, they claimed criminal jurisdiction over cases in which a clerk was accused, jurisdiction over religious offenses, and a broad corrective jurisdiction over clergy and laymen for the health of their souls. Religious offenses included heresy, witchcraft, blasphemy, abnormal sexual acts, drunkenness, slander, and usury. Under corrective jurisdiction came promises and contracts made under oath or pledge of faith; this explains their control over contract in the thirteenth century. Secondly, since marriage was one of the sacraments, the church courts claimed jurisdiction over matrimonial cases; they adjudicated such questions as annulment and legitimacy. Testamentary cases, because of their close relation to marriage, were also claimed; this entailed probating and administering wills and supervising testaments. All executors and administrators were under supervision of church courts. The movable goods of individuals dying intestate were distributed by the church. The origin of this right seems to stem from the Anglo-Saxon period when the church was urging men to make wills and was drawing them up for those who could not read or write. Such probating power, however, extended only to personal property after the Conquest. With the advent of the feudal system, land could not be willed; if it was not alienated before the holder's death, it had to pass to the legal heir. Finally, the church courts claimed jurisdiction over all matters of an ecclesiastical nature—ordination, consecration, celebration of divine services, status of ecclesiastical persons, and ecclesiastical property such as advowson, land held in free alms, and spiritual dues.

In regard to the last claim, relating to property and advowson, the church steadily lost ground. The policy of Henry II and his successors of forcing all litigation over land to be decided in royal courts deprived the church of determining, for example, disputed claims to clerical offices. Because church livings were endowed with land and tithes, they were regarded as real property and so treated. Although procedure stipulated under the writ *utrum* stated that land found to be held in free alms should be under jurisdiction of the church, this position had been reversed by the thirteenth century. By the end of this century the church courts had lost their jurisdiction over all causes connected with land.

The battle between royal and spiritual courts was caused by the underlying medieval struggle of state and church. Specifically it involved crown jealousy of any infringement of its prerogatives, an attitude which in the thirteenth century came to be associated with a growing spirit of nationalism. Most English subjects came to regard themselves as endowed with special laws and privileges that no outside power could infringe upon. They consequently supported the crown in its battle to whittle down the sphere of ecclesiastical justice; both kings and subjects were ably supported by the common law lawyers, who were professionally jealous of the church courts and who resented their claims in the peripheral fields of litigation. We can observe, therefore, a definite trend in the thirteenth century to oppose the international power of the papacy not only in the matter of taxation but also in that of justice.

Two royal enactments on these matters are noteworthy. One, the Statute *Circumspecte Agatis* of 1285, specifically defined the function of ecclesiastical courts and the limits of lay and spiritual jurisdiction. Though it definitely reserved all matters purely spiritual for the ecclesiastical courts, it enunciated the doctrine that the church should act circumspectly with other justice. This statute buttressed the writ of prohibition that, since the twelfth century, had forbidden a church court to hear a case over which a lay court had the proper jurisdiction. The Statute of Carlisle in 1306–1307, which was directed against the fiscal policy of the church and forbade the payment of certain taxes that would drain wealth out of the realm into the papal treasury, is important legally because it served as precedent for subsequent statutes that restricted papal authority over England. The kings resented, in particular, the appeal of cases to the papal *curia* and attempted to restrict or to end the custom. They succeeded in the fourteenth century by two statutes of Praemunire (premonish) that forbade appeal of cases above the court of the archbishop of Canterbury or outside England. The position of the church declined steadily in the fourteenth and fifteenth centuries as it was drained of prestige by the Babylonian Captivity, the Great Schism, and a general degeneration of spirit, and as England and other western states developed a spirit of nationalism that would tolerate little church interference in their internal affairs.

It should be emphasized that none of the special courts noted above were permitted to use jury trial; it was a monopoly of the common law courts. In the royal prerogative courts not governed by common law there was great flexibility in procedure and the judges decided the cases. This was true also with the other special courts. The church courts employed inquisitorial methods, often used on the Continent against heretics, in order to secure evidence from recalcitrant witnesses and litigants, and from this evidence the judges made their decisions. Such procedure was regarded as alien to the English legal tradition and accounts for the unpopularity of the courts that used it.

XXX

The Substance of the Law

THE legislation of Edward I profoundly influenced land law. And it took much legislation to untangle the problems created by the decline of feudalism in the thirteenth century, a decline that brought the disappearance of political and military interests in land and a magnification of economic interest. The transition from feudal to nonfeudal relations wrought by the recurrence of money was working in favor of the tenant and to the disadvantage of the lord. Under feudal law the tenant or vassal enjoyed no rights of ownership; he had only possession of a fief, which was held as long as certain military and political obligations were performed. The tendency of the thirteenth century, however, was to regard the tenant as an owner and to give him proprietary rights. Despite the ultimate triumph of this trend in land law, Edward I attempted to thwart it by legislation because he and the great barons stood to suffer if it continued unchecked. Edward's legislation caused the implanting of much feudal custom into English land law with the result that modern Anglo-American law is more feudalistic than are other law systems. In the struggle that formed between lord and tenant over rights to land in the thirteenth century, the lawyers and the common law courts supported the tenant and were matched against the king and barons in parliament.

1. THE LAND LAW

Before continuing with land law we must speak of tenure. Theoretically the king was the only real owner of land; he owned all his realm and all land was held of him. He was the lord of tenants or vassals who held land of him along with the right to use it in return for specified service. These were the tenants-in-chief. They in turn granted out portions of these lands to tenants or vassals in return for service, and these vassals in their turn could do likewise. Under feudal law this was subinfeudation and the lords and tenants once removed from the king were known as intermediary (mesne) lords and tenants. Most land was held by feudal tenure, although there were six different tenures, all of which required the tenant to render some service to the lord.

We may rapidly dispose of tenure in villeinage as it was unfree and under the jurisdiction of the local seignorial courts. It was, therefore, unaffected by the common law and by the changes wrought by Edward's statutes. Tenure in free alms also need not detain us. It was tenure under which land was granted to the church in return for the performance of some spiritual service and was somewhat exceptional in England. Most of the land in England was held by the tenure of knight service (feudal tenure), which we have previously examined in detail. We are interested at this point only in the so-called incidents of this tenure, rights which the lord had over his tenants. In addition to the customary feudal aids, the lord possessed the incidents of relief, escheat, wardship, and marriage, with all of which we are familiar. Lords also held the incident of consent, which was necessary when tenants desired to alienate land; when consent was given fines were customarily collected. There was also what is called primer seisin. This was the right of taking the first possession (seisin) after the tenant's death. Though there was much opposition against this lordly right, the king retained it in the thirteenth century and could keep the heirs of his deceased tenants out of their lands for a year or, in lieu of this, extort one year's profit from the land in addition to the relief. The other lords did not retain this right. They were deprived of it by the Statute of Marlborough (1267), which declared that no lord could seize the land of a deceased tenant but could make only formal entry upon it to show evidence of his lordship.

Two other tenures were those of grand and petty serjeanty. Under them the tenant held land in return for some service less than knight service. Grand serjeanty differed little from knight service and petty serjeanty came to be regarded as but a variation of another free tenure called free socage. Socage tenure specified the performance of some nonmilitary service, which customarily consisted of a rent in either money or kind payable to the lord, or the obligation to do so much plowing or hauling service for the lord. This tenure involved some incidents but not all the burdens involved with knight service. The three aids were owed, payment of relief was customary, and when a tenant died without heirs the land escheated to the lord. If the king was lord, he was entitled to a primer seisin and must give permission for alienation. The incidents of wardship and marriage did not pertain to socage tenure. Most land, as we have said, was held by knight service; the tenure of free socage was rare when land was held directly of the king, but many of the mesne tenants held by this tenure. All the tenures except that of villeinage were free and persons so holding were known as freeholders and were protected by the royal courts.

Complicating freehold tenure was a practice that had been customary since the Conquest. Land had been let for terms of varying duration to lessees (termors) in return customarily for some consideration such as a rent. For a long time custom had held that the lessees had no right in the land, that is, no real right; all they had was a personal right against the lessor, which meant that the contract must be honored. While this custom remained in force the lessees were not regarded as holding in freehold and so were not freeholders. Although before Edward I's reign the custom had changed and the lessees were given more rights in their land and more protection in the royal courts, still they were not considered freeholders and so had no right in the county court nor the right to vote; they did not acquire the franchise until the Reform Act of 1832.

With the various tenures in mind we can now turn to some of the statutes to see how they affected land tenure. As we proceed it must be understood that the lord was primarily interested in maintaining his right to all the incidents of tenure for they were essentially all that he had left of value in land; military and political service was no longer of any consequence. The tenant, on the other hand, was just as determined to escape these incidents and to gain more control over his land; he wanted full ownership.

Medieval lords were long confronted with the problem of their tenants' granting land to the church. Because the church never died, never married, and never had children, none of the incidents of tenure could apply to this land. The land had been granted into a dead hand, in "mortmain" as the records say. To remedy this situation Edward I finally enacted the Statute *De Viris Religiosis*, which forbade alienation of land to the church without the consent of the lord, on pain of forfeiture.[1] In practice this statute did not serve its intended purpose; lords too often gave their permission in return for a pecuniary consideration. Also, as we shall see, the lawyers developed legal means to defeat the purpose of the statute.

Another problem created by the decline of feudalism was subinfeudation. Originally a part of the logic of feudalism because it helped to provide lords with military service, by Edward I's reign the king and barons wished the practice had never existed. As subinfeudation operated, if V (vassal) who held of L (lord) enfeoffed MV (mesne vassal) with land and then V's land escheated or wardship was necessary, L lost all the incidents over and income from the land held by MV except the services which MV was obliged to render to V. Since military service had lost its value, the service was worthless. This was apparent to landholders in the thirteenth century and they therefore customarily granted land in return for very nominal services such as rendering a red rose upon a specified date. The principal reason for subinfeudation was the money received by the landlord as a purchase price from the tenant. The Statute of Westminster III, generally called *Quia Emptores*, was intended to save lords a loss of income. In effect, it ended subinfeudation. Applying this statute to the example cited above, we see that V may alienate his land to MV, but when he does, MV will not become his tenant but the tenant of L and will owe to L all the service, the incidents, that V formerly owed to L. All the feudal incidents accrue to L rather than to V, who has been removed from the equation. His only gain is the price

[1] SM, no. 52B.

received for alienating the land to MV. The result of this statute was eventually to bring all landholders into immediate relations with the king and thereby multiply greatly his tenants-in-chief. The statute killed subinfeudation and hastened the demise of the feudal system.[2]

The part of the Statute of Westminster II (1285) dealing with *De Donis Conditionalibus* (concerning conditional gifts) tackled the most complex problem of the land law; its provisions tremendously influenced the future course of the law. According to feudal law when a lord granted a fief to a vassal it was under certain conditions and the vassal secured only limited rights to the fief. The vassal held land by the tenure called "fee simple," fee because it was a fief, and simple to distinguish it from tenurial variations that developed. Under feudal law these fees could not be willed because that would destroy primogeniture, the very essence of the feudal system. In the thirteenth century, as feudalism was disappearing while its law remained in force, the tenure of fee simple became complicated; all sorts of adjustments had to be made as land sloughed off its feudal nature and became nonfeudal or became land to which proprietary right applied.

In the thirteenth century when a landlord conveyed land to a purchaser, the latter did not receive it in fee simple (now interpreted as conveying full ownership) but with limited rights of ownership. For economic rather than for military and political reasons, the lord now desired to hold all the traditional rights to the land so that there would be a good chance of its coming back to him by escheat. The purchaser, on the other hand, feared that this might happen and thereby deprive his descendants of land that he had labored to add to the family holdings. He feared also that the land, so dearly acquired, might be alienated after his death. Both seller and purchaser had become extremely nervous about the legal status of their land and did everything possible to guarantee that it would remain in their families.

Influenced by such considerations, powerful families possessing a great deal of land experimented with methods whereby their descendants would retain the landed wealth indefinitely, no matter what events or forces tended to drain it off. Such families holding land in fee simple endeavored to pass it on to heirs with certain conditions. The method customarily followed in the twelfth and thirteenth centuries took the form of selling the land to a living son on condition that he do the same and that it descend to his heir and so on indefinitely. Such an estate of land was called a fee simple conditional.

The royal courts, however, supported by the kings, who did not look kindly upon families' securing too tight a control over land, threw their influence on the side of free alienation and permitted individuals to alienate their land freely no matter under what condition they had received it. Generally the lawyers also favored this view because they felt that ancestors

[2] SM, no. 52G.

should not be allowed to control the destiny of land *ad infinitum*. In Edward I's reign the royal courts are found interpreting grants of land to an individual "and his heirs" as terms of limitation and not of purchase. However devious this interpretation might appear it meant that the only beneficiary of the alienation was the individual and that the phrase "and his heirs" merely defined the estate (interest) transferred to him. The heirs, so the interpretation ran, had not secured any right in the land and were merely mentioned to limit or describe the individual to whom the land was granted. It followed that as soon as an heir was born to the grantee the description or limitation was fulfilled and he could then grant his estate of land in fee simple to another party if he so desired.

This legal interpretation was viewed with alarm by the great barons and in the Statute of Westminster II they inserted a clause dealing with conditional gifts. It provided that land should always descend "according to the form expressed in the charter" (*secundum formam in carta expressam*) so that those to whom the land had been granted upon certain conditions should have no power to alienate it; free alienation was thereby thwarted. By this statute estates tail were created, so named because they were restricted (*taille* in French, meaning "cut down") to the line of descent specified in the original charter. For a while after the passage of this statute it was doubtful whether it prevented alienation only by the grantee or by the grantee and his heirs. Eventually the latter interpretation prevailed and the modern estate tail (fee tail) was created.

It soon became clear to lawyers that the donor of a fee tail had not granted away everything that he had to give. It was seen that the donor might give directions so that the land could "remain" to another person rather than "reverting" to himself. When such directions were given, interests in "remainder" or "reversion" had been created. The conditions enforced by the statute greatly increased the chances that granted land would revert to the donor, who came to look upon reversion as a valuable property right which he could sell to a third party if he desired. All sorts of arrangements for reversion came to be made. In a typical case L might grant land to V "and his heirs legally begotten" with a remainder to VB (V's brother) or to VD (V's daughter), with the same limitation on heirs. Upon the extinction of V and his line the land consequently does not revert or return, but remains to the second line VB or VD. In this manner a right of remainder and a line of remainder men were created. Such a right of remainder came to be termed an estate in expectancy and was considered real property just as much as the land. Such an estate was considered a freehold and the holder was legally protected in his rights.

By the end of Edward I's reign there were three basic freehold estates in possession: the fee simple, the fee simple conditional, and the fee tail. In addition there was the estate in expectancy and others which we can only summarize. A life estate was held only for the life of the holder. There was the dower right of a woman to receive one-third of her deceased husband's estate. There was the right of curtesy by which a husband enjoyed his deceased wife's estate until he died. And there was land mortgaged for a debt, land which the creditor received possession of until the debtor had repaid the loan. To protect this transaction the land was conveyed by debtor to creditor in fee simple with the provision that upon payment of the debt the land should be reconveyed back to the debtor. This arrangement created the estate defeasible (terminable) upon a subsequent condition (repayment of the loan at a specified time).

Such were the principal freehold estates and their legal protections and rules. Obviously the statutes dealing with mortmain and conditional gifts were resented by numerous landholders because their freedom of alienation was severely restricted. They and the lawyers, often abetted by the royal courts, looked for devices by which the intent of the statutes could be defeated. The statute against mortmain was soon neutralized by the technique of a collusive lawsuit called recovery. An example: L wishes to grant land to M, a monastery. By mutual agreement M sues L for the land, claiming a superior title to it; L allows the suit to go by default and thus surrenders the land to M by court judgment. A similar action, developed later in the fourteenth and fifteenth centuries and known as common recovery, grew out of the collusive lawsuit and was used to "break" or "bar" entailed estates. Basically, common recovery was a child of the old Anglo-Saxon custom of vouching to warranty. A purchaser P who desired to buy a fee tail from a landlord L would bring a collusive lawsuit against L, who, instead of defaulting, vouched to warranty a third party W from whom L claimed to have secured the land and whose obligation it was to warrant L's title. W would appear in court and accept the obligation, with the result that he took L's place in the case. W would then disappear, permitting the case to go by default and the land to be conveyed to P by court judgment. Once this had been done, L's heirs were barred from any inheritance since they must proceed for their rights against W rather than P. It was generally arranged so that W held no property, and later some minor officer of the court fulfilled W's role. Eventually the pretense of a lawsuit was dropped and the interested parties simply filed the necessary records with the court and paid the fees. The action of common recovery remained prominent down to the nineteenth century.

Another device for by-passing the statutes against free alienation was that of granting land to one individual for the use of another. The common law recognized the ownership of the individual granted the land but the use and benefits derived were enjoyed by the other party. Evolving after the restrictive legislation of Edward I, this practice founded the doctrine of uses, which later contributed its principles to the law of trusts. In a case where the intent was to avoid the Statute of Mortmain, L would convey the land to O, stating in the deed of conveyance that O should permit use of the land by the church. Though O has the legal ownership, he is trusted by L to let the church use the land and to derive all benefits from it. The common law recognized only the right of O and there was no legal remedy against him if he decided to withhold use of the land from the church. The trust given him was considerable; if he broke it, the only remedy was to petition the king and his council for equitable justice. Soon this device was applied to breaking entailed estates and to preserving land for heirs when a man was accused of treason and in danger of forfeiting all land to the crown. It was also used in making wills which named a trustee or several trustees who were given instructions on what to do with the deceased's lands. Often these trustees were empowered to appoint successors; in this way the individual making the will insured that his plans and rights would prevail. In the fourteenth and fifteenth centuries the king's council and chancery took notice of such proceedings and developed a new body of equitable law to see that justice was done.

2. PERSONAL PROPERTY AND RULES OF INHERITANCE

Although we have talked about immovable or real property and about the rights in real things (*in res*), or real actions as the law called them, we have said little about personal property. Not until the twelfth and thirteenth centuries did there develop a concept of personal property as different from real property. Previously the law had made no distinction between a cow and an estate of land. One brought the same action for recovery of a cow or a chair as he did for recovery of a piece of land. Such legal thinking and action could not continue as the money economy gained in vigor and caused men to evaluate their personal property or wealth in terms of money. It became ridiculous to sue for a cow or a chair when a payment of money would suffice. Men consequently began to sue for the recovery of money and there developed a real distinction between personal (movable) and real (immovable) property. Because originally a cow had been the most valuable form of personal property, all movable property came to be termed "chattels" which was but a variant of "cattle."

At first when movable property was recovered it had to be under the legal action of theft; the thief was hanged and the property restored. By the Angevin period the kings not only confiscated the thief's property but frequently appropriated the property he had stolen. Thus when the injured party sued, he generally recovered his property in the form of a money compensation. In the last years of Henry III's reign when the criminal action of trespass became common, a variant of it was employed to recover personal property. This variant was called the action of goods taken away (*de bonis asportatis*). Under this action the plaintiff sued for property compensation in the form of money; if successful, he received damages in the payment of money.

We shall say little about the inheritance laws of real and personal property.

According to the feudal custom of primogeniture all fiefs had to be inherited intact by the eldest son. As feudalism became less military and less rough, daughters were permitted to inherit fiefs. The eldest daughter was given little preference over younger daughters. By the thirteenth century lords were receiving homage from all the daughters and thereby acquiring marriage rights over more than one heiress. When this became common practice it also became customary to divide the property of a deceased man equally among his daughters. A man's daughters, therefore, were co-heiresses when a male heir was lacking, and they were termed coparceners (equal sharers).

A difficult inheritance problem arose when a landholder died without any direct heirs. Under feudal law wills were not recognized and no clear theory had evolved on the rights of collateral relatives. Eventually, around the middle of the thirteenth century, lawyers developed a theory which still partially holds today; this was the parentelic system. It was argued that upon a man's death his children could represent his claim. First the complete oldest surviving branch (*parentela*) of a family must be exhausted before an heir could be secured from the next oldest branch. After much debate over how far afield the search for an heir could go, it was finally decided that the limit of relationship should be sixth cousins. The accompanying table

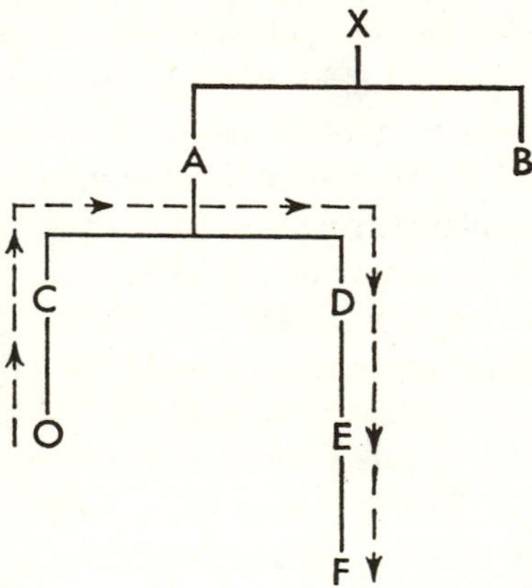

illustrates how the parentelic system worked. If O is taken as the *prepositus* (head), it is seen that he has no descendants. Then one looks to C for descendants; he has none so one then one goes to A and goes through his descendants in order. If D and E are dead, then F will inherit after O because neither A nor C can inherit as they are direct ascendants. Under the parentelic scheme F is also closer to O than B.

The inheritance laws governing personal property were fairly well defined by Edward I's reign. Real property was excluded from testaments or wills for feudal reasons, but personal property was not. For its disposition the church had always encouraged the making of a will. According to the rules that developed, a man could bequeath his personal property subject to certain family rights known as the *legitime*. If only the wife survived, she received half of the property. Similarly, if children survived, but no wife, they received half of the property. When the wife and children survived, each party received one third and it was hoped that the remaining fraction would go to the church as a reward for praying for the deceased's soul. An executor was named for the will, which was probated in the church courts, probably because the church from an early time had emphasized the importance of wills and the sinfulness of dying intestate (with no will). The church courts distributed the personal property according to the terms of the will.

3. CRIMINAL LAW

During the twelfth and thirteenth centuries there gradually developed a distinction between civil cases and serious social offenses which fell into the category of criminal cases. Though by Edward's death the distinction between civil and criminal cases was far from complete, much progress had been made. Along with this separation there arose a semicriminal action called the action of trespass which in turn led to the development of the law of tort. We must understand the details of these developments because they exerted a lasting influence over the common law.

Previously we have traced the growth of such concepts as the king's peace and the pleas of the crown and have noted how the types of offenses included constantly grew. Though we must use terms and concepts not yet fully developed in Edward's day, it should be pointed out that from the pleas of the crown grew three categories of crime—treason, felony, and misdemeanor. The law of Edward I had not clearly defined treason; it was ignorant of the concept of misdemeanor; and it had only come to an understanding of the meaning of felony. The threefold classification was just in its first stage.

The most serious offenses triable in the royal courts were known as felonies. The word "felony" was derived from the Latin word *fel* meaning "gall." A felony was, therefore, looked upon as venomous. By the reign of Edward I felony included such crimes as homicide, arson, rape, robbery, burglary, and larceny. These offenses could be prosecuted by way of indictment or by individual appeal. The penalties involved loss of life or limb or outlawry; a felon's goods were confiscated by the crown and his land was forfeited to the crown for a year and a day, thereafter escheating to the felon's lord. With these crimes we can note the beginning of ideas on criminal responsibility. Very young children, for example, could not be held guilty of felony and individuals of unsound mind or those who killed by misadventure or in self-defense were pardoned. Still, such individuals were liable to be sued by the injured party or his relatives. Different kinds of homicide were unknown. Murder still meant secret homicide and the term "manslaughter" had not yet appeared. Burglary was an offense committed feloniously in time of peace and consisted of breaking into churches, houses, and into the walls and gates of villages and boroughs. As yet it did not signify an offense committed during the night. In the case of theft a distinction was made between grand and petty larceny. Any offense involving stolen goods worth less than 12*d.* was considered petty larceny and not a felony. Theft was already being regarded as wrongfully taking something from another's possession. Treason was not yet clearly distinguished from felony but was regarded only as a most serious type of felony. It was later that treason was defined as breach of allegiance to the king.

During Edward I's reign a few forces were at work that led to the concept of misdemeanor. Individual appeal, although it survived the Middle Ages, was hastily retreating before indictment, which was found to be more efficient in bringing a man to justice. Still there had to be some procedure whereby an injured person could obtain a remedy by himself. By the late thirteenth century such a procedure appeared in the form of trespass, called by Maitland that "fertile mother of actions." The action of trespass was a quasi-criminal proceeding aimed at serious breaches of the peace. The guilty person was punished and the plaintiff compensated. A trespass was a tort (wrong); it was initiated by the injured person and was of a criminal nature. The importance of the trespass is explained by its penal and reparatory nature. From its penal side came the misdemeanor and from its reparatory side came the law of tort. Out of the miscellaneous and minor trespasses eventually developed the misdemeanors of later law, those minor offenses such as blows that did not draw blood or break bones. Though some were tried in the royal courts, increasingly they were shunted to local courts or the justices of the peace. It was the Statute of Westminster II that started trespass on the way to being a tort. The limited power granted to make new writs was used chiefly to expand the domain of trespass. Under a liberal interpretation practically any trespass, almost any cause of action, could be viewed as a kind of wrong (tort) by the plaintiff.

The law of tort under Edward I, however, was far from this stage of development. There was, for example, no action for defamation and the only action for perjury applied to a jury suspected of having perjured itself. In Edward's reign there were remedies only for personal violence, for forcible seizure of property, and for various frauds and offenses that came to the court's notice during the trial of a case. The real law of tort does not develop until such frauds and offenses, no matter where and when committed, became subject to legal actions.

Of the various personal actions entertained for recovery of personal property there were four principal ones: detinue, debt, covenant, and account. The writ of detinue was employed when there was wrongful detention of a chattel. The writ of debt, almost identical, sought the restoration of money. It was used for any money claim except money taken by force, which was covered by the writ of trespass. The action of covenant was used primarily to secure compliance with the terms of leases but the terms had to be in written form or the law would not recognize them. This action was soon extended to cover all sorts of personal property. The last action, that of account, was used to secure remedies against bailiffs of manors, guardians, and partners. It had been used throughout the thirteenth century but was improved by legislation in 1267 and 1285.

Mention of the actions of detinue and debt leads logically to the subject of contract because the line separating property, for which they were used, and contract was as yet very indefinite. Writs of detinue and debt were similar to the writ *praecipe* in that they asked for the restoration of something. But the problem in Edward I's day was whether these writs could be used to enforce a contract. The most we can say is that when a man sued to obtain restoration of a debt owed to him personally, the word *debet* must be used in the action of debt; but if the suit was brought by the creditor's executor the word *detinet* must be used. The theory seemed to be that the creditor could demand the money as his property whereas the executor could not; he could only ask that a prior agreement be honored. It would seem that the former action lay in the realm of the law of tort; the latter, in that of contract. But it is still too early to speak of a law of contract. No clear delineation between tort and contract was drawn during Edward I's reign; all that was known was certain forms of actions that could be used under specific circumstances. With contract, symbolic acts still loomed prominently. Contractual parties still clasped hands or made solemn Christian oaths. Not until foreign associations of Italian bankers lost control over banking and credit transactions would the English become their own bankers and become familiar with the concept of contract and with the rules necessary to insure good faith.

4. CONCLUSIONS

Though the legal historian Maitland would admit that the supreme achievement of the thirteenth century was parliament, he would place it only slightly above the far-reaching developments in the common law. The three great central law courts had definitely become separated and distinct, each with its special jurisdictions, routine, and records. What could not be done under the common law could be done by the king and his council or by the High Court of Parliament. To handle the fields of law that the common law would not touch after it narrowed its scope of jurisdiction by limiting the introduction of new legal remedies, courts of special jurisdiction developed or expanded their jurisdiction; these were the church courts, the courts merchant, and the courts of the constable and the marshal. Locally, the reorganization of the judicial eyres into judicial assizes linked with the routine of the three central courts at Westminster expedited the flow of the king's justice. This reform, plus the more rapid and reasonable justice offered by the royal courts, forced the retreat of both local public and franchisal courts to the rearguard area of minor civil and criminal justice.

While civil procedure and trial continued to grow along the lines drafted by Henry II in the twelfth century, criminal procedure and trial broke sharply with twelfth-century tradition and gave birth to the criminal trial jury. This was the most important legal change in the thirteenth century and perhaps the most significant for the future of Anglo-American law. But the less dramatic and colorful transformation of the civil law, especially in the realm of land law and real property, laid down more legal foundations used today than any other development in the common law. The fourteenth- and fifteenth-century advance in law was fundamentally a more detailed working out of the law as Edward I left it in 1307. Until the nineteenth century only Tudor legislation could effect any major remodeling of Edward I's master legal structure. The great lawyers like Coke and Blackstone wrote commentaries on a law basically medieval and derived from the thirteenth century. It took the Industrial Revolution to change England enough socially and politically to force modernization of the law.

BIBLIOGRAPHY

The most comprehensive treatment of thirteenth-century political history with valuable discussions of constitutional problems is F. M. Powicke, *King Henry III and the Lord Edward: Community of the Realm in the Thirteenth Century* (Oxford, 1947). L. F. Salzman's *Edward I* (London, 1968) fails to highlight the achievements of Edward I. For a good evaluation of Edward I see Geoffrey Templeman, "Edward I and the Historians," *Cambridge Historical Journal,* X (1950), 16–35. For some of the principal figures and baronial families see N. Denholm-Young, *Richard of Cornwall* (Oxford, 1947), Charles Bémont, *Simon de Montfort* (Oxford, 1930), M. W. Labarge, *Simon de Montfort* (London, 1961), Michael Altschul, *A Baronial Family of Medieval England: The Clares, 1217–1314* (Baltimore, 1965), and H. S. Snellgrove, *The Lusignans in England, 1247–1258* (Albuquerque, N.M., 1950).

The studies of Bertie Wilkinson cited previously in the General Bibliography are especially valuable for constitutional developments in this period. For the royal council J. F. Baldwin's *The King's Council* remains essential. For the last of the great justiciars see Clarence Ellis, *Hubert de Burgh: A Study in Constancy* (London, 1952). A good study on a typical household official is C. M. Fraser, *A History of Antony Bek, Bishop of Durham, 1283–1311* (Oxford, 1957). Also informative on central administration is Michael Prestwich, *War, Politics and Finance under Edward I* (London, 1972).

A thorough study on taxation is S. K. Mitchell, *Taxation in Medieval England,* Sidney Painter, ed. (New Haven, 1951). For the development of fractional taxation see J. F. Willard, *Parliamentary Taxes on Personal Property, 1290–1334* (Cambridge, Mass., 1934). A detailed account of royal finance and parliament is G. L. Harriss, *King, Parliament and Public Finance in Medieval England to 1369* (Oxford, 1975).

The two principal studies on the struggle between Henry III and the barons are still those by E. F. Jacob, *Studies in the Period of Baronial Reform and Rebellion, 1258–1267* (Oxford, 1925) and R. F. Treharne, *The Baronial Plan of Reform, 1258–1263* (Manchester, 1932). See also *Documents of the Baronial Movement of Reform and Rebellion, 1258–1267,* J. J. Sanders, ed. (Oxford, 1973). Bibliographical guides list the many studies on this subject. For the relations of England and the papacy and for church organization see J. T. Ellis, *Anti-Papal Legislation in Medieval England* (Washington, D.C., 1930). Geoffrey Barraclough, *Papal Provisions* (Oxford, 1935), C. R. Cheney, *English Synodalia of the Thirteenth Century* (Oxford, 1941), and W. E. Lunt, *Papal Revenues in the Middle Ages* (New York, 1934), 2 vols. and *Financial Relations of the Papacy with England to 1327* (Cambridge, Mass., 1939). See also C. R. Cheney, *Notaries Public in England in the Thirteenth and Fourteenth Centuries* (Oxford, 1972) and J. E. Sayers, *Papal Judges Delegate in the Province of Canterbury, 1198–1254* (London, 1971).

A provocative study on local government is A. B. White, *Self-Government by the King's Command* (Minneapolis, 1933). A good account of the sheriff's functions is Geoffrey Templeman, *The Sheriffs of Warwickshire in the Thirteenth*

Century (Oxford, 1948). For local preservation of law and order see R. Stewart-Brown, *The Sergeants of the Peace in Medieval England and Wales* (Manchester, 1936) and R. F. Hunnisett, *The Medieval Coroner* (Cambridge, 1962). See also T. F. T. Plucknett, *The Medieval Bailiff* (London, 1954). For excellent studies on various aspects of local government see H. M. Cam, *Studies in the Hundred Rolls* (Oxford, 1921), *The Hundred and the Hundred Rolls* (London, 1930), *Liberties and Communities in Medieval England* (Cambridge, 1944), and *Law-Finders and Law-Makers in Medieval England* (New York, 1963). See also Frank Barlow, *Durham Jurisdictional Peculiars* (Oxford, 1950). Books containing material on the thirteenth-century borough are H. E. Salter, *Medieval Oxford* (Oxford, 1936), J. W. F. Hill, *Medieval Lincoln* (Cambridge, 1948), H. A. Cronne, *The Borough of Warwick in the Middle Ages* (London, 1951), C. R. Young, *The English Borough and Royal Administration, 1130–1307* (Durham, N.C., 1961), and G. A. Williams, "London and Edward I, "*Transactions of the Royal Historical Society*, XI (1961), 81–99 and *Medieval London: From Commune to Capital* (London, 1963).

The decline of feudalism is studied by J. M. W. Bean, *The Decline of English Feudalism, 1215–1540* (Manchester, 1968). For manorial administration and justice see N. Denholm-Young, *Seignorial Administration in England* (Oxford, 1937), W. O. Ault, *Private Jurisdiction in England* (New Haven, 1923) and *Open Field Husbandry and the Village Community: A Study in Agrarian By-Laws in Medieval England, Transactions of the American Philosophical Society*, IV (Philadelphia, 1965). For an idea of the extensive literature on the decline of manorialism and related problems see R. H. Hilton, *The Decline of Serfdom in Medieval England* (London, 1969), J. Maddicott, *The English Peasantry and the Demands of the Crown, 1294–1341* (Oxford, 1974), J. Z. Titow, *English Rural Society, 1200–1350* (London, 1969), and M. M. Postan, *Essays on Medieval Agriculture and General Problems of the Medieval Economy* (Cambridge, 1973).

The following studies provide the principal explanations for the origin and nature of parliament. Stubbs gives his account of the rise of parliament in vol. II of his history. Ludwig Riess treats the petitory nature of parliament in *The History of the English Electoral Law in the Middle Ages* (Cambridge, 1940). For the judicial interpretation of parliament see F. W. Maitland, *Memoranda de Parliamento* (London, 1893), C. H. McIlwain, *The High Court of Parliament and Its Supremacy* (New Haven, 1910), A. F. Pollard, *The Evolution of Parliament*, 2d ed. (London, 1926), and G. O. Sayles, *The King's Parliament of England* (London, 1975). Good accounts of the representative element in parliament are D. Pasquet, *An Essay on the Origins of the House of Commons* (Cambridge, 1925), G. L. Haskins, *The Growth of English Representative Government* (Philadelphia, 1948), and May McKisack, *The Parliamentary Representation of the English Boroughs during the Middle Ages* (Oxford, 1932). The interpretation of Stubbs finds support in M. V. Clarke, *Medieval Representation and Consent* (London, 1936) and in the various works of Bertie Wilkinson. For a brief summary of Wilkinson's views see *The Creation of Medieval Parliaments* (New York, 1972). It is impossible to cite the scores of other monographs and articles on parliament by such scholars as Cam, Clarke, Edwards, Haskins, Jolliffe, Lapsley, Morris, Plucknett, Powicke, Richardson, Sayles, Stephenson, Wilkinson, and Wood-Legh. Their ideas and their studies are admirably summarized by Geoffrey

Templeman, "The History of Parliament to 1400 in the Light of Modern Research," *University of Birmingham Historical Journal*, I (1948), 202–231, reprinted in *The Making of English History*, R. L. Schuyler and Herman Ausubel, eds. (New York, 1952) and by Edward Miller, *The Origins of Parliament* (London, 1960), Peter Spufford, *Origins of the English Parliament* (London, 1967), J. G. Edwards, *The Commons in Medieval Parliaments* (London, 1958) and *Historians and the Medieval Parliament* (Glasgow, 1960), and G. P. Cuttino, *"Mediaeval Parliament Reinterpreted,"* *Speculum*, XLI (1966), 681–687. E. B. Fryde and Edward Miller, eds., have collected studies by many of the leading scholars in *Historical Studies of the English Parliament* (Cambridge, 1970), 2 vols. For the possible influence of ecclesiastical assemblies upon the organization of parliament see Ernest Barker, *The Dominican Order and Convocation* (Oxford, 1913). See also D. B. Weske, *Convocation of the Clergy: A Study of its Antecedents and its Rise with Special Emphasis upon its Growth and Activities in the Thirteenth and Fourteenth Centuries* (London, 1937). For a comparison of the English parliament with representative assemblies of the Continent see Antonio Marongiu, *Medieval Parliaments: A Comparative Study* (London, 1968), A. R. Myers, *Parliaments and Estates in Europe to 1789* (London, 1975), and Bryce Lyon, "Medieval Constitutionalism: A Balance of Power," *Album Helen Maud Cam* (Louvain, 1962), II, 155–183.

Some of the finest work on the courts, procedure, statutes, innovations, and legal writing is to be found in the introductions to the legal texts published by the Selden Society. There one may read such as Maitland, Vinogradoff, Holdsworth, Gross, Baildon, Turner, Bolland, Neilson, Plucknett, Sayles, D. M. Stenton, W.H. Dunham, and S. E. Thorne. Thorne has now completed his edition and translation of Bracton along with a valuable introduction on the problem of the text: *Bracton on the Laws and Customs of England* (Cambridge, Mass., 1968–1977), 4 vols. Other useful books on Bracton are Hermann Kantorowicz, *Bractonian Problems* (Glasgow, 1941) and H. G. Richardson, *Bracton: The Problem of his Text* (London, 1965). On the relation of Roman to common law see W. W. Buckland and A. D. McNair, *Roman Law and Common Law* (Cambridge, 1936), T. F. T. Plucknett, "The Relations between Roman Law and English Common Law down to the Sixteenth Century," *University of Toronto Law Review*, III (1939), 24–50. On legislation and law see T. F. T. Plucknett, *Legislation of Edward I* (Oxford, 1949) and *Edward I and Criminal Law* (Cambridge, 1960), and A. W. B. Simpson, *Introduction to the History of the Land Law* (Oxford, 1961). On the Year Books see W. C. Bolland, *Manual of Year Book Studies* (Cambridge, 1925), R. C. Palmer, "County Year Book Reports: The Professional Lawyer in the Medieval County Court," *English Historical Review*, XCI (1976), 776–801. For other aspects of the law see N. D. Hurnard, *The King's Pardon for Homicide before A.D. 1367* (Oxford, 1969), J. B. Given, *Society and Homicide in Thirteenth-Century England* (Stanford, 1977), and R. B. Pugh, *Imprisonment in Medieval England* (Cambridge, 1968).

Part Five

EDWARD II, EDWARD III, AND RICHARD II

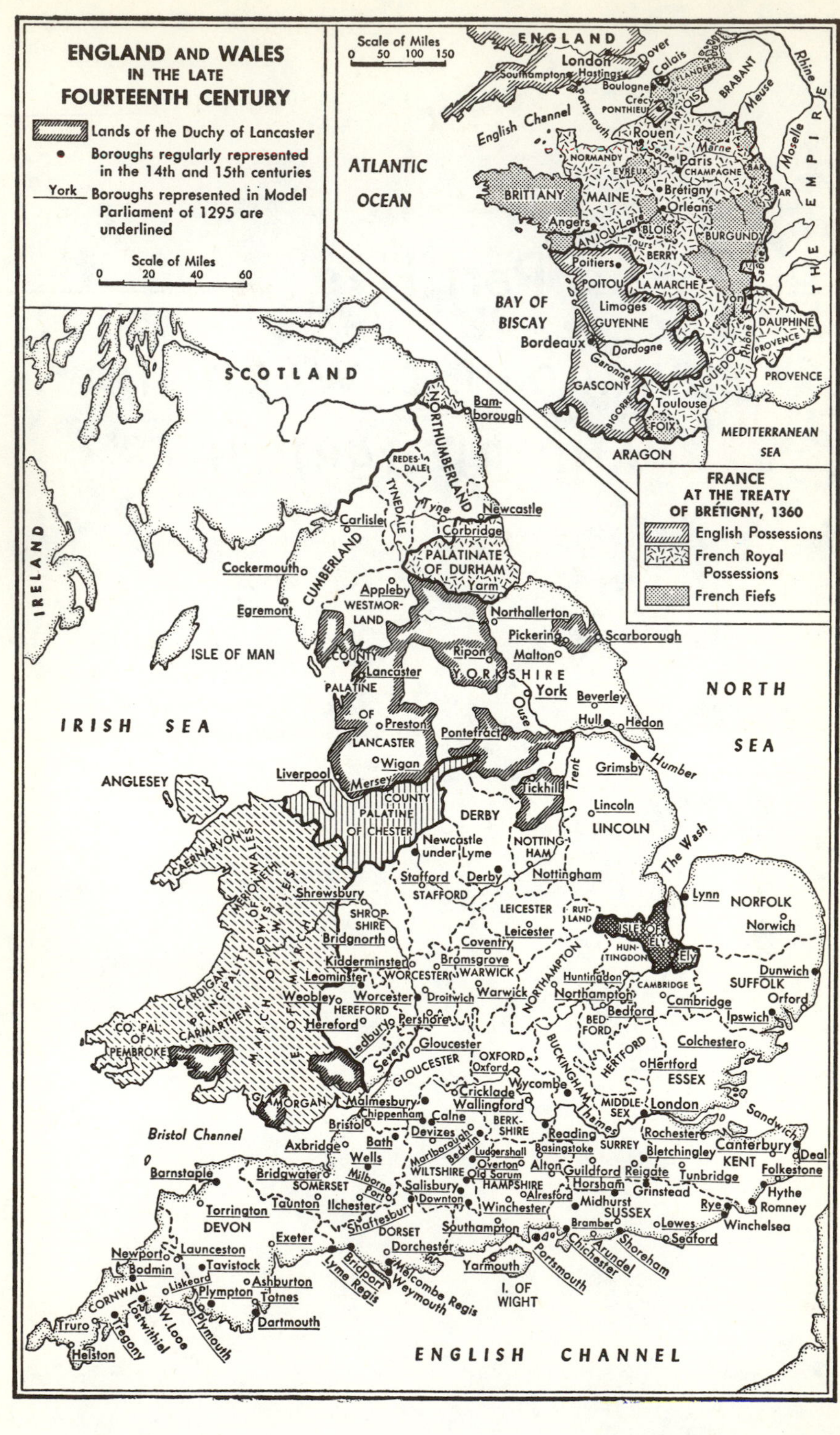
ENGLAND AND WALES IN THE LATE FOURTEENTH CENTURY
Lands of the Duchy of Lancaster
Boroughs regularly represented in the 14th and 15th centuries
York Boroughs represented in Model Parliament of 1295 are underlined
Scale of Miles
0 20 40 60
Scale of Miles
0 50 100 150
FRANCE AT THE TREATY OF BRÉTIGNY, 1360
English Possessions
French Royal Possessions
French Fiefs
ENGLAND
London
Dover
Calais
Southampton
Hastings
Boulogne
Crécy
PONTHIEU
ARTOIS
FLANDERS
BRABANT
Meuse
Rhine
English Channel
Portsmouth
Rouen
Seine
Marne
NORMANDY
EVREUX
Paris
CHAMPAGNE
BAR
Moselle
THE EMPIRE
ATLANTIC OCEAN
BRITTANY
MAINE
Brétigny
Orléans
Angers
ANJOU
Loire
BLOIS
Tours
BURGUNDY
BERRY
Poitiers
POITOU
LA MARCHE
Saône
Lyon
BAY OF BISCAY
Limoges
GUYENNE
DAUPHINÉ
Rhône
PROVENCE
Bordeaux
Dordogne
Garonne
GASCONY
LANGUEDOC
PROVENCE
BIGORRE
Toulouse
FOIX
MEDITERRANEAN SEA
ARAGON
SCOTLAND
IRELAND
ISLE OF MAN
IRISH SEA
ANGLESEY
NORTH SEA
Bamborough
NORTHUMBERLAND
REDESDALE
TYNEDALE
Tyne
Newcastle
Carlisle
Corbridge
CUMBERLAND
PALATINATE OF DURHAM
Yarm
Cockermouth
Appleby
WESTMORLAND
Egremont
Northallerton
Pickering
Scarborough
Malton
Ripon
COUNTY PALATINE OF LANCASTER
Lancaster
YORKSHIRE
York
Beverley
Ouse
Hull
Hedon
Preston
Pontefract
Wigan
Humber
Grimsby
Liverpool
Mersey
Trent
Tickhill
COUNTY PALATINE OF CHESTER
DERBY
Lincoln
LINCOLN
Newcastle under Lyme
NOTTINGHAM
The Wash
CAERNARVON
MERIONETH
PRINCIPALITY OF WALES
POWYS
Shrewsbury
Stafford
STAFFORD
Derby
Nottingham
Lynn
NORFOLK
SHROPSHIRE
LEICESTER
RUTLAND
ISLE OF ELY
Norwich
Bridgnorth
Leicester
Coventry
HUNTINGDON
Ely
Kidderminster
Bromsgrove
WARWICK
Dunwich
MARCH OF WALES
Leominster
WORCESTER
Warwick
Huntingdon
CAMBRIDGE
SUFFOLK
CARDIGAN
Weobley
Worcester
Droitwich
NORTHAMPTON
Northampton
Cambridge
Orford
HEREFORD
Bedford
Ipswich
CARMARTHEN
Hereford
Pershore
BEDFORD
CO. PAL. OF PEMBROKE
Ledbury
Gloucester
OXFORD
Oxford
HERTFORD
Colchester
BUCKINGHAM
Severn
GLOUCESTER
Hertford
ESSEX
Cricklade
Wycombe
GLAMORGAN
Malmesbury
Wallingford
MIDDLESEX
London
Chippenham
Calne
Thames
Sandwich
Bristol
BERKSHIRE
Bristol Channel
Devizes
Reading
Rochester
Axbridge
Bath
Marlborough
Bedwin
SURREY
Canterbury
Deal
Wells
Ludgershall
Basingstoke
Bletchingley
KENT
Overton
Alton
Barnstaple
Bridgwater
Milborne Port
WILTSHIRE
Old Sarum
Guildford
Reigate
Folkestone
SOMERSET
HAMPSHIRE
Tunbridge
Salisbury
Horsham
Hythe
Torrington
Taunton
Ilchester
Downton
Alresford
Grinstead
Romney
Midhurst
DEVON
Winchester
SUSSEX
Rye
Shaftesbury
Bramber
Lewes
Winchelsea
DORSET
Southampton
Exeter
Seaford
Launceston
Dorchester
Shoreham
Newport
Arundel
Chichester
Tavistock
Bridport
Yarmouth
Portsmouth
Bodmin
Liskeard
Ashburton
Weymouth
Melcombe Regis
CORNWALL
Plympton
Totnes
Lyme Regis
I. OF WIGHT
Lostwithiel
W. Looe
Truro
Plymouth
Dartmouth
Tregony
Helston
ENGLISH CHANNEL

XXXI

The Sources and History of the Fourteenth Century

SO EARLY had the English kings and their official servants developed records for the royal government that by the fourteenth century the principal series had long been in existence, some for well over two hundred years. One must account for only a few more records in the fourteenth century, records produced by innovation in royal justice, finance, and chancery procedure. The records of local government increase, particularly those of the boroughs. The chronicles and similar narrative sources continue to provide historical background, an occasional official record, and a stray fact; such authorities on the fourteenth century as V. H. Galbraith, Maude Clarke, and Bertie Wilkinson have used them with skill. Again we must emphasize the tremendous bulk of the English records; it is particularly evident to anyone who has worked also in the continental archives. Only in the fourteenth century do the records of such states as France begin to compare in quantity to the English. This may partially account for the fact that the history of this period has not received the attention devoted to earlier periods.

I. NONNARRATIVE SOURCES

Constitutionally the fourteenth century was especially significant for the development of parliamentary institutions. This story is told by the Parliament Rolls, which, beginning under Edward I, are a mine of information; they are the most important records of the fourteenth century.[1] Though devoid of great detail on parliament, the Parliamentary Writs inform us on the dates of parliament, the boroughs included, and the representatives returned. Next in value to the Parliament Rolls are the statutes. The statute-making power of parliament was recognized and used not only to give the king what laws he desired but to give the barons and commons the laws they desired. Similar to the statutes were the ordinances. They were, however, enacted by king and council and did not have the force of statutes. They merit attention because they were often enacted into statutes by parliament and because they initiated the chief reforms in central government.[2] Certain miscellaneous records also deal with parliament and king—as, for example,

[1] SM, nos. 61, 63.
[2] SM, nos. 62, 64.

the coronation oaths and documents relating to the depositions of Edward II and Richard II, and the anonymous fourteenth-century tract *Modus Tenendi Parliamentum*, which purported to give an account of the composition and proceedings of parliament.[3]

All the established records of the royal organs of administration continued in the fourteenth century and increased in size. Whereas a Pipe Roll of Henry II is barely a foot in diameter, one of Edward III is at least two feet in diameter. In that the king's council was an essential part of parliament, much of its activity was recorded on the Parliament Rolls. It was a court that could entertain all sorts of justice and the legal records pertaining to it are extremely important. They show the council acting as both a common law and an equitable court. Because the council did not keep a record of its proceedings until the reign of Richard II, the legal records dealing with the council must be dug out of other collections such as the Exchequer Accounts, Chancery Miscellanea, Close and Patent Rolls, and Original Petitions. Fortunately records of the proceedings of the council begin in 1390, and they greatly facilitate study of the judicial and administrative functions of the council. These records were actually minutes of the meetings.[4] Prior to their keeping, the proceedings of the council were scattered about in the Patent, Close, *Coram Rege*, and Parliament Rolls.

The administrative side of the chancery's work continued with little change. From it issued all the formal documents under the great seal such as charters. Here originated the letters patent and close, and here were kept the great series of Patent, Close, Liberate, Charter, and other such rolls. All original writs for judicial purposes were issued from the chancery, and the clerks of the chancery had charge of the records of parliament. The records most interesting, however, are the equity proceedings of the court of chancery; these begin under Richard II. During the fourteenth century the chancery was designated as a special court to hear petitions for equity in order that the council would be partially relieved of judicial work and could concentrate on politics and administration. Until the records of these proceedings begin, account of the chancery's rise as a court of equity must be derived from the Original Petitions and from the writs of *sub poena* by which the defendants were brought into the court. Occasionally the chancery enrollments also supply information on the judicial work of the chancery.

The household, and particularly its subdepartment the wardrobe, was closely associated with the chancery in much of its work. For some time the controller of the wardrobe was responsible for the issue of writs under the privy seal; not until the reign of Edward II did there definitely emerge a separate clerk of the privy seal whose responsibility was to initiate all warrants for documents issued by the chancery and for payments made out of the exchequer. The warrants or letters issued under the privy seal were less

[3] SM, nos. 53, 59.
[4] SM, no. 64D.

formal than those of the chancery and were normally in French during the fourteenth century. They are known as the Chancery Warrants and deal with virtually every aspect of government; they provide a clear picture of how royal policy was initiated. Referring again to the wardrobe, we need only to say that all the records which arose in the thirteenth century continued in the fourteenth. The Wardrobe Accounts and Debentures offer a good description of fourteenth-century finance and of diplomatic policy and military expeditions.

All the established exchequer records—the Pipe, Issue, Receipt, Originalia, Fine, and Memoranda Rolls—remain important in the fourteenth century. Only a few other financial documents need be described. There were all sorts of miscellaneous financial reports tendered by royal officers and servants to the exchequer that are known as the Exchequer Accounts. They consist of accounts rendered for crown lands, military expenses, and costs of diplomatic missions. Often these accounts along with all the pertinent vouchers were enclosed in a leather bag bearing a suitable description of the contents. They were enrolled upon the Pipe Rolls until Edward II's reign when they came to be enrolled on a separate series of rolls called the Foreign Accounts (foreign to the business of the sheriffs), which appear to be digests of the original accounts. Of particular value among these accounts are those containing surveys and records of rents due from royal manors.

Of the old established financial records there are those which relate to the tallages, those which record the feudal aids levied on the knights' fees, and the Scutage Rolls, which give the names of those who were exempt from payment of scutage because they had performed military service or had paid a fine in lieu of it. We have already noted that new taxes arose in the thirteenth century. The principal new tax was that of fractions upon movables and it was recorded upon the Taxation or Subsidy Rolls, which become especially valuable with the reign of Edward I and continue so for the rest of the Middle Ages. Another tax that began in the fourteenth century was the poll tax, which was levied at a certain rate per head. The Poll Tax Rolls are particularly valuable for the reigns of Edward III and Richard II because of the light they throw upon the mortality rate due to the Black Death and upon the causes of the Great Revolt of 1381.

There was little change in judicial records. All the Plea Rolls of the central and itinerant courts continued. The only development of importance was the more precise classification given to these records in the fourteenth century. The Plea Rolls of the central courts had long been distinct but this was not so with the eyre records, all of which were called Assize Rolls. From the reign of Edward I, however, they were broken up into separate categories such as gaol delivery, oyer and terminer, and the other assizes. We have already discussed the legal records of the king's council and the court of chancery. Of all the legal records of the fourteenth century surely the Year Books are the most valuable. As more of these marvelous records are published historians will be able to write a better account of legal and constitutional history. No important legal books, no ordinary legal treatises, except a few minor anonymous tracts, were written in the fourteenth century. One must wait until the fifteenth century to find the English law again described in treatises worthy of the subject.

The records of local royal government can be described most effectively by concentrating upon those connected with the principal officers. The Coroners' Rolls are one of the richest sources on local law enforcement and provide our best account of local English society. The Escheat Rolls or Inquisitions Post Mortem reported the findings of the royal escheators, who held investigations whenever royal vassals died in order to determine the feudal incidents due the king. From a local jury the escheator ascertained what lands the deceased vassal had held and their annual value, what services or rents were owed, who the next heir was, and the age of the heir. Depending upon the results of the inquest either a feudal relief was paid to the king, wardship was exercised, or the lands escheated to the crown. These records not only tell of the royal rights exercised but provide minute detail for genealogy of the feudal families and excellent descriptions of the various manors included in the fiefs. Lastly, there are the records connected with the justices of the peace, who became important officers for the local enforcement of law and order. Much of our evidence on their duties comes from a miscellaneous group of records such as statutes, parliamentary petitions, and the Patent and Close Rolls. But for the judicial proceedings conducted by these justices one must consult the records of the common law courts. Because the justices of the peace were assigned to deliver jails and to determine indictments, record of their activity is found in such series as those of Gaol Delivery and the *Coram Rege* Rolls. About 1340, however, the justices of the peace had become so important as local royal judges that their judicial sessions, the sessions of the peace, were recorded regularly upon the Peace Rolls.

The other local records are nonroyal and we are already familiar with most of them. The manorial records consisted of account rolls rendered by bailiffs and reeves who audited the manor accounts. Also in this category were the manorial court rolls and "extents," which were detailed descriptions of the manors, including such items as the names of the tenants, their services, and their rents.[5] The municipal records of the boroughs became substantial only in the fourteenth century. In many boroughs the oldest documents date from this period. The principal records preserved in the municipal archives are borough charters, financial records relating to receipts and expenditures of the town government, records of the council business, books containing the municipal ordinances, court rolls, and guild merchant rolls, which tell about the activities of the local burgess members. This fine group of records pro-

[5] SM, no. 65.

vides a good picture of the borough in the fourteenth century and supplements the royal records with material on the relations between the central government and the boroughs. Also of some value for constitutional history are the collections of private deeds, wills, and letters, which contribute information on the history of the great baronial families.

Though ecclesiastical records such as the monastic cartularies are less important than earlier for the evidence shed on constitutional developments, we must remember that they remain useful and that they were supplemented with a new class of records that began in the thirteenth century—the bishops' registers. These registers, of which the earliest date back to the early thirteenth century, became compendious in the fourteenth century. They recorded all the official acts of the bishop, all the bulls and privileges received from the popes, and all the pertinent business of the diocese. They are particularly useful for local history and for the relations of church and state. A source of even greater value for local history are the churchwardens' accounts which deal with the parish affairs. They provide vital statistics on population and on the smallest units of English society. Unfortunately most of those extant date later than 1485.

In addition to the records noted, it should be added that correspondence with foreign rulers, papal records, and diplomatic records of such countries as France, Germany, and Flanders supplement the main series. These records become especially important upon the outbreak of the Hundred Years' War when England became involved in military and political entanglements throughout western Europe.

2. NARRATIVE SOURCES

We are particularly fortunate in possessing a number of good accounts for the unhappy reign of Edward II that help to clear away the haze surrounding the character and personality of this misfit king who for twenty years was the target of bitter baronial attack. The Saint Albans tradition of historical writing was continued early in the fourteenth century by two writers. The first was John of Trokelowe, a monk of Saint Albans, who completed the *Annales* (*The Annals*) about the year 1330. An eyewitness to much of what he recorded, Trokelowe covered events between 1307 and 1323. His history must be used for the struggle between Edward II and Thomas, earl of Lancaster. Trokelowe's *Annals* were continued for another two years in the *Chronica* (*The Chronicle*) by another Saint Albans monk, Henry of Blaneford.

The principal account of Edward II is the *Vita Edwardi II* (*The Life of Edward II*) covering the years 1307 to 1325. Long attributed by historians to an anonymous monk of Malmesbury, it has recently been shown that the author was undoubtedly John Walwayn, canon of Hereford, who was a household servant of the earl of Hereford, as well as treasurer of England and an escheator. Apparently a member of the middle baronial party, Walwayn was close to the events he described. Though inclined to moralizing and somewhat incoherent, he gives a most human picture of Edward II. For constitutional history he is most useful for the events connected with the Ordinances of 1311.

Probably the other two most valuable accounts of Edward II's reign are the *Annales Londonienses* (*The London Annals*) and the *Annales Paulini* (*The Annals of Saint Paul's*). The first work covers the years 1301 to 1330 and deals principally with events centering around London; it was apparently written by Andrew Horn, a chamberlain of London, who had easy access to the municipal records. The second work, which is of greater value, was composed by someone associated with Saint Paul's. Though one recent critic has said that most of the work is "hardly worth reading," such a harsh conclusion does not seem warranted by the available evidence. The portion from 1307 to 1341 is reasonably accurate and must be used by anyone who hopes to understand the significance of Edward II's coronation oath in 1308.

Though not a first-rate history, the *Gesta Edwardi de Carnarvon* (*The Deeds of Edward of Caernarvon*), by a canon of the priory of Bridlington, is a good composition. It is of special value because the early portion used contemporary records and included much material on such key constitutional events as the coronation of Edward II, the Ordinances of 1311, and the Statute of York. The *Chronicon* (*Chronicle*) of Walter of Hemingburgh, who was a canon of the priory of Gisburn in Yorkshire, though useful for the period between 1048 and 1346, is particularly valuable for the reigns of the three Edwards because the material included is derived from contemporary evidence and personal knowledge. Important documents not found elsewhere have been inserted in this chronicle. The chronicles of Adam Murimuth and Geoffrey le Baker, though dealing principally with the reign of Edward III, also treat at some length that of Edward II. The *Continuatio Chronicarum* (*Continuation of the Chronicles*), covering the period from 1303 to 1347, was written by Murimuth, who was a canon of Saint Paul's, a doctor of civil law, and a diplomatic servant of Edward II entrusted with important missions to the papal court. His composition is rich with material on some of the constitutional crises of Edward III's reign, notably that of 1341. Geoffrey le Baker, who wrote the *Chronicon*, was a secular clerk from Oxfordshire. The portion of his chronicle from 1303 to 1341 relies mainly on Adam Murimuth but that down to 1356 is an independent account. The early part is noteworthy for the touching details of Edward II's fall and death, and the last part, for an excellent description of the Battle of Poitiers. Of merit chiefly because of its account of political events in northern England and Scotland is the *Chronicon de Lanercost*, written by an anonymous Franciscan friar of Carlisle. Though it begins with the year 1201 it is reliable only for the reigns of the three Edwards.

For the long reign of Edward III we have few chronicles or histories that deal with the constitutional issues. Robert of Avesbury, who wrote around the middle of the century, was a registrar of the court of the archbishop of Canterbury. His *De Gestis Mirabilibus Regis Edwardi Tertii* (*The Memorable Deeds of King Edward III*) concentrates on military history between 1339 and 1356 but also includes some valuable material on the constitutional crisis of 1341. Henry Knighton, a contemporary of Avesbury, was a canon from Leicester. His *Chronicon* is of value only for that part after 1336. The portion between 1377 and 1395 was continued by another writer. The Knighton chronicle is a good authority on the Black Death of 1348–1350 and on the constitutional struggles of 1386 and 1387 between Richard II and the barons which culminated in the Merciless Parliament of 1388. For the constitutional historian the most valuable chronicle of the fourteenth century is the *Anonimalle Chronicle*, written in French, probably by a monk of Saint Mary's Abbey in York. However the man got his information on the dramatic events of the famous Good Parliament of 1376, he provides a superb account. It is so lucid that one feels the writer may have been an eyewitness. His account of the proceedings in this parliament is the only extant description of the discussions and debates of a medieval parliament. The *Chronicon Angliae* (*The Chronicle of England*), written by a Saint Albans monk, is useful for the years 1376–1388 because of the vivid and personal narrative devoted to the role of John of Gaunt, duke of Lancaster, in the parliaments of 1376 and 1377. The *Historia Anglicana* (*The English History*) of Thomas Walsingham, who wrote in the early fifteenth century, is an original and contemporary account of the period between 1376 and 1422. For Edward III's reign it deals with the issues involved in the Good Parliament of 1376. For Richard II's reign it furnishes some of the best details on the Great Revolt of 1381 and on the deposition of Richard II in 1399. Likewise of value for the reigns of Edward III and Richard II is the celebrated *Chronicle* of Jean Froissart, which gives one of the chief accounts of the Hundred Years' War. Though primarily interested in the military action and the chivalrous deeds of the knights, Froissart included numerous sections on the internal history of England. He has, for example, a vivid account of the Great Revolt. Unfortunately he was a biased supporter of the king and feudal aristocracy and whitewashed all their actions. Much of what he says is inaccurate and one must read him with discretion and caution.

Though at least a dozen histories and chronicles deal with various periods of Richard II's reign, we shall concentrate on the five that treat extensively the constitutional struggles. The *Eulogium Historiarum* (*The Eulogy of Histories*) is a general history of England written by a monk of Malmesbury. The period from 1367 to 1413 was continued by an anonymous writer of the fifteenth century, and it is this which is interesting because it reports the proceedings of parliaments, particularly that of 1399 which deposed Richard II. The *Chronicon* of Adam of Usk is valuable for the critical years 1397–1399; his comments are significant because of his part in the deposition proceedings. A skilled lawyer who was a violent partisan of the Lancastrian faction, Usk was close to Archbishop Arundel of Canterbury, one of the principal leaders, and was a member of the commission constituted by Henry Bolingbroke to draw up the procedure to be used for the deposition of Richard. Another Lancastrian sympathizer was the author of the *Historia Vitae et Regni Richardi* (*The History of the Life and Reign of Richard*). The part describing the last three years of Richard II's reign is especially enlightening on the parliaments held at Westminster and Shrewsbury. Also writing with a Lancastrian bias was William Winterhill, a monk of Saint Albans, who composed the *Annales Ricardi Secundi et Henrici Quarti* (*The Annals of Richard II and Henry IV*). Covering the period between 1392 and 1406, this work is regarded by some historians as the most valuable narrative of Richard's deposition. Unfortunately, all the principal accounts of Richard II are pro-Lancastrian and depict this cryptic monarch in the blackest of terms. These and the official records such as the Parliament Rolls must be used with caution because they comprise an apologia for the Lancastrian Revolution of 1399. However impractical Richard II may have been, we must remember that there were two sides to this constitutional struggle as there were to all the political struggles of the Middle Ages, even that of King John and the barons.

3. THE REIGN OF EDWARD II (1307–1327)

The disastrous rule of Edward II cannot be attributed solely to his shortcomings. Even such an able ruler as Edward I would have found the problems overwhelming. By securing effective control over the government, Edward I had alienated the baronage. By pressing royal claims in all directions, he had plunged England into war in Wales, Scotland, and France. Wars were fought simultaneously, lines of communication and supply were overextended, and the payment of troops proved expensive. Also costly was the erection of imposing concentric castles in Wales and the foundation of *bastides* in Gascony. Edward I, like the Roman emperor Justinian, had exhausted his realm's resources on grandiose projects. In 1307 Edward II ascended a throne pressed with debt and awkward policies. He was faced with two dilemmas that were to continue until the strong rule of the Tudors. If he adhered to the policy of his father, he would further alienate the barons; if he compromised with them, he might lose what power his father had restored to the crown. If he fought aggressive war against Scotland, he would exhaust his realm's resources and put himself at the mercy of the barons; if he chose a policy of peace, he would lose prestige and encourage baronial opposition. The indecisive Edward played the hand dealt to him about as ineptly as possible. He chose to rule without the barons and secured their bitter opposition. He fought halfheartedly in Scotland and lost both reputation and money there.

However difficult the problems of Edward II, he was definitely not the man to solve them. Though handsome, attractive, and strong, and though a creditable fighter in four Scottish campaigns, Edward did not like martial life. Nor did he have a head for business. Like many a man he preferred sports, games, good fellowship, handicrafts, and plenty of relaxation. Though the judgment of Stubbs is overly stern, his famous characterization of Edward II is fundamentally correct: "He was a trifler, an amateur farmer, a breeder of horses, a patron of playwrights, a contriver of masques, a smatterer in mechanical arts; he was, it may be, an adept in rowing and a practised whip; he could dig a pit or thatch a barn; somewhat varied and inconsistent accomplishments, but all testifying to the skilful hand rather than the thoughtful head, and in some respects reminding us of the tastes of more modern and scarcely less fortunate princes, such as Louis XVI." The contrast between Edward I and his son was indeed striking, so striking that a pope described Edward II as a Rehoboam following a Solomon. Where Edward I loved to rule, Edward II disliked responsibility; he was simply not the man for the position to which he had been called.

Edward II might eventually have weathered the storm like his grandfather Henry III had he not quickly alienated the barons by the trust and affection showered upon Piers Gaveston, a young adventurer who was the son of a prominent Gascon knight and who had entered the household of Edward I as a squire. Realizing the evil influence wielded over his son by the ambitious Gaveston, the old king had banished him in 1307, but he came back in triumph within the year. It was not because Gaveston was not courageous or able that the barons hated him. It was because Edward II relied almost exclusively upon his advice and shut the barons out of his councils. Gaveston rejoiced in his triumph by using his caustic wit to good advantage against the stolid, serious, and grumpy barons. Whatever the attraction Gaveston held for Edward, whether or not there was unlawful intimacy between them, theirs was a highly magnetic relationship that plunged Edward immediately into difficulty. The barons felt that they could never trust Edward.

By forcing upon Edward II a coronation oath more stringent than the traditional one, the barons exhibited the strong resentment felt towards the autocratic Edward I. Within a year of the succession the barons proclaimed in parliament that their loyalty was due to the crown rather than to the royal person. In the same year, 1308, baronial resentment against Gaveston, who had been parading about splendidly in purple and pearls, forced Edward to send him to Ireland as royal lieutenant. But by 1309 Gaveston was back by Edward's side and became the scapegoat for the wretched mismanagement of the realm. In 1310 the barons came fully armed to a great council and forced Edward to agree to the appointment of a baronial committee to draw up ordinances for the reform of the realm. This the Lords Ordainer did and the famous Ordinances of 1311 were issued. For the present it is enough to say that the Ordinances put Edward under the control of a baronial council that was to reform central and local government. Edward chafed under this control and turned completely to Gaveston, who sought to release his royal master from so dishonorable a restraint. While Edward and Gaveston were in northern England at York the archbishop of Canterbury excommunicated Gaveston and the barons agreed that the realm would never be well ordered while the royal favorite remained alive. The barons went after Gaveston, whom they found behind the walls of Scarborough Castle. Lacking supplies and men, Gaveston agreed to surrender in return for his life. The barons agreed to this but as soon as they had their hands upon him they proceeded to do justice in the manner of the American wild west. He was routed out of bed by the earl of Warwick and a band of men, taken to Warwick Castle, and after a mock trial had his head cut off on Blacklow Hill just outside the town of Warwick.

The murder of Gaveston ended any hope of cooperation between Edward and the barons in the governance of the realm. For the moment, powerless to strike back, Edward had to acknowledge the control of the baronial opposition led by his first cousin, Earl Thomas of Lancaster, the richest and most powerful baron in the realm. Lancaster, though ambitious and selfish, was dull and incapable and did a more incompetent job of governing than Edward and Gaveston. To the north the Scots raided the bordering counties with impunity, and within the realm administration practically broke down. Finally in 1314 the Scottish situation became so desperate that Edward felt compelled to lead an army north to drive Robert Bruce and his levies out of the realm. Jealous of Edward and fearful that a victory would strengthen his reputation, Thomas and other barons failed to send troops to the royal banner. Mainly, however, it was the poor generalship of Edward that inflicted upon his army at Bannockburn one of the severest defeats suffered by an English army during the Middle Ages. Forgetting the lessons learned by Edward I, his son failed to protect his archers; they were driven back in confusion upon the ranks of men-at-arms, who were broken up and fled in terror from the field. Edward accompanied them and did not dismount until he reached Dunbar.

The nadir of Edward II's reign followed the disaster of Bannockburn. The independence of Scotland under the rule of Robert Bruce was assured and the Scots raided northern England at will. Edward, a defeated and fugitive king, returned home to a seething baronage. The Lords Ordainer piled new insults upon him; he was bound to a limitation of expenditure and Thomas of Lancaster was appointed commander against the Scots and chief councillor of the king. But again Thomas proved to be a total failure; the Scots continued their raids and the government foundered. By 1318 the situation was so grave that a group of moderate barons seized control from the Lords Ordainer and ousted Lancaster, who proceeded to sulk in his castles.

Government under the moderate middle party of barons was hardly more successful. It was more efficient in administration but this made control over Edward more restrictive and drove him the harder to regain independence from the barons. He worked to this end, helped by two favorites—the Despensers, father and son. Less capable than Gaveston, the Despensers were equally greedy for land, especially for land in the marcher lands of Wales. The favors extended to the Despensers in this region inflamed the turbulent marcher lords, who, though a powerful element in politics, had not previously thrown their weight behind Lancaster and the opposition. In 1321, however, when Lancaster roused himself from retirement and protested against the Despensers, the marcher lords and most of the moderate barons joined his standard. At a parliament held in 1321 in London the Despensers were denounced as "false and most evil counsellors" and banished from the realm. This stroke roused Edward to the most energetic action of his reign. He recruited forces quickly, recalled the Despensers, and marched against Lancaster and the opposition. In March 1322 the armies met at Boroughbridge not far from York. There the royal forces led by Sir Andrew Harclay defeated Lancaster in a desperate engagement. Lancaster surrendered immediately and was taken to Pontefract Castle where Edward awaited him. Here he and a number of his confederates were hastily condemned as rebels and traitors. Lancaster, mounted on a sorry steed, was conducted to a hill outside the castle where his head was cut off by two or three blows of the ax. Some twenty of the opposition paid the penalty of death. And so it was that Edward finally avenged the death of Piers Gaveston. The tragic end of Lancaster can arouse little sympathy; repeatedly given the opportunity to wield effective leadership, he invariably bumbled.

From 1322 until his fall in 1327 Edward II was master with but the help of the Despensers and the loyal support of a small clique of household administrators. Though greedy and ruthless, the Despensers had some capacity for politics. Immediately a parliament was held at York. There the Ordinances of 1311 were annulled and the royal authority was asserted. It was also vaguely proclaimed that great matters of state were to be ordered by all the community of the realm. In the next four years valuable reforms were made in the administration of the household, exchequer, and chancery. Government was improved somewhat but on the whole it was inept, wielded in practice by the household clique and the Despensers, to whom Edward donated lands and titles. Though Edward seemed to have triumphed, he little realized how small and tenuous was the foundation of his power and how hated were the Despensers, who occupied the same position as the despised Gaveston. Only a small nudge was needed to upset the unsteady "triumvirate." It came in 1326.

Since 1308 Edward had been married to Isabella, the daughter of Philip IV of France. The marriage had never been a success. It had been arranged to facilitate peace between England and France in the troubled land of Gascony. This it had done temporarily, but it had united two individuals who never were compatible. Isabella was considerably younger than Edward and their relationship steadily deteriorated. In the last few years of his reign Edward came to hate her. It was reported that he carried a knife in his hose with which to kill her and that he had said he would crush her with his own teeth if no weapon was handy. The feeling was mutual and Isabella resented the ascendancy of the Despensers. In 1325 Isabella was sent to Paris to negotiate a settlement over Gascony with her brother Charles IV. War had broken out in 1324 and in 1325 Gascony had been seized by the French. It was thought that Isabella could prevail upon her brother to return it to England. While in France she persuaded Edward to send their son, the future Edward III, to join her. Meanwhile she had met and had an affair with Roger Mortimer, a powerful marcher lord who had been in prison or exile since the Battle of Boroughbridge. The two now worked hand in hand against Edward. They betrothed the young Edward to Philippa, the daughter of the count of Hainaut, used her dowry to hire troops, and in the autumn of 1326 invaded England where many barons joined them. Edward was caught by surprise and deserted by all except the Despensers. They were hunted down and hanged as traitors. While attempting escape, Edward was captured and imprisoned in Kenilworth Castle.

In early 1327 the rebels held a parliament where it was decided that a delegation should ask Edward to abdicate. This he did when he realized the scope of the revolt, and his son was proclaimed Edward III. For nine months Edward endured imprisonment and torture until Isabella and Mortimer decided to remove him. On the night of 21 September 1327 he was cruelly murdered in his bed. It was reported that piercing shrieks came from the castle to tell the peasants outside of Edward's horrible death. The next day it was announced that Edward had died a natural death, but his corpse was buried before it could be viewed by the public. And so ended in tragedy the life of a king who had brought only tragedy to his realm for two decades.

4. THE REIGN OF EDWARD III (1327–1377)

Though the reign of Edward III began in 1327 he did not rule until 1330. England was ruled the first three years of his reign by the lovers Isabella and Mortimer. While Isabella was kept happy by amorous attentions, Mortimer acquired titles and vast power and land in Wales and Ireland. His greed and ruthlessness aroused internal opposition among the barons and his peace policy with Scotland and France made him unpopular with the realm. In the autumn of 1330 the short adventure of Mortimer and Isabella was abruptly ended. The earl of Lancaster and Edward III, who detested Mortimer and who was repelled by the scandalous behavior of Isabella, united forces. Mortimer was abruptly arrested one night and soon hanged. Isabella was placed in comfortable captivity and remained so for the next twenty-eight years. The personal rule of Edward III had begun.

In 1330 Edward III was an attractive young man of eighteen. Had he lived a century and a half earlier his reign might have been singularly successful, but in the fourteenth century his military and political dreams were antiquated. In personality and ability Edward III resembled Richard I. He was a good warrior, was chivalrous, and loved the display and pageantry of the joust and tournament. To promote the virtues of chivalrous behavior among his barons and military captains Edward founded the Order of the Garter in 1349. His dream was to reconquer the lost Angevin Empire, subdue Scotland, and make himself the most renowned warrior king of western Christendom. Such qualities and goals were admired by the barons, who with a few exceptions loyally supported him almost to the end of his reign. But these qualities which contributed so much to successful rule in the Middle Ages were no longer realistic in the fourteenth century. The French spirit of nationalism and loyalty to the French dynasty was too strong to permit any permanent English occupation of French soil. Nor were English resources equal to such an enormous military effort. These obstacles, however, were not apparent to Edward who, like Richard I, disliked routine administration and permitted servants to conduct the government so long as they kept him supplied with soldiers and money. It was Edward's great desire to be free to conduct war that caused him to make concessions to the barons and to the commons. Throughout most of his reign the barons controlled his council, and parliament achieved significant political power in return for grants of supply. When Edward died in 1377 all his wars had been in vain. England possessed little more on the Continent than she had in 1327, the realm was almost bankrupt, and his subjects had lost faith in the inefficient and corrupt royal administration. Edward III died a failure. The significance of his long reign lies in the remarkable progress made by parliament.

The first military projects of Edward III were in the north. Taking advantage of internal Scottish divisions after the death of Robert Bruce in 1329, Edward gave military support to a party of disaffected Scottish lords and won two striking victories at Dupplin Moor (1332) and at Halidon Hill (1333). As a result Edward obtained cession of some Scottish lands bordering England and some influence in Scottish politics. By 1341, however, these gains were lost and Scotland was completely independent again. But the Scottish failure was offset by the great French war which began in 1337. Though numerous causes can be listed for the outbreak of the Hundred Years' War, the fundamental reason for the strife was French determination to oust the English completely from the Continent and the equally strong determination of Edward III to regain what John had lost. All that may be said in Edward's behalf is that it would have been extremely unpopular for him to withdraw peacefully from Gascony. Such an expedient and politic act would have been regarded as cowardly and as unbecoming an English sovereign. Though the barons and commons resented high taxation for war, they would not have permitted Edward to conclude an enduring peace settlement with the French kings even if he had so desired. Edward, like Richard I, was eager for war and needed only some border incidents in Gascony and some conflicts between English and French sailors in the Channel to supply ample reason for hostilities.

Constructing a series of alliances with Low Country and Rhineland princes during the early 1330's, Edward secured the support of the great Flemish towns which were in revolt against the pro-French count and which were determined to maintain an entente with England because the raw wool for their thriving cloth industry came largely from there. It was Edward's hope to use Flanders as a base of operations in the north and to strike towards Paris from there with his allies while from the south English forces in Gascony would probe northward. When war broke out in 1337 Edward's only justification was that he wished to retake what English kings had once held and that he should rightfully rule France because he was the son of Isabella, daughter of Philip IV. The French, however, had declared that the crown could not descend through a woman and had recognized Philip VI of Valois as king in 1328 when the last Capetian died.

The first campaign, between 1338 and 1340, was conducted in the Low Countries and Picardy. Differences between Edward and his allies blocked an effective campaign and Edward was happy to conclude a truce and return to England. The one English success to show for the effort and money expended was a decisive naval victory over the French at Sluys off the Flemish coast in 1340. This victory insured control of the English Channel for many years. Upon his return to England Edward attributed his lack of success in France to improper and inadequate support from the treasurer and chancellor John Stratford, archbishop of Canterbury. In a parliament held in April 1341 the first constitutional crisis of Edward's reign was resolved. The barons defended Stratford against the charges of Edward and asserted that none of them should be tried in parliament except by their peers. They also demanded parliamentary control over audit of financial accounts and the appointment of baronial councillors before they would grant a tax. Edward reluctantly agreed and thereby paved the way for baronial control of the council down to 1369. In return he obtained baronial cooperation in the French wars.

By 1345 Edward felt ready to renew the war. He broke the truce of 1340 and invaded Normandy with a small force in 1346. While plundering the countryside he was forced to do battle with a vastly larger French army under Philip VI. In August 1346 Edward won a remarkable victory at Crécy. His skilled longbowmen smashed the charges of the lumbering French knights, who retreated in confusion and were slaughtered by dismounted English men-at-arms. Edward then proceeded to invest Calais, which he finally reduced after almost a year's siege. He expelled the French residents and replaced them with English colonists. Calais remained English until the reign of Mary Tudor. Edward, realizing that his army was too depleted for further campaigning, concluded a truce and came home loaded with glory and plunder. Never was his fame to be greater. While he had been in France hostilities had broken out with Scotland and the Scottish king had been defeated, captured, and stored in the Tower of London. For the moment all England thought that the millennium had arrived. The barons and soldiers secured plunder and glory, land in France had been conquered, and the war expenditure had brought a short boom to the economy. Within a year, however, the rosy hue disappeared under the onslaught of the Black Death that ravaged England between 1348 and 1350 and took almost a fourth of her population.

For a while the shock and economic dislocation caused by the plague made war impossible, but in 1355 Edward III allied himself with King Charles the Bad of Navarre, who was scheming for the French crown, and they agreed to partition France. This time the campaign was begun from Gascony under the leadership of Edward's eldest son, Edward the Black Prince. In September of 1356 while leading a plundering raid into Poitou, the Black Prince was brought to bay near Poitiers by a larger army under King John the Good. Using the same tactics as his father, the Black Prince won an equally crushing victory and for good measure took captive King John, who joined the Scottish king in the Tower of London. Edward III now meant to capitalize upon his good luck. In 1357 the Scottish king was released for a ransom of 100,000 marks. For the rest of his reign Edward was not bothered with the Scots. Though the indolent and incapable John enjoyed his captivity, the desperate condition of France forced him to come to terms. In 1360 the Treaty of Brétigny was concluded. By its terms Edward III renounced his claim to the French throne but received Calais and Ponthieu in northern France as well as all of Aquitaine. A ransom of 3,000,000 gold crowns was exacted for the release of King John.

Again, however, English success was ephemeral. Companies of unemployed mercenary troops pillaged and terrorized the French countryside, often with the backing of the English government. The Black Prince, still eager for military adventure, intervened in a Castilian civil war and won a victory over the rebel Henry of Trastamara and his French allies in 1367. This was at the cost, however, of dysentery in the English army, contraction of a fatal disease by the Black Prince, and arousal of French hatred. To defray the expense of the Castilian expedition the Black Prince levied a burdensome hearth tax on Aquitaine which incited the inhabitants to revolt and to request assistance from the French king Charles V. In 1369 war between England and France was resumed, this time with all the advantages on the side of the French. In Charles V they had a hardheaded king who understood the business of politics and war and who surrounded himself with able generals such as Bertrand du Guesclin. The French armies now followed guerrilla tactics, fighting an engagement only when circumstances favored them. The former *esprit de corps* of the English was lacking. Edward III was old, interested only in his mistresses and ignorant of happenings in the field. The Black Prince soon had to retire from active fighting to await death from dropsy. His younger brother John of Gaunt, duke of Lancaster, was an incompetent captain. Parliament became reluctant to vote money for war that consistently went against the English armies. In 1377 when Edward died only coastal areas around Calais, Cherbourg, Bordeaux, and Bayonne were still held.

The military reverses also had an unfavorable effect upon domestic politics, which had been relatively stable and calm since the crisis of 1341. Edward's advancing age and loss of prestige abroad ended the *modus vivendi* with the barons. Having secured extraordinary power as a result of the royal concessions made for their military support, the barons now balked at further war and controlled the government by dominating the council and parliament. While Edward became senile and spent his time with Alice Perrers, his mistress, and while the Black Prince wasted away with disease, the great lords competed for political ascendancy. The leading contender for power was John of Gaunt, Edward III's third eldest son and the most powerful lord of the realm. In 1369 he began to attack the royal ministers for their conduct of the war and in 1371 succeeded in ousting most of them from office. Though unsuccessful in prosecuting a winning war, John dominated the royal government until 1376. His administration was blatantly corrupt. Alice Perrers, royal favorites, and rich London financiers and merchants, who had backed John, were the beneficiaries of the political spoils and proceeded to siphon off the crown resources.

Finally, opposition to the Lancastrian party formed around the Black Prince and a relative of his through marriage—Edmund Mortimer, the earl of March and a powerful lord of the Welsh country. Skillfully building up its strength, the opposition succeeded in capturing control of the parliament of 1376—the famous Good Parliament. The commons, a large number of whom had been elected through the efforts of the opposition, now bitterly attacked John of Gaunt and his cronies. The leader was Peter de la Mare, steward of Edmund Mortimer and the first speaker of the commons. He accused various courtiers and councillors of corruption, in particular the chamberlain Lord Latimer and the London banker and merchant Richard Lyons. The lords of the parliament condemned them to imprisonment and to forfeiture of goods. They were the first royal servants to be impeached by a parliament. Next, Alice Perrers was driven from Edward III's side and the royal council was reshuffled to include nine barons and prelates, who were to approve all transactions. But with the death of the Black Prince in June 1376 the position of the Good Parliament weakened, and in July it was dissolved. John of Gaunt swept back into power, Alice Perrers returned to Edward III, Latimer and Lyons were freed, the nine councillors were removed, and the reforms of the Good Parliament were annulled. A new parliament of early 1377 was a willing instrument of John of Gaunt, who saw to it that his steward Sir Thomas Hungerford was elected speaker of the commons.

For the next six months neither baronial faction made any further move for power; both bided their time while Edward III's health rapidly declined. In June Edward lay dying while Alice Perrers concealed from him his true condition; she talked with him about hawking, hunting, and tournaments. When he reached his last hours Alice robbed him of all that she could, including the rings on his fingers, and then took flight along with other greedy courtiers. A simple priest administered the last rites to Edward, who was hardly capable of gasping, "Jesus have mercy." And so died a king whose rule had begun with high hope and glittering military success. Edward's great fault was lack of political capacity and perspective. What he attempted in the fourteenth century was politically infeasible. His drain upon the resources of England brought her to her knees politically, economically, and militarily and contributed to the unhappy reign of his grandson Richard II.

5. THE REIGN OF RICHARD II (1377–1399)

Richard II was another English king doomed to failure by adverse fortune and the historical temper of the age. Whereas Edward III could have been a reasonably successful king in the twelfth century, Richard would undoubtedly have achieved a good record as king in the sixteenth century when men and the age were ready for strong autocratic government and withdrawal from arid continental wars. Richard II's objectives were mainly those of the Tudors but their attainment in the fourteenth century was impossible; England was not ready for them. The character of Richard II was weak and unstable but this is no cause for historians to diagnose him as a schizophrenic hovering on the brink of insanity. That Richard was suspicious, lonely, imbued with a high sense of his royal authority, autocratic, alternately ambitious and lazy, and a devotee of culture rather than of war is explained by his Plantagenet inheritance and by the circumstances of his youth. The son of the Black Prince, he succeeded to the throne at the age of ten and was thereafter faced with problems and crises that would have tried mature men. He had seen little of his father or mother, and after he was king he was constantly surrounded by a council of twelve magnates representing the two baronial factions. Long tutelage under a domineering baronial council that worked for baronial interest imbued in Richard the overwhelming desire to make himself independent and to exalt the royal prerogative. That he carried his autocratic pretensions too far and became too vindictive can be explained by his long subservience to the barons and by their brutal and studied insults to him. Only an exceptionally able ruler such as Charles V of France might have overcome the steep obstacles that met Richard when he mounted the throne in June 1377.

During the first four years of Richard's reign all went badly. The French war was a record of defeats, and only the death of Charles V and his constable Du Guesclin spared what little land yet remained to the English. The new French king Charles VI was also a boy and France was plunged into civil war by two royal uncles, the duke of Burgundy and the duke of Orléans, who aspired to political supremacy. For many years France was in no position to wage energetic war. As for the English, the French wars had been such a drain upon their resources that parliament balked at further demands. The propertied classes that constituted parliament, weary of paying most of the taxes, resorted to a poll tax in 1380 assessed at so much per head. Now poor and wealthy alike were liable. This was the spark that lit the flame of revolt among the peasants and the poor inhabitants of the towns.

In the summer of 1381 the Peasants' Revolt erupted. Though various parts of England were affected, the revolt centered in the counties about London. There in May the peasants refused to pay the poll tax, formed armed bands, and went about killing royal officials and hated manorial lords, pillaging and burning, and destroying manorial records, especially those that recorded the servitude of the peasants. In spite of a few leaders such as the priest John Ball and the adventurers Wat Tyler and Jack Straw, the revolt was poorly planned and had no program. Fundamentally it was a protest against the economic and social misery left in the wake of war and the Black Death. Unable to protest through a legally constituted instrument, the peasants turned to violence. All that can be said about the objectives of the peasants is that those who were free demanded better working conditions, higher wages, and lower rents; those who were unfree demanded their freedom. Converging on London in the middle of June, the peasants gained entry into the city and terrorized and plundered for three days. Richard II and his councillors were happy to shield themselves in the Tower of London or in the Wardrobe. Still, the peasants found some of the hated officials and killed them. John of Gaunt's town house, the Savoy, was pillaged and burned, and other buildings shared a like fate. On the third day the death of Wat Tyler and promises by Richard II to accede to their demands for freedom caused the peasants to disperse and to return home. Of course none of the promises were honored and the ringleaders were captured, tried, and hanged. Like most such disturbances in the Middle Ages, the Peasants' Revolt ended in failure without accomplishing a single objective. It was a violent and blind protest against abominable conditions for which the royal government and aristocracy were blamed and for which they became the scapegoat.

From 1381 to 1388 Richard remained under the dominance of various baronial cliques that exploited the situation for their own aggrandizement. The leading baronial councillors were Richard's youngest uncle, Duke Thomas of Gloucester, and the earls of Arundel and Warwick. John of Gaunt retired from active politics after 1381 and concentrated on winning a title and land in Portugal. In 1386 the three lords compelled Richard to dismiss his able chancellor Michael de la Pole, earl of Suffolk, who was impeached by parliament and imprisoned. In 1387 the three raised an army, defeated some royal forces, and imposed further control upon Richard. In early 1388 they summoned the so-called Merciless Parliament, which under their direction saw to it that all Richard's supporters and servants were dismissed, imprisoned, exiled, or executed. The Lords Appellant (so named because they appealed the royal supporters) were now supreme and rewarded themselves with land and offices. By 1389, however, the Lords Appellant had alienated so much of their support by incompetent administration, by a defeat at the hands of the Scots, and by negotiating for peace with France that Richard finally regained some of his lost authority and retained it until his violent downfall.

For the next nine years Richard worked quietly and skillfully to consolidate his power. His reasonableness and leniency surprised even the Appellants. He made no attempt to recall his supporters exiled by the Merciless Parliament in 1388, and he even continued the Appellants on his council. But while he disarmed their fears, he built up a core of loyal household servants, cultivated the friendship of the moderate barons, and worked closely with John of Gaunt, who was now back in England, to neutralize the power of the duke of Gloucester. To free himself for domestic politics Richard concluded a truce with France that he cemented by marriage in 1396 to Isabella, the eight-year-old daughter of Charles VI. This marriage can be regarded only as a political move and was made possible by the death in 1394 of Richard's queen, Anne of Bohemia, for whom he had had real affection. In fact, some historians have argued that if Anne had lived to exert a restraining influence the violent and autocratic behavior of Richard during the last years of his reign might have been forestalled. In any event Richard extricated himself from war and secured the promise of French assistance against royal enemies in England. He further strengthened himself by conducting a short expedition to Ireland in 1394 where he buttressed sagging English authority and reasserted royal authority. At this time he began to forge a strong military force drawn primarily from the royal estates. Following the example of the great barons, who had built private armies by the system of indenture and retaining fee, Richard constructed a loyal force which wore the royal badge of the White Hart. He now had at his command a dependable army prepared for any task. By 1397 he felt strong enough politically and militarily to strike for his ultimate goal—royal absolutism.

In a parliament at Westminster in September 1397 Richard was in complete control. Through influencing the election of the commons he had a parliament packed with royal supporters. Present was the king's force of the White Hart, which, the chronicler Adam of Usk relates, was used to overawe the assembly. Because of repairs to Westminster Hall parliament met in an open-sided temporary structure; all around it, the members of parliament could see the royal retainers fully armed. With the stage thus prepared Richard began to act. All the royal opponents were impeached and suffered exile, imprisonment, confiscation, or execution. The earl of Warwick confessed his guilt, incriminated his confederates, and was sentenced to loss of goods and to exile. The hated duke of Gloucester had been previously arrested and imprisoned at Calais. Parliament was informed that he had died, but his murder was apparent to all. The earl of Arundel was condemned to death and executed. This much accomplished, Richard adjourned parliament and ordered it to meet again at Shrewsbury near Cheshire, which was the center of his military power. Having assembled in early 1398, parliament declared all acts of the Merciless Parliament invalid and annulled all actions against supporters of the royal authority, even as far back as the Despensers. The triumph of Richard seemed complete. Parliament granted him for life the customs on wool and leather. Moreover, Richard declared with a haughty countenance "that his laws were in his mouth" or "that they were in his breast." There is no doubt that he conceived of himself as an absolute monarch unrestricted by law or by parliament.

After working cleverly for nine years to achieve such power, Richard undid it all by several foolish acts. Feeling completely supreme in 1398, he banished from the realm Henry Bolingbroke, the eldest son of the old John of Gaunt. When Gaunt died in 1399 Richard exiled Henry for life and forbade him to inherit the Lancastrian lands. This was Richard's cardinal blunder. It brought him a bitter and able foe, soon supported by a large segment of the propertied classes who realized that no man's possessions were safe when the laws of the land could be thus voided by the royal will. Richard added fuel to this discontent when he forced the moneyed classes to give him large loans, when he terrorized persons suspected of being disloyal, when he favored the prerogative law courts over the common law courts, and when he exercised a tight surveillance over local government. Apparently unaware of the tension and widespread opposition to his rule, Richard went to Ireland to provide for a new lieutenant to succeed Roger Mortimer, the earl of March, who had been killed. While Richard was absent from the realm, Henry Bolingbroke landed with a force at Ravenspur on the Humber River and was quickly joined by a large number of barons including the powerful Percy and Neville families of the north country. Richard's lieutenants in England were speedily outmaneuvered so that they could raise no forces, and when Richard landed at Conway in North Wales, he found only a few men willing to fight for him. The last tragic moments of Richard's career were at hand.

From Conway Richard could easily have escaped by sea to a number of places—Gascony, Paris, or Ireland. But he surrendered to Henry. Apparently he was duped into this course by Henry's promise that he would remain king if the Lancastrian lands were restored and if Henry was appointed hereditary steward of England. Richard was immediately thrown into the

Tower of London and an abdication wrung from him the day before a parliament convened to deal with the *fait accompli* of Henry. The Lancastrian leaders first announced that Richard had voluntarily and cheerfully abdicated and then read out thirty-three charges against him. Henry then stepped forward and claimed the throne by descent and conquest, and because Richard had proved incapable of good rule. Henry's only right came from conquest; his argument that Richard's rule was incompetent was later turned against him and his dynasty. But Henry had the realm behind him and was crowned as Henry IV, the first of the Lancastrian dynasty.

In early 1400 after a revolt had occurred in behalf of Richard II, who was imprisoned in Pontefract Castle not far from York, Henry IV decided that Richard must be removed. The official Lancastrian story was that Richard starved himself to death after learning of the unsuccessful revolt. Some of the chroniclers tell what is more likely the true story. Richard was probably killed by systematic torture, cold, insufficient clothing and food, and heavy chains. Like his unfortunate predecessor Edward II, he was murdered and the Lancastrian Revolution had at last run its course. Although the first two Lancastrians were better rulers than the last of the Plantagenets, the revolution did not solve England's problems, namely, the need for strong and efficient rulers who could cooperate with parliament, the need to reduce the overmighty and factious barons, and the need to bring the exhausting French wars to an end. These were problems throughout the fifteenth century; they were not settled until England had been totally defeated in France, until the Wars of the Roses had ended, and until Henry Tudor took up the crown after Bosworth Field.

XXXII

Kingship and Council

THE struggle between king and barons for power in the central government, a struggle that dominated the reigns of Henry III and Edward I, continued more violently and bitterly in the fourteenth century. Whereas Henry III ultimately triumphed over the baronage and Edward I restored the English kingship to power and prestige, their successors of the fourteenth century steadily lost the powers that traditionally constituted the royal prerogative. Edward II and Richard II suffered ignominious defeats and paid the penalties of deposition and death. Despite his military prowess and victories, Edward III repeatedly had to make concessions that weakened his independence and authority. The fourteenth century was characterized by the decline of royal power, which was shared by the kings with the barons and parliament. By studying the principal elements of central government—kingship and royal council—we can observe this decline that was ultimately to transform the kings into limited monarchs.

I. KINGSHIP

Until the reign of John there had been little talk about the royal prerogative; the Norman and Angevin kings evidently saw no need to speak of something to which there was virtually no opposition. But after John's setback one hears more about royal prerogative because Henry III and his councillors felt compelled to define what they struggled to uphold against baronial opposition. Though Edward I recovered much authority lost by Henry III, the records abound in references to kingly prerogative and indicate that Edward was formulating what he considered his indefeasible rights. The more his three successors fell under attack by barons and commons, the more they elaborated upon their powers and attempted to assume new ones and to evade limitations. The strongest defense of the royal prerogative was made by Richard II, who formulated a theory of royal absolutism little different from that practiced by the Tudors. He believed that he was above positive law, that he could repudiate any obligation, that his subjects were bound to provide for him however he ruled, that the realm was his private property to do with as he saw fit, and that he could legislate by himself and annul and suspend statutes. Indeed, Richard felt that he could do anything that he willed. Despite this exalted concept of royal power, the facts of history made him a far weaker king than Edward I; nor was his power at all comparable to that of Henry II. Our task is to determine first what the kings of the fourteenth century could and did do and then to see how their power waned.

In the fourteenth century the kings were still the mainspring of the executive. Their prerogative remained undiminished in all matters not regulated by statute. But to their chagrin more matters were brought under statutory regulation. Though much of the central administration was well established and operated automatically and impersonally, the kings still paid careful attention to government and, when possible, ignored the traditional theory that the king and his officers were subject to the law of the land and to the statutes. All three kings were lax in observing statute law. They continued, for example, to pardon criminals despite statutes limiting this power. They often annulled common law procedure and took refuge behind privileged position when claims were made against them. They postponed pleas, delayed hearings, and pardoned royal debtors. Arrests were made by royal mandate and prisoners held in derogation of the existing requirements for bail. The regulation of commerce was exclusively in the hands of the king and his council. The prerogative to extend remedies and to dispense grace was regularly exercised; to king and council came a steady stream of those aggrieved by actions of administrative and judicial officers and those seeking the royal grace.

The fiscal battles of the crown were still extensive. The funds in the exchequer and wardrobe were largely at the king's disposal. Though only parliament could grant national taxes, the kings attempted to procure such grants from local assemblies or by individual negotiation. Men were pressed into granting loans and gifts and the evils of prise and purveyance continued. Throughout the fourteenth century the customs on wool and hides were collected and were occasionally increased. Over coinage and the mint the kings held exclusive control. Mines were private property of the crown, royal forests were specially administered, and royal lands were managed by custodians, escheators, and chamber officials.

The kings, it must be emphasized, were still feudal sovereigns to whom royal vassals were bound by homage and the oath of allegiance and to whom they owed feudal services. At times feudal military service was exacted and the kings zealously guarded their feudal rights of wardship, marriage, forfeiture, escheat, and such miscellaneous perquisites as allotting the dowers of widows and partitioning lands among heiresses of royal vassals. The kingly prerogative was yet tenacious. The archbishoprics, bishoprics, and numerous abbeys and priories were under royal patronage. During vacancy of office the temporal profits went to the king, his approval for election was required, and an oath of fealty was demanded from every new officeholder. For some church offices the kings made the appointments. Also, they held advowson of churches whose patrons were royal wards. All the kings were alert to the danger of papal jurisdiction and worked to limit appeals to the papal court. They were equally alert in protecting the royal court system against usurpations by the church courts.

The summons, administration, and command of feudal levies and the forces provided by commission of array were the responsibility of the king, his council, and his household staff. Commissioners of array and victualers were appointed; so were all the military commanders. War was as much a royal concern as were diplomacy, negotiation, and treaties. It was parliament that pared down the royal prerogative but, we must realize, only the king could summon parliament. The kings attended many of their parliaments and otherwise were represented by their council and household officers. Statutes could be enacted only by king and parliament. Often the king sat with the great magnates to hear and to adjudicate pleas. In spite of an increasing amount of parliamentary business introduced by the lords and commons, the dynamo of parliamentary business was yet the king and his council. Whether the king personally busied himself with the affairs of his realm or whether they were initiated and implemented by the central organs of administration, they were but agencies of the royal prerogative. In the England of 1399 the royal prerogative was far weaker than in the England of 1307, but there was still a wide range of powers that today we would consider absolutistic. The fourteenth century saw no rigid separation of the executive, legislative, and judicial; the kings could still pass from one domain to the other with comparative ease and act as they saw fit unless specifically regulated by law and custom.

The powers summarized above constituted what the kings considered their prerogative and what they struggled to exercise. But the political facts of the fourteenth century, unlike those of the twelfth, did not consistently support the theory. Richard II, who held the clearest and most exalted view of royal power, suffered the most decisive defeat and thereby helped to prepare the way for a century of weak kingship and ineffective central administration. To trace in detail how the kings suffered loss of their authority would prove too tedious; rather, we shall concentrate on a few key events that epitomize the royal retreat before baronial and parliamentary attack.

When Edward II was anointed and crowned on 25 February 1308 he took a new coronation oath that was to have future serious implications for him and his successors. Traditionally in their coronation oath the kings had sworn to "observe peace, honor and reverence to God, the church, and the clergy, to administer right justice to the people, to abolish the evil laws and customs, and to keep the good." Edward II, however, was asked in addition to make an affirmative reply to the following question: "Sire, do you grant to be held and observed the just laws and customs that the community of your realm shall determine, and will you, so far as in you lies, defend and strengthen them to the honour of God?"[1] The difficulty with this new promise is to determine what was expected of the king when he swore to abide by the just laws and customs ordained by the community of the realm. Though we must beware of attributing a comprehensive political plan to the barons, it would seem that fear of the resurgence of royal power under Edward I and distrust of what the unproved Edward II would do with it led them to insist that he swear to rule by laws which they would approve. The coronation promise was unprecedented and much more derogatory to royal power than the Provisions of Oxford. That the barons expected to hold Edward to his promise is revealed by their actions throughout the reign. A few years later, for example, when Edward resisted the appointment of barons to reform the royal government, they threatened to remove him because he would not fulfil his coronation oath. And in 1327 when Edward was forced to abdicate, one reason given why he was no longer capable of rule was that he had ignored his coronation oath.[2] We may conclude that the new promise incorporated in the traditional coronation oath more specifically limited royal authority and made it responsible to a community of the realm which, consisting in 1308 primarily of an aggrieved baronage, would gradually expand to include the commons in parliament. A more precise standard for good rule had been established, and the community of the realm demonstrated that it intended to hold the king to this standard.

That the baronage was determined to restrict Edward II in the exercise of his power was evinced by its famous declaration of the same year stating that there was a distinction between the crown and the royal person, and that homage and allegiance were due to the former and not to the latter. In effect the barons were saying that their loyalty was to the crown and that they would oppose the king if he acted against the welfare of the crown. The history of Edward II's reign is filled with the spirit of making the king accountable for the manner in which he wielded royal power. The decisive stroke against the royal dignity and authority came with the coup of 1327.

Immediately after their successful military stroke late in 1326, Isabella, Mortimer, and their baronial adherents summoned in Edward II's name a parliament for January 1327; it was to legalize what had not occurred since before 1066—deposition of a king. Having proclaimed Edward III king, parliament was then presented for approval six articles giving the reasons why Edward II should no longer be king. The articles said that he was incompetent and had accepted evil counsel; that he had rejected good counsel; that he had lost Scotland, Ireland, and Gascony; that he had injured the church; that he had imprisoned, exiled, disinherited, and killed numerous good men; that he had broken his coronation oath; and that his incapacity and incorrigibility had ruined the realm. These six charges were accepted as proven by common notoriety. Next it was decided to fortify what amounted

[1] SM, no. 55.
[2] SM, no. 59.

to deposition by securing Edward II's abdication. This was accomplished by a parliamentary deputation sent to Edward, who abdicated in favor of his son.[3] Our interest in the deposition lies in its effect upon the constitution and the royal power. What parliament did was unprecedented and illegal, but to question the legal justice of the deposition is academic. The successful coup of 1327 constituted the justification for what was done in parliament. There was no place for an unsuccessful king and parliament, as the center of political life and spokesman for the community of the realm, was the logical institution to deal with such a problem. Though it did not act as a properly constituted court of law, what it did was as effective as though accomplished in a regular court of law. The most striking effect of the deposition was to serve notice to the kings that they were expected by their subjects, represented by parliament, to govern by an established and recognized law of which parliament was becoming the vigilant custodian.

The constitutional crisis of 1341 was precipitated by Edward III's sudden return in late 1340 from the war in Flanders. Enraged by his military failure against the French, he attributed it to lack of funds and obstruction by various councillors, chiefly Archbishop Stratford of Canterbury, who was chancellor, head of the royal council, and a power in the exchequer. Stratford was the leader of the barons whose opposition to the king stemmed from the Lancastrian resistance of Edward II's reign. Although military failure was the immediate cause of Edward III's attack against Stratford and his supporters in the council, Edward hoped to accomplish more than making Stratford a scapegoat; he hoped to strengthen his royal authority and exert unchallenged control over his council. Immediately upon his return he removed Stratford and other councillors from their offices and imprisoned various royal justices and chancery clerks. In early 1341 he charged Stratford and his adherents with various offenses. He charged that Stratford was like a broken reed, that he obstructed the war, and that he had misappropriated funds. He announced an investigation into the funds which had disappeared. Edward acted on the principle that as it was his prerogative to appoint his councillors and officers it was also his prerogative and his own affair to remove and to punish them. But Stratford argued otherwise and stated that he would not answer the charges. He demanded trial by his peers, the lords, in parliament and in the presence of the commons. Neither Edward nor Stratford could achieve his demands. After debate in parliament, both agreed to a compromise which actually conceded more to Stratford, who was backed by the great lords. Edward conceded that Magna Carta should be kept and that any officer infracting its provisions should be tried by the lords in parliament. He also promised that no officer should be removed from office until so judged by parliament and that the royal councillors would be appointed only with the approval of the great lords.[4]

[3] SM, no. 59.

[4] SM, no. 61E.

These concessions damaged the royal prerogative as Edward clearly realized. Later in 1341 and in 1343 he revoked them, stating that they were prejudicial to the royal prerogative and contrary to the laws of the realm.[5] He was determined not to be deprived of what all his predecessors had claimed—the appointment and dismissal of officers and insistence upon complete loyalty to the royal person and his will. Despite this repudiation, the crisis of 1341 had set a precedent that was to weaken the royal power and that was to be appealed to in the future. Parliament was regarded as the proper and only institution capable of solving such disputes. What the crisis of 1341 did was to say that differences between the king and his officers were not a private but a public affair which could be solved only by investigation and judgment in parliament. It pointed to the day not far distant when officers would be impeached by parliament, a judicial process that made royal officers ultimately responsible to parliament rather than to the king.

The fortunes of the royal prerogative during the reign of Richard II revolve around three events—the crisis of 1386–1387, the Merciless Parliament of 1388, and the deposition of Richard in 1399. Although Richard ruled for a considerable time as a constitutional monarch, cooperating with barons and parliament, we know that his objective was absolutism. As early as 1382 we are told that he consulted with favorites in a secret council in an attempt to govern without baronial interference. And his last acts of 1397–1399 can be interpreted only as a desperate bid to rule over the realm unaided by barons or by parliament, to rule as an absolute monarch.

Numerous reasons have been advanced for the crisis of 1386–1387, among them the political ambitions of the duke of Gloucester, dissatisfaction with the prosecution of the French war, and aristocratic hatred against Richard's favorites and courtiers of the household. All these causes were involved but behind them lay the larger issue of sovereignty. The fundamental question was whether the king or the barons and commons in parliament were to be sovereign. The crisis arose chiefly because Richard II exalted the royal prerogative, worked to rewin lost power, and insisted upon employing his own councillors and officers. The answer was a bitter baronial attack upon Richard which was supported by the commons. He was faced in 1386 with a parliamentary deputation that made four declarations on royal and parliamentary authority. First it asserted that parliament was the supreme court of the realm; secondly, that parliament could rightfully order the affairs of the king as well as of the realm; thirdly, that the lords and commons had the right to supervise expenditures; and finally, that parliament could dissolve itself if the king absented himself for forty days, the intent being to demonstrate that parliament could meet and dissolve without the king. These assertions were violently denied by Richard. The result was an

[5] SM, no. 62c.

ultimatum from the deputation which declared in essence that Richard would be governed by the laws of the realm and by the advice of his faithful peers or that it would be lawful for them with the assent of the realm to depose him and substitute another. Richard surrendered and the opposition prevailed. Some of the principal councillors were removed and one of them, Michael de la Pole, earl of Suffolk, was impeached. The opposition put in its own councillors and forced Richard to accept a commission of reform to hold power for a year, during which it would reform the state of the realm and of the household.[6]

Richard's answer was typical. He protested that all done in parliament to the prejudice of the royal prerogative he considered null and void. He formed a party of opposition and went throughout the realm raising forces. In August 1387 five royal justices were rounded up at Nottingham and asked point-blank whether the proceedings of 1386–1387 were lawful. Obviously under pressure they replied that the commission of reform was illegal and contrary to the royal prerogative, that those responsible deserved execution, that the direction of procedure in parliament belonged to the king, and that parliament had no power to remove royal officials. But Richard, lacking the support necessary to execute what he considered his rightful power, was forced to submit to the duke of Gloucester and the opposition in late 1387. The stage was now set for the Merciless Parliament of 1388. The events of 1386 and 1387 show the great inroad made into royal authority since 1307. The lords with the support of the commons conceived of the High Court of Parliament as a body that not only could impeach royal officers but also could create commissions to reform the state of the realm and, if necessary, to depose the king. The crisis of 1386–1387 was an important step in the stairway leading to parliamentary sovereignty.

The Merciless Parliament of 1388 was the baronial reply to Richard's opposition in 1387.[7] In late 1387 Richard had been forced to accept the appeals brought against his leading councillors by the Lords Appellant and to summon a parliament to hear the appeals and to hand down a judgment. Parliament convened in February 1388. The five Lords Appellant—Gloucester, Derby, Nottingham, Warwick, and Arundel—appealed various of Richard's councillors of thirty-nine offenses which constituted high treason. Those appealed who had escaped from the realm were impeached *in absentia*, those present were executed, and those in holy orders were removed from their spiritual offices. Gloucester and his cronies remained in power for a year until their own incapacity forced them to step down and to cooperate with Richard, who then governed with their assistance until 1397.

We shall avoid the finely spun arguments on the intentions of the Lords Appellant and on the legality of the proceedings taken against Richard's councillors and state simply that the acts of the Merciless Parliament were

[6] SM, no. 63F.

[7] SM, no. 63G

excessive and cruel, pushed through by greedy, ambitious, and vindictive lords. They used parliament as an instrument with which to destroy their political enemies. Whatever their political theory or concept of government, they made the court and law of parliament supreme in the realm so that they could remove the servants of Richard and humiliate him. However transitory their victory, the Lords Appellant with the support of other lords and the commons had struck a hard blow at the royal prerogative. The actions of the Merciless Parliament made parliament the ultimate legal arbiter of the realm and attributed to it supreme political authority. For the moment Richard had to acknowledge this political settlement and to rule with parliament. But for a ruler of his temperament subordination was intolerable. His actions beginning in 1397 could be the only answer to what he considered high treason against the crown.

Richard II's deposition in 1399 was the last act in the drama of opposition between king, barons, and parliament. Though the deposition was forced by successful revolt, the fact remains that an absolutistic ruler was ousted and a dynasty was ushered in, destined by historical fortune to rule with prerogative limited by parliament. Between 1397 and 1399 Richard executed a counterrevolution that completely reversed the trend of the fourteenth century and made him absolute. He forced parliament to admit that the royal person was inviolable and beyond criticism and that any act against the royal prerogative was high treason. By forcing the Shrewsbury parliament to vote him a subsidy for life he buttressed his independence. And by forcing parliament to delegate its authority to a commission of eighteen he reduced that body to impotency.[8] That his actions were generally feared and disapproved of is shown in the support given by the realm to Henry of Bolingbroke when he raised the standard of revolt.

The two chief problems surrounding the deposition are whether it resulted from Richard's absolutism and whether it was parliamentary. From what we know about Richard it is likely that along with some partisan bias and falsity there was a large element of truth in the charges levied against him by the Lancastrian parliament, charges that represent what generally was thought of Richard. Whatever its inconsistencies and falsehoods, this denunciation must certainly be recognized as an eloquent and stinging rebuke to a king who flouted the law and conventions of his realm. Alone, it is a most effective attack against absolutism.

As to whether Richard was legally deposed by parliament opinion differs widely. Ultimately, as already noted, Lancastrian military force deposed Richard, but it was done through the medium of parliament. Richard's opponents had to remove him through parliament because, in previously using parliament to remove the royal councillors, they had set a precedent and now felt obliged to follow it. Though it may be argued that a real

[8] SM, no. 63H and I.

parliament was not convened because the king was absent, for all practical purposes a parliament assembled, deposed Richard, and recognized Henry Bolingbroke as king. This parliament was a landmark in English constitutional history because it transferred an extraordinary amount of power from the king to itself and made succeeding kings much more dependent upon parliament. Perhaps it is going too far to assert that Henry IV ruled by virtue of parliamentary title, but he did rule by a title secured through the legal process held in parliament and could claim and could appeal to a legal legitimacy beyond the claim of national and political expediency. Henry IV could claim no good heritable title but he could claim that he ruled by the grace of God and by the consent of the realm as expressed in parliament. The deposition of Richard II is the best barometer of how much the royal power had declined since the death of Edward I.

2. THE ROYAL COUNCIL

During the thirteenth century the sworn council had developed into a department of central administration distinct from such other organs as the chancery, exchequer, and law courts. As an agent of the royal prerogative through which funneled the king's will it was the core of central administration; those who controlled the royal council had a decisive part in the governance of the realm. To win control of it was the baronial objective throughout Henry III's reign. Against the masterful Edward I the barons achieved little success and had to acquiesce in a professional council selected and tightly controlled by Edward. Only in the last few years of his reign did Edward's grip loosen enough to give the barons an opportunity to secure a larger voice in the government. Exclusion from Edward I's council engendered in the barons a determination to win control of the council from the incompetent Edward II. With certain interruptions, notably during the reign of Edward III, the struggle between king and baronage for control of the council continued through the fourteenth century. Our primary interest lies in this struggle because it was an essential element in the transfer of power from king to parliament. But first we must briefly examine the principal characteristics and functions of the fourteenth-century council.

The effective core of the council, that part consistently in attendance on the king, consisted of the chancellor, treasurer, and keeper of the privy seal, all of whom were assisted by officers from the household departments of wardrobe and chamber, and from other organs of government such as the law courts. Although ecclesiastics had predominated down to the middle of Edward III's reign, thereafter educated laymen became increasingly prominent. The core of the council was supplemented by numerous other sworn councillors chosen from the greatest magnates of the realm and from men with specialized knowledge and training. The total number of sworn councillors was twenty-odd but no meeting of the council ever included them all.

Most gatherings consisted of about ten members, the principal councillors plus several others; few numbered more than fifteen. As the king moved about the realm the core of the council often accompanied him and acts are noted as approved by king and council. During war and when the king was outside the realm, the council was split. Generally such councillors as the chancellor and treasurer remained at Westminster supervising the business of government, particularly that of the chancery and the exchequer. Others of the council such as the keeper of the privy seal and household officers customarily went with the king. They assisted with on-the-spot business and sent out warrants for the execution of business both to the council at Westminster and to officers all over the royal possessions.

As for the functions of the council, its principal task was to help the king exercise his prerogative powers. Its duties, therefore, varied considerably. There were, for example, specialized council meetings quite departmental in nature; such were the council in chancery and in exchequer. A meeting in chancery might be held to dispose of petitions or to deal with some administrative or procedural reform in the chancery. The council in exchequer dealt with difficult financial problems, judicial cases, and sometimes with foreign relations involving the reception of foreign envoys and the dispatching of English agents to continental courts. However the council met—with the king, in the royal absence, or in a specialized session—it was the council that met. There was only one royal council.

Though we shall speak more in detail about the council and justice, it should be noted that it was a court which provided remedy and rectified grievances. Though a court of equity, the council was much more concerned with the administration of justice than with the pronouncement of judgments. Most often petitions were answered by directing some court or some department to see that justice was done. The council could hand down directives concerning the administration of law in the common law courts and governing the relations of these courts but it did not make or annul common law in reply to petitions. What law it made was equitable law. Closely related to judicial work were the various and constant investigations into the operations of royal government. Both local and central officers were summoned before the council to be questioned. Out of such investigations might come recommendation for ordinances or statutes reforming abuses or establishing procedure. The council was still an essential part of parliament. It normally took the initiative in the business and prepared the agenda for the discussion of great matters of state, legislation, and taxation. If parliament decided upon war, peace, reform of the government, or legislation and taxation, it was the duty of the council to carry out the decision. The council was responsible for wartime administration and military supply and for conducting negotiations with foreign powers. Except when parliament decided to interfere, the regulation of commerce rested with the king and council. This entailed trade treaties, regulations of the wool staple, and setting the rates on customs. One of the most important functions of the king and council was the enactment of ordinances. This legislation frequently laid the groundwork for statutes or supplemented in detail broad policy of statutes.

The functions noted so far were all of a consultative or administrative nature; the councillors gave advice, helped the king to fulfil his royal obligations, and carried out what he willed. There was, however, another function that grew in the fourteenth century—the executive. The whole tendency of royal government in the fourteenth century was to make the council more independent of the King. When the king appointed his own councillors and could count upon their devoted support, he granted them executive powers in a wide range of business. When the barons captured the council they seized executive power. No king, we must realize, could personally supervise every aspect of royal government as it continued to grow and spawn new departments. The increasing burden of government plus repeated baronial seizure of the council made it an executive organ which the kings voluntarily or involuntarily permitted a large sphere of executive initiative and authority. The formation of the executive council was one of the fundamental developments of the fourteenth century. By the reign of Richard II the executive powers of the council were firmly established. Under the privy seal it authorized most routine business and even important matters which but a century earlier only the king could order. Records of the council meetings began in 1392. In this year alone the council met forty-three times in the absence of Richard and transacted all sorts of business. This evolution in conciliar authority inevitably deprived the king of some of his authority and contributed to the political process that was making him into a constitutional monarch.

Of the council's functions we shall say more when we study the other central organs of administration. Our concern for the moment is with the attempts of the barons and parliament to control the council so that they could determine governmental policy and restrict the royal power. A notable step in this direction occurred during Edward II's reign. The first baronial seizure of the council came with the Ordinances of 1311, numerous clauses of which were inspired by the Provisions of Oxford. A committee of twenty-one barons—the Lords Ordainer—appointed by the baronage to reform the state of the realm, submitted forty-one articles that were approved by parliament and assented to by Edward II in October 1311.[9] The tone of the Ordinances was set in the preamble, which declared that the king and his subjects had been dishonored and the crown debased "through bad and deceitful counsel." This opening attack of the barons was against the favorites of Edward's council such as Piers Gaveston and declared in effect that the bad government of Edward was due to his councillors, a situation that could be remedied only if the council was composed of men approved

[9] SM. no. 56.

by the baronage and parliament. To this end the Lords Ordainer included three articles that dealt specifically with the council. In Article XIII it was ordained that all evil councillors should be removed and replaced by acceptable men. Article XIV provided for the appointment of councillors and other royal officials. Such councillors as the chancellor, treasurer, keeper of the privy seal, keeper of the wardrobe, and steward of the household were to be appointed by the king with "the counsel and assent of the baronage, and that in parliament." Should appointments be necessary while parliament was not in session, they should be made with the counsel of those near the king, that is, the Lords Ordainer. In Article XXXIX it was ordained that all councillors and officers should be sworn to keep and observe all the Ordinances. Finally, Article XL constituted a baronial commission of five barons to hear complaints against the councillors and officers who contravened the Ordinances. The Ordinances of 1311 sought no fundamental revision of royal government nor did they attack the administrative departments. They were designed to procure a greater influence of the barons in royal government, to restrict Edward II's authority, and to reform specific abuses in administration.

The Ordinances of 1311 were never fully implemented. Edward II struggled to free himself from their trammels and the Lords Ordainer headed by Thomas of Lancaster proved incapable of governing the realm. The result was that Edward rewon some of his power, the Lords Ordainer declined in prestige and authority, and a middle party of moderate barons headed by the earl of Pembroke moved in and held the balance of power. These barons stabilized the royal government until 1318 when Lancaster and Edward I quarreled violently and threatened the realm with civil war. Only the Scottish threat of invasion and the mediation efforts of the moderate barons produced a compromise sealed by the Treaty of Leake in August 1318. The Ordinances of 1311 were ratified and Edward was forced to agree to the appointment of a new council of magnates consisting of eight bishops, four earls, four barons, and a banneret to be named by Lancaster. Five of these councillors were to be in constant attendance on the king and only with their concurrence could any affair of state be settled. It was provided also that at the next parliament a standing council was to replace this interim council; this was done in the parliament of York held in October 1318. Actually the standing council, backed by the moderate barons and composed primarily of their men, was an expedient derived from the Provisions of Oxford. It kept out of the government the bitter baronial enemies such as Lancaster and made it possible for Edward to cooperate; he was, however, still supervised by the barons. This scheme, though the most useful one devised to control Edward, depended upon his good will and upon a precarious political balance of power. When this broke down in 1322 the moderates could not hold the realm together. The result was the Battle of Boroughbridge and the parliament of York, which revoked the Ordinances of 1311 and the Treaty of Leake and restored the royal prerogative.[10] Until his deposition in 1327 Edward exercised the prerogatives of his office and appointed men to the council whom he favored and trusted. The council was the king's domain and the baronial effort to capture and control it was, for the moment, at a standstill. Precedents for conciliar control, however, had been established; they would provide a guide for future action in the reigns of Edward III and Richard II.

Amidst the spirit of conciliation and amicable relations with the barons that characterized the first part of Edward III's reign, no major changes occurred in the council. Until the crisis of 1341 the council consisted of the chancellor, treasurer, keeper of the privy seal, and other key officers close to the king. The break between Edward and Archbishop Stratford in 1341 arose from Edward's feeling that the council must be completely loyal to him and to his military and political policies and that he must obtain more baronial support if his military objectives in France were to be successful. Though Stratford and his group of councillors were professionals, Edward was convinced that they were unsympathetic to the war and too closely bound to Lancastrian interests. This induced Edward to remove Stratford and his colleagues and to replace them with men drawn chiefly from among the barons.[11] Henceforth the council was staffed principally by prominent lay barons, with the ecclesiastics and the professionals of lower status becoming less numerous. Edward had voluntarily staffed his council with prominent barons so that the baronage would be more cooperative in his war against France. From this time down to the Tudors the barons obtained an influence in the council never before wielded. They were to increase their power until in the fifteenth century the weak kings became playthings in their hands. Though the appointment of lay barons was Edward's idea, he did not intend that all the principal councillors should be selected with the advice of the baronage. He soon repudiated this promise under the plea that it was against the royal prerogative and rights but at the same time wisely selected councillors acceptable to the baronage and so warded off attack.[12] He retained the prerogative of appointing his ministers but was careful to choose those who would get along with the baronage. Such was the composition of the council for the next thirty years, and Edward was free to campaign in France. Laymen of good education and training became more prominent in the council and many held posts for years. The council became a stable and secure organ of government; it was not to attain such political harmony again during the Middle Ages.

In 1371 the political stability of the council was destroyed by a parliamentary attack initiated by John of Gaunt, Edward III's third eldest son and duke of Lancaster. The reasons given for the attack were failure to prosecute

[10] SM, no. 58.
[11] SM, no. 61E.
[12] SM, no. 62C.

the French war successfully and incompetent government. The real causes were the declining powers of the aging Edward III and the political ambition of John of Gaunt to control the government. The baronial party of Gaunt forced Edward to dismiss all the old councillors and to install a council acceptable to Gaunt which remained in control until 1376. Meanwhile Edward devoted less and less attention to government. The council shake-up of 1371 did not involve a conflict between the king and magnates or a fight between the professionals and aristocrats for conciliar control. There was perhaps anticlericalism in the removal of some ecclesiastics from the council but it was greatly overshadowed by the personal political ambitions of John of Gaunt and his cronies. Gaunt perceived that the council was the center of power and that whoever controlled it would govern the realm, especially as Edward's declining health restricted him from active participation in the administration. Gaunt and some of his political allies such as Richard Lyons, who negotiated royal loans with the London merchants, and William Latimer, royal chamberlain and councillor, were thoroughly dishonest and mulcted the government of money, lands, and offices. The upshot was a counterattack against the Gauntian council in 1376.

The Good Parliament which assembled in April 1376 took its cue and its orders from a faction of moderate barons led by Edward the Black Prince and the earl of March. Many of the commons who had been elected to parliament through the political maneuvering of this faction were ready to do what was asked of them. Peter de la Mare, who spoke for the commons and launched a bitter attack against Gaunt and the council, was steward of the earl of March. There were similar connections and ties between other commons and this baronial faction. Consulting together on procedure and tactics, the lords and commons worked smoothly and warded off all opposition. Peter de la Mare delivered a devastating speech accusing the leading councillors of financial peculation and corrupt and inefficient government. As a result a detailed investigation was held in the House of Lords, and it was determined that the charges against the councillors were proven. So occurred the first impeachment of royal councillors by parliament. Lyons and Latimer were sentenced to imprisonment and forfeiture of goods. For the first time was established the principle that royal ministers were responsible not to the king alone but also to parliament. Immediately the council was reconstructed. Nine new baronial councillors were appointed by the king with the consent and advice of parliament. The commons then pressed for further reorganization of the council. They asked that it be enlarged by ten or twelve more lords, that no great matters should be decided except with the consent of the whole council, that lesser affairs should be approved by at least four councillors, and that from four to six councillors should be in constant attendance on the king.[13] The Good Parliament of 1376 left un-

[13] SM, no. 61I.

touched the royal prerogative and the system of administration. What it did attack was the councillors and their abuses. The great precedent that it established was the responsibility of royal councillors to parliament, which indirectly curtailed the royal prerogative.

The death of the Black Prince in June 1376 weakened the Good Parliament and it was dissolved in July. Meanwhile Gaunt labored to overturn the work of the Good Parliament. In January 1377 he secured the assembly of a parliament favorable to his interests. All the work of the Good Parliament was annulled and the council filled with Gaunt's men. This council was the government during the last few months of Edward III's life. Gaunt's men acted in the royal name but executed the commands of Gaunt. The year 1377 marks a decisive stage in the history of the royal council. Completely the instrument of the king in 1307, it had become seventy years later the instrument of the lords; they would control it and in effect the government until changed in the last quarter of the fifteenth century by Edward IV and Henry Tudor.

The conciliar arrangement during the first years of Richard II's minority was complicated. At the outset there was a great council of lords that met occasionally and a small council consisting of the principal officers that dealt daily with state business. This stopgap arrangement was soon changed by the establishment of a continual council. The great council named a council of twelve in July 1377. In October a second continual council was selected by parliament to supersede the former. It represented a balance of various political factions and remained in power until 1380 when the commons became dissatisfied and replaced it with five officers appointed in parliament. This experiment in appointing a continual council primarily responsible to parliament failed and the years between 1380 and 1386 saw the rise of a new court party of royal favorites from the household, nourished by Richard and appointed to the council. This political development alarmed the barons. Under the leadership of Thomas, duke of Gloucester, who was Richard's uncle, and Gaunt's son Henry Bolingbroke, they organized an opposition party.

The attack against Richard and his council of favorites was launched with fury in the parliament of October 1386.[14] Richard was faced with a demand for the dismissal of all his councillors and for the impeachment of his chancellor, Michael de la Pole, earl of Suffolk. At first Richard refused and haughtily replied that he would not dismiss the humblest servant of the royal kitchen at parliament's request. But a reminder of Edward II's fate led Richard to capitulate. The chief councillors were dismissed and replaced by partisans of the opposition. Suffolk was impeached. The opposition then demanded a reconstructed council invested with power to reform the government. Richard agreed to such a council for a year, yet when parliament

[14] SM, no. 63F.

dissolved he declared that he would surrender none of his power to the council. Nevertheless the council of reform came into being and temporarily removed Richard from direction of the government. His attempt to raise a party of opposition failed and he was reduced to further humiliation in 1387 and 1388. Gloucester and his chief supporters appealed the five principal advisers and favorites of Richard and forced the summoning of another parliament—the Merciless Parliament—which sat from February to June 1388. At this parliament a new council consisting of the five Lords Appellant was instituted. It took all initiative and discretion away from Richard and ruled the realm in his name. All orders and warrants were issued by king and council, by council, or by king and council in parliament.[15]

The regime of the Lords Appellant collapsed, as we have seen, in 1389. Richard came back into power and ruled with the assistance of a council consisting both of the Lords Appellant and of his own men. This solution continued down to 1397 and made these years the most fruitful and harmonious part of Richard's reign. Though Richard's control of the council was recognized, in actual fact much of the business was conducted by the council in his absence. An ordinance of 1390 acknowledged this as normal procedure.[16] The royal council had now arrived at the summit of royal government. It was the actual ruler of England. The core of the council met often during the week and consistently discharged routine business in the absence of the king. Occasionally it was afforced by other sworn councillors to deal with special problems. In theory the council carried out Richard's will; in practice it assumed most of his power.

With Richard's bid for absolutism we are familiar. The council was no longer a restriction upon his authority. All that restrained him was the bureaucratic routine and procedure of the various central organs of administration. Richard, to be sure, retained a council and acted upon its advice but it was a council composed of his men, men who would support his bid for absolute power. But even this council, despite its subservience to the king, was composed of professional experts upon whom Richard relied and to whom he delegated much authority. Richard's abrupt fall ended this brief interlude of absolutism and brought the Lancastrian dynasty to the throne.

3. CONCLUSIONS

The very circumstances of the Lancastrian accession to the throne dictated that the Lancastrian kings must respect the power of the barons who supported them and the parliament which veiled their rule in the cloak of legality. Yet even the Lancastrians did not intend to preside over the disintegration of the royal prerogative; they struggled tenaciously to exercise its main powers, chiefly the executive rights of the monarch. None were very

[15] SM, no. 63C.
[16] SM, no. 64D.

successful, however, because for almost a century there had been a steady growth in the powers of the royal council nourished by the repeated attacks of the barons. Even when a king controlled the council he was forced by the burden and complexity of government to delegate wide authority to it; when the king was not in control, as was frequently the case in the fourteenth century, the lords dominated it and ruled England. One of the two or three principal political issues at stake during the fourteenth century was whether the council was to be controlled by the king or by the baronial factions. Generally the barons prevailed and wielded a restrictive arm over the king. But limitation of the king by the lords was no permanent solution because ultimately it rested upon military persuasion. Constitutional limitation of the king that was enduring and peaceful could come only through the medium of parliament.

XXXIII

Central and Local Government

IN SPITE of the decline of royal power in the fourteenth century and the authority delegated to or usurped by the royal council, the king remained at the center of his government. Central government was highly personal and the king was still the most important part of it. Once this basic fact is understood one can see more clearly why the kings struggled to retain their personal control over the various departments which tended to slip out of the royal hand. That royal government in the fourteenth century was less personal than formerly is obvious, but this change, it must be realized, was not due wholly to baronial and parliamentary opposition and control of the royal council. Because of the expansion in government, personal supervision over every detail was no longer possible; each department became larger and more bureaucratic or spawned new departments to cope with administrative demands. As this happened government drifted farther from the kings, who attempted to counter the current by devising techniques that would still link their vast central bureaucracy to the royal person.

One must also realize that the repeated attacks against royal government aimed at capturing the royal council and exerting control over the king did not stem primarily from the urge to reform the government. Admittedly the opposition in many of its documents speaks of reforming the chancery, wardrobe, chamber, and exchequer, but there is little evidence of actual reform. Even when the baronial opposition captured the council and worked under the cloak of reform such as that blocked out by the Ordinances of 1311 or by the reform commission of 1388–1389, reform was negligible. Consistently the only result of such political upheaval was the removal of royal councillors and officers and the eradication of abuses particularly resented by the barons. All true reform and change in royal administration came from within the various departments. The barons, almost exclusively concerned with winning political power, had no thought of changing administrative procedure. The cry of reform was only a sort of "campaign slogan" to secure the support of the commons and the realm.

Locally, government continued to shift in the fourteenth century from royal officers such as the sheriff to the gentry, the knights and squires, who carried the major burden of government in the counties and hundreds. From these men came the justices of the peace, who deprived the sheriffs of most of their functions. Despite the varied constitutions of the boroughs, municipal government uniformly became a closed corporation dominated by a few wealthy merchants and industrial enterpreneurs who controlled the organs of local government and who represented the boroughs in parliament.

I. THE CENTRAL GOVERNMENT

A. The Chancery

Besides the council the principal organs of administration in the fourteenth century were the chancery, wardrobe, chamber, and exchequer. The chancery was the formal mouthpiece of the king; most state business funneled through it and was officially authorized by the great seal. The exchequer was the great central treasury which still received and expended most of the royal income. Behind these two departments, governed by a strict and traditional routine and often referred to by historians as state departments, lay the wardrobe and chamber plus an indeterminate area of administration that was never recorded or departmentalized. As the gulf between the chancery and exchequer and the king widened, the latter used his household organs as intermediaries. Generally close to him, they were used to transmit royal orders to chancery and exchequer, and for this purpose each got a seal. It could happen that the king would orally give an order to the chamber which would transmit it to the wardrobe which would transmit it to the chancery which would issue it under the great seal. In royal finance the wardrobe and chamber shared the same position. They were bridges between the exchequer and the king and served to expedite immediate and personal financial obligations. In addition to employing these departments for transmitting and implementing his will, the king carried on much business orally, communicating his orders by word of mouth to the chancellor and to the treasurer. This was possible, of course, only when these officers were at the royal court. We must note one more trend in fourteenth-century administration. The kings had narrowed the gulf between the exchequer and chancery and themselves in the thirteenth century by working through the chamber and wardrobe. In the fourteenth century they continued to do this but were forced also to devise means to supervise and to communicate with the wardrobe and chamber, which, like the chancery and exchequer, became more formal and less accessible to the royal person.

Two generalizations may be made on the fourteenth-century chancery. The first is that it developed into a court of equity; the second, that it continued to be the formal mouthpiece of the king, performing the same functions as in the twelfth and thirteenth centuries but sharing them more with the wardrobe and chamber so that it became less intimately connected with the king, who conducted much of his business with it through the wardrobe and chamber. We shall reserve discussion of the judicial development until later and shall turn now to the administrative functions of the chancery.

During Edward II's reign the bulk of royal administration was initiated by chancery writ under the great seal. The chancery was still close to the king and enough under his supervision so that he could orally communicate orders to the proper chancery officials. Though the chancellor was the leading officer of the royal government he was but one of four or five with whom the king transacted business and in no respect did he have a general supervision over all departments of central administration as had the justiciars. The chancery and chancellors, though not a part of the household, maintained a close relation with it; numerous chancellors and chancery officials had come from the wardrobe and chamber and were appointed and dismissed at the king's will. What must be understood is that although the chancery was not a part of the household it was as subordinate to the king as the wardrobe and chamber. Perhaps the barons and parliament viewed the chancery as more of a state department but the kings certainly did not. And it is safe to say that no one talked much about state and household government or separated it upon the basis of a logical division of labor. All government was the king's and he accomplished it by whatever department he desired. If the chancery was farther from the king than his household department it was not because the king willed it that way but because the growth of royal government and administrative operations made it that way. Though the chancellor was the most influential of the royal ministers he owed this elevated role not to the chancery but to his position in the royal council where he could influence state policy. This explains the struggle by the barons to fill the position with one of their men.

Cry for reform dominated Edward II's reign, but there was little in the chancery. The Ordinances of 1311 ordained that the chancellor should be appointed by the counsel and consent of the baronage in parliament, but this pertained to all royal officers; the chancellor was not singled out. The article ordering the chancellor to swear under oath to obey the laws of the realm was no innovation; every royal officer had sworn such an oath for years. Of the central departments the chancery was least affected by the Ordinances of 1311. The only change was substitution of a baronial man as chancellor.[1] If the chancery's administrative functions changed under Edward II they did so, we may conclude, principally as a result of reform effected in the wardrobe and chamber, most of it voluntarily initiated by the king and the interested officers.

During the reigns of Edward III and Richard II few administrative reforms directly affected the chancery. The most significant change was wrought by the Ordinances of Walton in 1338, considered by Tout "perhaps the most important administrative act of the reign of Edward III." These ordinances

[1] SM, no. 56.

seem to have been issued just prior to Edward's departure overseas for the French war with the intention of outlining administrative procedure in his absence for the central government and for some of the departments and key personnel. Some of the ordinances long remained in effect and guided future administrative procedure. The principal intent of the act was to coordinate the organs of central administration by insuring to the king and his personal ministers a tight supervision. Edward III wanted neither the chancery nor the exchequer to assume any initiative in his absence. It was ordained, therefore, that the chancery was to authorize no special payments of money unless so warranted under the privy seal. Furthermore, warrants under the privy seal were required for all business issued under the great seal except routine legal writs and administrative matters. Though a wartime measure, control of the great seal by warrants of the privy seal was to become increasingly prevalent and was to provide what all the kings desired—communication with and control over the chancery. The procedure ordained by the act of 1338, however, was not entirely new; the privy seal had for some time been the lever of royal executive action. The act of 1338 but applied the procedure with more system and rigor. During the rest of Edward III's reign there was little change in the chancery. The crisis of 1341 brought no reform, only the wholesale removal of officers, among them the chancellor Stratford, who was struck down not because of his administrative incapacity but because of his political opposition to Edward.

The principal reason for discussion of the chancery under Richard II stems from a better knowledge of its functions and routine provided by the records. By Richard's time the initiative of the chancery had perceptibly declined. Its work was mainly to issue under the great seal orders that had been decided upon elsewhere. The chancery was largely restricted to implementing what was authorized under the privy seal and other small seals employed by Richard and his household staff. There was, however, some initiative left to the chancery. All routine judicial writs—writs *de cursu*—were issued without authorization. Also, the chancery initiated various royal commissions, exercised some patronage such as appointments to ecclesiastical benefices worth less than 20 marks annually, and issued routine letters and orders regulating procedural relations with other central departments.

Except for the five-year period between 1332 and 1337 when Edward III was campaigning against the Scots and had moved most of the principal departments to York so that they would be readily accessible, the chancery was located at Westminster. With the outbreak of the Hundred Years' War it became the permanent capital of England. Besides being situated in the richest part of England, Westminster was most strategically located for the prosecution of the war and for the governance of the realm. Specifically, chancery headquarters was in Westminster Hall where the chancellor sat at the great bench and performed his judicial functions. Here letters were issued and sealed and important matters transacted. Routine business, not requiring the chancellor's presence, was conducted elsewhere. Though occasionally the chancery itinerated with the king, usually it stayed at its permanent headquarters at Westminster.

The chancellor headed a department consisting of two subdepartments and a staff of about sixty. The office of the rolls was the secretariat. Here all the documents were drawn up and enrolled for record. At least ten different enrollments were kept besides numerous miscellaneous records preserved without enrollment. The other department was the hanaper, which collected all the fees received for issuing judicial writs and similar documents under the great seal. The hanaper accounted for its receipts and periodically transferred them into the exchequer. The principal members of the chancery staff were the twelve clerks of the first grade, which included the keeper of the rolls (the lieutenant of the chancellor), the clerks of parliament, receivers of petitions, and judicial assistants of the chancellor. The minor and mechanical secretarial work fell to twelve clerks of the second grade, twenty-four cursitors who drew up routine writs, and a few other miscellaneous officers. Compared to chanceries on the Continent the English chancery was efficiently organized and accomplished a remarkable amount of work. It was nonetheless open to abuses and corruption which increased as the chancellors devoted less time to administration and more time and effort to the council and the growing judicial functions of the chancery. The chancellors of the fourteenth and fifteenth centuries had become foremost politicians and statesmen whose energies were consumed by the ebb and flow of national politics. As the council grew in executive power the chancellors grew in prestige and authority. The administrative departments of the chancery suffered; supervised mostly by subordinates, their work was often delegated to poorly paid functionaries whose economic plight invited bribes and corrupt practices.

B. The Exchequer

Edward II inherited an administrative procedure that gave him an even tighter control over the exchequer than over the chancery. Often even routine and formal business had to await the royal authorization communicated to the exchequer under writ of privy seal. Warrants were common for payments and grants of lands and offices made under the exchequer seal. A principal function of the exchequer was to keep the household furnished with adequate supplies for its frequent needs. Although funds were periodically transferred from the exchequer to the wardrobe, many subsidiary payments were ordered by writs of *liberate* issued from the wardrobe under privy seal. This tightly knit arrangement was scarcely affected by the Ordinances of 1311. Article VIII alone dealt specifically with exchequer reform; it reiterated a demand, previously made by the Provisions of Oxford, that all royal income should be paid directly into the exchequer and nowhere else.[2] Obviously the barons hoped to simplify the royal financial system so that

[2] SM, no. 56.

they could more easily check upon the condition of the royal pocketbook by making the exchequer the ultimate and only treasury of receipt and issue. They also planned to reduce the financial position of the wardrobe, which was more difficult to control and very closely tied to the king. But this ordinance never questioned the payments of the exchequer to the wardrobe, chamber, or other organs of government; it took for granted that they must be supplied. Fundamentally the barons were attempting to account for all the money the king received so that they would know how much he spent. If a great deal of his income was paid into the wardrobe or chamber it was difficult to check on the royal receipts. This ordinance did not remain in force long, and Edward and his successors continued to by-pass the exchequer and carry on much of their financial business through the wardrobe and chamber.

Effective reform in the exchequer was triggered by its officers and willingly accepted by the king. The principal reforms came between 1322 and 1326 during the treasurerships of Walter Stapledon, bishop of Exeter, and William Melton, archbishop of York. They were effected by a series of ordinances by king and council based upon a detailed investigation of exchequer administration ordered by Stapledon. A by-product of this examination was a partial inventory of the exchequer archives. The first reform came with the Cowick Ordinance of 1323. It dealt chiefly with the system of recordkeeping, now hopelessly antiquated. The records were in such disarray that no one knew accurately the state of royal finances. The principal bottleneck was the Pipe Rolls, upon which were enrolled, in addition to the county incomes, other miscellaneous crown incomes and debts. They had become so cluttered that no one could find what he wanted in them. Henceforth all foreign accounts and debts (income not received from the counties) were to be omitted and given separate enrollment. Debts owed to the king, for example, were to be enrolled on an exannual roll, one for each year. If any debts were unpaid, they were to be enrolled on a new roll for the following year. To cope with the new enrollments clerks were added and the barons of the exchequer were instructed that their primary duty was to examine the accounts of royal debtors. They were to hear pleas only when ordered to and only when the pleas concerned royal finances or exchequer officers.

The next exchequer reform came with the York Ordinance of 1323, suggested by exchequer officers. It was mainly concerned with regulating the accounts rendered to the exchequer by the wardrobe. The wardrobe had always accounted for the money received from the exchequer but had done so sporadically and inefficiently. The York Ordinance tightened up the accounting procedure and ordered that general wardrobe accounts should be compiled quarterly and incorporated in a yearly account submitted to the exchequer. Strict penalties were provided for officers who failed to produce their accounts promptly. The Ordinance of Westminster in 1324 enforced what had been instituted by Article VIII of the Ordinances of 1311. It ordered that the keeper of the wardrobe should receive no money except at the hands of the treasurer or chamberlains of the exchequer. The last reform, initiated by the Westminster Ordinance of 1326, was basically a restatement and summary of the three preceding ordinances. The chief innovation was to order the chancellor and keeper of the privy seal to enroll all writs that ordered payments by the exchequer. The total effect of these ordinances was to streamline administrative procedure and to make the accounting system functional. These reforms accomplished under Edward II influenced royal financial administration for the rest of the Middle Ages; it changed only with the extensive Tudor reorganization of central finance.

Though some historians have argued that the Ordinances of 1311, as well as the other four, were of constitutional importance in making the king strictly accountable for his receipts and expenditures to the realm, this conclusion is overdrawn. Edward II himself supported the most extensive and permanent reforms and in no way lost control over the royal financial administration. Admittedly the wardrobe was forced to a strict accountability to the exchequer, which could be more easily controlled by barons and parliament, but the exchequer was still the king's and his to command. What the financial reforms accomplished was to produce a more efficient financial system and to save the records and accounting procedure from absolute chaos. They had little constitutional significance.

Reform of the exchequer during the rest of the fourteenth century was inconsequential. The Ordinances of Walton in 1338 specified that all extraordinary payments must be warranted under the privy seal. To guarantee that this procedure was followed the exchequer chamberlains were to account for their payments before a special auditing committee which was to check every special payment against a roll containing a record of all issues warranted under the privy seal. But this was no innovation; it merely elaborated upon previous instructions. The only other exchequer procedure worthy of mention consisted of attempts to secure periodic estimates of the royal finances. Various extant accounts from Edward II and Edward III list the assets, liabilities, and debts. In 1362, for example, the first attempt was made to produce a balance sheet for the fiscal year. But few such accounts survive, perhaps because the king and interested officials thought it better to remain ignorant of the precarious state of the royal purse. The balance sheet for 1362–1363 showed a deficit of £55,000, which was more than the ordinary yearly income.

The chronic royal deficit is largely explained by the heavy cost of the French war, but also responsible was inefficiency of the exchequer in collecting crown debts. To provide the king with ready cash the exchequer resorted to borrowing huge sums from foreign and English merchants and to issuing tallies on anticipated receipts such as those from the wool customs. Often the revenue anticipated did not materialize or fell short, and frequently too many tallies were assigned on the same revenue. The exchequer was constantly writing too many checks and overdrawing its account. This resulted in dishonoring tallies and a consequent loss of faith in the royal solvency. Such unsound financing threw the records into confusion, a confusion made worse by lack of understanding basic principles of accounting and budgeting. The exchequer system had been efficient during the twelfth and thirteenth centuries but in the fourteenth and fifteenth it was archaic and unequal to the new demands of public finance. Financial order and stability would be restored only when Henry VII tackled the problem and revolutionized the 500-year-old system. When Henry accomplished his reform he did it through a revived chamber, not through the exchequer.

C. The Royal Income

Though royal taxation will be discussed when we investigate parliament, we must have some idea of the royal resources in the fourteenth century and of how they were collected and paid into the exchequer. The royal income may be conveniently broken down into three categories. First, there were the revenues received by the kings in their capacity as landlords and feudal lords. These revenues consisted of the county farm, the borough farm, incomes from royal estates, and receipts from escheats, wardships, and reliefs. Second, there were the revenues derived from government operations and services such as amercements, fines, profits of justice, and incomes from the royal mints. Third, there were the revenues which came to the king by virtue of the royal prerogative—export and import duties (indirect taxation), lay subsidies (direct taxation), and ecclesiastical tenths. During the reign of Edward III the first category of income averaged about £15,000 to £16,000 per annum; the second category about £14,000. Customs netted about £12,000 yearly, the ecclesiastical tenth approximately £19,000, and the lay subsidies around £35,000 to £40,000.

Anyone who studies the royal finances in the fourteenth century soon perceives that the above incomes were far from adequate; the government always had a deficit which forced the king and his officers to devise means of extracting more money out of the realm. Two techniques often employed were to increase the rate and frequency of the taxes and to raise the customs duties. The kings attempted this by negotiating with parliament and with separate assemblies of native and foreign merchants. Sometimes the kings achieved their objectives but invariably they incurred resentment from their subjects and increased resistance against direct and indirect taxation. When occasionally the kings experimented by negotiating for grants individually with county courts and boroughs, it proved unremunerative. Equally unsuccessful were attempts to revive obsolete royal taxes or incomes such as the tallage. Ultimately all three kings of the fourteenth century recognized that their best source of income were lay subsidies voted to them in parliament. Though not enthusiastic about any tax, the royal subjects at least paid a tax that had been voted in parliament and to which they were bound by the actions of their representatives. Naturally the kings never received enough in taxes but parliamentary taxation was the best solution to their dire financial needs.

How were these various revenues collected and paid into the exchequer? The principal royal revenues were generally collected by local men of some prestige and wealth, men who enjoyed financial independence and political influence in the community. This does not mean that the men who collected taxes were not royal officers but that the men appointed to offices were local residents of considerable social, economic, and political prestige. Such had been the tradition of English government and so it would continue for centuries. Local royal government was performed by local men at the royal command without remuneration.

The sheriffs were customarily knights though occasionally they were selected from the squires. They held the oldest and most important local financial office. They collected and paid the farm of the county, farms of some of the royal domains, the profits of justice, and miscellaneous county incomes. The assessors and collectors of the lay subsidies voted by parliament came from the same class as the sheriffs. Because the lay subsidy consisted of a certain percentage of a man's personal property, the assessors had to evaluate a man's property before the tax could be determined and collected. For each county chief taxers were appointed who then relied upon the information supplied to them by numerous subassessors from the hundreds and villages. When all the assessments had been made they were lumped together and their total represented the sum owed by each county to the exchequer. Obviously there was much room for dishonesty among the taxpayers and collectors, and the royal government repeatedly experimented with devices to check embezzlement. The assessors and chief collectors or taxers were, however, in a difficult position; they had to serve both local community and king, and apparently they tried to satisfy both. While not exacting the last pound from their neighbors, they came close enough to producing the anticipated income to escape undue royal suspicion. But numerous collectors were dishonest. They made deals with the taxpayer and pocketed money. The assessment and collection of taxes was not overly efficient in the Middle Ages, but then no system of taxation has ever been infallible.

Lands that escheated to the crown were evaluated by escheators, who accounted for the income from them as long as they were held by the king. Though the number and organization of escheators varied in the fourteenth century there were generally two chief escheators—one for the area south of the Trent River and another for the land north. These two were often helped by eight regional escheators, who in turn relied upon county escheators. The escheators, like the other collectors of royal revenue, were traditionally chosen from the local gentry. The officials who collected the customs were taken from the burgesses of the towns such as the merchants, industrial entrepreneurs, and shipowners. The customs were collected at designated ports where four types of officials performed their tasks. The collectors, numbering two or four in each port, collected the wool customs; the deputy butlers collected wine duties; the pesagers (tronagers) weighed merchandise that paid duties on weight and collected the duties; and the controllers checked these officials through a counterroll which was compared with the original tax records. Often these officials were appointed or elected by the town council or the burgesses, and invariably they came from leading families and owed the office to connections with influential merchants or with the town council. When the king appointed them he relied upon local advice and generally selected those nominated. The last category of tax collectors were those who secured the ecclesiastical tenths. The bishops were responsible for the collection of the tax in their dioceses but delegated the task to deputies, generally abbots and priors, who collected it and rendered it directly to the exchequer. It was a simple and routine procedure. They always collected a tenth which consistently remained the same. They knew what each property was to pay and simply collected the amount.

Collection of the royal income by unpaid local men, however inefficient, was the only workable and possible method in medieval England. The crown did not have the resources to establish the civil service necessary to accomplish all the tasks. Obviously checks and controls over these local men were hit and miss and the exchequer never received a lot of the revenue due it, but the age could produce no better system. In France where a royal bureaucracy collected and administered the royal money there was even greater inefficiency and corruption. In the final analysis the English kings had to trust their tax collectors and their taxpayers to provide for the royal necessity. How loyally they served and supported the king depended largely upon how well they thought they were governed. Good government, then as now, depended upon the good relations and spirit existing between central and local government.

D. The Wardrobe

Under Edward I the wardrobe attained its greatest power in central government. It competed with the exchequer as the principal treasury, it guarded the privy seal which initiated a major part of royal business, it served as a war office during campaigns, it provided intelligent and experienced men to negotiate the royal interest abroad, and it served as a training school for a large percentage of the leading Edwardian ministers. Though there were occasions in the fourteenth century, especially during war, when the wardrobe again became the nerve center of government, it never held for long the power it had exercised in the thirteenth century. Exchequer reform improved that department's efficiency and tightened its control over the wardrobe. The chamber, from which the wardrobe had grown, was revived as a financial and executive organ and deprived the wardrobe of much authority. And repeated baronial attacks against household government, though resulting in no significant reform, placed the wardrobe under closer scrutiny and thereby deprived it of power. The counterstrategy of the kings was to transfer the instruments of their executive power to other household departments and officers not exposed to the glare of baronial attack and suspicion.

During the early part of Edward II's reign the wardrobe operated as it had under Edward I. Its flexibility provided the administrative machinery that could give efficient and rapid expression to the royal will and that could work closely with the chancery and exchequer. It helped the chancery preserve documents and even guarded the great seal upon occasion. It received the bulk of its supply from the exchequer, paid three times a year under authorization of bills of wardrobe (writs of *liberate*) issued under the privy seal. Supplementary payments were also received under writs of *liberate*, and some revenue was collected directly without passing through the exchequer. At this time the hanaper paid its receipts into the wardrobe and the exchequer honored loans contracted for the king by wardrobe officials. The wardrobe, at the king's fingertips, was the logical department for him to use in dealing with the chancery and exchequer, both of which had gone out of court. The foundation of the wardrobe's strength, however, was custody of the privy seal, the principal instrument of the royal executive. Warrants under it set in motion machinery in all departments. The privy seal held by the controller of the wardrobe was behind most of the exchequer payments and documents issued by the chancery.

Like that of the chancery and exchequer, the organization of the wardrobe was basically unchanged by the Ordinances of 1311. But with household government as the butt of attack certain changes were attempted. The barons did not challenge the financial and executive functions of the wardrobe or the fact that skilled personnel were needed. What they attempted to correct was what they considered improper use of authority and abuses by some of the staff. For better control of the wardrobe staff Article XIV provided that the keeper and controller of the wardrobe were to be appointed with the consent of the baronage in parliament and that a capable clerk was to be named to keep the privy seal. This change was no different from what was made with the chancery and exchequer; the barons wanted to secure key positions for their men. Article XIII directed the removal of all evil councillors both within and without the household. The article that hit most tellingly at the wardrobe was XXXII; it stated that writs issued under the privy seal were not to be used to delay or to disturb the law of the land or common right. This provision was intended to stop royal interference with cases in the common law courts and to insure that a case would be decided according to the law in a proper court under the supervision of common law justices. The king's will expressed through writs of privy seal was not to change or supersede the law of the land under which the king governed. This article struck at the core of royal authority and established a precedent that would be used against succeeding monarchs, especially against the Stuarts in the seventeenth century. The only other provisions affecting the wardrobe were those that restricted it to exacting only the ancient and lawful prises under authorized commissions of purveyance.[3] Though determined to control the chief wardrobe offices and to correct abusive uses of authority, the barons did not question the right of the wardrobe to act as a treasury, to use the privy seal, or to purvey the traditional prises. They wanted to gain more influence in royal policy and possibly to reduce the expenditures of the household.

Though the wardrobe was the subject of numerous articles of the Household Ordinance of York in 1318, no drastic reform resulted. In the parliament of York (1318) the barons had insisted that the household be reformed. Accordingly a reform commission was established consisting of men named by the magnates and by Edward II, who cleverly included four household officers, among them the keeper and controller of the wardrobe. With such men on the commission it is not surprising that its report embodied in the Household Ordinance recommended no basic reform. This ordinance, modeled upon the Household Ordinance of 1279, resulted in a detailed codification of the rules and procedure of the household with special emphasis upon the wages and perquisites of the officers and upon a definition of their duties. In many respects it was like *The Establishment of the King's Household* that had outlined the functions and perquisites of the household staff of Henry I. The most interesting part is its reference to a keeper of the privy seal as an officer distinct from the controller of the wardrobe. It indicates that by 1318 the office of privy seal was no longer within the wardrobe but had become a department of the household headed by a clerk assisted by a staff of subclerks.[4] The only other changes in wardrobe administration during Edward II's reign occurred between 1322 and 1326 when its financial relations with the exchequer were modified so as to make it more strictly accountable.

The history of the wardrobe under Edward III is one of short revival followed by slow decline. Until the outbreak of the Hundred Years' War in 1337 the wardrobe operated on a limited scale. Then suddenly the demands of Edward's first continental campaign in the Low Countries catapulted it back to the activity and power exercised under Edward I. It accompanied Edward to Brabant and Flanders and served not only as a war office but as the center of his government overseas. The Ordinances of Walton, as we have seen, organized administrative procedure so as to control the central departments at home and abroad through writs of privy seal. Though controlled by the privy seal, the wardrobe financed the first campaign of Edward III. The exchequer supplied the bulk of money but when this proved inadequate the wardrobe resorted to contracting loans and

[3] SM, no. 56.
[4] SM, no. 57.

issuing bills of the wardrobe. The failure of the exchequer to honor these obligations was the root of the crisis of 1341.

The wardrobe performed its functions between 1337 and 1340 as efficiently as under Edward I, but its inability to finance the campaign indicates that the large-scale demands of war had antiquated the old system of military administration. It was soon apparent that the prolonged military operations on the Continent could be adequately financed only by more numerous and larger exchequer grants obtained from parliamentary taxation. For the rest of the century the French war was financed by grants from parliament collected and administered by the exchequer. This inevitably revived exchequer activity and authority and stimulated parliament to a close supervision of war finance. Gradually the wardrobe was excluded from war finance and declined as a treasury for public finance. It became but a court office concerned only with financing the domestic needs of the household. This was to be the role of the wardrobe until the end of the Middle Ages. Only for a short period under Henry V was it revived as a war office and treasury for his French campaigns. The exchequer assumed the burden of war finance and shared it with parliament, which appointed committees to audit the expenditures, and treasurers to insure that supply voted for war was spent for that purpose.[5]

Under Richard II the wardrobe was a minor household department. All its money came from the exchequer and its officers ceased playing a prominent role in administration and politics. No longer was it the department that produced the great royal officers and prominent bishops. Administrative power had shifted elsewhere leaving the wardrobe on the periphery. When the Tudors revived strong central government and sought to personalize their power they turned not to the wardrobe but to the chamber.

More than changing methods in financial administration account for the decline of the wardrobe in the fourteenth century. Since the reign of Henry III the mainspring of wardrobe power had been its custody of the privy seal. This it lost in the fourteenth century as central government continued the traditional and typical process of bifurcation. The Household Ordinance of York in 1318 provided for an officer called keeper of the privy seal. This officer was not a member of the wardrobe but headed a department of his own.[6] By 1323 the keepership of the privy seal was definitely recognized as an office quite different from that of the wardrobe controller. It was now considered a promotion for the controller to be named keeper of the privy seal. After 1360 it was the exchequer, and no longer the wardrobe, that paid the wages of the keeper and his staff. By this time the keepership had gone not only out of the wardrobe but out of the household to take its place beside the chancery and exchequer. Meanwhile the various administrative reforms centering executive initiative and control in the privy seal made its keeper

[5] SM, no. 61E.
[6] SM, no. 57.

one of the great royal ministers; he ranked directly after the chancellor and treasurer and became a leading member of the royal council. The capable William of Wykeham, bishop of Winchester, who held the office between 1363 and 1367, was the principal minister and adviser of the king. During the reign of Richard II the keeper of the privy seal was recognized by parliament as one of the five leading royal officers.

Having become the head of a separate department and one of the three most powerful ministers during the reigns of Edward II and Edward III, the keeper of the privy seal continued to occupy a position of authority in the royal council of Richard II. Indeed he became so closely associated with the council that the privy seal became an instrument of its executive initiative. The keeper took on administrative and judicial functions, which he initiated and executed under the privy seal. His judicial work, there is reason to believe, foreshadowed the Tudor court of requests. The department of the privy seal developed so rapidly that it acquired its own headquarters at Westminster during Edward III's reign. It was housed in a new structure between Westminster Hall and the palace not far from the new council chamber (the Star Chamber of Tudor times).

During the reigns of Edward III and Richard II most executive action was initiated by writs of privy seal; all the royal departments have left behind hundreds and thousands of such writs directing implementation of some policy or order. Though the kings were ultimately responsible for most of the orders, there was a growing tendency in this period to have the council initiate actions under the privy seal. This does not mean that the privy seal was the council's but that the keeper had become a key member of a council constantly delegated or usurping executive power. There is no denying that the keeper of the privy seal had lost his intimate relationship with the king. He had gone out of court and had become a member of the council, which was repeatedly captured and controlled by the baronage, who used it to coerce the king. Many measures initiated against the crown were germinated in the council under writ of privy seal. Whether used by king or council, the privy seal was the spark of royal government. It had become a prized possession and both king and barons vied to control it. Long past was the day when a king like Henry III or Edward I kept the privy seal by his side in the wardrobe, ever available for his personal use.

E. The Chamber

Though English medieval administrative history abounds in occasions when departments bifurcated and spawned others which supplanted or overshadowed the parents, there are few cases in which the parent revived to overshadow its offspring. This is, however, what the chamber did in the fourteenth century. Beginning in John's reign the chamber declined and during the thirteenth century all its functions were taken over by the wardrobe. Then, under Edward II, the chamber revived and assumed considerable importance in fourteenth-century finance and administration. The reasons for this revival are difficult to ascertain. Two seem plausible. The first is that although the wardrobe remained a household department it was occupied largely with administrative and financial matters of the realm. With little time to care for the royal personal and domestic needs, it became impersonalized and no longer had a close tie with the king. Edward II seems to have felt the need for a household department more intimately connected with him which would serve as a sort of privy treasury and execute or initiate matters of personal concern. The second reason for the revival of the chamber stems from the close scrutiny kept by barons and parliament over the exchequer, chancery, and wardrobe in order to restrict the royal authority. It seems likely that to thwart the irksome restraints of the barons Edward II and his close supporters turned to the chamber to execute some of the royal matters. It is well known that the chamber revived swiftly after 1322 when Edward's favorite, the Younger Despenser, was chamberlain and worked through the chamber to increase both the royal and his own power.

The steps in the revival of the chamber are easily traced. To bolster its supply of money numerous manors that had been accountable to the wardrobe were made accountable to the chamber, especially after the confiscations that followed the royal victory at Boroughbridge in 1322. The five earldoms of Thomas of Lancaster plus lands of other rebels were assigned to the chamber. Later many of these lands were transferred to the exchequer and the resources of the chamber were considerably reduced. It still had substantial funds, however, and accrued a sizable staff to administer the lands and money. So important did its business become that it acquired its own seal, the secret seal. No account of the receipts and issues was kept; the king wanted no record of how he expended the chamber money.

Though the financial transactions of the chamber during Edward II's reign were limited to the king's work, in the field of general administration the chamber assumed importance because of the use made of its secret seal. Not long after being employed in the administration of the chamber lands, the chamber seal also became used as the king's personal seal for initiating a wide range of business. Already it was beginning to replace the privy seal, not because the privy seal was unequal to administrative demands, but because is was not as convenient to use. It was going out of the wardrobe, it soon would be out of the household, and eventually it would be a separate department like the chancery and exchequer. Edward II and his successors needed a seal easily available to initiate the royal will; they found this in the secret seal of the chamber. By the end of Edward's reign the secret seal was initiating administrative action and authenticating royal correspondence. When the privy seal was captured by the Scots at Bannockburn the secret seal was used as a substitute. Frequently it was used to move the privy seal, which in turn moved the great seal. Although the chamber administration collapsed with Edward II's fall, there had been created in the secret seal a new instrument of executive power that would be used by succeeding kings.

Within a few years of his succession to the throne Edward III turned to the work of restoring the chamber to the position held under his father. All sorts of land—escheats, wardships, confiscations, and vacant benefices—were assigned to the chamber. Soon a large staff was occupied with administering the chamber lands, a task requiring so much attention that a second seal, the griffin seal, was created. This seal is first heard of in 1335 and eventually was used for all types of chamber business. It continued in use until 1356 when modification in the management of the chamber estates rendered it unnecessary. Meanwhile the military and administrative demands of the French war brought the chamber back into the center of public administration. In 1338 the Ordinances of Walton placed the chamber in a key position for controlling all central departments by assigning to the chamber clerk the duty of keeping a counterroll that recorded all payments and actions authorized by writ of privy seal. By referring to this roll the king could quickly check on the affairs of the wardrobe, chancery, and exchequer. During the campaigns of the 1340's the chamber was assigned a number of the wardrobe duties and bore the brunt of military, naval, and armament finance.

The renewed prominence of this household department and its fiscal immunity from the exchequer evoked fears among the barons that Edward III was attempting to free some of the key operations of royal government from their scrutiny. These fears were fanned by officers of the exchequer who felt that their position was being undermined. Pressures and criticism descended upon the chamber and Edward was forced to withdraw its resources and authority. Lands were gradually withdrawn until by 1356 all had been transferred to the exchequer. During the remainder of Edward's reign and during that of Richard II the chamber was limited to subventions from the exchequer and reverted to being a private treasury for household needs. This remained its status to the end of the Middle Ages. Modification in the custody of the secret seal also brought decline to the chamber as an organ of executive initiative. The chief role of the chamber under Richard II was to supply him with well-trained and loyal men to perform his confidential work. He relied heavily upon the chamberlain and underchamberlains and placed them in the royal council where they represented his interests and served as intermediaries between the king and the "outside" members of the council. Though the chamber continued to provide services for succeeding kings, it remained in administrative limbo until refurbished by the Tudors and converted into the financial keystone of their strong personal rule.

A few words must be said about the changes undergone by the secret seal of the chamber. When Edward III revitalized the chamber he revived the secret seal to initiate much of his business, and it became a primary instrument of the royal prerogative. But soon after it again came into prominence its name began to decline in usage and was supplanted by the term "signet seal." The legend encircling the seal more often came to read: "*Signetum Regis Anglie et Francie.*" By the end of Edward's reign the term "secret" was no longer used and the signet seal had become the personal instrument of the royal prerogative. Though the reasons for this change in terminology remain obscure, it seems that there was need for a seal more personal than that of the chamber, which had a less intimate relation with the king as soon as it assumed financial and administrative duties. In any event we know that Richard II substituted his finger signet ring for the privy seal and used it as his personal seal to initiate a large amount of government business. In fact so many matters did it initiate during his reign that it acquired an office of its own staffed with clerks. With Richard's reign there begins a collection of letters issued under the signet seal, letters warranting action in the chancery, in the office of the privy seal, or by individual officers. Only when the baronial opposition was in power, such as the Lords Appellant between 1386 and 1389, did the signet seal cease its work. When Richard resumed power it became the trusted instrument of his prerogative and so continued until his deposition. The barons repeatedly attacked the signet seal as Richard's personal instrument of tyranny and absolutism which flouted all law and convention. Yet when Henry IV mounted the throne in the presence of the assembled parliament of 1399 one of his first acts was to hold on high before all onlookers the signet seal of Richard II. To him and to parliament it symbolized the transfer of kingship from Richard II to Henry IV of Lancaster.

2. LOCAL GOVERNMENT

A. County Government

The theme of local government in the thirteenth century was decline of the sheriff's power and its gradual transference to local residents of the county. By the fourteenth century the sheriff no longer held the commanding position enjoyed by his predecessor during the twelfth century. By royal command many of his functions had been given to other local officers. There were the escheators, who looked after the royal feudal rights, the keepers of royal manors, who administered the king's estates, the collectors of subsidies, who collected the new taxes, the commissioners of array, who assembled those obliged to serve the king, the keepers of the peace (the future justices of the peace), who assumed police and judicial obligations, and finally the coroner, who since the reign of Richard I had performed judicial and administrative duties and had checked upon the shrieval actions. Except for the coroners, elected in the county court, the other officers were customarily appointed by the king. All, including the coroner, held an authority parallel to the sheriff's but performed functions different from his; they were not subordinates of the sheriff. There were in addition other officers whose authority and functions paralleled the sheriff's; these were the officers of great liberties or franchises. Finally, there were those officials who were the sheriff's subordinates and who assisted him.

Let us turn first to the officers who served in the liberties. It will be recalled that a number of great barons had received extensive royal franchises which largely removed their lands from royal administration. The lords of such liberties exercised regalian powers. Most of the liberties were modeled upon the royal administration and were managed by stewards, appointed by the lords, who supervised administration of the lands and fulfilled those obligations owed to the royal government. These officers were actually private sheriffs and were responsible for collecting and paying revenues owed to the exchequer. When royal justices came to hear pleas at the county court, liberties sent their own coroners to report all inquests and presentments made before them. If the king wished to communicate with the liberties, he did so through his sheriff. The latter delivered the royal writs or gave them to stewards of the small liberties, who went to the county court to receive them. All the officials of liberties were in frequent contact with royal officers and cooperated with them. Though they served their own lord, who appointed and dismissed them, in the last analysis they served the king and formed part of the king's local government.

We come now to the royal officers whose authority and duties paralleled those of the sheriff. The coroners, who had served as the principal checks upon shrieval authority in the thirteenth century, continued to occupy a prominent place in local government throughout the fourteenth century. Elected by full county court, they theoretically held office for life, although in practice their tenure of office depended upon how long they cared to exercise it and upon the good will of the county. Frequently the usual qualifications of knighthood and tenure of a specified amount of land in the county were ignored if the candidate's county and royal connections were good. The coroner's relations with the central administration were much closer than the sheriff's. From the chancery the coroners received requests for information, often to guide the royal government in making decisions on pardons. Frequently the exchequer ordered the coroners to check on the financial operations of the sheriff and his subordinates, to report their findings, and sometimes to replace temporarily a sheriff found guilty of financial irregularities. The relations of the coroners were closest, however, with the central courts. As keepers of the royal pleas they were responsible for a variety of preparatory judicial inquests and records. The coroners were constantly associated with the sheriff. They shared many of his functions—as, for example, sitting with him at every county court and accompanying him on his tourns. They complemented the sheriff in his obligations and at the same time checked upon his work.

In the fourteenth century there were normally four coroners for every county, each responsible for a part of the county. Their principal task was the keeping of records, of which the most important was the roll of inquisitions (Coroners' Rolls). It recorded all inquests into sudden deaths conducted by the coroners in their districts with the assistance of local juries. Then as now this was the main function of the coroner. When the coroner attended the county court he not only presented the roll of inquisitions but also kept a record of the inquests held by his fellow coroners as well as one of all the indictments made at the county court by juries of hundreds and liberties. In addition, he kept a record of all the presentments made on the sheriff's tourn. These records were extremely important because they were the legal records of indictment. The coroners likewise were responsible for a record of appeals made in the county court before themselves or the sheriff. Almost without fail such appeals were made by prisoners who had turned king's evidence with the hope that their sentences would be lightened if they informed on others who broke the law. Criminals who could not be brought to justice or civil litigants who would not appear in court could, after all other means failed, be outlawed. This was done by the judgment of the coroners and the county court. Criminals who had taken sanctuary and would not surrender to justice were often allowed to abjure the realm; this ceremony occurred before the coroner, who assigned the port to which the fugitive should go and from which he should abjure the realm. Along with the sheriff and the justices of the peace the coroners were the principal officers of local government. For most of the fourteenth century they were the main checks upon shrieval power and fulfilled their burdensome tasks with efficiency and honesty. Compared to the sheriffs', their record was one of high-principled administration.

The last group of local officials were the sheriff's subordinates. First, there were the constables of the royal castles, who, though appointed by the king and receiving orders directly from him, closely cooperated with the sheriff. The constable's duties consisted of recruiting, feeding, and commanding the castle garrison. If there was a jail at the castle, the constable was responsible for it. Occasionally he made arrests. Next, there were the constables of the hundreds, whose duties were mainly of a military and policing nature. They levied military forces of the hundred and checked to see that men possessed the requisite type of arms. As police officers they were the captains of the hundreds, the heads of police administration. They kept peace on the highways, enforced the hue and cry, and supervised watch and guard duty. Possibly the constables also received some indictments. Below the hundred constables were constables for the agrarian villages, who were elected annually. They commanded the village levies, were responsible for keeping the assize of arms, enforced the hue and cry, made arrests when necessary, and occasionally took and guarded property of fugitive felons for whom the village was responsible. Though accountable to hundred constable, sheriff, and coroner, these local constables acted largely on their own responsibility and were guided by common law and common sense.

Other local officers were tied more closely to the sheriff. There was the bailiff itinerant, who was appointed by the king and sent by the sheriff throughout the county on administrative business. He also executed royal writs received by the sheriff. There were the hundred bailiffs, assisted by such subordinates as subbailiffs, clerks, and bedels. Bailiffs of private hundreds were appointed by the lords but were, like the stewards of liberties, also officers of royal local government. In some hundreds the bailiffs were appointed by the king and in others by the sheriff. The appointments were for life or for a certain term. Most of the hundred bailiff's work came from commands of the sheriff. He had to execute all sorts of royal writs passed on to him by the bailiff itinerant and had to collect royal income in the hundred. Direct commands from the sheriff involved purveyance of carts and food supplies. The bailiff was a key figure in the collecting of royal subsidies. Many of his functions were connected with justice. From the county court came a variety of orders. He might be directed to have a certain person appear at the next county court, in which case a summons, attachment of goods, distraint, and even arrest might be involved. The bailiff was likewise responsible for empaneling juries and for presiding over the hundred courts, which met about every three weeks. He was always present at the sheriff's tourn and frequently held the tourn himself. The hundred bailiff was a much burdened man whose opportunities for evil and corrupt practices were numerous. That he often took advantage of his position is eloquently proven by the protests of local men which appear in the records of royal investigations. To help him with his duties the bailiff had assistants. The subbailiffs purveyed, attached, distrained, arrested, and collected money; they were bitterly hated. The clerks drew up the necessary documents. And the bedels —those inquisitive individuals still about in the nineteenth century and described so picturesquely by Dickens—delivered writs, summonses, and messages. These were the men who comprised the local officialdom. Whether they worked gratuitously at the royal command or whether they worked for remuneration and prestige, they worked for the king and were ultimately responsible to him through a long chain of command.

B. The Boroughs

Despite the assertions of some scholars that medieval borough government was democratic, we have seen that the evidence portrays an oligarchic system. The boroughs that attained self-government in the twelfth and thirteenth centuries were governed by a small, select group of the wealthiest and most powerful citizens who perpetuated themselves or others of their class in power. Where elections were held, qualifications for office were so high that only a few were eligible. Though in the fourteenth century one hears more of protest and demonstrations against government monopoly by the few, the municipal constitutions changed but slightly. There was some experimentation in the form of the town councils, but in no borough did government become even faintly democratic; it was merely spread more widely among the oligarchy and, as one historian has said, "did no more than broaden the base of civic oligarchy."

From the establishment of its commune in the late twelfth century London had been governed by a mayor and aldermen, who made all the decisions and chose the chief officials. When weighty decisions were to be made there was provision for consulting a few of the wealthier and more discreet men from each ward. Towards the end of the thirteenth century there were thirty-nine men who were occasionally consulted. In 1346 a quota of four, six, or eight men from each ward was ordained for deliberative assemblies, and in 1347 a record states that 133 men met at one of these meetings in the Guildhall. The chief modification in the London government came in 1376, seemingly as a reaction against various powerful London citizens found corrupt by the Good Parliament of 1376. The electoral unit was changed from the wards to the guilds (misteries), each of which was to elect from two to six men to give counsel to the mayor and aldermen. It was not a very democratic change because it was expressly stated that the guilds were to accept whatever the mayor, aldermen, and their representatives decided, and that only ordinances passed by the mayor and aldermen were to be valid. It was stipulated that the mayor and aldermen were to consult twice in a quarter with the representatives of the guilds, who were termed a "common council." The result of this modification was to give more oligarchic burgesses an opportunity to consult with the mayor and aldermen and to check their arbitrary authority. The arrangement, however, was short-lived; by 1385 the ward was again the electoral district and consultative meetings of the mayor and aldermen were reduced to one per quarter. From the evidence available it seems that the mayor and aldermen controlled elections in the wards in order to insure election of men sympathetic to their idea of government. The net gain of the fourteenth-century experiments was the addition of another council to that of the mayor and aldermen. Four times a year the small council of mayor and aldermen was bound to consult with a larger council of oligarchic citizens elected by the wards—the so-called common council. The government of London had simply been broadened to include a few more of the wealthy and discreet men of the community.

The addition of a larger common council to an older council of mayor and aldermen occurred also in Norwich and Lynn. During the fifteenth century two-council systems appeared in Winchester, Colchester, Leicester, Northampton, Shrewsbury, and Worcester. The result was always the same; participation in municipal government was but extended to a few more wealthy citizens. The mayor and aldermen of the old primary council who decided what business should come before the larger common council remained in control of the borough government.

Meanwhile other experiments were being tried. Some boroughs were broadening the executive power by enlarging the old primary council. In the middle of the fourteenth century at Bristol and Exeter single common councils of wealthy burgesses were established to curb the arbitrary actions of the mayor and bailiffs working through very small councils. At Bristol in 1344 provision was made for forty-eight of the *potentiores et discretiores* to be the councillors of the mayor and to assist him in expediting town affairs. In 1345 a similar council was established at Exeter where twelve "of the better and more discreet" citizens were to be elected annually along with the mayor and four stewards to assist these latter five officers with all the great affairs of the community. The enlargement of the single council represented no triumph of a popular party over the old oligarchs but simply the assertion of control by the wealthy over the town officers. Whatever the modification in borough government in the fourteenth century, we must conclude that it was not a period of democratic advance in urban government. Nothing resembling democratic government would come until 1835 when the borough close corporations were swept away by the Municipal Corporation Act.

Though this is not the place to sketch in detail the relations and obligations of the boroughs to the royal government, we may briefly summarize the situation in the fourteenth century. The boroughs were political islands that possessed administrative, economic, and judicial rights that made them semi-independent units of administration within the realm. Many were self-contained units to which royal officers were barred. Still, much of the royal administration extended to the boroughs and had to be recognized; all boroughs had obligations to the royal government. These were fulfilled in two ways; either the boroughs selected men to perform royal administrative tasks or borough officers were delegated by the central government to perform certain obligations. Thus were created borough sheriffs, coroners, escheators, and other officers who shouldered the royal obligations. Generally they were already members of the town council, the organ that in reality dealt with the royal government and fulfilled the responsibilities of the borough. The town council assessed and paid royal taxes, carried out royal inquests, administered royal lands, purveyed for the king, and maintained royal buildings, bridges, and highways. It was responsible for the return of representatives to parliament, however they may have been selected. And it executed royal orders and policies connected with domestic and foreign trade. The local political autonomy and the privileges and immunities of the boroughs in the fourteenth century, however extensive, did not spare them from royal interference and from civil and military responsibilities to the crown. The political, economic, and legal particularism of the boroughs had to bow before the sovereignty of a law and a government common to all the realm.

XXXIV

The Maturing of Parliamentary Institutions

WHEN Edward I died in 1307 there had been hewn, however roughly, the national institution called parliament. The representative element, though not always a part of assemblies called parliaments, was coming to be included more regularly because it spoke for that part of the community of the realm from which the king must obtain the bulk of his taxes. Parliaments without knights and burgesses still met with the king and accomplished a wide range of business, but the king had acknowledged incontrovertibly that no extraordinary tax could be levied without the consent of the community of the realm, which was understood to comprise the knights and burgesses.

A parliamentary framework had been constructed in the thirteenth century and there was rising a structure of which certain lines were becoming discernible. But much had yet to be added to the girders and ribs of this structure; this is what occurred in the fourteenth century. It was a century dominated by one great constitutional theme—the maturing of parliamentary institutions. The representative element became a regular component of parliaments that were convoked frequently, if not regularly. The representatives of the lower clergy ceased to attend parliament and met instead in their convocations. The unicameral parliament was then rapidly converted into a bicameral assembly consisting of the House of Lords and the House of Commons. Both houses developed a rudimentary organization. The House of Commons elected a speaker to act as its spokesman with the king and council. Meanwhile both counties and boroughs took a keener interest in parliament and began to regard representation as a privilege and political necessity rather than a burden to be escaped. Regulations and qualifications were established for the electorate and for the candidates. But, most important, the commons began to slough off their passive role in parliament and to acquire some essential powers. They began to represent the local interests of their constituencies and secured a firm grip on taxation. They came to introduce bills and thereby to initiate much legislation which, however introduced, must secure their approval. Finally, both lords and commons won certain privileges fundamental for the conduct of constitutional government.

Although it was to take five more centuries for parliamentary institutions and procedures to mature, the footings of parliament had been poured and the rough structure erected by 1399. Contrary to the contention of Hallam and Stubbs, parliament was not yet fully formed, nor would the House of Commons in parliament win sovereign power until the seventeenth century. But parliament was so firmly entrenched that not the civil and military disorder of the fifteenth century, nor Tudor absolutism of the sixteenth century, nor Stuart divine right of the seventeenth century could destroy it as the institution through which the community of the realm kept the king under law and shared with him the government.

I. PARLIAMENT: A REPRESENTATIVE INSTITUTION

Parliaments with or without the representative element had become an accepted means of transacting government during the reign of Edward I. After 1295 they became frequent. It was this frequency coupled with regularity that was to gain parliament broad acceptance and power. Fortunately, political and military circumstances of the fourteenth century made the summoning of parliaments with the representative element a frequent practice. The abnormal political strife of Edward II's reign and the extraordinary demands for money occasioned by the Hundred Years' War forced the kings to meet often with parliament. Although in the first two and a half years of Edward II's reign the commons were summoned to only three of seven parliaments, between 1310 and 1327 they were present in all the parliaments except two. During the reign of Edward III the presence of the commons was accepted; only a few parliaments or great councils consisting solely of barons were summoned. Four such great councils, styled *colloquium et tractatus*, convened between 1329 and 1332; thereafter they were rare.[1] By the middle of the fourteenth century and for the rest of the Middle Ages whenever a parliament assembled the commons were present.

Political and financial necessity forced the kings to summon parliaments frequently. Early in Edward II's reign enactments begin which decree regular meetings of parliament. The Ordinances of 1311, although baronially inspired and probably referring but to a baronial great council, ordained that there should be a parliament twice a year.[2] In 1322 after Edward II's victory over his baronial opponents at Boroughbridge, a parliament at York annulled the Ordinances of 1311 but provided by statute that great affairs of the realm "shall be considered, granted, and established in parliament by our lord the king and with the consent of the prelates, earls, and barons, and of the community of the kingdom." There is some doubt as to whether the "community of the kingdom" meant the commons, but that it did seems likely because most subsequent parliaments included the representative element.[3] Early in Edward III's reign, in 1330, a statute ordered annual

[1] SM, no. 60B.
[2] SM, no. 56.
[3] SM, no. 58.

parliaments. And in 1362 a statute ordained that "a parliament should be holden every year." Generally these statutes were adhered to although in 1364, 1367, 1370, 1373–1376, 1387, 1389, and 1396 no parliament convened. In many years, it should be realized, more than one parliament a year was summoned. In 1328 there were four; in 1340, three; and two parliaments a year were common. We may conclude that even if the statutes ordering annual parliaments were not rigorously obeyed, parliaments were held frequently throughout the fourteenth century and became the accepted instrument of the kings for transacting their business with the subjects of their realm. During the fifty-year reign of Edward III forty-eight parliaments were held.

Another feature of the fourteenth-century parliament was the short duration of its sessions. Parliaments actually sat longer than they did in the thirteenth century and more of the lords and commons remained throughout the entire session, but still the total time was short, being two to three weeks, or at the most several months. One of the longest parliaments, and it was exceptional, was the Good Parliament of 1376, which sat from 28 April to 6 July. Each of the parliaments was short; each was a new parliament requiring summonses and an election. The time had not yet come when one parliament would continue its life year after year by means of prorogations.

2. THE HOUSE OF LORDS

A typical parliament of Edward I, as we have seen, consisted of the spiritual and secular barons, representatives of the lower clergy, and representatives of the counties and boroughs. It was an assembly of the three estates without the division that characterized it fifty years later. After the assembled parliament had listened to a speech outlining the royal business and financial need, the king and his council departed from Westminster Hall for separate quarters where they could transact government business, the barons and knights remained in the hall to discuss the matter of a subsidy, and the burgesses of the boroughs retired to a neighboring building to decide upon their response. The representatives of the lower clergy, it seems, discussed their response in a separate meeting and then gave their answer to the king. When the responses were made, the barons customarily agreed on a tax of a certain percentage and the burgesses on a tax of a different percentage. The knights consulted and cooperated with the spiritual and secular barons of the first and second estates while the burgesses, the third estate, acted alone. Such an arrangement did not long continue and the fourteenth century saw the organization of parliament along lines that were to make it unique among the representative assemblies of western Europe.

The first development contributing to the formation of a two-house parliament was the withdrawal of the representatives of the lower clergy. We have noted that they were disinclined to attend parliament after 1295. A long church tradition of separation between spiritual and secular matters, a custom of accomplishing business in ecclesiastical convocations, and clerical prejudice against association with laymen dictated the reluctance to attend parliament. The clergy, feeling that the king could obtain taxes just as easily from their convocations, chose this way in which to vote taxes. For a time the kings were dubious about this development, feeling that it was insubordination and that it weakened their control. For some forty years they continued to summon the lower clergy through the *praemunientes* clause included in the writs to the bishops, and occasionally the clergy attended. But they had stopped doing so by the end of Edward III's reign. In fact, after 1332 there is no reference to the representatives of the lower clergy in the Parliament Rolls. Until 1340 the clergy, like the laity, had been summoned *ad faciendum et consentiendum* (for making and consenting). After this year they were summoned simply *ad consentiendum;* this formula became standard after 1377 and the clergy consented to matters ordained in parliament by their silence. What clergy remained in parliament were the great prelates, who did so because they were barons, because they were feudal vassals of the king.

The withdrawal of the clergy from parliament prepared the way for the next peculiar development. Except for the great prelates who were of the first estate, the second estate, consisting of the barons and knights, and the third, consisting of the burgesses, remained. During the first fifty years of the fourteenth century the barons were to be organized into the House of Lords while the knights ended their association with the barons and coalesced with the burgesses to form the House of Commons. Though that part of parliament constituted by the barons was not called the House of Lords until the early years of Henry VIII's reign, it had been such *de facto* since the reign of Edward III. During the course of the thirteenth century there slowly grew a distinction between the greater and lesser barons. The greater barons received individual writs of summons to great councils or parliaments; the lesser ones, general summonses. The lesser barons, though retaining the right to attend, seldom did so, and attendance was therefore dominated by the greater barons. But because there was as yet no sharply drawn distinction between greater and lesser barons and the summoning of great barons was still capricious into the reign of Edward III, confusion remained. Not until the reign of Edward III is there evidence of a well-defined group of barons who were always summoned to parliament and who composed a House of Lords.

The series of political crises in the fourteenth century and the constant demand for taxes partially account for the definite corporateness acquired by the barons in parliament. All the major barons had large political and economic stakes involved and considered attendance at parliament imperative. There they could protect their vested interests, consult and unite with other barons, and, if need be, join them in opposition to royal policy or demands for taxes. They began to regard attendance at parliament not simply as a matter of feudal tenure and obligation to perform suit to court but as a political privilege and an honor. Already in Edward II's reign the barons had referred to themselves as "peers of the realm." Literally peer simply meant a social equal, but the great barons regarded themselves as social equals above whom there were none higher with the sole exception of the king. Since the thirteenth century a baronial core had regularly received individual summonses to parliament and in the fourteenth century this core with the addition of a few other barons expected to be summoned regularly to parliament. Furthermore, these barons reasoned that the custom of regular attendance was a right which should be inherited by the eldest son. By the end of the fourteenth century, though a few relics of feudal tenure survived, regular attendance at parliament was almost exclusively based on hereditary right which had evolved out of individual summonses.

The barons who attended parliament in the fourteenth century were, first, barons by tenure and, secondly, greater barons by virtue of their writs of summons. These greater barons were the peers of the realm, a title and dignity which only the eldest son could inherit. Just as the rule of primogeniture had been applied to feudal inheritance, so was it applied to peerage. The peers, the greatest barons, constituted the lords of parliament who came to meet in their own assembly to discuss the matters presented to them by the king and his advisers.

The composition of this early body of peers, however, did not remain frozen. If, for example, a peer died without male heirs, his peerage could be inherited by a female heir. She could not, however, attend parliament and therefore customarily conferred upon her husband a presumptive right to the writ of summons that entitled him to sit in the House of Lords. A woman could thus be a peeress by heritable right but still could not sit in the House of Lords. The early close corporation that was the House of Lords was gradually loosened with the creation of new peers by royal grant. Towards the end of the fourteenth century it had become customary for the king to create peers with various titles of dignity by letters patent. This device had been used since the reign of Stephen in the twelfth century to elevate certain barons to the rank of earl. Then in the fourteenth century two more titles were added—duke and marquess. In the fifteenth century the title of viscount was created. Above the earls and barons were the marquesses and dukes; between the earls and barons were the viscounts. The first duke was created in 1337 when Edward III bestowed that title upon his eldest son. Later the dukedoms of Lancaster, Clarence, Gloucester, and York were created for other members of the royal house and in 1397 Richard II conferred dukedoms upon men unrelated to the royal family. It was also Richard who named Robert de Vere, his close favorite, as the first marquess. Legally these new titles were valueless and bore no relation to territorial power. What they did was to give some barons precedence over others and, if the newly titled peer was not already a baron entitled to sit in parliament, to give him that right with the privilege of passing it on to his eldest heir. In this manner were peers made; they owed their dignity to writs of summons or to letters patent. The latter has been the method used since the fifteenth century to create new peers. By letters patent a man received his peerage, be it a barony, earldom, or dukedom, and received it as a heritable right.

In creating peerages to reward close friends or to remunerate able men for loyal service to the crown the kings gained a control over the composition of the House of Lords. With no limit to the number of peers they could create, it was within their power to establish a new nobility that could constitute a House of Lords loyal unto them. Although Richard II moved in this direction after his coup of 1397 and although peers were created by the Lancastrians and Yorkists to obtain political allies in their bitter struggle, none of the kings in the Middle Ages created a new nobility. Experience with a few new peers taught them all that they might create a noble leviathan that would crush them.

In addition to the lay peers in the House of Lords there were the spiritual lords or peers, who were an important element of the house and who often constituted a majority. There were two archbishops and eighteen bishops as well as a fluctuating number of abbots. The latter cared little for parliament and tended to absent themselves. Whereas in 1305 seventy-five abbots attended parliament, at the end of the Middle Ages only twenty-odd were still attending. The spiritual peers attended parliament because they held land of the king and because of their administrative power in the church. Though these lords could not be created, the kings had much say as to what men became prelates. Generally they sent a letter to the electing clergy of a vacant benefice and nominated their man. The king's man was usually elected and approved by the pope. During the fourteenth century the House of Lords consisted of from forty to fifty lay peers and of a few more spiritual peers.

Let us now examine the organization and functions of the House of Lords. When parliament assembled at Westminster both lords and commons gathered in the Painted Chamber of Westminster Palace to hear a formal address by some distinguished prelate or officer on the causes for summoning parliament. After this, petitions were received and then parliament broke up into its various elements to discuss the matters that required action. The council adjourned to the council chamber; the commons departed for a different place of meeting; and the lords generally remained in Westminster Hall where they proceeded to dispose of their business. Though it was within the power of the lords to help the king in administration, this function was left largely to the royal council. The lords gave advice on great affairs of state, on war and peace. They had legislative powers, formulating and giving their consent to statutes. But their right to vote supply to the king was perhaps their most essential power. Throughout the fourteenth century they customarily voted a percentage of a fifteenth. When these matters had been decided, they were reported to the king by spokesmen.

A principal function of the House of Lords was the dispensation of justice. As the successor of the feudal great council it was a court of justice. It was in fact the High Court of Parliament, the supreme court of the realm, above all other courts. It had a supervisory jurisdiction over all inferior courts. It was recognized as the highest court of appeal in England, which meant not that a case was actually appealed to it, because the common law tradition opposed trying the same facts twice, but that it had a jurisdiction in error and corrected errors made in the law by lower courts. The House of Lords was also a court of first instance which could hear any case, criminal or civil, that the king decided to lay before it. Although the royal council and eventually the court of chancery received the bulk of petitions seeking redress of wrongs or beseeching equity, the House of Lords still received and acted upon such petitions. It was, however, as a feudal court, a court where royal vassals were triable under feudal law, that the House of Lords was most prominent. In the fourteenth century ordinary barons who were not members of the House of Lords were entitled to trial only in the ordinary courts, whereas the peers had the right of trial in the House of Lords, of being judged by their fellow peers, a custom that for centuries had been deeply embedded in feudal law. In practice, however, judgment by peers (*judicium parium*) pertained only to major crimes. For treason or felony a peer could be tried by the House of Lords, which constituted a court and adjudged both the facts of the case and the law. If parliament was not in session the peer was tried by a select body of peers, customarily twenty-three, named and presided over by the lord high steward appointed by the king. Towards the end of the fourteenth century the House of Lords became a court where royal ministers were impeached, that is, accused of crimes against the crown. The lords acted as the judges and the commons as the prosecutors who presented the charges.

Although the House of Lords constituted the supreme and High Court of Parliament, to regard parliament chiefly as an instrument for judicial work is erroneous. As noted above, the judicial work of the House of Lords became limited and specialized; most justice had been siphoned off to the common law courts, to the council, or to the court of chancery. Justice was but one of a number of functions of the House of Lords in the fourteenth century. As part of parliament the House of Lords handled whatever business came before it—counsel, taxation, legislation, and justice. We must not exalt the judicial role of the lords over their other responsibilities, or lose sight of the fact that each lord, though a judge, was also a powerful politician. It was as leading politicians of the realm that the lords opposed the kings and consistently urged and pushed the commons into supporting their political policies and objectives. The lords were in parliament because therein was power, and they were determined to control and use it.

3. THE HOUSE OF COMMONS

In the early parliaments when the knights and burgesses first attended, there is no evidence of corporate consciousness between the representatives of the counties and the boroughs. The knights remained with the great barons to discuss the business of parliament and voted taxes at the same rate. They considered themselves closer to the barons because the whole feudal tradition made their interests and backgrounds common. Later when the corporateness of the barons and knights began to break up and when the barons became a select group of peers constituting the House of Lords, it appeared for a time that the knights, feeling themselves socially and politically superior to the burgesses, might form a separate house or estate. This remained a possibility as long as the kings attempted to negotiate separately with the burgesses for taxes. As late as 1372 the burgesses were detained at parliament after the dismissal of the knights so that a separate grant could be negotiated. Despite these tendencies, which seemed to militate against the coalescence of the knights and burgesses, more powerful forces were working for a fusion into one estate or house. The final triumph of these forces which assured a union of the knights and the burgesses constituted one of the most crucial and important developments in the history of parliament. During the fourteenth century the political, economic, and social ties of the knights and burgesses tightened. They discovered that they had many problems and objectives in common. They cemented their relations through intermarriage. They found that on the question of taxation they profited by cooperation. Finally the knights realized that they did not belong with the lords and that their interests could be served best through unity with the burgesses. The knights contributed social prestige and political experience while the burgesses with their expanding economic resources possessed an asset that would gain repeated concessions from the kings. The fortuitous coalescence of the knights and burgesses into the House of Commons is a major cause for the phenomenal durability and success of the English parliament. The lack of similar fusions on the Continent partially accounts for the failure of its various representative assemblies in medieval and early modern history.

The first sign of cooperation between knights and burgesses is their joint presentation of petitions, which began during the reign of Edward II and became common under Edward III. The fact that they agreed upon common matters which were incorporated into *communes petitiones* certainly suggests common deliberation and agreement over problems of mutual interest. Quite likely the knights acted with the burgesses (*gentz de la commune*) in the parliament of 1332 which approved a grant of a tenth and a fifteenth instead of a requested tallage and which ended the tallage as a tax.[4] In the parliament of 1339 the knights and burgesses definitely met together and deliberated over the royal request for a grant. They agreed that the amount

[4] SM, no. 61B.

requested was so large as to necessitate consultation with their constituencies before a reply could be given. In the Parliament Rolls they are called "the men of the commons."[5] Thereafter the knights and burgesses met in their separate house, deliberated, presented common petitions, and voted taxes. The House of Commons had been born.

The first reliable information on the meeting place of the commons comes from the Easter parliament of 1341 which was the setting for the first great constitutional crisis of Edward III's reign. Here was enacted the dramatic quarrel of Edward and Archbishop Stratford. On the first day the assembled parliament of lords, knights, and burgesses gathered in the Painted Chamber of the Palace of Westminster and heard the chancellor's speech on the reasons for summoning parliament. The lords were then asked to assemble later in the White Chamber in order to discuss the matters demanding response. The knights and burgesses were also requested to meet another time in order to deliberate.[6] In the parliament of 1352 most of the commons were directed to meet in the Chapter House of Westminster Abbey while the rest were ordered to discuss the king's business with the lords in the Painted Chamber. In 1368 the commons were assigned the Little Hall of Westminster Palace for their deliberations. At the Good Parliament of 1376 and at the one of 1377 the commons met in the Chapter House. These two parliaments lasted so long and the commons deliberated at such length that they wore out the floor coverings of the Abbey's Chapter House.[7] Apparently the commons continued to use the Chapter House until 1395. Then for the next twenty years the commons met in the Refectory of Westminster Abbey. Thereafter their place of meeting remains unrecorded until 1547 when Henry VIII assigned the Chapel of Saint Stephen's in the Palace of Westminster to the commons for their regular hall of assembly. Here they met until Saint Stephen's was consumed by fire in 1834.

4. THE ELECTORAL SYSTEM

Evidence on the electorate, the elected, and the electoral procedure employed by the counties and boroughs is scanty; we will never know as much about these subjects as we should. The records of the central government primarily pertain to parliament and its functioning; only occasionally does a statute refer to electoral procedure and then not until the fifteenth century. Local records are uniformly mute on the details of election to parliament. In the counties it was a general requirement that representatives to parliament should be knights. This was not stipulated by law, but the kings repeatedly urged that men of knightly rank be returned and specified this class in the writs of summons. This requirement, however, could not be consistently fulfilled because there were not enough knights. Since 1224

[5] SM, no. 61C.
[6] SM, no. 61D, E, and F.
[7] SM, no. 61I.

when a series of enactments inaugurated the levying of fines upon men who, though qualified to become knights, did not because of the heavy government responsibilities required from this class, many willingly paid the fines rather than take the order of knighthood. These men, the squires of the counties, generally held as much land as knights and came from families of equal social standing. Though theoretically barred, in practice they were qualified and were returned to parliament. When the records speak of knights of the county they refer to the squires as well as to the knights. Other qualifications and disabilities, likewise not strictly enforced in the fourteenth century, were that the county representatives must reside in the county, that they must be men of considerable property, and that they must possess ability and experience. Furthermore, in spite of statutes in the fourteenth century barring sheriffs and lawyers from election to parliament on the grounds of what we would call conflict of interest, lawyers were elected and formed a prominent part of the commons in any parliament.

Though there was a marked reluctance in the counties at the beginning of the fourteenth century to send representatives to parliament, this feeling gradually yielded to a real appreciation of representation and the necessity of sending men to Westminster to advance and protect local interests. The men returned to parliament were generally the most prominent and powerful economic and political figures of the county and were repeatedly re-elected, partly because of their experience. By the end of the century these men realized the significance and honor of going to parliament and vied for the opportunity.

Although there were regulations on the qualifications of the electorate in the fifteenth century, we are uncertain about the men qualified to vote in the fourteenth century. About all we can say is that all knights, squires, and freemen who possessed some land could participate in the elections held at the county court. The knotty question concerns the nature of the county court. When the writs of summons were sent out they were addressed to the sheriffs, who were ordered to have elected in full county court two men and who were then to return the names of those elected to the chancery. A full county court could include all the resident freemen but we must assume that few elections were attended by all qualified. The summonses to parliament were customarily sent out forty days before it was to assemble, which meant that most elections occurred in the ordinary county court that convened monthly in the fourteenth century, and but few at the large courts convened to meet the royal justices when they came on the assizes. Obviously, therefore, not many men attended the county courts which elected the knights to parliament. The expression "full county court" must be understood as an occasion when the knights were elected to represent all the freemen of the county.

Popular election as we understand it seldom occurred at the county court. In general only the leading men of the county regularly attended the courts and they were usually influenced in their selection of representatives by the sheriff or by a powerful lord of the area who suggested suitable men. General acclamation then followed, though at times there were protest and dissent. In the later fourteenth century when there was more interest in representation and more contests among candidates, the electors had some choice. At this point, however, the system of retaining and maintenance employed by the great lords to secure private armies and political followings was brought to bear upon county elections with the intent of returning knights who would do the bidding of the lord in parliament. There is evidence that the sheriffs wielded undue influence over the elections as late as 1376 because the commons petitioned the king asking that knights be elected by the better men of the counties rather than by the sheriffs alone. It would take centuries before anything like popular elections occurred in the counties. The electorate of the Middle Ages was limited to an oligarchy of the leading residents, who in turn were persuaded or ordered to approve knights named by the sheriff or prominent political magnates. Often elections were not held; the sheriffs simply named their men and informed the chancery.

Though what we would term an election was not held, still a process of selection occurred and two knights from thirty-seven counties were given power of attorney to go to parliament and to bind by their decisions all freemen of the county. When legislation was approved it became the law of the land; when taxes were voted all were bound to pay them. This was real representation and the men who had to make the decisions were so aware of their heavy responsibility, both to the king and to those represented, that there was a marked reluctance to serve in the early parliaments. Then, too, expense was a factor, although in the reign of Edward II the cost of attending a parliament was partially defrayed by the practice of paying the knights 4s. per day.

Electoral procedure in the boroughs is more complicated to explain than that in the counties; it differed from borough to borough. The kings were not concerned how burgesses were elected as long as they were present at parliament to vote the taxes and to supply necessary information. Electoral procedure in the boroughs was often a matter of local arrangement between the sheriff who received the writs of summons and the borough officials. The question of which boroughs should send representatives to parliament was determined largely by the sheriffs. The great boroughs of southern England and the cathedral cities were invariably represented, but the establishment of a recognized group of represented boroughs was due largely to the sheriffs, who decided what boroughs should receive writs of summons. Possibly some boroughs fought representation in parliament because it entailed the payment of higher taxes. To be sure, when the tax of a tenth and fifteenth became fixed early in the fourteenth century, represented boroughs paid a tenth and unrepresented boroughs were lumped with the county and paid a fifteenth. But the latter boroughs were still liable to taxation and it is therefore wrong to argue as have some historians that boroughs fought representation to escape taxation. The sheriff dealt with the boroughs in three ways. He worked directly with the officers of the great boroughs and informed them to return two burgesses to parliament. With the boroughs in liberties he dealt with the stewards or bailiffs of the liberties and directed them to have the boroughs return burgesses. And with the boroughs of lesser status, not yet wholly independent of hundredal organization, he directed the bailiffs of the hundreds to order certain boroughs to return burgesses.

However the sheriff dealt with boroughs and whatever his basis for selecting some and not others for representation, he could manipulate borough representation in a variety of ways. He might arbitrarily fail to notify some boroughs. He might alter the names of the electees when the boroughs delivered the results to him for return to the chancery. Such opportunity for manipulation and corruption lessened towards the end of the fourteenth century when the boroughs comprehended the value of representation, fought to obtain it, and attempted to send competent men to Westminster. The manipulation of the sheriffs also came to be checked by petitions of the commons in parliament. Furthermore, some of the great boroughs like Bristol and York obtained charters incorporating them into counties; this guaranteed representation and put an end to shrieval interference. By the end of the fifteenth century eighteen boroughs had been recognized as counties.

The following figures testify to the unevenness of borough representation in the Middle Ages. Under Edward I the maximum number of boroughs represented was 146 while the average was 86. During the reign of Edward II the average dipped to 70, then rose to 75 under Edward III, and to 83 under Richard II. The number continued to rise in the fifteenth century. In the boroughs represented, the election procedure varied greatly. In London after the sheriffs received the writ of summons they turned it over to the mayor and aldermen, who nominated the candidates, generally aldermen, and then called an election in which the aldermen and prominent citizens of the wards participated. At Norwich elections to parliament were made by the assembly (*congregacio*), which in the fourteenth century was a small oligarchic body. It was the same at Northampton. In Lynn the process was quite complicated. On the appointed day of election the mayor summoned a general assembly of the most substantial citizens to the guildhall and read aloud the writ of summons. He then nominated four burgesses, who nominated four others, and these eight nominated four more. These twelve men, who came from the leading officers and citizens of Lynn, then withdrew from the main chamber of the guildhall to select the representatives. They handed the names written on a slip to the town clerk, who proclaimed the winners. And the winners, it is hardly necessary to add, were discreet, prominent, and worthy men of Lynn. These instances are but few of the many we could cite to show how election procedure differed and how oligarchic merchants invariably controlled the borough government as well as the elections. Such high-sounding phrases as elected by "the mayor and all the burgesses" were meaningless. A few of the same group of citizens regularly elected men who time and again were returned to parliament. In London between 1354 and 1399 were held 152 elections to thirty-eight parliaments but only seventy-six different persons were elected. A certain John Hadle was returned eleven times. Electoral results in the other large boroughs were similar. Admittedly the experience of such men must have been valuable to king and borough, but elections were by no means popular and democratic.

In examining the personnel who represented the boroughs one finds wealthy merchants, some small traders, local officials, and lawyers. But always the merchants were the typical representatives and their election was generally presupposed in the writs of summons. Among the merchants and financiers who represented London was the famous Sir John Philipot, mayor of London, who served Edward III in many capacities and who equipped a squadron of one thousand armed men in 1377 for the French war; John de Causton who owned a brewery as well as many houses and shops; Nicholas Brembre, a well-known goldsmith and financier. From other boroughs were Thomas Graa, mayor of York, who sat in twelve parliaments of Richard II and rendered prominent public services to the crown; and William de la Pole, who often represented Hull during the reign of Edward III and loaned him large sums, who was the founder of the great merchant family of De la Pole, was an ancestor of the earls of Suffolk, was mayor of Hull, king's butler, and a baron of the exchequer. Towards the end of the fourteenth century such men were joined by less prominent tradesmen and lawyers. All, however, were leading citizens of their boroughs and coveted election to parliament for the political, economic, and social benefits that inevitably came.

5. THE POWERS OF PARLIAMENT

Parliament was the most important institution that arose in medieval England; it was the medium through which the community of the realm limited the royal power and eventually established its sovereignty over the land. But one cannot speak of parliamentary sovereignty until the foundations upon which such political power rests have been established. At the outset of the fourteenth century it was by no means certain that the king in parliament was to be the ultimate victor in the struggle for sovereign power. It might well have been the king alone as it was in France; it might have been the king and the baronage; or it might have been the king and his council. It was the winning of financial, legislative, and political power that insured the triumph of parliament. And in particular, it was the winning of these powers by the House of Commons, the representative element, that paved the way for constitutional government and finally for democratic government.

The commons had become a regular element of parliament because the kings needed their money. It was in the area of taxation that parliament first secured power over the kings. As early as 1297 we saw the principle enunciated that the consent of the community of the realm was necessary for all taxation save ancient aids and customs. This meant that the king could not levy direct taxes upon his subjects without their consent and this came to be given in parliament. Meanwhile the traditional taxes were becoming obsolete. Scutage, for example, was no longer profitable and was forgotten. Tallages, however, continued to be levied for a while. In 1312 Edward II collected a tallage and in 1332 Edward III attempted to collect one but settled instead for a tenth and a fifteenth. This was the last attempt to collect a tallage.[8]

The older taxes that disappeared in the fourteenth century were found to be less remunerative than the fractional tax on personal property and it was this which became the standard form of taxation for the rest of the Middle Ages. Under Edward II it became established practice to ask parliament for a tenth from the boroughs and a fifteenth from the counties. Until 1332 assessments of personal property were made each time parliament voted the tax, but thereafter no new assessment was made because of the dissatisfaction with corrupt assessment and the high rate of the tax. In 1334 negotiations between tax collectors and the counties and boroughs resulted in the collection of £38,000. This sum was subsequently accepted as a standard charge and prorated between the counties and boroughs when parliament voted a tenth and a fifteenth. Occasionally dire necessity would move parliament to raise the percentage or to experiment with a new subsidy such as the poll tax of 1377, 1379, and 1380, assessed at so much per head, but the standard tax was the tenth and fifteenth.[9] In regard to direct taxation, it was firmly established early in Edward III's reign that such taxes must be consented to by the lords and the commons.

Although the objective of the barons, as stated in the Confirmation of the Charters, was to force the king to secure parliamentary approval to both direct and indirect taxation, there were enough loopholes in the wording to permit a contrary interpretation by the kings on indirect taxation. They felt that they could negotiate outside of parliament with groups of English and foreign merchants and obtain agreement to customs and duties on exports and imports. The kings veiled these indirect taxes under the cover of private agreements and encouraged the merchants to approve the assessments in return for special commercial privileges. In that England's export trade in wool and import trade in such commodities as wine was rapidly increasing in the fourteenth century, the kings were able to realize a large portion of their supply without the consent of parliament. If the practice had continued unchecked the kings would have achieved considerable financial independence from parliament.

[8] SM, no. 61B.
[9] SM, no. 63D.

We have noted the development of indirect taxation under Edward I, how in 1275 the old customs began and how it was superseded by the new customs of 1303 which considerably raised the rate. The new customs was extremely unpopular and was regarded as an evil toll (*maltote*). Soon after Edward II's accession to the throne parliament petitioned for relief from the new customs and the Ordinances of 1311 abolished it, but saved the old customs for Edward. Henceforth, the Ordinances said, new customs must be levied with the consent of the baronage.[10] After Edward II's victory in 1322, however, the new customs of Edward I was revived and a heavy subsidy was imposed upon wool exported by English and foreign merchants. Edward III levied the higher customs also and the baronage encouraged him to derive much of his income from this source, especially with the outbreak of the Hundred Years' War when he was annually in need of large amounts of money. King and the lordly part of parliament collaborated on this tax, ignoring for a time the will of the merchants, which could be expressed only by the commons. In 1332, for example, the magnates advised Edward to impose a half-mark on the wool sack and a pound upon the last of hides. In 1333 slightly higher customs were levied, and this happened again between 1337 and 1340. During this period the commons, conscious that they were not powerful enough to force the king to get their consent for such taxation, adopted the practice of formally voting the customs which had previously been arranged for by the king.[11] In so doing they were asserting the claim that no taxes could be imposed without their consent. Edward III permitted the commons this action as long as he got his money but by this indulgence he gave the commons the opportunity to establish a precedent.

In 1340 Edward III, desperate for increased income, resorted to levying a customs on wool comparable to the maltote of Edward I. This time, however, the commons did not approve the levy *ex post facto* but made a regular grant of the customs for a specified time with the added provision that at the termination of the grant no customs higher than the old customs of 1275 could be levied.[12] Parliament followed this stroke by the enactment of a statute that specifically regulated the royal right to levy taxes. It was stated that henceforth the king's subjects "shall be neither charged nor burdened to make common aid or to sustain charge except by the common assent of the prelates, earls, and barons, and of the other lords and commons of our said realm of England, and this in parliament."[13] This statute combined with the parliamentary action on taxes in 1340 marks a significant victory for the control of parliament over taxation. By 1343 it was specifically asserted that indirect taxation must have the assent of the commons in parliament. We

[10] SM, no. 56.
[11] SM, no. 61C.
[12] SM, no. 61D.
[13] SM, no. 62B.

can now say that the principle of parliamentary control of taxation was established.

Though occasionally Edward III attempted to deal privately with English and foreign merchants in order to negotiate indirect taxes, and succeeded in by-passing parliament by manipulation of the customs, he finally surrendered and acknowledged the authority of parliament to approve indirect as well as direct taxation. In 1362 he approved a statute that placed limitations on his taxing power, one being that "henceforth no subsidy or other charge shall be levied or granted on wool either by merchants or by any other persons without the assent of parliament."[14] In 1371 Edward confirmed this promise.

The reign of Edward III saw parliament establish control over taxation, a victory which meant that the approval of the commons was essential for every grant voted to the king. This advance was fundamental because it ended arbitrary taxation. And yet had parliament stopped at this point its victory would have borne no other fruit essential for controlling the king. While it is very well to control taxation, those who approve it should receive something tangible in return for their money and obtain some guarantee that the money approved will be spent wisely and be used for the welfare of the realm. Fortunately, parliament soon took interest in the purposes for which taxes were used and how they were expended. What parliament did in the fourteenth century, we must realize, was but the beginning of a centuries-long struggle between king and parliament in the field of financial administration. Also we must recognize that on the one hand the kings viewed any parliamentary attempt to supervise their use of funds as blatant invasion of royal prerogative and on the other hand parliament had no concept of how far it could interfere with powers that we today would term executive. Two hostile forces faced each other in the fourteenth century with no realization of what rights each should properly have or upon what issues they should compromise. While parliament wanted to eradicate royal abuses in finance, the kings feared any interference lest it represent an encroachment upon their prerogative and overly restrict their freedom of executive action in war and civil government. Yet the kings, whatever their feelings, had to surrender the most in their need for money; on each occasion it was the commons that gained.

Every parliament asked to approve a tax was informed of the purpose and was asked to deliberate and to give a favorable response. When, by the reign of Edward III, it was customary for the burgesses and knights to present common petitions asking for specific concessions that would benefit all subjects of the realm, it likewise became customary for the commons to bargain with the kings. The commons let it be known that they would approve a tax if the king would grant their common petitions. In effect, what they were saying was that they would consent to taxation only after their

[14] SM, no. 62J.

petitions were approved, and in fact they did not answer the king's request for supply until he had first approved their petitions. Herein lies the origin of the famous principle of redress before supply which, as a result of continuous advance in this direction, definitely became accepted procedure in the reign of Henry IV in the early fifteenth century. The feeling that a grant should be made only after the king had satisfied petitions can be discerned in the parliament of 1339. The commons presented six petitions asking redress and requested the summoning of a new parliament so that the representatives could consult with the counties and boroughs on the heavy tax demanded.[15] In the parliament that followed in 1340 the commons approved a tax on condition that the king accept the petitions. This he did, referring them to a parliamentary committee of judges, lords, and commons who were to redraft them in statutory form. After this was done the six petitions were enacted into four statutes.[16] The commons used the same technique in two parliaments of 1348. In the first they presented sixty-four petitions for redress of grievances, but there was no satisfactory response nor was a tax voted. In the second parliament most of the same petitions were presented with the proviso that if they were accepted the commons would grant a tenth and a fifteenth for three years.[17] Although Edward III got his grant by agreeing to approve most of the petitions, they were not incorporated into a statute. In a later parliament of 1373 the commons consulted with a committee of the lords, the first time such a procedure had occurred, and after consultation approved both a direct and an indirect tax contingent upon the king's according to them a number of petitions. By bargaining their money in return for redress of grievances and for desired changes in government and by withholding approval of a tax until the king agreed to the petitions, the commons were able to exert some influence on the course of government and to prepare for the day when under the Lancastrians redress before supply would become a regular and main procedure for parliamentary legislation. But the commons had yet to win further gains before they could be assured that their petitions, if accepted, would be put into statutes that faithfully repeated the content and expressed the spirit of the petitions.

Another step in parliamentary control of expenditure was taken when the commons insisted upon auditing royal accounts. In 1340 parliamentary commissioners were appointed to audit the accounts of the collectors of taxes recently approved.[18] In 1341 when the commons again demanded that commissioners be appointed for such auditing, the king again acceded.[19] In the parliament of 1377, one of the first of Richard II, the commons de-

[15] SM, no. 61C.
[16] SM, no. 61D.
[17] SM, no. 61G.
[18] SM, no. 61D.
[19] SM, no. 61E.

manded that "certain fit persons" be appointed to receive and expend the money voted for war. The king appointed William Walworth and John Philipot, merchants of London, who were "to render faithful account of their receipts and expenditures."[20] In 1379 the royal council took the initiative and ordered the accounts of a tax to be presented for examination to parliament.[21] Thereafter the parliament that granted the tax regularly appointed treasurers of the taxes who were to account to the succeeding parliament. But the principle, still not settled to the complete satisfaction of parliament, had to be contested repeatedly in the fifteenth century.

A further claim made by parliament in the fourteenth century was the right to appropriate the money granted so that it would be expended on specific projects and not commandeered by the king, his councillors, or his favorites for less important and frivolous purposes. The commons in the parliament of 1348 voted a fifteenth for three years with the proviso that "this aid shall be assigned and kept solely for the war of our lord the king" against Scotland.[22] In 1353 parliament voted another tax to be used expressly for the prosecution of war. In 1390 parliament made a more detailed appropriation. Forty shillings on the sack of wool had been voted and of this amount ten shillings were to be used for the present royal needs and thirty shillings for military expenditures in case war continued. Although elaborate appropriations were made in the fifteenth century, we may say that by 1399 the essential principles of parliamentary control over royal finance had been introduced. All direct and indirect taxation had to be approved by parliament. Parliament was more often insisting upon redress before supply. Parliament was auditing the taxes received and expended and was beginning to appropriate the taxes for specific purposes. All these gains were to aid parliament in its bid for a greater role in legislation and for participation in governmental policy.

Since the thirteenth century it had been recognized that legislation—the statutes—required general consent and support given to the king by the great council or by parliamentary assemblies including both the barons and the commons. Upon occasion laws had been enacted after consultation with the burgesses. During the reign of Edward II, when the commons attended parliament more consistently, they consented to more legislation and perhaps the Statute of York in 1322 intended that legislation on major matters should be assented to by the commons as well as by the baronage.[23] It was in the reign of Edward III, however, that regular attendance of the commons at parliament and their control over supply gave them the leverage needed to win a key part in making statutes. From this time on all statutes enacted by parliament had to be approved by the commons.

[20] SM, no. 63A.
[21] SM, no. 63C.
[22] SM, no. 61G.
[23] SM, no. 58.

Mere consent to legislation did not, however, give the commons legislative initiative. This they had yet to acquire. The initial move towards introducing and controlling legislation was made in the first parliament of Edward III in 1327. For the first time the commons as a body introduced a common petition that concerned matters of general interest for the community of the realm—the commons public bill in modern terminology. This was not the usual petition introduced on behalf of an individual or a community; it was a petition of public concern. This particular petition consisted of forty-one articles; sixteen articles were incorporated into two statutes and twenty-two less important articles were dealt with by ordinances or in specific orders directing appropriate action. Henceforth commons petitions or bills, as they came to be called, were introduced with greater regularity. Similar comprehensive bills were presented in 1333 and 1337 and in the year 1343 begins a series of long comprehensive commons petitions. Such petitions were introduced during the next ten parliaments, and we find them in numerous other parliaments of Edward III and in parliaments of Richard II. The commons petition was a momentous innovation. In place of the traditional officially drafted bills emanating from the king and his council, henceforth the bills consisted largely of commons petitions introduced into parliament, modified by responses of the king and his council and the lords, and finally enacted into statutes.[24]

Despite the legislative initiative acquired, the commons remained fundamentally petitioners; it was still within the authority of the king and lords to accept *in toto*, to modify, or to reject the petitions. The commons, finding that frequently the king would reject petitions or so modify them as to defeat their intent, resorted to various methods to make the petitions acceptable to him. The form of the enacting words of the statutes passed during Edward III's reign clearly indicates the subordinate position of the commons. The statutes were said to be enacted by the king "at the request of the commons and by the assent of the prelates, earls, and barons." What converted the commons from mere initiators into effective legislators with control over the ultimate statutory product was their position, made possible by the extraordinary financial demands occasioned by the Hundred Years' War, of being able to refuse supply until remedy had been provided for their petitions. By forcing redress before supply the commons secured the acceptance of their petitions and the enactment of many into statutes.

The commons' weapon of redress before supply did not guarantee, however, that they always obtained the legislation desired. The royal assent (*le roi le veut*) did not give the petition the force of law. It still had to be converted into an appropriate enactment, either a statute, an ordinance, or letters patent that ordered remedy or administrative action. The commons realized that not every petition deserved enactment into statute but what they wanted was the accurate conversion of their petitions, whatever the ultimate

[24] SM, no. 61F, G, H, and I.

form of enactment. Repeatedly they found that this was not done; the statute or enactment, drafted by the king's council after parliament was dissolved, often bore faint resemblance to the petition. The commons discovered that their control over legislation was still imperfect. They complained bitterly against this practice, particularly in 1341 and 1385. In the parliament of 1341 they forced the king and council to approve their petition while parliament was still in session and the statutes enacted were sealed with the great seal and delivered to the lords and the commons.[25] While the struggle of the commons to control the final form of their petitions did not meet with success until early in the fifteenth century, precedents had been established that ultimately forced the king to enact the petitions into law exactly as they had been presented.

We have noted the development under Edward I of a fundamental distinction between statute and ordinance. The ordinance, which was made not in parliament but by king and council, dealt with less important and less permanent matters. Ordinances were basically administrative orders and were generally regarded as transitory enactments which dealt with particular subjects and which could be terminated when no longer required.[26] Sometimes, as we have seen, the commons petitions were finally enacted as ordinances. The commons, aware that the redress sought did not always require a statute, did not object to this form of enactment unless important petitions were put into ordinances to evade the purpose of the petitions; they then objected strenuously. They also protested when their statutes were modified or annulled by ordinances specifically enacted by king and council to undo what the commons had forced the king in parliament to do. Another grievance of the commons was that the king and council issued ordinances which properly should have been statutes enacted by parliament. The kings were seeking to maintain legislative independence while parliament was striving to limit royal and conciliar action to routine administration.

A classic example of the clashes on these issues between king and parliament occurred during the crisis of 1341. Edward III was forced under threat of no tax to agree to a statute that limited many of the traditional royal powers, including the provision that all important officers and justices be appointed by parliament.[27] No sooner was parliament dissolved than Edward and his council annulled the statute by an ordinance which stated that the statute "was expressly contrary to the laws and customs of our kingdom of England, and to our royal rights and prerogatives."[28] This ordinance was considered unwarranted and the next parliament repealed it, in effect serving notice on the king that only parliament could make and unmake statutes.[29] In permitting this action, Edward admitted that he could not annul a statute

[25] SM, no. 61E.
[26] SM, nos. 62G and H, 64C and D.
[27] SM, no. 61E.
[28] SM, no. 62C.
[29] SM, no. 61F

and thereby acknowledged a legislative authority superior to king and council. Thus finally established was the principle that laws must be made by king in parliament with the assent of lords and commons and that laws could be annulled only in the same manner. No matter who introduced a bill—king, lords, or commons—the consent of all was necessary to convert it into statute law. If any of the three withheld assent, it was as though a veto had been cast. From the middle of the fourteenth century ordinances became less numerous and were regarded primarily as temporary or emergency enactments that would be superseded by statutes if there was need. In 1349, for example, king and council enacted the Ordinance of Laborers to regulate prices and wages during the Black Death. In 1351 it was incorporated into the Statute of Laborers, which was regarded as having more authority and permanence.[30] Ordinances continued throughout the medieval period and came to be known as orders-in-council. Enacted mostly when immediate action was required and when parliament was not in session, the orders-in-council never impinged upon statutes; in the fourteenth century parliament had established its legislative supremacy.

Ultimately unsuccessful in their attempt to annul and modify distasteful statutes by means of ordinances, the kings adopted other prerogative weapons which threatened to be equally dangerous to parliamentary statutes. These weapons are known as the "dispensing" and "suspending" powers. The theory behind them was that he who made a law could dispense with its force in individual cases or suspend it temporarily for certain cases. To a degree these powers were necessary and useful because often the law worked individual injustice and hardship which must be relieved by executive action. A common and unquestioned use of these powers was the pardoning of individuals convicted of crime. But unfortunately the kings came to use the powers to advance their selfish aims. They obstructed the process of justice by pardoning men before they were tried and by suspending the application of statutes to certain individuals. Even more serious, they used these powers to nullify the statutes of parliament. Some statutes were so riddled with suspension and dispensation as to be worthless.

Parliament had long been mindful of the dangers inherent in the dispensing and suspending powers and fought throughout the fourteenth century to limit them to their rightful use. As early as 1328 a parliament enacted the Statute of Northampton, which restricted the royal prerogative of dispensation. Still, in 1330, 1347, and 1351 the commons petitioned against the use of the dispensing power. Apparently the petitions were of little avail because in 1390 Richard II was forced to assent to a statute forbidding the issue of pardons to men who had perpetrated serious crimes unless the nature of the crime was specified and the name of the criminal given. But nothing beyond this statute was enacted in the fourteenth century to restrict the dispensing power of the king, which continued to be

[30] SM, no. 62D.

used to obstruct legislation. The suspending power, though seldom employed in the fourteenth century, was to be an effective weapon in the hands of later kings, especially the Stuarts of the seventeenth century, who used it in combination with the dispensing power.

In the reign of Edward III the commons had begun to initiate legislation and by the end of the century they were responsible for a major part of it. Also in the fourteenth century parliament destroyed the claim of the crown to levy taxes without its consent, which meant the consent of lords and commons. The commons were called to parliament to give assent to taxation and from this function, undoubtedly their most important in parliament, grew their other powers. By the end of the century the commons had acquired the sole right to originate parliamentary taxation. In 1395 grants were made in parliament for the first time "by the commons with the advice and assent of the lords"; thereafter this became the general formula when taxes were approved. The commons, upon whom the heavier burden of taxation fell, had seized the initiative with money grants. In the fifteenth century it became recognized that all money bills (grants were made in the form of bills which, if approved, became statutes) must originate in the House of Commons. This right, though occasionally challenged by the Tudors and Stuarts, has endured to the present and has enabled the House of Commons to win exclusive control over money matters.

The achievements of the commons in the fourteenth century were indeed remarkable; to propose and to assent to the laws by which they would be governed was a great victory. But until they could also control and share in governmental policy they had no means of enforcing proper administration of their laws. Occasionally by refusing supply they temporarily influenced or controlled royal policy, but they did not regularly wield any influence. They had come to parliament originally as assentors to taxation; counsel and advice were secured from the small council and the barons—the natural feudal advisers of the kings. The barons in parliament had often given advice to Edward I and Edward II on war, peace, and foreign policy, but the commons had been virtually ignored. Then, in the reign of Edward III the pressure of war and finance forced the king to call upon the commons for advice. In 1328 a treaty of peace with Scotland was concluded with the advice and consent of the commons. During the Hundred Years' War their counsel was frequently sought. In 1333 the chancellor asked the lords and commons whether a marriage agreement should be struck with the French king and the commons replied that they thought "the way of marriage the best." In 1343 the lord chamberlain told parliament that "as the war was begun by the common advice of the prelates, great men and commons, the king could not treat of, or make peace without the like assent." In the same year the chancellor asked the commons "to meet in the Painted Chamber in order to treat, consult, and agree among themselves" on relations with the papacy.

Strangely, however, in 1348 when the commons were asked for advice on war and peace they excused themselves from answering, pleading "ignorance and simplicity," and agreed to accept whatever course the king and lords should take. Later in a parliament of 1384 when asked a similar question the commons replied that they should not be regarded as counsellors or asked to give advice on questions of policy. What is apparent, therefore, from the evidence just surveyed is that during Edward III's reign the commons were frequently asked for advice on policy and they often gave definite answers. But under Richard II there was a marked tendency not to give advice. It appears that as yet the commons were not eager to claim a share in policy and did not comprehend the stakes involved in sharing and controlling policy. They seemed to feel that too close an association with the king on policy might embarrass them when he requested taxes for projects they had approved. Though only too eager to criticize the conduct of government and to avenge themselves upon those who conducted unpopular and unsuccessful government, the commons were not yet prepared to take a responsible role in policy. This was not to come until the late seventeenth and eighteenth centuries.

Although taxation, legislation, and policy are the principal themes of parliamentary history in the fourteenth century we must not ignore the other valuable functions of parliament. Both knights and burgesses transacted a variety of services for king and local constituencies. To the king they brought valuable information on county and borough. They were to further the community and individual interest of their constituency. They labored hard to secure royal assistance for public works, commercial concessions, and all sorts of privileges. While expected to obtain all that they could for their community, they were to commit it to a minimum of taxation. On the other hand, both counties and boroughs were interested in what was done by parliament and in what important matters were discussed at Westminster. Their representatives were expected to give a report of what had been accomplished at Westminster and were subjected to questions about their personal views on various issues. Though the knights always had a more dominant role in parliament by virtue of stature and experience and could give more comprehensive reports to their county constituents, the burgesses quickly acquired experience and became knowledgeable politicians who rendered good accounts of their activities at parliament. They regularly delivered reports at the guildhalls and enlightened their audiences on the great political issues of the day. Records of these reports made in the boroughs provide an excellent description of medieval politics. Early in the fifteenth century, for instance, two burgesses of Lynn reported on parliament to their brethren in the guildhall. After describing the fine sermon of the archbishop of Canterbury, whose text was "Justice and peace have kissed each other," they gave what is probably the earliest description we have of the procedure for choosing the speaker of the House of Commons. After these reports were given, frequently copies of statutes enacted and other pertinent commissions and orders were distributed. Gone was the age when the sheriffs or itinerant justices linked central to local government; this was now done by the knights and burgesses of parliament.

6. PRIVILEGE AND PROCEDURE

Fourteenth-century evidence on parliamentary privilege and procedure is scanty. Beyond what the main source, the Parliament Rolls, tell us there is only the *Anonimalle Chronicle's* description of the Good Parliament of 1376. Little is known about procedure until the Journals of the lords begin under Henry VIII and those of the commons under Edward VI. We know, however, that the commons secured certain privileges in the fourteenth century which helped to establish some of the conditions necessary for the House of Commons to set up a procedure.

Undoubtedly the principal privilege acquired was that of impeachment (accusation). Inasmuch as the House of Lords constituted the High Court of Parliament the commons eventually came to see that they could impeach (indict) royal ministers and other royal officials for public misconduct, that is, for offenses against the crown which constituted high treason. The House of Lords was the high court of the realm in which were tried great crown officers indicted by the commons acting in the capacity of a grand jury for the realm. The lords judged, as was their traditional custom, and the commons prosecuted. The first case of impeachment occurred in 1376 at the Good Parliament when the two royal ministers Lord Latimer and Richard Lyons were accused of financial malversation and found guilty by the House of Lords. Latimer was imprisoned, fined, and deprived of his position as king's chamberlain and councillor. Richard Lyons was condemned to imprisonment and forfeiture of goods.[31] In 1386 the commons impeached Michael de la Pole, earl of Suffolk, who was the chancellor of Richard II. Seven serious charges of public offense were brought against him. He was found guilty, sentenced to imprisonment, and ordered to pay a fine and to return misappropriated funds.[32] When Richard II came into power in 1397 he arranged for his supporters in the House of Commons to impeach his old enemies the Lords Appellant. Later that year the commons stated "before the king in full parliament that they intended by his leave to accuse and impeach any person or persons, as often as seemed to them good in the parliament then sitting."

Through the legal process of impeachment the commons had opened the door to control of the royal ministers. By bringing accusations before the House of Lords the commons assured themselves that there would be no royal intimidation as was so often the case in the ordinary courts. The

[31] SM, no. 61I.
[32] SM, no. 63F.

process of impeachment also brought to trial serious offenses technically not recognized by the ordinary courts. Impeachment was the first effective means devised to control the crown. Even if the king could do no wrong, his ministers who carried out royal orders could, and they were made responsible for their conduct. When they were impeached royal power and prestige were equally at stake and admitted a parliamentary control. But medieval impeachment was far from being an impartial judicial appeal of the commons. Too often the commons were tools of the king or powerful barons in their efforts to bring down political opponents. It would be some time before the commons would act independently when they impeached royal officers before the House of Lords.

At the very end of the fourteenth century we have our first glimpse of the commons' asserting the privilege of free speech. In the January parliament of 1397 a royal official, Sir Thomas Haxey, introduced a bill of complaints against the royal government and boldly attacked the administration and the king himself. Hearing of this, Richard II was infuriated; he demanded the name of the person who had made the speech and asked for his punishment. Haxey was adjudged by parliament to die as a traitor and his life was spared only when the archbishop of Canterbury saved him as a cleric.[33] Meanwhile the commons humbly apologized for the attack against the king and Richard accepted the apology. The fact remained, however, that Haxey had been found guilty of high treason for a speech attacking the king and it was not until the first parliament of Henry IV in 1399 that the judgment was reversed. The commons then asked for its reversal on the grounds that Haxey had been "adjudged traitor and forfeited everything that he had, in violation of right and of the usage that had hitherto prevailed in parliament (and to the undoing of the customs of the commons)." Henry IV granted this petition and Haxey stood exonerated.[34] Though Haxey was a royal official who but introduced the odious bill and was not technically a commoner, his exoneration and the claim of the commons can still be regarded as an assertion of the right of freedom of debate and of the principle that the proceedings of the House of Commons should be immune. This incident became a great precedent in future defense of the commons' right to freedom of speech.

We have already discussed the customary procedure of parliament in the fourteenth century. The king made known, generally by means of the chancellor, the cause of summoning parliament. When the speech was completed, the lords and commons were ordered to withdraw to their separate meeting chambers where they discussed the business presented to them. At the end of their deliberations they were to make known their answers to the king, and parliament was then ordinarily dissolved. The chief innovation in this procedure was the designation of a speaker of the House of Commons, who acted as an intermediary between the king and his council and the com-

[33] SM, no. 63H.
[34] SM, no. 66A.

mons and who, as spokesman, delivered the formal reply of the commons to the king and his council. There may have been such a spokesman during much of Edward III's reign but evidence of his existence first appears during the Good Parliament of 1376. At this parliament Sir Peter de la Mare, though not appointed at the outset to serve as a speaker, was selected on different occasions to act as spokesman for the commons. He, it will be remembered, led the bitter attack against John of Gaunt and his cronies on the royal council and was instrumental in pushing through a major portion of the parliamentary enactments.[35] In the parliament of 1377 Thomas Hungerford was the speaker, and thereafter all parliaments had a speaker of the House of Commons.

Though these speakers of the fourteenth century were the ancestors of the present speakers who preside over the House of Commons, their functions were quite different. The early speakers, as spokesmen and intermediaries of the commons, worked energetically in behalf of political programs and factions. One cannot say that they were freely elected; generally they were named by the commons following the suggestions of the lords or king. Peter de la Mare was the steward of the earl of March, who, with his political ally the Black Prince, masterminded the attack against John of Gaunt and his faction. On the other hand, Thomas Hungerford was the steward of John of Gaunt and did his bidding in the parliament of 1377. The first two speakers were but political managers of the commons for their lordly masters. This trend persisted. In later parliaments the great lords often imposed their men upon the commons. And when Richard II assumed independent direction of the government, he imposed his men upon the commons. One of them was Sir John Bussy, a devoted servant of Richard, who pushed through much of the absolutistic program between 1397 and 1399. In the fifteenth century the Lancastrians followed Richard's precedent; they consistently prevailed upon the commons to select loyal and experienced servants. The early speakers of the House of Commons, we may conclude, were not freely elected by the commons and did not often express the independent views of the commons. They served the king and the great lords and influenced the commons on behalf of their political masters. Royal and lordly influence would continue to be decisive until the late seventeenth and eighteenth centuries when, for a time, the speaker came to be primarily the servant of the House of Commons. Later he gave up his political activity and connection with party and became an impartial presiding officer.

7. CONCLUSIONS

With the possible exception of the seventeenth century, no century in the history of parliament equaled the fourteenth in achievement. It was then that the basic foundations of parliamentary government were laid. Parlia-

[35] SM, no. 61I.

ment became an accepted part of the government, constituted in part of representatives of the counties and boroughs. Thanks to a fortuitous combination of events it became a bicameral assembly divided into the House of Lords and the House of Commons. In spite of no marked enthusiasm for representation in parliament, both county and borough eventually saw the need for it and took a serious interest in the work of parliament. Two basic rights were acquired by parliament which did more than anything else to limit the power of the king and make him a constitutional monarch; these were consent to taxation and consent to legislation. In the acquisition of these rights the commons cooperated with the lords and eventually secured the initiative. The commons made no consistent attempt to share in and control policy, nor did they have a sense of responsibility for policy despite some sporadic starts in this direction. They had just begun to fight for the privilege of free speech. They established their right to impeach royal officers and thereby make the crown more responsible to parliament for its conduct of government. In the speaker, the House of Commons had an intermediary who reported its decisions and occasionally its sentiments to the king and his council. Though the early speakers were not independently elected by the commons and seldom represented the views of the commons, they were valuable in preparing the way for the modern speaker of the House of Commons.

All these powers, privileges, and procedures constituted the basic ingredients of the English parliament; they represented progress that would not be equaled until the seventeenth century. The fifteenth century would only see parliamentary privileges and powers worked out in greater detail. Though as yet the kings were not limited monarchs and still strove mightily to retain their independence and their prerogatives, they were no longer monarchs who taxed, legislated, and administered the realm arbitrarily. They recognized the power that was parliament and realized that they must govern under the laws of the realm, of which parliament was the supreme guardian. By 1399 parliament had survived the most precarious phase of its life. It was in England to stay.

BIBLIOGRAPHY

For the history of the fourteenth century see the works cited in the General Bibliography, especially those of McKisack and Wilkinson. For the reign of Edward II the best specialized study remains that by T. F. Tout, *The Place of the Reign of Edward II in English History*, 2d ed. (Manchester, 1936). Also useful for Edward II are Hilda Johnstone, *Edward of Carnarvon* (Manchester, 1947) and H. F. Hutchinson, *Edward II: The Pliant King* (London, 1971). J. C. Davies has studied the opposition to Edward in *The Baronial Opposition to Edward II: Its Character and Policy* (Cambridge, 1918). Studies on some of the principal figures are Alice Beardwood, *The Trial of Walter Langton, Bishop of Lichfield 1307–1312, Transactions of the American Philosophical Society*, LIV (Philadelphia, 1964), J. Maddicott, *Thomas of Lancaster* (Oxford, 1970), and J. R. S. Phillips, *Aymer de Valence: Earl of Pembroke, 1307–1324: Baronial Politics in the Reign of Edward II* (New York, 1972).

There are no modern studies on Edward III and his leading magnates except Kenneth Fowler's *The King's Lieutenant: Henry of Grosmont, First Duke of Lancaster, 1310–1361* (New York, 1969). There are many studies on Richard II, a much debated and misunderstood king. See Anthony Steel, *Richard II* (Cambridge, 1941), H. F. Hutchinson, *The Hollow Crown* (New York, 1961), R. H. Jones, *The Royal Policy of Richard II: Absolutism in the Later Middle Ages* (New York, 1968), Gervase Mathew, *The Court of Richard II* (London, 1968), Anthony Tuck, *Richard II and the English Nobility* (London, 1973), and F. R. H. Du Boulay and C. M. Barron, eds., *The Reign of Richard II: Essays in Honour of May McKisack* (London, 1971). Two key figures are studied by Joseph Dahmus, *William Courtenay: Archbishop of Canterbury, 1381–1396* (University Park, Pa., 1966) and by Margaret Aston, *Thomas Arundel: A Study of Church Life in the Reign of Richard II* (Oxford, 1967). See also Anthony Goodman, *The Loyal Conspiracy, the Lords Appellant under Richard II* (London, 1971).

In numerous articles such scholars as Wilkinson, Richardson, Lapsley, Sayles, Strayer, Plucknett, Chrimes, Clarke, Edwards, and Galbraith have discussed the baronial attempt to limit the royal prerogative and to control the royal council. For these and other studies see the bibliographical guides. See also G. L. Haskins, *The Statute of York and the Interest of the Commons* (Cambridge, Mass., 1935), T. F. T. Plucknett, "The Impeachments of 1376," *Transactions of the Royal Historical Society*, I (1951), 153–64, J. G. Bellamy, "Appeal and Impeachment in the Good Parliament," *Bulletin of the Institute of Historical Research*, XXXIX (1966), 35–46.

A detailed study of royal administration is *The English Government at Work*: vol. I, *Central and Prerogative Administration*, J. F. Willard and W. A. Morris, eds. (Cambridge, Mass., 1940) deals with the central departments of government and vol. II, *Fiscal Administration*, J. R. Strayer, ed. (Cambridge, Mass., 1947) deals with exchequer and royal revenue. For the chancery see Bertie Wilkinson, *The Chancery under Edward III* (Manchester, 1929). There are also valuable studies on household government in T. F. Tout, *Collected*

Papers (Manchester, 1932–1934). On the great seal see H. Maxwell-Lyte, *Historical Notes on the Use of the Great Seal* (London, 1926). On royal finance the following books are valuable: Anthony Steel, *The Receipt of the Exchequer, 1377–1485* (Cambridge, 1954), Stephen Dowell, *A History of Taxation and Taxes in England*, 3d ed. with new introduction (London, 1965), N. S. B. Gras, *The Early English Customs System* (Cambridge, Mass., 1918), R. L. Baker, *The English Customs Service, 1307–1343: A Study of Medieval Administration* (Philadelphia, 1961). E. B. Fryde has written many important articles on the subject.

Vol. III of *The English Government at Work: Local Administration and Justice*, W. H. Dunham, Jr., ed. (Cambridge, Mass., 1950) has chapters on local government. For the boroughs see Martin Weinbaum, *The Incorporation of Boroughs* (Manchester, 1937) and Ruth Bird, *The Turbulent London of Richard II* (London, 1949). See also N. Denholm-Young, *The Country Gentry in the Fourteenth Century* (Oxford, 1969).

A valuable study of the church is W. A. Pantin, *The English Church in the Fourteenth Century* (Cambridge, 1955). See also A. Hamilton Thompson, *The English Clergy and their Organization in the Later Middle Ages* (Oxford, 1947), L. C. Gabel, *Benefit of Clergy in the Later Middle Ages* (Northampton, 1929), and B. L. Woodcock, *Medieval Ecclesiastical Courts in the Diocese of Canterbury* (Oxford, 1952), 2 vols.

Supplementing the works on parliament cited previously are Faith Thompson, *A Short History of Parliament, 1295–1642* (Minneapolis, 1953) and Kenneth MacKenzie, *The English Parliament* (Harmondsworth, 1951). For the development of the House of Lords see J. H. Round, *Peerage and Pedigree* (London, 1910), L. O. Pike, *The Constitutional History of the House of Lords* (London, 1894), and J. E. Powell and K. Wallis, *The House of Lords in the Middle Ages* (London, 1968). The principal interpretations of parliament in the fourteenth century are in Bertie Wilkinson, *Studies in the Constitutional History of the Thirteenth and Fourteenth Centuries* (Manchester, 1937), M. V. Clarke, *Fourteenth-Century Studies* (Oxford, 1937), Gaillard Lapsley, *Crown, Community and Parliament in the Later Middle Ages: Studies in English Constitutional History*, H. M. Cam and Geoffrey Barraclough, eds. (Oxford, 1951), H. L. Gray, *The Influence of the Commons on Early Legislation* (Cambridge, Mass., 1932), H. M. Cam, *The Legislators of Medieval England* (London, 1945), and J. S. Roskell, *The Commons and their Speakers in English Parliaments, 1376–1523* (Manchester, 1965) and *The Knights of the Shire for the County Palatine of Lancaster, 1377–1460* (Manchester, 1937).

For the political role of the magnates, their influence in parliament, and their use of the indenture system the following studies of K. B. McFarlane are important: *The Nobility of Later Medieval England: The Ford Lectures for 1953 and Related Studies* (Oxford, 1973) and "Parliament and 'Bastard Feudalism'," *Transactions of the Royal Historical Society*, XXVI (1944), 53–79. Cf. H. M. Cam, "The Decline and Fall of English Feudalism," *History*, XXV (1940), 216–233, G. A. Holmes, *The Estates of the Higher Nobility in Fourteenth-Century England* (Cambridge, 1957).

Part Six

THE HOUSES OF LANCASTER AND YORK

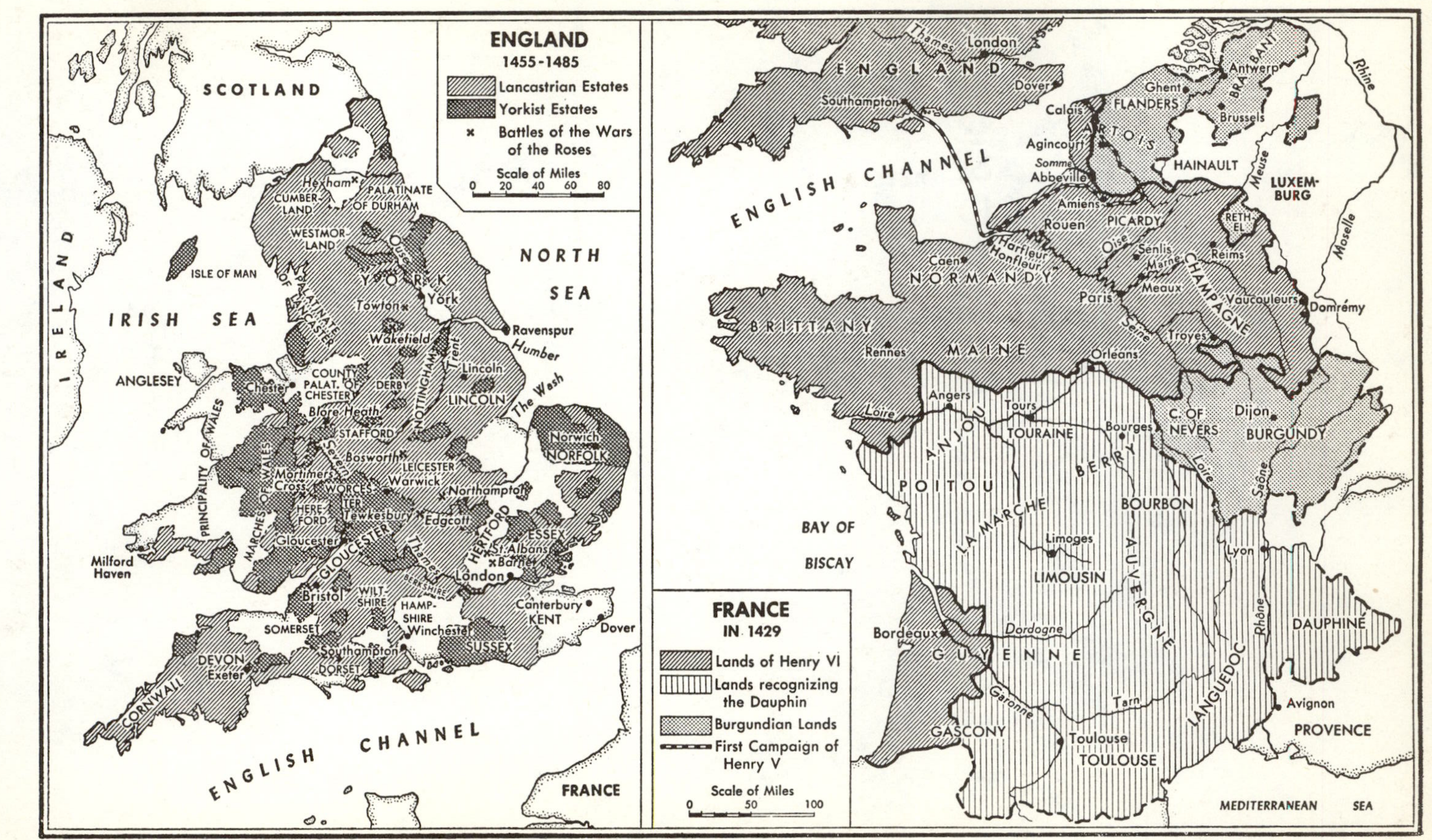

ENGLAND
1455-1485
Lancastrian Estates
Yorkist Estates
Battles of the Wars of the Roses
Scale of Miles
0 20 40 60 80
SCOTLAND
IRELAND
IRISH SEA
NORTH SEA
ISLE OF MAN
ANGLESEY
Milford Haven
CUMBERLAND
Hexham
PALATINATE OF DURHAM
WESTMORLAND
PALATINATE OF LANCASTER
YORK
York
Ouse
Towton
Wakefield
Ravenspur
Humber
NOTTINGHAM
Trent
Lincoln
LINCOLN
The Wash
COUNTY PALAT. OF CHESTER
Chester
DERBY
Blore Heath
STAFFORD
Bosworth
LEICESTER
Warwick
Northampton
PRINCIPALITY OF WALES
MARCHES OF WALES
Mortimers Cross
WORCESTER
HEREFORD
Tewkesbury
Edgcott
Severn
Gloucester
GLOUCESTER
HERTFORD
St. Albans
Barnet
Norwich
NORFOLK
ESSEX
Thames
London
BERKSHIRE
WILTSHIRE
Bristol
HAMPSHIRE
Winchester
Canterbury
KENT
Dover
SUSSEX
SOMERSET
Southampton
DORSET
DEVON
Exeter
CORNWALL
ENGLISH CHANNEL
FRANCE
FRANCE
IN 1429
Lands of Henry VI
Lands recognizing the Dauphin
Burgundian Lands
First Campaign of Henry V
Scale of Miles
0 50 100
ENGLAND
Thames
London
Dover
Southampton
ENGLISH CHANNEL
Calais
Ghent
FLANDERS
Antwerp
BRABANT
Brussels
ARTOIS
HAINAULT
Agincourt
Somme
Abbeville
Meuse
LUXEMBURG
Rhine
Moselle
Amiens
PICARDY
RETHEL
Rouen
Harfleur
Honfleur
Oise
Senlis
Marne
Reims
Caen
NORMANDY
Meaux
CHAMPAGNE
Paris
Vaucouleurs
Domrémy
BRITTANY
Rennes
MAINE
Seine
Troyes
Orléans
Loire
Angers
Tours
ANJOU
TOURAINE
Bourges
C. OF NEVERS
Dijon
BURGUNDY
BERRY
POITOU
BOURBON
Saône
BAY OF BISCAY
LA MARCHE
Limoges
LIMOUSIN
AUVERGNE
Lyon
Rhône
DAUPHINÉ
Bordeaux
GUYENNE
Dordogne
LANGUEDOC
Garonne
Tarn
Avignon
PROVENCE
GASCONY
Toulouse
TOULOUSE
MEDITERRANEAN SEA

XXXV

The Sources and History of Lancastrian and Yorkist England

THE fifteenth century forms a plateau in the growth of records valuable for institutional and legal history. Compared to the many new records appearing in each preceding century, the fifteenth brought forth only a few. The Lancastrians and Yorkists, no innovators, were satisfied with continuing the large number of records already in existence. Even this was a difficult task in a century characterized by kaleidoscopic shifts in political power and by lawlessness and sporadic warfare. Such chaos affected the records; some were destroyed or were no longer kept. The historian who labors in the fifteenth century soon discovers that this disorderly century is reflected in its disorderly records.

Some of the most useful records are those of the boroughs, which were beginning to understand the value of orderly records for municipal government. After the silence of legal writers on fourteenth-century law, two great lawyers, Sir John Fortescue and Sir Thomas Littleton, wrote classic descriptions of the law in the fifteenth century. There are in addition to the standard sources some valuable collections of royal letters as well as correspondence of noble families. A small number of reliable chronicles and biographies supplements these records.

I. NONNARRATIVE RECORDS

All that need be said about the royal records is that the Parliament Rolls, statutes, and ordinances constitute the prime sources for the fifteenth century.[1] From them is largely gleaned the account of the dominant constitutional theme—the evolution of parliamentary power and privilege. Far from rising in splendid isolation, parliament was closely tied to the political, legal, and financial problems of the age. For these aspects of constitutional history such legal records as the Plea Rolls and such financial records as the Receipt and Issue Rolls, the Subsidy Rolls, and the Wardrobe and Foreign Accounts help to explain why parliament enacted certain statutes regulating the common law and why the kings had to rely upon parliament for the bulk of their supply. Also significant are the royal charters granted to the boroughs because

[1] SM, nos. 66, 67, 68, 69.

they describe borough incorporation during its classic age in the fifteenth century.

Two types of records merit special attention. One tells the story of the royal council's fifteenth-century pre-eminence and the other that of the growth of the chancery as a court of equity. Separate records of the proceedings of the royal council did not begin until the reign of Richard II, probably not until the year 1390. From then until 1435 official records of the proceedings are extant. They then cease for over a century, not reappearing until 1540. These records were actually formal minutes of the council meetings and are of value for their description of the council when it was at the apogee of its power during the minority of Henry VI.[2] By the end of the fourteenth century the chancery had become a court of equity almost completely independent from the royal council, and during the fifteenth century it definitely established its judicial independence in the realm of equitable law. This development is reflected in the appearance of legal records which describe the equity proceedings in chancery. Customarily known as the Proceedings in Chancery, they begin in the reign of Richard II and continue down to the Tudor period.[3]

Most of the traditional local records continued in the fifteenth century, but only certain municipal records merit discussion. Though municipal records antedate the fifteenth century, few are older than the thirteenth century. In fact, in many boroughs the oldest muniments date only from the late fourteenth and fifteenth centuries. These records in the borough archives consist of urban charters, treasurers' financial accounts, borough assembly and council rolls, guild merchant rolls, and peculiar books containing municipal ordinances and miscellaneous records which go by such varied names as the White Book, the Red Book, and the Black Book. A good example is the *Little Red Book of Bristol*, which is typical of borough registers in the fourteenth and fifteenth centuries. In 1344 William de Colford, recorder of Bristol, had copied in this book all the ordinances, customs, and liberties of Bristol because, as he tells us, many customs had been abused and forgotten. For the rest of the fourteenth century and throughout the fifteenth this practice continued and the book became the official memoranda book of the mayor and community of Bristol. There are similar records for such boroughs as Reading, Leicester, and Nottingham; for London there are a number of excellent collections, chief of which is the *Munimenta Gildhallae Londoniensis* (*Muniments of the London Guildhall*). All these records are essential for our knowledge of local borough government; they throw valuable light on the boroughs at the very moment when they were taking a serious interest in parliamentary representation.[4]

Royal correspondence, though most valuable for war and diplomacy, also

[2] SM, no. 70.
[3] SM, no. 71.
[4] SM, no. 72.

gives information on some of the constitutional problems of the fifteenth century. We have collections of letters for all the kings of the fifteenth century, but probably the most helpful are those written by Thomas Beckington, secretary of Henry VI. That Beckington, a confidant of the king and an influential member of the royal council, exerted much authority over domestic and foreign policy is clearly manifest in his letters.

Of nonroyal correspondence the most remarkable and valuable collection comes from the Pastons, a family of industrious and sturdy squires whose lands lay in Norfolk. The letters written by various members of the family to each other as well as to individuals outside the family, many of high rank like Sir John Fastolf, extend from 1422 to 1509. Political history is little enhanced, but there are abundant details on the abuses of the indenture system, the constant litigation, the local feuds and clashes, the family debts and political fortunes, and the negotiations and agreements over lands and marriages. No other source can compare with these letters, which reflect the atmosphere of the fifteenth century and portray a typical county family of squires prominent in local politics and in parliament. They render insignificant such other fifteenth-century letters as the *Cely Correspondence* and the *Plumpton Correspondence*.

Since the great law book of Bracton in the thirteenth century no good histories or tracts on the common law had appeared. The lawyers seemed to be completely occupied by their practice in the law courts and by their training and camaraderie at the Inns of Court. During the fourteenth century mostly anonymous, short tracts were composed on restricted aspects of the law. In the reign of Edward III there was published a selection of judicial writs with a commentary under the title of *Natura Brevium* (*The Nature of Writs*). Another tract from the reign of Edward III entitled the *Novae Narrationes* (*The New Declarations*) consisted of precedents of pleading upon a number of writs commonly used in the courts. The *Articuli ad Novas Narrationes* (*The Articles on New Declarations*), a tract written during the first half of the fifteenth century, dealt with the jurisdiction of courts and the various forms of action. To these treatises should be added the so-called *Register of Writs*, which, though not drawn up by any single author or in any one century, contained all the writs usable in the common law courts. Chancellor after chancellor and justice after justice left their imprint upon the *Register* as they reorganized it and added new writs. A compendium of writs, it was reproduced by lawyers and large landholders for their use. To it the lawyer first went to choose the appropriate writ for bringing a legal action in the proper court. The Middle Ages were drawing to a close when finally there appeared two lawyers, Fortescue and Littleton, who saw the need and had the literary ability to write classic descriptions of the common law.

Details about Fortescue's date of birth and early life are vague. We know that his father served in the French war and was captain of the town of

Meaux and that Fortescue attended Oxford and received his legal training at Lincoln's Inn. By 1430 he was a serjeant-at-law and soon thereafter was a royal judge who rode the circuit of the western counties. In 1442 he was appointed chief justice of the king's bench and the following year he was knighted. Down to 1460 his life was that of a busy judge; then he was swept into the Wars of the Roses and became a staunch supporter of the Lancastrians. Forced into exile by the Yorkist victories of Edward IV, Fortescue accompanied the queen Margaret of Anjou and her son Edward to the Continent and resided in their household as tutor to the young prince until their return to England in 1471. The complete military collapse of the Lancastrians then forced Fortescue to make his submission to Edward IV. He was pardoned and made a member of the royal council, and by 1475 all his estates were restored to him. We hear no more of him after 1476 but assume that he lived to a ripe old age.

The fame of Fortescue rests mainly upon three treatises. The first, written between 1461 and 1463 and entitled *De Natura Legis Naturae* (*On the Nature of the Natural Law*), was intended to uphold the Lancastrian claim to the throne by appeal to natural law. Although chiefly a political pamphlet with a sprinkling of political theory, it holds value for law in its allusions to the condition of legal education, the constitutional position of the king, and the nature of equity. Fortescue's second composition, *De Laudibus Legum Angliae* (*In Praise of English Law*), was written in France. Composed to instruct Prince Edward in the fundamental principles of English law, this book contains the famous distinction of Fortescue between common and civil (Roman) law. He praises the English law as superior to all other laws and presents the earliest account of the Inns of Court, of legal education, and of the ranks of the legal profession. A particularly useful book because of its lucidity and simplicity, it was intended to instruct a layman in the elements of the law. This accounts for its richness of legal detail, a quality lacking in legal tracts meant only for the lawyer. It became extremely popular among lawyers, was copied frequently, and in the sixteenth century was printed and translated into English. Fortescue's third work, entitled the *Monarchia* or *The Governance of England*, was probably composed in 1470. It is similar to the *De Laudibus* in that it discusses the differences between limited and absolute government and contrasts English and French institutions, but it differs in that it probes the causes leading to the Wars of the Roses and masterfully analyzes the weaknesses of Lancastrian government with suggestions for removing them.

More the political theorist and political scientist than most legal writers, Fortescue worked out his ideas on law and government from years of experience. We have him to thank for an eloquent and high-minded defense of such principles as the rule of law and the supremacy of parliament which, at the same time, allows for a strong executive power founded upon the royal prerogative. One cannot fail to admire Fortescue, who acted upon his beliefs when the time of decision arrived. He risked his career and position for a cause in which he had faith. We are indebted to him for his skillful analysis of fifteenth-century government and for his fine description of the law and its profession.

Littleton, the other great legal writer, also has an uncertain date of birth. He received his legal education at the Inner Temple and by 1440 was often referred to as an able legal advocate. By 1453 he was a serjeant-at-law and in 1455 a royal judge of assize in the northern counties. Unlike Fortescue, Littleton did not become embroiled in the civil war, and the shifting political fortunes in no way affected his career. So removed was he from politics that he would give no opinion to the House of Lords on the legal merits of the duke of York's claim to the throne. In 1461 Edward IV made him a royal serjeant and in 1466 appointed him judge of the court of common pleas, a position he held until his death in 1481.

Littleton's great book on *Tenures* was the first text on English law not written in Latin; it was composed in law French and was wholly uninfluenced by the Roman law. Confined to one area of the common law, that of real property, which by the fifteenth century was the most important and complicated part of the law, the treatise was divided into three books and was in the form of a set of letters to his son, a student at Cambridge. The first two books dealt with estates and tenures at real property; the third discussed inheritance and alienation of land. The *Tenures*, the first in a series of textbooks on different branches of the common law, has served as a model of style and method for subsequent scholars. Based upon the Year Books, it went beyond a mere summary of decisions and got down to the "arguments and reasons of the law." It summed up the land law as it was at the end of the fourteenth century before it had been remodeled by the growth of new equitable principles in the chancery during the sixteenth century. This work of Littleton occupies a place comparable to that of the *Commentaries* of Blackstone in the eighteenth century. It is one of the classics in English law and was called by the famous seventeenth-century common law judge Sir Edward Coke "the ornament of the common law, and the most perfect and absolute work that ever was written in any humane science."

2. NARRATIVE SOURCES

During the fifteenth century no contemporary writer produced a comprehensive history of that period. We must rely for an account of the fifteenth century upon a number of short histories and biographies, many strongly partisan, which must be used with discrimination. To compensate for the lack of good histories there were certain noteworthy developments in historiography. At the beginning of the century history was still largely written by ecclesiastics upon the traditional medieval models; by the end of the century this was certainly not true. During the reign of Henry V history written in English was beginning to displace that written in Latin and French. Historical compositions began to exhibit a national consciousness, to speak in terms of national and general interest rather than of special and local interest. Many educated laymen turned their hands to history. Around the middle of the century, for example, various London citizens from the upper middle and commercial classes were writing fresh and spontaneous accounts of contemporary events which formed such London chronicles as *Gregory's Chronicle*, the *Short Chronicle*, and the *Main City Chronicle*.

Only two chronicles, both spotty and meager in their information, record events for the entire Lancastrian period. The *Chronicon Angliae Temporibus Ricardi II, Henrici IV, Henrici V, et Henrici VI* (*The Chronicle of England in the Times of Richard II, Henry IV, Henry V, and Henry VI*) is original and valuable only for the reigns of Henry IV and Henry VI. *An English Chronicle of the Reigns of Richard II and Henry IV, V, and VI* represents a continuation of the *Chronicle* of Brut and was written between 1461 and 1471 by one who was violently Yorkist. It is good only for Henry VI's reign, particularly for the events connected with Cade's rebellion in 1450. All the other writings deal merely with small periods of the century. For the reigns of Henry IV and Henry V, Adam of Usk's *Chronicon* provides some details on the Lancastrian revolution and the Welsh revolt led by Owen Glendower. Usk, a Welshman, who was a priest and lawyer, was violently partisan, first for Henry IV and then against him during the revolt of Glendower. There are only two other chronicles of any value for Henry IV. Capgrave, an Augustinian friar, completed a work entitled the *Illustrious Henries* between 1446 and 1453. The part relating to Henry IV, though a contemporary record, unfortunately provides little more than pious praise of the king. Thomas Otterbourne wrote a *Chronicon Regum Angliae* (*Chronicle of the Kings of England*) which is valuable principally for the first twenty years of the century because it is an independent account with details not found elsewhere.

For the reign of Henry V the most informed source is the *Gesta Henrici Quinti Angliae Regis* (*The Deeds of Henry V King of England*); unfortunately, it covers only the years 1413–1416. Written in an interesting style, it is an account by an anonymous chaplain of Henry V who witnessed the siege of Harfleur and the Battle of Agincourt. The *Vita et Gesta Henrici Quinti* (*The Life and Deeds of Henry V*) by Thomas of Elmham, a monk of Canterbury, is primarily an abridgment of the above work and has little independent value. Other histories which touch upon Henry V are useful mainly for the French campaigns.

Henry VI's long reign is as singularly barren in narrative sources as it was in accomplishment. William of Worcester, secretary to the celebrated Sir John Fastolf, included some useful details on the Wars of the Roses in his *Annals* but he must be used with caution because of his Yorkist leanings. Other histories that deal with Henry VI are chiefly interested in the Wars of the Roses and in the rise of the Yorkists. Only John Blackman's *Life of Henry VI* concentrates on the king and then but to describe the royal character rather than to discuss royal policy.

We are better informed about Edward IV. The *Continuation of the Croyland Chronicle* by an anonymous writer covers the period between 1459 and 1485 and is a detailed narrative of events from 1471 to Bosworth Field. Contemporary to the events he describes, the writer seems to have had some close connection with Edward IV, to whom he was extremely sympathetic, while on the other hand he was very hostile towards Richard III. The chronicle is especially useful for its material on the fall of the duke of Clarence. The *History of the Arrival of Edward IV* was an authorized Yorkist version of the struggle with the Lancastrians written by someone in the household of Edward IV. Though of the Yorkist camp, the author does a magnificent job of describing the various campaigns, notably those of Barnet and Tewkesbury. Two French works supplement these histories. The *Recueil des chroniques et anciennes histoires de la Grande Bretagne* by John de Wavrin, a member of a noble Artois family who fought in various campaigns of the French war, is original and contemporary for the period between 1444 and 1471. Wavrin seems to have met the earl of Warwick and to have secured from him some interesting episodes on the English civil war. There are lastly the celebrated *Mémoires* of Philip de Comines, councillor of both Charles the Rash of Burgundy and Louis XI of France. Comines met a number of the leading Yorkist and Lancastrian figures and was well informed about Edward IV, whom he held in low esteem.

One of the few contemporary accounts of Richard III's reign and an extremely hostile one is the *Continuation of the Croyland Chronicle*. Sir Thomas More's celebrated *History of King Richard III*, written in 1513, set the tone for all subsequent accounts of Richard. Violently Tudor, it painted an evil portrait of Richard. Most of what More wrote, however, is valuable because he secured his information from John Morton, bishop of Ely and a prominent Yorkist councillor, who was an eyewitness to the swift-moving events of Richard III's reign. Although the *Seventeen Books of English History* by the Italian historian Polydore Vergil is on the whole a scholarly work, critical of some aspects of English history, this cannot be said of the three books that cover the reigns of Edward IV, Edward V, and Richard III. Vergil, who lived in England from 1505 to 1550 as a sort of court historiographer for Henry VII, incorporated whatever information he could to blacken the reputation of Richard III. Of the same mold is Edward Hall's *Chronicle*, which was first published in 1542; it is fundamentally a glorification of the house of Tudor. The present-day historian who deals with Richard III and the events of his reign is almost completely at the mercy of hostile sources written subsequently under the Tudors. Only by delving into the official records can the historian hope to provide a more balanced account of England's royal arch villain.

We have not yet spoken of the chronicles of London. They are probably the most important source for English history in the fifteenth century, partly because of the paucity of other narrative sources but mostly because of their own intrinsic worth. Written in English, they give contemporary accounts and, in spite of recounting many trivialities, reflect popular opinion of the capital on some of the great political and military issues. The historian must remember, however, that this was local, not national, opinion; the two were not necessarily the same. The chronicles of London seem to have originated from the need for a record giving the names and dates of tenure of the municipal officers. Gradually it became customary to add notices of important civic events and great national events. Inasmuch as London was the center of the realm much local news was national news. The events which the compiler deemed worthy of inclusion were listed under the years of the mayoralty, each year being headed by the names of the mayor and sheriffs of London.

Seven of the London chronicles are of special interest for the fifteenth century; and of these, three provide a reasonably good account of England in the middle of the century. The *Great Chronicle*, a composite of a number of chronicles, gives a good summary of the parliaments between 1423 and 1428 and of the feud between Henry Beaufort, bishop of Winchester, and Duke Humphrey of Gloucester. It also includes descriptions of foreign affairs and texts of treaties and letters. *Gregory's Chronicle*, which owes its name to an entry of 1451–1452 referring to the mayor William Gregory, is excellent for the period between 1440 and 1470. The author had a pronounced sense of humor and wit which he projected upon various historical episodes. At one point in the chronicle while commenting upon the high prices and dearth of housing, he wrote that "Lyard my horse had more ease than some good yeomen; for my horse stood in the house, and the yeomen sometimes lay without in the street; for less than 4*d.* a man should not have a bed a night." The third major chronicle is *The Main City Chronicle*, which was the work of a number of writers and which deals with events between 1440 and 1485. Robert Fabyan, who was made sheriff of London in 1493, made use of a number of these London chronicles when he wrote *The New Chronicles of England and France* (also called *The Concordance of Histories*). He made no pretense to originality and admitted that his work was "gathered with small understanding." It is nothing more than a compilation and condensation of material taken from other chronicles with no attempt at harmonizing them or at criticizing their content. If Fabyan is valuable at all, it is for the reigns of Edward IV and Richard III, on which he has included some facts not found in other histories.

3. THE REIGN OF HENRY IV (1399–1413)

King of England by virtue of successful revolution, Henry IV, first of the Lancastrians, was known to his subjects more as a fighter than as a statesman.

While they were familiar with Henry's crusade against the heathen Lithuanians and with his fight against the Turks, they knew almost nothing about his political qualities, qualities that were to make his revolution a success. Thirty-four years of age when he mounted the throne, Henry was a stout, powerful, and handsome man imbued with extraordinary vitality. Though he had gained fame as a chivalrous knight and though he was courteous, tactful, and suave, he could be unscrupulous and cruel when necessary. From his father John of Gaunt he inherited a deep-seated ambition that accounts for his gamble for the throne. Generally in control of his emotions, Henry was a cold and unsympathetic man of business; efficiency was his great virtue. His murder of Richard II, an act not in character for a man usually moderate in political behavior, could be justified as necessary and politic. A man who made few friends and who was burdened with poor health after the first few years of his reign, Henry became gloomy, suspicious, and victim to epileptic fits which, worsened by political pressure, led to his death. But the practical, hardheaded Henry was endowed with the right qualities to make his revolution enduring; this was his greatest achievement.

Not until 1408 could Henry feel that his crown was secure. It took almost constant fighting to reduce those elements which would not have a Lancastrian as their king. Dispossessed and disaffected supporters of Richard II conspired and attempted to capture Henry at Windsor Castle. The plot was quickly discovered and snuffed out but it demonstrated to Henry that Richard was too dangerous to be left alive. In early February of 1400 murder ended Richard's cruel imprisonment in Pontefract Castle. Another serious threat to Henry's position was posed by France, which remained true to Isabella, the widow of Richard II. Then, too, there was Scotland, which always welcomed the opportunity to embarrass the English kings. Already in 1400 the Scots threatened the northern counties and an expedition against them ended in failure. Not until 1402 was the Scottish menace terminated by a brilliant victory won over the Scots at Homildon Hill by the Percies, a great northern noble family. Henceforth Scotland was too weakened by civil war to think of military interference, and in 1406 fortune smiled upon Henry IV. Prince James, heir to the Scottish throne, was captured by English seamen while en route to France and was retained by Henry to blackmail the Scots.

Meanwhile Henry had to face an even more formidable revolt in Wales. In 1400 there had occurred a local feud between an English marcher lord and a Welsh noble, Owen Glendower. Henry's support of the marcher lord forced Glendower into revolt which quickly spread throughout Wales. A talented soldier, Glendower defeated three armies sent against him and in 1403 gained as allies the formidable Percies, who felt that they had not been suitably rewarded for their support in the revolution and in the campaigns against the Scots. The Percies marched south to join forces with Glendower but Henry managed to intercept them before they reached Wales. At Shrewsbury Henry won a decisive victory over the Percies; Harry Hotspur, the son of the earl of Northumberland, was killed, and other influential Percies were captured. This was the battle that saved Henry's throne. Glendower, however, was still powerful; he defeated a fourth army and concluded a French alliance. The French now raided the southern coast, pirated in the English Channel, and in 1405 sent an expeditionary force to help Glendower. That same year the old Percy, the earl of Northumberland, still burning for revenge, conspired with the archbishop of York and accused Henry of usurpation and misgovernment. Prompt action on Henry's part resulted in the capture of the archbishop, who was summarily beheaded. Northumberland continued the fight until killed in 1408.

Despite the continuing revolt of Glendower, Henry was now secure. The French were no longer a menace. Their king Charles VI had become hopelessly insane and two factions of French nobles, one led by the duke of Burgundy and the other by the duke of Orléans, paralyzed France in their struggle for political power. Meanwhile Henry's eldest son, the future Henry V, was systematically reducing Wales and driving Glendower into a corner. Although Henry played the Burgundian faction off against the Orléanist faction, he had no intention of renewing the French war. He was therefore infuriated when in 1411 his son Henry secretly sent a small force of twelve hundred men to France in support of the Burgundians. It easily won a victory at Saint Cloud but Henry IV immediately recalled it and censured his insubordinate son. This disagreement over French policy deepened the rift between father and son and saddened the few years remaining to the sick king. Assisted by his father's half brothers the Beauforts, who were the bastard issue of John of Gaunt by Catherine Swyneford, Prince Henry worked against royal policy and such royal ministers as Archbishop Arundel of Canterbury, who supported the king. Already the ground was being sown with the seeds of aristocratic strife that were to sicken England for the next seventy years. In bad health and disillusioned by the vicious court politics, Henry IV declined rapidly in 1413. By March he could no longer ride a horse or take an intelligent part in the government. He wandered about London in a world of make-believe, convinced that he was about to depart on a great crusade. On 20 March he died. And as the chronicler said, "the unquiet time of Henry IV" had ended and "his first-born son began to reign."

4. THE REIGN OF HENRY V (1413–1422)

Henry V came to the throne at the age of twenty-five. He had demonstrated his military capacity but his ability in politics was less certain and his character was indeed dubious. The power-hungry Beauforts had easily used him in their shrewd political maneuvers and his unsteady and adolescent nature did not console those who desired stability and sobriety in their king. In body, mind, and personality the gods had smiled upon Henry. He had an abundance of physical stamina and excelled in sports; according to a chronicler, he could run faster than a buck. He was ambitious, hotheaded, and loyal to his companions, with whom he caroused and wasted much of his time. In the words of a contemporary writer "he was the fervent soldier of Venus as well as of Mars" and repeatedly became involved in unsavory adventures pursued in tavern and along dark London alleys. But like many men upon whom responsibility has fallen, Henry was transformed and became every inch the king. He immediately vowed a new life and resolved to do his duty. Everyone marveled at his sober and grave bearing, at his newfound piety, at his deep sense of responsibility. He was glorified by subsequent historians and Shakespeare as the model king. Unfortunately for England, however, a model king who worked for glory and military conquest was not what she required. Rather, she needed a long reign by one such as Henry IV. The legacy left by Henry V to later ages may have been the heroic epic of great feats of arms but the immediate legacy was sixty years of civil strife and drift.

From the outset of his reign Henry's chief concern and only preoccupation was the conquest of France. Despite the still weak hold of the Lancastrian dynasty, the aristocratic plots, and the disorder in west and north, Henry thought only of imperialist ventures in France and of winning military prestige for his family. Although he made a show of negotiating with the disunited French and was offered generous concessions, his claims were exorbitant. Henry was bent upon war and probably sincerely believed in his claims and in God's favor. While negotiating with the French, he secured parliamentary grants, forged an army, and looked to his transport and supplies; by the summer of 1415 he was prepared to strike.

In August 1415 Henry V sailed from Southampton with a small army of six thousand archers and two thousand men-at-arms, supplemented with various supporting units of specialists. Landing at Harfleur at the estuary of the Seine River, Henry laid siege to it and took it after five desperate weeks during which his army was reduced and weakened by dysentery. Realizing that he could do no more with his depleted forces, he determined to march quickly to Calais, return to England for more men, and then continue the campaign. But his march was delayed at the Somme River where he found his passage blocked by destroyed bridges; after much delay he found a bridge up the river and got across. By this time the French had collected a large army and blocked further advance at the village of Agincourt in Artois. Here Henry showed his great ability as a general. He not only held his depleted and exhausted army together but kept its morale at high pitch for the encounter with a huge force. When the battle ended Henry had won a victory greater than that of Crécy or Poitiers. The French knights had again been annihilated by a shrewd combination of archers and men-at-arms. There were seven thousand French casualties as against five hundred English.

Henry returned home a hero and received the grateful thanks of his enthusiastic subjects.

Henry realized that although he had gained a brilliant victory the war had yet to be won and that to reduce northern France would require hard campaigning. Not until 1417 was he ready to carry out the conquest of Normandy. After two years of steady campaigning, which consisted mostly of reducing towns and fortresses, Henry conquered Normandy. His success so alarmed the Burgundian and Orléanist leaders that they met in September 1419 on a bridge at Montereau to negotiate their differences and to plan a united front against the English. But when one of the Orléanists murdered Duke John the Fearless of Burgundy, any chance of a *rapprochement* ended. The new Burgundian duke Philip the Good immediately formed a military alliance with Henry and brought the unfaithful wife of Charles VI into a tripartite agreement sealed by the Treaty of Troyes in 1420. According to its terms the queen repudiated her son the dauphin as successor to Charles VI and agreed that Henry should succeed Charles as king of France upon the death of that unhappy monarch. To bind the agreement Henry was to marry Charles VI's daughter Catherine. Duke Philip the Good was to receive various territorial concessions in France.

The Treaty of Troyes marked the summit of Henry V's success. He had suddenly achieved more than he had even dreamed of or prayed for. But the permanent reduction of France was a political, military, and economic impossibility. England's resources were on the verge of complete exhaustion and France was too large and too hostile to permit foreign conquest and occupation. If Henry had ruled for another thirty years he would have tasted bitter defeat. France proved to be a bottomless hole into which English men and money were poured. Henry, however, immediately pushed southward and spent most of 1421 and part of 1422 reducing more French strongholds. After a six months' siege of Meaux, worn out by his exertions and dysentery, he died in August 1422 at the age of thirty-five. He died amidst military renown and success but at the price of misery for France and economic and political shipwreck for England. To Henry VI, his infant son of nine months, Henry V left only trouble, military and political, that was to haunt the Lancastrian dynasty down to its miserable end. When Charles VI of France shortly followed Henry in death, a sterile reign of forty-two years was ended.

5. THE REIGN OF HENRY VI (1422–1461)

Upon the succession of Henry VI to the English throne the chronicler might well quote the old adage: "Woe to the land when the king is a child." All England feared a minority and the political confusion that inevitably went with it. In the case of Henry VI there was to be a minority and chaos for almost forty years. Henry VI inherited the physical weaknesses of the Lancastrians and the mental infirmity of the Valois king Charles VI. In poor health all his life, Henry became subject to mental disturbances early in his manhood that eventually clouded his mind. Perhaps, if not subjected to the pressures and demands of kingship, he might have escaped insanity, but such a boon did not fall to this mild, honest, virtuous, and pious man. Poor Henry was as ill equipped for the crown as was Edward the Confessor; he loved literature, the arts, and the founding of university colleges and public schools such as Eton. This pitiful man was uncertain, unstable, overgenerous with his friends, and naïve towards his enemies. Shocked at the sight of bloodshed, he was fated to witness a succession of political executions. Essentially a figurehead, he was the helpless puppet of unscrupulous political factions who paraded him about in mockery. Captured three times in battle, he knew not how to fight and never raised a sword in anger. From a life of mental confusion and political failure in all that he attempted, Henry was released by murder in 1471 and sent on to a better world.

According to Henry V's deathbed instructions his two brothers were to direct the affairs of England and France during the minority. Duke Humphrey of Gloucester was to be protector and head of the royal council in England. This selection was unfortunate; Humphrey was untalented as a statesman and was consumed by greed, rashness, and jealousy. He attempted to become regent but was thwarted by the council, which distrusted his objectives and dishonest ways. It was the council, dominated by Henry Beaufort, bishop of Winchester, that controlled England during the early years of Henry VI's reign. Though no more scrupulous than Humphrey and equally ambitious for political power, Henry Beaufort (the son of John of Gaunt and his mistress Catherine Swyneford) was far more able and politic. By virtue of his enormous wealth he kept England in debt to him. The lines of political battle were drawn; strife flared up that sickened England for the rest of the century.

Henry V's choice of his brother Duke John of Bedford as administrator and military commander in France was wise. Bedford was a talented general and an able and conscientious administrator who achieved immediate success against obstacles that ultimately were to sweep the English from the Continent. He repeatedly won victories and though he gave northern France better and more honest government than the Valois he could not overcome the French hatred, their growing spirit of nationalism, and the lack of support from England. Bedford managed, however, to hold his own until 1429 when the spirit and strength of France were stimulated and unified by Joan of Arc. However one interprets the amazing success of Joan, he must admit that she accomplished a miracle. She inspired the French soldiers to relieve Orléans and to take the offensive against the English. She restored confidence to the dauphin and marched him across France to be crowned Charles VII in Reims Cathedral. She symbolized the soul of an awakened France. Her capture in 1430 and her death at the stake in 1431 did not stem the tide of French success. No man or army could henceforth stop a revived France.

Until his death in 1435 Bedford did everything possible to buttress the English cause. He took Henry to Paris and had him crowned king of France. He persuaded a reluctant parliament to vote him money. He held on to the Burgundian alliance as long as he could. But he struggled in vain. No Frenchman recognized Henry VI, parliament had no heart for a war that had lost its glamor and brought only financial loss, and in 1435 Duke Philip the Good of Burgundy made peace with Charles VII at Arras and the English were left to carry on the fight alone. Fortunately Bedford died in 1435 and was spared witnessing the disaster that followed.

Humphrey of Gloucester, who stood next in line of succession, argued that the French war must be prosecuted. He was opposed by Henry Beaufort, by Beaufort's two nephews John and Edmund Beaufort, and by William de la Pole, the earl of Suffolk, all of whom were convinced that England must conclude peace with France. Henry VI supported the Beaufort faction but in so feeble a manner that Humphrey was able to muster enough strength to continue the enervating war until he finally retired from active politics in 1444. By then the war was progressing so badly that the royal council, consisting entirely of the Beaufort party, tried to arrange peace by negotiating the marriage of Henry VI to Margaret of Anjou, a spirited and ambitious French princess of sixteen. In 1445 the marriage was celebrated. A brief truce ensued but at the price of surrendering more territory to France. By 1449 the war had been renewed by Charles VII and in 1450 Normandy was lost. The distraught English now vented their fury upon Henry VI's principal minister William de la Pole, recently created duke of Suffolk. His political enemies moved against him and he was impeached in parliament on the charges of misgovernment, malversation, and treasonable negotiations with the French. While attempting to escape by boat to France he was intercepted and beheaded in the English Channel. Three years later the ordeal ended. In 1453 the French captured the last English towns in Gascony; Calais alone remained to England. The Hundred Years' War had ended in the only way it could.

With the death of the duke of Suffolk in 1450 Henry VI was deprived of the services of his last loyal minister. Henceforth he was to be counseled by the incompetent Edmund Beaufort, duke of Somerset, and by the queen Margaret of Anjou, who became the real head of the Lancastrian house. But time was running out. Beaten on the Continent, incapable of preserving law and order at home, and without proper financial resources, Henry VI and his council became the targets for bitter attack. There arose in the late 1440's a new political leader against the Beaufort gang—Richard, duke of York. Descended from Duke Edmund of York, the fourth eldest son of Edward III, Richard could also claim descent through female inheritance from Edward III's second eldest son, Duke Lionel of Clarence. He could thus claim descent from a line senior to the Lancastrian, which came from John of Gaunt, Edward III's third eldest son. At first Richard had no royal ambitions but eventually his resentment against ineffective government and his shoddy treatment at the hands of Edmund Beaufort pushed him towards open opposition to Henry VI.

The year 1453 was crucial for the Lancastrian dynasty. It was marked by the loss of all territory in France, by the birth of a Lancastrian heir, Edward, and by the insanity of Henry VI. This combination of events was enough to trigger the civil strife—the Wars of the Roses—that gripped England down to 1485. Now that Henry VI had an heir, Margaret of Anjou's one consuming ambition was to protect the throne, especially against Richard, duke of York, who had the best claim and was the most popular leader of the opposition. Richard, who had waited patiently, hoping that there would be no Lancastrian heir, now realized that only force would secure the throne. Both sides jockeyed for power but Richard did not march upon London until he was convinced that Margaret of Anjou and Edmund Beaufort meant to destroy him. In May 1455 he and his supporters marched towards London and were met by a Lancastrian army at Saint Albans. Here Richard triumphed, killed Beaufort, and captured the king. Still Richard withheld making a bid for the crown and attempted to give England good government in his capacity of protector. Margaret and her party would not compromise with him, however, and in 1456 he was dismissed. Both parties now prepared for war, which broke out again in 1459. By 1460 the strife became so bitter that York claimed the throne. Then just after Christmas he and one of his strongest supporters, the earl of Salisbury, were defeated at the Battle of Wakefield by Margaret of Anjou and a Lancastrian army; York was slain and Salisbury beheaded. In February 1461 Margaret marched south and defeated the powerful Yorkist noble, the earl of Warwick, in the Second Battle of Saint Albans. Her great mistake was in not entering London. Warwick and Edward of York, the son of Richard, united the remnants of the Yorkist forces and slipped into London. In March 1461 at the age of nineteen Edward was crowned as Edward IV, the first king of the short-lived Yorkist dynasty.

6. THE REIGN OF EDWARD IV (1461–1483)

As soon as he was crowned, Edward IV marched north to engage the Lancastrian army under Margaret of Anjou. On Palm Sunday a bitter contest was fought in a blinding snowstorm; at its end Edward IV and Warwick had totally defeated the Lancastrians. Though Margaret attempted to carry on the fight from Scotland she was finally compelled in 1463 to flee to the Continent. She, her son Edward, and a small group of devoted followers settled in France where they remained in exile until 1471. For the moment Edward IV was master of England. He was content to relax from his exertions and to enjoy himself while Warwick "the kingmaker" managed the realm. During the first three years of his reign Edward IV appeared to be a man whose only exceptional quality was military leadership; he seemingly spent most of his time in merrymaking and drinking. Beneath this façade of indolence and pleasure-seeking, however, was considerable political skill. In 1464 without Warwick's knowledge Edward suddenly married the beautiful young widow Elizabeth Woodville, who came from a very ordinary family of Lancastrian connections. Warwick, in the midst of negotiating a marriage with a French princess, was infuriated. Soon thereafter Edward again showed his independence by going against Warwick's advice in concluding an alliance with Burgundy and marrying his sister Margaret to Duke Charles the Rash. Warwick, now realizing that his power was at an end, worked to foment revolt against Edward and won over to his side Edward's brother George, duke of Clarence. In 1470 Edward discovered the conspiracy and declared Warwick and Clarence traitors. They fled to France where through the skilled mediation of the French king Louis XI they were induced to parley with Margaret of Anjou and to unite in common opposition to Edward IV. To cement the alliance Warwick's youngest daughter Anne was to marry Margaret's son Edward.

With French backing Warwick suddenly invaded England in September 1470. Caught by surprise Edward IV took flight and went to the court of his brother-in-law Charles the Rash. Warwick occupied London, released Henry VI from the Tower of London, and placed him once again upon the throne. In all but name, however, Warwick was king. His success was brief. By March 1471 Edward IV had landed with an army fitted out by Charles the Rash. Warwick frantically appealed to Margaret of Anjou to come over from France with reinforcements but she procrastinated and arrived too late. On the very day of her landing in England, Easter Sunday, the fourteenth of April, Edward IV and Warwick fought a desperate battle at Barnet; Warwick was defeated and slain. Edward then moved rapidly to head off Margaret's march to the west country where she could count upon reinforcements. On 4 May he caught her at Tewkesbury and crushed her army. Most of the leading Lancastrian nobles were killed, Margaret was captured, and her son Edward was put to death. Edward IV returned in triumph to London and the day after his arrival news was given out that poor Henry VI had died in the Tower of London out "of pure displeasure and melancholy." After some years of captivity Margaret of Anjou was ransomed by the French king and she returned to France to die of a lingering illness.

Edward IV, finally secure, ruled in peace until he died in bed in 1483. Only the unstable and fickle duke of Clarence seemed unwilling to cooperate and he was finally executed in the Tower of London in 1478. Though he loved pleasure and devoted much time to his mistresses and to gratifying his physical appetites, Edward had some political capacity. He partially restored order to England, started the machinery of justice and administration functioning again, supported the economic aspirations of England's strong middle class, secured advantageous commercial concessions from such northern powers as the German Hanse and the Low Countries, buttressed the sagging finances, and restored power and dignity to the crown. Although in 1474 it looked as if he intended to join Charles the Rash in war against Louis XI of France, in 1475 he concluded the Treaty of Picquigny with the wily Louis XI, who persuaded him to drop his projected invasion of France in return for a large sum of money and an annual pension of fifty thousand gold crowns. This additional income further strengthened the royal position and freed Edward from depending upon parliamentary taxation. When he died in 1483 at the age of forty, worn out by his dissolute life, Edward IV had advanced England well along the road that might have ended in absolute monarchy. His principal failure was not to provide for an orderly succession.

7. THE REIGN OF RICHARD III (1483–1485)

Edward IV left two young sons, Edward the Prince of Wales, aged twelve, and Richard, aged nine, as well as several daughters. Edward IV had arranged for his brother Richard, duke of Gloucester, to be protector during the minority of Edward V. An able administrator and skilled warrior, the duke seemed the most logical man for the position of trust. Contrary to the usual picture derived from Tudor historians, he was no sinister, deformed monster but a respected man with a reputation for loyal service to his brother and efficient government in northern England. That he was ambitious and greedy will not be denied, but in the fifteenth century what English noble was not? Bitterly opposed to the arrangements for the minority, however, were the maternal relatives of Edward V, the Woodvilles and Greys, who were in charge of Edward and feared what Richard might do with him. That Richard despised the upstart relatives of Edward V was well known and there was good reason to distrust the new protector of the realm. A struggle for power developed at once and Richard quickly won. Undoubtedly from the outset Richard had planned to seize the royal power; his speedy triumph was aided by the almost psychopathic feeling of most Englishmen against a minority.

Richard's aim was to secure control of his nephew Edward V and to have the unpopular Woodvilles and Greys beheaded. Working closely with the unscrupulous duke of Buckingham, Richard soon had both Edward and his brother Richard behind the strong ramparts of the Tower of London and struck down those Yorkists such as Lord Hastings who opposed his ruthless climb to power. But nearly everyone seemed cowed or was reluctant to oppose Richard and to renew a dreaded civil war. He now had Edward and Richard and their sisters declared illegitimate and had his henchmen such as Buckingham drum up support for him as king. Though few enthusiastically backed him, no one offered any strong opposition, and he was accepted by parliament and crowned as Richard III on 26 June 1483. Because it was obviously dangerous to leave his two nephews alive in the Tower, two trusted servants murdered them one night in their chamber. By this cruel act Richard overstepped the limits of what most men could accept; no matter how much they abhorred civil strife and in spite of what Richard promised them, they could not condone an uncle's brutal murder of two innocent nephews.

Buckingham, dissatisfied with the spoils Richard had allotted to him, was the first to raise the standard of revolt. He was unsuccessful and paid with his life. Meanwhile both Yorkist and Lancastrian nobles cast about for a leader around whom they could rally. They found him in Henry Tudor, earl of Richmond, who was living in exile in France. On his mother's side Henry traced his descent back to the Beauforts, the bastard issue of John of Gaunt. On his father's side he traced his descent back to the Welsh noble Owen Tudor who had married Henry V's widow Catherine of France. While neither descent gave Henry a strong claim to the throne, some claim was better than none, and both Yorkist and Lancastrian men rallied around him. Elizabeth of York, the eldest daughter of Edward IV who was living in the sanctuary of Westminster Abbey, had the best claim, but few men could become enthusiastic about supporting a female ruler. To fuse the Yorkist and Lancastrian houses it was agreed that Henry Tudor and Elizabeth of York were to marry after Richard III had been removed. As for Richard, his qualities as an able soldier and administrator and a successful ruler were not enough to neutralize the evil he had done. His supporters drifted away from him and his position was worsened by the death of his only son in 1484. Standing almost alone, Richard made heroic efforts to save his crown. He levied a mobile army which was ready to strike in any direction, vigilantly defended the southern coast, and oversaw every detail. But his cause was hopeless; no mortal effort could stem the tide swelling against him.

In August 1485 Henry Tudor, with a small army composed partly of Yorkist and Lancastrian nobles and of some French troops, landed at Milford Haven in southwestern Wales. As he swiftly moved east into England men flocked to his banner and Richard's lieutenants failed to keep him bottled up in Wales. He continued to augment his army and marched into the Midlands close to Leicester where he met Richard's army at Bosworth Field. Though Richard had the larger army and was the abler commander, there was treachery on his side; at the critical moment of the battle large elements of his troops and their leaders deserted to Henry. Courageously facing death, Richard threw himself headlong into the fray and attempted to strike down Henry Tudor. He managed to slay Henry's standard bearer and another renowned warrior who was next to Henry. He even crossed swords with Henry but was then swept over by a mass of Tudor men and cut to pieces. The golden crown of Richard III which had fallen to the ground was retrieved and placed upon Henry's head by his triumphant troops. As the naked and battered corpse of Richard III, bloody and hideous for all to see, was slung across a horse and borne away to an obscure grave, Henry VII, the first of the strong Tudor dynasty, turned towards Westminster, to the task of delivering England from a gloomy century of strife and of setting the weary kingdom upon a course that was to take it through one of its grandest and most heroic centuries.

XXXVI

Administrative Council and Parliament

THE fifteenth century remains a trap for those who would uncover its contributions to English constitutional history. The records, numerous and difficult to work with, have only recently received the studious attention lavished upon the sources of preceding centuries. Some of the most important sources such as the Year Books and Plea Rolls have just begun to be edited and published. The dearth of printed material has hindered research on constitutional problems in the fifteenth century. Fortunately much work has been done in recent years enabling the constitutional history of the fifteenth century to be discussed with more accuracy and objectivity.

At present historians are freeing themselves from the shadow of interpretations propounded long ago by scholars working without adequate sources and without other studies to help chart their course. Inevitably these early historians arrived at distorted conclusions. Stubbs, the great pioneer, had to rely primarily upon the Parliament Rolls and the chronicles. The nature of the evidence (almost completely on parliament) and the era in which he wrote (the second half of the nineteenth century) obviously influenced his outlook and caused him to view the fifteenth century as a time of great constitutional experimentation. He believed that in this period there occurred a premature testing of the strength of parliament, that the Lancastrians ruled as constitutional monarchs, and that the Yorkists defied this precedent. Stubbs considered fifteenth-century constitutionalism almost modern in its practices and ideals; he attributed the delay in its further advance to the fact that it had outrun administrative order and that the strong-willed Yorkists and Tudors labored to impede it. This Stubbsian interpretation has been embraced by most historians; only in recent years has it been viewed critically. Although the history of parliament remains the dominant theme of the fifteenth century, increasingly attention is being diverted from it to the crown and other institutions, about which more is coming to be known. Particularly is this true with the king's council. We shall discuss, as fully and accurately as the evidence and state of knowledge permit, the two principal institutions of fifteenth-century England—council and parliament. But first we must inquire into the powers of kingship and its place in the government.

1. KINGSHIP

That the Lancastrian Revolution pared down the royal power is evident to anyone familiar with the dramatic events of 1399. It is not so apparent, however, that the practical powers of kingship, rather than the theoretical powers, were the ones weakened. In addition, the abnormal political, military, and financial situation that the Lancastrian kings had to meet continued to enforce a limitation upon their practical powers. Bereft of a sound claim to the throne, uncertain of their newly acquired power, dependent upon parliament for taxes to prosecute an ever less popular and less successful French war, unequal in political ability, and, in the cases of Henry IV and Henry VI, weak in body or mind, the Lancastrians were rarely in a position to wield what had traditionally been the royal powers, what contemporaries called the powers of the "estate of the king." The Lancastrian Revolution destroyed the abnormally high theoretical claims of Richard II but left untouched the prerogatives traditionally enjoyed by English kings. What was swept away had never been claimed even by such kings as William the Conqueror and Henry II.

Under all the Lancastrians, even Henry VI, men admitted to and believed in certain majestic powers comprising the "estate of the king," that highest estate temporal of the realm. Even in the last moments before the civil war in 1452 Richard, duke of York, swore not to attack the "roiall estate." The royal estate was a necessity to which no one could see an alternative; it was the heart of the body politic. Men believed in the sacrosanctity and miraculous powers of regality conferred by divine grace. Men pointed to three principal attributes of regality. The kings of England had "liberty" in order that they might enforce the laws and do justice. This liberty was a discretionary power to be used in the interest of law and justice and not for their own personal gain. By means of the "royal will" liberty was exercised and maintained. It was Archbishop Arundel of Canterbury who declared in the opening address of Henry IV's first parliament that it was the king's will that the liberties of the church as well as those of lords and boroughs be maintained and that there be justice and equity for all. Finally, the kings of England had "grace," by which they accepted political innovation. On one occasion when the commons petitioned Henry V to permit their bills to be engrossed without change, he granted the request out of his special grace. There was also a generally held conception that the king was a public person or prince who held the realm as real property which, however, was of a public character and could not be disposed of as private property. The royal proprietorship was public and must be shared with the community of the realm. Such was the fifteenth-century opinion of the royal estate. By the coronation oath the kings committed themselves to formal acceptance of the moral duties of their estate. The kings swore to keep the peace for church and for their subjects, to do justice in mercy and in truth, and to uphold the laws of the realm. By this oath they formally and publicly promised to discharge the duties of their kingly office to which God had called them. They bound themselves before God, as Fortescue said, to the observance of the laws. And the community of the realm was justified in removing them when they did not govern by the law.

Although Henry IV owed his crown to conquest and to parliamentary title he emphasized all the notions traditionally associated with royal succession. He claimed the realm, the crown, and all the appurtenant rights by virtue of descent of the true line, by divine grace, and by the right and duty of removing a king who had misgoverned the realm and failed to uphold its laws.[1] By such claims the Lancastrians hoped to eradicate the memory of conquest and parliamentary title, but they were never successful. As late as 1460 both the lords and lawyers vividly recalled that Henry VI owed his crown originally to parliamentary title, and for a time they were reluctant to admit the counterclaim of Richard of York. But the Yorkist cause was strong and both lords and lawyers were faced with deciding upon a claim to the crown put forward on the grounds of hereditary right alone. The lawyers cleverly pleaded their inability to meddle in such a matter and the lords were obliged to deal with the Yorkist claim by themselves. Despite the fact that their predecessors in parliament had given the royal title to the Lancastrians and despite their oath of allegiance to Henry VI, they realistically decided that the Yorkist claim could not be defeated. In so doing they admitted that the theory of parliamentary right to determine the succession to the throne was subordinate to the theory of the right of the divine law of inheritance. The Yorkists, therefore, claimed rule by heritable and legitimate right and by that only. To be sure, Richard III was declared king not only by right of consanguinity and inheritance but also by right of lawful election by parliament, consecration, and coronation. But he emphasized the force of legitimism and paid but lip service to the authority of parliament. Two years later when Henry Tudor mounted the throne neither the fiction of legitimism nor parliamentary election was raised. He had parliament enact a statute declaring that he was now king and that the crown should pass on to the heirs of his body. We must conclude that each dynasty used the claims and fictions that provided them with the most support; Henry Tudor was the most realistic of all because he understood and admitted that he was king by success in arms and that he would remain king only so long as he had sufficient power. There was no clear law of royal succession; only strong kings could perpetuate a dynasty.

In the sixteenth century a differentiation developed between the royal

[1] SM, no. 66A.

person and the royal office whereas in the fifteenth century no such distinction was drawn between the person of the king and the crown. Men thought it impossible to set up a dichotomy between the royal person and royal authority. Full responsibility fell upon the person, not the office, and the royal person was held fully accountable for his governance, the success of which, loyal subjects would admit, required taxation and counsel given in parliament. But to be effective in his governance the king must also have his prerogative, that is, a reservoir of undefined powers necessary for every ruler to deal with emergencies. The royal prerogative implied an amplitude of power, or what may be termed sovereignty.

This was not an unlimited sovereignty; it was good and accepted opinion that the king was limited in his prerogative power. In the great affairs of state the king was limited by the assent of the realm given in parliament. The fifteenth century held firmly to the traditional English medieval political opinion that ultimate sovereignty resided not in the king but in the law, that the king was below the law, and that for all lawful legislation and taxation the king must obtain the assent of those affected, and that in parliament. Fortescue truly expressed the political opinion of England when he proclaimed that the king of England "cannot at his pleasure change the laws of his kingdom," but that the laws of England "are established not only by the prince's will but by the assent of the whole kingdom." Although the theoretical powers of kingship remained in the fifteenth century, the actual powers of kingship were limited by the law and its guardian, parliament. England was a limited monarchy.

2. THE ADMINISTRATIVE COUNCIL

Despite the abrupt political and dynastic changes during the fifteenth century there were few fundamental modifications in the central administration. Royal administration was essentially the same as in the fourteenth century; that it was less efficient is attributable to the civil strife and weak kingship. Strong and effective government still depended upon the king, in whom supreme executive authority was invested. The success of royal government was so inextricably tied to the capacity of the king that, like a barometer, it reflected the strengths and weaknesses of the successive kings. The administrative machinery of medieval England could not operate properly without the vigorous exercise of royal authority. During the long and ineffective reign of Henry VI the system declined for lack of firm direction and because of the factional strife of the great magnates for power. With the partial revival of royal power under Edward IV and Richard III there was a concurrent revival of effective administration. Truly effective government would not return to England, however, until the strong Tudors had firmly imposed their will upon the realm.

During the fifteenth century the only substantial innovation in royal administration was the institutionalization of the royal council and the rise of the royal secretary to administrative power. All the other departments such as the chancery, exchequer, and privy seal continued unchanged. It is first to the council and then to the secretary that we must devote our attention because upon these two executive organs the Tudors were to revive strong government and through them to express their strong will.

Two types of council existed in the fifteenth century. One, the great council, may be disposed of quickly. Under the Lancastrian dynasty there is record of a number of great councils consisting of the leading magnates. The evidence indicates that such a council was convened by the Lancastrians to obtain advice from the magnates, who welcomed the occasion to exert their influence upon crown policy. The magnates regarded an assembly of the great council as an opportunity to enforce the dependence of the crown upon themselves; their aim was to obtain a voice in general policy and finance and to secure key posts in the central administration. Henry IV felt compelled to meet with such great councils in order to hold the support of the nobility. Henry V also brought the magnates into his confidence because he needed their backing for his French war. During the minority of Henry VI great councils continued to exert much influence. This ended, however, in 1437 when Henry VI assumed personal direction of his government and little is heard of great councils again until the outbreak of the civil war in the 1450's. They were then convened for different purposes, to arrange peace between the Lancastrians and Yorkists or to discuss military and political strategy. With the end of the war the great council ceased to wield as much power but was summoned frequently by Edward IV to consult the magnates without a full parliament and thereby escape the danger of parliamentary debate. Throughout the fifteenth century the great council was never a regular administrative organ; it assembled and exerted political influence only so long as the lords were more powerful than the kings and forced the latter to consult with and make concessions to them.

On the other hand, the royal administrative council was a regular organ of government and occupied a prominent place in administration down to the reign of Edward IV. We have seen that throughout the fourteenth century the royal council operated under two diametrically opposed theories of government. While the lords and commons called for a continual council which should be staffed by men appointed by the lords or by parliament, the kings and the professional ministers fought to retain the king's prerogative of naming his own councillors and consulting with whomsoever he desired. The lords, in particular, advocated a nonprofessional council composed of their men, through whom they could wield political influence; the kings wanted a professional council of skilled and loyal servants who would carry out the royal will and preserve its independence. But however constituted, the royal council was not in continual session and tended to degenerate into *ad hoc* meetings to dispatch business as it came along. Those who attended these meetings worked either for baronial interest or for the interest of the king. The royal council was thus the tool of political interests and the medium through which political spoils were dispensed; it was not a constant and stable executive organ that administered affairs of state in the interests of the whole realm. The great need of the council was to become an institution with a definite place in the government, independent of power politics and representative of the political desires of the realm. Under the Lancastrians some progress was made in this direction. For a time the council became more than the slavish servant of the royal will and the political captive of the magnates. It developed into an executive organ that neutrally guarded the interests of both king and realm. It came to have a professional and high-minded attitude towards the political issues of the realm and reserved its ultimate loyalty to the community of the realm rather than to king or lords.

The evolution of the council to this political position was not complete until the reign of Henry VI. The political dependence of Henry IV and the military and financial dependence of Henry V upon the magnates forced both to heed the advice given by great councils and parliament. For a while it appeared that continual councils consisting largely of baronial nominees would predominate. The first councillors of Henry IV were his appointees, but soon he was placed under pressure to name members of his council in the presence of parliament. At first he did not bow to the pressure but finally in 1404 he agreed to announce in parliament the names of his councillors. In the Long Parliament (1 March to 26 December) of 1406 he had to make substantial concessions in return for a parliamentary grant. He agreed to nominate in parliament his councillors and principal officers and he approved a list of articles defining the functions and procedure of the council.[2] The Articles of 1406 moved the continual council nearer to becoming an administrative body serving the general interest of the realm. They were intended to establish the council as an institutionalized department of government in which the king was to put more trust and which was to be so organized that he could rightfully have confidence in it. State secrets were to be known only to the councillors. Those absent from a meeting were to be informed of the business transacted. The king was advised to place equal trust in all the councillors and not be prejudiced against one or a group of them. Petitions for royal offices and favors were to be considered by the entire council and all matters were to be presented to the councillors. The king was to support his councillors and to permit no hindrance to the performance of their duties.

These articles were meant to instil greater royal and public confidence in the council and did not curtail the royal prerogative. A further provision, however, seems to have aimed at restricting the personal executive power of

[2] SM, no. 66D.

the king. It stipulated that all bills endorsed by the chamberlain and all letters under the signet seal, as well as warrants sent to the chancellor, treasurer, and keeper of the privy seal, except pardons and appointments to vacant offices, should be endorsed by the council or issued by its advice. The intent of this provision was to make the council an intermediary between king and administrative departments; it would screen every order of the king, who would be deprived of all independence. When Henry IV agreed to this provision he reduced his administrative power and became dependent upon the council.

How fully the Articles of 1406 were implemented under Henry IV and Henry V is difficult to say. It would seem that they were put into operation and remained in force until Henry VI assumed personal power in 1437. Henry IV may not have carried out every article but he cooperated sufficiently to assist in the institutionalization of the council. During the last years of his reign when poor health forced him to retire from active politics the burden of government fell to the council, which initiated or warranted almost all the affairs of state. Under the industrious Henry V government became more personal but this adventurous king, bored by administrative routine, was absent for long periods from the realm. The council therefore continued to administer the realm and assumed a key part in military finance and the supply of troops and war matériel. At the death of Henry V the council had become institutionalized as a regular organ of government. It was ready for the political role enforced by the long minority of Henry VI.

The general stature of the council and the confidence men had in it are demonstrated by the political arrangement following the death of Henry V. The bid of Humphrey, duke of Gloucester, for the regentship was defeated; he was allowed only the titles of protector and defender of the realm and principal councillor. During the minority of Henry VI the governing of the realm fell not to a regent but to the council, which had proven itself capable of the task during the reigns of Henry IV and Henry V. The council had, as Jolliffe has written, "provided the nation with a Council which could master the offices of State, reduce faction to manageable proportions, and conduct what was, in effect, if not in name, a regency of peers and great officers." This minority council appointed by the great lords in the king's name controlled the government from 1422 to 1437, a fifteen-year span that marks the apogee of the medieval administrative council. During this time it promulgated the Articles of 1423 and 1426, which elaborated further upon the conciliar functions defined in the Articles of 1406. In 1427 the council specifically formulated its constitutional position during the royal minority. It declared that the execution of royal power belonged to the lords when they were assembled in parliament or great council and at all other times to the lords of the continual council, who wielded the "politique reule and governaille" of the realm. This council maintained a remarkable coherence and collective responsibility but its efficiency was gradually impaired by the personal ambitions and interests of various councillors who were not content with subordinating their ambitions to the collective good of the realm. However well the council governed during Henry VI's minority, it had the weaknesses of an aristocratic council, which led to a reaction against conciliar government.

In 1437 when Henry VI began to attend council meetings and to assume his royal duties, the form and function of the council were modified; Henry and court followers were bent upon reviving the personal authority of the king and reducing the executive power of the council. Already in 1435 Henry VI had consulted with the council relative to royal grants and had begun to place the royal sign-manual to bills. In 1437 he sharply reminded the council of those powers specifically reserved to the king by the Articles of 1406, forbade the council to settle important matters without consulting him, and reserved for his decision cases over which there was disagreement. Henry thereby proclaimed that the council was not a law unto itself and followed up this initial action with moves that further buttressed his authority. In 1439 he appointed his secretary Thomas Beckington to the council and between 1440 and 1443 revised the Articles of 1406. It was ordained that the king could use the signet seal at his will and, with it or by the sign-manual or by the chamberlain's signature, warrant action under the privy seal. This considerably reduced the independence and authority of the privy seal because for some time it had been employed by the council to implement its decisions and the chancery had insisted upon warrants under the privy seal before it would initiate action under the great seal. The privy seal was further restricted in scope of authority by an article of 1444 stipulating that grants and warrants issued under the sign-manual or the signet seal or signed by the chamberlain or clerk of the council were as valid as those authorized by the privy seal. By these various acts Henry VI restored the royal initiative and prepared the ground for the personal government that followed under the Yorkists and Tudors.

The position of personal strength attained by Henry VI in 1444 could, with a forceful and capable king, have been the first act of a reign characterized by strong rule and full exercise of the traditional royal prerogative. The supremacy of the Lancastrian administrative council had ended and the lordly members ceased to attend, leaving the duties to professional administrators. The kingdom was Henry's to govern, the council his to control, but his physical and mental weakness brought the Lancastrian edifice down in collapse.

The principal avenue used by the Yorkists to reassert royal initiative was the signet seal. This course had been prepared by Henry VI when he established the validity of acts issued under the signet seal and appointed the vigorous Thomas Beckington as its custodian and royal secretary. An intimate of Henry VI, Beckington had a position of confidence that enabled him to elevate the position and authority of secretary and signet seal. But the secretary was still little more than a household officer whose strength was derived largely from the king himself. It was Edward IV who made the secretary into a public officer who was generally a member of the council. Under Edward IV and Richard III the business passing through the secretary's office and warranted by the signet seal greatly expanded. Though still but the office of the king's secretary and regarded as a part of the household, the signet office had its own archives, daily registered the royal instructions received, and preserved all warrants issued. The Yorkists saw the administrative potential of the secretary and the signet seal for expressing their personal will and relied primarily upon this combination in reviving royal authority. But they stopped short of making the secretary the principal officer of state as was eventually done by the Tudors. As yet the secretary was inferior to such household officers as the chamberlains and controller and was overshadowed by the chancellor and the keeper of the privy seal. As yet the secretary and the seal in his custody had not achieved administrative supremacy. But Henry VI and the Yorkists had poured the footings for the famous Tudor secretaryship. Already present were the royal confidence, membership in the council, and an organized office. Only the Tudor talents were needed to catapult the secretary to the position of chief executive officer of the king.

We are not certain what the Yorkists did with the council. That it foundered during the Wars of the Roses and that it failed to regain the authority exercised under the Lancastrians we know. Some historians have argued from the dearth of conciliar records that the Yorkists chose to do the bulk of their governing without a council. This assumption is probably correct if a continual council is meant because neither Edward IV nor Richard III worked with a council such as had characterized Lancastrian government. Edward had good reason to be apprehensive about a council that had exercised so great an authority and seems to have reverted to the type of council found in the pre-Lancastrian period when the kings took counsel as they saw fit from certain officers and magnates. Neither Edward nor the magnates who were his sworn councillors regularly attended meetings; they left routine administration to the professional staff drawn from the various royal departments. When Edward IV felt the need to deliberate on certain matters he convened a council composed of trusted magnates and the principal heads of the departments. Fewer decisions were warranted *per concilium* as formerly. But despite this conciliar decline evidence shows that the Yorkist kings made more use of the council than was formerly thought and that they began giving it special judicial work. It was constantly occupied with those difficult pleas that could be settled only by the royal judicial discretion.[3] It was becoming the council in Star Chamber and was little different from the Court of Star Chamber, that famous prerogative court established by Henry VII in 1487.

[3] SM, no. 70A and G.

Although the infirmity of Henry VI, the Wars of the Roses, and the personalized government of the Yorkists destroyed the continual administrative council of the Lancastrians, the precedents for the efficient Tudor privy council had been set. It took the political genius of the Tudors to remodel the Lancastrian council and make it serve their strong government. They realized that government was so complicated and burdensome that it must be shared with a continual council holding a large sphere of delegated authority. But their innovation was in the mastery they wielded over this body, which always remained the loyal instrument of their personal will. Also, the Tudors understood the significance of the conciliar personnel. They consciously guarded against filling their privy council with great magnates who might capture the continual council and use it as had their fathers in the fifteenth century. In the main, the Tudors staffed their privy council with skilled professionals whose first loyalty was to the king and whose second loyalty was to effective administration in behalf of the whole realm.

3. PARLIAMENT

A. The Nature of Parliament and Its Authority

Thanks to the remarkable amount of research devoted to the medieval parliament we are relatively certain of its functions and role in English politics. We are, however, less sure what men of the fifteenth century thought of it as an institution. At this stage in our investigation of parliament, when parliament had a century of history and had become an accepted institution of the realm, the latter problem is of special relevance. To understand the achievements of parliament we must first understand what parliament meant in the fifteenth century.

By the beginning of the fifteenth century parliament had matured enough as an institution so that various men engaged in parliamentary and legal work began to talk about the nature of parliament and formulate various theories. Though parliament had always been regarded as the king's high court, the High Court of Parliament, by the middle of the century the legal profession had developed a theory of parliament as the highest and supreme court of the land. Parliament was the king's court and was understood to be an afforced session of the king's council. Parliament was the supreme guardian of the laws of the realm, which all inferior courts merely executed. Along with this notion of parliament as a supreme court there also developed the idea that parliament was a representative political assembly with powers beyond those of a court. Parliament was, therefore, a unique court. It was considered a body that represented all men, who were privy to its every act. The acts of parliament were interpreted as binding all persons who were represented. The next step in such an interpretation was to regard an act of parliament as deriving its authority not so much from the sanction of the king in his court as from enactment by a body representative of the community of the realm. The acts of parliament were far more binding because parliament was representative than because they had the sanction of the highest court.

This fusion of ideas of parliament as a court and as a representative assembly was much influenced by the evolution of the concept of parliament as composed of the "estates of the realm." As the century progressed so too did the idea that parliament consisted of the three estates of the realm and possessed, therefore, an authority inherent in the three natural social orders as well as a power innate in the king's court. Towards the end of the fifteenth century the three estates were recognized as being the spiritual lords, the temporal lords, and the commons; these estates and the king were regarded as constituting parliament. Once this assimilation had occurred men realized that statutes had force not because they emanated from the king's court but because they came from the legislative authority of the three estates. By the time it was realized that parliament represented the three estates of the realm it came to be understood that the House of Lords and House of Commons were not simply places of meeting but institutions through which the will of the three estates was manifested. The commons, for example, were beginning to comprehend that they went to parliament to represent not merely the local constituencies but a whole estate—the commons of the realm. At the close of the fifteenth century we may say that men conceived of parliament as the highest court of the realm, in which were fused the royal assent, the assent of the lords spiritual and temporal, and the assent of the commons. In this assembly the king was expected to secure his taxes and to make his laws, taxes and laws to which all the realm was bound because they were assented to by the "three estates of the realm."

As far as we can determine from the available evidence these were the ideas on parliament held by the men associated with it and familiar with what it did. Let us now inquire into the powers, procedure, and privileges of parliament in the fifteenth century. Into the twentieth century most historians who wrote about the fifteenth-century parliament agreed with the classic theory propounded chiefly by Hallam and Stubbs that by 1400 the structure of the English parliament was complete and that no real progress in parliamentary government was achieved during the fifteenth century. Stubbs in particular decried this arid period of constitutional history and attributed it to the lethargy of the commons and to the selfish and power-hungry lords, who were vastly inferior to the lords dominating thirteenth- and fourteenth-century politics. Stubbs concluded that "if the only object of Constitutional History were the investigation of the origin and powers of Parliament, the study of the subject might be suspended at the deposition of Richard II."

Further research during the twentieth century, however, has modified

Stubbs' interpretation; it is now recognized that much progress occurred in the powers, procedure, and privileges of parliament. Still, this counterview must not be pushed too far because it is dangerous to assert, as have some historians, that the Lancastrian parliaments constituted a golden age of constitutionalism when king, council, and parliament amicably cooperated in the governance of the realm and when parliament had a truly sovereign power. To be sure, these historians argue, this Lancastrian constitutionalism was prematurely modern and soon succumbed before Yorkist legitimism and Tudor absolutism, but still there was a constitutional government in which parliament had the deciding vote. But even this qualification of "premature modern constitutional government" has not quieted the doubts of some historians, who challenge the idea of Lancastrian constitutionalism. They have, as Professor T. F. T. Plucknett has expressed it, an uneasy feeling about the "constitutionalism" of the Lancastrians. Some have argued that under the weak Lancastrians parliament wielded power not wielded previously nor to be wielded in the future until its sovereignty had been permanently established in the seventeenth century. Only abnormal royal weakness permitted such abnormal power to parliament, and parliament quickly lost it under the strong Yorkists and Tudors. Another group of historians has questioned whether fifteenth-century parliaments had independent power and initiative. They argue quite convincingly that the commons seldom acted on their own initiative but acted consistently as the tools of factions of great lords who struggled for political ascendancy. They further suggest that the great lords, acting in the role of political bosses, packed the House of Commons with their men, who did what they were told. These lords developed political and military followings (affinities) by means of the indenture system; they contracted with men to do their fighting and political bidding whether it be on a national or local level. For such service the indentured men received yearly fees, clothes, food, political spoils, and other favors that a strong political figure could bestow. According to this interpretation parliaments were the captives of the magnates and parliamentary power was more theoretical than real.

The divergent opinion of the fifteenth-century parliament certainly raises serious problems and warns us to proceed with caution in our investigation of parliament. All these views have undoubtedly been pushed so far that none can be entirely accepted. Stubbs and Hallam were wrong to argue that parliamentary progress ceased in 1399, because the evidence shows considerable advance. Other historians such as G. B. Adams are undoubtedly too positive in their argument that the fifteenth century was prematurely constitutional and that parliament attained almost modern political power. And those who look upon fifteenth-century parliaments simply as tools of various political factions of magnates have taken too cynical a view. For numerous parliaments they have enough evidence to substantiate their claim, but one cannot ignore the others where the commons acted independently and demonstrated real initiative. In the following examination of parliament the view taken is that there was considerable parliamentary progress in the fifteenth century but that the authority of parliament was often more apparent than real, owing to unusually weak Lancastrian kings and to magnate factions which frequently controlled parliament.

B. The Election of Parliaments

In the fourteenth century the tendency had been to hold parliaments annually, or oftener if needed. The dire royal need of money and the custom of voting taxes for only one year guaranteed frequent, though not necessarily annual, parliaments. Each parliament was new and required an election until near the end of the fourteenth century when parliaments were occasionally prorogued instead of dissolved, thus rendering unnecessary a new election for each new session. This practice and the fact that the kings never adhered strictly to the statutes ordaining annual parliaments contributed to a decline in annually elected parliaments. Lancastrian insecurity and need for financial and political support dictated that parliaments be relatively frequent, but under Henry VI as the civil strife worsened they became less numerous. The substantial financial success of Edward IV relieved him of frequent consultation with parliament; during his twenty-two-year reign only seven parliaments were summoned. It was the same under Henry VII, who had recourse to parliament but six times between 1485 and 1509. So long as laws were not made and taxes were not levied no element of the realm felt that infrequent parliaments meant a departure from an accepted and lawful manner of governing the realm. The royal subjects understood that the fewer the parliaments, the fewer the taxes.

In the latter part of the fourteenth century when a real interest in parliament arose, electoral qualifications and procedures became necessary to regulate the candidates and the electors in the interest of honest elections. The boroughs were not included in these regulations and were left to develop their own procedures and requirements. Fifteenth-century legislation concentrated upon the counties. Although the kings had specified that knights were to be returned to parliament from the counties, we have seen that they often had to be content with qualified squires. Finally, in 1445 a statute recognized that candidates could be knights or squires of the county. It stated that knights elected to parliament "shall be notable knights of the same county from which they are elected, or else notable squires of those counties, gentlemen by birth, as are able to be knights; and that no man who is of the rank of valet or lower is to be of such knight of the shire."[4] Despite a prohibition against the return of lawyers they were consistently elected and formed an influential element of all fifteenth-century parliaments.

The regulations for the electorate were more numerous and stringent. It could not be otherwise for, as men became more cognizant of the values of

[4] SM, no. 69F.

parliamentary representation, they vied to obtain votes in whatever way they could be obtained. It was particularly imperative to define who was qualified to vote in a county because the great lords used their affinities to pack the county courts and elect candidates who would carry out their orders at Westminster. The tendency was to reduce the number of men qualified to vote by introducing residence and property qualifications. This was necessary or the magnates would swamp the election with drifters and men of no standing and property. In 1406 a petition complaining of improper election of knights to parliament was answered by a statute that ordered all qualified suitors to participate freely and impartially in the election.[5] This may or may not have been a progressive step. We must allow that lords could still swamp the county court with their retainers because no definite qualifications were stipulated. An act of 1413 was more specific when it declared that electors in both counties and boroughs must be residents.[6] In 1430 came the famous statute regulating the county franchise for the next four centuries down to the Reform Act of 1832. This statute provided that electors must be resident in the county and that they must possess a freehold worth 40s. per annum. This requirement, the statute said, was necessary because the county elections were packed and overawed by improperly qualified men.[7] Definitely a "disfranchising statute" and extremely conservative in its limitations, it was undoubtedly a defense against the lawless conditions and political tactics of the great lords. It should be realized that the copyholder and leaseholder, however valuable their land might be, were disfranchised and remained so until 1832. Obviously the statute was repeatedly ignored as the lords took the law into their own hands but it nevertheless set a precedent for more peaceful ages and introduced the franchise as a political right dependent upon property. It also singled out the landed gentry as the class that would consistently supply the members of parliament well into the nineteenth century.

The electoral procedure of the counties was also the subject of numerous complaints which gave rise to a series of statutes. Invariably the complaints dwelled upon improper manipulation of elections, upon false returns by sheriffs, or upon the coercion and disorder spewed over county elections by the indentured bands of the "overmighty" subjects. A statute of 1406 spoke of grievous complaints about improper elections and "favouritism of the sheriffs" to the "great scandal of the counties." It provided for a "true return" by requiring the names of the two men elected to be written down in an indenture authenticated by the seals of the electors. The election was to be conducted in the first county court held after the receipt of the writ of summons.[8] In 1410 a statute placed the supervision of elections under the

[5] SM, no. 69C.
[6] SM, no. 69D.
[7] SM, no. 69E and F.
[8] SM, no. 69C.

justices of assize, who were empowered to inquire into the legality of returns and to impose a penalty of £100 upon any sheriff found guilty of sending in a false return. The statute of 1445 imposed an additional penalty on the sheriff; it provided that a candidate defrauded by a sheriff could secure damages by action of debt in the court of common pleas.[9] Such was the nature of the acts designed to eliminate dishonest electoral procedure. Though ultimately they served as valuable precedents, throughout most of the fifteenth century they were consistently flouted by the magnates and kings, especially after the outbreak of the Wars of the Roses. The House of Commons did not begin to claim jurisdiction over election disputes until the reign of Queen Elizabeth. When there were election disputes in the fifteenth century, individual communities or the commons petitioned the king and lords to take proper action; there are records that tell of penalties imposed upon sheriffs and other guilty persons.

C. The Powers of Parliament

With the separation of parliament into the House of Commons and the House of Lords in the fourteenth century the judicial powers of parliament resided in the latter house, and it constituted the High Court of Parliament. At the end of the century the House of Lords had the following jurisdiction: trial of peers for high treason and serious felony, appeals on writs of error from courts of the common law, and impeachment. The House of Lords thus constituted the highest common law court of the realm. As for trials of peers, many came before fifteenth-century parliaments but few were conducted in a proper and impartial legal manner. Most proceeded under the heat of factional strife when a victorious party was avenging itself against its political enemies. These were not judicial trials; they were political assassinations. The victim might protest that there had been no proper *judicium parium* as proclaimed by Magna Carta but such complaint was of no avail when force was the only law of the land. In regard to the second jurisdiction, review of error, it was definitely admitted by the fifteenth century that the House of Lords could correct errors in both criminal and civil cases but that these were errors in law, not in fact. Apparently there were few such appeals in the fifteenth century. The commons, though having disclaimed any role as judges in the fourteenth century, reiterated this stand more precisely in the famous parliament of 1399. They especially wanted to have it recorded that they had not constituted the court which had adjudged Richard II incapable of rule and deposed him. They were too uncertain of future political tides to become closely involved with any of the actions of Henry IV. The commons made it a matter of record that they were not "parties to any judgment . . . given in parliament," and Henry IV replied that the "commons are petitioners and demandants, and that the king and lords have always had and of right shall have the [rendering of] judgments in par-

[9] SM, no. 69F.

liament."[10] The procedure of impeachment remained the same as that developed in the fourteenth century. The commons constituted the accusers or prosecutors; the lords, the judges. Eventually we shall see the process of impeachment replaced by bills of attainder.

Neither Lancastrians nor Yorkists questioned parliament's control over extraordinary taxation, be it direct or indirect. The Lancastrians consistently went to parliament for their supply and became the financial captives of this body. Their abject financial dependence upon parliament principally accounts for the greater powers and privileges it obtained in the fifteenth century. Customarily all taxes were voted for a short term, generally a year. There were, however, some exceptions. In 1414 parliament granted to Henry V tunnage and poundage for life; it did the same for Henry VI in 1453, for Edward IV in 1463, and for Richard III in 1484.[11] This custom if applied to the other taxes could have resulted in the absolutism that characterized France. But the English kings either did not realize the political potential of such life grants or could not coerce parliament into extending the practice. By experimenting with a method already resorted to by Richard II, the Yorkists managed to develop a financial technique that reduced their requests to parliament for taxation. Richard had negotiated forced loans from rich subjects and, although promising repayment, seldom bothered to honor his obligations; from this practice Edward IV invented the benevolence. It was, according to theory, a gift freely given unto the king by his subjects; in practice it was a gift wrung from the wealthy subjects. The commons tended to wink at these benevolences because when the king secured his money in this fashion he found it less necessary to ask parliament for supply. But there was bitter complaint against Edward IV's benevolences and in the parliament of Richard III (1483) the commons complained of a "new imposition called benevolence" which had subjected many of them to servitude, penury, and wretchedness. To curry favor with parliament Richard replied that henceforth his subjects would not be burdened with benevolences or any like impositions.[12] But he was soon forced to collect such impositions to defend his realm against Henry Tudor, and the practice continued under the Tudors. It was fortunate for the growth of parliament that benevolences never supplied the kings with an adequate income and parliamentary taxation remained a necessity.

While parliamentary control over taxation marked a significant advance towards constitutional government, this power could contribute to progress only if used to exploit political concessions from the crown. Especially was this true with the principle of "redress before supply" which was slowly establishing itself as the normal method of financial negotiation between king and parliament in the fourteenth century and was acknowledged as

[10] SM, no. 66A.
[11] SM, no. 68.
[12] SM, no. 69H.

such by the Lancastrians in the fifteenth century. In the second parliament of Henry IV in 1401 the commons presented a petition which prayed that they might know the royal answers to their petitions before any taxes were granted. Henry emphatically refused the demand and declared that "such procedure had been unknown and unaccustomed in the time of his progenitors or predecessors."[13] But the commons had made their claim and Henry IV could not hold to his refusal. The commons soon adopted the practice of delaying grants until the last day of parliament and compelled the impoverished king to give redress before he was voted supply.

For some time the kings had conceded the right of the commons to audit the collection and disbursement of the royal income. This custom was not, however, so well established that the kings automatically conceded the right. In 1406 when Henry IV was met with a demand for audit, he proudly retorted that "kings do not render accounts."[14] This was his only refusal; in 1407 he wisely decided to imitate the example of his predecessors and voluntarily submitted an account of how his income had been expended.[15] Such procedure was followed until repudiated by the Yorkists and Tudors. It was not revived until 1624 and 1641 and did not become a regular practice until the reign of Charles II. Appropriation of taxes for specific purposes had developed during the reigns of Edward III and Richard II; under the Lancastrians it became an accepted practice. Large grants were generally appropriated for the defense of the realm while tunnage and poundage was used to safeguard the seas. The latter, granted to Henry VI in 1453, was appropriated for the navy. The income from the royal domain was reserved for the expenses of the household and was occasionally supplemented by appropriations from other sources. Calais was maintained by an appropriation from the poundage and the customs on wool. Early in Henry IV's reign the commons decided to separate royal household from state expenses and appropriated a special sum for the royal household. This continued to be done upon occasion and marks the beginning of a separation between the civil or king's list and the extraordinary expenses of the kingdom. Like the practice of auditing, however, that of appropriation fell into disuse under the Yorkists and Tudors and was not revived until the reign of James I.

The most fundamental gain of the commons in financial power was the establishment of the principle that all money bills should originate in the House of Commons. Though as early as 1395 the commons had granted a tax which was then approved by the lords, they did not secure definite control over the initiative in taxation until the reign of Henry IV. During the parliament of 1407 the king and lords had conferred about a tax and agreed upon a tenth and a fifteenth. The next step was to secure the assent of the commons, who were requested to send a committee of twelve to discuss the

[13] SM, no. 66B.
[14] SM, no. 66D.
[15] SM, no. 66E.

matter with the king and lords. The committee was informed of the decision and directed to report it to the commons and to secure their speedy consent. Told of this action, the commons were enraged and protested that it was against established procedure and in derogation of their liberties. They argued that each house should decide upon the amount of taxation to be approved and that after the houses were agreed on the amount their decision should be announced to the king. It was specifically declared that the decision should be announced "by the mouth of the speaker of the said commons" and that the grant should be "made by the commons and assented to by the lords."[16] This assertion shows that the commons intended to initiate all money grants. Henceforth it became the custom for all money bills to originate in the House of Commons. This was the key financial victory of the commons in the fifteenth century because it set off a line of thinking that interpreted the right of initiation as meaning that the House of Lords could not amend a money bill but must accept or reject it. The issue was not to be settled definitely until the year 1911. In the fifteenth century each house discussed taxation independently of the other and of the king but when the amount of the tax was settled it was introduced by the commons as a bill, approved by the lords, and became law if accepted by the king.

At least since the reign of Edward II the principle had been strongly imbedded that all legislation must be enacted by king in parliament and soon thereafter "in parliament" included the assent of the commons. By the end of Edward III's reign it was recognized that no statute could be made without the consent of the commons. Both Henry IV and Henry V acknowledged that no law could be made, revoked, or changed without the consent of the three estates in parliament. But as yet the place of the commons in the legislative process was subordinate. Although the king made his statutes "by the authority" of parliament, they were said to be made by the king with the assent of the prelates, earls and barons, and at the request of the commons. Rarely was it stated that the assent of the commons had been secured. It was only gradually in the fifteenth century that the commons attained an equal footing with the lords in legislation. As late as 1435 and 1436 statutes were passed by "the advice and assent of the lords at the special request of the commons." In 1439 and in the next few years there was legislation with the assent of the lords and commons. In 1450 only the "request of the commons" was referred to, but it was not until the reign of Henry VII that statutes were regularly enacted by the "assent of the lords spiritual and temporal and the commons" and by the "authority of parliament." Only then did the commons finally cast off their traditional role as petitioners and gain stature equal to that of the lords.

We have seen that in the fourteenth century the commons worried about

[16] SM, no. 66E.

the final form of their petitions, which were repeatedly tampered with before being published in statute form. Though the commons strongly protested and occasionally gained a point, they did not secure a lasting concession until 1414. Then the commons petitioned the king Henry V that "no law shall . . . be made and engrossed as a statute and a law with either additions or subtractions" or have any change made that would alter the intent of the law without the assent of the commons. Henry V replied that "nothing contrary to their request shall henceforth be enacted . . . without their assent."[17] In the future if the king accepted a petition he then had it engrossed as submitted and published in statute form.

In their struggle to secure the engrossment of their petitions as submitted the commons were basically right in their charges that the royal intent in altering petitions had been to defeat their purpose. But it must be pointed out that the rough and ill-conceived petitions of the commons required considerable revision by legal experts before they could be published as statutes. The commons could not complain about such revision and it taught them that their petitions must be drafted in a more formal and precise manner. It also did not escape their attention that when the king and council introduced a bill to parliament it was in finished form and, if approved, engrossed just as it had been initiated. After their victory of 1414 the commons gradually ceased the introduction of rough and unfinished petitions and sent up to the king and council bills drawn in the form of a finished statute so that the king need only assent or dissent. This practice became customary during the reign of Henry VI and was invariably followed under Henry VII. If the king accepted the bill he signified his approval by the phrase *le roi le veut* ("the king so wills it"); if he refused assent he signified so by the response *le roi s'avisera* ("the king will deliberate"). The commons had surely won a point by the concession of 1414 and by the innovation in bill procedure, but the kings still retained and exercised the power of withholding consent to bills that they did not want to become statutes.

It was in such a manner that public bills became law. By the fifteenth century the numerous private petitions introduced into every parliament were transformed into private bills. They could be presented by the petitioners in either house but most were initiated in the House of Commons. Public bills, on the other hand, could initiate from three sources: king and council, House of Lords, and House of Commons. Under the Lancastrians the commons dominated the initiation of legislation; they initiated almost all legislation during the reign of Henry IV. During the reign of Henry V only one statute was introduced by the king. In fact, we may say that the commons controlled legislation between 1399 and 1453 and that most of it was enacted with but slight amendment. Also during the reigns of Henry IV and Henry V more petitions and bills were accepted as the basis of statutes

[17] SM, no. 66F.

than at any other time during the Middle Ages. With the outbreak of the Wars of the Roses the legislative mastery of the commons waned and thereafter they had a serious rival in the crown. Increasingly king and council introduced official bills into parliament for the assent of both houses; there is no evidence that the bills were amended or refused assent. Most of the legislation inspired by king and council reflected the personal interest of the crown. An act of 1455, for example, appropriated £3000 for the royal household. Throughout the civil war the crown introduced a large number of bills asking for the attaint of political enemies, for the resumption and confiscation of land, and for the revocation of privileges. In the period after 1450 the commons also lost their influence over general legislation. Increasingly what few bills they introduced were rejected, particularly during the reigns of Edward IV and Richard III. Under Richard official bills definitely predominated over commons' bills and it was the same under Henry VII. Finally, it must be noted that under the Lancastrians and Yorkists legislation was less frequent and less important than in the thirteenth and fourteenth centuries. What statutes were enacted generally lacked the permanent and basic value that characteristized those of Edward I. Only under Henry VII were fundamental statutes enacted and they were concerned with the amendment of medieval law badly in need of revision.

Except with money bills the lords maintained an equality with the commons in legislation. Both could initiate bills and had the power to amend or reject a bill. Difficulty arose only when one house rejected or amended a bill of the other. There was frequently disagreement over taxation and in the last quarter of the fourteenth century differences were settled by conferences. Generally a committee of lords selected by the House of Lords, or occasionally by the commons, would confer with the whole House of Commons. But the lords came to resent having to deal through a committee with the entire commons and during the reign of Henry IV persuaded the commons to appoint a committee to confer on problems that arose over taxation and legislation. After 1407 conferences between select committees of the houses began to be held and became the normal solution for settling differences between the lords and commons.[18]

During the first three quarters of the fourteenth century parliament had struggled against bitter royal opposition to secure some continual voice in government policy and administration. Then, in the last quarter of the century the House of Commons had seemed to back away from sharing responsibility for various policies. Under the Lancastrians the commons reversed this trend and asserted surprising control over royal policy and administration. This they did by means of the usual financial methods, by control of the royal council through appointment and nomination of members, and by impeachment of royal servants. In the last resort parliament could de-

[18] SM, no. 66E.

pose the king, as it did Richard II in 1399. During the Lancastrian period when the commons took a lively interest in royal government and exercised a surprising influence, one questions if they consistently did so on their own initiative. We can assume that being vitally interested in taxation, in the French war, in relations with the church, and in economic policy, they must at times have acted on their initiative. But much of the time they must also have acted on behalf of the magnates, who forced them to do their political bidding. This would seem to be especially true when Henry VI lost control over the government in the 1450's and when the struggle for ascendancy degenerated into war. Then the commons, often the political captives of great lords, attacked the existing government, introduced bills intended to embarrass the king and his council, and initiated impeachment proceedings. In 1450, for example, the commons, acting for the magnates, instigated the vicious attack against and impeachment of William de la Pole, duke of Suffolk.

The impeachment of Suffolk was to be one of the last notable cases of impeachment. During the swift succession of parliaments and the bitter political feuds that dominated England in the civil war, impeachment was supplanted by bills of attainder (from the verb "attaint," which literally means "to prove guilty"), a more rapid and efficient technique of bringing down unpopular ministers or political foes. A bill of attainder resembled any other bill introduced into parliament to receive assent as law. It was fundamentally a private bill, however, and was partly legislative and legal in nature. He who introduced such a bill included accusations against a specific person or persons and provided for the punishment. If parliament assented to the bill and it was accepted by the king, it became law. The specified person or persons were then guilty of breaking a law and could be punished. There was no introduction of evidence nor any court procedure such as there was with impeachment and the person accused was condemned without the opportunity of defending himself. Although the common law courts were critical of such legislative trial, they were unable to block acts of the High Court of Parliament. Bills of attainder were obviously a swift and practical method of dealing with great men of evil reputation against whom no satisfactory evidence could be produced or who were too powerful to be punished by customary legal procedure in the common law courts or even in the High Court of Parliament. Bills of attainder certainly punished royal ministers, brought down whole governments, and controlled policy and administration, if this method is to be understood as "control," but as used in the fifteenth and sixteenth centuries they were definitely an abuse. All parliament, and in a sense all the realm, was involved in the attaint, thereby giving the impression that the attainted had been punished because he had committed a crime against the whole community. Yet it is difficult to justify punishing men by legislation when employed as it was in the second half of the fifteenth century and under the Tudors to strike down political enemies or remove ministers no longer considered useful.

In the fifteenth century two notable cases of this legislative punishment occurred. In 1459 a Lancastrian parliament accepted a bill of attainder introduced by Lancastrian leaders and proceeded to attaint the duke of York and all prominent Yorkist leaders, who were declared guilty of high treason and had all their goods confiscated. In 1461 after Edward IV's victories a Yorkist parliament did the bidding of the revengeful Yorkist magnates. It attainted Henry VI, Margaret of Anjou, leading Lancastrian lords, and a number of prominent commons. Guilty of high treason, they faced death and loss of all goods. Their only action could be flight into exile.[19] Attaint was too arbitrary and vengeful a means of controlling or threatening a government to develop into an effective instrument for the limitation of policy and administration. Control would ultimately come in the seventeenth century with the sovereignty of parliament.

D. The Privileges and Procedure of Parliament

In sixteenth-century parliaments, especially those of Elizabeth, the speaker of the House of Commons regularly made a formal request of the sovereign to recognize certain customary privileges of the commons. Three of these privileges had their origin in the fifteenth century and were immunities or fundamental rights which the commons fought for because they recognized them to be essential for the preservation of independence and political power. The first and most important was freedom of speech, that is, free, independent, and private discussion of the commons in their house. The attainment of this privilege meant that the people of the realm had a voice in the government because their political opinions were expressed and often acted upon. We must realize, however, that complete freedom of speech in the House of Commons did not come until the seventeenth century and that the fight for it did not begin until the fifteenth century. Though the privilege was not won in this century, the struggle towards it established a precedent for later ages.

The clashes between the kings and commons over the right to free speech centered around three problems. First, the kings maintained that the commons should not deviate from the agenda of business presented to them for discussion by the royal government. The commons took the view that they could deviate from the agenda and discuss other matters. Secondly, the commons argued that the king should be informed of their discussions and decisions only through approved and responsible channels; they resented the leakage of information which might be distorted and which might offend the king. Finally, the commons contended that they should not be punished for what they said as long as it was not treasonable. Throughout the fifteenth century there were numerous celebrated incidents that tested these claims and helped the commons to establish precedents for free speech.

[19] SM, no. 69G.

The first clash over this privilege came, as we have seen, with the critical speech of Thomas Haxey in 1397. Although not an elected member of the House of Commons, Haxey was a royal officer who introduced a bill for the reform of the royal household. That Haxey could plead benefit of clergy was all that saved his life. In securing Haxey's imprisonment and the confiscation of his goods Richard II definitely won the first round of the battle. Then in the first parliament of Henry IV in 1399 the commons petitioned the king for the exoneration of Haxey and asked that his judgment as a traitor be reversed and that he be returned all his confiscated titles and goods. This Henry granted.[20] The commons had at least asserted the claim for free speech and made it a matter of parliamentary record, even though they had not yet won a test of strength with one of their own elected members.

In the second parliament of 1401 the commons made further claims to free speech through the speaker of the house, Sir Arnold Savage, an eloquent and able parliamentarian who served in five parliaments and whose family had represented Kent for six generations. The first speech of Savage delivered to the king resembled those of Elizabethan speakers asking for the customary privileges of the commons. Savage requested that "the said commons should have their liberty in parliament as they had had before this time and that this protestation should be recorded in the roll of parliament." Henry IV agreed to this. Savage then beseeched the king that the commons might have "good advice and deliberation" on matters presented to them rather than having to give an immediate reply. Henry IV agreed to this. Finally, Savage made one of the basic requests for free debate, that the king would entertain no reports of proceedings in the House of Commons unless they came to him through official channels. Henry IV also granted this request, which marked a distinct advance towards the right of free and full deliberation by the commons.[21]

We hear little more about the privilege of free speech until 1453 when the speaker Thomas Thorpe, a staunch Lancastrian and a baron of the exchequer, was arrested for what he had said against the duke of York. Thorpe was put in Fleet prison and the commons sent a delegation to the king and lords asking for his release on the basis that a man could be arrested only for treason or felony. The lords under the influence of York replied that Thorpe should "remayne stille in prison for the causes above-said, the privelegge of the parlement, notwithstandying." While the commons did not achieve a satisfactory settlement in this case, they won a theoretical victory because their claim was supported by the common law judges who were consulted during the proceedings. In 1451 Thomas Young, burgess for Bristol, was imprisoned and suffered loss of property because he had suggested Richard, duke of York, for the next king of England if Henry VI should have

[20] SM, no. 66A.
[21] SM, no. 66B.

no heirs. He was released from prison in 1452 but was not compensated for damages until 1455. He then presented a petition to the commons which was sent to the king, asking for compensation. In the petition he made the most effective claim for free speech yet advanced. He stated that the commons "in any parliament ought to have their freedom to speak and say in the house of their assembly whatever they think convenient or reasonable without in any way incurring any sort of challenge, charge, or punishment." At the royal order compensation was given to Thomas Young.

Despite some victories and a number of eloquent claims for the privilege of free speech, it would be incorrect to say that at the end of the fifteenth century the commons could look upon it as one of their established rights. Their claims and assertions were a step in the right direction and were precedents, but they ultimately depended upon the will of the king, which was largely determined by his strength. The issue remained unsettled in the sixteenth century despite more gains of the commons. It was not definitely settled in their favor until 1689 when guaranteed in the Bill of Rights.

A close corollary to free speech was the commons' freedom of access to the king through their speaker. The lords had access to the king because this right came from feudal custom, which united king and tenants-in-chief in a highly personal bond. By virtue of feudal law and of prescriptive usage the lords were deemed the hereditary counsellors of the king and always had access to him. But the commons had no such relationship with the king and this seems to explain why the speaker developed as a commons officer. He became an intermediary between commons and king. He spoke for the commons and the king spoke through him to them. Eventually as the lords and commons cooperated in taxation and legislation the speaker became an intermediary between the two houses. This position could be perilous, as many early speakers recognized, and they began to claim immunity from what was said in their speeches on the plea that they were but spokesmen of the commons. The first definite request for immunity came from the speaker Sir Arnold Savage in 1401 when he prayed that the king would excuse him for any words he might say displeasing to the royal person. The essential claim involved here was freedom of speech of the commons through their speaker.[22] They wished to have the privilege of petitioning, counseling, or differing with the king through the speaker and to have a favorable interpretation given to the speaker's words. Such a claim, however, would not be firmly established until after the fifteenth century.

The third important privilege claimed by the commons was freedom from arrest. This concept of immunity from legal process probably developed out of the idea of royal safe-conduct, that certain individuals were under the special protection of the king while performing various services for him. Such protection had been known since the Anglo-Saxon period. It had been

[22] SM, no. 66B.

traditional to place assemblies that were to meet with the king under his special peace. All members of parliament were under this peace and by the fifteenth century seldom had to worry that physical harm would befall them except during periods of violence. What they did have to worry about was molestation by means of some process of law. It became obvious to the members of parliament that they would have to immunize themselves from outside interference and protect themselves if parliament was to accomplish effectively its work. Members who said unpopular things or introduced bills disliked by certain persons or groups of men should not have to fear legal retaliation which had no connection with what had been done or said in parliament. Early in Henry IV's reign, in 1404, the commons asked that triple damages be exacted from a person assaulting a member of parliament going to and returning from parliament. They claimed freedom from arrest for debt, trespass, and contract, not only for themselves but for their servants. The king would not grant this request, replying that sufficient protection was already being extended to members of parliament.[23]

Famous test cases leading to freedom from arrest began in the parliament of 1429. A certain William Larke, servant of William Melrede, member of parliament, had been arrested. The commons asked for his release, arguing that during sessions of parliament all members of parliament and their servants were immune from arrest except for treason, felony, or surety of the peace. The commons emphasized that this was "by the privilege of your court of parliament." They then petitioned the king that none of the commons or their servants should "be arrested or detained in prison during the time of your parliaments, except for treason, felony, or surety of the peace, as aforesaid." Henry VI agreed to release Larke from prison but denied the remainder of the petition.[24] In 1453 and 1455 came the famous cases of the speaker Thomas Thorpe and of Thomas Young, burgess of Bristol. Both, as we have noted, were arrested and proceeded against by legal actions because of unpopular political speeches in parliament. Thorpe was not released and the commons had to elect a new speaker. Young, however, was vindicated when the council accepted his petition for damages and took steps to remunerate him. Young was a prominent representative, merchant, and lawyer. He eventually became king's serjeant and justice of both the court of common pleas and king's bench. Young specifically stated in his petition that he had been imprisoned and suffered loss of property "without any indictment, presentment, appeal, due original, accusation, or lawful cause held or sworn against him." Redress was granted and this decision became a precedent for numerous other cases involving freedom from arrest.[25] By the end of the reign of Edward IV it may be said that this privilege had definitely been established and that it protected all members of parliament

[23] SM, no. 66C.
[24] SM, no. 67C.
[25] SM, no. 67F.

except when they were involved in treason, felony, or breach of security of the peace.

It has been noted that few accounts of parliamentary procedure exist from the Middle Ages. Not until the sixteenth century do we begin to have adequate records. We must therefore rely upon a stray chronicle, a report of a commoner to his borough or county, or the Parliament Rolls, which are not particularly descriptive. What has been said on parliamentary procedure for the fourteenth century largely holds true for the fifteenth and, during the course of our discussion of the powers and privileges of parliament, we have frequently referred to procedure. All that need be added is a few remarks on the speakership in the fifteenth century.

The speaker of the House of Commons became an established fixture in the last quarter of the fourteenth century when for the most part he was the political manager of baronial politicians and helped to control and to direct the House of Commons. Though he was presented to the king by the commons as their spokesman, it is doubtful that he often represented solely the sentiments of the House of Commons. It was Richard II who learned from baronial example the value of controlling the speaker and who began to impose his trusted servants upon the commons. During the fifteenth century the speakers were regularly men who had been in the royal service and who could be trusted as royal political managers. As the century progressed and entered into the chaos of political feud and civil war it was evident that the speakers were no mere spokesmen or intermediaries for the commons but were active politicians working for either the Lancastrian or the Yorkist interest. They accepted the political vicissitudes and hazards of their office and a notable number including William Tresham, Thomas Tresham, Thorpe, Wenlock, and Catesby came to a violent end on the scaffold, on the battlefield, or by assassination. Some suffered imprisonment and loss of rights and property. Despite these perils the speakers of the fifteenth century did act as spokesmen and intermediaries and requested such privileges as access to the sovereign and freedom of speech. The speaker as a skilled and experienced chairman of the House of Commons was still many years in the future but precedents and functions were accruing which, once divested of the strong political hues, would contribute to his emergence.

4. CONCLUSIONS

What may we conclude about the paradoxical politics of the fifteenth century? We certainly are not justified in looking upon this century as one in which a modern constitutional monarchy emerged only to be submerged at the end by the Yorkists and Tudors. Neither the men, nor the institutions, nor the society was ready for the constitutional government England got in the seventeenth century. Some powers and privileges having the ring of modernity were but temporary constitutional advances permitted only by long years of exceedingly weak kings; they were terminated rapidly with the return of strong kings. But should the temporary constitutional advance and the precedents that did not survive be written off as so much wasted history? Certainly not. The advance and the precedents were recorded in the historical memory and tradition of England and in such records as the Parliament Rolls and the statutes to be read by future generations who were prepared to convert them into a permanent constitutional scheme. In spirit, innovation, and accomplishment the fifteenth century does not equal the thirteenth and fourteenth centuries but it should not be disparaged as a century of little constitutional development. If it promised more than it delivered in permanent parliamentary sovereignty, it was followed by a century that provided no more permanent solution to England's ultimate constitutional structure. Not until the seventeenth century was there permanent progress towards true limited monarchy and the sovereignty of parliament. And the men who won the victory, the parliamentarians and common law lawyers, turned for their precedents and their inspiration not to the sixteenth century but to the fifteenth century and to those that preceded it.

XXXVII

The Common Law and Its Elaboration

THE history of the common law in the fourteenth and fifteenth centuries is one of development and elaboration along the lines marked out by the great statutes and innovations of Edward I. There was not in these two centuries the innovation or rapid expansion that characterized law in the twelfth and thirteenth centuries. Fundamental statutes were few and what change occurred was outside the common law system. The last two centuries of medieval England witnessed the elaboration of the machinery of process and of the rules of pleadings and a refinement of legal principles previously established. No longer was the law dominated and molded by legislation but by a skilled, learned, proud, and jealous legal profession.

What innovation occurred in the law did so outside the common law framework and because the common law had become so rigid and inflexible that it failed to provide adequate justice. New legal developments and demands in the realm of civil law went unrecognized by the common law courts and eventually had to be provided for by a new prerogative court, the court of chancery, which forged an equitable law. Maitland has written that "The sky might fall, the Wars of the Roses might rage, but they [the lawyers] would pursue the even course of their argumentation." Yet despite these lawyers and despite the legal records that pour out a story of the law without reference to the chaos about, the law of England did not thrive in a political vacuum. It was inevitable that the courts and their law should be affected by a decay in the coercive strength of the government and by practices that twisted the processes of law and disregarded its authority. The decay in "the integrity of royal justice" rendered the common law and its courts ineffective in the dispensation of justice. Overmighty men respectful of their own law seemed bent upon destroying the legal edifice of the realm. It took severe legal measures under the Yorkists and Tudors to save the common law and the state. They had to use their council, the Court of Star Chamber, which executed a tough, summary, and unEnglish law and procedure, to restore respect for the law of the land. With all justification it can be said that the court of chancery with its equity "saved the common law" and that the Court of Star Chamber saved the "constitution."

I. THE COURTS

Though none of the generalizations that follow on the courts are completely valid for the two centuries under review, they indicate what jurisdictions and powers the courts exercised at the end of the fifteenth century. Starting at the peak of the legal pyramid and descending the legal steps, one first meets the High Court of Parliament, the supreme court of the realm. The jurisdiction of this court was exercised by the House of Lords and consisted of three types. First, the House of Lords had jurisdiction over peers accused of treason or of felony. All lesser criminal and civil cases of the peers were triable in the ordinary common law courts. Secondly, the House of Lords held a jurisdiction in error and could correct errors in law of all lower common law courts. In the fifteenth century it was definite that there could be a correction of legal error but this must not be understood as errors in fact. Medieval law would not try the same facts twice and made no provision for appeal such as existed in the canon law courts. During the fourteenth century there is considerable evidence of errors corrected but in the fifteenth century the practice declined; from the reign of Henry V to the end of the century there was only one case. The third jurisdiction of the lords was over impeachment, which along with felony and treason constituted the only occasion when the High Court of Parliament acted as a court of first instance. After the middle of the fifteenth century, as we have noted, impeachment was superseded by the act of attainder and the House of Lords did not again exercise this jurisdiction until the reign of James I

The king's council by the end of the fifteenth century no longer concerned itself primarily with justice as it had under Edward I. Though it could entertain difficult pleas it had become primarily an executive organ, delegating legal matters to two prerogative courts that had branched off from it. During the course of the fourteenth century council and parliament broke away from the cooperation they had shared under Edward I, when it was even difficult to distinguish their functions, and became bitter rivals in every sphere of government. This was especially true with conciliar legal jurisdiction, which parliament fought to limit.

The council had traditionally corrected errors in law of the ordinary common law courts but in the fourteenth century lost this jurisdiction to the House of Lords. When in 1365 the council reversed a judgment of the justices of assize the court of common pleas would not recognize the reversal; it argued that the council had no authority to reverse common law court judgments. Nevertheless the council attempted to correct errors until 1402 when parliament enacted a statute declaring that the council could not correct errors in law of the common law courts. Meanwhile parliament and council had been feuding over the latter's jurisdiction as a court of the first instance. As early as 1331 parliament attempted by statute to restrict all legal proceedings to the common law courts. This statute was followed by similar ones in 1351, 1354, 1363, 1364, and 1368, all of which curbed the original jurisdiction of the council and sanctioned common law court procedure, indictment, and original writs as the only recognized legal procedure. But these statutes were not successful; in the fifteenth century the commons were still petitioning the kings to terminate the legal jurisdiction of the council.

It was just as well that parliament was not successful in destroying the original jurisdiction of the council because both lords and commons, though opposed to its legal authority, still had to admit that such authority was often necessary. It was recognized that the formal common law and procedure were not equal to all the legal demands and that the council with its flexible and informal procedure was often more capable of dealing with special legal problems. Parliament grudgingly and informally admitted that the council had a certain sphere of jurisdiction. In 1363 parliament decreed that individuals who failed to abide by the Statutes of Provisors and Praemunire, two antipapal enactments, were to be summoned before the council and to receive punishment according to the discretion of the council. In 1388 parliament passed a statute directing the holding of regular quarterly sessions by the justices of the peace; justices not abiding by the statute were to be punished according to conciliar discretion. During the disorderly fifteenth century parliament admitted the legality of writs ordering persons responsible for riot, oppression, and extortion to appear before the council. Those who ignored the writs were punished by forfeiture of goods. Parliament was, therefore, acknowledging that special cases of justice, particularly forceful acts against the state, could be handled most expeditiously by the council. In effect, parliament said this in 1430 when it approved certain conciliar articles dealing with judicial authority. It was agreed that all petitions addressed to the council should be sent to the common law courts unless the council felt that one party to the case was too powerful and held undue influence or that certain other circumstances would hinder justice in ordinary courts; the council could then retain jurisdiction. Here parliament admitted the legality of conciliar jurisdiction over criminal offenses which the common law courts were incapable of punishing. In a lawless century the very lawful common law courts had to be backed up by the council, which regularly handled nonfelonious offenses (because it did not want to pronounce the death penalty) such as the hindrance of justice, riot, bribery of jurors, and other acts of physical violence. However much parliament proclaimed that all men were entitled to due process of law and trial by jury in common law courts it admitted that these courts were not able to deal out justice to magnates and indentured retainers who considered themselves above the law. In such cases jury trial was a mockery and injustice because no juror dared hand down a verdict of guilty. Over such men and their offenses it was conceded that the royal prerogative justice must have jurisdiction and that it must be wielded by king and council, who could employ hard and summary punishment.

Though the legal jurisdiction just described came to be exercised after

1487 by the Court of Star Chamber, which was first the judicial part of the privy council and then broke off into a distinct prerogative court, it was still held under Henry VI and Edward IV by the council. By the end of Edward IV's reign, however, the procedure had been developed that was to characterize the famous Court of Star Chamber.[1] With its ordaining power the council ordained offenses and punished infractions. Its procedure was swift and informal. There was no trial by jury; the accused was examined on his oath and was, in reality, forced to accuse himself. Under Edward IV torture was introduced to secure confession. Accusation could be made against the defendant without proper substantiation and without his knowing the source. Such procedure, alien to the common law system, was introduced and used regularly by the council. Under the abnormal conditions of the second half of the fifteenth century this procedure is probably defensible on the grounds that it was one of the few sure means of punishing the overmighty subject and preserving respect for the state and its tradition of law and order. But while the criminal jurisdiction of the council saved the common law, it became bitterly hated and regarded as alien to the English legal tradition. The iniquities of the later Star Chamber were infamous and most subjects were relieved when the Long Parliament abolished it in 1641.

We have spoken mainly of the criminal jurisdiction of the council and how that part of its justice came to be wielded in the Court of Star Chamber. But, as we know, the council also had a civil jurisdiction which came to reside in the court of chancery. While speaking of the law in the thirteenth century we saw that when no remedy was obtainable in the ordinary common law courts an individual could petition for legal action by parliament or by council. We observed also that by the reign of Edward I the council was receiving and acting upon most petitions seeking legal remedy and that the chancellor with the assistance of his underclerks assumed most of the responsibility for dealing with the petitions. There were many reasons why this work devolved upon the chancellor. He was the most important member of the council and was its unofficial president. He was almost always a prominent ecclesiastic who from experience and tradition would be interested in justice. As chancellor he was responsible for issuing the original writs that initiated actions in the common law courts and was therefore familiar with what justice was obtainable from the common law. As an ecclesiastic he was well versed in canon and Roman law and could draw upon legal principles from these two great bodies of law and employ them to give legal remedy when it was unobtainable under the existing judicial system. By position and by training, the chancellor was well equipped to administer the royal prerogative justice and under its elastic coverage to give legal remedy. In the fourteenth century when it was established that the council could not judge in common law and thus had to surrender its com-

[1] SM, no. 70G.

mon law powers to parliament, the council, and especially the chancellor, came to specialize in noncommon law justice, which came to be known as equitable law.

At the beginning of the fourteenth century the chancellor was presiding over special sessions of the council, or parts of it, in order to give remedy. As early as 1319 the records speak of the "council of the chancery," and we may say that the chancellor was beginning to develop a formalized jurisdiction of his own and was setting forth on a path that was to place his successors over a court distinct from the council. When the chancellor could not give a plaintiff a writ that would provide remedy under common law, he would give informal justice. The council deferred to the superior legal knowledge of the chancellor and permitted him to select assistants to help him dispose of a mounting litigation. He chose prominent justices, serjeants, and learned legal men to sit with him in court and began to establish a procedure and to follow rules. He and his assistants rapidly increased the scope and amount of their special justice until by the reign of Richard II there existed in all but name a separate court of chancery. An ordinance of 1390 for the regulation of the king's council specified that "matters touching the office of chancellor are to be sent for determination before him in chancery"; but matters of common law were to go before the common law justices.[2] Both parliament and council encouraged the flow of all special justice into chancery and the majority of petitioners addressed their petitions for remedy directly to the chancellor. Perhaps it is inaccurate to say that there was a distinct court of chancery until the reign of Henry VII, and yet one functioned throughout the fifteenth century. Seldom did the council deal with justice.[3] Under Henry IV it had judicial sessions but twice a week and under Henry VI but once a week; in many weeks justice never appeared on the agenda. The council devoted itself to the business of state while the chancellor and his court dealt with justice. A definite body of chancery law was evolving and there can be discerned a definite chancery procedure. Under Henry VI the court of chancery consisted of the chancellor, the master of the rolls, two other justices, and four masters of chancery. The members of the court increased rapidly. By Henry VII's reign there were twelve clerks to assist the chancellor and during the sixteenth century a large staff of underclerks and minor officials mushroomed to handle the mountain of petitions. In the fifteenth century all petitions requesting civil relief came to the chancellor and assistants, who invariably disposed of them; rarely was the council bothered with legal problems. Just as the council had created a court of special criminal jurisdiction, so too did it give birth to a court of special civil jurisdiction.

The civil litigation coming to the chancery was variable. Individuals who

[2] SM, no. 64D.
[3] SM, no. 70A.

considered themselves injured and who believed that they could obtain no remedy in ordinary courts petitioned for extraordinary relief. All sorts of requests were made which based their appeal for justice upon the royal favor or conscience. The royal boon was humbly requested, asked for out of love of God, or sought because of charity. A typical petition of the fifteenth century requested writs that would summon two men to appear before the chancellor "in the king's chancery, which is a court of conscience, there to make answer in this matter, as is demanded by reason and conscience; otherwise the said petitioner is and shall be without remedy—which God forbid!" Frequent reasons given for asking remedy were that the petitioner was poor, or that he was too old, or sick, or that his adversary was too rich and powerful and would bribe and coerce jurors of a common law court. Or perhaps by accident, luck, or trick an adversary had won an advantage that could be redressed only by special legal action of the chancery.[4]

The increasing rigidity of the common law, noted previously, continued in the fourteenth and fifteenth centuries. Common law courts recognized just so much justice and stopped; the general opinion was that the common law courts gave enough justice and should not expand their jurisdiction. It was this inflexible legal attitude that contributed most to the rise of the equitable jurisdiction of the court of chancery. While the common law courts refused to take any part in the vast developing area of uses and trusts, it was to such law that the chancery devoted much of its time. We have seen that in the thirteenth century it became common in real estate transactions for a possessor of land to convey legal ownership to another party with the understanding that this party would hold the land in trust or confidence for the possessor and permit him to use it. All sorts of legal arrangements developed around the principle of the use and trust and such devices increased in the fourteenth and fifteenth centuries. To evade various statutes of mortmain men granted ownership of land to individuals with the understanding that ecclesiastical establishments should enjoy the use. Often during the troubled fifteenth century when numerous men lived under constant fear of being convicted of high treason and sentenced to forfeiture of their land, the use was employed to save the family inheritance. Men conveyed their land to another party with the agreement that the party was to hold it in trust or for their use. If they were then convicted of high treason their land could not be confiscated because legal ownership resided in the other party; heirs of men convicted of treason could therefore still enjoy the use of the land. The same device was employed to escape feudal burdens and to defraud creditors. When services, payments, or debts were demanded, the responsible person would default. If attempt was made to seize his land it was discovered that legal ownership resided in another person and that there was no legal remedy. None of these transactions were sanctioned by the common law.

[4] SM, no. 71.

When A granted legal title of his land to B for A's use or for the use of a third party C, and B failed in his trust and would not permit use of the land, there was no remedy for A or for C in the common law courts. The common law recognized only the legal ownership of B and would not look behind him and inquire into his obligations to A or C.

The use and trust, though unrecognized by common law, were enforced by the royal council. When use or trust agreements were not fulfilled, the council would accept petitions asking remedy and enforce the obligation. By the early fifteenth century the chancellor and his assistants were handling most of these petitions and by the reign of Henry V the chancery can be said to have had jurisdiction over uses, trusts, and confidences. It became established custom for the court of chancery to enforce uses. When A granted legal title of land to B under agreement of a use or trust and B failed to honor the agreement, A then petitioned the chancery for remedy. The chancery would order B to do with the land as directed by A and if B refused would imprison him for contempt of court. Under writ of *sub poena* (under punishment) B was ordered to fulfil his bargain. In the name of equity or conscience the chancery intervened to uphold an agreement unrecognized by common law. Because of the convenience of uses and trusts the practice was widespread in the fifteenth century and much litigation arose in this field.[5] The court of chancery, which had established its jurisdiction over uses and trusts, developed a body of equitable law to deal with such litigation. It may be that eventually the common law courts would have been forced to modify their law and to recognize the principle of the use but this would not have come for some time because the common law was so cumbersome and complicated that it could be changed only slowly and with much labor. The chancellor and his court, knowledgeable in the law and unrestricted by rules and procedure, were eminently equipped to give quick remedy in this field of civil law and greatly eased the task of the common law courts when finally they accepted the use and trust. Meanwhile the court of chancery served an important function in supplementing the common law and enforcing justice that had to be enforced. The court of chancery, like the Court of Star Chamber, was never popular and was only grudgingly accepted but, while the common law courts remained reluctant to expand their justice, it was a much needed institution.

Little need be said about the three traditional and superior courts of common law—the king's bench, the court of common pleas, and the court of exchequer. They continued to grow in strength and prestige and came to be staffed by experienced and learned justices. Among them they handled most of the civil litigation. The king's bench was the supreme court for criminal causes. The court of common pleas specialized in civil cases between private parties. The court of exchequer held a monopoly over revenue cases relevant

[5] SM, no. 71c.

to the royal government. The three were all characterized by conservative practices and followed inflexible rules and procedure.

During the fourteenth century there was bitter competition among these three courts for more justice. The justices, living primarily from legal fees, concentrated upon increasing the volume of business in their courts and manufactured all sorts of legal fictions in order to steal justice from their competitors. In this legal thievery the court of common pleas naturally suffered the greatest loss because it adjudicated the civil cases, which netted the most profitable fees. The suitors, it must be realized, also became involved in this competition and helped to influence its course. They wished to secure the swiftest and most effective justice possible and took their cases to the court that operated the most efficiently.

One of the largest inroads upon the court of common pleas was made by the court of exchequer. Though the exchequer had been forbidden by statutes and ordinances to hear common pleas, in the fourteenth century it ignored such legislation and secured a lucrative jurisdiction over private debts. Private creditors, knowing that the procedure of the exchequer to collect royal debts was quick, maneuvered to place their debts or claims under the exchequer's jurisdiction. The favorite stratagem was for a private creditor to allege that he was a crown debtor but was having difficulty paying his debts because he could not collect a private debt. By reason of the private debt, so the creditor argued, he was the less (*quo minus*) able to pay what he claimed was due the exchequer. This court was only too eager to enter the game and immediately placed its procedure at the disposal of the creditor so that he could quickly collect his debt. The justification was, of course, that the crown was suffering financial loss because of an uncollected private debt and that the exchequer should do everything possible to aid rapid collection. The legal device of *quo minus* was well developed in the first half of the fourteenth century and gave to the court of exchequer a rich area of litigation.

As though it was not enough to lose cases to the court of exchequer the court of common pleas was also assailed by the king's bench, which occupied the highest position of the three courts. The king's bench, likewise desiring to dip into the civil cases of the common pleas court, did so by the devious method of ensnaring litigants to civil causes in its prison, the marshalsea. By means of a falsified criminal charge the king's bench would secure the incarceration of a defendant in the marshalsea prison and then assume jurisdiction over the civil cause. In the vicinity of Westminster and London such imprisonment was secured by a bill of Middlesex, which consisted of an order to the sheriff of Middlesex County to arrest a defendant to a civil action on a criminal charge such as trespass and place him in the marshalsea. When a defendant did not reside in Middlesex County the king's bench achieved its end by addressing a writ *latitat* ("he lurks") to the sheriff of the defendant's county which stated that the latter, a criminal suspect, was lurking in the county and that he should be apprehended and placed under jurisdiction of the court. Once this had been accomplished, the king's bench forgot about the trumped-up criminal charge and proceeded to try the civil case. Despite vociferous protest of the common pleas' justices the king's bench continued this usurpation and thereby acquired a share of original civil jurisdiction.

Below the three central common law courts were those of the itinerant justices. They continued without much modification in the fourteenth and fifteenth centuries. The itinerant justices of assize operated under the *nisi prius* system introduced by Edward I. Twice a year they visited the counties and made the justice of Westminster available through the length and

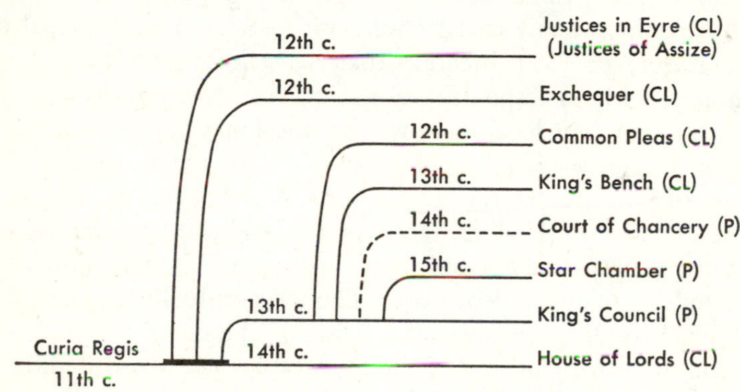

The Descent of the Common Law and Prerogative Courts from the *Curia Regis*. Adapted from G. B. Adams, "The Descendants of the *Curia Regis*," *American Historical Review*, XIII (1907), 11.

breadth of the realm. Under their commission they were empowered to try civil cases pending at the Westminster courts, to hear all criminal cases not disposed of locally by justices of the peace, and to deliver the jails (gaols). After the judicial reforms of Edward I the itinerant justices no longer went out on general eyres but limited themselves to purely judicial business; they no longer had administrative tasks. By the end of the fourteenth century when they went around on their circuits they did not meet with the whole county court. Instead of having grand juries from each hundred, borough, and agrarian village, a single grand jury represented all the county and made the indictments.

But while the heavy burden of the itinerant justices had been lightened by relieving them of their general administrative duties, their judicial work still remained heavy. In the fourteenth century, therefore, they were relieved further by the transference of much criminal justice to local justices of the peace. The institution of the justice of the peace had its origin, as we have seen, in the keeper of the peace of Edward I's reign. The keeper of the peace was, however, primarily a local assistant of the sheriff who devoted his time to preserving the peace and to apprehending criminals; he was a local police officer until the fourteenth century. The transformation of the keeper of the peace into the justice of the peace began in the reign of Edward III. In 1327 a statute ordered that good and lawful men should be appointed to keep the peace in each county.[6] A statute of 1330 repeated this provision and added to it the instructions that men were to be indicted before them and to be imprisoned. Moreover, the keepers of the peace were to send the indictments to the justices of gaol delivery. This was an essential step because the keepers now exercised certain judicial functions along with the police. They received indictments from grand juries and committed those indicted to prison to await trial by itinerant justices. The principal change came in a statute of 1360 directing that in each county there should be appointed a lord whose responsibility was to keep the peace. He was to be assisted by three or four local men, worthy and knowledgeable in legal matters. They were empowered to make arrests, to receive indictments, and to hear and to determine "at the king's suit" all felonies and trespasses. By this statute and one of 1361 the keepers of the peace were converted into justices of the peace; they not only could receive indictments but could try those indicted for felony and trespass.[7] Though eventually all justices of the peace would be leading squires and knights of the county, at this stage of their development many officers of the royal court were appointed; the kings were not yet certain that they could trust local men with such important criminal justice.

During the rest of the fourteenth century further statutes defined and added to the powers of the justices of the peace. A statute of 1362 directed that justices of the peace should hold four judicial sessions a year to try criminal cases; this was the origin of the famous quarter sessions. Soon they heard complaints against local bailiffs, sheriffs, and mayors of boroughs and thus came to acquire a supervisory and restraining power over local administrators. In an ordinance of 1380 they were granted jurisdiction of the Statutes of Winchester, Northampton, and Westminster for the preservation of the peace, power to bind persons to abide by the peace, powers of search and inquest, and power to hear and to determine all criminal cases except treason. By this time the justices of the peace had almost replaced the criminal jurisdiction of the itinerant justices; only the most difficult cases were reserved for the latter. In a statute of 1388 the custom of holding quarter sessions was reaffirmed and the number of justices for each county limited to six or eight. This limitation, however, was generally disregarded and the number tended to increase. In 1392 the justices of the peace were empowered

[6] SM, no. 62A.
[7] SM, no. 62I.

to raise county levies in order to keep law and order and to suppress the acts of violence perpetrated by indentured retainers of the magnates. On such occasions even the sheriffs were to be under their orders. Meanwhile the justices had been permitted to hold emergency judicial sessions when they deemed it necessary and, after the abolition of the special justices of the laborers, to enforce the Statute of Laborers, which in 1351 had specified official wages and prices in order to control the inflation following the Black Death of 1348–1350.[8] By the end of the fourteenth century the administrative duties of the justice of the peace had become almost as important as his judicial work. He superseded local officers in their duties, he checked on powerful officials such as the sheriffs and coroners, and he was the chief medium of communication between central and local government. The quarter sessions of the justice of the peace had superseded the county court as the governing body of the county.

Although local men appointed justices of the peace were either knights or squires, there were no definite qualifications for office until 1439. A statute then provided that no man was eligible unless he had an annual income worth £20. This sum was the value of the old knight's fee and so the office of the justice of the peace was associated with the landed and moneyed class—the aristocratic gentry. Like the sheriff, the justice of the peace was always an appointive office. By the fifteenth century all the men selected were from the counties; men from Westminster no longer received appointment. With the reign of Richard II the justices were granted a fee of 4s. per day for their services and this continued to be standard remuneration to the end of the Middle Ages. Also under Richard II a form of commission was developed which continued down to modern times. The king appointed certain men as justices in each county and empowered all of them to keep the peace and to make arrests; two men were empowered to hold sessions for trying individuals indicted.

By the fifteenth century the justices of the peace had three main functions. The first was to conserve the peace by putting down rioters and arresting malefactors. The second was judicial. They received indictments and at their quarter sessions tried indicted men by a trial jury. All criminal cases except treason were triable although the more knotty cases were reserved for the itinerant justices. They were also receiving statutory power to hold summary trials for petty offenses. This meant that they tried specified offenses without jury trial. In 1433, for example, a statute empowered the justices to punish summarily individuals using false weights and measures. A statute of 1464 which established regulations for the manufacture of cloth provided summary punishment for offenders. Such statutes were numerous. They instructed the justices of the peace to call suspected persons before them, to examine them, and to fine them if found guilty. The third function

[8] SM, no. 62D.

of the justices was administrative and under this rubric fell the duties of helping in local government and checking upon the other local officers. By the middle of the fifteenth century the justices of the peace had developed into the most efficient and powerful local officers of justice and administration. Again the kings by their command had placed local men in a position of trust and power and forced them to assist in the governance of the realm. Again the aristocratic gentry, the rural middle class, had been made an instrument of self-government and by experience gained further political stature and wisdom. The kings in parliament had to deal with these skilled politicians and administrator-justices, men of their own making. They had truly created an experienced body politic of the realm.

The phenomenal expansion of royal justice in the twelfth and thirteenth centuries had reduced the local public courts to insignificance. By the early fourteenth century they heard only cases involving not more than 40s. Hardly any of the freeholders attended the county court; they discharged their obligation of suit to court through attorneys. It seems likely that the sheriff disposed of most of the legal business by himself. None of the local public courts was permitted to use jury trial; they still used the old system of compurgation.

The history of feudal courts is the same. They lost their jurisdiction to the royal courts. Most that still existed by the reign of Henry VII did so only in name; the private feudal court was dead. In the fifteenth century, however, when royal justice could not be upheld against the overmighty subject there was some danger that the great lords might again acquire extensive judicial power. They usurped royal justice and substituted their law and their courts for the king's in numerous areas of the realm. Some magnates were able to establish their own conciliar courts, to try cases, to issue writs counter to the king's, and to force men to show cause why they had recourse to royal courts rather than to theirs. The magnates, ignoring the royal jurisdiction and writs, divided up the realm into judicial and political spheres which they controlled with their indentured bands. This development was, however, but temporary and was ended by Edward IV and Henry VII. Still, if strong kings had not replaced the weak Lancastrians it is possible that three hundred years of legal progress and centralization might have been undone.

By Henry VII's reign the manorial court had ceased to have much judicial importance. Most peasants were now free and had access to the royal courts. Furthermore, the royal courts had begun to protect peasants still holding land in villeinage. Such tenants were acquiring the name of copyholder because they held their land according to terms of tenure copied on the manorial court roll. In the fifteenth century the royal courts, deciding that copyholders should be given more protection than their copyhold gave them in the manorial court, assumed jurisdiction over them. If a lord arbitrarily dispossessed a copyholder of his tenements, the latter was permitted to initiate an action of trespass in the royal courts to recover his land. As early as 1457 we hear of such action and by 1481 it is definitely established that a copyholder can initiate an action against his lord if deprived of his holding contrary to manorial court custom. This meant that manorial court custom was incorporated into the royal law and enforced by the king's courts. Henceforth the manorial court was essentially a place where transfers in tenancy occurred. Tenants who wished to leave their land paid what obligations were due to the lord and sold their right to the tenement to another party who was accepted as tenant. Also when a tenant died his heir was accepted as the tenant.

2. THE LEGAL PROFESSION

During the reign of Edward I a distinct legal profession was taking form. Men called pleaders who were learned and experienced in the common law were becoming a legal group quite separate from the attorneys and apprentices. But this was only a beginning. It was during the fourteenth and fifteenth centuries that the legal profession became highly organized and obtained a monopoly over the law. It was the legal profession that completed the system of the medieval common law, that gave it its peculiar characteristics, and that worked out its detailed system of rules. It was this learned, skilled, and tough legal profession that molded and practiced a tough common law that withstood all competition and attempts to weaken it and emerged triumphant under the legal principle that the law of the realm is the supreme master, above both king and parliament.

Our first concern is with the training of the legal profession. We have seen that Edward I realized the necessity of a trained profession and made some provision for the education of apprentices. But not until the fourteenth century did a definite system of legal education develop, and then informally and by the efforts of those who desired to learn and to practice the law. As early as the thirteenth century young men aspiring to the legal profession had gone to Westminster to observe the working of the law and to study the texts and famous cases. They lived in a tavern or inn conveniently located near the courts and, drawn together by their legal interests, began to discuss the law in their chambers and to eat together. Eventually they became numerous enough to take over an inn or tavern and to use it as their headquarters. They then seemed to have formed clubs or associations which invited and hired practicing lawyers to lecture to them. Thus, just as the universities had arisen to teach the liberal arts and professional fields and just as the guilds had taken form to give economic strength and security to merchants and craftsmen, societies developed to learn the law. And so arose the Inns of Court. As the societies became larger, more prosperous, and better organized, they came to be directed by experienced lawyers who established training requirements and set the qualifications for permission to practice the law. Just as the halls of the universities were absorbed into colleges controlled by masters, so the inns and taverns were absorbed into legal inns controlled by experienced practitioners of the law.

The Inns of Court, concentrated between the city of London and Westminster, were thus strategically located midway between the source of most of the clients and the courts. In this area developed the four principal Inns of Court. Although some scholars have conjectured that Lincoln's Inn derived its name from the earl of Lincoln, who supposedly was a founder and patron, this was probably not the case. The name appears to have been derived from a king's serjeant named Thomas de Lincoln who owned property which was the earliest headquarters of the society of Lincoln's Inn. This was about the middle of the fourteenth century and seems to mark the beginning of the society of Lincoln's Inn. Early in the fifteenth century the society moved into better and more commodious quarters in the house of the bishop of Chichester. The society of Gray's Inn derived its name from Lord Gray of Wilton, whose house it rented. Gray's Inn probably was organized in the same period as Lincoln's Inn. The other two chief inns, the Middle and Inner Temple, were located in buildings that originally had belonged to the crusading order of the Knights Templars. During the reign of Edward II in 1324 the order was dissolved by church decree and its buildings were temporarily occupied by the Knights Hospitalers, who later rented them to young apprentices at law. By the year 1347 apprentices were renting part of the complex of buildings called the Temple and were organized into a society. Before the middle of the fifteenth century there were two societies occupying the buildings of the Temple within the corporation of London in contrast to that part of the Temple outside the city boundaries of London, the Outer Temple, which was never occupied by lawyers. This explains the origin of the names Inner Temple (buildings innermost to London) and Middle Temple (buildings next to the corporation boundary but between the Inner and Outer Temples).

Eventually there were associated with the four principal inns subsidiary inns occupied by new societies of students who wished to have a connection with older established inns. These associated inns were called the Chancery Inns because they were preparatory schools in which the junior apprentice was expected to master all the legal writs that issued out of the chancery. When he had completed this training he normally moved up to one of the four inns. Each of the four inns had at least two junior Chancery Inns associated with it; the Inner Temple had three—Clifford's Inn, Clement's Inn, and Lyon's Inn.

The Inns of Court were governed by committees of distinguished lawyers called benchers because when they dined in the commons or great dining hall they sat together on a bench at a table (high) placed on a raised platform at one end of the hall. The benchers educated and controlled the apprentices. They co-opted new members when necessary and gave instruction. They seem to have rotated the responsibility of instruction and taught only at certain times. When serving in this capacity they were called readers because they read in the law. In the fifteenth century we know that the readers lectured on the "old" laws, that is, the statutes prior to Edward III. The great statutes of Edward I constituted a substantial part of all fifteenth-century readings. From the readings that are extant we can observe that the readers taught simply and accurately and strove to explain the content and effect of the fundamental statutes upon which a large part of the law rested. It was only in the sixteenth century that readers tried to impress their colleagues with their great learning and erudition. Between term times of the courts when there was no opportunity for the students to attend the courts and to observe the pleadings and procedure, the readers lectured on the law and held discussions.

During the summer vacation and the long winter evenings the students held informal discussions and practice (moot) courts in which they tried difficult cases concocted for them by the benchers and readers. The moot courts afforded the best preparation for pleading because the students could not practice in the royal law courts. Using the benches and tables of the dining hall the participants arranged them as they would be in a court. Low benches (forms) were placed before the high bench so as to form a dividing barrier of the court known as the bar. On this bar sat the counsel for defendant and plaintiff. Experienced members would sit at the outer ends of the bar while the beginners would sit between them. Those who sat at the ends of the benches were full members of the inn who had been admitted to plead at its bar. Actually senior apprentices, they were eventually called utter or outer barristers because they sat at the outer end of the bar, and then later simply barristers. The junior apprentices were known as inner barristers. The outer barristers bore the brunt of the pleading while the inner barristers took minor parts. As they conducted their mock trial both outer and inner barristers were observed by the benchers and readers, who decided when the inner barristers were qualified to become outer barristers entitled to practice law in the royal courts. When an inner barrister was made an outer barrister and became a full member of the inn, he was said to be called to the bar. This was the only qualification necessary for a lawyer to practice law in the common law courts. The judges recognized full membership in one of the four inns as sufficient proof of a man's ability to plead in the courts and so long as a lawyer retained his membership he could practice the law. If he was deprived of membership, he lost the right to plead in the courts and was disbarred. This meant that all the legal standards were controlled by the inns and that the caliber of the members was largely set by the level of the standards.

The inns worked zealously to improve their training and standards and to surpass each other in the product that they admitted to the bar. This intense competition accounts for the high degree of competency that has always characterized the English legal profession. And the tradition is still maintained. One has but to read the novels of Charles Dickens, who was learned in the law, to see how rigid and difficult was the legal training of the Inns of Court in the middle of the nineteenth century. Dickens' observations on the Inns of Court in the *Pickwick Papers* are no imaginary flight of a novelist but a firsthand and realistic description. The following remarks addressed to Mr. Pickwick were as true in the nineteenth century as in the fifteenth: "What do you know of the time when young men shut themselves up in those lonely rooms, and read and read, hour after hour, and night after night, till their reason wandered beneath their midnight studies; till their mental powers were exhausted; till morning's light brought no freshness or health to them; and they sank beneath the unnatural devotion of their youthful energies to their dry old books?"

Once the aspiring lawyer had become a barrister he had placed his foot only on the first rung of a ladder with many higher legal grades and honors. He still had to prove himself and to gain professional recognition. The most capable and experienced barristers formed an inner clique or circle of lawyers called serjeants. They were an elite group who may originally have been selected by the judges of the court of common pleas. Eventually the judges named men nominated by the serjeants. The serjeants held a monopoly over the legal business in the Westminster courts and participated in the most complicated and lucrative cases. They had their own societies or inns known as serjeants' inns and were entitled to wear a distinctive headdress called a coif which was a white silk skullcap. From these men the king selected his serjeants—the king's serjeants—who, the most distinguished lawyers in the realm, represented the crown in all its actions and tendered expert legal advice to the king. Normally the justices of the common law courts were selected from these renowned serjeants.

In addition to the barristers who did the pleading in the common law courts there were lesser legal practitioners known as attorneys. They appeared in court for litigants and accomplished the bulk of the routine legal work such as drawing up necessary papers. During the fourteenth century they were accepted as members of the Inns of Court but with a rank equivalent only to that of the inner barristers. Nevertheless this association with full-fledged barristers gave them the opportunity to discuss legal business of mutual interest and to keep themselves informed about the most recent developments in the law. With the formation of the court of chancery during the late fourteenth and fifteenth centuries a new group of lawyers arose to handle its legal business. They were known as solicitors because originally they were chancery clerks who solicited additional work by assisting litigants with the papers necessary in the court of chancery. Gradually many clerks found this business so lucrative and demanding that they resigned their positions and devoted all their time to legal work for litigants in chancery. Thus originated the solicitors who practiced law in the chancery.

3. LEGISLATION

The golden age of legislation occurred during the reign of Edward I; then did king and great council or king and parliament enact the great statutes that determined the course of English common law. The legislation of Edward I contributed more than any other development to the legislative supremacy of parliament acknowledged by all in the fourteenth and fifteenth centuries. Only occasionally did lawyers and justices claim the right of disregarding statutes which were at variance with the common law, with God's law, or with the royal prerogative. But this sporadic and ineffective defiance had no effect upon the statutes. Ultimately the legal profession became the staunch ally of parliament and regarded it as the guardian of the fundamental law of the land. This fundamental law was ideally considered a perfect body of law which represented the work of God; the common law, man's law, was supposed to be but a reflection of it. When it did not reflect this law it was the duty of king and parliament to make adjustments in the common law by statutes. Such adjustment had been accomplished in so masterful a fashion under Edward I that little was done in the following two centuries. It almost appeared that parliament had abandoned its control over the development of the common law. Few fundamental adjustments were made and for the most part the common law was left to be molded by the justices and the lawyers. When statutes did deal with the law, generally they were concerned with making it more specific, defining it more closely, or reaffirming and expanding its scope; they were concerned with details rather than with principles. A casual reading of the fourteenth- and fifteenth-century statutes leaves the impression, as Maitland has said, that "if for a moment the Parliament of Edward IV can raise its soul above defective barrels of fish and fraudulent gutter tiles this will be in order to prohibit 'cloish, kayles, half-bowl, hand-in-hand and hand-out, quekeboard' and such other games as interfere with the practice of archery."

Except for a few key statutes we can rapidly summarize the nature of late medieval legislation. A long series of statutes dealt with the function and obligations of the executive, from the king down to the humblest royal officers. Most of the statutes were concerned with specific infractions but, collectively, they did contribute to the growth of the common law principle that executive officers who act beyond their powers are liable for prosecution. Eventually this principle was to be transformed into the famous constitutional doctrine of ministerial responsibility. By far the most important statute dealing with criminal law, and one of which we shall say more, was that of Edward III in 1352. It clearly distinguished treason from felony and specified what constituted high treason.[9] In the areas of criminal law the list of felonies was enlarged, the boundary line between criminal and civil liability was drawn more distinctly, and more was said about crime and tort. Unfor-

[9] SM, no. 62F.

tunately, little that was clear was enacted on crime and tort and the distinction between them became hopelessly blurred. Finally, statutes attempted to shore up the writs and to protect them from the legal abuses that were all too current, as well as to reinforce the courts against the flagrant attacks upon their procedure, law, and sentences.[10]

Besides these statutes that adjusted the law there were others enacted to regulate the political, economic, social, and religious needs of the realm. We have already referred to the acts of attainder and to those which repealed attaint. Numerous statutes concentrated upon the regulation of domestic industry and commerce. Price and wage regulations were established. Standards of quality were introduced in the woolen industry. In the wake of the Black Death workers were frozen to their jobs and all aspects of the economy were regulated to combat the disastrous effect of the epidemic. The Statute of Laborers (1351) was a comprehensive list of economic regulations. Import and export restrictions were imposed on international trade. Both alien and English merchants were restricted as to the countries where they could buy and sell and as to the ports where they could transact their business. At times the legislation seems to indicate a policy of royal protectionism. Certain English products could not be exported, certain foreign goods were prohibited entry, goods had to be shipped in English bottoms, and the amount of gold and silver that could be taken out of the realm was strictly regulated.[11] When the evils of the indenture system had become apparent statutes were enacted to prohibit maintenance and livery.[12]

The statutes of the fourteenth and fifteenth centuries that dealt with the church are of great interest because of their relation to the Reformation in the sixteenth century. Most were intended to reduce the power of the church and to define more precisely the boundaries between secular and spiritual authority. We must skip over the numerous statutory clauses dealing with the jurisdiction of English ecclesiastical courts and with the rights of criminal clergy and comment upon a few of the statutes that affected the relations between England and the papacy. We are already familiar with the development of a spirit of English nationalism and with the concomitant rise of anticlericalism and antipapalism. We have noted the issues of contention between Edward I and the papacy. And in the fourteenth and fifteenth centuries we saw these and other issues drive an ever widening wedge between the English church and the papacy. The kings would brook no interference with their prerogative authority and the English subjects became increasingly restive and defiant because of what was considered unjustified papal authority and interference in their realm. From this feeling sprang the statutes restricting ecclesiastical authority.

[10] SM, no. 64B.
[11] SM, no. 62D, H, and J.
[12] SM, no. 64C.

The first was that of Provisors in 1351.[13] It attempted to carry farther what had been begun by the Statute of Carlisle in 1307. It directed that all men receiving papal provisions (appointments) would be liable to imprisonment. It stated that election for ecclesiastical office should be freely held and that the advowsons held by king and lords should be respected. This statute was never effectively enforced because the king too often connived with the pope to secure the appointment of a royal favorite. Despite a papal promise in 1377 that there would be no interference in ecclesiastical elections, interference continued. In 1388, for example, the pope on his own authority transferred Alexander Neville from York to Saint Andrews and Thomas Arundel from Ely to York. Then in 1390 the Statute of Provisors was re-enacted and confirmed and for a while observed. But by 1396 the pope was again making key appointments and he continued to do so in the fifteenth century. Italians and other foreigners were appointed and administered their offices, many without ever going to England. Though the popes, often with royal support, were the victors, they ultimately lost control over ecclesiastical appointments under such strong kings as Henry VII and Henry VIII, who nominated and secured the selection of their candidates without consulting the papacy.

Two other statutes enacted against papal jurisdiction were more successful; they were the Statutes of Praemunire ("to premonish" or "warn"). The first, enacted in 1353, was to end the tradition of appealing cases outside England to the papal court. It declared forfeiture and outlawry upon those who appealed a case in foreign courts (meaning the papal court) that was adjudicative in the royal courts.[14] In 1365 another statute was passed which specifically prohibited taking a case to the papal court. In 1393 came the great Statute of Praemunire which imposed forfeiture of goods as the penalty for anyone who "purchases or pursues, or causes to be purchased or pursued, in the court of Rome" bulls or instruments that would take justice out of England or in any way infringe upon the royal authority and justice.[15] While this did not end papal jurisdiction in minor matters, it ended papal influence in great affairs of the state. The ground had been broken for the breach with Rome under Henry VIII and for the total destruction of papal authority in England.

Other statutes regarding the church are less significant. In 1391 a statute on the restriction of uses confirmed the Statute of Mortmain enacted in 1279, extended the scope of its provisions, and provided for forfeiture to the king of land alienated for the use of the church.[16] In 1401 a statute providing for the punishment of heretics was enacted. This was a concession of Henry IV to secure the support of the church and was the only secular law enacted

[13] SM, no. 62E.
[14] SM, no. 62G.
[15] SM, nos. 64F, 69A.
[16] SM, no. 64E.

in medieval England against heresy. It stated that all heretics (this meant Lollards) who refused to recant their doctrinal errors or those individuals who relapsed into heresy should be turned over to the state to be "burned before the people in some prominent place."[17] Fortunately few men were punished under the statute and England escaped the persecution that characterized some of the continental states. Burning at the stake was always unpopular in England and remained so even during the Reformation of the sixteenth century.

4. CRIMINAL LAW

Criminal law in the fourteenth and fifteenth centuries is primarily a history of further elaboration of principles established in the reign of Edward I. Except for the Statute of Treasons in 1352 no fundamental change in criminal law came by legislation. And it was by parliamentary legislation that criminal law had to be enlarged or modified because there was widespread feeling against any extension of criminal law by judicial decision. But even though criminal law was developed more by statute than any other branch of the law, fear of change halted further legislation in this area. A plateau was reached and a law that became ever more archaic was not radically changed until the nineteenth century, and even then there were still such outmoded survivals as trial by battle, deodands, and benefit of clergy.

The most serious of all crimes was treason as defined by the Statute of Treasons in 1352.[18] This statute specified seven offenses which were to be regarded as high treason. They fell under three principal categories: (1) imagining the king's death, which involved an intention to kill the king and a display of the intent by some overt act; (2) participating in war against the king; and (3) supporting the king's enemies. To the present day this statute has provided the foundation of the law of treason. By clearly specifying seven offenses as treason it distinguished treason from felony. It also separated high treason from petty treason. High treason was defined as an offense against the king and petty treason as an offense against a lord.

There were a few other statutes listing more offenses under treason, such as that of 1397, which stated that it was treasonable to compass the death of the king and to depose him, but not until the reign of Henry VIII did legislation significantly increase the number of new treasons. Throughout the Middle Ages the concept of treason was principally modified by stretching the definition of the statute of 1352. The following case illustrates how treason could be loosely interpreted. Report has it that Edward IV killed a white buck of a certain Thomas Burdett, who was so angry that he expressed the wish that the buck, horns and all, were in the belly of him who advised

[17] SM, no. 69B.
[18] SM, no. 62F.

the king to do it. This expressed wish was adjudged high treason. Whether or not the story is accurate we know that by the end of the fifteenth century any attempt shown by an overt act to depose the king, or to compel him by force to govern in a certain way, was considered as imagining the king's death. It was in this manner, by broad interpretation of the statute of 1352, that "constructive treasons" were created. And most of them have remained treasons to the present day.

The next most serious crime was felony. The traditional felonies, the common law felonies, were those crimes deemed especially serious when the common law was evolving—homicide, arson, burglary, robbery, rape, and larceny. These were capital crimes punishable by death. There were other various crimes declared felonies by statute that were also punishable by death. After the felonies came the minor crimes, punishable by fine and imprisonment, known as misdemeanors. Such crimes had formerly been called trespasses but this term was taken and used to denote civil wrongs. Often an act could be both a trespass and a misdemeanor. If, for example, an individual assaulted another person, he could be sued for trespass in a civil court and the assailed person could recover damages. This assault was also a misdemeanor; it was an indictable offense and could be punished by fine and imprisonment. The least serious crimes were known as petty offenses and were designated by statute. They might involve drunkenness, noise-making, or a scuffle in an alehouse and were punishable upon summary conviction by justices of the peace without jury trial. The usual sentence was a small fine or short period of imprisonment.

5. CIVIL LAW

There is not time to enter the intricate labyrinth that was the civil law in the late Middle Ages; we can but describe the general features of the land law, comment upon some of the innovations in legal actions dealing with real property, and note the development of the law to cover contract. We should bear in mind that by real property is meant land. The legal actions used to recover land were classified as real actions; they demanded specific real things which could be recovered.

In our discussion of the thirteenth-century land law we have seen that the kings were opposed to the legal devices developed to give a family control over estates of land indefinitely. Although the barons persuaded Edward I to consent to the insertion of the clause *De Donis Conditionalibus* (Concerning Conditional Gifts) in the Statute of Westminster II (1285) which created the estates tail and provided that land should descend according to the conditions imposed upon it, both the kings and royal courts fought the intent of the statute and tried to defeat the creation of estates in perpetuity. We have described how the lawyers and justices cooperated in developing the collusive lawsuit called recovery and a similar action called common recovery in order to circumvent the statute and to bar the entailed estate.

By the middle of the fifteenth century common recovery had been fully perfected and recognized in the common law courts. The judges would permit S who held an estate tail (subject to conditions restricting alienation) to alienate his estate of land in fee simple (no conditions on alienation) to a purchaser P in the following manner. Having purchased the land, P would initiate a suit against S, who immediately replied that his title to the land had come from a third party TP whom he vouched to warranty. TP would acknowledge that he had granted the land to S but would then fail to appear in court to defend the title. By default the court would then award the land to P in fee simple. In this manner the entailed estate was broken up or, as the courts said, barred. Once P had been awarded the land there was nothing that other parties with claims on the land could do. If there were heirs (issues in tail) and remainder men they were deprived of their rights. If they initiated an action to recover the land they were informed that they must initiate the action against TP because he had held the legal title. But it was always arranged so that TP was a humble court official or some obscure figure who possessed so little property that it was useless to sue him. When common recovery was approved by the justices in the celebrated case of Taltarum in 1472 it was definitely established as the accepted method for recovering land that was entailed. This legal action, however unfair to the heir (issue in tail) and to the remainder men, was justified on the grounds that no man could establish conditions over land that would restrict what was done with it in perpetuity.

The other noteworthy advance in civil law was the extension of the common law to contract. We have seen that the common law virtually ignored contracts in the thirteenth century; when they were enforced it was in the church courts. When the court of chancery developed, however, it began to enforce contracts. Gradually the common law justices realized that they were depriving themselves of valuable fees by refusing to enforce contracts and so they cooperated with lawyers to devise legal remedies for contract. The remedies consisted of extending the meaning of trespass to cover broken contracts. The writ of trespass, essentially meaning that a defendant with "force and arms" and "against the peace of our lord the king" had interfered with a plaintiff's lands or goods, was extended to mean any interference with possession, however small the possession. But interference in the plaintiff's possession had to be proven or the writ of trespass would not hold.

After the invention of the writ of trespass it became evident that in numerous circumstances the plaintiff suffered serious loss when no trespass was involved. At this juncture obviously some remedy was needed and therefore the writ of trespass came to be extended to contracts. Lawyers began to argue that when an individual assumed (in Latin, *assumpsit*) an obligation to do something for another individual and then did not fulfil it, he had trespassed against the peace of mind of the second party and was consequently liable for damages. But in the fourteenth century when trespass began to be so interpreted, only one form of the writ of trespass, that of *assumpsit*, was accepted by the courts and only upon those occasions when the plaintiff had been injured by the defendant's malfeasance (wrongdoing in respect of a physical object by the defendant from which the plaintiff suffered loss). A Year Book of 1348 relates that a Humber ferryman so overloaded his ferry that the plaintiff's horse, which was being ferried across, was drowned. Although there was obviously no trespass involved because the plaintiff had freely parted with possession of his horse when he put it on the defendant's ferry, the writ was allowed to lie and damages were awarded because malfeasance could be proven. There is record of similar cases in which damages were awarded because of malfeasance. In one, a blacksmith lamed a horse entrusted to him for shodding; in another, a leech did his work so negligently that a horse died; and in still another, a plaintiff's hand was damaged by a surgeon. Whereas in these cases malfeasance could be proven and damages were awarded by the court, where the defendant's malfeasance could not be demonstrated the judges did not permit him to be sued under the writ of trespass.

By the middle of the fifteenth century judges were allowing the introduction of the writ of trespass when it was shown that the defendant had done nothing to carry out an agreement. But in these cases of nonfeasance (failure to fulfil a promise) damages were not awarded unless the plaintiff had paid some money to bind the agreement. Herein we detect the origin of the famous doctrine of consideration. It was argued that when nude contracts (*nuda pacta*) were struck they could not be enforced; only when a consideration was involved could a plaintiff sue the defendant. It became established that without consideration no simple contract was valid. The consideration was known as a *quid pro quo* (something for something) which, when received by an individual, obliged him to fulfil an agreement and made him liable for damages. The status of the person to whom the obligation was owed altered when he underwrote the agreement with a consideration. The doctrine of consideration was closely related to the action of debt developed originally to recover something of the plaintiff's which had been bailed to the defendant (*quid pro quo*).

We must realize that in areas of the law other than those cited above the common law was beginning to expand and to relax its rigid attitude. Common law justices decided that they would have to become more flexible if their courts were to withstand the competition of the new court of chancery where law and procedure were extremely elastic and where any unusual case was accepted. We may repeat what was said earlier, that the court of chancery with its equitable law forced the common law to take stock of its position and to respond to the new legal demands of a changing society. This expansion and modification was necessary if the common law was to remain vital and not become a vestigial legal system. And yet we can be thankful that there was rigidity and continuity of principle in the common law because no legal system can survive constant flux. To retain the faith and atmosphere of security essential for striking real estate agreements or entering into contracts, men have to feel that next year or twenty-five years hence the law will be the same as it is today or was ten years ago. They cannot act under the shadow of an ever changing law. The equitable law of the chancery lacked this legal stability and had it been permitted to make too great an inroad into the English law, legal chaos would have resulted and the whole edifice of the majestic common law system might have collapsed. The common law with its rigid defense of age-old principles and procedure could command what men in any age must have—faith and respect for the law.

6. PROCEDURE

In that branch of the law known as procedure the extensive innovations in royal justice combined with the new ideas sown by the legal renaissance of the twelfth and thirteenth centuries to effect fundamental and decisive change during the Middle Ages. In criminal law there was the new technique of indictment. In civil law there was the system of royal writs, a growth in the complexity of the rules of process, and an elaboration of the rules of pleading characterized by the numerous exceptions and replications granted to the litigants. In both civil and criminal law there emerged trial by jury. These developments contributed to making the royal courts and their procedure more elaborate and more rational. With the principal lines of procedure thus laid down what little change occurred in the fourteenth and fifteenth centuries was piecemeal under the direction of the judges, who adapted old procedure to new demands in civil and criminal litigation. Much of the change was stimulated by the rival courts, whose procedure, frequently more expeditious, forced the common law judges to improve their procedure in order to remain competitive. But procedural change in this period, being fragmented and uncoordinated, became also very complex and intricate. In fact, because of the unscrupulous litigation permitted and the litigiousness of the age, procedure became more and more irrational. There were, then, two procedural currents in the fourteenth and fifteenth centuries. On the one hand there was a modernization of procedure and the embracement of new legal ideas; on the other hand, a tendency to cling to old procedure that was archaic. Behind both tendencies was the shrewd lawyer with his unscrupulous litigiousness to complicate both old and new procedure. At the end of the Middle Ages legal procedure was a tangled skein which only an experienced lawyer could unravel. In this brief summary we can but emphasize the chief characteristics of late medieval procedure.

Let us speak first of criminal procedure. We will begin with process, the machinery used for securing the appearance in court of a person suspected of or charged with a crime. Into the fourteenth century arrests of individuals not yet indicted were customarily made by local men acting under the frankpledge system. In the next two centuries the tendency was to rely on royal officials such as the sheriff and coroner. The arrest of persons indicted was the responsibility of the sheriff and other officers entrusted with the conservation of the peace. It remained, however, the duty of all to help make an arrest when called upon. A person appealed or indicted of treason or felony who attempted to evade arrest was outlawed. Such a person was summoned at five successive courts and if he did not appear the sentence of outlawry was pronounced. This meant that besides having all his goods forfeited he was put outside the king's peace and, into the early fourteenth century, could be slain with impunity by any man. The weapon of outlawry was a brutal custom because it worked injustice upon many innocent men. There thus arose the tendency to permit the reversal of outlawry when a man could show that it had been unjustly placed over him.

Turning now to court procedure we see that it customarily involved two juries. First there was the grand jury that did the indicting. It consisted of a body of twenty-three men representing the county, men sworn to indict all criminals who had committed indictable offenses, that is, treason, felony, and misdemeanor. Into the fifteenth century the grand jury accused men on the basis of its own knowledge. It was supposed to be conversant with the facts of the crime. Only at the end of the century did it cease to be primarily a body of men who knew the criminal facts and become a body examining criminal evidence presented to it. A man who believed an individual guilty of a crime would go before the grand jury and in a bill of indictment state that this individual committed a particular crime. The grand jurors then heard the evidence for the prosecution. If they thought it sufficient, they would recommend trial by jury; if they thought it insufficient, they ignored the bill and the accused person went free. Only a majority decision of the grand jury was necessary to settle whether or not the bill was to be ignored.

Though trial by jury was the standard criminal trial we must recognize that it was still opposed by many men who refused consent to such trial. Under such circumstances consent was extorted by torture, by *peine forte et dure*. Some men, however, died under pressure of heavy weights rather than risk conviction and the forfeiture of their lands and chattels. As late as 1658 a man was pressed to death. In 1726 a man was pressed into pleading. *Peine forte et dure* was not abolished until 1772.

The petty jury consisted of twelve men who, after 1352, could not be members of the grand jury that had indicted the person under trial. This change in the composition of the petty jury still did not render it impartial; men who served on it continued to be prejudiced in one way or another. Until the late fifteenth century a majority verdict ruled, but by Henry VII's reign the law demanded a unanimous verdict. Criminal suspects, though still forbidden legal assistance, were somewhat compensated by the allowance of numerous technical pleas that could result in the court's dismissal of the indictment. There were, however, certain alternatives to this normal criminal procedure. Petty offenses, we have seen, were nonindictable and could be tried summarily by justices of the peace. Also, the appeal still existed. An appellee could claim trial by battle or submit to trial by jury. Though trial by battle was becoming quite unusual, appeal remained common and did not end until 1819.

As to punishment we shall speak mainly of that given for high treason. Once this crime had been set apart from all other crimes and had been branded as the most serious, the sentence of mere hanging was regarded as too light. Various indignities were therefore added to it. At first the convicted person was dragged through the streets to the scaffold. Later he was taken on a hurdle (wooden frame). After execution the body was quartered and beheaded and sections of it were displayed at prominent places in London such as London Bridge to serve as a reminder of the fate suffered by treasonable men. The victim's land was forfeited to the crown. At times petty treason was punished by burning at the stake. For felonies and lesser crimes the common sentences were mutilation, imprisonment, and fines.

The principal change in civil procedure took place with the jury. The twelve jurors, originally regarded as witnesses, were by the fifteenth century considered judges of fact. No longer was it assumed that the civil jury, before sitting in court, would become familiar with the facts of the case to be tried. Rather, the jurors came to court and then the parties placed evidence before them and brought in witnesses to testify publicly in court. In the fifteenth century the civil jury was assuming its modern form, a jury that tried questions of fact. But the transformation was not yet complete because jurors were still selected from the region in which the case had originated. They were familiar with the facts and were expected to use this knowledge in settling the case. If a civil jury should give a false verdict it was liable to be attainted. When this occurred a new jury of twenty-four tried the case again; if its verdict differed from the former verdict the first jury was severely punished. By the fifteenth century few were the occasions when other forms of civil trial were held. At times there was trial by battle for property cases and occasionally there was compurgation.

During the fourteenth and fifteenth centuries the lawyers continued to be fertile in the discovery of new techniques to delay a trial and to avoid immediate pleading of the basic issues involved. Essoins were perfected and became more complicated. The records tell of frequent recourse to confession and avoidance (special traverse or special plea). One becomes fatigued and confused reading the records telling of repeated essoins and tortuous pleading. Certainly many bewildered litigants must have felt themselves to be in a legal no man's land and must have doubted whether they would ever extricate themselves.

The most significant change in the system of writs resulted from a clause in the Statute of Westminster II (1285) which provided that an old established writ could be issued by the chancery "in a similar case (*in consimili casu*) falling under similar law." This enactment was interpreted as a general authority for the expansion of legal remedies. The scope of old writs was enlarged and new writs were formed on the analogy of the older ones. In the case of the writ of trespass its scope was greatly extended. It was argued that any personal injury amounted to trespass and a writ known as "trespass on the case" (the word "case" was taken from the phrase "in a similar case") was used to recover civil damages in cases formerly regarded as criminal actions. Because this writ initiated a sort of semicriminal action it made possible arrest in a civil action. We have seen that another form of trespass on the case known as *assumpsit* was used to enforce contracts. This was but the beginning of an extension that was to make the action of trespass applicable in a wide range of civil cases.

7. CONCLUSIONS

Admittedly, if one looks back over the two centuries of legal history between the death of Edward I and the accession of Henry VII he cannot point to legal achievements, to judicial monuments of such a nature as those cast by Henry II and Edward I. But achievement there was. And we should not overlook the contribution of these two centuries to English law. The judges and lawyers who dominated the common law in the late Middle Ages had by legal hook and crook, by piecemeal adaptation, and by shrewd litigation woven the common law into a distinct and compact system of law. They had tied together the local Anglo-Saxon law, the great universal legal principles which the accomplished lawyers of the twelfth and thirteenth centuries had introduced as practice in the royal courts, and the remarkable statutes of the thirteenth century which helped to channel the development of the principles of law, and had adapted these laws and principles to new demands. This was no mean accomplishment and it should be weighed in the balance when criticizing the archaic law and procedure that were permitted to live on and to clutter up the rational and efficient growth of the law. It should also be taken into account when reproving the arid, tangled, and incredibly tedious litigation that was seemingly the delight of judge and lawyer.

Whatever may be said against the rigidity of the common law and its failure to adapt itself willingly to changing legal needs, it must be acknowledged that a tough-minded legal profession had developed the common law into an extremely tough system of law. Despite the challenge of despotism, of Roman law, and of other new movements of the Renaissance and Reformation the common law had been forged into such a strong law that it repulsed these rivals and maintained its supremacy. Not only did it emerge from the sixteenth century victorious but it was able to influence the new ideas and currents of the Renaissance. No Tudor, not even Henry VIII, thought of challenging the sovereignty of the common law. The fourteenth and fifteenth centuries were not the golden legal age of medieval England but throughout this period, that may be labeled sterile, technical, and superficial, it was never forgotten that the common law and its procedure had been developed to protect the frailties and needs of man. The good and sound principles of the common law so outweighed its deficiencies that the common law system had by the end of the Middle Ages established itself as a legal way of life. It was to become the core and essence of Anglo-American law.

XXXVIII

The Success of English Medieval Constitutionalism

DURING the course of this survey of English medieval institutions we have repeatedly come to conclusions about local and central government, about the common law, and about parliament. There is no need to recapitulate or to summarize these conclusions. Nor for the intelligent and curious student should there be any reason to explain the value of the constitutional and legal institutions that developed in medieval England. Certainly the great debt of English and American government to English medieval institutions is apparent to all. What needs to be asked at this point is why English medieval constitutionalism became successful and why England, of all the medieval western states, emerged into the modern world as a constitutional monarchy.

Why was the constitutionalism of medieval England different? The answer to this difficult question depends upon our understanding of parliament. It is evident that the principal studies on parliament have concentrated upon why it arose and how it functioned. Few historians have seen the need to explain why it continued to grow and to become a thriving institution. Actually, there has been only one serious effort devoted to fathoming the success of parliament, and this by Stubbs, whose views on parliament have for some time been deemed outmoded. We need not concern ourselves with Stubbs' explanation for the origin of parliament or with his opinions on the nature and role of parliament in the fourteenth and fifteenth centuries. With all this we are familiar. We know that much of the Stubbsian "system" has been repudiated by historians. We know also that his explanation for the origin of parliament goes no farther towards explaining the success of English medieval constitutionalism than do scores of other theories on parliament. What is unique in the history of Stubbs is the relation he saw between local units of English government and parliament. The emphasis placed upon this relation indicates Stubbs' deep comprehension of English medieval politics.

Stubbs argued that the phrase *quod omnes tangit ab omnibus approbetur* ("that which concerns all should be approved by all") appearing in the writs of summons for the Model Parliament of 1295 was a résumé of the political policy of Edward I. To summon representatives of the counties and boroughs to parliament was but to implement this theory or political idea. To particularize, Stubbs believed that the county court was already a little parliament. Here periodically assembled various classes of freemen of the county. And these men were representatives of someone or something. This system of representation long employed for local county government was but appropriated by Edward I and used for the governance of the realm. He summoned to a national parliament representatives of the county gentry and of the burgesses of the boroughs and thereby transformed little county parliaments into large national parliaments. What Stubbs sensed but did not elaborate upon was the fundamental importance of the relation between king and the estates of the realm—the clergy, baronage, and the third estate. Without saying so or without proving it, he was suggesting that the English parliament functioned successfully because in the critical period of its formation—1215 to 1399—there was a balance of power, especially among king, barons, and third estate. To paraphrase the Greek political thinkers, there was such a nice balance of power that no king, however capable and powerful, could become a tyrant. The barons, though they tried repeatedly, could not transform the government into an oligarchy. And the commons, though they labored industriously to make the representative element of parliament—the House of Commons—the sovereign power, could not change the government into a democracy, much less an ochlocracy. Thus checked and checkmated the great trinity of English government gave and took, cooperated and compromised themselves into a state of constitutionalism that neither the fifteenth century of wars, nor the Tudors, nor the Stuarts could destroy.

While the theory of Stubbs that county parliaments coalesced into a national parliament under the guiding genius of Edward I is not historically defensible, the balanced relations he saw among king, baronage, and commons is of real merit and is entitled to serious reflection. It may be said that English history at least since 1066 was endowed by fortune with an exceptionally delicate balance of political power. In the Norman and Angevin period when England's need was for powerful and centralized government to combat the centrifugal forces that often accompanied feudalism the kings gave their realm the centralized institutions and law that became common to all the kingdom. By the middle of the twelfth century a royal department of finance, a law, a local system of administration, and a military organization were common to the realm and were directed by professional ministers selected by the kings. Early, therefore, England was a unified community of the realm in which the kings and their government maintained effective control over the feudal vassals, who instead of opposing efficient government were compelled to strengthen it by their services. On the other hand, the feudal aristocracy did not become so anemic that it lost the will or ability to bridle despotism; for this it did when John pushed Angevin efficiency too far. Magna Carta, a feudal document, expressed the feudal ideal that both lord and vassal are under law and bound to honor mutual obligations. Down to 1215 England was characterized by strong central government which could have become absolute but did not because held in check by a yet vigorous feudal baronage.

Meanwhile there were important economic and social developments. By the middle of the eleventh century the economic revival in western Europe had sparked the rise of commerce and this contributed to the growth of towns and bourgeois inhabitants. In the eleventh and throughout the twelfth century the practical bourgeois were winning economic, legal, and social privileges that indeed freed them from the seignorial routine of the countryside but did not give them self-government. It was the 1190's before London permanently became a commune, that is, obtained the right of self-government, and it was the thirteenth century before boroughs achieved the political powers that have for so long characterized them. Compared to many areas of the Continent municipal growth was retarded. This seems to be explained by the slower commercial and industrial development of England as well as by the fearful reluctance of the Angevin kings to give the bourgeois too much power. Like the feudal aristocracy, the burgesses were kept in check and did not become a force in national politics until the later thirteenth century. And yet the kings could not completely ignore the bourgeoisie because its financial resources increasingly had to be tapped; this involved a give-and-take on both sides that is well seen in the transactions accompanying individual royal negotiation with the boroughs in the twelfth century for tallages, aids, and *dona*.

The thirteenth century witnessed the last key development in the political configuration that preceded the formation of parliament—the separation of the great feudal aristocrats (the barons) from the lesser aristocrats. The former became the lords, who first received individual writs of summons to great council or parliament and then eventually came to attend by prescriptive and heritable right; they became the House of Lords. Blocked from sitting in that body, the petty aristocrats—the knights and squires—by virtue of their common political and economic interests coalesced with the burgesses of the boroughs and eventually were summoned to parliament to represent the counties as the burgesses did the boroughs. Thus arose the House of Commons. Working together in parliament, the representatives of town and country developed an entente that broke down the traditional sharp division between rural and urban society. By the middle of the fourteenth century the knights and burgesses regularly attended parliament because their money was so often needed. Though king and lords still held most of the political power, the commons held the economic power and could not be written out of national politics. By the end of the fourteenth century such a political balance of power had been achieved that no element of it could be disbanded.

The kings, particularly the Normans and Angevins, had by political and military ability hammered out a strong, unified, and centralized state that provided the foundation essential for constitutional growth. Feudal war was almost nonexistent; king and vassal had learned how to get along and to compromise. This peace and stability enabled the towns and their bourgeois to develop into a powerful element of the realm. But having forged the most effective state of western Europe, the kings found themselves stuck with their handiwork. In a unified state the great feudal aristocrats learned cooperation on a national level and so, too, did the knights and burgesses. Both elements became such powerful national pressure groups that the kings could neither destroy them nor get along without them. And neither pressure group, however much it disliked the other, could dismantle it. Often the two groups cooperated in opposition to the king. Sometimes the king cooperated with one element against the other. But no member of the trinity could win a real ascendancy. The early strong kings and central government in a unified realm produced the type of feudal aristocracy and third estate that characterized England in the thirteenth and fourteenth centuries. Because of strong kingship neither element became too powerful, nor was either so weak that the kings could run roughshod over it; each had a national unity which the kings could not destroy. Three national elements balanced themselves off and had to make the best of their inextricable triangle in parliament. Each, to protect its interests and to win something for itself, had to have parliament. So sovereign had it become that it dominated lords, commons, and king.

If this discussion of English constitutionalism should terminate at this point about all that could be claimed for it would be its emphasis upon certain political and economic developments that led to a balance of power in English government. But to determine the validity of this suggestion we must apply it to various states on the Continent. The lack of constitutionalism in Italy and Germany is so easily explained that we need not tarry long in either area. Lack of strong centralized government and political unity made impossible any form of constitutional life. Political anarchy and particularism do not breed constitutionalism on a national level. For short periods here and there in Italy and Germany one can find democratic government in the city-states and free cities, but this is the exception rather than the rule. It is scarcely legitimate to speak of national assemblies. There were German diets between 1125 and 1247 but they contained only lay and spiritual lords. The diet of 1255 at Oppenheim was the first to which classes other than the aristocracy were summoned; it was attended by delegates from the cities of the Rhenish League. Thereafter the burghers were occasionally summoned and, after the Golden Bull of 1356, were considered one of the recognized estates. But so impotent were the German emperors of the thirteenth and fourteenth centuries that the towns and princes determined the great political affairs invariably to their own advantage. The powerful leagues of cities as well as the princes had no respect for imperial authority and used the diets as a forum for advancing their own particularistic objectives. It is farcical to speak, as do some German apologists, of German constitutionalism. The diets were merely a form of concentrated anarchy. In Italy and Sicily the situation was fundamentally the same. Representatives of the towns were summoned only twice by Frederick II—in 1232 and 1234; the dismal end of the Hohenstaufen in southern Italy and Sicily precluded the growth there of constitutional government. The lesson derived from both Germany and Italy is that there must be a unified state controlled by strong central authority in order for constitutionalism to take root. The ruler cannot be pushed around at will by the nobles and the towns.

The failure of the estates general in France is a somewhat more knotty problem. It is generally agreed that the institutional development of France lagged about a century behind that of England. France under Philip Augustus was about as advanced as England under Henry I. The France of Philip the Fair can be compared to the England of Henry III. Why, then, if French institutions around 1300 were on a par with those of England in the thirteenth century when parliament was taking form, did the estates general, for all practical purposes, cease to exist during the reign of Charles V (1360–1380) and thereby open the door for France to become an absolute monarchy? The key to the answer is the ever mighty king with no effective opposition. In England, though the king had been extremely powerful, the feudal aristocracy had blocked his advance to absolutism. In Germany and southern Italy the kings and emperors had never been powerful enough to wield effective authority. In France throughout the long period extending from Hugh Capet (987) to Philip the Fair (1285–1314) when the Capetians were expanding their authority and pushing the borders of the Île de France outward to form a greater France, the one institution common to the various counties and duchies absorbed was kingship. There was no common law, no uniform administrative system. From area to area custom, law, and institutions varied; in each there was a high degree of provincialism. It is a tribute to the Capetians that except for a few peripheral areas they were ultimately successful in unifying France.

When by the reign of Philip the Fair this had been accomplished, military, political, and financial necessity compelled Philip to do what had been done in England and Spain—convene an assembly of the three estates to secure broad backing for opposition to the papacy, for fighting the Flemish, and for a vote of supply. But despite the fact that Philip and some of his successors generally got what they wanted from the estates general, the great experiment failed because the nobility and third estate were too weak and inexperienced to make it work. The experience of the nobility in cooperation and opposition to the king had always been on a local level and they could not transfer it to a national level. Though the French towns had obtained a greater measure of political freedom earlier than the English boroughs, they too were handicapped by provincialism. It was unthinkable that towns of Poitou would cooperate with towns of Anjou, of Normandy, or Toulouse. In France, unified bit by bit over a period of three hundred years, an *esprit* of the community of the realm could not exist. England, it will be remembered, was unified in 1066. The French kings of the fourteenth century, seeing the inherent danger of large assemblies, played region against region and secured their supply from provincial estates. They could dispense with the estates general. As revolt in 1314 demonstrated, the feudal aristocracy was incapable of organizing more than provincial leagues. In vain did the Leagues of Burgundy, Champagne, and Vermandois protest against royal autocracy. French kingship by the year 1314 had become too strong to be shaken by feudal leagues. And yet an English king, equally powerful, had been decisively defeated in 1215 by the baronage of the realm. There was in France no balance of power; all power resided in the king.

Were one to investigate the reasons for the failure of the *cortes* in Castile and Aragon, he would undoubtedly arrive at conclusions similar to those obtained for France. The history of both Castile and Aragon resembled that of France. Both kingdoms were unified and expanded slowly at the expense of the Moors, a situation not conducive to the growth of a real and solid feeling of cooperation among the nobles and middle class. The balance of power concept can be much better tested in the Low Country states of Flanders and Brabant.

In the twelfth century few states of western Europe could boast a more efficient government or richer economy than the county of Flanders. It was a miniature kingdom long unified under able and strong counts who had introduced efficient comital institutions common to the whole county. Both Professors F. L. Ganshof and Jan Dhondt have argued that as early as the first quarter of the twelfth century the towns had a sense of the community of the realm. Their argument seems to be justified. Among such great towns as Ypres, Lille, Ghent, and Bruges there was a common bond. But between the towns and the countryside or between the towns and the feudal aristocracy there was no bridge of feeling or understanding. In fact, the divisions between urban and rural inhabitant were extremely bitter. The towns had much better relations with the counts, who adhered to an enlightened policy of granting them social, economic, legal, and political liberties. Cooperation between towns and counts was remarkable throughout the twelfth century.

But with the thirteenth century internal political conditions changed rapidly. The rulers of Flanders were either weak countesses or incompetent counts bullied by the French kings. The Flemish nobility had almost vanished as an estate owing to the precipitate decline of feudalism and seignorialism before the onrush of industry and trade. Without a noble estate to rely upon and no longer able or strong, the Flemish rulers had to deal with a group of towns whose power steadily increased in the thirteenth century and whose goal in the late thirteenth and early fourteenth centuries was to win a political independence that would make them self-governing republics like the cities of Germany and Italy. They bitterly opposed each other for economic and political advantage and upon occasion even sacrificed Flemish interests to the French kings to gain a selfish objective. As the principal source of financial supply, the towns struck hard bargains with the early fourteenth-century counts, who became merely puppets in their hands. Comital pleas for extraordinary taxation resulted each time in more political power for the towns. Until the dukes of Burgundy with the support of the French kings obtained the county of Flanders in 1385 the towns were the real political masters and, if given more time, would have converted Flanders into a mosaic of petty city-states.

What seems apparent, if this analysis of Flemish history is accurate, is that the advanced economy of Flanders stimulated the growth of urban life too fast for it to be properly assimilated. The second estate had virtually disappeared from the stage of history by 1200 and the counts, like Frankenstein, having nurtured their urban monsters, could no longer control them unaided. Whereas in the twelfth century, before it was necessary for the counts to call comital assemblies, a sort of balance of power existed, in the thirteenth century, when the counts had to ask for extraordinary taxation, they were pitted against the all-powerful towns, which were beyond negotiation and control.

While the swift flow of economic life was producing a political unbalance in Flanders, in the duchy of Brabant, less advantageously located for trade, history moved at a slower pace. Brabançonne economic development lagged far behind that of Flanders; not until the fourteenth century did such towns as Brussels, Louvain, and Antwerp begin to compete with the Flemish communes. The economic growth of these towns paralleled that of the English boroughs, which did not become centers of large-scale industry until the growth of cloth production during the fourteenth century. Meanwhile, the dukes of Brabant retained a strong grip over a relatively well-organized administration and the feudal aristocracy retained its strength well into the fourteenth century. Except for some territory won in the late thirteenth century the duchy had long been a unified state. Like England, then, Brabant had astute rulers with authority, a strong feudal aristocracy, and a middle class that slowly but steadily achieved economic and political power. At the outset of the fourteenth century there was, one could say, a political balance of power in Brabant. But at this point the dukes had to make the first demands for large sums of money from their subjects.

By the early fourteenth century Duke John II was enmeshed in the same financial difficulties as his English and French brethren. Deeply in debt to Italian bankers, he finally became insolvent and defaulted on his debts. Now his subjects also suffered; the creditors began to seize their property and rents and to confiscate their cloth and wool. Faced with financial ruin, the nobles and men of the towns collaborated and agreed to pay off the ducal creditors in return for certain concessions that would give them a share in the government and reaffirm certain cherished privileges. Thus Duke John II was forced to grant the Charter of Cortenberg in 1312. Of the numerous concessions made to the nobles and bourgeois most important was the promise that all new laws and amendments would be made only with the advice and consent of a council of the good men of the land which was to be composed of nobles and bourgeois from the leading towns of Brabant. The decisions of the council were to be sovereign; if the duke failed to abide by them, both nobles and bourgeois could renounce their allegiance and use force to obtain right and law. Two years later further concessions gave the council the power to approve ducal councillors and to examine ducal receipts and expenditures. Then in 1356 the joint rulers Jeanne and Wenceslas were forced to concede the *Joyeuse Entrée*, a group of privileges which in the history of Belgium became as fundamental to her law and constitution as did Magna Carta for England. By this grant the council of nobles and bourgeois received control over war, alliances, ducal appointments, legislation, and taxation. Subsequent dukes confirmed the *Joyeuse Entrée*. The Burgundian dukes accepted it when they acquired the duchy of Brabant, and even the Hapsburgs had to swear to uphold it.

Meanwhile the council of nobles and bourgeois increased in size until it became the estates of Brabant, in which the representatives of the towns were preponderant. The *Joyeuse Entrée* with its form of constitutional government was gradually extended over the sprawling Low Country state that Duke Philip the Good forged in the fifteenth century. Brussels became his capital and here assembled the estates general of all the Low Countries; here the provinces and the dukes were guided by the principles of the *Joyeuse Entrée*. Though such Hapsburg rulers as Philip II often violated its constitutional principles, legislating and taxing without the consent of the estates, they could never destroy the estates. The Austrian Hapsburgs had to negotiate with the estates of the ten southern provinces. It was Joseph II's attempt to suppress the estates and to annul the *Joyeuse Entrée* that sparked the Brabançonne Revolution of 1787–1790. After the Revolution of 1830, when the members of the Belgian congress assembled to draw up a constitution for the new Belgian state, the spirit of the *Joyeuse Entrée* was behind the great rights inscribed into the constitution—individual liberty, inviolability of the home and of property, and equality before the law and in taxation.

Though more feeble than English constitutionalism and though lacking the opportunity for independent growth, Brabanconne constitutionalism flourished in the fourteenth and fifteenth centuries and bequeathed so strong a heritage to the southern provinces in the succeeding centuries that no amount of Hapsburg despotism could destroy it. The *Joyeuse Entrée* became the battle cry of the Brabanconne Revolution just as Magna Carta became the symbol of parliamentary opposition to the Stuarts in the seventeenth century. In medieval Brabant and in medieval England only an extraordinary political balance of power among ruler, nobles, and third estate explains the success of parliament and the estates general.

What this brief comparative study seems to indicate is that a fortuitous combination of political and economic forces was basically responsible for the constitutional fortunes of the various states of medieval western Europe. It is most unrealistic, at least for the Middle Ages, to argue that some people have a greater capacity and flair for creating and supporting constitutional government than others. Certainly few historians would care to support Stubbs in his assertion that the growth of the English constitution can be largely attributed to the "national character" of the English people, an assertion which is in effect a subtle way of saying that English institutions are the result of Anglo-Saxon political genius.

The facts, which no amount of finely spun philosophical, economic, or legal theory can sophisticate, say that in 1066 England was happily unified under able kings who imposed strong centralized government upon the realm. In this large political community the feudal aristocracy was too strong to be destroyed and too weak to destroy strong government. It was, however, unified and powerful enough to block the ultimate goal of the Angevins—despotism. Meanwhile the English economy dictated so gradual a growth in the political and economic stature of the burgesses that their dynamic force, instead of destroying effective government as it did in Flanders and to some extent in Germany and Italy, was assimilated into the national political scheme of the thirteenth century. The success of English and Brabanconne constitutionalism depended upon chance, political and economic chance, that produced a balance of power in the body politic which was indeed the *sine qua non* of medieval constitutionalism.

BIBLIOGRAPHY

The fifteenth century, long the neglected century of medieval England, has during the past twenty years been the subject of many fine studies. Good general works are F. R. H. Du Boulay, *The Age of Ambition: English Society in the Late Middle Ages* (London, 1970), J. R. Lander, *Conflict and Stability in Fifteenth-Century England* (New York, 1969), *Fifteenth-Century England, 1399–1509: Studies in Politics and Society*, S. B. Chrimes, C. D. Ross, and R. A. Griffiths, eds. (New York, 1972), S. B. Chrimes, *Lancastrians, Yorkists and Henry VII* (London, 1964), K. B. McFarlane, *Lancastrian Kings and Lollard Knights* (Oxford, 1972). For the Lancastrian kings see J. L. Kirby, *Henry IV of England* (London, 1970), C. T. Allmand, *Henry V* (London, 1968), H. F. Hutchinson, *Henry V: A Biography* (London, 1967), and R. L. Storey, *The End of the House of Lancaster* (London, 1966). The two best books on kings are C. D. Ross, *Edward IV* (Berkeley, 1974) and S. B. Chrimes, *Henry VII* (Berkeley, 1972). Less reliable is P. M. Kendall, *Richard the Third* (London, 1955). Cf. A. R. Myers, "Richard III and Historical Tradition," *History*, LIII (1968), 181–202. For the nobility and some of the principal figures see J. R. Lander, *Crown and Nobility, 1450–1509* (London, 1976), P. M. Kendall, *Warwick the Kingmaker* (London, 1957), J. J. Bagley, *Margaret of Anjou, Queen of England* (London, 1948), E. F. Jacob, *Archbishop Henry Chichele* (London, 1967), K. H. Vickers, *Humphrey, Duke of Gloucester* (London, 1907), and W. H. Dunham, Jr., *Lord Hastings' Indentured Retainers, 1461–1483* (New Haven, 1955). On the Wars of the Roses see J. R. Lander's collection of pertinent sources, *The Wars of the Roses: History in the Making* (London, 1965), C. D. Ross, *The Wars of the Roses: A Concise History* (London, 1976), and K. B. McFarlane, "The Wars of the Roses," *Proceedings of the British Academy*, L (1964), 87–119.

A basic study of kingship, council, parliament, and the law is S. B. Chrimes, *English Constitutional Ideas in the Fifteenth Century* (Cambridge, 1936). For the council see the works cited above including Wilkinson on the fifteenth century and T. F. T. Plucknett, "The Place of the Council in the Fifteenth Century," *Transactions of the Royal Historical Society*, I (1918), 157–189, J. Otway-Ruthven, *The King's Secretary and Signet Office in the XVth Century* (Cambridge, 1939), and A. L. Brown, *The Early History of the Clerkship of the Council* (Glasgow, 1969). For financial administration see Steel, *Receipt of the Exchequer* and B. P. Wolffe, *The Crown Lands 1461 to 1536: An Aspect of Yorkist and Early Tudor Government* (New York, 1970). There are also articles on kingship, council, and central government by Chrimes, Plucknett, Wilkinson, Ross, Lander, Wolffe, McFarlane, and C. A. J. Armstrong.

Parliament is well scrutinized by Wilkinson and others cited in the Bibliography for the previous section. See also G. R. Elton, *The Body of the Whole Realm: Parliament and Representation in Medieval and Tudor England* (Charlottesville, Va., 1969), J. S. Roskell, *The Commons in the Parliament of 1422: English Society and Parliamentary Representation under the Lancastrians* (Manchester, 1954), J. C. Wedgwood and A. D. Holt, *History of Parliament, 1439–*

1509: Biographies of the Members of the Commons House (London, 1936). For a description of parliamentary procedure see Henry Elsynge, *Expedicio Billarum Antiquitus. An Unpublished Chapter of the Second Book of the Manner of Holding Parliaments in England*, C. S. Sims, ed. (Louvain, 1954).

For law and legislation in the fourteenth and fifteenth centuries see Plucknett, *Statutes and their Interpretation in the First Half of the Fourteenth Century* (Cambridge, 1922), Geoffrey Barraclough, "Law and Legislation in Medieval England," *Law Quarterly Review*, LVI (1940), 75–92, J. G. Bellamy, *The Law of Treason in England in the Later Middle Ages* (New York, 1970), and A. W. B. Simpson, *A History of the Common Law of Contract: The Rise of the Action of Assumpsit* (New York, 1975). For the development of impeachment see Plucknett, "The Origin of Impeachment," *Transactions of the Royal Historical Society*, XXIV (1942), 47–72.

A good study of a central common law court is Margaret Hastings, *The Court of Common Pleas in Fifteenth Century England: A Study of Legal Administration and Procedure* (Ithaca, N.Y., 1947). On the development of equitable law and procedure in the court of chancery see F. W. Maitland, *Equity: A Course of Lectures* (Cambridge, 1936), W. T. Barbour, *The History of Contract in Early English Equity* (Oxford, 1914), H. D. Hazeltine, "The Early History of English Equity," in *Essays in Legal History*, Paul Vinogradoff, ed. (Oxford, 1913), and M. E. Avery, "The History of the Equitable Jurisdiction of Chancery before 1460," *Bulletin of the Institute of Historical Research*, XLII (1969), 129–144 and "An Evaluation of the Effectiveness of the Court of Chancery under the Lancastrian Kings," *Law Quarterly Review*, LXXVII (1970), 84–97.

On the justice of the peace C. E. Beard's *The Office of the Justice of the Peace in England* (New York, 1904) has been mostly superseded by the studies of B. H. Putnam, *The Enforcement of the Statute of Labourers* (New York 1908), *Early Treatises on the Practices of the Justices of the Peace in the Fifteenth and Sixteenth Centuries* (Oxford, 1924), "The Transformation of the Keepers of the Peace into the Justices of the Peace, 1327–80," *Transactions of the Royal Historical Society*, XII (1929), 19–48, "Shire Officials: Keepers of the Peace and Justice of the Peace," in *English Government at Work*, III, 185–217, and *Proceedings Before the Justices of the Peace in the Fourteenth and Fifteenth Centuries* (London, 1938). See also John Bellamy, *Crime and Public Order in England in the Later Middle Ages* (Toronto, 1973) and E. G. Kimball, *A Cambridgeshire Gaol Delivery Roll, 1332–1334* (Cambridge, 1978) which has a good introduction on local criminal justice.

Valuable studies on Fortescue are John Fortescue, *The Governance of England*, Charles Plummer, ed. (Oxford, 1885), Sir John Fortescue, *De Laudibus Legum Anglie*, S. B. Chrimes, ed. and trans. (Cambridge, 1942), Chrimes, "Sir John Fortescue and his Theory of Dominion," *Transactions of the Royal Historical Society*, XVII (1934), 117–147, and Felix Gilbert, "Sir John Fortescue's Dominium Regale et Politicum," *Medievalia et Humanistica*, II (1944), 88–97.

For legal education see Gerald Hurst, *A Short History of Lincoln's Inn* (London, 1946), William Ball, *Lincoln's Inn: Its History and Traditions* (London, 1947), *Readings and Moots at the Inns of Court in the Fifteenth Century*, S. E. Thorne, ed., Selden Society, vol. LXXII (London, 1954), and W. C. Richardson, *A History of the Inns of Court* (Baton Rouge, La., 1975). On the legal profession see T. F. T. Plucknett, "The Place of the Legal Profession in the History of English Law," *Law Quarterly Review*, XLVIII (1932), 328–340, G. O. Sayles, "Medieval Judges as Legal Consultants," *ibid.*, LVI (1940), 247–254, E. L. G. Stones, "Sir Geoffrey le Scrope (c. 1280–1340), Chief Justice of the King's Bench," *English Historical Review*, LXIX (1954), 1–17, B. H. Putnam, *The Place in Legal History of Sir William Shareshull, Chief Justice of the King's Bench, 1350–1361: A Study of Judicial and Administrative Method in the Reign of Edward III* (London, 1950), and E. W. Ives, "Promotion in the Legal Profession of Yorkist and Early Tudor England," *Law Quarterly Review*, LXXV (1959), 348–363.

INDEX